THE UNITED STATES IN GLOBAL PERSPECTIVE

THE UNITED STATES IN GLOBAL PERSPECTIVE

A Primary Source Reader

Julie K. deGraffenried and Stephen M. Sloan

editors

BAYLOR UNIVERSITY PRESS

Book and cover design by Kasey McBeath
Cover image: Shutterstock/pio3

Paperback ISBN: 978-1-4813-1265-3
Library of Congress Control Number: 2020936971

The United States in Global Perspective: A Primary Source Reader offers a wide range of historical materials, some of which may contain offensive language or negative stereotypes. It is essential to view these materials in the context of the period in which they were created. Baylor University Press does not endorse the views expressed in such materials.

Printed in the United States of America on acid-free paper.

BRIEF CONTENTS

CONTENTS

3 | The Early Republic and the World   69

360 | Indigenous Peoples   71

Foreign Policy   78

Encountering the Other   91

5 | Making a Nation   137

6 | Western Expansion and Empire   187

360 | Motives for Empire   189

To the West   195

The United States in the Age of Imperialism   204

7 | Constructing the Urban Landscape   231

9 | Wrestling with the Modern Age   315

360 | The Modern Woman   317

Postwar Unrest   325

Culture and Society in the Interwar Period   331

10 | The Search for Solutions   349

11 | World War II   389

12 | The Bipolar World   441

Globalization   591

ACKNOWLEDGMENTS

This publication would not have been possible without the support of a host of outstanding organizations, colleagues, students, and partners that assisted in identifying, researching, translating, and publishing these resources. At Baylor University, these include the Department of History, the College of Arts & Sciences, the Institute for Oral History, the University Libraries, and Baylor University Press. While we framed this reader to support a number of college-level history courses, the impetus for its creation was a new core course in the College of Arts & Sciences at Baylor University, HIS1300: The United States in Global Perspective.

Within the College, Associate Dean Blake Burleson and Director of the Core Lauren Poor supported the creation of a primary source reader for this course, Christopher Richmann from the Academy of Teaching and Learning led collaborative sessions and provided useful deadlines, and Dean Lee Nordt provided essential funding at key moments in the reader's production. Fellow travelers Derek Dodson, Doug Weaver, Elizabeth Dell, and Joe Fulton offered great advice and encouragement.

Within the Department of History, we are grateful for collective discussions on history pedagogy, form, structure, and themes, and particularly for colleagues who drew on their own expertise to suggest potential sources. We appreciate the team of instructors (and their students) that used the beta phase reader in fall 2019 and offered us feedback, especially Adina Kelley, Lauren Poor, and Dan Watkins. Regina Wenger managed the Sisyphean task of coordinating texts, images, sourcing information, and notes with grace, often serving as the middlewoman between us and Baylor University Press. Regina and Adina Kelley helped with discussion questions, and Patrick Leech aided in proofreading and editing texts. Colleagues and students who assisted with translations include Dan Barish, Katerin Collazo, George Gawrych, Elisa Gonzalez, Michael Long, Charley Ramsey, Eric Rust, and Dan Watkins. At every step, Barry Hankins, Chair of the Department of History, offered his support in a variety of ways.

In the Institute for Oral History, we acknowledge and thank the entire staff and student worker corps, but most especially Dianne Reyes. The Institute afforded this reader a welcoming home base of operations. Students who worked on parts of the project include Layton Coker, Will deGraffenried, Elisa Gonzalez, Shannon Sepanski, and Amelia Tidwell. In the University Libraries, Becky Parton helped us envision the electronic version of the reader.

The staff of Baylor University Press advocated for this project from its inception. David Aycock and Jenny Hunt provided enthusiasm for and labor on the reader, for which we are appreciative. Thanks also to Maya Adams, Lindsey Keller, Kasey Mc-Beath, Stephanie Hoffman, Hannah Dyar, Carey Newman, and Savanah Landerholm.

Last but never least, we remain indebted to our families for their patience, support, and encouragement.

NOTE TO STUDENTS

Why This Reader

This morning when I woke up, I grabbed my iPhone—made of components designed in Taiwan, Germany, Japan, China, Switzerland, South Korea, and assembled in China—and scanned the headlines from a dozen international news sources, read about events in at least six locations around the world, flipped through photos of friends in Mendoza (Argentina), Tbilisi (Georgia), and Waco (Texas, U.S.) on social media, and noticed that I had missed a call from a telemarketer in Sierra Leone. After answering an email from a friend in the military posted in the Canary Islands, I wrote two others destined for colleagues in Canada and Kazakhstan. I put on an outfit made by workers in Colombia, Bangladesh, and Mexico, got in my Honda Pilot, and drove to work while listening to music by The Chieftains, an Irish band, picking up coffee sourced in Kenya along the way. Later, I ate Thai food prepared by a man who recently immigrated to the U.S. while having a conversation about the influence of protests in Hong Kong on Disney's stock prices, mulling over the effects Brexit might have on our university's study abroad program in London, and pondering an article written by a Russian historian. All this by 11 a.m.!

In unprecedented ways, today's technology has enabled us to see and experience the connection between the United States and the world. These connections are interwoven into our daily lives and activities, often in ways we do not notice or take for granted. Consider how differently my morning might have unfolded had nothing in my life been made in, part of, or related to the rest of the world.

Likewise, the history of the United States cannot be fully told without recognizing and understanding the many ways that it not only links to a broader history of the world, but also intersects with dozens of other national histories. Put simply, the events of the collective past in the U.S. involved areas beyond its borders. The U.S., from its beginnings as a European colonizing venture in an already inhabited North America to its modern-day role as world power in an international community, has never existed or acted in a vacuum. The world has influenced the U.S., and the U.S. has influenced the world. What we see at the micro-level in our daily lives is the reality of national and global history. U.S. national history is part of a broader global narrative about the past.

This way of viewing U.S. history explains our idea in putting together the reader of primary sources you are holding. The various sources included demonstrate some essential, representative connections between the United States and the rest of the world. These links and relationships have always existed, and without them, the story of the U.S. is incomplete. We hope you encounter both the expected and the unexpected as you use this book, and that it enriches your understanding of both U.S. and world history.

Primary Sources

History is a story that we tell about the past based on evidence. Though the past cannot change, history can; you can't change what happened in your life yesterday, but over time, you may interpret those events differently, based on the information you have, its meaning, and its context. In most cases, the best evidence historians can use to construct a high-quality, reliable narrative is provided by the people who lived the moment in the past being investigated. A **primary source** is any source of information, in any form—a treaty, a birth certificate, a diary, a photograph, an advertisement, an artifact, a video, a social media post, etc.—that is left behind by those who experienced an event in the past. This firsthand evidence is invaluable in puzzling out the past and providing a legitimate interpretation of it.

Historians seek out primary source materials about a particular topic in the past and then face the difficult task of locating, comparing, compiling, selecting, sometimes translating, and interpreting them—a series of actions usually encapsulated by the single word "research"—in order to build a story about the past. That work is then reviewed by other trained historians, who decide if the evidence is adequate in amount and type and if the story, built on analyzing the evidence, is legitimate and reasonable. Whether or not these historians *agree* with their colleague's interpretation is another story entirely!

Thinking Historically and Why It Matters

It will not come as a surprise to you to learn that historians look at things differently than, say, theologians or scholars of literature . . . or maybe it will! The way we, as historians, approach a primary source document is very much a product of years of training in asking particular sorts of questions for particular purposes. That is not to say you must train for years before being able to use this reader. It simply means that to read primary sources effectively, as a historian, takes *practice.*

A number of tools have been developed to help us practice reading primary sources, some of which are listed at the end of this note under "For Further Reading." Here is a quick guide to getting the most out of a primary source.

- *Start with the basics.* What is it? Identify the type of primary source and its general contents. Who created it? Figure out who the creator was, looking for clues about age, gender, class, race, nationality, religion, position in society, and so on. How reliable is he, she, or this group? When was it created? Think about the relationship between the creation of the primary source and past events. Where was it created? Reflect on the significance of place in the making of this account or artifact and the places it might have traveled. Make sure that you are familiar with words, places, and names mentioned.

- *Dig a little deeper.* What was the purpose of this source? Think about the context in which the creator existed. Can you tell if the creator was reacting to another person, idea, or event? Who might the audience(s) have been? Is the source reflective of a particular set of ideas, politics, traditions, values, or culture? How representative is it? Are there any unspoken messages to decipher? Is possible that language has changed over time, so that what the author meant by a certain word or phrase at that time means something different now? If the source is an image, what might symbols or colors represent? Might the way figures are positioned, dressed, or drawn mean something important?
- *Answer the big questions.* How does this source help us understand this time, place, and society? What might the producer's argument and/or point of view be, and does it demonstrate a change from past ideas, values, actions, roles, or traditions? How does it fit with other sources generated by others on the same or related topics? Does this source demonstrate cause and/or effect? In what ways might the source challenge or affirm or modify existing narratives about the past?

Each of the primary sources in this reader has been carefully chosen to highlight a variety of voices, both international and national, commenting on issues, both international and national, of the United States' past. Some of the primary sources include outdated language or images that are offensive, while others may feature text and visual content that seem comfortable and harmless; we encourage you to confront each source with the critical eye of the historian. Moving through the questions above will help you develop good habits of historical thinking and historical question-asking.

Five of the most important aspects of thinking historically are (1) Change and continuity: how have ideas/relationships/events changed or remained the same over time? To make useful and reliable comparisons, historians constantly need to ask "How is this different than or similar to what came before it and what came after it?" (2) Context: how are time, place, and conditions significant? The environment in which evidence was created matters immensely to historians in order to adequately grasp the reasons for its creation and the meaning of its message. A second aspect of context involves placing a primary source in conversation with other sources produced at approximately the same time or context in order to assess how representative (or not) the source was of a particular time, place, and group. (3) Causality: what can be learned about causes and consequences from the past? Though historians are often accused of obsessing over dates, this is a misunderstanding; what historians really get excited about is chronology. Understanding the chronological relationship of past events reveals cause-and-effect, the key to making connections between people, places, and ideas and unraveling motives and consequences. (4) Contingency: what conditions needed to be in place for this past event to occur as it did? Historians rarely, if ever, concede that an event was inevitable. We recognize that many preconditions must exist to create the opportunity for each past event. Speculating about the absence or presence of specific conditions lets us play the "what if" game, an exercise in which historians occasionally dabble but don't often dwell. (5) Complexity: humans and their civilizations are messy and, thus, so is the past. Any attempt to distill the past into a neat, one-size-fits-all package pretends that all people acted in predictable ways with the same motives and goals, that the "good life" for one group was the "good life" for every group, and that there are simple explanations for the way of the world. Rejecting this, historians embrace the complicated and revel in nuance. Because we continually strive to construct a fuller and more complete narrative that accounts for the complex, history—the story we tell about the past—changes. History is dynamic, not static.

These characteristics highlight what make a historian's interests different from those of other scholars. Think about Dr. Martin Luther King's 1963 "Letter from Birmingham Jail," a primary source that could be read in a variety of college departments, for a number of reasons. While all scholars would be interested in establishing basic who-what-when-where facts, people of different disciplines then ask specific questions tailored to the contours of that discipline. For example, a historian would be interested in the significance of King's document for the U.S. civil rights movement and its place in a longer history of nonviolent resistance in order to understand the ways in which the African American freedom struggle had evolved by the 1960s, what influences from around the world inspired King's argument, what consequences King's letter and message had for civil rights movements in the U.S. and beyond, and how it differed from methods and goals of other prominent figures of the civil rights movement. A theologian would highlight the biblical references in King's letter, seeking to understand their function and interpretation, or analyze how references to God or religious themes reflected a particular religious tradition and that tradition's interaction with the civil rights movement. A scholar of literature would be concerned with genre, the use of language tools and rhetoric, literary movements, theme, and ways of reading the text; so, King's nonfiction essay might be read for its stunning use of ethical appeal in a writing course or as an example of protest literature or an example of African American literature employing themes of conscience, justice, and human rights in a literature course. Scholars of the humanities and social sciences differ even further in their use of primary sources. A sociologist, political scientist, or psychologist might read King's letter and use it to make a broad statement about humanity or political theory or group behavior. Historians, however, do not look for what the letter tells us about all people in all times, but for what it tells us about a specific person or group (King, his audience) in a particular time (1963) and place (Birmingham, Alabama, U.S.). Though there is some overlap, even this brief description shows how differently the disciplines look at the same primary source.

Good things come from studying history: it develops critical thinking skills, habits of good question-asking, and confidence in the ability to find answers, assess evidence, and build an argument all while bringing new life to the past. Learning to view the past through someone else's eyes, from another person's point of view, is one of the most important things that learning to think historically can do for us. It is not easy, nor should we expect it to be. We must be willing to step outside ourselves and "the now." Too many times we read something from the past with our present-day glasses on, forgetting that political systems and parties, geographies, cultural expressions, language, and ideas about race, class, gender, childhood, science, religion, education—almost everything!—have changed over time; if we do so, we risk misinterpreting evidence and creating a story that does not accurately reflect the reality of past lives. Acknowledging and casting off the "now" glasses takes some humility: not only must we be willing to allow that our way of seeing isn't necessarily a *superior* way of seeing, but also, more fundamentally, we have to be willing—collectively and individually—to admit that the way we see today isn't the *only* way of seeing. The art of viewing the past through others' eyes translates to daily life. The more practice you can get in thinking historically through reading, reflecting on, and interpreting primary sources, the better you will become at appreciating complicated present-day issues from multiple perspectives. History matters!

For Further Reading

Andrews, Thomas, and Flannery Burke. "What Does It Mean to Think Historically?" *Perspectives on History* 45, no. 1 (2007).

Fea, John. *Why Study History? Reflecting on the Importance of the Past*. Grand Rapids: Baker Academic, 2013.

Wineburg, Sam. *Historical Thinking and Other Unnatural Acts: Charting the Future of Teaching the Past*. Philadelphia: Temple University Press, 2001.

NOTE TO INSTRUCTORS

As demonstrated in the "Note to Students," we truly live in a global era. To meet the needs of our students and our discipline, instructors must meet this new age with fresh models for teaching the American past. Twentieth-century frames for U.S. history instruction are inadequate, can be overly narrow, and are often unsuited for the demands of the new millennium. With this publication, the editors have crafted a tool that can support this necessary shift to a broader global historical perspective. Whether the need be to teach an introductory course on the United States from an international perspective, to globalize a U.S. survey course, or simply to bring U.S. elements into a class on world history or Western civilization, this reader can be a useful device in developing a new approach.

For more than two decades now, historians have discussed the importance of moving away from a strictly national frame and internationalizing the teaching of American history.[1] This shift provides a history that is both more connected to the present and more representative of the past, intertwined with the larger processes and forces that shaped both the development of the United States and the broad paths of world history. As historian Peter N. Stearns argues, "even those aspects of the American history course designed to provide a sense of national experience and identity—a staple of the survey course since its inception in the nineteenth century—are vastly improved through a global perspective. In what ways has the nation moved in rhythms shared with other parts of the world? In what institutions and values does national distinctiveness rest?"[2] The rewards of shifting our pedagogical focus can reap a host of positive outcomes for both instructors and students.

Envisioning teaching a survey of United States history from a global perspective can be a daunting task. Choosing to narrow the course thematically offers a wealth of avenues to both understand and learn aspects of the topic. The editors organized this publication to support a variety of themes that instructors can use as a concentration, including encountering the other, environment, foreign policy, women's history, war and society, and immigration. Within these pages, instructors will find

---

1 An important early effort is encapsulated in Thomas Bender's "The LaPietra Report: A Report to the Profession," the outcome of a four-year series of discussions among historians from a host of different countries sponsored by the Organization of American Historians. The full report can be found here: https://www.oah.org/insights/archive/the-lapietra-report-a-report-to-the-profession/.
2 Peter N. Stearns, "Whys and Hows of Globalizing," in *Globalizing American History: The AHA Guide to Re-Imagining the U.S. Survey Course*, ed. Noralee Frankel and Peter N. Stearns (Washington, D.C.: American Historical Association, 2008), 23.

some entries here that will be new to them and some that may be quite familiar. Even familiar texts or images, however, take on new meaning when framed and analyzed in a global context.

A special feature that begins each chapter is the 360. This section offers a collection of sources organized around a discrete theme, such as the rights of the individual (chapter 2), motives for empire (chapter 6), or the digital world (chapter 15). These pieces position assorted primary sources around a topic, are less strictly chronological, and place items in conversation with one another. The 360 discussion questions will prove useful in encouraging students to explore the relationship between these sources from disparate contexts and periods.

Discussion questions are included for all items in the reader. These are designed to encourage analysis of primary sources through in-class discussions or short student writing assignments. As this reader will often be used in college and university general survey courses, the text may also offer some students one of their sole experiences to understand the historian's work. This compilation includes a rich mix of primary sources for undergraduates to analyze and interpret. In our "Note to Students," your students are provided suggested pathways and approaches for working with primary source material. The issues raised through the discussion questions and primary source analysis should be enriched by the specialized methodologies and interests of each individual instructor.

As is quickly evident, a distinctive feature of this primary source reader is its extensive visual content. Students will find it of added benefit to have the opportunity to work with these images in and out of class. The publishers took additional steps to provide these images in color, as it offers a fuller representation of the original image and reveals additional layers for inquiry and interpretation.

A priority in planning the volume was also to include a diverse mix of perspectives and materials. About 60 percent of the pieces in the reader originate outside the U.S. This makes this publication distinctive from many texts which have primarily consisted of domestic looks outward rather than more inclusive global viewpoints on the U.S. To broaden students' understanding of where historians get their source material, you will also find an array of types of primary sources, including memoirs, statistical reports, oral histories, government documents, ephemera, maps, and political cartoons.

The exciting developments in transnational research and publication in history over the past two decades have been impressive. It is time that our undergraduate students benefit from this important historiographical turn. As it has done in research, this shift can reinvigorate the teaching of U.S. history at the undergraduate level. As historian John R. Gillis maintains, "the internationalization of American history provides an opportunity to restore history to its position at the core of a civic education by connecting it to that which really matters in the lives of people caught in the force field of transnational rather than purely national events."[3] As you embrace this challenge in your classroom, we, the editors, hope you find this volume useful in your efforts.

3   John R. Gillis, "What Will It Take to Globalize American History?" in Frankel and Stearns, *Globalizing American History*, 114.

1

Contact and Colonization

360 | Columbian Exchange

Early Contact

Colonial Politics and Society

COLUMBIAN EXCHANGE

Scholars have long since shed the image of Christopher Columbus as the discoverer of America—after all, the Americas were full of people when the sailor showed up in 1492—but agree that his voyage from Europe to the Caribbean and back to Europe set in motion one of the most momentous events of the modern era. The Columbian Exchange—named after Columbus—refers to the two-way transfer of plants, animals, microbes, ideas, and peoples between the Old World and the New World. It was the knitting together of dramatically different ecosystems, with all the ruptures and variations that resulted. This exchange significantly influenced cuisines, nutrition, and agriculture worldwide, but led to massive depopulation in the New World due to virgin soil epidemics from the introduction of Old World diseases. The examples collected here focus on evidence of the effects of crop transfer from the New World to the Old World.

Painting by Giuseppe Arcimboldo, *Vertumnus* (Rudolf II as Vertumnus), Milan, 1590

SEE COLOR INSERT

Encyclopedia entry on chocolate, *Encyclopédie*, France, 1750s

Chocolate, a type of cake or bar prepared with different ingredients but whose basic element is cocoa. . . . The beverage made from this bar retains the same name; the cocoa nut originates from the Americas: Spanish travelers established that it was much used in Mexico, when they conquered it around 1520. . . .

Spaniards, who learned about this beverage from the Mexicans and were convinced, through their own experience that this beverage, though unrefined, was good for the health, set out to correct its defaults by adding sugar, some ingredients from the Orient, and several local drugs that it is unnecessary to list here, as we only know their name and as, from all these extras, only the vanilla leaf traveled to our regions (similarly, cinnamon was the only ingredient that was universally approved) and proved to resist time as part of the composition of chocolate.

The sweet scent and potent taste it imparts to chocolate have made it highly recommended for it; but time has shown that it could potentially upset one's stomach, and its use has decreased; some people who favor the care of their health to the pleasure of their senses, have stopped using it completely. In Spain and in Italy, chocolate prepared without vanilla has been termed the healthy chocolate; and in our French islands in the Americas, where vanilla is neither rare nor expensive, as it can be in Europe, it is never used, when the consumption of chocolate is as high as in any other part of the world. . . .

When the cocoa paste has been well shredded on the stone, sugar can be added once it has been filtered through a silk-cloth sifter; the secret to the true proportion of cocoa and sugar is to put equal quantity of both: one could in fact subtract one quarter out of the dosage of sugar, as it might dry up the paste too much, or render it too sensitive to changes in the air, or endanger it even more to the apparition of worms. But that suppressed quarter of sugar must be used when chocolate, the beverage, is being prepared.

Once sugar is well mixed with the cocoa paste, a very thin powder can be added, made with vanilla seeds and cinnamon sticks finely cut and sifted together; this new mixture shall be mixed on the stone; once every ingredient is well incorporated, the mixture shall be poured into chocolatière pots, the shape of which it will take, and where it will harden. When one loves scents, one could add some amber essence into the pots.

Ottoman men smoking hookah at a Turkish café, Ottoman Empire, between 1880 and 1900

SEE COLOR INSERT

Recipe for salsa di pomodoro, Italy, 1891

There once was a priest in a city of Romagna who stuck his nose into everything, and inserted himself into families, desiring to have a hand in every domestic affair. On the other hand, he was an honest man, and since more good than bad came from his eagerness, people let him do it. But the witty christened him Don Pomodoro (Father Tomato), to show that tomatoes were everywhere. Therefore a good tomato sauce will be a valuable help in the kitchen.

> Make a battuto with a quarter of an onion, a clove of garlic, a finger-length stalk of celery, some basil leaves and enough parsley. Season with a little olive oil, salt, and pepper, and mash 7 or 8 tomatoes and put everything together on the stove. Stir from time to time and once you see the sauce condensed like a creamy liquid, pass it through a strainer and serve.

> This sauce is fit for very many uses, as I shall indicate accordingly. It is good with boiled meat, and goes best with pasta topped with butter and cheese, as well as for making risotto (recipe 77).

First known reference to the peanut, Huang Hsing-tsêng, China, early 16th c.

There is another [kind of tuber] whose skin is yellow and whose flesh is white. It is delicious and highly edible. Its stem and leaves are like those of the broad bean but slimmer. It is called *hsiang-yü* (fragrant taro). There is yet another kind whose flowers are on the vinelike stem. After the flowers fall, [the pods] begin to develop [underground]. It is called *lo-hua-sheng*. Both are produced in Chia-ting country (near Shanghai).

Adam Smith on the potato, *Wealth of Nations*, England, 1776

Book 4, Chapter 7, Of Colonies
The vegetable food of the inhabitants, though from their want of industry not very abundant, was not altogether so scanty. It consisted in Indian corn, yams, potatoes, bananas, etc. plants which were then altogether unknown in Europe, and which have never since been very much esteemed in it, or supposed to yield a sustenance equal to what is drawn from the common sorts of grain and pulse, which have been cultivated in this part of the world time out of mind.

Book 1, Chapter 11, Part I: Of the Produce of Land which Always affords Rent
The food produced by a field of potatoes is not inferior in quantity to that produced by a field of rice, and much superior to what is produced by a field of wheat. Twelve thousand weight of potatoes from an acre of land is not a greater produce than two thousand weight of wheat. The food or solid nourishment, indeed which can be drawn from each of those two plants, is not altogether in proportion to their weight, on account of the watery nature of potatoes. Allowing, however, half the weight of this root to go to water, a very large allowance, such an acre of potatoes will still produce six thousand weight of solid nourishment, three times the quantity produced by the acre of wheat. An acre of potatoes is cultivated with less expense than an acre of wheat; the fallow, which generally precedes

the sowing of wheat, more than compensating the hoeing and other extraordinary culture which is always given to potatoes. Should this root ever become in any part of Europe, like rice in some rice countries, the common and favourite vegetable food of the people, so as to occupy the same proportion of the lands in tillage which wheat and other sorts of grain for human food do at present, the same quantity of cultivated land would maintain a much greater number of people, and the labourers being generally fed with potatoes, a greater surplus would remain after replacing all the stock and maintaining all the labour employed in cultivation. A greater share of this surplus, too, would belong to the landlord. Population would increase, and rents would rise much beyond what they are at present.

The land which is fit for potatoes, is fit for almost every other useful vegetable. If they occupied the same proportion of cultivated land which corn does at present, they would regulate, in the same manner, the rent of the greater part of other cultivated land.

In some parts of Lancashire it is pretended, I have been told, that bread of oatmeal is a heartier food for labouring people than wheaten bread, and I have frequently heard the same doctrine held in Scotland. I am, however, somewhat doubtful of the truth of it. The common people in Scotland, who are fed with oatmeal, are in general neither so strong nor so handsome as the same rank of people in England who are fed with wheaten bread. They neither work so well, nor look so well; and as there is not the same difference between the people of fashion in the two countries, experience would seem to show, that the food of the common people in Scotland is not so suitable to the human constitution as that of their neighbours of the same rank in England. But it seems to be otherwise with potatoes. The chairmen, porters, and coal-heavers in London, and those unfortunate women who live by prostitution, the strongest men and the most beautiful women perhaps in the British dominions, are said to be, the greater part of them, from the lowest rank of people in Ireland, who are generally fed with this root. No food can afford a more decisive proof of its nourishing quality, or of its being peculiarly suitable to the health of the human constitution. It is difficult to preserve potatoes through the year, and impossible to store them like corn, for two or three years together. The fear of not being able to sell them before they rot, discourages their cultivation, and is, perhaps, the chief obstacle to their ever becoming in any great country, like bread, the principal vegetable food of all the different ranks of the people.

. . .

The circumstances of the poor through a great part of England cannot surely be so much distressed by any rise in the price of poultry, fish, wild fowl, or venison, as they must be relieved by the fall in that of potatoes.

360 DISCUSSION QUESTIONS

1   Do the sources gathered here seem to suggest that new crops from the Americas were received positively in the Old World?

2   How might the Columbian Exchange challenge the idea of "traditional" or "national" cuisines being timeless?

3   How might the documents here provide evidence of increasing globalization as far back as the sixteenth century?

EARLY CONTACT

1–1 | Paolo Toscanelli, map of Atlantic Ocean, Florence, 1474

Paolo dal Pozzo Toscanelli (1397–1482) was an Italian astrologer, mathematician, and cosmographer who, in 1474, proposed a plan to King Afonso V of Portugal for sailing westward to reach the Spice Islands and Asia. Later, a transcript of this letter outlining the strategy and a version of the map below were sent to Christopher Columbus, who took them on his first voyage to the New World. For reference, the 1911 publication by British cartographer John George Bartholomew superimposed Toscanelli's chart on a more modern atlas.

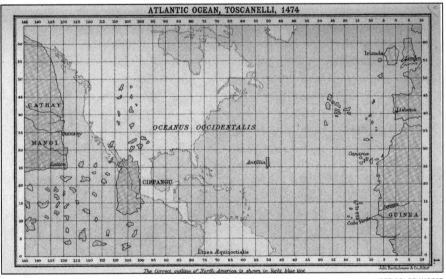

SEE COLOR INSERT

DISCUSSION QUESTIONS

1 What does Toscanelli's map signal about the extent of European knowledge of world geography in 1474?

2 Cipangu (Japan) and Cathay (China) are indicated on the map. Why would European explorers be seeking a route to those places?

1–2 | Council of Castile for Spanish-claimed Americas, *The Requerimiento* (Requirement), Spain, 1510

The Requerimiento [Requirement] (1510) was authored by the Council of Castile, the ruling body of the Crown of Castile, and was intended to be read aloud as notice to indigenous populations in the New World of the Spanish right to conquest. It draws on the 1493 papal bull (decree) that split the territory of the western hemisphere between Spain and Portugal. In many cases, *The Requerimiento* was proclaimed in Latin to American peoples without an interpreter or even read from aboard ship to an empty beach.

On the part of the King, Don Fernando, and of Doña Juana, his daughter, Queen of Castile and León, subduers of the barbarous nations, we their servants notify and make known to you, as best we can, that the Lord our God, Living and Eternal, created the Heaven and the Earth, and one man and one woman, of whom you and we, all the men of the world, were and are descendants, and all those who came after us. But, on account of the multitude which has sprung from this man and woman in the five thousand years since the world was created, it was necessary that some men should go one way and some another, and that they should be divided into many kingdoms and provinces, for in one alone they could not be sustained.

Of all these nations God our Lord gave charge to one man, called St. Peter, that he should be Lord and Superior of all the men in the world, that all should obey him, and that he should be the head of the whole human race, wherever men should live, and under whatever law, sect, or belief they should be; and he gave him the world for his kingdom and jurisdiction.

And he commanded him to place his seat in Rome as the spot most fitting to rule the world from; but also he permitted him to have his seat in any other part of the world, and to judge and govern all Christians, Moors [Muslims], Jews, Gentiles, and all other sects. This man was called Pope, as if to say, Admirable Great Father and Governor of men. The men who lived in that time obeyed that St. Peter and took him for Lord, King, and Superior of the universe; so also they have regarded the others who after him have been elected to the pontificate, and so has it been continued even till now and will continue till the end of the world.

One of these Pontiffs [popes] who succeeded that St. Peter as Lord of the world, in the dignity and seat which I have before mentioned, made donation of these isles and Tierra-firme to the aforesaid King and Queen and to their successors, our lords, with all that there are in these territories, as is contained in certain writings which passed upon the subject as aforesaid, which you can see if you wish.

So their Highnesses are kings and lords of these islands and land of Tierra-firme by virtue of this donation: and some islands, and indeed almost all those to whom this has been notified, have received and served their Highnesses, as lords and kings, in the way that subjects ought to do, with good will, without any resistance, immediately, without delay, when they were informed of the aforesaid facts. And also they received and obeyed the priests whom their Highnesses sent to preach to them and to teach them our Holy Faith; and all these, of their own free will, without any reward or condition, have become Christians, and are so, and their Highnesses have joyfully and benignantly received them, and also have commanded them to be treated as their subjects and vassals; and you too are held and obliged to do the same. Wherefore, as best we can, we ask and require you that you consider what we have said to you, and that you take the time that shall be necessary to understand and deliberate upon it, and that you acknowledge the Church as the Ruler and Superior of the whole world, and the high priest called Pope, and in his name the King and Queen Doña Juana our lords, in his place, as superiors and lords and kings of these islands and this Tierra-firme by virtue of the said donation, and that you consent and give place that these religious fathers should declare and preach to you the aforesaid.

If you do so, you will do well, and that which you are obliged to do to their Highnesses, and we in their name shall receive you in all love and charity, and shall leave you, your wives, and your children, and your lands, free without servitude, that you may do with them and with yourselves freely that which you like and think best, and they shall not compel you to turn Christians, unless you yourselves, when informed of the truth, should wish to be converted to our Holy Catholic Faith, as almost all the inhabitants of the rest of the islands have done. And, besides this, their Highnesses award you many privileges and exemptions and will grant you many benefits.

But, if you do not do this, and maliciously make delay in it, I certify to you that, with the help of God, we shall powerfully enter into your country, and shall make war against you in all ways and manners that we can, and shall subject you to the yoke and obedience of the Church and of their Highnesses; we shall take you and your wives and your children, and shall make slaves of them, and as such shall sell and dispose of them as their Highnesses may command; and we shall take away your goods, and shall do you all the mischief and damage that we can, as to vassals who do not obey, and refuse to receive their lord, and resist and contradict him; and we protest that the deaths and losses which shall accrue from this are your fault, and not that of their Highnesses, or ours, nor of these cavaliers who come with us. And that we have said this to you and made this Requisition, we request the notary here present to give us his testimony in writing, and we ask the rest who are present that they should be witnesses of this Requisition.

DISCUSSION QUESTIONS

1 What choices and consequences did the Spaniards place before the indigenous peoples?

2 Why did the Spaniards feel justified in treating Native Americans this way?

3 What connections were made between exploration, conquest, and religion?

1–3 | Jacques Cartier, excerpt from *The First Voyage*, France, 1534

In 1534, navigator Jacques Cartier (1491–1557) led an expedition to the New World under the authority of France's King Francis I. For this voyage, he was to explore the "northern lands," as the east coast of North America had been well defined at that point. In April of that year, he set out with two ships and explored the western coast of Newfoundland and the Gulf of St. Lawrence. From this expedition, he is also credited with the discovery of what became known as Prince Edward Island.

On account of the continuous bad weather with over-cast sky and mist, we remained in that harbour and river, without being able to leave, until [Saturday], the twenty-fifth of the said month [of July]. During that time there arrived a large number of savages, who had come to the river [Gaspé basin] to fish for mackerel, of which there is a great abundance. They [the savages] numbered, as well men, women as children, more than 300 persons, with some forty canoes. When they had mixed with us a little on shore, they came freely in their canoes to the sides of our vessels. We gave them knives, glass beads, combs and other trinkets of small value, at which they showed many signs of joy, lifting up their hands to heaven and singing and dancing in their canoes. This people may well be called savage; for they are the sorriest folk there can be in the world, and the whole lot of them had not anything above the value of five sous, their canoes and fishing-nets excepted. They go quite naked, except for a small skin, with which they cover their privy parts, and for a few old furs which they throw over their shoulders. They are not at all of the same race or language as the first we met. They have their heads shaved all around in circles, except for a tuft on the top of the head, which they leave long like a horse's tail. This they do up upon their heads and tie in a knot with leather thongs. They have no other dwelling but their canoes, which they turn upside down and sleep on the ground underneath. They eat their meat almost raw, only warming it a little on the coals; and the same with their fish. On St. Magdalen's day, we rowed over in our long-boats to the spot on the shore where they were, and went on land freely among them. At this they showed great joy, and the men all began to sing and dance in two or three groups, exhibiting signs of great pleasure at our coming. But they made all the young women retire into the woods, except two or three who remained, to whom we gave each a comb and a little tin bell, at which they showed great pleasure, thanking the captain by rubbing his arms and his breast with their hands. And the men, seeing we had given something to the women that had remained, made those come back who had fled to the woods, in order to receive the same as the others. These, who numbered some twenty, crowded about the captain and rubbed him with their hands, which is their way of showing welcome. He gave them each a little tin ring of small value; and at once they assembled together in a group to dance; and sang several songs. We saw a large quantity of mackerel which they had caught near the shore with the nets they use for fishing, which are made of hemp thread, that grows in the country where they ordinarily reside; for they only come down to the sea in the fishing-season, as I have been given to understand. Here likewise grows Indian corn like pease, the same as in Brazil, which they eat in place of bread, and of this they had a large quantity with them. They call it in their language, *Kagaige*. Furthermore they have plums which they dry for the winter as we do, and these they call, *honnesta*; also figs, nuts, pears, apples and other fruits, and beans which they call, *sahe*. If one shows them something they have not got and they know not what it is, they shake their heads and say, *nouda*, which means, they have none of it and know not what it is. Of the things they have, they showed us by signs the way they grow and how they prepare them. They never eat anything that has a taste of salt in it. They are wonderful thieves and steal everything they can carry off.

On [Friday] the twenty-fourth of the said month [of July], we had a cross made thirty feet high, which was put together in the presence of a number of Indians on the point at the entrance to this harbor, under the cross-bar of which we fixed a shield with three *fleurs-de-lys* in relief, and above it a wooden board, engraved in large Gothic characters, where was written, LONG LIVE THE KING OF FRANCE. We erected this cross on the point in their presence and they watched it being put together and set up. And when it had been raised in the air, we all knelt down with our hands joined, worshipping it before them; and made signs to them, looking up and pointing towards heaven, that by means of this we had our redemption, at which they showed many marks of admiration, at the same time turning and looking at the cross.

When we had returned to our ships, the chief, dressed in an old black bear-skin, arrived in a canoe with three of his sons and his brother; but they did not come so close to the ships as they had usually done. And pointing to the cross he [the chief] made us a long harangue, making the sign of the cross with two of his fingers; and then he pointed to the land all around about, as if he wished to say that all this region belonged to him, and that we ought not to have set up this cross without his permission. And when he had finished his harangue, we held up an axe to him, pretending we would barter it for his fur-skin. To this he nodded assent and little by little drew near the side of our vessel, thinking he would have the axe. But one of our men, who was in our dinghy, caught hold of his canoe, and at once two or three more stepped down into it and made the Indians come on board our vessel, at which they were greatly astonished. When they had come on board, they were assured by the captain that no harm would befall them, while at the same time every sign of affection was shown to them; and they were made to eat and to drink and to be of good cheer. And then we explained to them by signs that the cross had been set up to serve as a land-mark and guide-post on coming into the harbor, and that we would soon come back and would bring them iron wares and other goods; and that we wished to take two of his [the chief's] sons away with us and afterwards would bring them back again to that harbour. And we dressed up his two sons in shirts and ribbons and in red caps, and put a little brass chain round the neck of each, at which they were greatly pleased; and they proceeded to hand over their old rags to those who were going back on shore. To each of these three, whom we sent back, we also gave a hatchet and two knives at which they showed great pleasure. When they returned on shore, they told the others what had happened. About noon on that day six canoes came off to the ships, in each of which were five or six Indians, who had come to say good-bye to the two we had detained, and to bring them some fish. These made signs that they would not pull down the cross, delivering at the same time several harangues which we did not understand.

DISCUSSION QUESTIONS

1 What kind of observations were the French making about the people they encountered?

2 How did the French interpret the chief's response to the French cross?

3 Why might Native Americans be receptive to the presence of the French? What signs of tension can be observed?

1–4a | Engraving by Theodor de Bry of a watercolor by John White, *The arriual of the Englishemen in Virginia*, England and Germany, 1590

John White (ca. 1540-ca. 1593) was an English artist and colonist that participated in six expeditions to the New World during his lifetime, including a 1585 expedition to found a settlement at Roanoke Island. That same year, he was commissioned to sketch the natural bounty and inhabitants of the area. Published in an illustrated 1590 edition of Thomas Harriot's *A Briefe and True Report of the New Found Land of Virginia*, the image below is an engraving by Belgian Theodor de Bry (1528–1598) of White's watercolor depicting the arrival of the English in Virginia. Roanoac (Roanoke Island) is a central feature of the image.

SEE COLOR INSERT

1–4b | John Smith, excerpt from *Advertisements for the Unexperienced Planters of New-England, or Anywhere*, 1633

Captain John Smith (1580–1631) was an explorer, colonial governor, and author. He played an important role in the establishment of the first permanent English settlement in North America, Jamestown, and was an early leader of that colony. He also mapped the Chesapeake Bay area. Published the year he died, this piece, like many of his works, encouraged and supported colonization of the New World by the English.

Many good religious devout men have made it a great question, as a matter in conscience, by what warrant they might goe to possesse those Countries, which are none of theirs, but the poore Salvages. Which poore curiosity will answer it selfe; for God did make the world to be inhabited with mankind, and to have his name knowne to all Nations, and from generation to generation: as the people increased they dispersed themselves into such Countries as they found most convenient. And here in *Florida*, *Virginia*, *New-England*, and *Cannada*, is more land than all the people in Christendome can manure, and yet more to spare than all the natives of those Countries can use and culturate. And shall we here keepe such a coyle for land, and as such great rents and rates, when there is so much of the world uninhabited, and as much more in other places, and as good, or rather better than any wee possesse, were it manured and used accordingly. If this be not a reason sufficient to such tender consciences; for a copper kettle and a few toyes, as beads and hatchets, they will sell you a whole Countrey; and for a small matter, their houses and the ground they dwell upon; but those of the *Massachusets* have resigned theirs freely.

Now the reasons for plantations are many; *Adam* and *Eve* did first begin this innocent worke to plant the earth to remaine to posterity, but not without labour, trouble, and industry: *Noah* and his family began againe the second plantation, and their seed as it still increased, hath still planted new Countries, and one Country another, and so the world to that estate it is; but not without much hazard, travell, mortalities, discontents, and many disasters: had those worthy Fathers and their memorable off-spring not beene more diligent for us now in those ages, than wee are to plant that yet unplanted for after-livers. Had the seed of *Abraham*, our Saviour Christ Jesus and his Apostles, exposed themselves to no more dangers to plant the Gospell wee so much professe, than we, even we our selves had at this present beene as Salvages, and as miserable as the most barbarous Salvage, yet uncivilized. The *Hebrewes*, *Lacedemonians*, the *Goths*, *Grecians*, *Romans*, and the rest, what was it they would not undertake to inlarge their Territories, inrich their subjects, and resist their enemies. Those that were the founders of those great Monarchies and their vertues, were no silvered idle golden Pharisies, but industrious honest hearted Publicans, they regarded more provisions and necessaries for their people, than jewels, ease and delight for themselves; riches was their servants, not their masters; they ruled as fathers, not as tyrants; their people as children, not as slaves; there was no disaster could discourage them; and let none thinke they incoun- tered not with all manner of incumbrances, and what hath ever beene the worke of the best great Princes of the world, but planting of Countries, and civilizing barbarous and inhumane Nations to civility and humanity, whose eternall actions fils our histories with more honour than those that have wasted and consumed them by warres.

Lastly, the *Portugals* and *Spaniards* that first began plantations in this unknowne world of *America* till within this 140. yeares, whose everlasting actions before our eyes, will testifie our idlenesse and ingratitude to all posterity, and neglect of our duty and religion wee owe our God, our King, and Countrey, and want of charity to those poore Salvages, whose Countries we challenge, use, and possesse, except wee be but made to mar what our forefathers made, or but only tell what they did, or esteeme our selves too good to take the like paines where there is so much reason, liberty, and action offers it selfe, having as much power and meanes as others: why should English men despaire and not doe so much as any? Was it vertue in those Heros to provide that doth main- taine us, and basenesse in us to doe the like for others to come? Surely no; then seeing wee are not borne for our selves but each to helpe other, and our abilities are much alike at the howre of our birth and minute of our death: seeing our good deeds or bad, by faith in Christs merits, is all wee have to carry our soules to heaven or hell: Seeing hon- our is our lives ambition, and our ambition after death, to have an honourable memory of our life: and seeing by no meanes wee would be abated of the dignitie and glorie of our predecessors, let us imitate their vertues to be worthily their successors, or at least not hinder, if not further them that would and doe their utmost and best endevour.

DISCUSSION QUESTIONS

1   What features did the artist choose to highlight in his etching?

2   Why did Smith deem colonies necessary? How did Smith employ religion to promote colonization?

3   What, according to Smith, was the purpose of land and its acquisition? How does the image reinforce his view of the land?

1–5 | *Waniyetu Wowapi* (Nakota Winter Count), Lone Dog, first recorded 1800–1871

Lone Dog, a member of the Yanktonai Nakota community, was the last known keeper of the winter count included below. With pictorial symbols on a buffalo hide, this winter count provided mnemonic devices that recorded notable events from the winter of 1800 to 1871. The keeper, often a position that passed from father to son, painted a new pictograph each year. Symbols begin in the center and spiral counterclockwise outward.

DISCUSSION QUESTIONS

1   How does this piece challenge a definition of history that privileges written texts?

2   What types of images appear most frequently? What can that tell us about Nakota culture?

3   Why would the use of a single image be a useful way to capture the events of an entire year?

COLONIAL POLITICS AND SOCIETY

1-6 | Governor Glen on the role of Native Americans in the rivalry between France, Spain, and England, South Carolina, 1761

James Glen (1701-1777) was appointed Royal Governor of South Carolina in 1738 but arrived in the province in December 1743. Indian affairs were a key issue during his governorship. In Glen's view, the French were the primary enemy, and Glen worked, with mixed results, to unite all local tribes to tip the colonial balance of power in the English favor. His term as governor lasted until June 1756.

The people of most experience in the affairs of this country, have always dreaded a French war; from an apprehension that an Indian war would be the consequence of it; for which reasons, I have ever since the first breaking out of the war with France, redoubled my Attention to Indian affairs: and I hope, not without Success.

For notwithstanding all the intrigues of the French, they have not been able to get the least footing among our Nations of Indians; as very plainly appears by those Nations still continuing to give fresh proofs of their attachment to us: and I have had the happiness to bring over and fix the Friendship of the Chactaw Nation of Indians in the British Interest.

This powerful Engine, which the French for many years past, played against us and our Indians, even in times of Peace, is now happily turned against themselves, and I believe they feel the force of it.

For according to last accounts, which I have received from thence, by the Captain of a Sloop that touched at Mobile about two months ago, the Chactaw Indians had driven into the Town of Mobile all the French Planters who were settled either upon the river bearing the same name or in the Neighbouring Country, and there kept them in a manner besieged, so that a few of the French who ventured out of the Town to hunt up Cattle were immediately scalped.

Monsieur Vaudreuille the Governor of Louisiana was then in Mobile endeavoring to support his people, and trying to recover the friendship of those Indians. At the same time there were some head men with about Twenty of their People in Charles-Town.

I have been the fuller in my Relation of this matter, because I humbly conceive it to be a very delicate Affair, for these Chactaw Indians, have formerly and even so lately as I have been in this Province, at the instigation of the French and assisted and headed by them, in time of Peace, murdered our Traders in their Way to the Chickasaw Indians, and Robbed them of their goods: but I hope the French Governors will never have it in their power to charge us with such unfair Practises.

I shall be particularly cautious of doing any thing inconsistent with the peace so lately concluded: but I think it incumbent on me to say, that it will be impossible to retain those Indians, or any other, in his Majesty's interest unless we continue to trade with them.

And since war and hunting are the business of the lives, both Arms and Ammunition as well as Cloaths other necessaries, are the goods for which there is the greatest demand among them—I therefore hope to receive instructions in this particular, as a rule of my conduct.

There are a pretty many Indians among the Kays, about the cape of Florida, who might be easily secured to the British Interest: but as they have little communication with any others on the main Land, and have not any goods to trade for, they could not be of any advantage either in peace or war.

There are also a few Yamasees, about twenty men near St. Augustine: and these are all the Indians in this part of the world that are in the Interest of the Crown of Spain.

The French have the Friendship of some few of the Creek Indians, such as inhabit near the Holbama Fort: and some of the Chactaw Indians have not as yet declared against them: They have also some tribes upon Mississippi River, and Ouabash, and in other parts: but most of these and all other Indians whatsoever, inhabit above a Thousand miles from Charles-Town; and yet it may be proper to give attention even to what happens among those who are so far from us; for to an Indian, a thousand miles is as one mile their Provisions being in the Woods, and they are never out of the way: they are slow, saying the Sun will rise again to-morrow, but they are steddy.

We have little intercourse with the French; but unless there have been alterations lately, the Accounts I have formerly sent may be relied on, there are not above six hundred men (Soldiers) in what they call Louisiana, and those thinly spread over a widely extended Country: some at New Orleans some at Mobile, and some as far up as the Ilinois.

They had a Fort at the Mouth of the Mississippi river called the Balise, but they found it was not of any service, and therefore they have built another farther up, where it commands the passage: their Forts Holbama, Chactawhatche, Notche, Notchitosh, and another on Ouabash are all inconsiderable stockadoed Forts, garrisoned by 40 and some by only 20 men each. If ever the French settlements on the Missippi grow great, they may have pernicious effects upon South Carolina, because they produce the same sorts of Commodities as are produced there, viz: Rice and Indigo: but hitherto, the only Inconvenience that I know of, is, their attempting to withdraw our Indians from us, and attacking those who are most attached to our interest.

I beg Leave to assure you that I shall never do any thing inconsistent with that good faith which is the basis of all his Majesty's Measures, but it is easy for me at present to divert the French in their own way, and to find them business for double the number of men they have in that Country.

However, this, and even the Tranquility of South Carolina will depend upon preserving our Interest with the Indians, which it will be very difficult to do, unless the presents are continued to them, and those Forts built which I have formerly proposed, or at least, one of them, and that to be in the Country of the Cherokees. . . .

DISCUSSION QUESTIONS

1   What was Governor Glen's goal in relating to Native Americans, particularly the Chactaw? How did the governor think this goal could be best accomplished?

2   Why were alliances with Native Americans important to European colonial powers?

1–7a | John Nathan Hutchins, woodcut, *Prospect of the City of New-York* from *New York Almanac*, 1771

Hugh Gaine (1726–1807), an eighteenth-century American printer, bookseller, and newspaper publisher, began the *New-York Mercury* in 1752. Although a patriot early on, he supported accommodation with England between 1768 and 1774. After Lexington and Concord in April 1775, he supported the revolutionary effort fully, with the *Mercury* as an instrument of that cause. Below is a published image of a woodblock depicting the 1771 New York skyline. Note the diversity of religious meetinghouses in this emerging city of approximately 20,000.

SEE COLOR INSERT

1–7b | Andrew Burnaby, description of colonial Philadelphia, England, 1759

Andrew Burnaby (1732–1812), an English reverend and travel writer, published his celebrated travelogue, *Travels Through the Middle Settlements in North America, In the Years 1759 and 1760*, in 1775. It reached a second edition and was published in an expanded form in 1798. His work contains close observations but avoids discussions of political developments in the colonies. Here, Burnaby reflects on the development of the city of Philadelphia.

Philadelphia, if we consider that not eighty years ago the place where it now stands was a wild and uncultivated desert, inhabited by nothing but ravenous beasts, and a savage people, must certainly be the object of every one's wonder and admiration. It is situated upon a tongue of land, a few miles above the confluence of the Delaware and Schuylkill; and contains about 3,000 houses, and 18 or 20,000 inhabitants. It is built north and south upon the banks of the Delaware; and is nearly two miles in length, and three quarters of one in breadth. The streets are laid out with great regularity in parallel lines, intersected by others at right angles, and are handsomely built: on each side there is a pavement of broad stones for foot passengers; and in most of them a causeway in the middle for carriages. Upon dark nights it is well lighted, and watched by a patrol: there are many fair houses, and public edifices in it. The stadt-house is a large, handsome, though heavy building; in this are held the councils, the assemblies, and supreme courts; there are apartments in it also for the accommodation of Indian chiefs or sachems; likewise two libraries, one belonging to the province, the other to a society, which was incorporated about ten years ago, and consists of sixty members. Each member upon admission, subscribed forty shillings; and afterward annually ten. They can alienate their shares, by will or deed, to any person approved by the society. They have a small collection of medals and medallions, and a few other curiosities, such as the skin of a rattlesnake killed at Surinam twelve feet long; and several Northern Indian habits made of furs and skins. At a small distance from the stadt-house, there is another fine library, consisting of a very valuable and chosen collection of books, left by a Mr. Logan; they are chiefly in the learned languages. Near this there is also a noble hospital for lunatics, and other sick persons. Besides these buildings, there are spacious barracks for 17 or 1800 men; a good assembly-room belonging to the society of Free Masons; and eight or ten places of religious worship; viz. two churches, three Quaker meeting-houses, two Presbyterian ditto, one Lutheran church, one Dutch Calvinist ditto, one Swedish ditto, one Romish chapel, one Anabaptist meeting-house, one Moravian ditto: there is also an academy or college, originally built for a tabernacle for Mr. Whitefield. At the south end of the town, upon the river, there is a battery mounting thirty guns, but it is in a state of decay. It was designed to be a check upon privateers. These, with a few alms-houses, and a school-house belonging to the Quakers, are the chief public buildings in Philadelphia. The city is in a very flourishing state, and inhabited by merchants, artists, tradesmen, and persons of all occupations.

DISCUSSION QUESTIONS

1   Burnaby is from England. How does that influence what and how he describes colonial Philadelphia and its people?

2   Why might the religious diversity present in Philadelphia and New York be remarkable? What does this illustrate about differences between the colonies and imperial powers?

1–8a | Advertisement, Rolls's Best Virginia tobacco, England, 18th c.

Tobacco cultivation and processing dominated the economy of Virginia for more than three centuries. A strain of tobacco, introduced by John Rolfe (1585–1622), became very popular in Europe and competed well with other Spanish sources of the crop. Demanding of the soil and labor-intensive to produce, tobacco reshaped the colonial landscape and led the initial drive to import indentured servants and, in the second half of the seventeenth century, the commitment to using enslaved peoples from Africa as labor.

1–8b | Jasper Danckaerts, journal entry, Netherlands, 1679

Jasper Danckaerts (1609–1702/1704) founded a Protestant religious community in the Labanist movement of the seventeenth century. From this settlement, along the Bohemia River in present-day Maryland, Danckaerts traveled throughout the middle colonies, providing some of the earliest descriptions of life in the region. His diary was not published in English until 1867.

Maryland, 1679

As to the present government of Maryland, it remains firm upon the old footing, and is confined within the limits before mentioned. All of Maryland that we have seen, is high land, with few or no meadows, but possessing such a rich and fertile soil, as persons living there assured me that they had raised tobacco off the same piece of land for thirty consecutive years. The inhabitants, who are generally English, are mostly engaged in this production. It is their chief staple, and the money with which they must purchase every thing they require, which is brought to them from other English possessions in Europe, Africa and America. There is, nevertheless, sometimes a great want of these necessaries, owing to the tobacco market being low, or the shipments being prevented by some change of affairs in some quarter, particularly in Europe, or indeed to both causes, as was the case at this time, whereby there sometimes arises a great scarcity of such articles as are most necessary, as we saw when there. So large a quantity of tobacco is raised in Maryland and Virginia, that it is one of the greatest sources of revenue to the crown by reason of the taxes which it yields. Servants and negroes are chiefly employed in the culture of tobacco, who are brought from other places to be sold to the highest bidders, the servants for a term of years only, but the negroes forever, and may be sold by their masters to other planters as many times as their masters choose, that is, the servants until their term is fulfilled, and the negroes for life. These men, one with another, each make, after they are able to work, from 2,500 pounds to 3,000 pounds and even 3,500 pounds of tobacco a year, and some of the masters and their wives who pass their lives here in wretchedness, do the same. The servants and negroes after they have worn themselves down the whole day, and come home to rest, have yet to grind and pound the grain, which is generally maize, for their masters and all their families as well as themselves, and all the negroes, to eat. Tobacco is the only production in which the planters employ themselves, as if there were nothing else in the world to plant but that, and while the land is capable of yielding all the productions that can be raised anywhere, so far as the climate of the place allows.

DISCUSSION QUESTIONS

1   Describe several ways, according to Danckaerts, that tobacco functioned for a colonial plantation.

2   What are some characteristics of the colonial economy shown in the Rolls tobacco advertisement and Danckaerts' observations?

3   How do these sources illustrate the complexities of race and racial hierarchies in a colonial economy?

1–9a | Phillis Wheatley, poem, "On Being Brought from Africa to America," New England, 1773

Phillis Wheatley (ca. 1753–1784), the first African American woman to publish a book of poetry, arrived in the colonies in approximately 1760 after being sold into slavery in West Africa. Her owners, the Wheatley family of Boston, taught her to read and write and encouraged her poetry. Wheatley's *Poems on Various Subjects, Religious and Moral,* first published in 1773, received acclaim in the colonies and England. She was emancipated soon after the publication of her book.

'Twas mercy brought me from my *Pagan* land,
Taught my benighted soul to understand
That there's a God, that there's a *Savior* too:
Once I redemption neither sought nor knew.
Some view our sable race with scornful eye,
"Their color is a diabolic die."
Remember, *Christians*: *Negros*, black as *Cain,*
May be refin'd, and join th'angelic train.

1–9b | Ottobah Cugoano, excerpt from *Narrative of the Enslavement of Ottobah Cugoano, a Native of Africa; published by himself, in the Year 1787,* England, 1787

Ottobah Cugoano (1757–unknown) was, as a child, kidnapped by slave traders and placed on a slave ship bound for the West Indies. He endured the Middle Passage and then was sold to plantation owners in Grenada and worked in the Caribbean until his purchase by an English merchant in 1772, when he was set free and baptized "John Stuart." A leader in London's black community, he, with the aid of his friend Olaudah Equiano, published an account of his experiences in 1787, *Narrative of the Enslavement of Ottobah Cugoano, a Native of Africa.* This publication revealed the horrors of the international slave trade, a traffic that over a period of more than three hundred years displaced over 12 million souls from Africa to the New World. Approximately 400,000 of those arrivals came to North America.

I was early snatched away from my native country, with about eighteen or twenty more boys and girls, as we were playing in a field. We lived but a few days' journey from the coast where we were kidnapped, and as we were decoyed and drove along, we were soon conducted to a factory, and from thence, in the fashionable way of traffic, consigned to Grenada. Perhaps it may not be amiss to give a few remarks, as some account of myself, in this transposition of captivity.

I was born in the city of Agimaque, on the coast of Fantyn; my father was a companion to the chief in that part of the country of Fantee, and when the old king died I was left in his house with his family; soon after I was sent for by his nephew, Ambro Accasa, who succeeded the old king in the chiefdom of that part of Fantee, known by the name of Agimaque and Assince. I lived with his children, enjoying peace and tranquillity, about twenty moons, which, according to their way of reckoning time, is two years. I was sent for to visit an uncle, who lived at a considerable distance from Agimaque. The first day after we set out we arrived at Assinee, and the third day at my uncle's habitation, where I lived about three months, and was then thinking of returning to my father and young companion at Agimaque; but by this time I had got well acquainted with some of the children of my uncle's hundreds of relations, and we were some days too venturesome in going into the woods to gather fruit and catch birds, and such amusements as pleased us. One day I refused to go with the rest, being rather apprehensive that something might happen to us; till one of my playfellows said to me, "Because you belong to the great men, you are afraid to . . . venture your carcase, or else of the bounsam," which is the devil. This enraged me so much, that I set a resolution to join the rest, and we went into the woods, as usual but we had not been above two hours, before our troubles began, when several great ruffians came upon us suddenly, and said we had committed a fault against their lord, and we must go and answer for it ourselves before him.

Some of us attempted, in vain, to run away, but pistols and cutlasses were soon introduced, threatening, that if we offered to stir, we should all lie dead on the spot. One of them pretended to be more friendly than the rest, and said that he would speak to their lord to get us clear, and desired that we should follow him; we were then immediately divided into different parties, and drove after him. We were soon led out of the way which we knew, and towards evening, as we came in sight of a town, they told us that this great man of theirs lived there, but pretended it was too late to go and see him that night. Next morning there came three other men, whose language differed from ours, and spoke to some of those who watched us all the night; but he that pretended to be our friend with the great man, and some others, were gone away. We asked our keeper what these men had been saying to them, and they answered, that they had been asking them and us together to go and feast with them that day, and that we must put off seeing the great man till after, little thinking that our doom was so nigh, or that these villains meant to feast on us as their prey. We went with them again about half a day's journey, and came to a great multitude of people, having different music playing; and all the day after we got there, we were very merry with the music, dancing, and singing. Towards the evening, we were again persuaded that we could not get back to where the great man lived till next day; and when bed-time came, we were separated into different houses with different people. When the next morning came, I asked for the men that brought me there, and for the rest of my companions; and I was told that they were gone to the sea-side, to bring home some rum, guns, and powder, and that some of my companions were gone with them, and that some were gone to the fields to do something or other. This gave me strong suspicion that there was some treachery in the case, and I began to think that my hopes of returning home again were all over. I soon became very uneasy, not knowing what to do, and refused to eat or drink, for whole days together, till the man of the house told me that he would do all in his power to get me back to my uncle; then I eat a little fruit with him, and had some thoughts that I should be sought after, as I would be then missing at home about five or six days.

I inquired every day if the men had come back, and for the rest of my companions, but could get no answer of any satisfaction. I was kept about six days at this man's house, and in the evening there was another man came, and talked with him a good while and I heard the one say to the other he must go, and the other said, the sooner the better; that man came out and told me that he knew my relations at Agimaque, and that we must set out to-morrow morning, and he would convey me there. Accordingly we set out next day, and travelled till dark, when we came to a place where we had some supper and slept. He carried a large bag, with some gold dust, which he said he had to buy some goods at the sea-side to take with him to Agimaque. Next day we travelled on, and in the evening came to a town, where I saw several white people, which made me afraid that they would eat me, according to our notion, as children, in the inland parts of the country. This made me rest very uneasy all the night, and next morning I had some victuals brought, desiring me to eat and make haste, as my guide and kidnapper told me that he had to go to the castle with some company that were going there, as he had told me before, to get some goods. After I was ordered out, the horrors I soon saw and felt, cannot be well described; I saw many of my miserable countrymen chained two and two, some handcuffed, and some with their hands tied behind. We were conducted along by a guard, and when we arrived at the castle, I asked my guide what I was brought there for, he told me to learn the ways of the browfow, that is, the white-faced people. I saw him take a gun, a piece of cloth, and some lead for me, and then he told me that he must now leave me there, and went off. This made me cry bitterly, but I was soon conducted to a prison, for three days, where I heard the groans and cries of many, and saw some of my fellow-captives. But when a vessel arrived to conduct us away to the ship, it was a most horrible scene; there was nothing to be heard but the rattling of chains, smacking of whips, and the groans and cries of our fellow-men. Some would not stir from the ground, when they were lashed and beat in the most horrible manner. I have forgot the name of this infernal fort; but we were taken in the ship that came for us, to another that was ready to sail from Cape Coast. When we were put into the ship, we saw several black merchants coming on board, but we were all drove into our holes, and not suffered to speak to any of them. In this situation we continued several days in sight of our native land; but I could find no good person to give any information of my situation to Accasa at Agimaque. And when we found ourselves at last taken away, death was more preferable than life; and a plan was concerted amongst us, that we might burn and blow up the ship, and to perish all together in the flames: but we were betrayed by one of our own countrywomen, who slept with some of the headmen of the ship, for it was common for the dirty filthy sailors to take the African women and lie upon their bodies; but the men were chained and pent up in holes. It was the women and boys which were to burn the ship, with the approbation and groans of the rest; though that was prevented, the discovery was likewise a cruel bloody scene.

But it would be needless to give a description of all the horrible scenes which we saw, and the base treatment which we met with in this dreadful captive situation, as the similar cases of thousands, which suffer by this infernal traffic, are well known. Let it suffice to say that I was thus lost to my dear indulgent parents and relations, and they to me. All my help was cries and tears, and these could not avail, nor suffered long, till one succeeding woe and dread swelled up another. Brought from a state of innocence and freedom, and, in a barbarous and cruel manner, conveyed to a state of horror and slavery, this abandoned situation may be easier conceived than described. From the time that I was kidnapped, and conducted to a factory, and from thence in the brutish, base, but fashionable way of traffic, consigned to Grenada, the grievous thoughts which I then felt, still pant in my heart; though my fears and tears have long since subsided. And yet it is still grievous to think that thousands more have suffered in similar and greater distress, Under the hands of barbarous robbers, and merciless task-masters; and that many, even now, are suffering in all the extreme bitterness of grief and woe, that no language can describe. The cries of some, and the sight of their misery, may be seen and heard afar; but the deep-sounding groans of thousands, and the great sadness of their misery and woe, under the heavy load of oppressions and calamities inflicted upon them, are such as can only be distinctly known to the ears of Jehovah Sabaoth.

This Lord of Hosts, in his great providence, and in great mercy to me, made a way for my deliverance from Grenada. Being in this dreadful captivity and horrible slavery, without any hope of deliverance, for about eight or nine months, beholding the most dreadful scenes of misery and cruelty, and seeing my miserable companions often cruelly lashed, and, as it were, cut to pieces, for the most trifling faults; this made me often tremble and weep, but I escaped better than many of them. For eating a piece of sugar-cane, some were cruelly lashed, or struck over the face, to knock their teeth out. Some of the stouter ones, I suppose, often reproved, and grown hardened and stupid with many cruel beatings and lashings, or perhaps faint and pressed with hunger and hard labour, were often committing trespasses of this kind, and when detected, they met with exemplary punishment. Some told me they had their teeth pulled out, to deter others, and to prevent them from eating any cane in future. Thus seeing my miserable companions and countrymen in this pitiful, distressed, and horrible situation, with all the brutish baseness and barbarity attending it, could not but fill my little mind horror and indignation. But I must own, to the shame of my own countrymen, that I was first kidnapped and betrayed by some of my own complexion, who were the first cause of my exile, and slavery; but if there were no buyers there would be no sellers. So far as I can remember, some of the Africans in my country keep slaves, which they take in war, or for debt; but those which they keep are well fed, and good care taken of them, and treated well; and as to their clothing, they differ according to the custom of the country. But I may safely say, that all the poverty and misery that any of the inhabitants of Africa meet with among themselves, is far inferior to those inhospitable regions of misery which they meet with in the West-Indies, where their hard-hearted overseers have neither Regard to the laws of God, nor the life of their fellow-men.

Thanks be to God, I was delivered from Grenada, and that horrid brutal slavery. A gentleman coming to England took me for his servant, and brought me away, where I soon found my situation become more agreeable. After coming to England, and seeing others write and read, I had a strong desire to learn, and getting what assistance I could, I applied myself to learn reading and writing, which soon became my recreation, pleasure, and delight; and when my master perceived that I could write some, he sent me to a proper school for that purpose to learn. Since, I have endeavoured to improve my mind in reading, and have sought to get all the intelligence I could, in my situation of life, towards the state of my brethren and countrymen in complexion, and of the miserable situation of those who are barbarously sold into captivity, and unlawfully held in slavery

FINIS.

DISCUSSION QUESTIONS

1 How would each of these texts be useful in ongoing abolitionist movements?
2 Who first captured and enslaved Cugoano? Why is this information important to understanding the global slave trade?
3 How does faith play into both Wheatley's and Cugoano's reflections on their experiences?

1–10 | Natalia Alekseevna Shelikhova, excerpts from "Explanations of the Successes of the American Company," Russian America (Alaska), 1798

Natalia Alekseevna Shelikhova (1762–1810) was a Russian businessperson and entrepreneur. Born in Okhotsk, in 1775 she married seafarer, merchant, and fur trader Grigory Shelikhov. Together they founded the Shelikhov-Golikov Company in 1782. She handled much of the affairs of the company and its business relations, taking full control upon the death of her spouse in 1795. Officially, this controversial development led to a legal process that lasted several years; it was not until 1799 that a final deal with the Russian government secured her position and resulted in the creation of the Russian-American Company.

The late Shelikhov, my husband, on his visit to America with three ships in the years 1784, 1785, and 1786, having civilized the Alaska Natives, Kodiak and Afognak island-ers, and likewise various tribes on the American mainland from Kenai Bay or Cook River to fifty-seven degrees north latitude to Lituya Bay, made more than 120,000 souls Russian subjects, but only chose who themselves voluntarily desired this. Trade has been established with those peoples, and a fur-trading company founded. And all that has been grounded on firm and reliable rules.

Upon his return from there, Shelikhov instructed his company assistants to carry out the operations noted below. As a result, the following has been done:

1. The Alaska Peninsula has been well surveyed and a very short and con-venient passage has been found across it on the north side to Bristol Bay without going around the cape and through the dangerous strait between it and Unimak Island. The Alaska Natives have become better known and more subordinated.

2. In Kenai Bay, where there is a river bearing Cook's name, an outpost of Russian *promyshlenniki* has been set up for trading, who affably did favors for the inhabitants and carried on trade and every kind of communication with them.

3. An outpost has also been set up in Chugach Bay, and in 1794 three ships were built there from local timber as an experiment: one excellent frigate, the *Phoenix*, of twenty-four guns, and two smaller ships. . . . An acquaintance has been made with many Natives, and a connection has been established.

4. A small fortress was constructed at Cape St. Elias on Montague or Siukliu Island.

5. On Kodiak a school has been established in which American [Native] boys learn, in the Russian language, reading, writing, arithmetic, and navigation. Ten boys were sent to Irkutsk and instructed on various musical instruments, and sent back to Kodiak in 1793, to the delight of the local residents, who have a liking for gaieties.

6. Some exploration has been carried out on the mainland in Yakutat and Lituya bays, where the Natives are more primitive. There was little success in civilizing chem up to 1795, but the situation is not hopeless, for they engage in barter without fear.

    Lituya Bay is a little beyond fifty-five degrees north latitude, in the vicinity of the English settlement of Nootka, and should be the boundary of the Russian dominions in America.

7. In all these bays and in other places, copper plaques with the inscription "Land of the Russian Dominions" have been buried in the ground for political reasons.

8. Many of the subject Americans and islanders have been baptized without a priest, and many have adopted the way of life of the Russian people; and from distant places whole tribes have moved near to places where the Russian trading posts are located, defending these from attack by their own peoples, who have the hateful habit of robbing and killing each other over the smallest trifles.

9. When, therefore, the local inhabitants had begun to become adherents of the Russians and of our law, my husband in 1793 requested missionaries . . . sent . . . at the expense of the company. In the winter of I 794 and the spring of I 795, they baptized on Kodiak more than eight thousand souls and remarried a large number of the Americans, as well as marrying Russians to American women, and showed them how one should live peaceably and decently. A church has been built on Kodiak by the company . . .

10. My husband, when he himself was on Kodiak, made experiments in grow-
     ing local grains and vegetables with success; and when requesting mission-
     aries, he also requested twenty families of unfortunates to serve as agricul-
     turists, as well as ten for shipbuilding. . . .

     In 1795, these settlers were sent with a clerical mission from Kodiak to
     the mainland to search for a place, and news is now being awaited of where
     and how they have settled. In this settlement my husband ordered the con-
     struction of another church, a fortress, dwellings, storehouses, and every-
     thing necessary for a secure and pleasant life in the first instance, naming
     the village, and through it the whole country, "Slavorossiia."

11. He also established a settlement, agriculture, and a company outpost on the
     eighteenth Kurile Island, not far from Japan, so that in time a commercial
     connection can also be established with that country.

12. He set up a company with a special detachment consisting of two hundred
     men on the northern Aleutian "Zubov" [Pribilof] Islands for hunting sea
     lions and walrus, and established the headquarters of the company on Un-
     alaska Island.

     His intention in establishing this company was to claim with it all the
     Aleutians and the islands lying to the north toward Bering Strait, as well as
     the Asiatic Chukotsk lands and the American mainland lying opposite each
     other. . . .

14. For the better governance of all these enterprises, he founded a company
     office in Irkutsk in 1794 and, calculating the entire company capital in all
     properties and goods at around 1.5 million rubles. . . .

In the midst of all such enterprises, he died in 1795. I began to run those companies in
accordance with his will.

DISCUSSION QUESTIONS

1   What was the primary method of establishing the Russian presence in North
    America? Provide evidence from the source to support your statement.

2   How did the Russians demonstrate their claims upon this land?

3   Why, at this time, might Shelikhova be making a case for the successes of the
    company?

2

The United States in the Age of Revolution

360 | Rights of the Individual

Making Revolution

Responses to Revolution

RIGHTS OF THE INDIVIDUAL

One of the most striking developments of the modern era is the recognition and extension of individual rights by governments. These rights can take a variety of forms: civil, political, social, economic, and cultural rights are among those most commonly acknowledged and have roots in the premodern era. The concepts of individual civil rights emerging from the American and French Revolutions, for example, derived from Roman law, Christian theology, and English tradition. The Enlightenment influenced the revolutionaries' thinking about natural rights—rights held simply through existence—and the role of governments in protecting them, and the development of democracy has necessitated definitions of political rights and citizenship.

Declaration of the Rights of Man, France, 1789

Approved by the National Assembly of France, August 26, 1789

The representatives of the French people, organized as a National Assembly, believing that the ignorance, neglect, or contempt of the rights of man are the sole cause of public calamities and of the corruption of governments, have determined to set forth in a solemn declaration the natural, unalienable, and sacred rights of man, in order that this declaration, being constantly before all the members of the Social body, shall remind them continually of their rights and duties; in order that the acts of the legislative power, as well as those of the executive power, may be compared at any moment with the objects and purposes of all political institutions and may thus be more respected, and, lastly, in order that the grievances of the citizens, based hereafter upon simple and incontestable principles, shall tend to the maintenance of the constitution and redound to the happiness of all. Therefore the National Assembly recognizes and proclaims, in the presence and under the auspices of the Supreme Being, the following rights of man and of the citizen:

Articles:

1. Men are born and remain free and equal in rights. Social distinctions may be founded only upon the general good.

2. The aim of all political association is the preservation of the natural and imprescriptible rights of man. These rights are liberty, property, security, and resistance to oppression.

3. The principle of all sovereignty resides essentially in the nation. No body nor individual may exercise any authority which does not proceed directly from the nation.

4. Liberty consists in the freedom to do everything which injures no one else; hence the exercise of the natural rights of each man has no limits except those which assure to the other members of the society the enjoyment of the same rights. These limits can only be determined by law.

5. Law can only prohibit such actions as are hurtful to society. Nothing may be prevented which is not forbidden by law, and no one may be forced to do anything not provided for by law.

6. Law is the expression of the general will. Every citizen has a right to participate personally, or through his representative, in its foundation. It must be the same for all, whether it protects or punishes. All citizens, being equal in the eyes of the law, are equally eligible to all dignities and to all public positions and occupations, according to their abilities, and without distinction except that of their virtues and talents.

7. No person shall be accused, arrested, or imprisoned except in the cases and according to the forms prescribed by law. Any one soliciting, transmitting, executing, or causing to be executed, any arbitrary order, shall be punished. But any citizen summoned or arrested in virtue of the law shall submit without delay, as resistance constitutes an offense.

8. The law shall provide for such punishments only as are strictly and obviously necessary, and no one shall suffer punishment except it be legally inflicted in virtue of a law passed and promulgated before the commission of the offense.

9. As all persons are held innocent until they shall have been declared guilty, if arrest shall be deemed indispensable, all harshness not essential to the securing of the prisoner's person shall be severely repressed by law.

10. No one shall be disquieted on account of his opinions, including his religious views, provided their manifestation does not disturb the public order established by law.

11. The free communication of ideas and opinions is one of the most precious of the rights of man. Every citizen may, accordingly, speak, write, and print with freedom, but shall be responsible for such abuses of this freedom as shall be defined by law.

12. The security of the rights of man and of the citizen requires public military forces. These forces are, therefore, established for the good of all and not for the personal advantage of those to whom they shall be intrusted.

13. A common contribution is essential for the maintenance of the public forces and for the cost of administration. This should be equitably distributed among all the citizens in proportion to their means.

14. All the citizens have a right to decide, either personally or by their representatives, as to the necessity of the public contribution; to grant this freely; to know to what uses it is put; and to fix the proportion, the mode of assessment and of collection and the duration of the taxes.

15. Society has the right to require of every public agent an account of his administration.

16. A society in which the observance of the law is not assured, nor the separation of powers defined, has no constitution at all.

17. Since property is an inviolable and sacred right, no one shall be deprived thereof except where public necessity, legally determined, shall clearly demand it, and then only on condition that the owner shall have been previously and equitably indemnified.

Bill of Rights, United States, 1791

Congress of the United States begun and held at the City of New-York, on Wednesday the fourth of March, one thousand seven hundred and eighty nine.

THE Conventions of a number of the States, having at the time of their adopting the Constitution, expressed a desire, in order to prevent misconstruction or abuse of its powers, that further declaratory and restrictive clauses should be added: And as extending the ground of public confidence in the Government, will best ensure the beneficent ends of its institution.

RESOLVED by the Senate and House of Representatives of the United States of America, in Congress assembled, two thirds of both Houses concurring, that the following Articles be proposed to the Legislatures of the several States, as amendments to the Constitution of the United States, all, or any of which Articles, when ratified by three fourths of the said Legislatures, to be valid to all intents and purposes, as part of the said Constitution; viz.

ARTICLES in addition to, and Amendment of the Constitution of the United States of America, proposed by Congress, and ratified by the Legislatures of the several States, pursuant to the fifth Article of the original Constitution.

Article the first . . . After the first enumeration required by the first article of the Constitution, there shall be one Representative for every thirty thousand, until the number shall amount to one hundred, after which the proportion shall be so regulated by Congress, that there shall be not less than one hundred Representatives, nor less than one Representative for every forty thousand persons, until the number of Representatives shall amount to two hundred; after which the proportion shall be so regulated by Congress, that there shall not be less than two hundred Representatives, nor more than one Representative for every fifty thousand persons.

Article the second . . . No law, varying the compensation for the services of the Senators and Representatives, shall take effect, until an election of Representatives shall have intervened.

Article the third . . . Congress shall make no law respecting an establishment of religion, or prohibiting the free exercise thereof; or abridging the freedom of speech, or of the press; or the right of the people peaceably to assemble, and to petition the Government for a redress of grievances.

Article the fourth . . . A well regulated Militia, being necessary to the security of a free State, the right of the people to keep and bear Arms, shall not be infringed.

Article the fifth . . . No Soldier shall, in time of peace be quartered in any house, without the consent of the Owner, nor in time of war, but in a manner to be prescribed by law.

Article the sixth . . . The right of the people to be secure in their persons, houses, papers, and effects, against unreasonable searches and seizures, shall not be violated, and no Warrants shall issue, but upon probable cause, supported by Oath or affirmation, and particularly describing the place to be searched, and the persons or things to be seized.

Article the seventh . . . No person shall be held to answer for a capital, or otherwise infamous crime, unless on a presentment or indictment of a Grand Jury, except in cases arising in the land or naval forces, or in the Militia, when in actual service in time of War or public danger; nor shall any person be subject for the same offence to be twice put in jeopardy of life or limb; nor shall be compelled in any criminal case to be a witness against himself, nor be deprived of life, liberty, or property, without due process of law; nor shall private property be taken for public use, without just compensation.

Article the eighth . . . In all criminal prosecutions, the accused shall enjoy the right to a speedy and public trial, by an impartial jury of the State and district wherein the crime shall have been committed, which district shall have been previously ascertained by law, and to be informed of the nature and cause of the accusation; to be confronted with the witnesses against him; to have compulsory process for obtaining witnesses in his favor, and to have the Assistance of Counsel for his defence.

Article the ninth . . . In Suits at common law, where the value in controversy shall exceed twenty dollars, the right of trial by jury shall be preserved, and no fact tried by a jury, shall be otherwise re-examined in any Court of the United States, than according to the rules of the common law.

Article the tenth . . . Excessive bail shall not be required, nor excessive fines imposed, nor cruel and unusual punishments inflicted.

Article the eleventh . . . The enumeration in the Constitution, of certain rights, shall not be construed to deny or disparage others retained by the people.

Article the twelfth . . . The powers not delegated to the United States by the Constitution, nor prohibited by it to the States, are reserved to the States respectively, or to the people.

ATTEST,

Frederick Augustus Muhlenberg, Speaker of the House of Representatives
John Adams, Vice-President of the United States, and President of the Senate
John Beckley, Clerk of the House of Representatives.
Sam. A Otis, Secretary of the Senate

Declaration of the Rights of Woman, Marie-Olympe de Gouges, France, 1791

Man, are you capable of being just? It is a woman who asks you the question; you will, at least, not deprive her of that right. Tell me—what gave you the supreme control to oppress my sex? Your strength? Your talents? Observe the Creator in His wisdom; roam through nature in all her grandeur, to which you seem to want to grow closer, and give me, if you dare, an example of this tyrannical rule.

Only Man has carved a principle out of this exception. Peculiar, blind, swollen with science and degenerated, in this century of understanding and wisdom, into the most crass ignorance, he wants to rule like a despot over a sex that has full intellectual capacity; he claims to enjoy the Revolution, and demands his rights, and says no more.

Declaration of the Rights of Woman and of the Female Citizen

To be decreed by the National Assembly in its final sessions or in that of the next legislature.

Preamble. Mothers, daughters, sisters, representatives of the nation, ask to be incorporated into a national assembly. Judging that ignorance, oblivion or contempt for the rights of women are the sole causes of public misfortune and the corruption of governments, [women] have resolved to set out in a solemn declaration the natural rights, inalienable and sacred, of woman, so that this declaration, constantly set before all members of the social body, will perpetually remind them of their rights and their duties, in order that women's legislative instruments and men's, being able to be compared at any given moment with the aim of any political institution, may be more respected, so that the demands of citizens, henceforth based on simple and indisputable principles, will always turn toward the maintenance of the Constitution, good morals, and the happiness of all.

Consequently, the sex higher in both beauty and courage, in maternal hardship, recognizes and declares, in the presence and under the auspices of the Supreme Being, the following Rights of Woman and of the Female Citizen.

The first article. Woman is born free and remains equal to man in rights. Social distinctions may not be founded on anything other than the common good.

Article 2. The aim of any political association is the conservation of the natural and indissoluble rights of Woman and Man. These rights are freedom, property, security, and above all resistance to oppression.

Article 3. The principle of all sovereignty essentially resides in the Nation, which is nothing but the union of Woman and Man: no body, no individual, can exercise authority that does not expressly emanate from it.

Article 4. Liberty and justice consist in returning everything that belongs to others; thus the exercise of the natural rights of woman has no limits other than the perpetual tyranny with which man opposes her; these limits must be redrawn by the laws of nature and reason.

Article 5. The laws of nature and reason forbid all actions harmful to society; everything that is not forbidden by these laws, wise and divine, cannot be prevented, and no one can be forced to do what these laws do not command.

Article 6. The law must be an expression of the general will; all female citizens and male citizens must participate, personally or via their representatives, in its crafting; it must be the same for everyone: all female citizens and male citizens, being equal in its eyes, must be equally eligible for all honors, positions and public employment, according to their abilities, and without other distinctions than those of their virtues and their talents.

Article 7. No woman is an exception; she is accused, arrested, and detained in cases determined by law: women obey this strict law just as men do.

Article 8. The Law must establish only those penalties that are strictly and obviously necessary, and no one can be punished except in accordance with a Law established and promulgated prior to the offense and legally applied to women.

Article 9. Any woman who is declared guilty is subject to the full rigor of the law.

Article 10. No one should be bothered over his or her fundamental opinions. Woman has the right to mount the scaffold; she must have equally the right to mount the platform, as long as her protests do not disrupt public order as established by law.

Article 11. The free communication of thoughts and opinions is among the most precious of a woman's rights, as this freedom assures children's legitimacy in the eyes of their fathers. Any female citizen may thus say freely, "I am the mother of a child who belongs to you," without barbaric prejudice forcing her to hide the truth; except to answer for the abuse of this freedom in cases determined by the Law.

Article 12. The guarantee of women's and female citizens' rights involves a great benefit; this guarantee must be instituted for the advantage of all, and not for the particular benefit of those to whom it is entrusted.

Article 13. For the maintenance of law enforcement, and for administrative expenses, the contributions of women and men are equal; she participates in all chores, in all difficult tasks; she must thus have the same share in the distribution of positions, jobs, offices, honors and industry.

Article 14. Female citizens and male citizens have the right to verify, on their own or through their representatives, the need for public funds. Female citizens cannot participate in this unless they are granted an equal share not only of wealth, but also of public administration, and in the determination of the portion, basis, collection, and duration of the tax.

Article 15. The general populace of women, united to that of men in terms of taxation, has the right to demand from any public official an account of his administration.

Article 16. Any society in which the security of rights is not assured, nor the separation of powers determined, has no constitution; the constitution is void if the majority of individuals who compose the Nation have not collaborated in its drafting.

Article 17. Property belongs to both sexes, united or separated: it is for each an inviolable and sacred right; no one can be deprived of it as a true patrimony of nature, unless legally certified public need clearly dictates it, and on the condition of just compensation beforehand.

Postscript

Woman, wake up; the alarm bell of reason is making itself heard throughout the universe; recognize your rights. The mighty empire of nature is no longer surrounded by prejudice, fanaticism, superstition and lies. The torch of truth has dissipated all the clouds of foolishness and usurpation. The male slave has multiplied his strength, [but] has needed to seek yours to break his chains. Having become free, he became unjust toward his companion. O women! Women, when will you cease to be blind? What benefits have you reaped in the revolution? A more marked contempt, a more pronounced disdain. Over the centuries of corruption you have ruled over no more than men's weakness. Your empire is destroyed; what is left to you? The belief in men's injustice. The demand for your inheritance, based on the wise decrees of nature; what would you have to fear from such a beautiful undertaking? . . .

Whatever barriers confront you, it is in your power to liberate yourselves from them. You have only to want to do so.

Universal Declaration of Human Rights, United Nations, 1948

Preamble

Whereas recognition of the inherent dignity and of the equal and inalienable rights of all members of the human family is the foundation of freedom, justice and peace in the world,

Whereas disregard and contempt for human rights have resulted in barbarous acts which have outraged the conscience of mankind, and the advent of a world in which human beings shall enjoy freedom of speech and belief and freedom from fear and want has been proclaimed as the highest aspiration of the common people,

Whereas it is essential, if man is not to be compelled to have recourse, as a last resort, to rebellion against tyranny and oppression, that human rights should be protected by the rule of law,

Whereas it is essential to promote the development of friendly relations between nations,

Whereas the peoples of the United Nations have in the Charter reaffirmed their faith in fundamental human rights, in the dignity and worth of the human person and in the equal rights of men and women and have determined to promote social progress and better standards of life in larger freedom,

Whereas Member States have pledged themselves to achieve, in cooperation with the United Nations, the promotion of universal respect for and observance of human rights and fundamental freedoms,

Whereas a common understanding of these rights and freedoms is of the greatest importance for the full realization of this pledge,

Now, therefore,

The General Assembly,

Proclaims this Universal Declaration of Human Rights as a common standard of achievement for all peoples and all nations, to the end that every individual and every organ of society, keeping this Declaration constantly in mind, shall strive by teaching and education to promote respect for these rights and freedoms and by progressive measures, national and international, to secure their universal and effective recognition and observance, both among the peoples of Member States themselves and among the peoples of territories under their jurisdiction.

Article 1

All human beings are born free and equal in dignity and rights. They are endowed with reason and conscience and should act towards one another in a spirit of brotherhood.

Article 2

Everyone is entitled to all the rights and freedoms set forth in this Declaration, without distinction of any kind, such as race, colour, sex, language, religion, political or other opinion, national or social origin, property, birth or other status. Furthermore, no distinction shall be made on the basis of the political, jurisdictional or international status of the country or territory to which a person belongs, whether it be independent, trust, non-self-governing or under any other limitation of sovereignty.

Article 3

Everyone has the right to life, liberty and security of person.

Article 4

No one shall be held in slavery or servitude; slavery and the slave trade shall be prohibited in all their forms.

Article 5

No one shall be subjected to torture or to cruel, inhuman or degrading treatment or punishment.

Article 6

Everyone has the right to recognition everywhere as a person before the law.

Article 7

All are equal before the law and are entitled without any discrimination to equal protection of the law. All are entitled to equal protection against any discrimination in violation of this Declaration and against any incitement to such discrimination.

Article 8

Everyone has the right to an effective remedy by the competent national tribunals for acts violating the fundamental rights granted him by the constitution or by law.

Article 9

No one shall be subjected to arbitrary arrest, detention or exile.

Article 10

Everyone is entitled in full equality to a fair and public hearing by an independent and impartial tribunal, in the determination of his rights and obligations and of any criminal charge against him.

Article 11

1. Everyone charged with a penal offence has the right to be presumed innocent until proved guilty according to law in a public trial at which he has had all the guarantees necessary for his defence.

2. No one shall be held guilty of any penal offence on account of any act or omission which did not constitute a penal offence, under national or international law, at the time when it was committed. Nor shall a heavier penalty be imposed than the one that was applicable at the time the penal offence was committed.

Article 12

No one shall be subjected to arbitrary interference with his privacy, family, home or correspondence, nor to attacks upon his honour and reputation. Everyone has the right to the protection of the law against such interference or attacks.

Article 13

1. Everyone has the right to freedom of movement and residence within the borders of each State.

2. Everyone has the right to leave any country, including his own, and to return to his country.

Article 14

1. Everyone has the right to seek and to enjoy in other countries asylum from persecution.

2. This right may not be invoked in the case of prosecutions genuinely arising from non-political crimes or from acts contrary to the purposes and principles of the United Nations.

Article 15

1. Everyone has the right to a nationality.

2. No one shall be arbitrarily deprived of his nationality nor denied the right to change his nationality.

Article 16

1. Men and women of full age, without any limitation due to race, nationality or religion, have the right to marry and to found a family. They are entitled to equal rights as to marriage, during marriage and at its dissolution.

2. Marriage shall be entered into only with the free and full consent of the intending spouses.

3. The family is the natural and fundamental group unit of society and is entitled to protection by society and the State.

Article 17

1. Everyone has the right to own property alone as well as in association with others.

2. No one shall be arbitrarily deprived of his property.

Article 18

Everyone has the right to freedom of thought, conscience and religion; this right includes freedom to change his religion or belief, and freedom, either alone or in community with others and in public or private, to manifest his religion or belief in teaching, practice, worship and observance.

Article 19

Everyone has the right to freedom of opinion and expression; this right includes freedom to hold opinions without interference and to seek, receive and impart information and ideas through any media and regardless of frontiers.

Article 20

1. Everyone has the right to freedom of peaceful assembly and association.

2. No one may be compelled to belong to an association.

Article 21

1. Everyone has the right to take part in the government of his country, directly or through freely chosen representatives.

2. Everyone has the right to equal access to public service in his country.

3. The will of the people shall be the basis of the authority of government; this will shall be expressed in periodic and genuine elections which shall be by universal and equal suffrage and shall be held by secret vote or by equivalent free voting procedures.

Article 22

Everyone, as a member of society, has the right to social security and is entitled to realization, through national effort and international co-operation and in accordance with the organization and resources of each State, of the economic, social and cultural rights indispensable for his dignity and the free development of his personality.

Article 23

1. Everyone has the right to work, to free choice of employment, to just and favourable conditions of work and to protection against unemployment.

2. Everyone, without any discrimination, has the right to equal pay for equal work.

3. Everyone who works has the right to just and favourable remuneration ensuring for himself and his family an existence worthy of human dignity, and supplemented, if necessary, by other means of social protection.

4. Everyone has the right to form and to join trade unions for the protection of his interests.

Article 24

Everyone has the right to rest and leisure, including reasonable limitation of working hours and periodic holidays with pay.

Article 25

1. Everyone has the right to a standard of living adequate for the health and well-being of himself and of his family, including food, clothing, housing and medical care and necessary social services, and the right to security in the event of unemployment, sickness, disability, widowhood, old age or other lack of livelihood in circumstances beyond his control.

2. Motherhood and childhood are entitled to special care and assistance. All children, whether born in or out of wedlock, shall enjoy the same social protection.

Article 26

1. Everyone has the right to education. Education shall be free, at least in the elementary and fundamental stages. Elementary education shall be compulsory. Technical and professional education shall be made generally available and higher education shall be equally accessible to all on the basis of merit.

2. Education shall be directed to the full development of the human personality and to the strengthening of respect for human rights and fundamental freedoms. It shall promote understanding, tolerance and friendship among all nations, racial or religious groups, and shall further the activities of the United Nations for the maintenance of peace.

3. Parents have a prior right to choose the kind of education that shall be given to their children.

Article 27

Everyone has the right freely to participate in the cultural life of the community, to enjoy the arts and to share in scientific advancement and its benefits.

1. Everyone has the right to the protection of the moral and material interests resulting from any scientific, literary or artistic production of which he is the author.

Article 28

Everyone is entitled to a social and international order in which the rights and freedoms set forth in this Declaration can be fully realized.

Article 29

1. Everyone has duties to the community in which alone the free and full development of his personality is possible.

2. In the exercise of his rights and freedoms, everyone shall be subject only to such limitations as are determined by law solely for the purpose of securing due recognition and respect for the rights and freedoms of others and of meeting the just requirements of morality, public order and the general welfare in a democratic society.

3. These rights and freedoms may in no case be exercised contrary to the purposes and principles of the United Nations.

Article 30

Nothing in this Declaration may be interpreted as implying for any State, group or person any right to engage in any activity or to perform any act aimed at the destruction of any of the rights and freedoms set forth herein.

360 DISCUSSION QUESTIONS

1   Who qualified (or qualifies) for guaranteed rights in these sources? Why?

2   How are the rights enumerated in the sources here tied to historical events? How important is context in understanding justifications for and types of rights described in each source?

3   How have the rights of the individual evolved over time?

MAKING REVOLUTION

2–1a | John Locke, excerpt from *Two Treatises of Government*, England, 1690

John Locke (1632–1704), English philosopher and leading thinker of the Enlightenment, is considered the father of modern liberalism. His work influenced Voltaire and Jean-Jacques Rousseau and inspired American revolutionaries, and is even reflected in the United States Declaration of Independence. His major work, *Two Treatises of Government*, published in 1689, offered a strong argument against absolute monarchy and for individual consent of the governed. His work on natural rights and government were revolutionary for the period.

The Preface

Reader.

Thou hast here the beginning and end of a discourse concerning government; what fate has otherwise disposed of the papers that should have filled up the middle, and were more than all the rest, it is not worth while to tell thee. These which remain I hope are sufficient to establish the throne of our great restorer, our present king William; to make good his title in else consent of the people; which being the only one of all lawful governments, he has more fully and clearly than any prince in Christendom; and to justify to the world the people of England, whose love of their just and natural rights, with their resolution to preserve them, saved the nation when it war on the very brink of slavery and ruin.

Chapter II. Of the State of Nature

4. To understand political power aright, and derive it from its original, we must consider what estate all men are naturally in, and that is, a state of perfect freedom to order their actions, and dispose of their possessions and persons as they think fit, within the bounds of the law of Nature, without asking leave or depending upon the will of any other man.

A state also of equality, wherein all the power and jurisdiction is reciprocal, no one having more than another, there being nothing more evident than that creatures of the same species and rank, promiscuously born to all the same advantages of Nature, and the use of the same faculties, should also be equal one amongst another, without subordination or subjection, unless the lord and master of them all should, by any manifest declaration of his will, set one above another, and confer on him, by an evident and clear appointment, an undoubted right to dominion and sovereignty.

. . .

6. But though this be a state of liberty, yet it is not a state of license; though man in that state have an uncontrollable liberty to dispose of his person or possessions, yet he has not liberty to destroy himself, or so much as any creature in his possession, but where some nobler use than its bare preservation calls for it. The state of Nature has a law of Nature to govern it, which obliges every one, and reason, which is that law, teaches all mankind who will but consult it, that being all equal and independent, no one ought to harm another in his life, health, liberty or possessions; for men being all the workmanship of one omnipotent and infinitely wise Maker; all the servants of one sovereign Master, sent into the world by His order and about His business; they are His property, whose workmanship they are made to last during His, not one another's pleasure. And, being furnished with like faculties, sharing all in one community of Nature, there cannot be supposed any such subordination among us that may authorise us to destroy one another, as if we were made for one another's uses, as the inferior ranks of creatures are for ours. Every one as he is bound to preserve himself, and not to quit his station wilfully, so by the like reason, when his own preservation comes not in competition, ought he as much as he can to preserve the rest of mankind, and not unless it be to do justice on an offender, take away or impair the life, or what tends to the preservation of the life, the liberty, health, limb, or goods of another.

7. And that all men may be restrained from invading others' rights, and from doing hurt to one another, and the law of Nature be observed, which willeth the peace and preservation of all mankind, the execution of the law of Nature is in that state put into every man's hands, whereby every one has a right to punish the transgressors of that law to such a degree as may hinder its violation. For the law of Nature would, as all other laws that concern men in this world, be in vain if there were nobody that in the

state of Nature had a power to execute that law, and thereby preserve the innocent and restrain offenders; and if any one in the state of Nature may punish another for any evil he has done, every one may do so. For in that state of perfect equality, where naturally there is no superiority or jurisdiction of one over another, what any may do in prosecution of that law, every one must needs have a right to do.

8. And thus, in the state of Nature, one man comes by a power over another, but yet no absolute or arbitrary power to use a criminal, when he has got him in his hands, according to the passionate heats or boundless extravagancy of his own will, but only to retribute to him so far as calm reason and conscience dictate, what is proportionate to his transgression, which is so much as may serve for reparation and restraint. For these two are the only reasons why one man may lawfully do harm to another, which is that we call punishment. In transgressing the law of Nature, the offender declares himself to live by another rule than that of reason and common equity, which is that measure God has set to the actions of men for their mutual security, and so he becomes dangerous to mankind; the tie which is to secure them from injury and violence being slighted and broken by him, which being a trespass against the whole species, and the peace and safety of it, provided for by the law of Nature, every man upon this score, by the right he hath to preserve mankind in general, may restrain, or where it is necessary, destroy things noxious to them, and so may bring such evil on any one who hath transgressed that law, as may make him repent the doing of it, and thereby deter him, and, by his example, others from doing the like mischief. And in this case, and upon this ground, every man hath a right to punish the offender, and be executioner of the law of Nature.

. . .

27. He that is nourished by the acorns he picked up under an oak, or the apples he gathered from the trees in the wood, has certainly appropriated them to himself. Nobody can deny but the nourishment is his. I ask, then, when did they begin to be his? when he digested? or when he ate? or when he boiled? or when he brought them home? or when he picked them up? And it is plain, if the first gathering made them not his, nothing else could. That labour put a distinction between them and common. That added something to them more than Nature, the common mother of all, had done, and so they became his private right. And will any one say he had no right to those acorns or apples he thus appropriated because he had not the consent of all mankind to make them his? Was it a robbery thus to assume to himself what belonged to all in common? If such a consent as that was necessary, man had starved, notwithstanding the plenty God had given him. We see in commons, which remain so by compact, that it is the taking any part of what is common, and removing it out of the state Nature leaves it in, which begins the property, without which the common is of no use. And the taking of this or that part does not depend on the express consent of all the commoners. Thus, the grass my horse has bit, the turfs my servant has cut, and the ore I have digged in any place, where I have a right to them in common with others, become my property without the assignation or consent of anybody. The labour that was mine, removing them out of that common state they were in, hath fixed my property in them.

28. By making an explicit consent of every commoner necessary to any one's appropriating to himself any part of what is given in common. Children or servants could not cut the meat which their father or master had provided for them in common with-

out assigning to every one his peculiar part. Though the water running in the fountain be every one's, yet who can doubt but that in the pitcher is his only who drew it out? His labour hath taken it out of the hands of Nature where it was common, and belonged equally to all her children, and hath thereby appropriated it to himself.

. . .

31. But the chief matter of property being now not the fruits of the earth and the beasts that subsist on it, but the earth itself, as that which takes in and carries with it all the rest, I think it is plain that property in that too is acquired as the former. As much land as a man tills, plants, improves, cultivates, and can use the product of, so much is his property. He by his labour does, as it were, enclose it from the common. Nor will it invalidate his right to say everybody else has an equal title to it, and therefore he cannot appropriate, he cannot enclose, without the consent of all his fellow-commoners, all mankind. God, when He gave the world in common to all mankind, commanded man also to labour, and the penury of his condition required it of him. God and his reason commanded him to subdue the earth—i.e., improve it for the benefit of life and therein lay out something upon it that was his own, his labour. He that, in obedience to this command of God, subdued, tilled, and sowed any part of it, thereby annexed to it something that was his property, which another had no title to, nor could without injury take from him.

. . .

50. But since gold and silver, being little useful to the life of man, in proportion to food, raiment, and carriage, has its value only from the consent of men—whereof labour yet makes in great part the measure—it is plain that men have agreed to a disproportionate and unequal possession of the earth—I mean out of the bounds of society and compact; for in governments the laws regulate it; they having, by consent, found out and agreed in a way how a man may, rightfully and without injury, possess more than he himself can make use of by receiving gold and silver, which may continue long in a man's possession without decaying for the overplus, and agreeing those metals should have a value.

2–1b | Jean-Jacques Rousseau, excerpt from *On the Social Contract*, France, 1762

Jean-Jacques Rousseau (1712–1778) was a Genevan philosopher and composer who was a highly influential thinker of the eighteenth-century Enlightenment in Europe. In his seminal publication, *The Social Contract,* he laid out an argument that based legitimate political order on a framework of classical republicanism, which included concepts such as civil society, civic virtue, and mixed government. Through surrendering inherent natural rights, individuals can form a social contract where the general will of the people rules as sovereign. His political philosophies affected the American and French Revolutions and shaped thinking on the central foundations of democratic government.

I suppose man arrived at a point where obstacles, which prejudice his preservation in the state of nature, outweigh, by their resistance, the force which each individual can employ to maintain himself in this condition. Then the primitive state can no longer exist; and mankind would perish did it not change its way of life.

Now, as men cannot engender new forces, but can only unite and direct those which exist, they have no other means of preservation than to form by aggregation a sum of forces which could prevail against resistance, and to put them in play by a single motive and make them act in concert.

This sum of forces can be established only by the concurrence of many; but the strength and liberty of each man being the primary instruments of his preservation, how can he pledge them without injury to himself and without neglecting the care which he owes to himself? This difficulty as related to my subject may be stated as follows:

"To find a form of association which shall defend and protect with the public force the person and property of each associate, and by means of which each, uniting with all, shall obey however only himself, and remain as free as before." Such is the fundamental problem of which the *Social Contract* gives the solution.

The clauses of this contract are so determined by the nature of the act that the least modification would render them vain and of no effect; so that, although they may, perhaps, never have been formally enunciated, they are everywhere the same, everywhere tacitly admitted and recognized until, the social compact being violated, each enters again into his first rights and resumes his natural liberty,—thereby losing the conventional liberty for which he renounced it.

These clauses, clearly understood, may be reduced to one: that is, the total alienation of each associate with all his rights to the entire community,—for, first, each giving himself entirely, the condition is the same for all; and the conditions being the same for all, no one has an interest in making it onerous for the others.

Further, the alienation being without reserve, the union is as complete as it can be, and no associate has anything to claim: for, if some rights remained to individuals, as there would be no common superior who could decide between them and the public, each, being in some point his own judge, would soon profess to be so in everything; the state of nature would subsist, and the association would necessarily become tyrannical and useless.

Finally, each giving himself to all, gives himself to none; and as there is not an associate over whom he does not acquire the same right as is ceded, an equivalent is gained for all that is lost, and more force to keep what he has.

If, then, we remove from the social contract all that is not of its essence, it will be reduced to the following terms: "Each of us gives in common his person and all his force under the supreme direction of the general will; and we receive each member as an indivisible part of the whole."

Immediately, instead of the individual person of each contracting party, this act of association produces a moral and collective body, composed of as many members as the assembly has votes, which receives from this same act its unity,—its common being, its life and its will. This public personage, thus formed by the union of all the others, formerly took the name of city, and now takes that of republic or body politic. This is called the *state* by its members when it is passive; the *sovereign* when it is active; and a *power* when comparing it to its equals. With regard to the associates, they take collectively the name of *people*, and call themselves individually *citizens*, as participating in sovereign authority, and *subjects*, as submitted to the laws of the state. But these terms are often confounded and are taken one for another. It is enough to know how to distinguish them when they are employed with all precision.

DISCUSSION QUESTIONS

1   How does Locke define freedom (equality) and the limits placed upon it by Nature?
2   What does Rousseau envision as the relationship between the individual and the collective?
3   How does the concept of the "common" function for each writer?

2–2 | Jonathan Mayhew, excerpt from "A Discourse Concerning Unlimited Submission and Non-Resistance to the Higher Powers," Massachusetts, 1750

Jonathan Mayhew (1720–1766) was a well-known congregational minister at the Old West Church in Boston, Massachusetts. Mayhew openly opposed the Stamp Act and encouraged a colonial union to secure liberty for the colonies. Mayhew delivered this sermon, a "Discourse Concerning Unlimited Submission," on the one hundredth anniversary of the execution of Charles I. He argued that monarchs rule through the voluntary consent of the people and should be opposed when liberties are infringed. Many argued Mayhew offered one of the first intellectual and spiritual justifications for rebellion.

The hereditary, indefeasible, divine right of kings, and the doctrine of non-resistance, which is built upon the supposition of such a right, are altogether as fabulous and chimerical, as transubstantiation; or any of the most absurd reveries of ancient or modern vissionaries. These notions are fetched neither from divine revelation, nor human reason; and if they are derived from neither of those sources, it is not much matter from *whence they come, or whither they go*. Only it is a pity that such doctrines should be propagated in society, to raise factions and rebellions, as we see they have, in fact, been both in the *last*, and in the *present* REIGN.

. . .

THE next question which naturally arises, is, whether this resistance which was made to the king *by the Parliament*, was properly *rebellion*, or not? The answer to which is plain, that it was not; but a most righteous and glorious stand, made in defense of the natural and legal rights of the people, against the unnatural and illegal encroachments of arbitrary power. Nor was this a rash and too sudden opposition: The nation had been patient under the oppressions of the crown, even to *long suffering*;—for a course of many years; and there was no rational hope of redress in any other way.—Resistance was absolutely necessary, in order to preserve the nation from slavery, misery and ruin. And who so proper to make this resistance, as the Lords and Commons;—the whole representative body of the people;—guardians of the public welfare; and each of which, was, in point of legislation, vested with an equal, co-ordinate power, with that of the crown? Here were *two* branches of the legislature against *one*;—two of which, had law and equity, and the constitution on their side, against one which was impiously attempting to overturn law and equity, and the constitution; and to exercise a wanton licentious *sovereignty* over the properties, consciences and lives of all the people:—Such a *sovereignty* as some inconsiderately ascribe to the Supreme Governor of the world.—I say, inconsiderately; because God himself does not govern in an absolutely arbitrary and despotic manner. The power of this Almighty King (I speak it not without caution and reverence; the power of this Almighty King) is *limited by law*; not, indeed, by *acts of Parliament*, but by the eternal *laws* as of truth, wisdom and equity; and the *everlasting tables* of right reason;—tables that cannot be *repealed*, or *thrown down* and *broken* like those of Moses. . . .

DISCUSSION QUESTIONS

1   Against which two philosophies did Mayhew speak? Why?
2   What distinguished resistance from rebellion according to Mayhew?
3   How did Mayhew employ Christianity to argue against the power of an absolute monarch?

2–3a | William Pitt, excerpt from speech on the Stamp Act, England, 1766

William Pitt, First Earl of Chatham (1708–1778), was a British leader of the Whigs and served as Prime Minister of Great Britain in the mid-eighteenth century. He led Great Britain during the Seven Years' War, a victory which solidified England's leading position among European states. He sought to find compromise on the escalating tensions with the American colonies. His arguments—for no taxation without consent, independent judges, trial by jury, recognition of the American Continental Congress—found little support amongst his peers. Because of his views, Pitt was a popular figure in the American colonies.

Gentlemen, Sir, I have been charged with giving birth to sedition in America. They have spoken their sentiments with freedom against this unhappy act, and that freedom has become their crime. Sorry I am to hear the liberty of speech in this House imputed as a crime. But the imputation shall not discourage me. It is a liberty I mean to exercise. No gentleman ought to be afraid to exercise it. It is a liberty by which the gentleman who calumniates it might have profited. He ought to have desisted from this project.

The gentleman tells us, America is obstinate; America is almost in open rebellion. I rejoice that America has resisted. Three millions of people so dead to all feelings of liberty, as voluntarily to submit to be slaves, would have been fit instruments to make slaves of the rest.

. . .

I am no courtier of America; I stand up for this kingdom. I maintain, that the parliament has a right to bind, to restrain America. Our legislative power over the colonies is sovereign and supreme. When it ceases to be sovereign and supreme, I would advise every gentleman to sell his lands, if he can, and embark for that country. When two countries are connected together, like England and her colonies, without being incorporated, the one must necessarily govern; the greater must rule the less; but so rule it, as not to contradict the fundamental principles that are common to both. If the gentleman does not understand the difference between external and internal taxes, I cannot help it; but there is a plain distinction between taxes levied for the purpose of raising a revenue, and duties imposed for the regulation of trade, for the accommodation of the subject; although, in the consequences, some revenue might incidentally arise from the latter.

The gentleman asks, when were the colonies emancipated? But I desire to know, when were they made slaves. But I dwell not upon words. When I had the honour of serving his Majesty, I availed myself of the means of information which I derived from my office: I speak, therefore, from knowledge. My materials were good; I was at pains to collect, to digest, to consider them; and I will be bold to affirm, that the profits to Great Britain from the trade of the colonies, through all its branches, is two millions a year. This is the fund that carried you triumphantly through the last war. . . . You owe this to America: this is the price America pays for her protection. And shall a miserable financier come with a boast, that he can bring a peppercorn into the exchequer, to the loss of millions to the nation? I dare not say, how much higher these profits may be augmented. Omitting the immense increase of people by natural population, in the northern colonies, and the emigration from every part of Europe, I am convinced the whole commercial system of America may be altered to advantage. You have prohibited where you ought to have encouraged, and encouraged where you ought to have prohibited. Improper restraints have been laid on the continent, in favour of the islands. You have but two nations to trade with in America. Would you had twenty! Let acts of parliament in consequence of treaties remain, but let not an English minister become a custom-house officer for Spain, or for any foreign power. Much is wrong; much may be amended for the general good of the whole. . . .

. . .

A great deal has been said without doors of the power, of the strength, of America. It is a topic that ought to be cautiously meddled with. In a good cause, on a sound bottom, the force of this country can crush America to atoms. I know the valour of your troops. I know the skill of your officers. There is not a company of foot that has served in America, out of which you may not pick a man of sufficient knowledge and experience to make a governor of a colony there. But on this ground, on the Stamp Act, when so many here will think it a crying injustice, I am one who will lift up my hands against it.

In such a cause, your success would be hazardous. America, if she fell, would fall like the strong man. She would embrace the pillars of the state, and pull down the constitution along with her. Is this your boasted peace? Not to sheathe the sword in its scabbard, but to sheathe it in the bowels of your countrymen? Will you quarrel with yourselves, now the whole House of Bourbon is united against you? . . .

The Americans have not acted in all things with prudence and temper. The Americans have been wronged. They have been driven to madness by injustice. Will you punish them for the madness you have occasioned? Rather let prudence and temper come first from this side. I will undertake for America, that she will follow the example. There are two lines in a ballad of Prior's, of a man's behaviour to his wife, so applicable to you and your colonies, that I cannot help repeating them:—

> "Be to her faults a little blind
> Be to her virtues very kind."

Upon the whole, I will beg leave to tell the House what is really my opinion. It is, that the Stamp-act be repealed absolutely, totally, and immediately; that the reason for the repeal should be assigned, because it was founded on an erroneous principle. At the same time, let the sovereign authority of this country over the colonies be asserted in as strong terms as can be devised, and be made to extend every point of legislation whatsoever: that we may bind their trade, confine their manufactures, and exercise every power whatsoever—except that of taking money out of their pockets without their consent.

2–3b | Political cartoon, "The Colonies Reduced," England, 1767

Possibly created by Benjamin Franklin, this cartoon published in Great Britain warned of the consequences of the Stamp Act. Here, Britannia, the national personification of the United Kingdom, considers her reduced empire. The banner translates "Give a farthing to Belisarius," referring to a well-known story about the Byzantine general Belisarius. In this tale, Belisarius, who had garnered many victories over the enemies of his country, was reduced to such extreme poverty that, in his old age and blinded, he sat on the highway begging for charity, imploring each passerby with this same phrase. Here, an olive branch has fallen from one of Britannia's hands and idle ships sit in the harbor.

DISCUSSION QUESTIONS

1   How did Pitt affirm the power of Parliament over the colonies while also denouncing the Stamp Act?

2   What symbols and images are used by the artist of the cartoon to represent the consequences of the Stamp Act?

3   What connection do these pieces show between colonial trade and peace?

2–4a | *The London Magazine*, frontispiece, "Britain, America, at length be friends . . . ," England, 1774

This etching and engraving offers depictions of a native woman (America) and Britannia (Great Britain) shaking hands with Concordia, the Roman goddess of harmony and concord, looking on. Concordia holds a globe and olive branch. Ships operating out of a busy port are in the background, and a lion, lamb, and cornucopia are in the foreground.

FRONTISPIECE.   Lon.Mag.1774.

Britain, America, at length be Friends,
Accept the terms which Concord, recommends!
Be ye but steady to each others Cause,
Protect, defend, and not infringe the Laws;
Ye may together - come the World in Arms.
Bear the brunt Shock of hostile, dire alarms.
'Tis Peace, Trade, Navigation, will support
The poor with bread - in Dignity the Court.
Rush to each others Arms, be firm and true:
One Faith, one Fame, one Intrest, makes the TWO.
E.T.

2–4b | John Adams, excerpt from "Novanglus letter III," Massachusetts, 1775

John Adams (1735–1826) was an American political leader, attorney, diplomat, and, later in his career, the second President of the United States. He rose to prominence with his opposition to the Stamp Act of 1765. Adams argued that it denied two fundamental rights guaranteed to all Englishmen, taxation with consent and trial by jury. Although more conservative than many of the leaders of dissent in the colonies, his views moved away from peaceful petition to necessary separation. Writing under the pen name Novanglus (New England), Adams answered essays by Massachusettensis (Daniel Leonard) published in the *Boston Gazette*. Adams rebuffs Massachusettensis's legalistic defense of the Loyalist opposition to the American colonies' push for independence.

"If the colonies are not subject to the authority of parliament, Great-Britain and the colonies must be distinct states, as completely so as England and Scotland were before the union, or as Great-Britain and Hanover are now." There is no need of being startled at this consequence. It is very harmless. There is no absurdity at all in it. Distinct states may be united under one king. And those states may be further cemented and united together, by a treaty of commerce. This is the case. We have, by our own express consent contracted to observe the navigation act, and by our implied consent, by long usage and uninterrupted acquiescence, have submitted to the other acts of trade, however grievous some of them may be. This may be compared to a treaty of commerce, by which those distinct states are cemented together, in perpetual league and amity.

DISCUSSION QUESTIONS

1   According to Adams, what truly draws together and unites states?
2   What symbols of peace and prosperity do you observe in the engraving?
3   Why might the artist have depicted the colonies this way, particularly in relation to the depiction of Great Britain?

2–5a | Oneida Declaration of Neutrality, 1775

Here, the Oneida people, one of the five founding nations of the Iroquois Confederacy, respond to Colony of Connecticut Governor Jonathan Trumbull siding with the colonial cause in the American Revolution. Despite the appeal for the Indians "to be all of one mind," Native Americans fought on both sides of the conflict in disruptive and shifting allegiances.

The Oneida Indians Address Governor Turnbull

The Indians, in return, dispatched Captain Solomon Ahhaunnauwaumut, their chief sachem, to the Congress, to make a reply, and on the 11th of April he delivered the following speech:

"BROTHERS: We have heard you speak by your letter—we thank you for it—we now make answer.

"BROTHERS: You remember when you first came over the great waters, I was great and you was little, very small. I then took you in for a friend, and kept you under my arms, so that no one might injure you; since that time we have ever been true friends; there has never been any quarrel between us. But now our conditions are changed. You are become great and tall. You reach to the clouds. You are seen all around the world, and I am become small, very little. I am not so high as your heel. Now you take care of me, and I look to you for protection.

"BROTHERS: I am sorry to hear of this great quarrel between you and Old England. It appears that blood must soon be shed to end this quarrel. We never till this day understood the foundation of this quarrel between you and the country you came from.

"BROTHERS: Whenever I see your blood running, you will soon find me about to revenge my brother's blood. Although I am low and very small, I will gripe hold of your enemy's heel, that he cannot run so fast, and so light, as if he has nothing at his heels.

"BROTHERS: You know I am not so wise as you are, therefore I ask your advice in what I am now going to say. I have been thinking, before you come to action, to take a run to the westward, and feel the mind of my Indian brethren, the Six Nations, and know how they stand—whether they are on your side or for your enemies. If I find they are against you, I will try to turn their minds. I think they will listen to me, for they have always looked this way for advice, concerning all important news that comes from the rising of the sun. If they hearken to me, you will not be afraid of any danger behind you. However their minds are affected, you shall soon know by me. Now I think I can do you more service in this way, than by marching off immediately to Boston, and staying there; it may be a great while before blood runs. Now, as I said, you are wiser than I; I leave this for your consideration, whether I come down immediately or wait till I hear some blood is spilled.

"BROTHERS: I would not have you think by this that we are falling back from our engagements. We are ready to do any thing for your relief, and shall be guided by your counsel.

"BROTHERS: One thing I as of you, if you send for me to fight, that you will let me fight in my own Indian way. I am not used to fight English fashion, therefore you must not expect I can train like your men. Only point out to me where your enemies keep, and that is all I shall want to know."

2–5b | Lenape Chief Buckongahelas, selections from "Address to Christian Native Americans at Gnadenhutten," 1781

Buckongahelas (ca. 1720–1805), Lenape chief and warrior, was active from the period of the French and Indian War (1754–1763) through the Northwest Indian War (1785–1795). During the American Revolution, he broke away from the neutral and pro-American Lenape alliance that was led by White Eyes (ca. 1730–1778) and led his followers against the colonists. He argued that American militia would disregard their status as fellow Christians. On March 8, 1782, state militia from Pennsylvania did attack and kill ninety-six Lenape in what became known as the Gnadenhutten massacre.

Friends!—Listen to what I have to say to you! You see a great and powerful nation divided! You see the father fighting against the son, the son against the father!—The father has called on his Indian children, to assist him in punishing his children, the Americans, who have become refractory!—I took time to consider what I should do—whether or not I should receive the hatchet of my father, to assist him!—At first, I looked upon it as a family quarrel, in which I was not interested—However, at length it appeared to me, that the father was in the right; and his children deserved to be punished a little!—That this must be the case, I concluded from the many cruel acts his offspring had committed from time to time on his Indian children; in encroaching on their lands, stealing their property, shooting at, and murdering without cause, men, women, and children—Yes! even murdering those, who at all times had been friendly to them, and were placed for protection under the roof of their father's house—The father himself standing centry at the door, at the time. . . .

Look back at the murders committed by the Long-Knives on many of our relations, who lived peaceable neighbors to them on the Ohio! Did not they kill them without the least provocation?—Are they, do you think, better now than they were then?

DISCUSSION QUESTIONS

1   What reasons did the Oneida provide for their neutrality in the conflict between Britain and America?

2   Why did Chief Buckongahelas choose to support the British?

3   How did the familial relationships ascribed to Britain and the colonies by these indigenous groups influence the position taken by each respective tribe?

2–6 | Noël Le Mire, engraving, Marquis de Lafayette and African American man, France, 1781

Noel De Mire (1724–1801) created this engraving of Marquis de Lafayette (1757–1834) titled *Conclusion de la Campagne Liberté de 1781 en Virginie*, based on a painting by French artist Jean-Baptiste Le Paon (1738–1785). The Marquis de Lafayette and his black attendant, most likely intended to be James Lafayette, stand in the foreground as the Battle of Yorktown rages in the background. James Lafayette was born into slavery in Virginia but received permission to enlist in Lafayette's French Allied units, where he spied on the British. The Marquis de Lafayette's participation in the Revolutionary War was an expression of the Franco-American Treaty of Alliance formalized in 1778. It promised mutual military support should fighting break out between French and British forces. This image, dedicated to General George Washington, was widely distributed both in the colonies and in Europe.

CONCLUSION DE LA CAMPAGNE LIBERTÉ DE 1781 EN VIRGINIE.
LE MARQUIS DE LA FAYETTE,
Maréchal de Camp des Armées du Roi, et Commandant de la Garde Nationale Parisienne.

L'Amérique était asservie, | Ses forces au dela des Mers
Ce Héros vint briser fes fers; | Préfageroient ceux de fa Patrie.

DISCUSSION QUESTIONS

1   Who might have been the intended audience for this engraving?

2   What reasons would Americans have had for welcoming international support?

RESPONSES TO REVOLUTION

2–7a | Newspaper, notices about runaway indentured servants and apprentices, British colonies, 1770–1771

Below are notices posted by masters seeking the return of runaway indentured servants or apprentices. These items appeared in colonial newspapers in 1770 and 1771. Unfree labor was common at the time of the American Revolution, including approximately 20 percent of the population that were enslaved. Indentured servants represented almost half of all European immigrants to the American colonies. A broker would pay for their passage and then sell the individual to the highest bidder, where they were then bound to serve the contract purchaser for several years, often seven. Indentured servants, as well as apprentices, could not sever these contracts at will as the notices below attest.

Trenton Goal [*sic*], December 28, 1769.

This is to give notice, there was committed to my custody, by William Clayton, Esq., as a runaway apprentice on the 24th day of October last, THOMAS SANDAMAN. This is to inform his master or sheriff that he run away from, that they come and pay charges and take him away, *or he will be sold* to pay cost and charges, on Saturday the 20th day of January, 1770, by me

PETER HANKINSON, *Goaler* [*sic*].

—*The Pennsylvania Journal, No. 1413, January 4, 1770.*

Three Pounds Reward

Run-away on Friday the 12th Inst. from the Subscriber at Hunterdon County, in New-Jersey, an Apprentice, named David Cox, about Twenty Years of Age, a Carpenter and Joiner by Trade, but its likely he may pass for a Mill-Wright, as he has two Brothers of that Trade, that works near Albany. He is about 5 Feet 10 Inches high, large boned, knock kneed, of a dark Complexion, down Look, black Eyes, black Hair, and wears it tied. Had on when he went away, a grey coloured Coat and Jacket, pretty much worn, with Horn Buttons on them, new Leather Breeches, with black Horn Buttons, Russia Shirt, black Yarn Stockings, new Shoes, also a rusty Castor Hat, wears it cocked: It is also suspected he has stole his Indentures, and will very likely show them for a Pass, as he is near of Age. Whoever apprehends said Apprentice, and secures him in any Goal [*sic*], so that his Master may have Notice thereof, shall have the above Reward, paid by me.

JAMES TAYLOR.

N. B. Perhaps he may changes his Cloaths, that he may not be discovered.

—*The N. Y. Gazette, or Weekly Post Boy, No. 1412, January 22, 1770.*

New Jersey, November 24, 1769.

Run-away the 22d September, from the Subscriber, living in Monmouth County, in the Township of Shrewsbury, in the Province of East New-Jersey; an indented Servant Man, named Walter Clark, born *in the Jerseys*, about Twenty-four Years of Age, a Black-Smith by trade, and understands farming Business; he is about six Feet high, has black curled Hair, and keeps his Mouth much open: He took several Suits of Apparel with him, all of a brownish Colour, some Broad Cloth, and some thin Stuff; also one striped double-breasted Jacket. Whoever takes up the above said Servant and delivers him to me the Subscriber, shall have Three Pounds Reward, and reasonable Charges paid, by me.

BENJAMIN JACKSON.

—*The N. Y. Journal or General Advertiser, No. 1412, January 25, 1770.*

2–7b | Petition for freedom to the Massachusetts Council and the House of Representatives, 1777

Unfree slave labor was a foundational fixture of the colonial period in America. Here, "A Great Number of Blackes" of Massachusetts state their case for freedom, arguing that it is the natural right of all people. Attributed to Prince Hall (ca. 1735–1807), the African American abolitionist and leader of the free black community in Boston, the official petition was submitted to the legislature signed by Hall and seven other free black men. The text was inspired by the radical rhetoric of the revolution.

To the Honorable Counsel & House of [Representa-]tives for the State of Massachusette Bay in General Court assembled, Jan 13 1777—

The petition of A Great Number of Blackes detained in a State of Slavery in the Bowels of a free & christian Country Humbly shuwith that your Petitioners Apprehend that Thay have in Common with all other men a Natural and Unaliable Right to that freedom which the Grat [Great]—Parent of the Unavese [Universe] hath Bestowed equalley on all menkind [mankind] and which they have Never forfuted [forfeited] by Any Compact or Agreement whatever—but thay [they] wher [were] Unjustly Dragged by the hand of cruel Power from their Derest frinds [friends] and sum of them Even torn from the Embraces of their tender Parents—from A popolous [populous] Plasant

[Pleasant] And plentiful cuntry [country] And in Violation of Laws of Nature and off Nations And in defiance of all the tender feelings of humanity Brough [Brought] hear [here] Either to Be sold Like Beast of Burthen & Like them Condemnd to Slavery for Life—among A People Profesing the [mild?] Religion of Jesus A people Not Insensible of the Secrets of Rationable Being Nor without spirit to Resent the unjust endeavours of others to Reduce them to A state of Bondage and Subjection your honouer [honor] Need not to be informed that A Life of Slavery Like that of your Petioners Deprived of Every social Priviledge of Every thing Requiset [Requisite] to Render Life Tolable [Tolerable] is far [. . .] worse then [than] Nonexistance.

[In imita]tion of [the] Lawdable [Laudable] Example of the Good People of these States your petiononers have Long and Patiently waited the Evnt [Event] of petition after petition By them presented to the Legislative Body of this state And cannot but with Grief Reflect that their Sucess [Success] hath ben [been] but too similar they Cannot but express their Astonisments [Astonishments] that It has Never Bin [Been] Considered [Considered] that Every Principle from which Amarica has Acted in the Cours [Course] Of their unhappy Deficultes [Difficulties] with Great Briton Pleads Stronger than A thousand arguments in favowrs [favors] of Your petioners thay [they] therfor [therefore] humble [humbly] Beseech your Honours to give this petion [petition] its due weight & consider-ration and cause an act of the Legislatur to be past Wherby they may Be Restored to the Enjoyments of that Which is the Naturel [Natural] Right of all men—and their—Children who wher [were] Born in this Land of Liberty may not be heald [held] as Slaves after they arive [arrive] at the age of Twenty one years so may the Inhabitance [Inhabitants] of thes [this] State No longer chargeable with the inconsistancey of acting themselves the part which thay condem and oppose in Others Be prospered in their present Glorious Struggle for Liberty and have those Blessing to them.

DISCUSSION QUESTIONS

1 How do these notices illustrate the type and regulation of labor in a colonial economy?

2 What arguments were made against slavery by the free men of Massachusetts?

3 Who held the power in the colonial economy? How did laborers try to exercise their agency?

2–8 | Thomas Jefferson, excerpts from letter on education to J. Banister Jr., 1785

Thomas Jefferson (1743–1826), statesman, diplomat, lawyer, and architect, was a lifelong advocate of public education. To Jefferson, "no other foundation can be devised for the preservation of freedom and happiness." The failure to provide a public education would "leave the people in ignorance." His philosophy on education would evolve throughout his public life: the capstone project in that thinking was the founding of the University of Virginia in 1819.

But why send an American youth to Europe for education? What are the objects of a useful American education? Classical knowledge, modern languages, chiefly French, Spanish, and Italian; Mathematics, Natural philosophy, Natural history, Civil history, and Ethics. In Natural philosophy, I mean to include Chemistry, and Agriculture, and in Natural history, to include Botany, as well as the other branches of those departments. It is true that the habit of speaking the modern languages, cannot be so well acquired in America; but every other article can be as well acquired at William and Mary college, as at any place in Europe. . . .

Let us view the disadvantages of sending a youth to Europe. To enumerate them all, would require a volume. I will select a few. If he goes to England, he learns drinking, horse racing and boxing. These are peculiarities of English education. The following circumstances are common to education in that, and the other countries of Europe. He acquires a fondness for European luxury and dissipation, and a contempt for the simplicity of his own country; he is fascinated with the privileges of the European aristocrats, and sees, with abhorrence, the lovely equality which the poor enjoy with the rich, in his own country; he contracts a partiality for aristocracy or monarchy; he forms foreign friendships which will never be useful to him, and loses the season of life for forming in his own country, those friendships, which, of all others, are the most faithful and permanent; he is led by the strongest of all the human passions, into a spirit for female intrigue, destructive of his own and others' happiness, or a passion for whores, destructive of his health, and, in both cases, learns to consider fidelity to the marriage bed as an ungentlemanly practice, and inconsistent with happiness; he recollects the voluptuary dress and arts of the European women, and pities and despises the chaste affections and simplicity of those of his own country; he retains, through life, a fond recollection, and a hankering after those places, which were the scenes of his first pleasures and of his first connections; he returns to his own country, a foreigner, unacquainted with the practices of domestic economy, necessary to preserve him from ruin, speaking and writing his native tongue as a foreigner, and therefore unqualified to obtain those distinctions, which eloquence of the pen and tongue ensures in a free country; for I would observe to you, that what is called style in writing or speaking, is formed very early in life, while the imagination is warm, and impressions are permanent. I am of opinion, that there never was an instance of a man's writing or speaking his native tongue with elegance, who passed from fifteen to twenty years of age, out of the country where it was spoken. This, no instance exists of a person's writing two languages perfectly. That will always appear to be his native language, which was most familiar to him in his youth. It appears to me then, that an American coming to Europe for education, loses in his knowledge, in his morals, in his health, in his habits, and in his happiness. I had entertained only doubts on this head, before I came to Europe: what I see and hear, since I came here, proves more than I had even suspected. Cast your eye over America: who are the men of most learning, of most eloquence, most beloved by their countrymen, and most trusted and promoted by them? They are those who have been educated among them, and whose manners, morals and habits, are perfectly homogenous with those of the country.

Did you expect by so short a question, to draw such a sermon on yourself? I dare say you did not. But the consequences of foreign education are alarming to me, as an American. I sin, therefore, through zeal, whenever I enter on the subject. You are sufficiently American to pardon me for it.

DISCUSSION QUESTIONS

1   What areas of study did Jefferson believe compose an "American education"?

2   How, according to Jefferson, was a European education detrimental to an American youth?

3   Why would Jefferson speak against a European education? What clues does that give for how he understood the purpose of education?

2–9a | Excerpt from lyrics of "Ça Ira!", France, 1790

First heard in May 1790, "Ça Ira" became a popular song of the French Revolution. It first became popular as a work song during preparation for the *Fête de la Fédération* (Festival of the Federation) held in honor of the French Revolution, but eventually was recognized as the unofficial revolutionary anthem. The title and theme were reportedly inspired by Benjamin Franklin, commissioner to France from the Continental Congress. When asked about the American revolution, supposedly Franklin answered in broken French "Ça ira, ça ira" ("It'll be fine, it'll be fine").

Ça Ira! (It'll be okay)

Refrain:

Oh. It'll be okay, be okay, be okay,
Hang the aristocrats from on high!
Oh. It'll be okay, be okay, be okay,
The aristocrats, we'll hang 'em all.

Despotism will breathe its last,
Liberty will take the day,
Oh. It'll be okay, be okay, be okay,
We don't have any more nobles or priests,
Oh. It'll be okay, be okay, be okay,
Equality will reign everywhere,
The Austrian slave will follow him,
To the Devil will they fly.
Oh. It'll be okay, be okay, be okay,
To the Devil will they fly.

Refrain

2–9b | Excerpt from the Levée en Masse (Draft), France, 1793

During the French Revolution (1789–1799), the dangers of a foreign war led the Committee of Public Safety to establish mass conscription. This move enlisted and trained an army of 800,000 soldiers in less than a year, much larger than any competing army in a European state. It was integral to the formation of a democratic national identity, laid a foundation for the rise of Napoleon, and made war the business of citizens.

1. From this moment until that in which the enemy shall have been driven from the soil of the Republic, all Frenchmen are in permanent requisition for the service of the armies.

The young men shall go to battle; the married men shall forge arms and transport provisions; the women shall make tents and clothing and shall serve in the hospitals; the children shall turn old linen into lint; the aged shall betake themselves to the public places in order to arouse the courage of the warriors and preach the hatred of kings and the unity of the Republic.

2. The national buildings shall be converted into barracks, the public places into workshops for arms, the soil of the cellars shall be washed in order to extract therefrom the saltpetre.

3. The arms of the regulation calibre shall be reserved exclusively for those who shall march against the enemy; the service of the interior shall be performed with hunting pieces and side arms.

4. The saddle horses are put into requisition to complete the cavalry corps; the draught-horses, other than those employed in agriculture, shall convey the artillery and the provisions.

5. The Committee of Public Safety is charged to take all the necessary measures to set up without delay an extraordinary manufacture of arms of every sort which corresponds with the ardor and energy of the French people. It is, accordingly, authorised to form all the establishments, factories, workshops, and mills which shall be deemed necessary for the carrying on of these works, as well as to put in requisition, within the entire extent of the Republic, the artists and workingmen who can contribute to their success. . . .

6. The representatives of the people sent out for the execution of the present law shall have the same authority in their respective districts, acting in concert with the Committee of Public Safety; they are invested with the unlimited powers assigned to the representatives of the people to the armies.

7. Nobody can get himself replaced in the service for which he shall have been requisitioned. The public functionaries shall remain at their posts.

DISCUSSION QUESTIONS

1   How could "Levée en Masse," mass conscription, be seen as a unifying and democratic action?

2   How do both of these documents illustrate the social and political reorientation caused by the French Revolution?

3   How do these French expressions of revolution compare or contrast with expressions of the American Revolution?

2–10 | Illustrated frontispiece, *Incendie du Cap* (Burning of Cap-Français, Haiti), France, 1815

Cap-Français (now Cap-Haïtien) was a wealthy port city and the commercial center of Saint-Domingue (Haiti) for much of the eighteenth century. The foundational structure of the profitable French colony was built on the enslaved, and in the late 1780s, as the population of Saint-Domingue approached half a million, 425,000 of that number were enslaved and 28,000 were free blacks and mulattos. A large and organized slave revolt met a colonial power also dealing with revolution at home in the summer of 1791. As the rebellion intensified, burnings and massacres in Cap-Français in 1793 virtually destroyed the city. The Haitian Revolution would last for thirteen years, crowned by the Haitian Declaration of Independence in 1804 (included in the 360 for chapter 12, "The Bipolar World"). Haiti became the first black-ruled nation in the Americas.

Incendie du Cap.

Révolte générale des Nègres. Massacre des Blancs.

SEE COLOR INSERT

DISCUSSION QUESTIONS

1   How might this image have capitalized on white fears about enslaved peoples?

2   What might a Haitian interpretation of this event look like?

3   How does the Haitian Revolution broaden or complicate the ideals of revolution in this age?

2-11 | Simón de Bolívar, excerpt from message to the Congress at Angostura, 1819

Simón de Bolívar (1783–1830) was the most important leader of Latin America's independence movement from Spain. Militarily, he opposed Spanish forces in northern South America, and politically, he was a central figure in the formative years of republics that rose to replace Spanish rule. He convened the Congress of Angostura during the wars of Independence of Columbia and Venezuela to reassert the autonomy of New Granada (present-day Columbia, Panama, Venezuela, and parts of Ecuador) and establish a political system to sustain the new republic. In his message, he lays the foundation for Gran Colombia (1819–1831), which he envisioned as democratically governed and free from slavery and racial inequality. The new state included the territories of New Granada along with additional territory in Ecuador, and parts of northern Peru, western Guyana, and northwestern Brazil.

The continuation of authority in the same person has frequently proved the undoing of democratic governments. Repeated elections are essential to the system of popular government, because there is nothing so dangerous as to suffer Power to be vested for a long time in one citizen. The people become accustomed to obeying him, and he becomes accustomed to commanding, hence the origin of usurpation and tyranny. A proper zeal is the guarantee of republican liberty, and our citizens must very justly fear that the same Magistrate who has governed them for a long time, may continue to rule them forever. . . .

Only democracy, in my opinion, is susceptible of absolute freedom. But where is there a democratic government that has united at the same time power, prosperity and permanence? Have we not seen, on the contrary, aristocracy, monarchy rearing great and powerful empires for centuries and centuries? What government is there older than that of China? What republic has exceeded in duration that of Sparta, that of Venice? The Roman Empire, did it not conquer the world? Does not France count fourteen centuries of monarchy? Who is greater than England? These nations, however, have been, or still are, aristocracies and monarchies. . . .

The more I admire the excellence of the Federal Constitution of Venezuela, the more I am persuaded of the impossibility of its application in our State. And, in my opinion, it is a wonder that its model in North America may endure so successfully, and is not upset in the presence of the first trouble or danger. Notwithstanding the fact that that people is a unique model of political virtues and moral education; notwithstanding that it has been cradled in liberty, that it has been reared in freedom and lives on pure liberty, I will say more, although in many respects that people is unique in the history of humanity, it is a prodigy, I repeat, that a system so weak and complicated as the federal system should have served to govern that people in circumstances as difficult and delicate as those which have existed. But, whatever the case may be, as regards the American Nation, I must say that nothing is further from my mind than to try to assimilate the conditions and character of two nations as different as the Anglo-American and the Spanish-American. Would it not be extremely difficult to apply to Spain the Code of political, civil and religious liberty of England? It would be even more difficult to adapt to Venezuela the laws of North America. Does not the *Spirit of Laws* state that they must be suited to the people for whom they are made; that it is a great coincidence when the laws of one nation suit another; that laws must bear relation to the physical features of a country, its climate, its soil, its situation, extension and manner of living of the people; that they must have reference to the degree of liberty that their constitution may be able to provide for the religion of the inhabitants, their inclinations, wealth, number, trade, customs and manners? Such is the Code that we should consult, not that of Washington! . . .

We must bear in mind that our population is not the people of Europe, not of North America, that it is rather a composite of Africa and America, which is an offspring of Europe. Spain herself ceases to be European on account of her African blood, her institutions and her temperament. It is impossible to point out with preciseness to what human family we belong. The greater portion of the natives has been annihilated, the European has mixed with the native American and the African, and this has mixed again with the Indian and the European. All having been born of the same mother, our parents, of different origin and blood, are foreigners, and all differ visibly in color of skin. This dissimilarity is in hindrance of the greatest importance. . . .

A republican government has been, is and must be that of Venezuela, based on the sovereignty of the people, the division of power, civil liberty, proscription of slavery, abolition of monarchy and privileges. We need equality to recast, so to speak, in a single mass the classes of men, political beliefs and public customs. . . .

In order to bring our rising republic out of this chaos, all our moral power will not be sufficient unless we cast the entire mass of the people in one single body, the composition of the government in one single body, legislation in one single body, and national spirit in one single body. Union, Union, Union, must be our motto. Our citizens are of different blood, let us mix it for the sake of union; our constitution has divided the powers, let us bind them together for the sake of union; our laws are sorry relics of all the ancient and modern despotisms; let us demolish such an awful structure. Let it fall, and discarding even its ruins let us create a temple to Justice, and under the auspices of its holy inspiration, let us frame a code of Venezuelan laws. If we wish to consult monuments and models of legislation, Great Britain, France, North America have admirable ones.

Popular education should be the paramount care of the paternal love of Congress. Morals and enlightenment are the poles of a republic; morals and enlightenment are our prime necessities. . . .

The merging of New Granada and Venezuela into one Great State, has been the unanimous wish of the peoples and the government of both republics. The fortunes of war have effected this union so earnestly desired by all Colombians; in fact, we are incorporated. These sister countries have already entrusted to you their interests, their rights and their destinies. In contemplating the union of these countries my soul rises to the heights demanded by the colossal perspective of such a wonderful picture. Soaring among the coming ages my imagination rests on the future centuries, and seeing from afar with admiration and amazement the prosperity, the splendor and the life which have come to this vast region, I feel myself carried away, and I see her in the very heart of the universe, stretching along her lengthy shores between two oceans which Nature has separated, but which our country unites through long wide channels. I can see her as the bond, as the center, as the emporium of the human family. I can see her sending to all the corners of the globe the treasure hidden in her mountains of silver and gold; I see her sending broadcast, by means of her divine plants, health and life to the sufferers of the old world; I see her confiding her precious secrets to the learned who do not know how much her store of knowledge is superior to the store of wealth bestowed by Nature upon her; I can see her sitting on the throne of liberty, the scepter of justice in her hand, crowned by glory, showing the old world the majesty of the modern world.

Deign, Legislators, to accept with indulgence the profession of my political faith, the highest wishes of my heart and the fervent prayer which on behalf of the people I dare address you: Deign to grant to Venezuela a government preeminently popular, preeminently just, preeminently moral, which will hold in chains oppression, anarchy and guilt. A government which will allow righteousness, tolerance, peace to reign; a government which will cause equality and liberty to triumph under the protection of inexorable laws.

Gentlemen, commence your duties; I have finished mine.

DISCUSSION QUESTIONS

1   What reasons did Bolívar give for favoring democracy? What elements must this government include?

2   Why did Bolívar state that—though both democratic in structure—Gran Colombia should not model its government after the United States?

2–12 | The Gulhane Proclamation, Ottoman Empire, 1839

The Tanzimât (1839–1876) was a period of reform in the Ottoman Empire that began with a purpose of modernizing the state and securing its territory from internal nationalist movements and increasingly aggressive external powers. In the Edict of Gulhane of

1839, the rule of law was enforced for all subjects, including non-Muslims. It sought to establish social and legal equality throughout the empire. It also called for a system of state schools to be established, a modern financial system to be created, and the expansion of communication and transportation networks.

All the world knows that in the first days of the Ottoman Monarchy, the glorious precepts of the Koran and the Laws of the Empire were always honored. The Empire in consequence increased in strength and greatness, and all her Subjects, without exception, had risen in the highest degree to ease and prosperity. In the last 150 years a succession of accidents and divers causes have arisen which have brought about a disregard for the sacred code of Laws, and the Regulations flowing therefrom, and the former strength and prosperity have changed into weakness and poverty: an Empire in fact loses all its stability so soon as it ceases to observe its Laws.

These considerations are ever present to our mind, and, ever since the day of our advent to the Throne, the thought of the public weal, of the improvement of the state of the Provinces, and of relief to the peoples, has not ceased to engage it. If, therefore, the geographical position of the Ottoman Provinces, the fertility of the soil, the aptitude and intelligence of the inhabitants are considered, the conviction will remain that, by striving to find efficacious means, the result, which by the help of God we hope to attain, can be obtained within a few years. Full of confidence, therefore, in the help of the Most High, assisted by the intercession of our Prophet, we deem it right to seek by new institutions to give to the Provinces composing the Ottoman Empire the benefit of a good Administration.

These institutions must be principally carried out under three heads, which are:

1. The guarantees insuring to our subjects perfect security for life, honour, and fortune.

2. A regular system of assessing and levying Taxes.

3. An equally regular system for the levy of Troops and the duration of their service. . . .

From henceforth, therefore, the cause of every accused person shall be publicly judged in accordance with our Divine Law, after inquiry and examination, and so long as a regular judgment shall not have been pronounced, no one can, secretly or publicly, put another to death by poison or in any other manner.

No one shall be allowed to attack the honor of any other person whatsoever.

Each one shall possess his Property of every kind, and shall dispose of it in all freedom, without let or hindrance from any person whatever; thus, for example, the innocent Heirs of a Criminal shall not be deprived of their legal rights, and the Property of the Criminal shall not be confiscated.

These Imperial concessions shall extend to all our subjects, of whatever Religion or sect they may be; they shall enjoy them without exceptions. We therefore grant perfect security to the inhabitants of our Empire, in their lives, their honor, and their fortunes, as they are secured to them by the sacred text of our Law. . . .

As all the Public Servants of the Empire receive a suitable salary, and that the salaries of those whose duties have not, up to the present time, been sufficiently remunerated, are to be fixed, a rigorous Law shall be passed against the traffic of favoritism and of appointments (*richvet*), which the Divine Law reprobates, and which is one of the principal causes of the decay of the Empire.

DISCUSSION QUESTIONS

1   What were the motivations for making these changes?
2   How are the practice of religion and the rule of law related in this piece?
3   What similarities and differences do you observe in the changes made by the sultan and changes enacted by the new governments in America and France?

3

The Early Republic and the World

INDIGENOUS PEOPLES

Indigenous peoples—also known as Aboriginal peoples, First Nations, or Native peoples—are those who self-identify as members of communities that originally inhabited a land, in contrast to those who came later as a result of colonization, settlement, or occupation. They hold distinct traditions and institutions passed down through generations. Though many indigenous communities are in Eurasia, European exploration and colonization in the Americas, Australia, and Oceania created new contact zones between Old World peoples and indigenous peoples, with the general outcome being negative for the latter. The negotiation of the relationship between indigenous people and settlers over questions of citizenship, legal and property rights, and cultural differences have been a constant feature not only of U.S. history, but the history of many nation-states. There are more than 370 million indigenous peoples around the world today, belonging to more than five thousand native communities, living on every inhabited continent.

Cherokee, *Cherokee Nation v. State of Georgia*, United States, 1831

Mr. Chief Justice Marshall delivered the opinion of the Court:

This bill is brought by the Cherokee Nation, praying an injunction to restrain the state of Georgia from the execution of certain laws of that state, which, as is alleged, go directly to annihilate the Cherokees as a political society, and to seize, for the use of Georgia, the lands of the nation which have been assured to them by the United States in solemn treaties repeatedly made and still in force.

If courts were permitted to indulge their sympathies, a case better calculated to excite them can scarcely be imagined. A people once numerous, powerful, and truly independent, found by our ancestors in the quiet and uncontrolled possession of an ample domain, gradually sinking beneath our superior policy, our arts and our arms, have yielded their lands by successive treaties, each of which contains a solemn guarantee of the residue, until they retain no more of their formerly extensive territory than is deemed necessary to their comfortable subsistence. To preserve this remnant the present application is made.

Before we can look into the merits of the case, a preliminary inquiry presents itself. Has this court jurisdiction of the cause?

The third article of the constitution describes the extent of the judicial power. The second section closes an enumeration of the cases to which it is extended, with "controversies" "between a state or the citizens thereof, and foreign states, citizens, or subjects." A subsequent clause of the same section gives the supreme court original jurisdiction in all cases in which a state shall be a party. The party defendant may then unquestionably be sued in this court. May the plaintiff sue in it? Is the Cherokee nation a foreign state in the sense in which that term is used in the constitution?

The counsel for the plaintiffs have maintained the affirmative of this proposition with great earnestness and ability. So much of the argument as was intended to prove the character of the Cherokees as a state, as a distinct political society, separated from others, capable of managing its own affairs and governing itself, has, in the opinion of a majority of the judges, been completely successful. They have been uniformly treated as a state from the settlement of our country. The numerous treaties made with them by the United States recognize them as a people capable of maintaining the relations of peace and war, of being responsible in their political character for any violation of their engagements, or for any aggression committed on the citizens of the United States by any individual of their community. Laws have been enacted in the spirit of these treaties. The acts of our government plainly recognize the Cherokee nation as a state, and the courts are bound by those acts.

A question of much more difficulty remains. Do the Cherokees constitute a foreign state in the sense of the Constitution?

The counsel have shown conclusively that they are not a state of the Union, and have insisted that individually they are aliens, not owing allegiance to the United States. An aggregate of aliens composing a state must, they say, be a foreign state. Each individual being foreign, the whole must be foreign.

This argument is imposing, but we must examine it more closely before we yield to it. The condition of the Indians in relation to the United States is perhaps unlike that of any other two people in existence. In the general, nations not owing a common allegiance are foreign to each other. The term *foreign nation* is, with strict propriety, applicable by either to the other. But the relation of the Indians to the United States is marked by peculiar and cardinal distinctions which exist nowhere else.

The Indian Territory is admitted to compose a part of the United States. In all our maps, geographical treatises, histories, and laws, it is so considered. In all our intercourse with foreign nations, in our commercial regulations, in any attempt at intercourse between Indians and foreign nations, they are considered as within the jurisdictional limits of the United States, subject to many of those restraints which are imposed upon our own citizens. They acknowledge themselves in their treaties to be under the protection of the United States; they admit that the United States shall have the sole and exclusive right of regulating the trade with them and managing all their affairs as they think proper; and the Cherokees in particular were allowed by the treaty of Hopewell, which preceded the Constitution, "to send a deputy of their choice, whenever they think fit, to congress." Treaties were made with some tribes by the state of New York, under a then unsettled construction of the confederation, by which they ceded all their lands to that state, taking back a limited grant to themselves, in which they admit their dependence.

Though the Indians are acknowledged to have an unquestionable, and, heretofore, unquestioned right to the lands they occupy, until that right shall be extinguished by a voluntary cession to our government; yet it may well be doubted whether those tribes which reside within the acknowledged boundaries of the United States can, with strict accuracy, be denominated foreign nations. They may more correctly, perhaps, be denominated domestic dependent nations. They occupy a territory to which we assert a title independent of their will, which must take effect in point of possession when their right of possession ceases. Meanwhile, they are in a state of pupilage. Their relation to the United States resembles that of a ward to his guardian.

They look to our government for protection; rely upon its kindness and its power; appeal to it for relief to their wants; and address the president as their great father. They and their country are considered by foreign nations, as well as by ourselves, as being so completely under the sovereignty and dominion of the United States that any attempt to acquire their lands, or to form a political connexion with them would be considered by all as an invasion of our territory and an act of hostility.

These considerations go far to support the opinion that the framers of our constitution had not the Indian tribes in view when they opened the courts of the union to controversies between a state or the citizens thereof and foreign states.

In considering this subject, the habits and usages of the Indians, in their intercourse with their white neighbors ought not to be entirely disregarded. At the time the constitution was framed, the idea of appealing to an American court of justice for an assertion of right or a redress of wrong had perhaps never entered the mind of an Indian or of his tribe. Their appeal was to the tomahawk, or to the government. This was well understood by the statesmen who framed the Constitution of the United States, and might furnish some reason for omitting to enumerate them among the parties who might sue in the courts of the Union. Be this as it may, the peculiar relations between the United States and the Indians occupying our territory are such that we should feel much difficulty in considering them as designated by the term *foreign state*, were there no other part of the constitution which might shed light on the meaning of these words. But we think that in construing them, considerable aid is furnished by that clause in the 8th Section of the 3rd Article, which empowers Congress to "regulate commerce with foreign nations, and among the several states, and with the Indian tribes."

In this clause they are as clearly contradistinguished by a name appropriate to themselves from foreign nations, as from the several states composing the Union. They are designated by a distinct appellation; and as this appellation can be applied to neither of the others, neither can the appellation distinguishing either of the others be in fair construction applied to them. The objects to which the power of regulating commerce might be directed are divided into three distinct classes—foreign nations, the several states, and Indian tribes. When forming this article, the convention considered them as entirely distinct. We cannot assume that the distinction was lost in framing a subsequent article, unless there be something in its language to authorize the assumption. . . .

Foreign nations is a general term, the application of which to Indian tribes, when used in the American constitution, is at best extremely questionable. In one article in which a power is given to be exercised in regard to foreign nations generally, and to the Indian tribes particularly, they are mentioned as separate in terms clearly contra-distinguishing them from each other. We perceive plainly that the constitution in this article does not comprehend Indian tribes in the general term "foreign nations;" not we presume because a tribe may not be a nation, but because it is not foreign to the United States. When, afterward, the term "foreign state" is introduced, we cannot impute to the convention the intention to desert its former meaning, and to comprehend Indian tribes within it, unless the context force that construction on us. We find nothing in the context and nothing in the subject of the article which leads to it.

The court has bestowed its best attention on this question and, after mature deliberation, the majority is of opinion that an Indian tribe or nation within the United States is not a foreign state in the sense of the constitution, and cannot maintain an action in the courts of the United States.

A serious additional objection exists to the jurisdiction of the court. Is the matter of the bill the proper subject for judicial inquiry and decision? It seeks to restrain a state from the forcible exercise of legislative power over a neighboring people, asserting their independence; their right to which the state denies. On several of the matters alleged in the bill, for example on the laws making it criminal to exercise the usual powers of self government in their own country by the Cherokee nation, this court cannot interpose; at least in the form in which those matters are presented.

That part of the bill which respects the land occupied by the Indians, and prays the aid of the court to protect their possession, may be more doubtful. The mere question of right might perhaps be decided by this court in a proper case with proper parties. But the court is asked to do more than decide on the title. The bill requires us to control the legislature of Georgia, and to restrain the exertion of its physical force. The propriety of such an interposition by the court may be well questioned. It savors too much of the exercise of political power to be within the proper province of the judicial department. But the opinion on the point respecting parties makes it unnecessary to decide this question.

If it be true that the Cherokee nation have rights, this is not the tribunal in which those rights are to be asserted. If it be true that wrongs have been inflicted, and that still greater are to be apprehended, this is not the tribunal which can redress the past or prevent the future.

The motion for an injunction is denied.

Māori, Native Land Court Act, New Zealand, 1865

Whereas it is expedient to amend and consolidate the laws relating to the lands in the Colony which are still subject to Maori proprietary customs and to provide for the ascertainment of the persons who according to such customs are the owners thereof and to encourage the extinction of such proprietary customs and to provide for the conversion of such modes of ownership into titles derived from the Crown and to provide for the regulation of the descent of such lands when the title thereto is converted as aforesaid and to make further provisions in reference to the matters aforesaid

. . .

XXI. Any Native may give notice in writing to the Court that he claims to be interested in a piece of Native Land specifying it by its name or otherwise describing it and stating the name of the tribe or the names of the persons whom he admits to be interested therein with him and that he desires that his claim should be investigated by the Court in order that a title from the Crown may be issued to him for such piece of land.

. . .

XXIII. At such sitting of the Court the Court shall ascertain by such evidence as it shall think fit the right title estate or interest of the applicant and of all other claimants to or in the land respecting which notice shall have been given as aforesaid and the Court shall order a certificate of title to be made and issued which certificate shall specify the names of the persons or of the tribe who according to Native custom own or are interested in the land describing the nature of such estate or interest and describing the land comprised in such certificate or the Court may in its discretion refuse to order a certificate to issue to the claimant or any other person. Provided always that no certificate shall be ordered to more than ten persons. Provided further that if the piece of land adjudicated upon shall not exceed five thousand acres such certificate may not be made in favor of a tribe by name.

Ainu, Hokkaido Former Natives Protection Law, Japan, 1899

Article 1

Those Former Natives of Hokkaido who are engaged, or wish to engage, in agriculture shall be granted free of charge no more than 12 acres of land per household.

Article 2

The land granted under the preceding Article is subject to the following conditions on rights of ownership.

1. It may not be transferred except by inheritance.

2. No rights of pledge, mortgage, lease or perpetual lease can be established.

3. No easement can be established without the permission of the Governor of Hokkaido.

4. It cannot become the object of a lien or preferential right. The land granted in the preceding Article shall not be subject to land tax or local taxes until 30 years from the date of grant. Land already owned by Former Natives shall not be transferred except by inheritance, nor shall any of the real rights (*jus in rem*) referred to in paragraphs 1 to 3 be established upon it without the permission of the Governor of Hokkaido.

Article 3

Any part of the land granted under Article 1 shall be confiscated if it has not been cultivated within 15 years from the date of the grant.

Article 4

Hokkaido Former Natives who are destitute will be provided with agricultural implements and seeds.

Article 5

Hokkaido Former Natives who are injured or ill but cannot afford medical treatment shall be provided with medical treatment or expenses for medicine.

Article 6

Hokkaido Former Natives who are too injured, ill, disabled, senile or young to provide for themselves shall be granted welfare under existing legislation and if they should die at or during the period of assistance funeral expenses will be provided.

Article 7

Children of destitute Hokkaido Former Natives who are attending school will be provided with tuition fees.

Article 8

Expenses incurred under Articles 4 to 7 shall be appropriated from the proceeds of the communal funds of Hokkaido Former Natives, or if these are insufficient, from the National Treasury.

Article 9

An elementary school will be constructed with funds from the National Treasury in areas where there is a Former Native village.

Article 10

The Governor of Hokkaido will manage the communal funds of the Hokkaido Former Natives.

The Governor of Hokkaido, subject to the approval of the Home Minister, may dispose of the communal funds in the interests of the owners of the communal funds or may refuse to expend them if he deems it necessary.

The communal funds managed by the Governor of Hokkaido shall be designated by the Governor of Hokkaido.

Article 11

The Governor of Hokkaido may issue police orders with regard to the protection of the Hokkaido Former Natives and may impose a fine of over 2 yen but no more than 25 yen or a period of imprisonment of over 11 days but no more than 25 days.

By-law
Article 12

This Law will become effective from April 1, 1899.

Article 13

Regulations relevant to the implementation of this Law shall be set by the Home Minister.

Image of Ainu people, Japan, 1904

Sami, Norway, Amendment to Norway's Constitution of 1814, Norway, 1988

Article 108

It is the responsibility of the authorities of the State to create conditions enabling the Sami people to preserve and develop its language, culture and way of life.

United Nations Declaration on the Rights of Indigenous Peoples, 2007

Important Themes in the Declaration (Articles 1–6)

The main themes are: (i) the right to self-determination; (ii) the right to be recognized as distinct peoples; (iii) the right to free, prior and informed consent; and (iv) the right to be free of discrimination. These themes are important to keep in mind as you read the Declaration.

The right to self-determination

The right of indigenous peoples to self-determination is fundamental to UNDRIP. While there are different interpretations, self-determination generally means that indigenous peoples have the right to decide what is best for them and their communities. For example, they can make their own decisions on issues that concern them and carry them out in the way that will be meaningful to indigenous peoples, while being respectful of the human rights of their community members (including children) and other peoples as well.

Indigenous peoples have the right to be independent and free. They have the right to be citizens of the country they live in and at the same time to be members of their indigenous communities. As citizens, they have the right to choose to build relationships with other peoples and to take active roles in the country in which they are living.

The right to cultural identity

Indigenous peoples are equal to all other peoples, but they also have the right to be different, for example in the way they dress, the food they eat and in the language they speak.

The right to free, prior and informed consent

Free, prior and informed consent means that indigenous peoples have the right to be consulted and make decisions on any matter that may affect their rights freely, without pressure, having all the information and before anything happens.

Protection from discrimination

The right to be free from discrimination means that governments must ensure that indigenous peoples and individuals are treated the same way as other people, regardless of sex, disability or religion.

360 DISCUSSION QUESTIONS

1   What do these documents tell about the relationship between governments and indigenous communities?

2   Why might a declaration of human rights specifically for indigenous peoples be considered necessary by the United Nations in 2007?

3   How do these sources represent an evolution in governmental policies toward indigenous peoples?

FOREIGN POLICY

3-1 | George Washington, selections from Farewell Address, 1796

George Washington (1732–1799), a third-generation colonial, Virginian planter and statesman, veteran of the French and Indian War, and commander in chief of the Continental Army in the Revolutionary War, was elected the first President of the United States in 1789. Largely responsible for shaping the office of President, Washington chose to refrain from seeking a third term in office. James Madison and Alexander Hamilton helped Washington draft his Farewell Address, a last word of counsel and personal reflection, published in the *American Daily Advertiser* in 1796. The excerpt below focuses on his views on "foreign entanglements."

Observe good faith and justice towards all nations; cultivate peace and harmony with all. Religion and morality enjoin this conduct; and can it be, that good policy does not equally enjoin it? It will be worthy of a free, enlightened, and at no distant period, a great nation, to give to mankind the magnanimous and too novel example of a people always guided by an exalted justice and benevolence. Who can doubt that, in the course of time and things, the fruits of such a plan would richly repay any temporary advantages which might be lost by a steady adherence to it? Can it be that Providence has not connected the permanent felicity of a nation with its virtue? The experiment, at least, is recommended by every sentiment which ennobles human nature. Alas! is it rendered impossible by its vices?

In the execution of such a plan, nothing is more essential than that permanent, inveterate antipathies against particular nations, and passionate attachments for others, should be excluded; and that, in place of them, just and amicable feelings towards all should be cultivated. The nation which indulges towards another a habitual hatred or a habitual fondness is in some degree a slave. It is a slave to its animosity or to its affection, either of which is sufficient to lead it astray from its duty and its interest. Antipathy in one nation against another disposes each more readily to offer insult and injury, to lay hold of slight causes of umbrage, and to be haughty and intractable, when accidental or trifling occasions of dispute occur. Hence, frequent collisions, obstinate, envenomed, and bloody contests. The nation, prompted by ill-will and resentment, sometimes impels to war the government, contrary to the best calculations of policy. The government sometimes participates in the national propensity, and adopts through passion what reason would reject; at other times it makes the animosity of the nation subservient to projects of hostility instigated by pride, ambition, and other sinister and pernicious motives. The peace often, sometimes perhaps the liberty, of nations, has been the victim.

So likewise, a passionate attachment of one nation for another produces a variety of evils. Sympathy for the favorite nation, facilitating the illusion of an imaginary common interest in cases where no real common interest exists, and infusing into one the enmities of the other, betrays the former into a participation in the quarrels and wars of the latter without adequate inducement or justification. It leads also to concessions to the favorite nation of privileges denied to others which is apt doubly to injure the nation making the concessions; by unnecessarily parting with what ought to have been retained, and by exciting jealousy, ill-will, and a disposition to retaliate, in the parties from whom equal privileges are withheld. And it gives to ambitious, corrupted, or deluded citizens (who devote themselves to the favorite nation), facility to betray or sacrifice the interests of their own country, without odium, sometimes even with popularity; gilding, with the appearances of a virtuous sense of obligation, a commendable deference for public opinion, or a laudable zeal for public good, the base or foolish compliances of ambition, corruption, or infatuation.

As avenues to foreign influence in innumerable ways, such attachments are particularly alarming to the truly enlightened and independent patriot. How many opportunities do they afford to tamper with domestic factions, to practice the arts of seduction, to mislead public opinion, to influence or awe the public councils? Such an attachment of a small or weak towards a great and powerful nation dooms the former to be the satellite of the latter.

Against the insidious wiles of foreign influence (I conjure you to believe me, fellow-citizens) the jealousy of a free people ought to be constantly awake, since history and experience prove that foreign influence is one of the most baneful foes of republican government. But that jealousy to be useful must be impartial; else it becomes the instrument of the very influence to be avoided, instead of a defense against it. Excessive partiality for one foreign nation and excessive dislike of another cause those whom they actuate to see danger only on one side, and serve to veil and even second the arts of influence on the other. Real patriots who may resist the intrigues of the favorite are liable to become suspected and odious, while its tools and dupes usurp the applause and confidence of the people, to surrender their interests.

The great rule of conduct for us in regard to foreign nations is in extending our commercial relations, to have with them as little political connection as possible. So far as we have already formed engagements, let them be fulfilled with perfect good faith. Here let us stop. Europe has a set of primary interests which to us have none; or a very remote relation. Hence she must be engaged in frequent controversies, the causes of which are essentially foreign to our concerns. Hence, therefore, it must be unwise in us to implicate ourselves by artificial ties in the ordinary vicissitudes of her politics, or the ordinary combinations and collisions of her friendships or enmities.

Our detached and distant situation invites and enables us to pursue a different course. If we remain one people under an efficient government, the period is not far off when we may defy material injury from external annoyance; when we may take such an attitude as will cause the neutrality we may at any time resolve upon to be scrupulously respected; when belligerent nations, under the impossibility of making acquisitions upon us, will not lightly hazard the giving us provocation; when we may choose peace or war, as our interest, guided by justice, shall counsel.

Why forego the advantages of so peculiar a situation? Why quit our own to stand upon foreign ground? Why, by interweaving our destiny with that of any part of Europe, entangle our peace and prosperity in the toils of European ambition, rivalship, interest, humor or caprice?

It is our true policy to steer clear of permanent alliances with any portion of the foreign world; so far, I mean, as we are now at liberty to do it; for let me not be understood as capable of patronizing infidelity to existing engagements. I hold the maxim no less applicable to public than to private affairs, that honesty is always the best policy. I repeat it, therefore, let those engagements be observed in their genuine sense. But, in my opinion, it is unnecessary and would be unwise to extend them.

Taking care always to keep ourselves by suitable establishments on a respectable defensive posture, we may safely trust to temporary alliances for extraordinary emergencies.

Harmony, liberal intercourse with all nations, are recommended by policy, humanity, and interest. But even our commercial policy should hold an equal and impartial hand; neither seeking nor granting exclusive favors or preferences; consulting the natural course of things; diffusing and diversifying by gentle means the streams of commerce, but forcing nothing; establishing (with powers so disposed, in order to give trade a stable course, to define the rights of our merchants, and to enable the government to support them) conventional rules of intercourse, the best that present circumstances and mutual opinion will permit, but temporary, and liable to be from time to time abandoned or varied, as experience and circumstances shall dictate; constantly keeping in view that it is folly in one nation to look for disinterested favors from another; that it must pay with a portion of its independence for whatever it may accept under that character; that, by such acceptance, it may place itself in the condition of having given equivalents for nominal favors, and yet of being reproached with ingratitude for not giving more. There can be no greater error than to expect or calculate upon real favors from nation to nation. It is an illusion, which experience must cure, which a just pride ought to discard.

DISCUSSION QUESTIONS

1   According to Washington, what elements make good foreign policy? Why?

2   Why was the United States able to take this new foreign policy approach?

3   How might other countries react to Washington's position on international affairs?

3–2a | James Mackay, excerpt from instructions for explorer John Thomas Evans, Louisiana Territory, 1796

During the seventeenth to early nineteenth centuries, explorers sponsored by European states sought to stake claims to and establish trade in the North American continent. James Mackay (1761–1822) was a Scottish trader-explorer, employed by the Spanish-funded but French-run Missouri Company. John Thomas Evans (1770–1799), a Welsh dreamer seeking a lost tribe of Welsh Indians, was hired by the Company to head an expedition from the Missouri River to the Pacific Ocean to counter the moves of the British and to gain scientific and geographic knowledge of the land. When Lewis and Clark set out on their famous trek in 1804, they set out well-informed by the findings and maps created by previous explorers. The excerpt below is from Mackay's instructions to Evans.

If you discover some animals which are unknown to us, you will see that you procure some of this kind, alive if possible. There is, they say, on the long chain of the Rockies which you will cross to go to the Pacific Ocean, an animal which has only one horn on its forehead. Be very particular in the description which you will make of it if you will be unable to procure one of this kind.

When you will have crossed the sources of the Missouri and will have gone beyond the Rockies, you will keep as far as possible within the bounds of the 40th degree of north latitude until you will find yourself nearly within the 111th to 112th degree of

longitude west meridian of London. Then you will take a northerly direction to the
42nd degree of latitude always keeping the same longitude in order to avoid the waters
which probably are destined to fall in California. This might induce you to take a route
away from the Pacific Ocean. After all, you cannot travel over so great an expanse of
land without finding some nations which can inform you about rivers which go toward the setting sun. Then you can build some canoes to descend these rivers, and will
watch carefully since there may be some waterfalls on them which can carry you away,
since the distance in longitude from the Rockies to the Pacific Ocean ought not to be
above 290 leagues, perhaps less, which condition makes it necessary for the rivers to
be very rapid or else to have great falls, in comparison with the distance which exists
between the sources of the Missouri which runs over a space of about 1000 leagues to
come to the sea by entering the Mississippi whose waters are very violent. This is so
if it is true that this chain of mountains serves to divide the waters of the west from
those of the east.

Mark your route in all places where there will be a portage to pass from one river to
another or from one waterfall to another by cutting or notching some trees or by some
piles of stones engraved and cut; and take care to place in large letters Charles IV King
of Spain and below [that] Company of the Missouri, the day, the month, and the year
when you do this in order to serve as unquestionable proof of the journey that you are
going to make.

There is on the coast of the Pacific Ocean a Russian Settlement that they say is
north of California, but there is reason to believe that it is not the only one and that
the nations of the interior of the continent ought to have knowledge of it. Then, when
you will have discovered the places that they inhabit, you will cease to make any sign
of taking possession, for fear of having spring up with these foreigners any jealousy
which would be prejudicial to the success of your journey. You will not neglect any interesting observation on the sea-shore and, although there may be some things which
do not appear to merit the least attention, nevertheless, in the journey of this nature,
everything is sometimes of great importance. Do not fail to measure the rise of the sea
in its ebb and flow.

As soon as you will have visited the sea-shore sufficiently, you will return from it
immediately, with as much vigilance as you can to this place, or to the spot where I
may be at the time, either among the Mandanes or elsewhere. You will take steps to
return by a different route from that which you have taken on your way out if you
believe it practical; but mind that if you find the route by which you will have passed
rather straight and easy for traveling by water in a canoe or other craft, it will be wiser
to return by the same route, and, in case there are portages to make from one river to
another or from one rapids to another, see whether the place permits the forming of a
settlement. . . .

In your orders be strict with your detachment and take care that no offense is committed against the nations through which you pass, especially by the connection that
they may seek to have with the women, a thing which is ordinarily the origin of dissatisfaction and discord with the savages. . . .

Take care, above all, to bring with you a collection of the products of the sea-shore:
animals, vegetables, minerals, and other curious things that you find, especially some

skins of sea-otters and other sea animals and shell-fish which cannot be found in any fresh water. A portion of each will be an unquestionable proof of your journey to the sea-shore; but, if you can find there any civilized people who wish to give you an affidavit of your journey in whatever language they speak, this will be an additional proof of the validity of your journey.

3–2b | Samuel Lewis, map of Louisiana, 1804

This map of the Louisiana Territory was published by American cartographer Samuel Lewis (ca. 1753–1822) and British cartographer Aaron Arrowsmith (1750–1823) in their *New and Elegant General Atlas* (Philadelphia, 1804). Their atlas promised the most current maps available at the time, and this engraved, uncolored map covers most of modern-day North America, noting natural features, people groups, and settlements, some of which—for example, the source of the Mississippi and the Missouri, the nature of the Rockies—were speculative ideas based on information gathered from explorers and native peoples.

SEE COLOR INSERT

DISCUSSION QUESTIONS

1   Which geographic features are prominent on the map? How does that demonstrate the map's purpose?

2   Why was it important for Evans to record his route as well as natural phenomena?

3   In the land being explored and mapped, whose claims were in competition? What constituted a claim?

3-3 | Tecumseh, excerpt of speech to General William Henry Harrison, 1810

Tecumseh (1768–1813), Shawnee chief and leader of a confederation of Native Americans outraged by U.S. expansion, met with Harrison, Governor of the Indiana Territory (1801–1812) and later President of the U.S. (1841), in a tense meeting at Vincennes. As governor, Harrison had negotiated eleven treaties with tribal leaders, leading to the federal government's acquisition of over sixty million acres of land. Tecumseh and his younger brother Tenskwatawa ("The Prophet") led a spiritually inspired military campaign of resistance to these treaties, leading to conflicts associated with the War of 1812, during which Tecumseh was killed. Several versions of his speech on August 11, 1810, one of which is excerpted here, have been passed down.

Brother, I wish you to listen carefully, as I do not think you understand what I so often have told you. Brother, since the peace was made you have killed some of the Shawanoes [Shawnee], the Winnebagos, the Delawares and the Miamis, and have taken our lands. We cannot long remain at peace if you persist in doing these things. The Indians have resolved to unite to preserve their lands, but you try to prevent this by taking tribes aside and advising them not to join the Confederacy. The United States has set us an example by forming a union of their Fires. We do not complain. Why, then, should you complain if the Indians do the same thing among their tribes? You buy lands from the village chiefs who have no right to sell. If you continue to buy lands from these petty chiefs, there will be trouble, and I cannot foretell the consequences. The land belongs to all the Indians, and cannot be sold without the consent of all. We intend to punish these village chiefs who have been false to us. It is true I am a Shawanoe, but I speak for all the Indians—Wyandottes, Miamis, Delawares, Kickapoos, Ottawas, Pottawatomies, Winnebagos and Shawanoes, for the Indians of the Lakes and for those whose hunting-grounds lie along the Mississippi, even down to the salt sea. My forefathers were warriors. Their son is a warrior. From them I take only my existence. From my tribe I take nothing. I am the maker of my own fortune. Oh, could I but make the fortune of my red people as great as I conceive when I commune with the Great Spirit who rules the universe! The voice within me communing with past ages tells me that once, and not so long ago, there were no white men on this continent. It then belonged to the red men, who were placed there by the Great Spirit to enjoy it, both they and their children. Now our once happy people are miserable, driven back by the white men, who are never contented but always encroaching. The way, the only way, to check this evil is for the red men to unite in claiming a common and equal right in the land as it was at first, and should be yet, for it was the gift of the Great Spirit to us all, and therefore the few cannot cede it away forever. What! Sell a country! Why not sell the air, the clouds and the great sea, as well as the earth? Backward have the Americans driven us from the sea, and on towards the setting sun are we being forced, *nekatacushe katopolinto*—like a galloping horse—but now we will yield no further, but here make our stand. Brother, I wish you would take pity on the red people and do what I have requested. The Great Spirit has inspired me, and I speak nothing but the truth to you.

DISCUSSION QUESTIONS

1 What charges did Tecumseh levy against Harrison and other Americans?

2 Why did he suggest the purchase of Indian lands by whites be invalidated?

3 How did Tecumseh's view of the natural world connect to his strategy to combat the encroachment of whites?

3–4 | James Gillray, political cartoon, "The Plumb-pudding in danger;—or— State Epicures taking un Petit Souper," England, 1805

James Gillray's engraving appeared in the midst of the Napoleonic Wars (1803–1815), just before Napoleon began his continental march east across Europe in late 1805. Britain had declared war on France in 1803, alarmed by French expansion and its implications for their trading post empire abroad. In this cartoon, British Prime Minister William Pitt, wearing a regimental uniform and hat, sits at table with French Emperor Napoleon Bonaparte. The caption in the upper right reads, "The Plumb-pudding in Danger;—or— State Epicures taking un Petit Souper," and under it: "the great Globe itself and all which it inherit" [a reference to *The Tempest*] is too small to satisfy such insatiable appetites'— Vide Mr W-d-m's [Windham's] eccentricities, in ye Political Register.'

SEE COLOR INSERT

DISCUSSION QUESTIONS

1 What does this cartoon imply about power in the western hemisphere?

2 What might be some American reactions to this cartoon?

3–5 | John Quincy Adams, excerpt of diary entry, November 16, 1819

John Quincy Adams (1767–1848), statesman and future president (1825–1829), served as Ambassador to the Netherlands, Prussia, Russia, and the United Kingdom. These key diplomatic posts culminated in his being named U.S. Secretary of State by James Monroe, a position Adams held from 1817 to 1825. A keen observer of global politics in a fledgling nation-state, he helped devise what would later be known as the Monroe Doctrine, first articulated in 1823 (see chapter 3, item 6a), and advocated territorial expansion in order to maintain U.S. security.

I said I doubted whether we ought to give ourselves any concern about it. Great Britain, after vilifying us twenty years as a mean, low-minded, peddling nation, having no generous ambitions and no God but gold, had now changed her tone, and was endeavoring to alarm the world at the gigantic grasp of our ambition. Spain was doing the same; and Europe, who, even since the commencement of our Government under the present Constitution, had seen those nations intriguing with the Indians and negotiating to bound us by the Ohio, had first been started by our acquisition of Louisiana, and now by our pretension to extend to the South Sea, and readily gave credit to the envious and jealous clamor of Spain and England against our ambition. Nothing that we could say or do would remove this impression until the world shall be familiarized with the idea of considering our proper dominion to be the continent of North America. From the time when we became an independent people it was as much a law of nature that this should become our pretension as that the Mississippi should flow to the sea. Spain had possessions upon our southern and Great Britain upon our northern border. It was impossible that centuries should elapse without finding them annexed to the United States; not that any spirit of encroachment or ambition on our part renders it necessary, but because it is a physical, moral, and political absurdity that such fragments of territory, with sovereigns at fifteen hundred miles beyond sea, worthless and burdensome to their owners, should exist permanently contiguous to a great, powerful, enterprising, and rapidly-growing nation. Most of the Spanish territory which had been in our neighborhood had already become our own by the most unexceptionable of all acquisitions—fair purchase for a valuable consideration. This rendered it still more unavoidable that the remainder of the continent should ultimately be ours. But it is very lately that we have distinctly seen this ourselves; very lately that we have avowed the pretension of extending to the South Sea; and until Europe shall find it a settled geographical element that the United States and North America are identical, any efforts on our part to reason the world out of a belief that we are ambitious will have no other effect than to convince them that we add to our ambition hypocrisy.

DISCUSSION QUESTIONS

1   How had American expansion been perceived by Europe?

2   What territorial gains did Adams envision for the United States?

3   Why did Adams assume America would continue to expand?

3-6a | James Monroe, excerpts from "Seventh Annual Message" (the Monroe Doctrine), 1823

James Monroe (1758–1831), lawyer and plantation owner, enjoyed a long career in government posts, serving as U.S. Senator, Ambassador to France as well as the United Kingdom, governor of Virginia, Secretary of War, and Secretary of State, culminating in the presidency (1817–1825). Monroe recognized the newly independent Latin American states to the south and initiated one of the most momentous—and audacious—policies in the history of U.S. foreign affairs: the Monroe Doctrine. This is an excerpt of his 1823 address to Congress, in which he articulated the policy of European non-intervention in the western hemisphere for the first time.

Fellow-Citizens of the Senate and House of Representatives:

Many important subjects will claim your attention during the present session, of which I shall endeavor to give, in aid of your deliberations, a just idea in this communication. I undertake this duty with diffidence, from the vast extent of the interests on which I have to treat and of their great importance to every portion of our Union. I enter on it with zeal from a thorough conviction that there never was a period since the establishment of our Revolution when, regarding the condition of the civilized world and its bearing on us, there was greater necessity for devotion in the public servants to their respective duties, or for virtue, patriotism, and union in our constituents. . . . A precise knowledge of our relations with foreign powers as respects our negotiations and transactions with each is thought to be particularly necessary. . . .

It was stated at the commencement of the last session that a great effort was then making in Spain and Portugal to improve the condition of the people of those countries, and that it appeared to be conducted with extraordinary moderation. It need scarcely be remarked that the result has been so far very different from what was then anticipated. Of events in that quarter of the globe, with which we have so much intercourse and from which we derive our origin, we have always been anxious and interested spectators. The citizens of the United States cherish sentiments the most friendly in favor of the liberty and happiness of their fellow-men on that side of the Atlantic. In the wars of the European powers in matters relating to themselves we have never taken any part, nor does it comport with our policy so to do. It is only when our rights are invaded or seriously menaced that we resent injuries or make preparations for our defense. With the movements in this hemisphere we are of necessity more immediately connected, and by causes which must be obvious to all enlightened and impartial observers. The political system of the allied powers is essentially different in this respect from that of

America. This difference proceeds from that which exists in their respective Governments; and to the defense of our own, which has been achieved by the loss of so much blood and treasure, and matured by the wisdom of their most enlightened citizens, and under which we have enjoyed unexampled felicity, this whole nation is devoted. We owe it, therefore, to candor and to the amicable relations existing between the United States and those powers to declare that we should consider any attempt on their part to extend their system to any portion of this hemisphere as dangerous to our peace and safety. With the existing colonies or dependencies of any European power we have not interfered and shall not interfere. But with the Governments who have declared their independence and maintained it, and whose independence we have, on great consideration and on just principles, acknowledged, we could not view any interposition for the purpose of oppressing them, or controlling in any other manner their destiny, by any European power in any other light than as the manifestation of an unfriendly disposition toward the United States. In the war between those new Governments and Spain we declared our neutrality at the time of their recognition, and to this we have adhered, and shall continue to adhere, provided no change shall occur which, in the judgment of the competent authorities of this Government, shall make a corresponding change on the part of the United States indispensable to their security.

The late events in Spain and Portugal shew that Europe is still unsettled. Of this important fact no stronger proof can be adduced than that the allied powers should have thought it proper, on any principle satisfactory to themselves, to have interposed by force in the internal concerns of Spain. To what extent such interposition may be carried, on the same principle, is a question in which all independent powers whose governments differ from theirs are interested, even those most remote, and surely none more so than the United States. Our policy in regard to Europe, which was adopted at an early stage of the wars which have so long agitated that quarter of the globe, nevertheless remains the same, which is, not to interfere in the internal concerns of any of its powers; to consider the government *de facto* as the legitimate government for us; to cultivate friendly relations with it, and to preserve those relations by a frank, firm, and manly policy, meeting in all instances the just claims of every power, submitting to injuries from none. But in regard to those continents circumstances are eminently and conspicuously different. It is impossible that the allied powers should extend their political system to any portion of either continent without endangering our peace and happiness; nor can anyone believe that our southern brethren, if left to themselves, would adopt it of their own accord. It is equally impossible, therefore, that we should behold such interposition in any form with indifference. If we look to the comparative strength and resources of Spain and those new Governments, and their distance from each other, it must be obvious that she can never subdue them. It is still the true policy of the United States to leave the parties to themselves, in the hope that other powers will pursue the same course.

If we compare the present condition of our Union with its actual state at the close of our Revolution, the history of the world furnishes no example of a progress in improvement in all the important circumstances which constitute the happiness of a nation which bears any resemblance to it. At the first epoch our population did not exceed

3,000,000. By the last census it amounted to about 10,000,000 and, what is more extraordinary, it is almost altogether native, for the immigration from other countries has been inconsiderable. At the first epoch half the territory within our acknowledged limits was uninhabited and a wilderness. Since then new territory has been acquired of vast extent, comprising within it many rivers, particularly the Mississippi, the navigation of which to the ocean was of the highest importance to the original States. Over this territory our population has expanded in every direction, and new states have been established almost equal in number to those which formed the first bond of our Union. This expansion of our population and accession of new States to our Union have had the happiest effect on all its highest interests. That it has eminently augmented our resources and added to our strength and respectability as a power is admitted by all. But it is not in these important circumstances only that this happy effect is felt. It is manifest that by enlarging the basis of our system and increasing the number of States the system itself has been greatly strengthened in both its branches. Consolidation and disunion have thereby been rendered equally impracticable. Each Government, confiding in its own strength, has less to apprehend from the other, and in consequence each, enjoying a greater freedom of action, is rendered more efficient for all the purposes for which it was instituted. It is unnecessary to treat here of the vast improvement made in the system itself by the adoption of this Constitution and of its happy effect in elevating the character and in protecting the rights of the nation as well as of individuals. To what, then, do we owe these blessings? It is known to all that we derive them from the excellence of our institutions. Ought we not, then, to adopt every measure which may be necessary to perpetuate them? . . .

3–6b | Simón Bolívar, excerpt from "Letter to Colonel Patrick Campbell," Gran Colombia, 1829

Six years after James Monroe called for an end to European intervention in the Americas, Simón Bolívar (1783–1830), President of Gran Colombia (1819–1830), wrote this letter to a British diplomat in Bogotá concerning the question of succession. Bolívar, a Venezuelan *criollo* and renowned military leader, led successful wars of independence against the Spanish Empire (ca. 1808–1825), resulting in a dozen new states in today's South America. An admirer of the U.S. and French Revolutions, Bolívar hoped to create a united Hispanic America able to counter moves by both Europe and the United States.

To Colonel Patrick Campbell, British charge d'affaires, Bogotá Guayaquil, August [5], 1829.

My esteemed friend and Colonel:

I have the honor of acknowledging receipt of your kind letter, dated May 31, at Bogotá.

I can only begin by thanking you for the many fine things that you say in your letter respecting Colombia and myself. Yet do you not have every right to our gratitude? I am abashed when I recall how much thought you have given and how much you have done, since you came among us, to assist this nation and uphold her leader's glory

The British minister resident in the United States does me too much honor in saying that he has hopes only for Colombia because Colombia alone has Bolívar. But he does not know that Bolívar's physical and political existence is seriously weakened and soon will end.

What you are good enough to tell me regarding the latest plan for appointing a European prince as successor to my authority does not take me by surprise. I had been informed of it in part, although with no little mystery and some trepidation, because my thoughts on the subject are well known.

I know not what to say to you about this plan, which is surrounded by a thousand drawbacks. You must know there is no objection on my part, as I am determined to resign at the next Congress. But, who will appease the ambitions of our leaders and the dread of inequality among the lower classes? Do you not think that England would be displeased if a Bourbon were selected? Will not all the new American nations, and the United States, who seem destined by Providence to plague America with torments in the name of freedom, be opposed to such a plan? I seem to foresee a universal conspiracy against our poor Colombia, which is already greatly envied by all the American republics. Every newspaper would issue a call for a new crusade against the ringleaders in the betrayal of freedom, those supporters of the Bourbons and wreckers of the American system. The Peruvians in the South, the Guatemalans and the Mexicans at the Isthmus, the peoples of the Antilles, Americans and liberals everywhere would kindle the flame of discord. Santo Domingo would not remain inactive; she would call upon her brothers to make common cause against a prince of France. Everyone would become our enemy, and Europe would do nothing to help us, for the New World is not worth the price of a Holy Alliance. We have good cause to think this way, judging from the indifference which greeted our launching and maintaining of the struggle for the liberation of half the world, which is soon to become the richest source of Europe's prosperity.

In short, I am far from being opposed to a reorganization of Colombia that conforms to the tested institutions of sagacious Europe. On the contrary, I would be delighted and inspired to redouble my efforts to aid an enterprise that might prove to be our salvation, one that could be accomplished without difficulty if aided by both England and France. With such powerful support we could do anything; without it we could not. I, therefore, reserve my final opinion until we hear the views of the English and French governments respecting the above-mentioned change in our system and the selection of a dynasty.

I assure you, my esteemed friend, with the utmost sincerity, that I have told you my thoughts fully. I have concealed nothing. You may use this statement as your duty and Colombia's welfare may require. That is my only condition, and so I bet you to accept the personal assurances of affection and regard of your very obedient servant,

    BOLÍVAR

A true copy.—Urdaneta.

DISCUSSION QUESTIONS

1 According to Monroe's speech to Congress, what was U.S. foreign policy toward Europe in the early 1820s? Toward Latin America? How were the two positions connected?

2 What appears to be President Bolívar's opinion of the Monroe Doctrine?

3 Under what conditions did Bolívar desire Gran Colombia to relate to Europe? How would the U.S. likely interpret this European influence?

ENCOUNTERING THE OTHER

3–7 | Hirata Atsutane, on "The Land of the Gods" and "The Art of Medicine," Japan, ca. 1820

Hirata Atsutane (1776–1843), prominent Shintō theologian and writer, contributed to the Edo Period's *kokugaku* (Native Learning) movement, which sought to elevate the ancient traditions of Japan over those of foreign influencers such as China, India, or the West. Confucianism and Buddhism had long been established in Japan via Korean texts and despite Tokugawa Japan's "closed country" policies, the study of Western science—which Atsutane admired—had been allowed since 1720. Most notably, he popularized an ethnocentric nationalism influential in modern Japan.

The Land of the Gods

All people are referring to this country, Japan, as the Land of the Gods and calling us, the people of Japan, the descendants of the gods. What they say is absolutely true. The heavenly gods particularly blessed us and descended to our land. There is no comparison of how blessed we are: in fact, Japan is worlds apart from all other countries. It must be understandably the Land of the Gods. Therefore, even the lowliest of men and women here are the descendants of the gods. . . . How deplorable not to fully understand one's origin. Only the people of Japan are truly superior and far from the people of all countries on earth such as China, India, Russia, Holland, Thailand, and Cambodia. We did not start calling Japan the Land of the Gods. If I may tell you the origin, all the lands were created by the divine gods from the time of the Japanese myths. And these gods, all of them, were formed in Japan. Therefore, Japan is the homeland of the gods. It is the universal and public view of why Japan is the Land of the Gods. You cannot dispute that. Even in the countries where no one has heard of our ancient traditions, they will naturally know Japan as the Land of the Gods from its gleaming majesty. Originally, when the current Korea was divided into three kingdoms of Shilla, Goguryeo, and Baekje, people there spread rumors that Japan was extremely superior, marvelously blessed. People of Korea said that in the east was the Land of the Gods called Japan as Japan is located east of Korea. They feared and spread the rumor throughout the world. Now, everyone, even the ones who do not know Japan, calls Japan the Land of the Gods.

The Art of Medicine

Among the things brought to Japan from abroad, the art of medicine appears to have been taught abroad early by our divine gods for a specific purpose. It has been practiced widely and has become our own again in the process. Just because it came from a foreign country does not mean we should dislike it. It's no wonder that China has naturally become proficient in medicine because they had to respond to difficult sicknesses due to the ill characteristics of China or because they only had ancient medicine available under their diverse climate. Since the *Heian* Period, Confucianism and Buddhism spread in Japan as well, and things became more troublesome, and the people more calculating. There are more things to worry about and more illnesses that are difficult to treat. That is when the Chinese medicine became the perfect response and people started practicing the Chinese medicine. Just like a country must enforce harsher laws when the number of robberies increase, a wise man emerges when more difficult illness develops. You tend to find more doctors in the areas with more difficult illnesses. Likewise, gradually doctors become more proficient and illness more troublesome.

DISCUSSION QUESTIONS

1   How would you describe Hirata Atsutanes's characterization of Japan?

2   What was Atsutanes's main argument regarding the development of medicine in Japan?

3   Compare Atsutanes's opinion of Japan with characterizations of the United States. How do you think these attitudes impacted the foreign relations of each country?

3–8a | Gordon Hall and Samuel Newell, excerpt from *The Conversion of the World*, 1818

This excerpt is from a booklet produced by the American Board of Commissioners for Foreign Missions (est. 1810). The ABCFM, in the context of the Second Great Awakening (ca. 1790–1840) and inspired by missionary associations in Great Britain, was the first successful U.S. organization to sponsor Christian missions overseas. While initial discussions focused on missions to Native Americans and India, the ABCFM quickly made its gaze global and, indeed, sponsored missions to all continents and a number of islands in Oceania.

That the number of Missionaries at present employed in preaching the gospel among unevangelized nations is nothing like an adequate supply will be evident from a moment's attention to the following general survey.

Let the population of the globe be computed at eight hundred millions.

Asia	500,000,000
Africa	90,000,000
Europe	180,000,000
America	30,000,000
Total	800,000,000

The number who bear the Christian name throughout the whole world may be ascertained with a sufficient degree of accuracy for the present purpose.

Europe, we know, contains the greatest part of the Christian population of the globe. After deducting about three millions of Mahometans, we may allow the whole remaining population of that quarter of the globe to be Christian in a very general acceptation of that term.

In the United States of America there are about eight millions that may also be reckoned Christians. The Christian population of the European possessions in North and South America is not accurately determined; but it probably is not far from ten millions. If we include Abyssinia in the list of Christian nations, we may allow about three millions of Christians for the continent of Africa.

The late Rev. H. Martyn, one of the English chaplains in Bengal, computed the Christians of all denominations in India and Ceylon at nine hundred thousand. If we allow one hundred thousand more for the islands in the Indian Ocean, and one million for Western Asia, we shall have a total in the whole of Asia, of two millions.

According to the foregoing estimate the Christian population of the world will stand as follows:

In Asia	2,000,000
Africa	3,000,000
Europe	177,000,000
America	18,000,000
In all the world	200,000,000

This amount deducted from the whole population of the earth leaves us six hundred millions of the human race, to whom Christ has not yet been preached. If this calculation is at all correct, it demonstrates the melancholy fact that in eighteen hundred years only about one fourth part of the world has been evangelized; and that, if the progress of the gospel should be no more rapid in future, than it has been hitherto, it will not be spread through the world in five thousand years to come. How distressing must this prospect be to every benevolent mind, to all who have been taught to say from the heart, "*Thy kingdom come.*" Let us hope, however, and let us pray, that God in mercy to our miserable and guilty world, may cut short the reign of sin, and speedily establish the holy and peaceful kingdom of his Son over all the earth.

But what exertions is the church of Christ now making for the advancement of the kingdom of her Lord? What means are Christians using tor the conversion of these six hundred millions of their fellow beings, for whom Christ died, and to whom he commanded that his gospel should be preached? What number of preachers have they sent forth to instruct this great multitude? The number of Missionaries actually labouring for the conversion of six hundred millions of people is only about three hundred and fifty in all the world, that is, one preacher of the gospel to one million seven hundred thousand souls.

The following is a pretty accurate list of all the Missionaries in the world, who have been sent by the churches in Europe and America to preach the gospel to the Heathen; not including native Missionaries, or persons converted from heathenism, now preachers of the gospel.

1. Asia

Danish Missionaries in India	7
Baptist Missionaries, Do.	20
From the London Missionary Society, in India and China	22
From Do. in the islands of Otaheite and Eimeo	16
Wesleyan Methodist Missionaries in India	6
From the church Missionary Society in India	10
From the American Board of Commissioners for Foreign Missions, Do.	9
From the American Baptist Board of Foreign Missions, Do.	4
From the Edinburgh Missionary Society, in Russian Asia	6
United Brethren in Do.	2
Total in Asia	**102**

2. Africa

The United Brethren	21
The London Missionary Society	30
The church Missionary Society	8
Wesleyan Methodists	2
Total in Africa	**61**

3. America

In the W. Indies, Wesleyan Methodists	40
The London Society	5
Baptist Society, (Eng.)	3
The United Brethren have in the W. Indies	63
Do. South America	15
Do. Greenland	19
Do. Labrador	28
Do. Canada and United States	10
American Board of Commissioners &c. to the Aborigines	4
Other Missionaries from different Societies	7
Total in America	**194**

Total in America	197
Africa	61
Asia	102
Total in the world*	**357**

*From this estimate it appears that while America has only about one sixteenth part of the unevangelical population of the globe, she has the labours of more than one half of all the Missionaries in the world. This fact should bar the objection to the American churches sending Missionaries to the Heathen in the East.

It claims attention also that the United Brethren, (Moravians) few and feeble as they are, supply nearly one half of the Missionaries now in the field! Only let other denominations do as much in proportion to their number and ability, and the gospel will soon be preached to every creature.

Six hundred millions of the human race who want the gospel, and less than four hundred Missionaries to impart it to them! It is thus, O ye disciples, of Jesus, that you repay the debt of gratitude, which you owe to your Redeemer! He died for you and all mankind. He called you by his grace, delivered you from sin and hell, restored you to God, and inspired you with the blessed hope of everlasting life. Now he calls you to his service, and requires that henceforth you should live not to yourselves, but to him, who loved you and gave himself for you and washed you from your sins in his own blood. He confers upon you the singular honor, the high privilege of going as heralds before him into all the world, to proclaim his approaching reign and call the nations to repentance. And is it so, that among the millions that bear the Saviour's name, only three or four hundred can be found who are willing to accept of this service? It cannot be. There are, there must be, if the gospel is not a fable, if religion is not a dream, there must be thousands, in different parts of the Christian world, who are ready, whenever the churches shall call them forth to embark for any part of the world to spend their lives in preaching the gospel to the Heathen, who are ready and willing "to endure all things for the elect's sake, that they also may obtain the salvation that is in Christ Jesus with eternal glory."

Let the churches then consider the part that belongs to them in the business of evangelizing the world. It is their business to send forth preachers.

If the church should at length come to the resolution fully and immediately, to obey the Saviour's command, to teach all nations, what number of teachers must she send forth in order to accomplish the object?

If we allow only one Christian Missionary to every twenty thousand souls throughout the unevangelized parts of the world, the claims of the different quarters of the globe will be as follows.

Heathen	population	Number of missionaries required
Asia	498,000,000	24,900
Africa	87,000,000	4,350
Europe	3,000,000	150
America	12,000,000	600
Total	**600,000,000**	**30,000**

Thirty thousand Missionaries for the whole world. Thus it appears that the number of Missionaries now in the field is to the number required, but little more than one to one hundred. With how much propriety may we say, "the harvest truly is plenteous, but the laborers are few!" and how much occasion is there for praying the Lord of the harvest that he would send forth more labourers into his harvest.

3–8b | Lam Qua, paintings for Dr. Peter Parker, China, 1830s

Peter Parker (1804–1888), Massachusetts native and the first Protestant medical missionary to Qing Dynasty China, opened a hospital in Canton (Guangzhou) in 1835, a year after his ordination by the Presbyterian church. Though a specialist in eye diseases, Parker also treated a number of patients for tumors causing deformities. While in China, he met Lam Qua (1801–1860), a highly skilled Chinese artist trained in Western portraiture. Parker commissioned Lam Qua to paint dozens of his patients in the 1830s, recording notes about many of them in his journals, and used the medical paintings to advance his missions work when in the U.S.

DISCUSSION QUESTIONS

1   Why might medicine be a skill that pairs well with the aim of missionary work?

2   Where were the most missionaries serving? What areas seem to be underserved?

3   What impact might missionary work have on indigenous populations? What effects
    might this endeavor have on missionaries?

3–9 | Domingo Faustino Sarmiento, excerpts from *Travels in the United States in 1847*, Argentina, 1847

Argentine Domingo Faustino Sarmiento (1811–1888) was a prolific writer, accomplished statesman, and world traveler who, as President of Argentina (1868–1874), argued against strongman politics and for modernization in Latin America. Like the better-known work of Alexis de Tocqueville, Sarmiento's reflections on his journey to the U.S. reveal penetrating observations of life in the mid-nineteenth-century United States by one determined to understand the "moral geography" of American society.

November 12, 1847

Don Valentin Alsina,

I am leaving the United States, my dear friend, in that state of excitement caused by viewing a new drama. . . . I want to tell you that I am departing sad, thoughtful, pleased, and humbled, with half of my illusions damaged while others struggle against reason to reconstitute again that imagery with which we always clothe ideas not yet seen. . . . The United States is without precedent, a sort of extravaganza that at first sight shocks and disappoints one's expectations because it runs counter to preconceived ideas. Yet this inconceivable extravaganza is grand and noble, occasionally sublime, and always follows its genius. It has, moreover, such an appearance of permanence and organic strength that ridicule would ricochet from its surface like a spent bullet off the scaly hide of an alligator. . . .

You and I, my friend, having been educated under the iron rod of the sublimest of tyrants . . . have prided ourselves and taken renewed courage from the aureola of light shining over the United States in the midst of the leaden night that broods over South America. At last we have said to each other in order to steel ourselves against present evils: "The Republic exists, strong and invincible, and its light will reach us when the South reflects the North." It is true, the Republic exists! However, on studying it at close range, one finds that in many respects it does not correspond to the abstract idea which we had formed of it. . . .

Why did the Saxon race happen upon this part of the world, so admirably suited to its industrial instincts? And why did South America, where there were gold and silver mines and gentle, submissive Indians, fall to the lot of the Spanish race—a region made to order for its proud laziness, backwardness, and industrial ineptitude? Is there not order and premeditation in all these cases? Is there not a Providence? . . .

I do not propose to make Providence an accomplice in all American usurpations, nor in its bad example which, in a more or less remote period, may attract to it politically, or annex to it, as the Americans say, Canada, Mexico, etc. Then the union of free men will begin at the North Pole and, for lack of further territory, end at the Isthmus of Panama. . . .

The American village . . . is a small edition of the whole country, with its civil government, its press, schools, banks, municipal organization, census, spirit, and appearance. Out of the primitive forests, the stagecoaches or railroad cars emerge into small clearings in the midst of which stand ten or twelve houses of machine-made bricks held together by mortar laid in very fine, straight lines, which gives their walls the smoothness of geometrical figures. The houses are two stories high and have painted, wooden roofs. Doors and windows, painted white, are fastened by patent locks. Green shades brighten and vary the regularity of the façade. I pay much attention to these details because they alone are sufficient to characterize a people and to give rise to a whole train of reflections. . . .

Westward, where civilization declines and in the far west where it is almost nonexistent because of the sparseness of the population, the aspect, of course, changes. Comfort is reduced to a bare minimum and houses become mere log cabins built in twenty-four hours out of logs set one on top of the other and crossed and dove-tailed at the corners. But even in those remote settlements, there is an appearance of perfect equality among the people in dress, manner, and even intelligence. The merchant, the doctor, the sheriff, and the farmer all look alike. . . . Gradations of civilization and wealth are not expressed, as among us, by special types of clothing. Americans wear no jacket or poncho, but a common type of clothes, and they have even a common blunt-ness of manner that preserves the appearance of equality in education. . . .

They have no kings, nobles, privileged classes, men born to command, or human machines born to obey. It is not this result consonant with the ideas of justice and equality which Christianity accepts in theory? Well-being is more widely distributed among them than among any other people. . . . They say that this prosperity is all due to the ease of taking up new land. But why, in South America, where it is even easier to take up new land, are neither population nor wealth on the increase, and cities and even capitals so static that not a hundred new houses have been built in them during the past ten years? . . .

The American male is a man with a home or with the certainty of owning one, be-yond the reach of hunger and despair, able to hope for any future that his imagination is capable of conjuring up, and endowed with political feelings and needs. In short, he is a man who is his own master, and possessed of a mind elevated by education and a sense of his own dignity. . . .

God has at last permitted the concentration in a single nation of enough virgin territory to permit society to expand indefinitely without fear of poverty. He has given it iron to supplement human strength, coal to turn its machines, forests to provide material for naval construction, popular education to develop the productive capacity of every one of its citizens, religious freedom to attract hundreds of thousands of for-eigners to its shores, and political liberty which views despotism and special privilege with abhorrence. It is the republic, in short—strong and ascendant like a new star in the firmament. . . .

The approach to New Orleans is marked by visible changes in the type of cultivation and the architecture of the buildings. . . . Alas slavery, the deep, incurable sore that threatens gangrene to the robust body of the Union! . . . A racial war of extermina-tion will come within a century, or else a mean, black, backwards nation will be found alongside a white one—the most powerful and cultivated on earth!

   Domingo Faustino Sarmiento

DISCUSSION QUESTIONS

1 What characteristics of life in the U.S. towns and villages did Sarmiento note? How did he account for variances?

2 To which forces did Sarmiento attribute the prosperity and growth of the United States?

3 How did he perceive the impact of slavery on American society?

3–10 | Xu Jiyu, *Ying-huan zhi-lüe* (*Short Account of the Oceans around Us*) on George Washington and the American political system, China, 1848

Xu Jiyu (1795–1873), a scholar-elite in Qing Dynasty China, witnessed the Chinese defeat by the British in the Opium Wars firsthand and, as governor of Fujian province, supervised two ports opened to foreigners as a consequence. Convinced that he needed to know more about the West, he gathered information from foreign missionaries, merchants, and available books. Xu Jiyu compiled this information in the *Short Account*. The excerpt here focuses on what he had learned about the U.S. and especially George Washington, whom he much admired.

America (A-mo-li-jia) is not connected with the other three continents. It is divided into two sections, one northern and one southern. The northern section is shaped like a flying fish, while the southern section looks like a person's thigh in loose trousers. A narrow strip, like a waist, connects the two sections. . . .

America has been separated from all other lands since time immemorial. The people are normal looking, similar to Chinese people, though with purplish red to brownish coppery skin. They leave several inches of hair when cutting it, tying it atop their heads. . . .

During the reign of the Hongzhi emperor (1487–1505) in the Ming dynasty, a Spanish official named Columbus (also called Columbo) sailed large ships westward in search of new lands. He first arrived at the islands of the Caribbean Sea, where he learned about the massive land of America. . . .

The United States is a large country in America. It is called the "Flower Flag Country" by the Cantonese because its ships hang flags with flowers. (Its flag is square with red and white interspaced stripes. In the left corner is another small black square with white dots in a constellation shape.) . . .

There was one among the people of the United States called Washington, born in the ninth year of the Yongzheng emperor (1731) [George Washington was actually born in 1732—*translator's note*]. When Washington was ten years of age, his father passed away, so he was raised and taught by his mother. He was an ambitious youth, talented in scholarly and military endeavors, with bravery surpassing all other. As an officer of the English military, he deftly overcame French raiders in the south. His superiors did not record his successes, but the villagers wished him to be their chief. Washington declined, falling ill and returning home. Later when the people rose up against England, they insisted that Washington be their commander in chief. . . .

After solidifying the nation, Washington resigned from the army and wanted to return home, but the people were unwilling to part with him, wanting him to become the nation's sovereign. Washington told the people that to take the nation and pass it down to his descendants would be selfish. It should be up to the common people to choose a leader of virtue to shoulder this responsibility. The former territory was divided into smaller states [The original word used is *guó*, referring more to a "nation-state" than "state" in the modern American sense—*translator's note*]. Each state has one commander and a vice-commander (some states have one vice-commander, others have several), serving terms of four years (there are also some that change every one or two years). If the people find the commander worthy, he may serve for another four years, but is not permitted to remain after the eighth year. Otherwise, he may be replaced by his vice-commander, and if either of them does not satisfy the people's wants, they may not be chosen again. Elders from towns and villages all may select a commander. The person's name is written down and cast into a box, from which whoever is recommended the most times is appointed. There is no restriction on whether only government officials or commoners can be recommended. After a person ends their term of service, they return to civilian life, being no different from other ordinary people. Among the commanders of the states, one is chosen to be the country's leader who is in charge of alliances and warfare, and all the states listen to him. The rules for selecting this leader are the same as in selecting the state commanders. He serves a term of four years, and may be reappointed up to a total of eight years. . . .

Washington was an exceptional man. In carrying out his tasks he was braver than Sheng or Guang; in conquering the land he was more heroic than Cao or Liu [These four names refer, respectively, to Chen Sheng, Wu Guang, Cao Cao, and Liu Bei, famous military strategists from the Qin dynasty (221–207 BC) and Three Kingdoms era (220–280 AD)—*translator's note*]. After taking up the sword and expanding the boundaries of the nation, he did not abuse his power or pass power on to his heirs. Rather, he invented a new method to choose leaders. He rapidly created an equal world for all, as idealized in the Three Eras [This refers to the ancient Xia (~2070–1600 BC), Shang (~1600–1046 BC), and Zhou (~1046–256 BC) dynasties—*translator's note*]. He idealized good behaviors rather than warfare, surely a leader unlike in any other nation. I have seen his portrait; his bearing was heroic and steadfast beyond measure. How could he not be called outstanding among men?

The weather in America is pleasant. The north is similar to Hebei or Shanxi province, while the south is similar to Jiangsu or Zhejiang. The land is flat and rich with no deserts, and the air is crisp and refreshing—although the air in the south can be humid and stifling, but it is still bearable. The soil is level and fertile, suitable for any crop, with the most widely grown being cotton. Both England and France acquire fruits and vegetables there, as well as tobacco, of which America's is the finest. Products coming from the deep mountainous areas include coal, salt, iron, and zinc. There are many rivers in the interior, and the Americans have carved out several canals for ease of travel. They have also created fire-wheel vehicles [China did not yet have trains at this time, so the word in modern Chinese for "train" (literally "fire car/vehicle") did not exist yet—*translator's note*]. They use stone to lay roads, then fill them with melted iron to facilitate the fire-wheel vehicle's movement. In one day, these vehicles can travel over three hundred *li* [A traditional unit of measurement roughly equal to half a kilometer—*translator's note*]. There is a particularly large amount of fire-wheeled ships coming and going between the rivers and seas, which is possible due to the coal that the land produces (fire-wheeled ships must burn coal because wood is too weak to power them . . .).

The United States government is the simplest, and taxes are also light. A census is taken every ten years. Every two years, one knowledgeable person among the populace is chosen among every 47,700 people to live in the capital and participate in the government. In the capital where the country's leader lives there is also an assembly, and two distinguished scholars from each state participate in the assembly. Here they discuss the most important government matters such as alliances, warfare, defense, and government paychecks. They serve for six years. Each state has six judges in charge of deciding legal matters and sentencing people to jail. . . .

The people of every state believe in Christianity. They enjoy discussing scholarly matters, and have established universities everywhere. There are three types of scholars: the academics, who research astronomy, geography, and Christianity; the physicians, who are in charge of curing illnesses; and the lawyers, who are in charge of judicial matters.

North and South America are separated by thousands of miles, but the greatest land there is the United States. The agreeability of the weather and the fertility of the land are no different than China. The people crossed thousands of miles of ocean from England to claim this shining pearl of a land. In just over two hundred years they have overcome this land, and their wealth has overflowed to the rest of the world. . . . The United States of America covers over ten thousand *li*. It has set no titles of king or other nobility, nor does it adhere to any rules of succession. Its system of rule through public governance and discussion has never been seen at any time in the ancient or modern world; it is a wonder. Among all Westerners from any time, how could Washington not be called the foremost?

DISCUSSION QUESTIONS

1   What characteristics about Washington and the American political system did Xu Jiyu most admire?

2   Why might the figure of Washington appeal to the Chinese?

3   According to this excerpt, what other features of American life did Xu Jiyu see as noteworthy? Why?

4

Forging a New Industrial Order

COMPARATIVE INDUSTRIALIZATION

The Industrial Revolution had repercussions far beyond the inside of a factory: industrialized societies faced unprecedented social, economic, political, cultural, and environmental change. Over time, agrarian societies became industrialized societies. Increased production provided new economic power—a power so potent that industrialized states could dictate terms to non-industrialized states—while new kinds of work created shifts in populations and work-life rhythms. A new working class demanded political voice and stretched traditional gender roles. Urban areas strained to accommodate thousands of new inhabitants drawn by opportunity and entertainment. The world became smaller with each innovation in transportation and communication.

Industrialization began in Great Britain in the eighteenth century and spread to Western Europe, the United States, and Japan in the nineteenth century. Several dozen nation-states are in the process of industrializing today, while fewer and fewer remain dependent on agriculture. Whereas nature used to be the predominant factor around which humans organized society, industrialization created a world in which humans adapt to and influence the environment.

Convention of commerce, Balta Liman, Ottoman Empire, August 16, 1838

ARTICLE I. All rights, privileges, and immunities which have been conferred on the suspects or ships of Great Britain by the existing Capitulations and Treaties, are confirmed now and for ever, except in as far as they may be specifically altered by the present Convention: and it is moreover expressly stipulated, that all rights, privileges, or immunities which the Sublime Porte now grants, or may here after grant, to the ships and subjects of any other foreign Power, or which it may suffer the ships and subjects of any other foreign Power, or which it may suffer the ships and subject of any other foreign Power to enjoy, shall be equally granted to, and exercised and enjoyed by, the subjects and ships of Great Britain.

II. The subjects of Her Britannic Majesty, or their agents, shall be permitted to purchase, at all places in the Ottoman Dominions, (whether for the purposes of internal trade or exportation) all articles, without any exception whatsoever, the produce, growth, or manufacture of the said Dominions; and the Sublime Porte formally engages to abolish all monopolies of agricultural produce, or of any other articles whatsoever, as well as all *Permits* from the local Governors, either for the purchase of any article, or for its removal from one place to another when purchased; and any attempt to compels the subjects of Her Britannic Majesty to receive such *Permits* from the local Governors, shall be considered as an infraction of Treaties, and the Sublime Porte shall immediately punish with severity any Vizirs and other Officers who shall have been guilty of such misconduct, and render full justice to British subjects for all injuries or losses which they may duly prove themselves to have suffered.

III. If any article of Turkish produce, growth, or manufacture, be purchased by the British merchant or his agent, for the purpose of selling the same for internal consumption in Turkey, the British merchant or his agent shall pay, at the purchase and sale of such articles, and in any manner of trade therein, the same duties that are paid, in similar circumstances, by the most favored class of Turkish subjects engaged in the internal trade of Turkey, whether Mussulmans or Rayas.

IV. If any article of Turkish produce, growth, or manufacture, be purchased for exportation, the same shall be conveyed by the British Merchant or his agent, free of any kind of charge or duty whatsoever, to a convenient place of shipment, on its entry into which it shall be liable to one fixed duty of nine per cent. *ad valorem*, in lieu of all other interior duties.

Subsequently, on exportation, the duty of three per cent, as established and existing at present, shall be paid. But all articles bought in the shipping ports for exportation, and which have already paid the interior duty at entering into the same, will only pay the three per cent. export duty.

V. The regulations under which Firmans are issued to British merchant vessels for passing the Dardanelles and the Bosphorus shall be so framed as to occasion to such vessels the least possible delay.

VI. It is agreed by the Turkish Government, that the Regulations established in the present Convention shall be general throughout the Turkish Empire, whether in Turkey in Europe or Turkey in Asia, in Egypt, or other African possessions belonging to the Sublime Porte, and shall be applicable to all the subjects, whatever their description, of the Ottoman Dominions; and the Turkish Government also agrees not to object to other foreign Powers settling their trade upon the basis of this present Convention.

. . .

Done at Balta-Liman, near Constantinople, on the 16th day of August, 1838.

Woodblock print by Inoue Tankei, *Famous Places in Tokyo: Picture of Azuma Bridge and a Distant View of a Torpedo Explosion*, Japan, 1888

SEE COLOR INSERT

Sergei Witte memorandum on the industrialization of imperial Russia, Russia, 1899

Russia remains even at the present essentially an agricultural country. It pays for all its obligations to foreigners by exporting raw materials, chiefly of an agricultural nature, principally grain. It meets its demand for finished goods by imports from abroad. The economic relations of Russia with western Europe are fully comparable to the relations of colonial countries with their metropolises. The latter consider their colonies as advantageous markets in which they can freely sell the products of their labor and of their industry and from which they can draw with a powerful hand the raw materials necessary for them. This is the basis of the economic power of the governments of western Europe, and chiefly for that end do they guard their existing colonies or acquire new ones. Russia was, and to a considerable extent still is, such a hospitable colony for all industrially developed states, generously providing them with the cheap products of her soul and buying dearly the products of their labor. But there is a radical difference between Russia and a colony: Russia is an independent and strong power. She has the right and the strength not to want to be the eternal handmaiden of states which are more developed economically. She should know the price of her raw materials and of the natural riches hidden in the womb of her abundant territories, and she is conscious of the great, not yet fully displayed, capacity for work among her people. She is proud of her great might, by which she jealously guards not only the political but also the economic independence of her empire. She wants to be a metropolis herself. On the basis of the people's labor, liberated from the bonds of serfdom, there began to grow our own national economy, which bids fair to become a reliable counterweight to the domination of foreign industry.

The creation of our own national industry—that is the profound task, both economic and political, from which our protectionist system arises. The advantages derived from the successful completion of this system are so numerous that I select here only the principal ones.

National labor, which at present is intensively employed only for a short agricultural season, will find full application and consequently become more productive. That, in turn, will increase the wages of the entire working population; and that again will cause an improvement of the physical and spiritual energy of the people. The welfare of Your Empire is based on national labor. The increase of its productivity and the discovery of new fields for Russian enterprise will always serve as the most reliable way for making the entire nation more prosperous.

The demand not only for raw materials but also for other articles will be met to a considerable extent by the work of the people themselves. And consequently the payment to foreigners, which at present consumes a considerable part of our national revenue, will be reduced. The import of foreign goods will then be determined not by the weakness of our industry but by the natural division of labor between nations, by which an industrially developed nation buys abroad only what it cannot advantageously produce at home; purchase abroad then enriches rather than exhausts it. Thanks to that, the accumulation of new capital from national savings is considerably facilitated, and that, in turn, promotes a further growth of productivity.

Within the country, exchange between the products of the soil and of labor will expand and give greater purchasing power to the grain market, which then can afford to pay higher prices for agricultural goods, thanks to which export prices also will rise. As a result, the income derived from land will also increase. And that, in turn, will make it possible for land cultivators, small and large, to improve their agricultural techniques and to raise the productivity of the land. The improvement of agricultural techniques will inevitably reduce the extreme fluctuation of harvests, which at present imposes such a heavy strain upon our national prosperity.

The gradual growth of industry in the country, always accompanied by falling prices for manufactured goods, will make it possible for our export trade to deal not only in raw materials, as at present, but also in industrial goods. Our present losses in the European trade can then be converted into profits in the Asiatic trade.

Graph of comparative primary school enrollment, United Kingdom, China, India, Japan, Turkey, Egypt, United States, and Senegal, 1820 to 2010

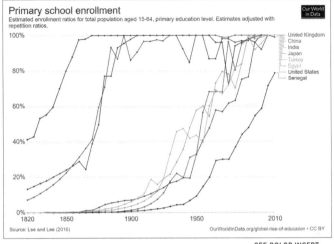

SEE COLOR INSERT

Chart showing percentage distribution of the world's manufacturing production, United States, Germany, UK, France, Russia, Italy, Canada, Belgium, Sweden, Japan, and India, 1870 and 1913

Table 1. PERCENTAGE DISTRIBUTION OF THE WORLD'S MANUFACTURING PRODUCTION

Period	United States	Germany	United Kingdom	France	Russia	Italy	Canada
1870	23.3	13.2	31.8	10.3	3.7	2.4	1.0
1881/85	28.6	13.9	26.6	8.6	3.4	2.4	1.3
1896/1900	30.1	16.6	19.5	7.1	5.0	2.7	1.4
1906/10	35.3	15.9	14.7	6.4	5.0	3.1	2.0
1913	35.8	15.7	14.0	6.4	5.5	2.7	2.3
1913*	35.8	14.3	14.1	7.0	b4.4	2.7	2.3
1926/29	42.2	11.6	9.4	6.6	b4.3	3.3	2.4
1936/38	32.2	10.7	9.2	4.5	b18.5	2.7	2.0

Period	Belgium	Sweden	Finland	Japan	India	Other countries	World
1870	2.9	0.4	—		11.0		100.0
1881/85	2.5	0.6	0.1		12.0		100.0
1896/1900	2.2	1.1	0.3	0.6	1.1	12.3	100.0
1906/10	2.0	1.1	0.3	1.0	1.2	12.0	100.0
1913	2.1	1.0	0.3	1.2	1.1	11.9	100.0
1913*	2.1	1.0	0.3	1.2	1.1	13.7	100.0
1926/29	1.9	1.0	0.4	2.5	1.2	13.2	100.0
1936/38	1.3	1.3	0.5	3.5	1.4	12.2	100.0

* The second line for 1913 represents the distribution according to the frontiers established after the 1914–18 war.
b U.S.S.R.

360 DISCUSSION QUESTIONS

1   What evidence of change caused by industrialization can be drawn from the sources listed here? What tensions or opportunities might be created by such change?

2   How might industrialization relate to imperialism? How could industrialization create the means and the motive for empire-building?

SLAVERY

4–1 | "A Planter's Letter," *The Gentleman's Magazine*, England, 1789

Heated debate surrounded the abolition of slavery and the slave trade. In Great Britain, abolitionists, armed primarily with moral arguments and grim evidence of abuses, were opposed by the powerful planters of the British Caribbean (or West Indies) who foregrounded economic and social—often racist—arguments. The following is an example of the latter, a letter to the editor dated April 1789 by the anonymous "No Planter. Mr.," printed in a pro-slavery news and gossip journal. *(Note the old-style printing of the letter "s.")*

Mr. URBAN,   *April* 23.

THE scheme for the abolition of the slave-trade is, in every view of it, absurd and impolitic. It is founded on a mistaken notion of humanity, or rather on ignorance, folly, and enthusiasm. The Negroes of Africa, in their native country, are apparently useless in the great scale of human society; they are totally incapable of refinement, arts, or sciences. The only way to promote their civilization, to make them serviceable in their generation, and happy in themselves, is to introduce them into a state of activity and industry. Man was not designed for a life of idleness. An idle man is a wretched creature. A Negro, removed to the West Indies, is placed in a climate much more agreeable to a labourer than the burning plains of Africa. His work in the Plantations is not harder, or more oppressive, than that of our common labourers in England, such as miners, blacksmiths, founders, paviours, scavengers, coal-heavers, and many others, whose situation is viewed, by those very humane and compassionate people who are advocates for their African brethren, without the least concern! Yet most of these drudges in this country have been *compelled* by necessity to leave the place of their nativity.

The vulgar are influenced by names and titles. Instead of SLAVES, let the Negroes be called ASSISTANT-PLANTERS; and we shall not then hear such violent outcries against the slave trade by pious divines, tender-hearted poetesses, and short-sighted politicians.

Yours, &c.   NO PLANTER.

Mr.

DISCUSSION QUESTIONS

1 How did the planter justify the enslavement of African people?

2 What assumptions did he make about the nature of labor?

3 Why did the planter suggest calling enslaved Africans "assistant planters" instead of slaves?

4–2a | Election handbill, "A Few Plain Questions to Plain Men," England, 1820s

Great Britain was the first major slave trading nation-state to end the transatlantic slave trade (1807), after which most other major slave traders followed suit by the 1830s. Ending slavery in the Atlantic world, however, took much longer because of the ways several centuries of slavery had become part of economic, social, cultural, political, and religious systems in the Americas and Europe. This handbill was published in London after the abolition of the slave trade, but before the abolition of slavery.

A Few Plain Questions to Plain Men.

Can a slave marry without his owner's consent? If so, quote the law : *give chapter and verse.*

Can a slave prevent the sale of his wife if the owner pleases? If so, quote the law.

Can a slave prevent the sale of his own child if his owner pleases? If so, quote the law.

Can a slave with impunity refuse to flog his wife, with her person all exposed, if his owner pleases to command him ?   If so, quote the law.

Can a slave obtain redress if *his master* deprives him of his goods? If so, quote the law.

Can a slave attend either public or private worship, without the risk of punishment, if his master forbids him? If so, quote the law.

These are plain questions, which every slave-owner knows can only be truly answered in one way.

When then any Englishman gets up to tell you how well the slaves are treated, or how happy under such circumstances slaves may be, tell him that he insults your understanding, that he outrages your British feeling, and that he dishonours God.

A HUSBAND AND A FATHER.

S. Bagster, Jun., Printer, 14, Bartholomew Close, London.

NO. 1.

4–2b | Broadside, "The Negro Woman's Appeal to Her White Sisters," England, ca. 1850

Published in London by abolitionist Richard Barrett (1784–1855), this widely distributed poem was intended for an American audience. Slavery had been abolished in Great Britain and its colonies in the 1830s, but British abolitionists remained active, supporting anti-slavery movements around the world for the remainder of the century. In the verse, Barrett adopts a female voice, using sentimental, religious, and gendered language to encourage sympathy among free and enslaved women in the U.S.

This Book tell man not to be cruel. Oh! that massa would read this Book.

THE NEGRO WOMAN'S APPEAL

TO HER WHITE SISTERS.

Ye wives, and ye mothers, your influence extend—
Ye sisters, ye daughters, the helpless defend—
These strong ties are severed for one crime alone,
Possessing a colour less fair than your own.
Ah! why must the tints of complexion be made
A plea for the wrongs which poor Afric invade?
Alike are his children in his holy sight,
Who formed and redeems both the black and the white.
In the good book you read, I have heard it is said,
For those of all nations the Saviour has bled,—
No "respecter of persons" is he I am told,
All who love and obey him he ranks in his fold;
His laws, like himself, are both pure and divine—
Ah! why bear his name and his precepts decline.

"Do justly," I hear is the sacred command—
Then why steal poor negro from his native land?
Can they violate this, and "love mercy?" Oh! no,
These chains, and these wounds, and these tears plainly show
That, assuming a power our God never gave,
The practice of sin will the heart more deprave.
That man, when rejecting his Maker's control,
His feelings and passions like billows will roll,
And spread desolation wherever he reigns
Behold it, alas! in this land of sweet canes.

'Tis the nature of crime so prolific its source;
To delude,—to mislead,—and to strengthen their force;
Then pity dear ladies and send me relief,
This poor heart is breaking with sorrow and grief:
Could you see my affliction your tears they would flow,
For women are tender by nature you know.
In health and in sickness I daily must toil
From sunrise to sunset, to hoe the rough soil,
My fevered head aching and throbbing with pain,
My fragile limbs torn, but I must not complain.
No voice of compassion its solace bestows,
If sinking with anguish I court some repose,

The wounds of fresh tortures will rouse me again,
For I must not one moment forgetful remain.
My babies are crying beneath the tall trees,
Their loud sobs come borne on the soft passing breeze,
To her whose rent bosom most keenly can feel,
Though she dare not her thoughts nor her wishes reveal,
While pierced with the knowledge they're roving alone,—
No hand to conduct them, and keep them at home—
To feed them—to sooth them, and hush them to peace
On that bosom of love, where their sorrows would cease.
Their smooth glossy cheeks, which as lovely I view
As are the mixed tints of the roses to you,
Are stained with the tears I would soon kiss away,
Could I see my sweet infants the long sunny day.
On their soft jetty locks hang the dew-drops of morn,
Which like pearls their bright ebony clusters adorn,
As they wander about round the green plantain tree,
Their little hands clasped, they keep asking for me—
Surprised that by her whom our nature has taught
To cherish and guard, they should now be forgot;
Alas! could they tell how my bleeding heart aches,
They would know that maternal love never forsakes:

The tide of affection that tinges *your* skin
With beauty's vermillion, proclaims it within;
But ladies believe me no warmer it glows
Because that through lilies and roses it flows.
The same holy hand which created *you* fair,
Has moulded *me* too in the hue that I wear;
No partial hand formed us, our title's the same—
'Tis inscribed on the Christian, whatever his name;
No sable can veil when his light from on high
Illumines the soul he has made for the sky,
To dwell in his courts, and be present with him,
When freed and redeemed from the bondage of sin.
Oh! fair Christian ladies, you bear a high name;
Your works of benevolence loudly proclaim
The mercy and kindness you show to distress;
Ah! pity dear ladies, our Saviour will bless.

Richard Barrett, Printer, Mark Lane.

DISCUSSION QUESTIONS

1 How did the handbill utilize contrast to argue against slavery?

2 What similarities did Barrett's "Appeal" rely upon to support abolition?

3 Note the audience and form of each source. What differences does gender make?

4-3 | David Walker, excerpts from *Walker's Appeal, in Four Articles; Together with a Preamble, to the Coloured Citizens of the World, but in Particular, and Very Expressly, to Those of the United States of America*, 1829

Abolitionist, businessman, and journalist David Walker (1796–1830) published his *Appeal*, a radical call to action that predated the organized anti-slavery movement in the U.S. Unabashedly criticizing the institution of slavery, Walker urged the black community to take action against it. Widely distributed by 1830, Walker's *Appeal* terrified some readers while stimulating others. Slaveholding states tried to prevent its dissemination; in fact, Georgia placed a bounty on Walker's head. Many abolitionists found its rhetoric too inflammatory, yet it inspired William Lloyd Garrison and Frederick Douglass, among others.

PREAMBLE.

My dearly beloved Brethren and Fellow Citizens.

Having travelled over a considerable portion of these United States, and having, in the course of my travels, taken the most accurate observations of things as they exist—the result of my observations has warranted the full and unshaken conviction, that we, (coloured people of these United States,) are the most degraded, wretched, and abject set of beings that ever lived since the world began; and I pray God that none like us ever may live again until time shall be no more. They tell us of the Israelites in Egypt, the Helots in Sparta, and of the Roman Slaves, which last were made up from almost every nation under heaven, whose sufferings under those ancient and heathen nations, were, in comparison with ours, under this enlightened and Christian nation, no more than a cypher—or, in other words, those heathen nations of antiquity, had but little more among them than the name and form of slavery; while wretchedness and endless miseries were reserved, apparently in a phial, to be poured out upon our fathers, ourselves and our children, by *Christian* Americans!

These positions I shall endeavour, by the help of the Lord, to demonstrate in the course of this *Appeal*, to the satisfaction of the most incredulous mind—and may God Almighty, who is the Father of our Lord Jesus Christ, open your hearts to understand and believe the truth.

The *causes*, my brethren, which produce our wretchedness and miseries, are so very numerous and aggravating, that I believe the pen only of a Josephus or a Plutarch, can well enumerate and explain them. Upon subjects, then, of such incomprehensible magnitude, so impenetrable, and so notorious, I shall be obliged to omit a large class of, and content myself with giving you an exposition of a few of those, which do indeed rage to such an alarming pitch, that they cannot but be a perpetual source of terror and dismay to every reflecting mind.

I am fully aware, in making this appeal to my much afflicted and suffering brethren, that I shall not only be assailed by those whose greatest earthly desires are, to keep us in abject ignorance and wretchedness, and who are of the firm conviction that Heaven has designed us and our children to be slaves and *beasts of burden* to them and their children. I say, I do not only expect to be held up to the public as an ignorant, impudent and restless disturber of the public peace, by such avaricious creatures, as well as a mover of insubordination—and perhaps put in prison or to death, for giving a superficial exposition of our miseries, and exposing tyrants. But I am persuaded, that many of my brethren, particularly those who are ignorantly in league with slave-holders or tyrants, who acquire their daily bread by the blood and sweat of their more ignorant brethren—and not a few of those too, who are too ignorant to see an inch beyond their noses, will rise up and call me cursed—Yea, the jealous ones among us will perhaps use more abject subtlety, by affirming that this work is not worth perusing, that we are well situated, and there is no use in trying to better our condition, for we cannot. I will ask one question here.—Can our condition be any worse?—Can it be more mean and abject? If there are any changes, will they not be for the better, though they may appear for the worst at first? Can they get us any lower? Where can they get us? They are afraid to treat us worse, for they know well, the day they do it they are gone. But against all accusations which may or can be preferred against me, I appeal to Heaven for my motive in writing—who knows that my object is, if possible, to awaken in the breasts of my afflicted, degraded and slumbering brethren, a spirit of inquiry and investigation respecting our miseries and wretchedness in this *Republican Land of Liberty!!!!!!*

The sources from which our miseries are derived, and on which I shall comment, I shall not combine in one, but shall put them under distinct heads and expose them in their turn; in doing which, keeping truth on my side, and not departing from the strictest rules of morality, I shall endeavour to penetrate, search out, and lay them open for your inspection. If you cannot or will not profit by them, I shall have done *my* duty to you, my country and my God.

And as the inhuman system of *slavery,* is the *source* from which most of our miseries proceed, I shall begin with that *curse to nations*, which has spread terror and devastation through so many nations of antiquity, and which is raging to such a pitch at the present day in Spain and in Portugal. It had one tug in England, in France, and in the United States of America; yet the inhabitants thereof, do not learn wisdom, and erase it entirely from their dwellings and from all with whom they have to do. The fact is, the labour of slaves comes so cheap to the avaricious usurpers, and is (as they think) of such great utility to the country where it exists, that those who are actuated by sordid avarice only, overlook the evils, which will as sure as the Lord lives, follow after the good. In fact, they are so happy to keep in ignorance and degradation, and to receive the homage and the labour of the slaves, they forget that God rules in the armies of heaven and among the inhabitants of the earth, having his ears continually open to the cries, tears and groans of his oppressed people; and being a just and holy Being will at one day appear fully in behalf of the oppressed, and arrest the progress of the avaricious oppressors; for although the destruction of the oppressors God may not effect by the oppressed, yet the Lord our God will bring other destructions upon them—for not unfrequently will he cause them to rise up one against another, to be split and divided, and to oppress each other, and sometimes to open hostilities with sword in hand. Some may ask, what is the matter with this united and happy people?—Some say it is the cause of political usurpers, tyrants, oppressors, &c. But has not the Lord an oppressed and suffering people among them? Does the Lord condescend to hear their cries and see their tears in consequence of oppression? Will he let the oppressors rest comfortably and happy always? Will he not cause the very children of the oppressors to rise up against them, and oftimes put them to death? "God works in many ways his wonders to perform."

DISCUSSION QUESTIONS

1 In what ways did Walker differentiate the ancient practice of slavery from its current American form?
2 From whom did he expect a reaction? Why?
3 Describe how Walker characterized God. How might this depart from white Christian interpretations?

4–4a | Solomon Northup, excerpt from *Twelve Years a Slave*, 1841

Popularized recently by the 2013 award-winning film of the same name, *Twelve Years a Slave* is the memoir of Solomon Northup (1807/1808–unknown). Northup was a free black man from New York kidnapped and sold into slavery. After twelve years of labor for several slaveholders in Louisiana, Northup was freed through the efforts of family, sympathizers, and the state of New York in 1853. His memoir, published soon after, was widely used by abolitionists. Here he describes the sale of slaves in New Orleans in 1841, not as a disinterested observer, but as part of the "lot" to be auctioned off.

In the first place we were required to wash thoroughly, and those with beards, to shave. We were then furnished with a new suit each, cheap, but clean. The men had hat, coat, shirt, pants, and shoes; the women frocks of calico, and handkerchief to bind about their heads. We were now conducted into a large room in the front part of the building to which the yard was attached, in order to be properly trained, before the admission of customers. The men were arranged on one side of the room, the women at the other. . . .

Next day many customers called to examine Freeman's "new lot." The latter gentleman was very loquacious, dwelling at much length upon our several good points and qualities. He would make us hold up our heads, walk briskly back and forth, while customers would feel of our hands and arms and bodies, turn us about, ask us what we could do, make us open our mouths and show our teeth, precisely as a jockey examines a horse which he is about to barter for purchase. Sometimes a man or woman was taken back to the small house in the yard, stripped, and inspected more minutely. Scars upon a slave's back were considered evidence of a rebellious or unruly spirit, and hurt his sale. . . .

The same man also purchased Randall. The little fellow was made to jump, and run across the floor, and perform many other feats, exhibiting his activity and condition.

All the time the trade was going on, Eliza was crying aloud, and wringing her hands. She besought the man not to buy him, unless he also bought herself and Emily. She promised, in that case, to be the most faithful slave that ever lived. The man answered that he could not afford it, and then Eliza burst into a paroxysm of grief, weeping plaintively. Freeman turned round to her, savagely, with his whip in his uplifted hand, ordering her to stop her noise, or he would flog her. He would not have such work—such snivelling; and unless she ceased that minute, he would take her to the yard and give her a hundred lashes. Yes, he would take the nonsense out of her pretty quick—if he didn't, might he be d—d. Eliza shrunk before him, and tried to wipe away her tears, but it was all in vain. She wanted to be with her children, she said, the little time she had to live. All the frowns and threats of Freeman, could not wholly silence the afflicted mother. She kept on begging and beseeching them, most piteously, not to separate the three. Over and over again she told them how she loved her boy. A great many times she repeated her former promises—how very faithful and obedient she would be; how hard she would labor day and night, to the last moment of her life, if he would only buy them all together. But it was of no avail; the man could not afford it. The bargain was agreed upon, and Randall must go alone. Then Eliza ran to him; embraced him passionately; kissed him again and again; told him to remember her—all the while her tears falling in the boy's face like rain.

4-4b | Ship's manifest of the schooner *Thomas Hunter*, 1835

The U.S. Customs Service provides this document from November 11, 1835—a ship's manifest detailing the ship's name, site and date of departure, site and date of arrival, and a list of its human cargo by name. Congress outlawed the slave trade in 1807 (effective in 1808), but did not extend its prohibition to the internal slave trade. Despite the ban, the number of enslaved peoples in the U.S. continued to rise, doubling from the time of the slave trade ban to 1830 and doubling again from 1830 to 1860.

DISCUSSION QUESTIONS

1 To what activity did Northup compare the slave auction? Why?

2 What does the manifest reveal about the U.S. slave trade in this era?

3 Why would the phrase "chattel slavery" be used to describe the reality presented by these sources?

4–5 | Chart, imports of raw cotton into Great Britain, 1856 to 1870

The chart below, drawn from British statistical reports for 1856–1870 and published in 1871, shows the dramatic influence of British industrialization on world markets. Leaders in mechanized textile manufacturing in the 1800s, Britain's factories not only dominated the global market but also radically increased demand for raw materials such as cotton.

Table 3. *Imports of raw cotton into Great Britain* (in 000s of 400-lb bales)

Calendar year	Source						
	US[a]	W Indies[b]	Egypt[c]	Brazil	E India[d]	Other	Total
1856	1,950.1	1.5	86.5	54.6	451.2	15.8	2,559.7
1857	1,639.7	1.4	62.2	74.8	625.9	19.4	2,423.3
1858	2,083.1	1.1	95.6	46.5	331.8	27.7	2,585.9
1859	2,404.3	1.5	95.3	56.2	480.8	26.9	3,065.0
1860	2,791.2	1.7	110.1	43.2	510.4	20.8	3,477.3
1861	2,048.8	1.6	103.7	43.2	922.6	22.6	3,142.5
1862	55.1	4.7	163.1	58.3	986.1	42.6	1,309.9
1863	138.6	13.0	268.4	56.5	1,165.0	32.5	1,674.0
1864	204.5	19.3	367.7	95.0	1,505.2	41.5	2,233.3
1865	475.7	41.9	510.0	138.5	1,212.0	66.9	2,444.9
1866	1,303.1	36.8	324.4	171.3	1,553.0	54.2	3,442.8
1867	1,323.4	33.3	332.4	176.1	1,247.1	44.0	3,156.3
1868	1,436.3	18.6	339.7	247.0	1,234.3	44.2	3,320.2
1869	1,144.6	24.3	434.9	198.5	1,203.4	46.4	3,052.0
1870	1,791.9	16.4	388.0	160.5	853.7	135.2	3,345.8

Notes: [a] US includes Bahamas and Mexico (during the war US cotton was smuggled through these regions); [b] West Indies includes British West India Islands, New Granada, and Venezuela; [c] Egypt includes cotton from other Mediterranean ports; [d] East India includes China and Japan (mostly for 1862-6).
Source: Great Britain, *Statistical abstract for the United Kingdom*, vol. 18 (1856-70), pp. 58-9

DISCUSSION QUESTIONS

1 In which years did Great Britain import the least amount of cotton from the United States? Why?

2 From where did Great Britain import its cotton during the years that imports from the U.S. declined? What did most of these places have in common?

3 What was fueling Great Britain's importation of cotton? Why might they require it in increasing amounts?

INDUSTRIALIZATION

4–6 | Adam Smith, excerpts from *Wealth of Nations*, 1776

The Industrial Revolution not only changed the way goods were manufactured through mechanization, but also saw mercantilism replaced by industrial capitalism. Scotsman Adam Smith (1723–1790), economist and philosopher of the Enlightenment, led the way by challenging existing mercantilist policies and, in so doing, developed concepts foundational to modern free market economic theory. In this excerpt from his influential 1776 work, he describes division of labor, the role of self-interest in the public good, the invisible hand of the market, and laissez-faire government policy.

Book 1, Chapter 1.

The greatest improvement in the productive powers of Labour, and the greater skill, dexterity, and judgement with which it is anywhere directed, or applied, seem to have been the effects of the division of labor. . . . To take an example, therefore, from a very trifling manufacture; but one in which the division of labour has been very often taken notice of, the trade of the pin-maker; a workman not educated to this business (which the division of labour had rendered a distinct trade), nor acquainted with the use of the machinery employed in it (to the invention of which the same division of labour has probably given occasion), could scarce, perhaps, with his utmost industry, make one pin a day, and certainly could not make twenty. But it the way in which this business is now carried on, not only the whole work is a peculiar trade, but it is divided into a number of branches, of which the greater part are likewise peculiar trades. One man draws out the wire, another straights it, a third cuts it, a fourth point it, a fifth grinds it at the top for receiving the head: to make the head requires two or three distinct operations; to put it on is a peculiar business, to whiten the pins is another; it is even a trade by itself to put them into the paper; and the important business of making a pin is, in this manner, divided into about eighteen distinct operations, which, in some manufactories, are all performed by distinct hands, though in others the same man will sometimes perform two or three of them. I have seen a small manufactory of this kind where ten men only were employed, and where some of them consequently performed two or three distinct operations. But though they were very poor, and therefore but indifferently accommodated with the necessary machinery, they could, when they exerted themselves, make among them twelve pounds of pins in a day. There are in a pound upwards of four thousand pins of a middling size. Those ten persons, therefore, could make among them upwards of forty-eight thousand pins in a day. Each person, therefore, making a tenth part of forty-eight thousand pins, might be considered as making four thousand eight hundred pins a day. But if they had all wrought separately and independently, and without any of them having been educated to this particular business, they certainly could not each of them have made twenty, perhaps not one pin a day. . . .

Book 1, Chapter 2.

The division of labor, from which so many advantages are derived, is not originally the effect of any human wisdom, which foresees and intends that universal opulence to which it gives occasion. It is the necessary, though very slow and gradual consequence of a certain propensity in human nature which has in view no such extensive utility; the propensity to truck, barter, and exchange one thing for another. . . .

Man has almost constant occasion for the help of his brethren, and it is in vain for him to expect it from their benevolence only. He will be more likely to prevail if he can interest their self-love in his favour, and show them that it is for their own advantage to do for him what he requires of them. Whoever offers to another a bargain of any kind, proposes to do this. Give me that which I want, and you shall have this which you want, is the meaning of every such offer; and it is in this manner that we obtain from one another the far greater part of those good offices which we stand in need of. It is not from the benevolence of the butcher, the brewer, or the baker that we expect our dinner, but from their regard to their own interest. . . .

As it is by treaty, by barter, and by purchase, that we obtain from one another the greater part of those mutual good offices which we stand in need of, so it is the same trucking disposition which originally gives occasion to the division of labor. In a tribe of hunters or shepherds a particular person makes bows and arrows, for example, with more readiness and dexterity than any other. He frequently exchanges them for cattle or for venison with his companions; and he finds at last that he can in this manner get more cattle and venison, than if he himself went to the field to catch them. From a regard to his own interest, therefore, the making of bows and arrows grows to be his chief business, and he becomes a sort of armorer. . . .

Book 4, Chapter 2.

As every individual, therefore, endeavors as much as he can both to employ his capital in the support of domestic industry, and so to direct that industry that its produce may be of the greatest value, every individual necessarily labours to render the annual revenue of the society as great as he can. He generally, indeed, neither intends to promote the public interest, nor knows how much he is promoting it . . . he intends only his own security; and by directing that industry in such a manner as its produce may be of the greatest value, he intends only his own gain, and he is in this, as in many other cases, led by an invisible hand to promote an end which was no part of his intention. Nor is it always the worse for the society that it was no part of it. By pursuing his own interest he frequently promotes that of the society more effectually than when he really intends to promote it. I have never known much good done by those who affected to trade for the public good. . . .

The statesman who should attempt to direct private people in what manner they ought to employ their capitals, would not only load himself with a most unnecessary attention, but assume an authority which could safely be trusted, not only to no single person, but to no council or senate whatever, and which would nowhere be so dangerous as in the hands of a man who had folly and presumption enough to fancy himself fit to exercise it. . . .

Book 4, Chapter 3.

Each nation has been made to look with an invidious eye upon the prosperity of all nations with which it trades, and to consider their gain as its own loss. Commerce, which ought naturally to be, among nations, as among individuals, a bond of union and friendship, has become the most fertile source of discord and animosity.

DISCUSSION QUESTIONS

1 In what ways did Smith's ideas challenge existing ideas about industry, markets, and economics?

2 What would the adoption of Smith's ideas mean for global commerce?

4–7a | Yorkshire Cloth Workers Petition, England, 1786

Published as a broadsheet in 1791, this address from dozens of cloth merchants in Leeds details arguments in favor of the mechanization occurring across Great Britain in the textile industry. Compare their arguments with those of the workers in the same industry.

At a time when the People, engaged in every other Manufacture in the Kingdom, are exerting themselves to bring their Work to Market at reduced Prices, which can alone be effected by the Aid of Machinery, it certainly is not necessary that the Cloth Merchants of Leeds, who depend chiefly on a Foreign Demand, where they have for Competitors the Manufacturers of other Nations, whose Taxes are few, and whose manual Labour is only Half the Price it bears here, should have Occasion to defend a Conduct, which has for its Aim the Advantage of the Kingdom in general, and of the Cloth Trade in particular; yet anxious to prevent Misrepresentations, which have usually attended the Introduction of the most useful Machines, they wish to remind the Inhabitants of this Town, of the Advantages derived to every flourishing Manufacture from the Application of Machinery; they instance that of Cotton in particular, which in its internal and foreign Demand is nearly alike to our own, and has in a few Years by the Means of Machinery advanced to its present Importance, and is still increasing.

If then by the Use of Machines, the Manufacture of Cotton, an Article which we import, and are supplied with from other Countries, and which can every where be procured on equal Terms, has met with such amazing Success, may not greater Advantages be reasonably expected from cultivating to the utmost the Manufacture of Wool, the Produce of our own Island, an Article in Demand in all Countries, almost the universal Clothing of Mankind?

In the Manufacture of Woollens, the Scribbling Mill, the Spinning Frame, and the Fly Shuttle, have reduced manual Labour nearly One third, and each of them at its first Introduction carried an Alarm to the Work People, yet each has contributed to advance the Wages and to increase the Trade, so that if an Attempt was now made to deprive us of the Use of them, there is no Doubt, but every Person engaged in the Business, would exert himself to defend them.

From these Premises, we the undersigned Merchants, think it a Duty we owe to ourselves, to the Town of Leeds, and to the Nation at large, to declare that we will protect and support the free Use of the proposed Improvements in Cloth-Dressing, by every legal Means in our Power; and if after all, contrary to our Expectations, the Introduction of Machinery should for a Time occasion a Scarcity of Work in the Cloth Dressing Trade, we have unanimously agreed to give a Preference to such Workmen as are now settled Inhabitants of this Parish, and who give no Opposition to the present Scheme.

> Appleby & Sawyer
> Bernard Bischoff & Sons
> [and 59 other names]

4–7b | Letter from Leeds Cloth Merchants, England, 1791

The primary characteristic of the Industrial Revolution was the shift from human and animal power to machine power, starting initially in Britain and moving to other Western states—including the U.S.—in the early to mid-1800s. This change radically increased productivity, yet it caused significant dislocation and anxiety in society as well. This proclamation, published in two Leeds newspapers on June 13, 1786, demonstrates some of the reasons that workers opposed the process of mechanization. Leeds was a major textile mill town in West Yorkshire, England.

To the Merchants, Clothiers and all such as wish well to the
Staple Manufactory of this Nation.

The Humble ADDRESS and PETITION of Thousands, who labour in the Cloth Manufactory.

SHEWETH, That the Scribbling-Machines have thrown thousands of your petitioners out of employ, whereby they are brought into great distress, and are not able to procure a maintenance for their families, and deprived them of the opportunity of bringing up their children to labour: We have therefore to request, that prejudice and self-interest may be laid aside, and that you may pay that attention to the following facts, which the nature of the case requires.

The number of Scribbling-Machines extending about seventeen miles south-west of LEEDS, exceed all belief, being no less than *one hundred and seventy!* and as each machine will do as much work in twelve hours, as ten men can in that time do by hand, (speaking within bounds) and they working night-and-day, one machine will do as much work in one day as would otherwise employ twenty men.

As we do not mean to assert any thing but what we can prove to be true, we allow four men to be employed at each machine twelve hours, working night and day, will take eight men in twenty-four hours; so that, upon a moderate computation twelve men are thrown out of employ for every single machine used in scribbling; and as it may be supposed the number of machines in all the other quarters together, nearly equal those in the South-West, full four thousand men are left to shift for a living how they can, and must of course fall to the Parish, if not timely relieved. Allowing one boy to be bound apprentice from each family out of work, eight thousand hands are deprived of the opportunity of getting a livelihood.

We therefore hope, that the feelings of humanity will lead those who have it in their power to prevent the use of those machines, to give every discouragement they can to what has a tendency so prejudicial to their fellow-creatures.

This is not all; the injury to the Cloth is great, in so much that in Frizing, instead of leaving a nap upon the cloth, the wool is drawn out, and the Cloth is left thread-bare.

Many more evils we could enumerate, but we would hope, that the sensible part of mankind, who are not biassed [sic] by interest, must see the dreadful tendancy [sic] of their continuance; a depopulation must be the consequence; trade being then lost, the landed interest will have no other satisfaction but that of being *last devoured*.

We wish to propose a few queries to those who would plead for the further continuance of these machines:

Men of common sense must know, that so many machines in use, take the work from the hands employed in Scribbling,—and who did that business before machines were invented.

How are those men, thus thrown out of employ to provide for their families;—and what are they to put their children apprentice to, that the rising generation may have something to keep them at work, in order that they may not be like vagabonds strolling about in idleness? Some say, Begin and learn some other business.—Suppose we do; who will maintain our families, whilst we undertake the arduous task; and when we have learned it, how do we know we shall be any better for all our pains; for by the time we have served our second apprenticeship, another machine may arise, which may take away that business also; so that our families, being half pined whilst we are learning how to provide them with bread, will be wholly so during the period of our third apprenticeship.

But what are our children to do; are they to be brought up in idleness? Indeed as things are, it is no wonder to hear of so many executions; for our parts, though we may be thought illiterate men, our conceptions are, that bringing children up to industry, and keeping them employed, is the way to keep them from falling into those crimes, which an idle habit naturally leads to.

These things impartially considered will we hope, be strong advocates in our favour; and we conceive that men of sense, religion and humanity, will be satisfied of the reasonableness, as well as necessity of this address, and that their own feelings will urge them to espouse the cause of us and our families—

> Signed, in behalf of THOUSANDS, by
> Joseph Hepworth, Thomas Lobley
> Robert Wood, Thos. Blackburn.

DISCUSSION QUESTIONS

1   According to the workers, what were the adverse effects of the mechanization of the textile industry?

2   How did the merchants say mechanization improved the textile market?

3   What were the respective priorities of the workers and merchants? How were they in tension with one another?

4–8a | Winslow Homer, sketch, "The Bobbin Girl," 1871

Considered by many to be the greatest American artist of the nineteenth century, Winslow Homer (1836–1910) worked early in his career as a freelance illustrator and produced one of the few extant images of working conditions in textile mills before the 1880s. This version, published in 1871 to accompany William Cullen Bryant's *Song of the Sower*, takes as its subject one of the many female mill workers and the machine she tends.

Fling wide the grain for those who throw
The clanking shuttle to and fro,
In the long row of humming rooms,

And into ponderous masses wind
The web that, from a thousand looms,
Comes forth to clothe mankind.

4–8b | Harriet H. Robinson, excerpt from *Early Factory Labor in New England*, 1883

Lowell, Massachusetts, was a planned factory town established in the early 1820s utilizing a management and labor system replicated throughout New England. Factory owners recruited the thousands of textile mill workers needed from agricultural areas, employing primarily young women and children. For most women, factory jobs provided freedom and income, yet the job itself both challenged traditional gender norms, creating family and social tension, and entailed long hours and difficult working conditions, a hardship for those employed. In this excerpt, former Lowell mill girl Harriet Robinson discusses motivations for work.

In what follows, I shall confine myself to a description of factory life in Lowell, Massachusetts, from 1832 to 1848, since, with that phase of Early Factory Labor in New England, I am the most familiar—because I was a part of it.

In 1832, Lowell was little more than a factory village. Five "corporations" were started, and the cotton mills belonging to them were building. Help was in great demand and stories were told all over the country of the new factory place, and the high wages that were offered to all classes of work-people; stories that reached the ears of mechanics' and farmers' sons and gave new life to lonely and dependent women in distant towns and farm-houses. . . . Troops of young girls came from different parts of New England, and from Canada, and men were employed to collect them at so much a head, and deliver them at the factories. . . .

The most prevailing incentive to labor was to secure the means of education for some *male* member of the family. To make a *gentleman* of a brother or a son, to give him a college education, was the dominant thought in the minds of a great many of the better class of mill-girls. I have known more than one to give every cent of her wages, month after month, to her brother, that he might get the education necessary to enter some profession. I have known a mother to work years in this way for her boy. I have known women to educate young men by their earnings, who were not sons or relatives. There are many men now living who were helped to an education by the wages of the early mill-girls.

It is well to digress here a little, and speak of the influence the possession of money had on the characters of some of these women. We can hardly realize what a change the cotton factory made in the status of the working women. Hitherto woman had always been a money *saving* rather than a money earning, member of the community. Her labor could command but small return. If she worked out as servant, or "help," her wages were from 50 cents to $1.00 a week; or, if she went from house to house by the day to spin and weave, or do tailoress work, she could get but 75 cents a week and her meals. As teacher, her services were not in demand, and the arts, the professions, and even the trades and industries, were nearly all closed to her.

As late as 1840 there were only seven vocations outside the home into which the women of New England had entered. At this time woman had no property rights. A widow could be left without her share of her husband's (or the family) property, an "incumbrance" to his estate. A father could make his will without reference to his daughter's share of the inheritance. He usually left her a home on the farm as long as she remained single. A woman was not supposed to be capable of spending her own, or of using other people's money. In Massachusetts, before 1840, a woman could not, legally, be treasurer of her own sewing society, unless some man were responsible for her.

The law took no cognizance of woman as a money-spender. She was a ward, an appendage, a relict. Thus it happened, that if a woman did not choose to marry, or, when left a widow, to re-marry, she had no choice but to enter one of the few employments open to her, or to become a burden on the charity of some relative.

In almost every New England home could be found one or more of these women sitting "solitary" in the family; sometimes welcome, more often unwelcome; leading joyless, and in many instances, unsatisfactory lives. The cotton factory was a great opening to these lonely and dependent women. From a condition of almost pauperism they were placed at once above want. They could earn money and spend it as they pleased. They could gratify their tastes and desires without restraint and without rendering an account to anybody.

At last they had found a place in the universe, and were no longer obliged to finish out their faded lives a burden to their male relatives.

DISCUSSION QUESTIONS

1   How does the image of the bobbin girl characterize her work?
2   What effects did mill work have on women and their families?
3   Why might mill owners hire women as workers?

4–9 | Growth of mobility

One of the consequences of the Industrial Revolution was the dramatic change in mobility due to ongoing innovations in transportation technology and capabilities. Initially, transport improvements addressed the need to get goods from one place to another more effectively, but the transformation soon influenced the mobility of people as well. Below is an advertisement from the first scheduled transatlantic service, the Black Ball Line, founded in 1817, as well as a map by cartographer Charles Paullin depicting how technology influenced travel times across the U.S.

4–9a | *Evening Post*, advertisement, line of American packets between New York and Liverpool, 1817

In order to furnish frequent and regular conveyances for Goods and Passengers, the subscribers have undertaken to establish a line of vessels between New-York and Liverpool, to sail from each place on a certain day in every month throughout the year.

The following vessels, each about four hundred tons burthen, have been fitted out for this purpose:

- Ship *Amity*, John Stanton, master
- Ship *Courier*, Wm. Bowne, master
- Ship *Pacific*, Jno. Williams, master
- Ship *James Monroe*,———

And it is the intention of the owners that one of these vessels shall sail from New-York on the 5th, and one from Liverpool on the 1st of every month.

These ships have all been built in New-York, of the best materials, and are coppered and copper fastened. They are known to be remarkably fast sailers, and their accommodations for passengers are uncommonly extensive and commodious. They are all nearly new except the *Pacific*; she has been some years in the trade, but has been recently throughly examined, and is found to be perfectly sound in every respect.

The commanders of them are all men of great experience and activity; and they will do all in their power to render these Packets eligible conveyances for passengers. It is also thought, that the regularity of their times of sailing, and the excellent condition in which they deliver their cargoes, will make them very desirable opportunities for the conveyance of goods.

It is intended that this establishment shall commence by the departure of the *James Monroe*, from New-York on the 5th, and the *Courier* from Liverpool on the 1st, of First Month (January) next; and one of the vessels will sail at the same periods from each place in every succeding month.

- Isaac Wright & Son
- Francis Thompson
- Benjamin Marshall
- Jeremiah Thompson

4–9b | Map, Paullin Transportation, 1932

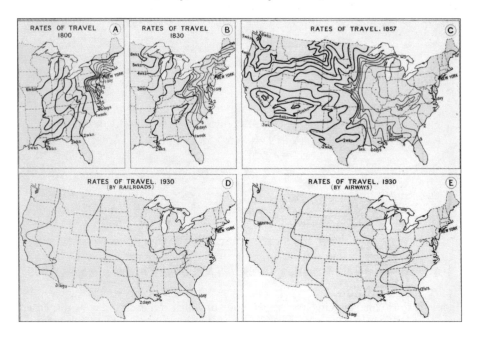

DISCUSSION QUESTIONS

1   What influence did industrialization have on the mobility of goods and people?

2   What kinds of changes would these developments have on life in industrialized societies?

4–10 | Mechanizing agriculture

Sometimes referred to as the Father of Modern Agriculture, inventor and businessman Cyrus McCormick (1809–1884) revolutionized farming. In an era when agriculture was dominated by small family farms relying upon scythe-swinging men to harvest wheat, McCormick, a blacksmith from Virginia, first patented a mechanical horse-drawn reaper in 1834. He later took an improved design to Chicago, where his McCormick Harvesting Machine Company became the largest farm equipment company in the U.S. and drew international acclaim at London's Great Exhibition of 1851. Below is an image of the 1845 McCormick reaper and a 1909 account of the reaper's success produced by Wisconsin's State Historical Society.

4−10a | Patent sketch, Cyrus McCormick mechanical reaper, 1845

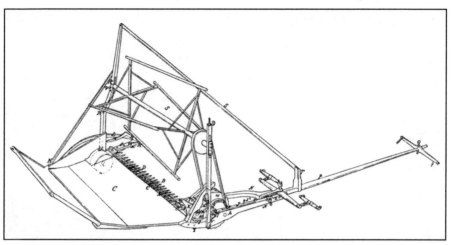

4−10b | Reuben Gold Thwaites, *Cyrus Hall McCormick and the Reaper*, 1909

There are four vital elements in a reaper, none of which can even today be dispensed with; and yet all four were successfully embodied in the machine which Cyrus H. Mc-Cormick introduced to the world in the harvest of 1831:

I. A platform, or grain deck, one end of which is flexibly affixed to the master-wheel, while the other is supported by a small "grain" wheel, so that the platform may readily accommodate itself to the irregularities of the surface.

II. A reciprocating knife (operated directly from the master-wheel) having a ser-rated edge, with stationary teeth or guards projecting forward from the platform, im-mediately over the inner edge of the knife and bent backward beneath it—so that, as the knife reciprocates through them, the stalks will be sustained by the fixed teeth and sheared off.

III. A horizontal and adjustable reel, so situated as to rotate in the direction of the master-wheel, serving to sweep the standing grain towards the cutting apparatus, and delivering the several stalks parallel upon the platform, in a swath adapted to be raked off into bundles, ready for the binders.

IV. A divider, serving, as McCormick stated in his original description, to "divide and keep separate the grain to be cut from that to be left standing"—an operation in which the reel also takes part.

. . . In after years McCormick stated that, living in the then isolated Valley of Virgin-ia, he had never seen or heard of any experiments in the mechanical reaping of grain save those made by his father. Such experiments were at the time not infrequently alluded to in English agricultural magazines, but none of these publications had as yet penetrated to Walnut Grove. Without doubt there was in this isolation a certain ad-vantage, for the young inventor was free to approach the subject from a comparatively fresh and original point of view. Probably this was the reason why, contemplating only the failures of his father, he made a radical and most essential departure from all his predecessors, inventing a machine along entirely new lines.

As is usually the case with the first form of an invention, the McCormick reaper of 1831 was crude in construction; but there is nothing on record indicating that any prior invention embodied such a scheme of construction, or indeed any scheme that succeeded or survived; and despite all subsequent invention, and it has been lavish, no one has contrived a successful substitute for McCormick's original plan. From it has proceeded in unbroken succession, and with remarkable adherence to the primary arrangement—although subsequently enriched with many refinements in details and supplemental improvements—the reaper that has taken and still holds possession of the markets of the world.

DISCUSSION QUESTIONS

1   How was the reaper powered? What makes it "mechanical"?

2   What are some reasons farmers would embrace mechanization?

3   Why would a mechanical reaper dramatically change the productivity and practice of agriculture?

4–11a | William Lovett of the London Working Men's Association, cover of *The People's Charter*, England, 1838

The changes wrought by the Industrial Revolution raised a number of questions about the newly created working class, from practical issues of wages and working conditions to political issues of voice and vote to social issues of class and mobility. As Britain industrialized first, it was also the site of many "firsts" related to labor reform movements, many of which spread to the rest of the industrialized world. The Chartists, or supporters of *The People's Charter*, sought reforms intended to increase and protect workers' participation in politics. Despite its garnering 1.2 million signatures, Parliament refused to consider it, leaving the issues of labor and political reform for later decades.

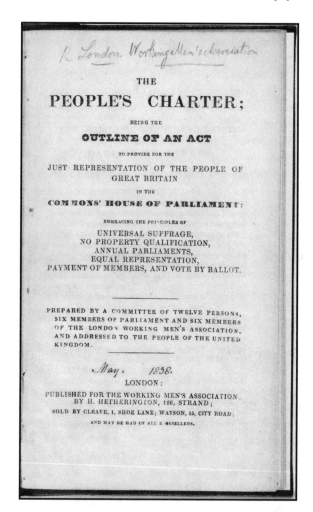

4-11b | Karl Marx and Friedrich Engels, excerpt from
Manifesto of the Communist Party, **UK, 1848**

The *Communist Manifesto*, written by philosopher, economist, and historian Karl Marx (1818–1883) and philosopher, sociologist, and businessman Friedrich Engels (1820–1895), was a political pamphlet—written in German, published in London—for an international audience: the working class of the industrialized world. Considered one of the most influential political writings of the modern world, this brief work presents the underlying theory and agenda of Marx's ideas on socialism (or Marxism) and includes a call for worker revolution. A critique of the capitalist system at a time when industrialization was in its infancy in the West, Marx's work only gained popularity in the late nineteenth century, translated into dozens of languages and circulated globally.

Modern bourgeois society, with its relations of production, of exchange and of property, a society that has conjured up such gigantic means of production and of exchange, is like the sorcerer who is no longer able to control the powers of the nether world whom he has called up by his spells. For many a decade past the history of industry and commerce is but the history of the revolt of modern productive forces against modern conditions of production, against the property relations that are the conditions for the existence of the bourgeois and of its rule. . . .

In proportion as the bourgeoisie, i.e., capital, is developed, in the same proportion is the proletariat, the modern working class, developed—a class of labourers, who live only so long as they find work, and who find work only so long as their labour increases capital. These labourers, who must sell themselves piecemeal, are a commodity, like every other article of commerce, and are consequently exposed to all the vicissitudes of competition, to all the fluctuations of the market.

Owing to the extensive use of machinery, and to the division of labour, the work of the proletarians has lost all individual character, and, consequently, all charm for the workman. He becomes an appendage of the machine, and it is only the most simple, most monotonous, and most easily acquired knack, that is required of him. . . .

Modern Industry has converted the little workshop of the patriarchal master into the great factory of the industrial capitalist. Masses of labourers, crowded into the factory, are organised like soldiers. As privates of the industrial army they are placed under the command of a perfect hierarchy of officers and sergeants. Not only are they slaves of the bourgeois class, and of the bourgeois State; they are daily and hourly enslaved by the machine, by the overlooker, and, above all, by the individual bourgeois manufacturer himself. The more openly this despotism proclaims gain to be its end and aim, the more petty, the more hateful and the more embittering it is.

The less the skill and exertion of strength implied in manual labour, in other words, the more modern industry becomes developed, the more is the labour of men superseded by that of women. Differences of age and sex have no longer any distinctive social validity for the working class. All are instruments of labour, more or less expensive to use, according to their age and sex.

No sooner is the exploitation of the labourer by the manufacturer, so far, at an end, that he receives his wages in cash, than he is set upon by the other portions of the bourgeoisie, the landlord, the shopkeeper, the pawnbroker, etc.

The lower strata of the middle class—the small tradespeople, shopkeepers, and retired tradesmen generally, the handicraftsmen and peasants—all these sink gradually into the proletariat, partly because their diminutive capital does not suffice for the scale on which Modern Industry is carried on, and is swamped in the competition with the large capitalists, partly because their specialised skill is rendered worthless by new methods of production. Thus the proletariat is recruited from all classes of the population. . . .

In the condition of the proletariat, those of old society at large are already virtually swamped. The proletarian is without property; his relation to his wife and children has no longer anything in common with the bourgeois family relations; modern industry labour, modern subjection to capital, the same in England as in France, in America as in

Germany, has stripped him of every trace of national character. Law, morality, religion, are to him so many bourgeois prejudices, behind which lurk in ambush just as many bourgeois interests. . . .

The essential conditions for the existence and for the sway of the bourgeois class is the formation and augmentation of capital; the condition for capital is wage-labour. Wage-labour rests exclusively on competition between the labourers. The advance of industry, whose involuntary promoter is the bourgeoisie, replaces the isolation of the labourers, due to competition, by the revolutionary combination, due to association. The development of Modern Industry, therefore, cuts from under its feet the very foundation on which the bourgeoisie produces and appropriates products. What the bourgeoisie therefore produces, above all, are its own grave-diggers. Its fall and the victory of the proletariat are equally inevitable. . . .

The immediate aim of the Communists is the same as that of all other proletarian parties: formation of the proletariat into a class, overthrow of the bourgeois supremacy, conquest of political power by the proletariat. . . .

We Communists have been reproached with the desire of abolishing the right of personally acquiring property as the fruit of a man's own labour, which property is alleged to be the groundwork of all personal freedom, activity and independence.

Hard-won, self-acquired, self-earned property! Do you mean the property of petty artisan and of the small peasant, a form of property that preceded the bourgeois form? There is no need to abolish that; the development of industry has to a great extent already destroyed it, and is still destroying it daily. . . .

You are horrified at our intending to do away with private property. But in your existing society, private property is already done away with for nine-tenths of the population; its existence for the few is solely due to its non-existence in the hands of those nine-tenths. You reproach us, therefore, with intending to do away with a form of property, the necessary condition for whose existence is the non-existence of any property for the immense majority of society. . . . Communism deprives no man of the power to appropriate the products of society; all that it does is to deprive him of the power to subjugate the labour of others by means of such appropriations. . . .

The Communists are further reproached with desiring to abolish countries and nationality.

The working men have no country. We cannot take from them what they have not got. Since the proletariat must first of all acquire political supremacy, must rise to be the leading class of the nation, must constitute itself the nation, it is so far, itself national, though not in the bourgeois sense of the word.

National differences and antagonism between peoples are daily more and more vanishing, owing to the development of the bourgeoisie, to freedom of commerce, to the world market, to uniformity in the mode of production and in the conditions of life corresponding thereto.

The supremacy of the proletariat will cause them to vanish still faster. United action, of the leading civilised countries at least, is one of the first conditions for the emancipation of the proletariat. . . .

In short, the Communists everywhere support every revolutionary movement against the existing social and political order of things.

In all these movements, they bring to the front, as the leading question in each, the property question, no matter what its degree of development at the time.

Finally, they labour everywhere for the union and agreement of the democratic parties of all countries.

The Communists disdain to conceal their views and aims. They openly declare that their ends can be attained only by the forcible overthrow of all existing social conditions. Let the ruling classes tremble at a Communistic revolution. The proletarians have nothing to lose but their chains. They have a world to win.

Working Men of All Countries, Unite!

DISCUSSION QUESTIONS

1 How did the principles of the People's Charter aim to broaden representation in government to include the working class? What would lead the Chartists to believe it should be broadened?

2 According to Marx and Engels, what effect(s) had industrial capitalism had on workers?

3 What was the agenda and endgame of Marx's party? Why?

4–12a | Map of the submarine telegraph between America and Europe, 1858

In addition to the transformation in transportation, the Industrial Revolution engendered a similar transformation in communication technology and accessibility. Initially intended to expedite commerce, the ability to communicate more quickly and easily changed politics, societies, cultures, military operations, and intellectual communities in industrialized states. The transatlantic telegraph cable, laid from Ireland to Newfoundland in 1858, reduced communication time between North America and Europe from ten days to a few hours. An improved cable, laid in 1866, resulted in messages in minutes.

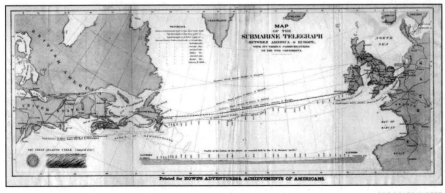

SEE COLOR INSERT

4–12b | General Postal Union Treaty, Switzerland, 1874

The 1874 Treaty of Bern, originally advocated by the U.S., created a General Postal Union to facilitate and regulate standards for international mail services. Prior to the GPU's establishment, each state had to negotiate mail agreements with every other state separately, with little guarantee of reliable delivery or rate exchange, and the need for complicated stamping and addressing.

Treaty Concerning the Formation Of A General Postal Union, Concluded Between Germany, Austria-Hungary, Belgium, Denmark, Egypt, Spain, The United States Of America, France, Great Britain, Greece, Italy, Luxemburg, Norway, The Netherlands, Portugal, Roumania, Russia, Servia, Sweden, Switzerland, and Turkey.

The undersigned, plenipotentiaries of the Governments of the countries above enumerated, have by common consent, and subject to ratification, agreed upon the following Convention:

ARTICLE 1

The countries between which the present treaty is concluded shall form, under the title of *General Postal Union*, a single postal territory for the reciprocal exchange of correspondence between their post-offices.

ARTICLE 2

The stipulations of this treaty shall extend to letters, post-cards, books, newspapers, and other printed papers, patterns of merchandise, and legal and commercial documents originating in one of the countries of the Union and intended for another of those countries. They shall also apply to the exchange by post of the articles above mentioned between the countries of the Union and countries foreign to the Union whenever such exchange takes place over the territory of two at least of the contracting parties.

ARTICLE 3

The general Union rate of postage is fixed at 25 centimes for a single prepaid letter.

Nevertheless, as a measure of conversion, the option is reserved to each country, in order to suit its monetary or other requirements, of levying a rate higher or lower than this charge, provided that it does not exceed 32 centimes or go below 20 centimes.

Every letter which does not exceed 15 grammes in weight shall be considered a single letter. The charge upon letters exceeding that weight shall be a single rate for every 15 grammes or fraction of 15 grammes.

The charge on unpaid letters shall be double the rate levied in the country of destination on prepaid letters.

The prepayment of post-cards is compulsory. The postage to be charged upon them is fixed at one-half of that on paid letters, with power to round off the fractions.

For all conveyance by sea of more than 300 nautical miles within the district of the Union, there may be added to the ordinary postage an additional charge which shall not exceed the half of the general Union rate fixed for a paid letter.

ARTICLE 4

The general Union rate for legal and commercial documents, patterns of merchandise, newspapers, stitched or bound books, pamphlets, music, visiting cards, catalogues, prospectuses, announcements and notices of various kinds, whether printed, engraved, lithographed, or autographed, as well as for photographs, is fixed at 7 centimes for each single packet.

Nevertheless, as a measure of conversion, the option is reserved to each country, in order to suit its monetary or other requirements, of levying a rate higher or lower than this charge, provided that it does not exceed 11 centimes or go below 5 centimes.

Every packet which does not exceed 50 grammes in weight shall be considered a single packet. The charge upon packets exceeding that weight shall be a single rate for every 50 grammes or fraction of 50 grammes.

For all conveyance by sea of more than 300 nautical miles within the district of the Union, there may be added to the ordinary postage an additional charge which shall not exceed the half of the general Union rate fixed for articles of this class.

The maximum weight of the articles mentioned above is fixed at 250 grammes for patterns of merchandise, and at 1000 grammes for all the others.

There is reserved to the Government of each country of the Union the right to refuse to convey over its territory or to deliver articles specified in the present Article with regard to which the laws, orders, and decrees which regulate the conditions of their publication and circulation have not been observed.

DISCUSSION QUESTIONS

1   How did these advances streamline communication?

2   Why would these communication efforts need to be cooperative?

3   What impact did these technological advancements have on globalization?

4–13 | Advertisement, "All nations use Singer sewing machines," ca. 1892

The Singer Company, first established in 1851 in the U.S., developed a number of innovations that made its version of Elias Howe's 1846 invention the most dominant in the world, including vigorous international advertising, the first installment-payment plans, door-to-door sales, glitzy showrooms, and traveling demonstrations. Singer controlled its own secondary market by buying up old models and rolling out new ones consistently. One of the first multinational companies, Singer built factories and regional headquarters around the world, often with landmark architectural features.

SEE COLOR INSERT

DISCUSSION QUESTIONS

1   Consider the people in this image, their appearance, positioning, gender, etc. How does the Singer ad envision its international consumers?

2   What messages does it seem that Singer was trying to communicate with this advertisement?

3   Why might the globalization of an American product be a domestic selling point?

5

Making a Nation

NATIONAL ANTHEMS

A national anthem can be defined as a patriotic song of praise and commitment that expresses national identity through its music, lyrics, narrative, and values. With the rise of the nation-state in the West during the nineteenth century—and the subsequent globalization of the concept of the nation-state in the twentieth century—came the desire to institutionalize national identity through symbols, lore, and language. The national anthem can often give insight into all of these. As you read the following, consider the dates of creation, the lyrics and story of each, and the use of language (when noted).

"La Marseillaise," France, 1792

Allons enfants de la Patrie,	Arise, children of the Fatherland,
Le jour de gloire est arrivé!	The day of glory has arrived!
Contre nous de la tyrannie,	Against us tyranny's
L'étendard sanglant est levé, (bis)	Bloody banner is raised, *(repeat)*
Entendez-vous dans les campagnes	Do you hear, in the countryside,
Mugir ces féroces soldats?	The roar of those ferocious soldiers?
Ils viennent jusque dans vos bras	They're coming right into your arms
Égorger vos fils, vos compagnes!	To cut the throats of your sons, your women!
Aux armes, citoyens,	To arms, citizens,
Formez vos bataillons,	Form your battalions,
Marchons, marchons!	Let's march, let's march!
Qu'un sang impur	Let an impure blood
Abreuve nos sillons!	Soak our fields!
Que veut cette horde d'esclaves,	What does this horde of slaves,
De traîtres, de rois conjurés?	Of traitors and conspiratorial kings want?
Pour qui ces ignobles entraves,	For whom are these vile chains,

Ces fers dès longtemps préparés? (bis)
Français, pour nous, ah! quel outrage
Quels transports il doit exciter!
C'est nous qu'on ose méditer
De rendre à l'antique esclavage!

Aux armes, citoyens . . .

Quoi! des cohortes étrangères
Feraient la loi dans nos foyers!
Quoi! Ces phalanges mercenaires
Terrasseraient nos fiers guerriers! (bis)
Grand Dieu! Par des mains enchaînées
Nos fronts sous le joug se ploieraient
De vils despotes deviendraient
Les maîtres de nos destinées!

Aux armes, citoyens . . .

Tremblez, tyrans et vous perfides
L'opprobre de tous les partis,
Tremblez! vos projets parricides
Vont enfin recevoir leurs prix! (bis)
Tout est soldat pour vous combattre,
S'ils tombent, nos jeunes héros,
La terre en produit de nouveaux,
Contre vous tout prêts à se battre!

Aux armes, citoyens . . .

Français, en guerriers magnanimes,
Portez ou retenez vos coups!
Épargnez ces tristes victimes,
À regret s'armant contre nous. (bis)
Mais ces despotes sanguinaires,
Mais ces complices de Bouillé,
Tous ces tigres qui, sans pitié,
Déchirent le sein de leur mère!

Aux armes, citoyens . . .

Amour sacré de la Patrie,
Conduis, soutiens nos bras vengeurs
Liberté, Liberté chérie,
Combats avec tes défenseurs! (bis)
Sous nos drapeaux que la victoire
Accoure à tes mâles accents,
Que tes ennemis expirants

These long-prepared irons? *(repeat)*
Frenchmen, for us, ah! What outrage
What fury it must arouse!
It is us they dare plan
To return to the old slavery!

To arms, citizens . . .

What! Foreign cohorts
Would make the law in our homes!
What! These mercenary phalanxes
Would strike down our proud warriors! *(repeat)*
Great God! By chained hands
Our brows would yield under the yoke
Vile despots would have themselves
The masters of our destinies!

To arms, citizens . . .

Tremble, tyrants and you traitors
The shame of all parties,
Tremble! Your parricidal schemes
Will finally receive their reward! *(repeat)*
Everyone is a soldier to combat you
If they fall, our young heroes,
The earth will produce new ones,
Ready to fight against you!

To arms, citizens . . .

Frenchmen, as magnanimous warriors,
Bear or hold back your blows!
Spare those sorry victims,
Who arm against us with regret. *(repeat)*
But not these bloodthirsty despots,
These accomplices of Bouillé,
All these tigers who, mercilessly,
Rip their mother's breast!

To arms, citizens . . .

Sacred love of the Fatherland,
Lead, support our avenging arms
Liberty, cherished Liberty,
Fight with thy defenders! *(repeat)*
Under our flags, may victory
Hurry to thy manly accents,
May thy expiring enemies,

Voient ton triomphe et notre gloire!	See thy triumph and our glory!
Aux armes, citoyens . . .	To arms, citizens . . .
(Couplet des enfants)	(Children's Verse)
Nous entrerons dans la carrière	We shall enter the (military) career
Quand nos aînés n'y seront plus,	When our elders are no longer there,
Nous y trouverons leur poussière	There we shall find their dust
Et la trace de leurs vertus (bis)	And the trace of their virtues *(repeat)*
Bien moins jaloux de leur survivre	Much less keen to survive them
Que de partager leur cercueil,	Than to share their coffins,
Nous aurons le sublime orgueil	We shall have the sublime pride
De les venger ou de les suivre	Of avenging or following them
Aux armes, citoyens . . .	To arms, citizens . . .

"Marcha Patriótica (Himno Nacional Argentino)," Argentina, 1812

### Marcha Patriótica (1813)	### English translation
Oíd, mortales el grito sagrado	Hear, mortals, the sacred cry:
Libertad, libertad, libertad:	"Freedom, freedom, freedom"
Oíd el ruido de rotas cadenas,	Hear the sound of broken chains,
Ved en trono a la noble igualdad.	See noble equality enthroned.
Se levanta en la faz de la tierra	On the face of the earth rises
Una nueva gloriosa nación,	A glorious new nation.
Coronada su cien de laureles,	Her head is crowned with laurels,
Y a sus plantas rendido un Leon.	And a Lion lies defeated at her feet.

CORO	**CHORUS**
Sean eternos los laureles,	*May the laurels be eternal,*
Que supimos conseguir:	*That we knew how to win.*
Coronados de gloria vivamos,	*Let us live crowned with glory,*
O juremos con gloria morir.	*Or swear to die gloriously.*

De los nuevos campeones los rostros	The faces of the new champions
Marte mismo parece animar;	Seem animated by Mars himself
La grandeza se anida en sus pechos:	Greatness nestles in their breasts:
A su marcha todo hacen temblar.	As they march everything trembles.
Se conmueven del Inca las tumbas,	The tombs of the dead Inca are shaken up,
Y en sus huesos revive el ardor,	And in their bones the ardour revives
Lo que vé renovando a sus hijos	Which renews their children
De la Patria el antiguo esplendor.	Of the Fatherland the ancient splendour.
Sean eternos los laureles &c.	*May the laurels be eternal etc.*
Pero sierras y muros se sienten	But hills and walls are heard
Retumbar con horrible fragor:	To echo with awful clamour:

Todo el país se conturba por gritos
De venganza, de guerra, y furor.
En los fieros tiranos la envidia
Escupió su pestífera hiel,
Su estandarte sangriento levantan
Provocando a la lid más cruel.
Sean eternos los laureles &c.

¿No los veis sobre México, y Quito
Arrojarse con saña tenaz?
¿Y quál lloran, bañados en sangre
Potosí, Cochabamba, y La Paz?
¿No los veis sobre el triste Caracas
Luto, y llanto, y muerte esparcir?
¿No los veis devorando qual fieras
Todo pueblo que logran rendir?
Sean eternos los laureles &c.

A vosotros se atreve Argentinos,
El orgullo del vil invasor.
Vuestros campos yá pisa contando
Tantas glorias hollar vencedor.
Mas los bravos, que unidos juraron
Su feliz libertad sostener,
A estos tigres sedientos de sangre
Fuertes pechos sabrán oponer.
Sean eternos los laureles &c.

El valiente Argentino á las armas
Corre ardiendo con brío y valor:
El clarín de la guerra, qual trueno
En los campos del Sud resonó.
Buenos—Ayres se opone á la frente
De los pueblos de la ínclita union,
Y con brazos robustos desgarran
Al ibérico altivo Leon.
Sean eternos los laureles &c.

San José, San Lorenzo, Suipacha,
Ambas Piedras, Salta, y Tucumán,
La Colonia y las mismas murallas
Del tirano en la banda Oriental.
Son letreros eternos que dicen:
Aquí el brazo argentino triunfó:
Aquí el fiero opresor de la Patria
Su cerviz orgullosa dobló.
Sean eternos los laureles &c.

The whole country is shaken by cries
Of revenge, of war, and fury.
On fierce tyrants envy
Spat its pestilential bile;
Their bloody standard they raise
Provoking the most cruel fighting.
May the laurels be eternal etc.

Do you not see them on Mexico and Quito
Throwing themselves with tenacious cruelty?
And how weep, soaked in blood,
Potosí, Cochabamba and La Paz?
Do you not see them over sad Caracas
Spread mourning, and tears, and death?
Do you not see them devouring as wild beasts
All peoples who they defeat?
May the laurels be eternal etc.

It dares face you, Argentines,
The pride of the vile invader.
Your lands it tramples, boasting
Of many glories as victor.
But the brave, who united swore
Their happy freedom to sustain,
These blood-thirsty tigers
They will confront with strong chests.
May the laurels be eternal etc.

The valiant Argentine to arms
Runs burning with zest and valour,
The bugle of war, as thunder,
In the fields of the South resounded.
Buenos Aires puts itself in the lead of
The people of the illustrious Union,
And with strong arms they tear to pieces
The arrogant Iberian lion.
May the laurels be eternal etc.

San José, San Lorenzo, Suipacha,
Both Piedras, Salta and Tucumán,
La Colonia and even the walls
Of the tyrant on the Eastern bank.*
They are eternal signboards that say:
"Here Argentine hands triumphed,
Here the fierce oppressor of the Fatherland
His proud neck bent."
May the laurels be eternal etc.

La victoria al guerrero argentino	Victory enveloped the Argentine warrior
Con sus álas brillantes cubrió,	With its shining wings,
Y azorado á su vista el tirano	And stunned at this sight the tyrant
Con infamia á la fuga se dió.	With infamy took to flight.
Sus banderas, sus armas se rinden	His flags, his arms surrendered
Por trofeos a la libertad,	As trophies to freedom,
Y sobre alas de gloria alza el pueblo	And on wings of glory the people raise
Trono digno a su gran majestad.	A throne worthy of its great majesty.
Sean eternos los laureles &c.	*May the laurels be eternal etc.*
Desde un polo hasta el otro resuena	From pole to pole resounds
De la fama el sonóro clarín,	The sonorous bugle of fame,
Y de América el nombre enseñando	And showing the name of America
Les repite, mortales, oíd:	It repeats "Mortals, hear!:
Yá su trono dignísimo abrieron	Their noble throne have now opened
Las provincias unidas del Sud.	The united provinces of the South."
Y los libres del mundo responden	And the free people of the world reply:
Al gran pueblo argentino salud.	"To the great Argentine people, hail!"
Sean eternos los laureles &c.	*May the laurels be eternal etc.*

* "Eastern bank" of the Uruguay River.

Es copia Dr Bernardo Velez Secretario del Gobierno de Intendencia. Buenos Ayres mayo 14 de 1813. Imprenta de Niños Expósitos.

"The Star-Spangled Banner," United States, 1814

O say can you see, by the dawn's early light,
What so proudly we hailed at the twilight's last gleaming,
Whose broad stripes and bright stars through the perilous fight,
O'er the ramparts we watched, were so gallantly streaming?
And the rockets' red glare, the bombs bursting in air,
Gave proof through the night that our flag was still there;
O say does that star-spangled banner yet wave
O'er the land of the free and the home of the brave?

"Kimigayo (His Imperial Majesty's Reign)," Japan, 1880

Official	Rōmaji	English translation
君が代は 千代に八千代に さざれ石の いわおとなりて こけのむすまで	Kimigayo wa Chiyo ni yachiyo ni Sazareishi no Iwao to narite Koke no musu made	May your reign Continue for a thousand, eight thousand generations, Until the pebbles Grow into boulders Lush with moss

Poetic English translation by Chamberlain

Thousands of years of happy reign be thine;
Rule on, my lord, until what are pebbles now
By ages united to mighty rocks shall grow
Whose venerable sides the moss doth line.

"An-Našīd al-Waṭaniyy (The National Anthem)," Saudi Arabia, 1984

Hasten
To glory and supremacy,
Glorify the Creator of the heavens!
And raise the green flag
Carrying the written light reflecting guidance,
Repeat: Allahu Akbar!
O my country!
My country,
Live as the pride of Muslims!
Long live the King
For the flag
And the homeland!

"Hatikvah (The Hope)," Israel, 1948

As long as in the heart, within,
A Jewish soul still yearns,
And onward, towards the ends of the east,
An eye still gazes toward Zion.

Our hope is not yet lost,
The hope two thousand years old,
To be a free nation in our land,
The land of Zion and Jerusalem.

"Warrior," Palestine, 1972

Warrior, warrior, warrior,
Oh my land, the land of the ancestors
Warrior, warrior, warrior,
Oh my people, people of eternity

With my determination, my fire and the volcano of my vendetta
With the longing in my blood for my land and my home
I have climbed the mountains and fought the wars
I have conquered the impossible, and crossed the frontiers

With the resolve of the winds and the fire of the weapons
And the determination of my nation in the land of struggle
Palestine is my home, and the path of my triumph
(Palestine is my home, Palestine is my fire,)
Palestine is my vendetta and the land of withstanding

By the oath under the shade of the flag
By my land and nation, and the fire of pain
I will live as a warrior, I will remain a warrior,
I will die as a warrior—until my country returns,
A warrior.

"National Anthem of South Africa," South Africa, 1997

First verse, first two lines in Xhosa
Nkosi sikelel' iAfrika
Maluphakanyisw' uphondo lwayo

Translation
Lord bless Africa
May His glory be lifted high,

First verse, last two lines in Zulu
Yizwa imithandazo yethu,
Nkosi sikelela, thina lusapho lwayo.

Translation
Hear our prayers
Lord bless us, your children.

Second verse in Sesotho
Morena boloka setjhaba sa heso,
O fedise dintwa le matshwenyeho,
O se boloke, O se boloke setjhaba sa heso,
Setjhaba sa, South Afrika, South Afrika.

Translation
Lord we ask you to protect our nation,
Intervene and end all conflicts,
Protect us, protect our nation,
The nation of South Africa, South Africa.

Third verse in Afrikaans
Uit die blou van onse hemel,
Uit die diepte van ons see,
Oor ons ewige gebergtes,
Waar die kranse antwoord gee,

Translation
Ringing out from our blue heavens,
From the depths of our seas,
Over everlasting mountains,
Where the echoing crags resound,

Fourth verse in English
Sounds the call to come together,
And united we shall stand,
Let us live and strive for freedom
In South Africa our land.

360 DISCUSSION QUESTIONS

1   Consider the narrative of each anthem: what story does it tell? To whom and to what is it meant to appeal? What is the purpose of telling a story in a national anthem?

2   Choose a few anthems to compare: how might these anthems be intended to reflect the values—what is important to—members of that nation-state? What similarities or differences do you observe? How might they exclude members of the nation-state, intentionally or unintentionally?

3   Finally, look at the South African national anthem. In what ways is their national anthem meant to reflect their national identity, society, and history?

EXPANSION

5–1a | José María Sánchez, diary entry on the mounting fears about the influx of Anglo-Americans into Texas, Mexico, 1828

José Maria Sánchez was a sublieutenant in Mexico's artillery corps, cartographer, and artist. He accompanied General Manuel Mier y Terán (1789–1832) on his investigations of conditions in Texas in 1828 and 1829. This endeavor, which traveled as far as Nacogdoches in present northeast Texas, was related to a commission establishing a boundary between the Republic of Mexico and the United States. In his report on the commission, Mier y Terán advocated strong measures to stop American encroachment, including new garrisons, closer trade ties to Mexico, and encouraging Mexican and European settlement of the territory. The Mexican government incorporated his recommendations into the Law of April 6, 1830, which called for the prohibition of slavery and closed Texas borders to Americans.

The Americans from the north have taken possession of practically all the eastern part of Texas, in most cases without the permission of the authorities. They immigrate constantly, finding no one to prevent them, and take possession of the *sitio* [location] that best suits them without either asking leave or going through any formality other than that of building their homes. Thus the majority of inhabitants in the Department are North Americans, the Mexican population being reduced to only Bejar, Nacogdoches, and La Bahía del Espíritu Santo, wretched settlements that between them do not number three thousand inhabitants, and the new village of Guadalupe Victoria that has scarcely more than seventy settlers. The government of the state, with its seat at Saltillo, that should watch over the preservation of its most precious and interesting department, taking measures to prevent its being stolen by foreign hands, is the one that knows the least not only about actual conditions, but even about its territory. . . .

The population [of Nacogdoches] does not exceed seven hundred persons, including the troops of the garrison, and all live in very good houses made of lumber, well built and forming straight streets, which make the place more agreeable. The women do not number one hundred. The civil administration is entrusted to an *Alcalde*, and in his absence, to the first and second *regidores*, but up until now, they have been, unfortunately, extremely ignorant men more worthy of pity than of reproof. From this fact, the North American inhabitants (who are in the majority) have formed an ill opinion of the Mexicans, judging them, in their pride, incapable of understanding laws, arts, etc. They continually try to entangle the authorities in order to carry out the policy most suitable to their perverse designs. . . .

The Mexicans that live here are very humble people, and perhaps their intentions are good, but because of their education and environment they are ignorant not only of the customs of our great cities, but even of the occurrences of our Revolution, excepting a few persons who have heard about them. Accustomed to the continued trade with the North Americans, they have adopted their customs and habits, and one may say truly that they are not Mexicans except by birth, for they even speak Spanish with marked incorrectness.

5–1b | A member of the Tejano elite makes comments in favor of Anglo-American immigration into Texas, Mexico, 1832

The push for reform among a group of members of the Mexican elite based primarily in San Antonio was expressed in a series of declarations made in a long memorial that dealt with one of the principal concerns of the group, the continued immigration of American settlers into Texas. These charges of abuse of state and federal administration of Texas followed a meeting with empresario Stephen F. Austin regarding what he called "the evils retarding the progress of Texas."

What shall we say of the law of April 6, 1830? It absolutely prohibits immigrants from North America coming into Texas, but there are not enough troops to enforce it; so the result is that desirable immigrants are kept out because they will not violate the law, while the undesirable, having nothing to lose, come in freely. The industrious, honest North American settlers have made great improvements in the past seven or eight years. They have raised cotton and cane and erected gins and sawmills. Their industry has made them comfortable and independent, while the Mexican settlements, depending on the pay of the soldiers among them for money, have lagged far behind. Among the Mexican settlements even the miserable manufacture of blankets, hats and shoes has never been established and we must buy them either from foreigners or from the interior, 200 or 300 leagues distant. We have had a loom in Bexar for two years, but the inhabitants of Goliad and Nacogdoches know nothing of this ingenious machine, nor even how to make a sombrero.

The advantages of liberal North American immigration are innumerable: (1) The colonists would afford a source of supply for the native inhabitants. (2) They would protect the interior from Indian invasions. (3) They would develop roads and commerce to New Orleans and New Mexico. (4) Moreover, the ideas of government held by North Americans are in general better adapted to those of the Mexicans than are the ideas of European immigrants.

DISCUSSION QUESTIONS

1   What practices of Anglo-American immigrants concerned Sanchez?
2   How did the member of the Tejano elite believe Anglo-American immigration to Texas would be beneficial?
3   What were the pros and cons of trying to regulate Anglo-American immigration into Texas?

5-2 | Etching, the USS *Peacock* in contact with the ice on the Wilkes Expedition (United States Exploring Expedition), Antarctica, 1840

Peacock was a sloop-of-war in the United States Navy during the War of 1812 and served until decommissioned in 1827. At that date, she was rebuilt as an exploration ship. She served as part of the seven-ship flotilla that comprised the United States Exploring Expedition (1838–1842). Also known as the "U.S. Ex. Ex." or "Wilkes Expedition" after its leader, Navy Lieutenant Charles Wilkes, the mission was of major importance to the growth of science in the United States, particularly the early years of oceanography. Many of the items found by the expedition formed the basis of collections in the new Smithsonian Institution. Here, the USS *Peacock* is depicted trapped in ice, an event which occurred shortly after the first confirmed sighting of the Antarctic by a U.S. Navy ship.

DISCUSSION QUESTIONS

1   Why might it be important for the U.S. to sponsor an international exploration venture?

2   What benefits might emerge from new lands and waters?

5–3a | James K. Polk, message on expansion and values, 1845

President James K. Polk (1795–1849) gave this message on the issue of American expansion just a few weeks before Texas was admitted to the union on December 29, 1845. Texas had been receiving settlers from the United States for decades, even prior to 1821, when it was a remote northern territory of New Spain. In his message, Polk addresses the notion of European efforts to keep the continent divided in this age of heightened notions of "manifest destiny."

Fellow-citizens of the Senate and House of Representatives:—

. . . In performing, for the first time, the duty imposed on me by the constitution, of giving to you information of the state of the Union, and recommending to your consideration such measures as in my judgment are necessary and expedient, I am happy that I can congratulate you on the continued prosperity of our country. Under the blessings of Divine Providence and the benign influence of our free institutions, it stands before the world a spectacle of national happiness. . . .

A constitution for the government of the state of Texas, formed by a convention of deputies, is herewith laid before Congress. It is well known, also, that the people of Texas at the polls have accepted the terms of annexation, and ratified the constitution. . . .

This accession to our territory has been a bloodless achievement. No arm of force has been raised to produce the result. The sword has had no part in the victory. We have not sought to extend our territorial possessions by conquest, or our republican institutions over a reluctant people. It was the deliberate homage of each people to the great principle of our federative union.

If we consider the extent of territory involved in the annexation—its prospective influence on America—the means by which it has been accomplished, springing purely from the choice of the people themselves to share the blessings of our union—the history of the world may be challenged to furnish a parallel. . . . We may rejoice that the tranquil and pervading influence of the American principle of self-government was sufficient to defeat the purposes of British and French interference, and that the almost unanimous voice of the people of Texas has given to that interference a peaceful and effective rebuke. From this example, European governments may learn how vain diplomatic arts and intrigues must ever prove upon this continent, against that system of self-government which seems natural to our soil, and which will ever resist foreign interference. . . .

I regret to inform you that our relations with Mexico, since your last session, have not been of the amiable character which it is our desire to cultivate with all foreign nations. On the 6th day of March last, the Mexican envoy extraordinary and minister plenipotentiary to the United States made a formal protest . . . against the joint resolution passed by Congress "for the annexation of Texas to the United States," which he chose to regard as a violation of the rights of Mexico, and, in consequence of it, he demanded his passports. . . . Thus, by the acts of Mexico, all diplomatic intercourse between the two countries was suspended.

Since that time Mexico has, until recently, occupied an attitude of hostility towards the United States—has been marshalling and organizing armies, issuing proclamations, and avowing the intention to make war on the United States, either by an open declaration, or by invading Texas. . . . The independence of Texas is a fact conceded by Mexico herself, and she had no right or authority to prescribe restrictions as to the form of government which Texas might afterwards choose to assume.

But though Mexico cannot complain of the United States on account of the annexation of Texas, it is to be regretted that serious causes of misunderstanding between the two countries continue to exist, growing out of unredressed injuries inflicted by the Mexican authorities and people on the persons and property of citizens of the United States, through a long series of years. Mexico has admitted these injuries, but has neglected and refused to repair them. . . . Such a continued and unprovoked series of wrongs could never have been tolerated by the United States, had they been committed by one of the principal nations of Europe. Mexico was, however, a neighboring sister republic, which, following our example, had achieved her independence, and for whose success and prosperity all our sympathies were early enlisted. . . . We have, therefore, borne the repeated wrongs she has committed, with great patience, in the hope that a returning sense of justice would ultimately guide her councils, and that we might, if possible, honorably avoid any hostile collision with her. . . .

The rapid extension of our settlements over our territories heretofore unoccupied—the addition of new States to our confederacy—the expansion of free principles, and our rising greatness as a nation, are attracting the attention of the powers of Europe; and lately the doctrine has been broached in some of them, of a "balance of power" on this continent, to check our advancement. The United States, sincerely desirous of preserving relations of good understanding with all nations, can not in silence permit any European interference on the North American continent; and should any such interference be attempted, will be ready to resist it at any and all hazards. . . . The American system of government is entirely different from that of Europe. Jealousy among the different sovereigns of Europe, lest any one of them might become too powerful for the rest, has caused them anxiously to desire the establishment of what they term the "balance of power." It can not be permitted to have any application on the North American continent, and especially to the United States. We must ever maintain the principle, that the people of this continent alone have the right to decide their own destiny. Should any portion of them, constituting an independent state, propose to unite themselves with our confederacy, this will be a question for them and us to determine, without any foreign interposition. . . .

5–3b | Map, *Mapa de los Estados Unidos Méjico*, 1847

This map created by John Disturnell (1801–1877), *Mapa de los Estados Unidos de Méjico*, was used by the United States as its primary cartographic reference for the peace settlement to end the Mexican-American War (1846–1848), the Treaty of Guadalupe Hidalgo. The U.S. gained ownership of California and an area including approximately half of modern-day New Mexico, the majority of modern-day Arizona, Nevada, Utah, and Colorado. Mexicans living in those areas had a choice: they could relocate to Mexico's new borders or they could be granted full U.S. citizenship. The U.S. paid fifteen million dollars to Mexico and promised to settle American claims against the Mexican government up to five million. The use of Disturnell's map complicated negotiations due to its many errors, including the location of El Paso. The disagreements and tensions ultimately contributed to the Gadsden Purchase (1854), the U.S. acquisition of a 29,670 square mile portion of modern-day southern Arizona and New Mexico from Mexico for ten million dollars.

SEE COLOR INSERT

DISCUSSION QUESTIONS

1   How did Polk describe the U.S. view of the annexation of Texas? How did he portray Mexico's response?

2   Which territories on Disturnell's map are well defined? Unclear? Why?

3   What elements of U.S. self-perception—as articulated by Polk—contributed to its territorial conflicts with Mexico?

5–4 | William Walker, selections from *The War in Nicaragua*, 1860

William Walker (1824–1860) was an American physician, lawyer, journalist, and mercenary who served as President of Nicaragua from 1856 to 1857. He engaged in an effort known then as "filibustering," organizing several private expeditions particularly into Latin America in attempts to establish English-speaking colonies under private control. This effort was a phenomenon of the mid-nineteenth century and participants had a wide range of motivations, including financial gain, political ideology, or a spirit of adventure. Walker's short-lived success in Nicaragua ended when he was ousted by a coalition of Central American armies. On his attempt to regain control, he was captured and executed by the Honduran government in 1860.

[T]here are many who, while admitting the advantage of slavery to Nicaragua, think it was impolitic to have attempted its re-establishment at the time the decree of the 22d of September was published. This brings us to consider the decree in its relation with the question of slavery in the United States.

. . . The decree, re-establishing slavery while it declared the manner in which the Americans proposed to regenerate Nicaraguan society made them the champions of the Southern States of the Union in the conflict truly styled "irrepressible" between free and slave labor. The policy of the act consisted in pointing out to the Southern States the only means, short of revolution, whereby they can preserve their present social organization. . . .

If there, then, be yet vigor in the South—and who can doubt that there is—for further contest with the soldiers of anti-slavery, let her cast off the lethargy which enthrals her, and prepare anew for the conflict. . . . The true field for the exertion of slavery is in tropical America; there it finds the natural seat of its empire and thither it can spread if it will but make the effort, regardless of conflicts with adverse interests. The way is open and it only requires courage and will to enter the path and reach the goal. Will the South be true to herself in this emergency?

. . . That which you ignorantly call "Filibusterism" is not the offspring of hasty passion or ill-regulated desire; it is the fruit of the sure, unerring instincts which act in accordance with laws as old as the creation. They are but drivellers who speak of establishing fixed relations between the pure white American race, as it exists in the United States, and the mixed Hispano-Indian race, as it exists in Mexico and Central America, without the employment of force. The history of the world presents no such Utopian vision as that of an inferior race yielding meekly and peacefully to the controlling influence of a superior people. Whenever barbarism and civilization, or two distinct forms of civilization, meet face to face, the result must be war. Therefore, the struggle between the old and the new elements in Nicaraguan society was not passing or accidental, but natural and inevitable. The war in Nicaragua was the first clear and distinct issue made between the races inhabiting the northern and the central portions of the continent. But while this contest sprang from natural laws, I trust the foregoing narrative shows that the stronger race kept throughout on the side of right and justice; and if they so maintained their cause in Central America let them not doubt of its future success. Nor kings nor presidents can arrest a movement based on truth and conducted with justice; and the very obstacles they place in the way merely prepare those who are injured for the part they are to play in the world's history. He is but a blind reader of the past who has not learned that Providence fits its agents for great designs by trials, and sufferings, and persecutions. "By the cross thou shalt conquer" is as clearly written in the pages of history as when the startled emperor saw it blazing in letters of light athwart the heavens. In the very difficulties with which the Americans of Nicaragua have had to contend I see the presage of their triumph. Let me, therefore, say to my former comrades, be of good cheer: faint not, nor grow weary by the way, for your toils and your efforts are sure in the end to win success. With us there can be no choice; honor and duty call on us to pursue the path we have entered, and we dare not be deaf to the appeal. By the bones of the mouldering dead at Masaya, at Rivas, and at Granada, I adjure you never to abandon the cause of Nicaragua. Let it be your waking and your sleeping thought to devise means for a return to the land whence we were unjustly brought. And, if we be but true to ourselves, all will yet end well.

DISCUSSION QUESTIONS

1   What was Walker's purpose for re-establishing slavery in Nicaragua?

2   How did he use race to argue for expansion?

3   Why did he believe the U.S. should settle colonists in Central America?

CIVIL WAR AND RECONSTRUCTION

5–5a | Political cartoon, "Caesar Imperator!" UK, 1861

Published in the British satirical magazine *Punch*, just over a month after the firing on Fort Sumter, the cartoon below provided a clear message on the relationship between the U.S. Civil War and slavery. On the left side, the combatant represents the North, opposed by the gladiator of the South on the right, which bears a close resemblance to Confederate President Jefferson Davis. The audience is exclusively enslaved blacks, with one seated high on a cotton bale throne, like the emperor presiding over the Roman Coliseum. The British press published this astute image while assertions were being made by many in both the North and the South that the conflict was not about slavery.

PUNCH, OR THE LONDON CHARIVARI.—May 18, 1861.

"CÆSAR IMPERATOR!"

OR,

THE AMERICAN GLADIATORS.

5–5b | English discussion on "Is the Secession of the Southern States of America from the Union Desirable?" UK, 1861

A primary feature of *The British Controversialist and Literary Magazine* was to put forth topics of the day and then "outline debates, embodying the varied thoughts of many minds on matters of present, though not necessarily of passing interest." Of great international interest in 1861 was the state of the union, or disunion, of the United States. Here, many contributors, each granted a paragraph to state their views, respond to two topics related to the American Civil War.

The Topic: Is the Secession of the Southern States of America from the Union Desirable?

Affirmative. Certainly! It is the surest way to abolish the slave trade thoroughly. The time taken up in reconstituting the revolting States into a tyranny would interfere with plantation labour and the cotton supplies; meanwhile, the Indian and African trade would be stimulated, and the Southern States would be outmarketed. Slavery would thus become unprofitable, and, therefore, would be abolished by the very act intended for its perpetuation. So be it.—N. R. S.

Secession? Yes. Let the clean be separated from the unclean. Where are the nations of Europe that would fraternize and make alliances with the States that had banded themselves together in iniquity the most iniquitous? Weakness and wickedness would thus be companions, and the detestation of Europe and Europeanized Indian and America would spurn the slave-traders from the confederations of civilization. The slaves would find more friends than ever, surely, if a nation should so outrage the convictions of men as to found itself upon the grossest abuse of power of which humanity has heard. Good always comes out of seeming evil.—E. M.

The Southern States are an obstacle in the way of the moral and political progression of the Union on many grounds; the principal and underlying cause being the corrupt institution of the South, which exerts a most deleterious influence upon the whole of the States. It is unnecessary to detail the effects produced by this terrible cause, these being obvious to every reflecting mind. The obstacle should be removed, and this can be done only by abolition or secession. In the present circumstances, secession appears to be most desirable.—T. C.

Taking slavery alone into consideration, we believe the secession of the Southern States from the Union to be desirable. Conservative spirits may mourn over the disruptions of old and well-tried constitutions; and in the present case their principles are very much in harmony with those of the strictest reformers, for a rupture of the union of the States must necessarily tend to weaken each party considerably. But, eventually, the North has nothing to fear; and her anxiety, for the most part, is groundless. Without the rust of the negro's chains upon her hands, she shall still increase in intellectual greatness and moral power, absolved, as she must be, from the crimes of human traffic, with which she has hitherto been unavoidably connected. For the Southern States we tremble. They may separate, and form a Southern Confederacy; but the 4,000,000 slaves are fostering a germ that, sooner or later, will cause a fearful retribution for the sufferings they have endured. While for many reasons, we deplore the disunion and want of confidence that are equally apparent in the two great bodies in America, we firmly believe that the secession movement, if consummated, will be the death-blow of slavery.–Harwood

Negative. The secession of the Southern States of America from the Union is not desirable, because that secession is not likely to be effected without war and bloodshed; or, if contention does not proceed to this length, yet strife, more or less, must take place, and angry and unbrotherly feelings be drawn forth, which feelings would probably continue after the effectuation of the disruption, the separate powers or nations having opposite interests. . . .

Man's nature is composed of two ingredients, good and bad; and were he to be separated wholly from either, he would be more of less than a man. In the Southern part of the United States there exists a confessed evil—slavery—which bears to the constitution of that country the same similarity as bad bears to the good of our natures. The Northern States represent the good; and we are asked if secession of the bad from the good is desirable? Were there no fellow-beings concerned so vital in the matter, we would answer in he affirmative; but as it is, we reply, No; and for these reasons:—The conjunction of the Northern and Southern States under one government is calculated to operate beneficially, the Northern restraining by their example, the Southern States from utter abandonment of their hideous traffic in the unfortunate slave, the one part exerting the same influence upon the other as good upon evil. The recent election of President proves that a majority of the Union are against the evil practiced by the minority; and I submit that if the secession of the Southern States of America becomes absolute, it cannot but have a prejudicial effect upon the seceding states, as they would then be under no authority opposite to their sinful traffic.—J. C.

Setting aside the question whether, in seceding, the Southern States have any right to appropriate the property of the Federal Government, we think it undesirable, inasmuch as the nation having elected a Republican President, the minority ought to submit to the will of the majority; and if they be allowed to secede, what will prevent other States from following their example on different questions, and setting up governments, each independent of the other? The inconvenience of this must be evident to all. The division of the Union would probably be the cause of much ill-will and border quarrels; and if either pursued a narrower and more illiberal line of policy, it would probably give rise to vast amount of smuggling, which, from the length of boundary, would be difficult to prevent. The African slave trade, also, would most likely be revived, with all its attendant horrors. But rather than any compromise should be effected, the Federal Government ought to keep or lose all.–Sagamore

Upon mature consideration I venture to pronounce against the secessionists' movement, as a measure calculated to produce no beneficial results to either party. In the first instance, the Northerners will ever be suspicious of, and even indignant at, the growing power of the seceders. Secondly, the Southerners will ever be bloating with the pernicious envy of slavery, so as to augment their greed for supremacy, thus generating contention and strife instead of a desire to promote universal greatness. . . . "Union is strength;" and the objects of division are such as will never benefit the parties; for in a divided condition they are weakened, and incapable of sustaining the national character. . . . What are the results of the secession cause, as to the progress of commerce? Let us review the statements of customs' authorities, Charleston, S.C. The returns, as published by them touching the trade of that port since secession, show that the value of exports is 905,717 dollars, against 3,095,618 dollars for the same period last year. These are startling accounts for secessionists to contemplate. But the rebellious measures now move with a halting pace; and the future measures of Mr. Lincoln, if judiciously executed, and with energy, may effectually destroy the now smouldering embers of discord, and restore the seceding members of the national family.—S. F. T.

DISCUSSION QUESTIONS

1   Why would the British have a clear early view of the centrality of the slavery question in the U.S. Civil War?

2   Summarize, in general, the positive and negative British perspectives on the desirability of Southern secession.

3   How could this domestic conflict in the states have repercussions for the British and their foreign policy?

5–6a | Alexander Gorchakov, letter to Bayard Taylor, Russia, 1862

Alexander Gorchakov (1798–1883) was a highly influential Russian diplomat and statesman and member of the Gorchakov princely family. He served as Foreign Minister of the Russian Empire from 1856 to 1882. In 1867, he oversaw the sale of Russian Alaska to the United States, a transaction that had begun through careful and secret negotiations in the mid-1850s. Bayard Taylor (1825–1878) was a writer and diplomat who, from 1862–1863, served as acting minister to Russia. Here, Gorchakov expresses his concern to Union officials. After stating "Russia alone has stood by you from the first . . . ," he continues:

You know the sentiments of Russia. We desire above all things the maintenance of the American Union, as one indivisible nation. We cannot take any part more than we have done. We have no hostility to the southern people. Russia has declared her position and will maintain it. There will be proposals for intervention. We believe that intervention could do no good at present. Proposals will be made to Russia to join in some plan of interference. She will refuse any invitation of the kind. Russia will occupy the same ground as at the beginning of the struggle. You may rely upon it, she will not change. But we entreat you to settle the difficulty. I cannot express to you how profound an anxiety we feel—how serious are our fears.

5–6b | Illustration, Russian battleships in New York Harbor, 1863

In September 1863, a fleet of six battleships sailed from the Russian Empire to anchor off the east coast of the U.S. for seven months, patrolling the New York region. A similarly sized Russian flotilla based in San Francisco watched areas of the west coast. Each contingent stood as a show of strength and support for important Union ports, underlining Russian support for the Union and countering British and French sympathies for the Confederacy. Tsar Alexander II—the "Tsar Liberator"—had recently freed the serfs in Russia (1861), part of a reform package instituted in the wake of Russia's loss in the Crimean War (1853–1856) to a British, French, and Ottoman alliance, a move that would later connect him with Lincoln, the "Great Emancipator." His decision to send the Russian Navy to the U.S. demonstrates a global expression of the British-Russian rivalry, a major factor in European politics that was playing out not only in the U.S., but in the Middle East, South Asia, and Eastern Europe.

Vilna.   Alexander Naselt.

THE RUSSIAN FLEET, COMMANDED BY ADMIRAL L

665

Pennent.   Steam-tugs.   Varieg.   Galiote.

N THE HARBOR OF NEW YORK.—[See Page 651.]

DISCUSSION QUESTIONS

1   The U.S. Civil War did not occur in a vacuum. How do the above sources suggest this domestic conflict related to international rivalries?

2   Why might Russia support the Union? Why might Britain and France be sympathetic to the Confederacy?

5–7 | Excerpts from A Habituate's *Opium Eating: An Autobiographical Sketch*, 1876

The anonymous author of one of the earliest accounts of opiate addiction by an American user was a Civil War veteran. Having joined up at age 16, he shed his drum for a gun, but was captured by Confederates at Chickamauga in 1863. Incarcerated at Richmond, Danville, and Andersonville, he suffered scurvy, dysentery, and lasting digestive problems due to starvation. The development of opium-based drugs such as morphine, laudanum, and heroin, combined with the newly developed hypodermic needle, led to widespread use during—and after—the war. Freed in a prisoner exchange in 1865, the author describes his injury and attempts at treatment.

On commencing to get better at Annapolis, I found my greatest trouble was with my stomach. It seemed contracted into a space no larger than my fist, and everything I ate seemed to irritate it; and I could apparently feel the exact size of any meal I had eaten, as it lay deposited in my stomach. Everything I took into my stomach seemed to weigh like lead, and constantly bear down so hard, that it made me continually miserable and unwell. . . . My stomach was much worse than ever, and my headache became worse in proportion with my stomach. My body was very much debilitated; I suffered fearfully, wretchedly. From the ravages made on my entire physical system by constant headaches, and the terrible agonies and torments of my stomach, my mind became debilitated.

. . .

I tried different physicians and remedies without avail. Nothing seemed to benefit me, and I quit trying. At last a physician in the town where I resided, in whom I had but little confidence, and who for six months past had been endeavoring to get my consent to allow him to treat my case, induced me to place myself under his professional care. None of the rest had benefited me, and he could but fail, and might do me some good. I would die if there were not a change soon, and I could but do this at the worst under his treatment. Besides, I wanted present relief from the most distracting pain. I was suffering daily torment and torture, with a body weak and wasted, and a constitution whose resisting power, before persistent and repeated assaults, had at last given way; my mind was become greatly impaired, and my spirits had sunk into a black midnight of despair.

"'Tis no time now to stickle over means and remedies; let him cure me who can, or let me die if I must," I thought. Nevertheless, in going into this physician's office, I emphatically charged him not to administer to me any opium or morphia, as I had a horror of such things.

I perceived that he was going to use, in my case, what was a new instrument in the practice there at that time, viz., the hypodermic syringe. "Oh, have no fear," he replied, holding up at the same time a phial of clear and colorless fluid; "this is no opium or morphia; it is one of the simplest and most harmless things in the world; but it is a secret, and no one in the town knows anything about it except myself." On this assurance, I allowed him to inject a dose into my arm. This first dose was too large, and nearly killed me or scared me to death, and I determined not to go back to him again. And I would have adhered to my determination, had he not accosted me at a hotel, about two weeks thereafter, and asked me why I had remained away; and on my telling him the reason, he entreated me to come back, saying, that as soon as he had ascertained the right dose for me, he would certainly cure me. God in heaven knows I wanted to be cured, and reasonably. I recommended taking the injections then, and allowed him full liberty to do what he could for me.

. . .

I continued the hypodermical treatment, taking about the same number of injections for a couple of months, when I found myself getting better, and in a much more substantial condition of health than I had been for many a long day, or even year.

I felt, indeed, better; but I observed one peculiarity in my case that was not comforting. It raised my suspicions, not having unlimited confidence in my physician. But should my suspicions turn out well founded, I argued, the great improvement in my health has justified my treatment, and I cannot see yet that I am in any danger. Let me go on a little while longer, until my health becomes permanently established, and then I will drop this doctor and his treatment. I found that the taking of my medicine had settled down into something like regularity, and when the time came around that I was restless, lacking spirit, and unable to do anything to any purpose till I had an injection. . . .

My fears were confirmed some time after by my coming in upon the doctor whilst he was preparing the solution, and thus detecting him. I exclaimed: "Ah ha, doctor, you have been giving me morphia." "Yes," he replied, "a little; but the main part was *cannabis indicus*" (Indian hemp). I don't know that he ever gave me a particle of *cannabis indicus*, for I know that some time after, and from *that* period on, he did not disguise the fact that he was giving me the unadulterated sulphate of morphia. The doctor soon found he had an elephant on his hands,—saw that I was in the habit; became tired of my regular calls for hypodermical injections, and endeavored to shake me off. After giving him fully to understand his culpability in the matter, we parted.

Knowing, then, that I was simply an opium eater, I purchased my own morphia at the drug-stores, and took it per mouth instead of by a hypodermic syringe. . . .

After I had come to take the drug daily, I often passed sleepless nights, the brain in uncontrollable action during the whole night. . . . After a time, when my body became more benumbed and deadened by opium, and consequently less susceptible to its stimulating influence, I could, and did, so regulate my taking of the drug as to insure sleep at night, and the best digestion possible under the circumstances at meals. But as to sleep, I could not do this in the first stages; the effect was too powerful, and extended over too long a time. . . . Days upon days my head has felt as though it were encircled by an iron helmet, which was gradually becoming more and more contracted, until it would literally crush my skull. Add to this the distress so often experienced in the region of the epigastrium (pit of the stomach), which, perhaps, more at one time than another, but which does always, impair the working of the brain for the time being, and often cuts off almost totally the use of the mind, and what is left of a man mentally is very little indeed.

. . .

I am no physician, and not learned in physiology, therefore I cannot enter into a learned analysis of the opium appetite. Neither have I read any books upon the subject. I know nothing about the matter save from my own observation or experience. But whether I know *why this* is true, or *that* is *so*, or not, one fact I am entirely conscious of, and that is, that in this appetite abides the enslaving power of opium. The influences of opium in the latter stages would not have such an attraction for the habituate but that he could easily forego them; but the appetite comes in and makes him feel that he *must* have opium if he has existence, and there is an end to all resistance. Here dwell the Circean spells of opium. Should one become accustomed to large doses, or rather a large quantity per diem, it is almost impossible to induce the mind to take less, for fear of falling to pieces, going into naught, etc. It seems in such a state that existence would be insupportable were a reduction made. An intense fear of being plunged into an abyss of darkness and despair besets the mind. Hence the opium eater goes on ever increasing until his final doom.

Opium as a medicine is a grand and powerful remedy, and without a substitute, though as imperfectly understood in its complex action and far-reaching consequences by the mass of the medical profession as by the people at large. Its abstruser mysteries and remoter effects are yet to be discovered and developed by the science of physic.

When the true nature of opium becomes generally known (and by the word nature I mean all the possibilities for good and evil embraced in the medical properties of the drug), the poor victim of its terrors will be taken by the hand and sympathized with by his fellow-man, instead of being ostracized from society, and treated with contempt and reprehension, as he now is.

. . .

I have not for a number of years made an effort to renounce opium. I know that my unaided efforts would prove fruitless. My constitution would no more stand the test than it would the abstinence from food. Death would follow sooner from want of opium than it would from want of food. Seventy-two hours' abstinence from opium would, I think, prove fatal in my case; and I believe that I would die by the expiration of that time. It may be impossible to conceive, without actual experience, the singular effect opium has upon the system in making itself a necessity. Being no physician, I am unable to give a technical description of that effect, but, with the reader's indulgence, I shall try, however, to describe it in my own language.

When opium is not taken by the *habitué* for twenty-four hours, his whole body commences to sag, droop, and become unjointed. The result is precisely like taking the starch out of a well-done-up shirt. The man is as limp as a dish-rag, and as lifeless. He perspires all over,—feels wet and disagreeable. To take opium now is to brace the man right up; it tightens him up like the closing of a draw-string. Such is the effect in the internal man, and it pervades thence the entire system. His mortal machine is screwed up and put in running order. The opium not taken at the expiration of the twenty-four hours, rheumatic pains in the lower limbs soon set in, gradually extending to the arms and back; these grow worse as time passes, and continue to grow worse until they become unendurable. Contemporaneously with the pain, all the secretions of the system, but more notably those of the stomach and bowels, are unloosed like the opening of a flood-gate, and an acrid and fiery diarrhœa sets in, which nothing but opium can check. All the corruption engendered and choked up there for years comes rushing forth in a foul and distempered mass. The pain and diarrhœa continue until the patient is either cured, if he has sufficient will and constitution to withstand the torture, or is compelled by his sufferings to return to opium.

During the period of time endured without opium, the body is fiery hot and painfully sensitive to every touch or contact. So exquisite is the sensibility, that to touch a hair of the head or beard, is like the jagging of needles into the body. The mouth continually dreuls, and in some instances is ulcerated and sore. As to eating, it is hardly to be thought of; a mouthful satisfies. Of the suffering hardest to withstand, is the *apparent* stationary position of time, which arises, I presume, from the rigid, intense condition, and intense sensitiveness, of the whole system, and the hopelessness of the thoughts which march like funeral processions through the mind; this, in connection with the sinking state of the spirits, and the awful aching of the heart, places a man in a predicament which no other earthly suffering can parallel. There is no prospect in life; opium has so transformed the human body, that it no longer has natural feelings; there is no expectancy, no hope, for a different future. The appetite for opium at this time is generally master of the man; it rages like the hunger of a wild beast.

If a person when in this condition had any human feelings or aspirations, he might resist and go on, if of constitution sufficient; but the difficulty is, it is necessary for the poor wretch to take opium to have natural feelings, or to place any reliance upon the future. It is generally the case, at this stage, that the opium eater would wade through blood for opium. All else in the world is nothing to him without it, and for it he would exchange the world and all there is in it. He yields to the irresistible demand for his destroyer; and with a heart the depth of whose despair the plummet of hope never sounded.

DISCUSSION QUESTIONS

1   What can we learn about nineteenth-century medical treatment from this passage?
2   Why describe drug addiction in such detail? What might be the author's purpose?
3   How might a source like this expand the ways in which we think about the Civil War and its legacies?

5-8 | Address of the International Working Men's Association to Abraham Lincoln, UK, 1865, and response by United States Ambassador to the UK Charles Francis Adams, 1865

The International Working Men's Association (IWMA), established in London in September 1864, was a sociopolitical movement of workers whose goal was the emancipation of the working class. Though Karl Marx was a part of the IWMA—and likely drafted this letter—he did not found it nor was it created as a Marxist organization; instead it was an organization for workers of any nation, of any political persuasion, who desired to work together to represent and forward labor interests and the rights of workers. International in outlook, they would have been keenly aware of the U.S. Civil War and national politics, as this communiqué demonstrates.

The International Workingmen's Association 1864
Address of the International Working Men's Association to Abraham Lincoln, President of the United States of America
Presented to U.S. Ambassador Charles Francis Adams
January 28, 1865

Sir:
We congratulate the American people upon your re-election by a large majority. If resistance to the Slave Power was the reserved watchword of your first election, the triumphant war cry of your re-election is Death to Slavery.

From the commencement of the titanic American strife the workingmen of Europe felt instinctively that the star-spangled banner carried the destiny of their class. The contest for the territories which opened the dire epopee, was it not to decide whether the virgin soil of immense tracts should be wedded to the labour of the emigrant, or prostituted by the tramp of the slave driver?

When an oligarchy of 300,000 slaveholders dared to inscribe, for the first time in the annals of the world, "Slavery" on the banner of armed revolt—when on the very spots where hardly a century ago the idea of one great Democratic Republic had first sprung up—whence the first declaration of the rights of man was issued, and the first impulse given to the European revolution of the eighteenth century—when on those very spots counter-revolution, with systematic thoroughness, gloried in rescinding "the ideas entertained at the time of the formation of the old constitution", and maintained "Slavery to be a beneficent institution", indeed, the only solution of the great problem of "the relation of capital to labour", and cynically proclaimed property in man "the cornerstone of the new edifice"—then the working classes of Europe understood at once, even before the fanatic partisanship of the upper classes, for the Confederate gentry had given its dismal warning, that the slaveholders' rebellion was to sound the tocsin for a general holy crusade of property against labour, and that for the men of labour, with their hopes for the future, even their past conquests were at stake in that tremendous conflict on the other side of the Atlantic. Everywhere they bore therefore patiently the hardships imposed upon them by the cotton crisis, opposed enthusiastically the pro-slavery intervention of their betters—and, from most parts of Europe, contributed their quota of blood to the good cause.

While the workingmen, the true political powers of the North, allowed Slavery to defile their own Republic, while before the negro, mastered and sold without his concurrence, they boasted it the highest prerogative of the white-skinned labourer to sell himself and choose his own master, they were unable to attain the true freedom of labour, or to support their European brethren in their struggle for emancipation; but this barrier to progress has been swept off by the red sea of civil war.

The workingmen of Europe feel sure, that as the American War of Independence initiated a new era of ascendancy for the middle class, so the American Anti-slavery War will do for the working classes. They consider it an earnest of the epoch to come that it fell to the lot of Abraham Lincoln, the single-minded son of the working class, to lead his country through the matchless struggle for the rescue of an enchained race and the reconstruction of a social world.

Signed on behalf of the International Workingmen's Association, the Central Council: *Longmaid, Worley, Whitlock, Fox, Blackmore, Hartwell, Pidgeon, Lucraft, Weston, Dell, Nieass, Shaw, Lake, Buckley, Osbourne, Howell, Carter, Wheeler, Stainsby, Morgan, Grossmith, Dick, Denoual, Jourdain, Morrissot, Leroux, Bordage, Bocquet, Talandier, Dupont, L. Wolff, Aldovrandi, Lama, Solustri, Nusperli, Eccarius, Wolff, Lessner, Pfander, Lochner, Kaub, Bolleter, Rybczinski, Hansen, Schantzenbach, Smales, Cornelius, Petersen, Otto, Bagnagatti, Setacci;*
George Odger, President of the Council; P. V. Lubez, Corresponding Secretary for France; Karl Marx, Corresponding Secretary for Germany; G. P. Fontana, Corresponding Secretary for Italy; J. E. Holtorp, Corresponding Secretary for Poland; H. F. Jung, Corresponding Secretary for Switzerland; William R. Cremer, Honorary General Secretary.
      18 Greek Street, Soho.

Ambassador Adams Replies

Legation of the United States
London, 28th January, 1865

Sir:
I am directed to inform you that the address of the Central Council of your Association, which was duly transmitted through this Legation to the President of the United [States], has been received by him.

So far as the sentiments expressed by it are personal, they are accepted by him with a sincere and anxious desire that he may be able to prove himself not unworthy of the confidence which has been recently extended to him by his fellow citizens and by so many of the friends of humanity and progress throughout the world.

The Government of the United States has a clear consciousness that its policy neither is nor could be reactionary, but at the same time it adheres to the course which it adopted at the beginning, of abstaining everywhere from propagandism and unlawful intervention. It strives to do equal and exact justice to all states and to all men and it relies upon the beneficial results of that effort for support at home and for respect and good will throughout the world.

Nations do not exist for themselves alone, but to promote the welfare and happiness of mankind by benevolent intercourse and example. It is in this relation that the United States regard their cause in the present conflict with slavery, maintaining insurgence as the cause of human nature, and they derive new encouragements to persevere from the testimony of the workingmen of Europe that the national attitude is favored with their enlightened approval and earnest sympathies.

I have the honor to be, sir, your obedient servant,
Charles Francis Adams

DISCUSSION QUESTIONS

1   What did the IWMA see as the economic conflict at the center of the Civil War?
2   Who did they support in the Civil War? Why?
3   How does Adams' quick response suggest he interpreted the meaning of the Civil War?

WHO IS AN AMERICAN?

5–9a | Declaration of Sentiments from the Seneca Falls Convention, 1848

Conceived by Lucretia Mott and Elizabeth Cady Stanton after they had been denied the right to speak or vote at an international anti-slavery convention in London, the Seneca Falls Convention marked the birth of the women's rights movement. The Declaration of Sentiments, drafted primarily by Stanton, included a demand for political rights, an issue so controversial that some attendees refused to endorse it. Emboldened and inspired by the European revolutions of 1848, women's rights activists in North America and Europe became particularly active in the 1850s.

When, in the course of human events, it becomes necessary for one portion of the family of man to assume among the people of the earth a position different from that which they have hitherto occupied, but one to which the laws of nature and of nature's God entitle them, a decent respect to the opinions of mankind requires that they should declare the causes that impel them to such a course.

We hold these truths to be self-evident: that all men and women are created equal; that they are endowed by their Creator with certain inalienable rights; that among these are life, liberty, and the pursuit of happiness; that to secure these rights governments are instituted, deriving their just powers from the consent of the governed. Whenever any form of government becomes destructive of these ends, it is the right of those who suffer from it to refuse allegiance to it, and to insist upon the institution of a new government, laying its foundation on such principles, and organizing its powers in such form, as to them shall seem most likely to effect their safety and happiness. Prudence, indeed, will dictate that governments long established should not be changed for light and transient causes; and accordingly all experience hath shown that mankind are more disposed to suffer, while evils are sufferable, than to right themselves by abolishing the forms to which they were accustomed. But when a long train of abuses and usurpations, pursuing invariably the same object evinces a design to reduce them under absolute despotism, it is their duty to throw off such government, and to provide new guards for their future security. Such has been the patient sufferance of the women under this government, and such is now the necessity which constrains them to demand the equal station to which they are entitled.

The history of mankind is a history of repeated injuries and usurpations on the part of man toward woman, having in direct object the establishment of an absolute tyranny over her. To prove this, let facts be submitted to a candid world.

He has never permitted her to exercise her inalienable right to the elective franchise.

He has compelled her to submit to laws, in the formation of which she had no voice.

He has withheld from her rights which are given to the most ignorant and degraded men—both natives and foreigners.

Having deprived her of this first right of a citizen, the elective franchise, thereby leaving her without representation in the halls of legislation, he has oppressed her on all sides.

He has made her, if married, in the eye of the law, civilly dead.

He has taken from her all right in property, even to the wages she earns.

He has made her, morally, an irresponsible being, as she can commit many crimes with impunity, provided they be done in the presence of her husband. In the covenant of marriage, she is compelled to promise obedience to her husband, he becoming, to all intents and purposes, her master—the law giving him power to deprive her of her liberty, and to administer chastisement.

He has so framed the laws of divorce, as to what shall be the proper causes, and in case of separation, to whom the guardianship of the children shall be given, as to be wholly regardless of the happiness of women—the law, in all cases, going upon a false supposition of the supremacy of man, and giving all power into his hands.

After depriving her of all rights as a married woman, if single, and the owner of property, he has taxed her to support a government which recognizes her only when her property can be made profitable to it.

He has monopolized nearly all the profitable employments, and from those she is permitted to follow, she receives but a scanty remuneration. He closes against her all the avenues to wealth and distinction which he considers most honorable to himself. As a teacher of theology, medicine, or law, she is not known.

He has denied her the facilities for obtaining a thorough education, all colleges being closed against her.

He allows her in Church, as well as State, but a subordinate position, claiming Apostolic authority for her exclusion from the ministry, and, with some exceptions, from any public participation in the affairs of the Church.

He has created a false public sentiment by giving to the world a different code of morals for men and women, by which moral delinquencies which exclude women from society, are not only tolerated, but deemed of little account in man.

He has usurped the prerogative of Jehovah himself, claiming it as his right to assign for her a sphere of action, when that belongs to her conscience and to her God.

He has endeavored, in every way that he could, to destroy her confidence in her own powers, to lessen her self-respect, and to make her willing to lead a dependent and abject life.

Now, in view of this entire disfranchisement of one-half the people of this country, their social and religious degradation—in view of the unjust laws above mentioned, and because women do feel themselves aggrieved, oppressed, and fraudulently deprived of their most sacred rights, we insist that they have immediate admission to all the rights and privileges which belong to them as citizens of the United States.

In entering upon the great work before us, we anticipate no small amount of misconception, misrepresentation, and ridicule; but we shall use every instrumentality within our power to effect our object. We shall employ agents, circulate tracts, petition the State and National legislatures, and endeavor to enlist the pulpit and the press in our behalf. We hope this Convention will be followed by a series of Conventions embracing every part of the country.

5–9b | Ernestine Polowski Rose, excerpts from "An Address on Woman's Rights," 1851

The Polish-born Ernestine Polowski Rose (1810–1892) was one of the most influential figures in the early women's rights movement. She lived in England before emigrating to the U.S. in 1836 and immediately began speaking on behalf of women's rights and against slavery. Representative of the international nature of the women's movement, Rose's speech to an American audience makes repeated reference to European events. Travelling widely and speaking frequently, Rose gained the moniker "Queen of the Platform."

My Friends:—The observing and reflecting mind that casts its vision far beyond the panoramic scenes of every-day life, must perceive that our present age is fast ripening for the most important changes in the affairs of man. The desire for freedom had shaken Europe to its very centere. The love of Liberty has convulsed the nations like the mighty throes of an earthquake. The oppressed are struggling against the oppressors. . . .

Yet great as these signs of the times are, they are not new. From the time of absolute despotism to the present hour of comparative freedom, the weak had ever to struggle against the strong, right against might. But a new sign has appeared in our social zodiac, prophetic of the most important changes, pregnant with most beneficial results that have ever taken place in the annuals of human history. And to him who can trace the various epochs in human life, it is as a cheering as it is interesting to mark the onward movement of the race towards a higher state of human progression—that while nations strive against nations, people against people, to attain the same amount of freedom already possessed in this country, WOMAN is rising in the full dignity of her being to claim the recognition of *her* rights. And though the first public demonstration has been here, already has the voice of Woman in behalf of her sex been carried as it were on her wings of lightning to all parts of Europe, whose echo has brought back the warmest and most heartfelt responses from our sisters there.

Among the many encouraging letters received at the recent Woman's Convention at Worcester, there was one exceeding all the rest in the soul-stirring interest it created. It spoke, through the dungeon walls, the cheering and encouraging words of sympathy from two incarcerated women of Paris, to the hearts of their sisters in America. The cause of their imprisonment was their practically claiming the fulfillment of that glorious motto, "Liberty, Equality and Fraternity," destined to shake the thrones, break the scepires, and bow down the mitres of Europe. One of them presented herself as candidate for Mayor of an Arrondissement, the other (to the honor of the genuine Republicans of Paris, be it said,) was nominated by the Industrial Union, consisting of two hundred and twenty Societies, as member of the Assembly. For these offenses they were cast into prison. Oh! France, where is the glory of thy revolutions? Is the blood thy children poured out on the altar of freedom so effaced, that thy daughters dare not lift their voices in behalf of their rights? But so long as might constitutes right, every good cause must have its martyrs. Why then, should woman not be a martyr to *her* cause?

But how can we wonder that France, governed as she is by Russian and Austrian despotism, does not recognize the higher laws of humanity in the recognition of the rights of woman, when even here, in this far-famed land of freedom and of knowledge, under a republic that has inscribed on its banner the great truth that all men are created free and equal and are endowed with inalienable rights to life, liberty, and the pursuit of happiness—a Declaration wafted like the voices of Hope on the breezes of heaven to the remotest parts of earth, to whisper freedom and equality to the oppressed and down trodden children of men—a Declaration that lies at the very foundation of human freedom and happiness, yet in the very face of that eternal truth, woman, the mockingly so-called "better half of man," has yet to plead for her rights, nay, for her life; for what is life without liberty? and what is liberty without equality of rights; and as for the pursuit of happiness, she is not allowed to pursue any line of life that might promote it; she has only thankfully to accept what man, in the plentitude of his wisdom and generosity, decides as proper for her to do, and that is, what he does not choose to do himself.

Is woman then not included in the Declaration? Answer, ye wise men of the nation, and answer truly; add not hypocrisy to your other sins. Say she is not created free and equal, and therefore, (for the sequence follows on the premises) she is not entitled to life, liberty and the pursuit of happiness. But you dare not answer this simple question. With all the audacity arising from an assumed superiority, you cannot so libel and insult humanity as to say she is not; and if she is, then what right has man, except that of might, to deprive her of the same rights and privileges he claims for himself? And why, in the name of reason and justice, I ask, why should she not have the same rights as man? Because she is woman? Humanity recognizes no sex—mind recognizes no sex—virtue recognizes no sex—life and death, pleasure and pain, happiness and misery, recognize no sex. Like him she comes involuntarily into existence; like him she possesses physical, mental, and moral powers, on the proper cultivation of which depends her happiness; like him she is subject to all vicissitudes of life; like him she has to pay the penalty for disobeying nature's laws, and far greater penalties has she to suffer from ignorance of her far more complicated nature than he; like him she enjoys or suffers with her country. Yet she is not recognized as his equal. In the laws of the land she had no rights; in government she has no voice, and in spite of another principle recognized in this republic, namely, that taxation without representation is tyranny, woman is taxed without being represented; her property may be consumed by heavy taxes, to defray the expenses of that unholy and unrighteous thing called war, yet she cannot give her veto against it. From the cradle to the grave, she is subject to the power and control of man, father, guardian, and husband. One conveys her like some piece of merchandize over to the other. . . .

But it will be said that the husband provides for the wife, or, in other words, he is bound to feed, clothe, and shelter her. Oh! the degradation of that idea! Yes, he keeps her, so he does his horse. By law both are considered his property; both can, when the cruelty of the owners compels them to run away, be brought back by the strong arm of the law; and according to a still extant law of England, both may be led by the halter to the market place and sold. This is humiliating, indeed, but nevertheless true, and the sooner these things are known and understood the better for humanity. . . .

And therefore, while I feel it my duty—aye, a painful duty, to point out the wrong done to woman and its evil consequences, and would do all in my power to aid her in deliverance . . . hence the necessity for active, earnest endeavors to enlighten their minds; hence the necessity to protest against the wrong and claim our rights, and in doing our duty we must not heed the taunts, ridicule, and stigma cast upon us. We must remember we have a crusade before us far holier and more righteous than led a warrior to Palestine—a crusade not to deprive anyone of his rights, but to claim our own; and as our cause is a better one, so also must be the means to achieve it. We therefore must put on the armor of charity, carry before us the banner of truth, and defend ourselves with the shield of right against the invaders of our liberty. . . .

To achieve this great victory of right over might, woman has much to do. She must not sit idle and wait till man inspired by justice and humanity will work out her redemption. It has well been said, "He that would be free, himself must strike the blow." It is with nations as with individuals, if they do not strive to help themselves no one will help them. Man may, and in the nature of things will, remove the legal, political, and civil disabilities from woman, and recognize her as his equal with himself, and it will do much towards her elevation; but the laws cannot compel her to cultivate her physical and mental powers, and take a stand as a free and independent being. All that, *she* has to do. She must investigate and take an interest in everything on which the welfare of society depends, for the interest and happiness of every member of society is connected with that of society. She must at once claim and exercise those rights and privileges with which the laws do not interfere, and it will aid her to obtain all the rest. She must, therefore, throw off that heavy yoke that like a nightmare weighs down her best energies, viz., the fear of public opinion. . . .

The priests well know the influence and value of women when warmly engaged in any cause, and therefore as long as they can keep them steeped in superstitious darkness, so long are they safe; and hence the horror and anathema against every woman that has intelligence, spirit, and moral courage to cast off the dark and oppressive yoke of superstition. But she must do it, or she will ever remain a slave, for of all tyranny that of superstition is the greatest, and he is the most abject slave who tamely submits to its yoke. Woman, then, must cast it off as her greatest enemy; and the time I trust will come when she will aid man to remove the political, civil, and religious evils that have swept over the earth like some malignant courage to lay waste and destroy so much of the beauty, harmony, and happiness of man; and the old fable of the fall of man through a woman will be superseded by the glorious fact that she was instrumental in the elevation of the race towards a higher, nobler, and happier destiny.

DISCUSSION QUESTIONS

1   Why did Seneca Falls attendees feel compelled to agitate for women's rights?

2   What responses did Rose state women should employ towards their cause?

3   How did each of these sources utilize the Declaration of Independence to make their argument for women's rights?

5–10a | Frederick Douglass, excerpts from "What to the Slave Is the Fourth of July?" 1852

A giant in the struggle against slavery and for human rights, Frederick Douglass (1818–1895) gave this powerful speech on July 5, 1852, to the Rochester (N.Y.) Ladies' Anti-Slavery Society. Born into slavery and escaping around age 20, Douglass dedicated his life to activism, becoming one of the best-known orators and public intellectuals in the country. His travels to Europe provided him an international audience, and his reputation meant he was tapped to serve in several public offices, even garnering support for a presidential run. Douglass' autobiographical works remain widely read today.

Fellow Citizens, I am not wanting in respect for the fathers of this republic. The signers of the Declaration of Independence were brave men. They were great men too—great enough to give fame to a great age. It does not often happen to a nation to raise, at one time, such a number of truly great men. The point from which I am compelled to view them is not, certainly, the most favorable; and yet I cannot contemplate their great deeds with less than admiration. They were statesmen, patriots and heroes, and for the good they did, and the principles they contended for, I will unite with you to honor their memory.

. . .

Fellow-citizens, pardon me, allow me to ask, why am I called upon to speak here to-day? What have I, or those I represent, to do with your national independence? Are the great principles of political freedom and of natural justice, embodied in that Declaration of Independence, extended to us? and am I, therefore, called upon to bring our humble offering to the national altar, and to confess the benefits and express devout gratitude for the blessings resulting from your independence to us?

Would to God, both for your sakes and ours, that an affirmative answer could be truthfully returned to these questions! Then would my task be light, and my burden easy and delightful. For who is there so cold, that a nation's sympathy could not warm him? Who so obdurate and dead to the claims of gratitude, that would not thankfully acknowledge such priceless benefits? Who so stolid and selfish, that would not give his voice to swell the hallelujahs of a nation's jubilee, when the chains of servitude had been torn from his limbs? I am not that man. In a case like that, the dumb might eloquently speak, and the "lame man leap as an hart."

But, such is not the state of the case. I say it with a sad sense of the disparity between us. I am not included within the pale of this glorious anniversary! Your high independence only reveals the immeasurable distance between us. The blessings in which you, this day, rejoice, are not enjoyed in common.—The rich inheritance of justice, liberty, prosperity and independence, bequeathed by your fathers, is shared by you, not by me. The sunlight that brought life and healing to you, has brought stripes and death to me. This Fourth [of] July is *yours*, not *mine*. *You* may rejoice, *I* must mourn. To drag a man in fetters into the grand illuminated temple of liberty, and call upon him to join you in joyous anthems, were inhuman mockery and sacrilegious irony. Do you mean, citizens, to mock me, by asking me to speak to-day? If so, there is a parallel to your conduct. And let me warn you that it is dangerous to copy the example of a nation whose crimes, lowering up to heaven, were thrown down by the breath of the Almighty, burying that nation in irrecoverable ruin! I can to-day take up the plaintive lament of a peeled and woe-smitten people!

"By the rivers of Babylon, there we sat down. Yea! we wept when we remembered Zion. We hanged our harps upon the willows in the midst thereof. For there, they that carried us away captive, required of us a song; and they who wasted us required of us mirth, saying, Sing us one of the songs of Zion. How can we sing the Lord's song in a strange land? If I forget thee, O Jerusalem, let my right hand forget her cunning. If I do not remember thee, let my tongue cleave to the roof of my mouth."

Fellow-citizens; above your national, tumultuous joy, I hear the mournful wail of millions! whose chains, heavy and grievous yesterday, are, to-day, rendered more intolerable by the jubilee shouts that reach them. If I do forget, if I do not faithfully remember those bleeding children of sorrow this day, "may my right hand forget her cunning, and may my tongue cleave to the roof of my mouth!" To forget them, to pass lightly over their wrongs, and to chime in with the popular theme, would be treason most scandalous and shocking, and would make me a reproach before God and the world. My subject, then fellow-citizens, is AMERICAN SLAVERY. I shall see, this day, and its popular characteristics, from the slave's point of view. Standing, there, identified with the American bondman, making his wrongs mine, I do not hesitate to declare, with all my soul, that the character and conduct of this nation never looked blacker to me than on this 4th of July! Whether we turn to the declarations of the past, or to the professions of the present, the conduct of the nation seems equally hideous and revolting. America is false to the past, false to the present, and solemnly binds herself to be false to the future. Standing with God and the crushed and bleeding slave on this occasion, I will, in the name of humanity which is outraged, in the name of liberty which is fettered, in the name of the constitution and the Bible, which are disregarded and trampled upon, dare to call in question and to denounce, with all the emphasis I can command, everything that serves to perpetuate slavery—the great sin and shame of America! "I will not equivocate; I will not excuse;" I will use the severest language I can command; and yet not one word shall escape me that any man, whose judgment is not blinded by prejudice, or who is not at heart a slaveholder, shall not confess to be right and just.

But I fancy I hear some one of my audience say, it is just in this circumstance that you and your brother abolitionists fail to make a favorable impression on the public mind. Would you argue more, and denounce less, would you persuade more, and rebuke less, your cause would be much more likely to succeed. But, I submit, where all is plain there is nothing to be argued. What point in the anti-slavery creed would you have me argue? On what branch of the subject do the people of this country need light? Must I undertake to prove that the slave is a man? That point is conceded already. Nobody doubts it. The slaveholders themselves acknowledge it in the enactment of laws for their government. They acknowledge it when they punish disobedience on the part of the slave. There are seventy-two crimes in the State of Virginia, which, if committed by a black man, (no matter how ignorant he be), subject him to the punishment of death; while only two of the same crimes will subject a white man to the like punishment. What is this but the acknowledgement that the slave is a moral, intellectual and responsible being? The manhood of the slave is conceded. It is admitted in the fact that Southern statute books are covered with enactments forbidding, under severe fines and penalties, the teaching of the slave to read or to write. When you can point to any such laws, in reference to the beasts of the field, then I may consent to argue the manhood of the slave. When the dogs in your streets, when the fowls of the air, when the cattle on your hills, when the fish of the sea, and the reptiles that crawl, shall be unable to distinguish the slave from a brute, then will I argue with you that the slave is a man!

For the present, it is enough to affirm the equal manhood of the Negro race. Is it not astonishing that, while we are ploughing, planting and reaping, using all kinds of mechanical tools, erecting houses, constructing bridges, building ships, working in metals of brass, iron, copper, silver and gold; that, while we are reading, writing and cyphering, acting as clerks, merchants and secretaries, having among us lawyers, doctors, ministers, poets, authors, editors, orators and teachers; that, while we are engaged in all manner of enterprises common to other men, digging gold in California, capturing the whale in the Pacific, feeding sheep and cattle on the hill-side, living, moving, acting, thinking, planning, living in families as husbands, wives and children, and, above all, confessing and worshipping the Christian's God, and looking hopefully for life and immortality beyond the grave, we are called upon to prove that we are men!

Would you have me argue that man is entitled to liberty? that he is the rightful owner of his own body? You have already declared it. Must I argue the wrongfulness of slavery? Is that a question for Republicans? Is it to be settled by the rules of logic and argumentation, as a matter beset with great difficulty, involving a doubtful application of the principle of justice, hard to be understood? How should I look to-day, in the presence of Americans, dividing, and subdividing a discourse, to show that men have a natural right to freedom? speaking of it relatively, and positively, negatively, and affirmatively. To do so, would be to make myself ridiculous, and to offer an insult to your understanding.—There is not a man beneath the canopy of heaven, that does not know that slavery is wrong *for him*.

What, am I to argue that it is wrong to make men brutes, to rob them of their liberty, to work them without wages, to keep them ignorant of their relations to their fellow men, to beat them with sticks, to flay their flesh with the lash, to load their limbs with irons, to hunt them with dogs, to sell them at auction, to sunder their families, to knock out their teeth, to burn their flesh, to starve them into obedience and submission to their masters? Must I argue that a system thus marked with blood, and stained with pollution, is *wrong*? No! I will not. I have better employments for my time and strength than such arguments would imply.

What, then, remains to be argued? Is it that slavery is not divine; that God did not establish it; that our doctors of divinity are mistaken? There is blasphemy in the thought. That which is inhuman, cannot be divine! *Who* can reason on such a proposition? They that can, may; I cannot. The time for such argument is past.

At a time like this, scorching irony, not convincing argument, is needed. O! had I the ability, and could I reach the nation's ear, I would, to-day, pour out a fiery stream of biting ridicule, blasting reproach, withering sarcasm, and stern rebuke. For it is not light that is needed, but fire; it is not the gentle shower, but thunder. We need the storm, the whirlwind, and the earthquake. The feeling of the nation must be quickened; the conscience of the nation must be roused; the propriety of the nation must be startled; the hypocrisy of the nation must be exposed; and its crimes against God and man must be proclaimed and denounced.

What, to the American slave, is your 4th of July? I answer; a day that reveals to him, more than all other days in the year, the gross injustice and cruelty to which he is the constant victim. To him, your celebration is a sham; your boasted liberty, an unholy license; your national greatness, swelling vanity; your sounds of rejoicing are empty and heartless; your denunciations of tyrants, brass fronted impudence; your shouts of liberty and equality, hollow mockery; your prayers and hymns, your sermons and thanksgivings, with all your religious parade, and solemnity, are, to him, mere bombast, fraud, deception, impiety, and hypocrisy—a thin veil to cover up crimes which would disgrace a nation of savages. There is not a nation on the earth guilty of practices, more shocking and bloody, than are the people of these United States, at this very hour.

Go where you may, search where you will, roam through all the monarchies and despotisms of the old world, travel through South America, search out every abuse, and when you have found the last, lay your facts by the side of the everyday practices of this nation, and you will say with me, that, for revolting barbarity and shameless hypocrisy, America reigns without a rival. . . .

5–10b | Excerpts from "The Black Code of St. Landry Parish," 1865

The Black Codes refer to any laws passed in Southern states in the immediate aftermath of the Civil War that were designed to curb the freedom of black people, particularly in terms of mobility and employment. As slavery had been abolished during the war, these laws were intended to replace the institution and enforce white supremacy through legal means. This example is from St. Landry Parish in Louisiana, a Black Code (or *Code Noir*) that had its roots in French laws concerning enslaved peoples from the eighteenth century.

Whereas it was formerly made the duty of the police jury to make suitable regulations for the police of slaves within the limits of the parish; and whereas slaves have become emancipated by the action of the ruling powers; and whereas it is necessary for public order, as well as for the comfort and correct deportment of said freedmen, that suitable regulations should be established for their government in their changed condition, the following ordinances are adopted, with the approval of the United States military authority commanding in said parish, viz:

SECTION 1. *Be it ordained by the police jury of the parish of St. Landry,* That no negro shall be allowed to pass within the limits of said parish without a special permit in writing from his employer. Whoever shall violate this provision shall pay a fine of two dollars and fifty cents, or in default thereof shall be forced to work four days on the public road, or suffer corporeal punishments as provided hereinafter.

SECTION 2. *Be it further ordained,* That every negro who shall be found absent from the residence of his employer after 10 o'clock at night, without a written permit from his employer, shall pay a fine of five dollars, or in default thereof, shall be compelled to work five days on the public road, or suffer corporeal punishments as provided hereinafter.

SECTION 3. *Be it further ordained,* That no negro shall be permitted to rent or keep a house within said parish. Any negro violating this provision shall be immediately ejected and compelled to find an employer; and any person who shall rent, or give the use of any house to any negro, in violation of this section, shall pay a fine of five dollars for each offence.

SECTION 4. *Be it further ordained*, That every negro is required to be in the regular service of some white person, or former owner, who shall be held responsible for the conduct of said negro. But said employer or former owner may permit said negro to hire his own time by special permission in writing, which permission shall not extend over seven days at any one time. Any negro violating the provisions of this section shall be fined five dollars for each offence, or in default of the payment thereof shall be forced to work five days on the public road, or suffer corporeal punishment as hereinafter provided.

SECTION 5. *Be it further ordained*, That no public meetings or congregations of negroes shall be allowed within said parish after sunset; but such public meetings and congregations may be held between the hours of sunrise and sunset, by the special permission in writing of the captain of patrol, within whose beat such meetings shall take place. This prohibition, however, is not intended to prevent negroes from attending the usual church services, conducted by white ministers and priests. Every negro violating the provisions of this section shall pay a fine of five dollars, or in default thereof shall be compelled to work five days on the public road, or suffer corporeal punishment as hereinafter provided.

SECTION 6. *Be it further ordained*, That no negro shall be permitted to preach, exhort, or otherwise declaim to congregations of colored people, without a special permission in writing from the president of the police jury. Any negro violating the provisions of this section shall pay a fine of ten dollars, or in default thereof shall be compelled to work ten days on the public road, or suffer corporeal punishment as hereinafter provided.

SECTION 7. *Be it further ordained*, That no negro who is not in the military service shall be allowed to carry fire-arms, or any kind of weapons, within the parish, without the special written permission of his employers, approved and indorsed by the nearest or most convenient chief of patrol. Any one violating the provisions of this section shall forfeit his weapons and pay a fine of five dollars, or in default of the payment of said fine, shall be forced to work five days on the public road, or suffer corporeal punishment as hereinafter provided.

SECTION 8. *Be it further ordained*, That no negro shall sell, barter, or exchange any articles of merchandise or traffic within said parish without the special written permission of his employer, specifying the articles of sale, barter or traffic. Any one thus offending shall pay a fine of one dollar for each offence, and suffer the forfeiture of said articles, or in default of the payment of said fine shall work one day on the public road, or suffer corporeal punishment as hereinafter provided.

SECTION 9. *Be it further ordained*, That any negro found drunk within the said parish shall pay a fine of five dollars, or in default thereof shall work five days on the public road, or suffer corporeal punishment as hereinafter provided.

SECTION 10. *Be it further ordained*, That all the foregoing provisions shall apply to negroes of both sexes.

SECTION 11. *Be it further ordained*, That it shall be the duty of every citizen to act as a police officer for the detection of offences and the apprehension of offenders, who shall be immediately handed over to the proper captain or chief of patrol.

SECTION 12. *Be it further ordained*, That the aforesaid penalties shall be summarily enforced, and that it shall be the duty of the captains and chiefs of patrol to see that the aforesaid ordinances are promptly executed.

SECTION 13. *Be it further ordained*, That all sums collected from the aforesaid fines shall be immediately handed over to the parish treasurer.

SECTION 14. *Be it further ordained*, That the corporeal punishment provided for in the foregoing sections shall consist in confining the body of the offender within a barrel placed over his or her shoulders, in the manner practiced in the army, such confinement not to continue longer than twelve hours, and such time within the aforesaid limit as shall be fixed by the captain or chief of patrol who inflicts the penalty.

SECTION 15. *Be it further ordained*, That these ordinances shall not interfere with any municipal or military regulations inconsistent with them within the limits of said parish.

SECTION 16. *Be it further ordained*, That these ordinances shall take effect five days after their publication in the *Opelousas Courier*.

5–10c | Photograph, sharecropper Sam Williams with family members and laborers in cotton field, 1908

This photograph, probably taken in Alabama (despite the handwritten label), shows a white sharecropper, Sam Williams; his wife, Diccie Williams (center, in the white dress); their youngest son Sidney (in front of Sam); and a number of farm workers. Sharecropping, a system where a tenant is allowed to use land in exchange for a share of his crop, arose in the postwar period as a substitution for the plantation system. About two-thirds of sharecroppers were white, like Williams, though nearly all sharecroppers faced difficulties with indebtedness and repressive landlords.

DISCUSSION QUESTIONS

1   In your own words, how does Douglass answer his question, "What to the Slave Is the Fourth of July?"

2   For what types of offenses could blacks in St. Landry Parish be prosecuted?

3   Consider the photograph. How might it suggest that conditions in the new South were similar to the antebellum South? How might it complicate your interpretation to know Williams' wife and child are in the photograph?

5–11 | Chinese immigration and exclusion

With the British defeat of China in the Opium Wars of the mid-nineteenth century, Western states began signing "unequal treaties" with China to avail themselves of China's markets, resources, and population. The U.S. negotiated the first equal treaty with China in 1868—the Burlingame Treaty—granting China most favored nation status and free immigration and travel rights for Chinese in the U.S. (and vice versa), a move intended to protect U.S. trade in China and ensure Chinese immigrant labor for U.S. businesses. Eventually widespread anti-Chinese feeling, as demonstrated by the Keller cartoon from 1881, led to the renegotiation of the treaty and subsequent legislation.

5–11a | Treaty regulating immigration from China, 1880

November 17, 1880

. . . Whereas the Government of the United States, because of the constantly increasing immigration of Chinese laborers to the territory of the United States, and the embarrassments consequent upon such immigration, now desires to negotiate a modification of the existing Treaties which shall not be in direct contravention of their spirit: . . .

ART. I. Whenever in the opinion of the Government of the United States, the coming of Chinese laborers to the United States, or their residence therein, affects or threatens to affect the interests of that country, or to endanger the good order of the said country or of any locality within the territory thereof, the Government of China agrees that the Government of the United States may regulate, limit, or suspend such coming or residence, but may not absolutely prohibit it. The limitation or suspension shall be reasonable and shall apply only to Chinese who may go to the United States as laborers, other classes not being included in the limitations. Legislation taken in regard to Chinese laborers will be of such a character only as is necessary to enforce the regulation, limitation or suspension of immigration, and immigrants shall not be subject to personal maltreatment or abuse.

ART. II. Chinese subjects, whether proceeding to the United States as teachers, students, merchants, or from curiosity, together with their body and household servants, and Chinese laborers who are now in the United States, shall be allowed to go and come of their own free will and accord, and shall be accorded all the rights, privileges, immunities and exemptions which are accorded to the citizens and subjects of the most favored nation.

ART. III. If Chinese laborers, or Chinese of any other class, now either permanently or temporarily residing in the territory of the United States, meet with ill treatment at the hands of any other persons, the Government of the United States will exert all its power to devise measures for their protection and to secure to them the same rights, privileges, immunities and exemptions as may be enjoyed by the citizens or subjects of the most favored nation, and to which they are entitled by treaty. . . .

5–11b | "Chinese Exclusion Act," 1882

May 6, 1882

An act to execute certain treaty stipulations relating to Chinese.

Whereas, in the opinion of the Government of the United States the coming of Chinese laborers to this country endangers the good order of certain localities within the territory thereof: Therefore,

Be it enacted . . . That from and after the expiration of ninety days next after the passage of this act, and until the expiration of ten years next after the passage of this act, the coming of Chinese laborers to the United States be, . . . suspended; and during such suspension it shall not be lawful for any Chinese laborer to come, or, having so come after the expiration of said ninety days, to remain within the United States.

SEC. 2. That the master of any vessel who shall knowingly bring within the United States on such vessel, and land or permit to be landed, any Chinese laborer, from any foreign port or place, shall be deemed guilty of a misdemeanor, and on conviction thereof shall be punished by a fine of not more than five hundred dollars for each and every such Chinese laborer so brought, and may be also imprisoned for a term not exceeding one year.

SEC. 3. That the two foregoing sections shall not apply to Chinese laborers who were in the United States on the seventeenth day of November, eighteen hundred and eighty, or who shall have come into the same before the expiration of ninety days next after the passage of this act, . . .

SEC. 6. That in order to the faithful execution of articles one and two of the treaty in this act before mentioned, every Chinese person other than a laborer who may be entitled by said treaty and this act to come within the United States, and who shall be about to come to the United States, shall be identified as so entitled by the Chinese Government in each case, such identity to be evidenced by a certificate issued under the authority of said government, which certificate shall be in the English language or (if not in the English language) accompanied by a translation into English, stating such right to come, and which certificate shall state the name, title, or official rank, if any, the age, height, and all physical peculiarities former and present occupation or profession and place of residence in China of the person to whom the certificate is issued and that such person is entitled conformably to the treaty in this act mentioned to come within the United States. . . .

SEC. 12. That no Chinese person shall be permitted to enter the United States by land without producing to the proper office of customs the certificate in this act required of Chinese persons seeking to land from a vessel. Any Chinese person found unlawfully within the United States shall be caused to be removed therefrom to the country from whence he came, by direction of the President of the United States, and at the cost of the United States, after being brought before some justice, judge, or commissioner of a court of the United States and found to be one not lawfully entitled to be or remain in the United States.

SEC. 13. That this act shall not apply to diplomatic and other officers of the Chinese Government traveling upon the business of that government, whose credentials shall be taken as equivalent to the certificate in this act mentioned, and shall exempt them and their body and household servants from the provisions of this act as to other Chinese persons.

SEC. 14. That hereafter no State court or court of the United States shall admit Chinese to citizenship; and all laws in conflict with this act are hereby repealed.

SEC. 15. That the words "Chinese laborers," whenever used in this act, shall be construed to mean both skilled and unskilled laborers and Chinese employed in mining.

5–11c | George Frederick Keller, political cartoon, "A Statue for *Our* Harbor," 1881

SEE COLOR INSERT

DISCUSSION QUESTIONS

1   How did the Chinese Exclusion Act limit immigration but still operate within the bounds of the 1880 (Angell) Treaty?

2   Why and how did the artist use the image of the Statue of Liberty to critique Chinese immigration?

3   What was the reason(s) many Americans wanted to limit immigration from China? Provide examples of this sentiment from the sources.

5–12 | New Mexico and statehood

Involved for decades in the antebellum fight over the extension of slavery in newly admitted states, the path to statehood for the New Mexico Territory was delayed for decades longer in the post–Civil War era by prejudice and misinformation. This editorial ran in *Harper's Weekly*, a highly influential, nationally distributed, New York–based magazine, and displays some of the attitudes that blocked New Mexico's admittance into the union—a delay lasting longer than any other petitioning territory. New Mexico was not admitted until 1912, as suggested by the date of the state constitution, a document that thoroughly reflects the rights guaranteed for Mexican citizens in the 1848 Treaty of Guadalupe Hidalgo.

5–12a | Reactions to the passage of a statehood bill for New Mexico, 1876

By a vote of thirty-five to fifteen—and we are glad to see Messrs. EDMUNDS, FRELING-HUYSEN, ALLISON, and the MORRILLS in the minority—the Senate has passed a bill to admit New Mexico as a State, and adding two Senators to the Chamber. Mr. MOR-RILL, of Maine, in a speech full of facts and good sense, showed the impolicy of the bill at this time. We have other authentic information in the letter of two gentlemen residents in the Territory, with the best opportunities of knowing what they say. Of the present population, which is variously estimated, and at the last census was 111,000, nine-tenths are Mexicans, Indians, "greasers," and other non-English-speaking people. About one-tenth or one-eleventh part of the population speak the English language. The nine-tenths are under the strictest Roman Catholic supervision. The Legislature lately in session was composed of ten Mexicans and three Americans in the Senate, and twenty-four Mexicans with two Americans in the House. The House, under the eye of a Roman priest, defeated a non-sectarian school bill, and passed an act incorporating the Jesuits and exempting their property from taxation. The improbability of an increase of the population was shown by Mr. MORRILL, of Maine, from the fact that hardly one acre in a hundred of the land of the Territory is arable, and such a limitation does not justify the expectation of an agricultural population or of any rapid increase of people.

The proposition of the admission of New Mexico as a State is, that such a population, in such a condition of civilization, of industries, and intelligence, and with such forbidding prospects of speedy improvement or increase—a community almost without the characteristic and indispensable qualities of an American State—shall have a representation in the national Senate as large as New York, and in the House shall be equal to Delaware. It is virtually an ignorant foreign community under the influence of the Roman Church, and neither for the advantage of the Union nor for its own benefit can such an addition to the family of American States be urged. There are objections to a Territorial government, but in this case the Territorial supervision supplies encouragement to the spirit of intelligent progress by making the national authority finally supreme, while, as a State, the sparse and scattered and foreign population would be used by the dominant ecclesiastical power for its own purposes. The State would grow up very slowly and under influences which would regard the Church and its infallible foreign head as superior to the State. The patriotism of such a community, its supreme devotion to its native land and the Union and their welfare, would necessarily be subordinated to other preferences. The inevitable result could not be advantageous to the State itself nor desirable for the Union.

The only arguments that were offered for admission were that under a Territorial government a community is in a state of pupilage, and does not advance as when it is a State, and secondly, that New Mexico has as fair a claim for admission as Colorado. The obvious reply to such remarks is that the comparative advantages of the two forms of government can be ascertained only by a careful consideration of the actual facts of the situation. It can not be said abstractly and absolutely that under our system a State government is necessarily better for a community than the Territorial, for this is one of the cases in which the allegation is not true. The same kind of consideration applies to the second remark. The admission of one community as a State can not fairly be made an argument for the admission of another, first, because the circumstances may be very different, and second, because if the proposition be allowed, a blunder might become an imperative precedent. Senator MORRILL, of Vermont, had asked the number of the Anglo-Saxon population of the Territory, and whether there was sufficient wealth to support the government. Such questions were very proper, but Senator HARVEY, of Kansas, seemed to think that they covertly assailed the fundamental American principle of the capacity of the people of all races for self-government, and implied that rich people only have that capacity. Mr. MORRILL did not appear to think that such arguments were very cogent or important, and left them unnoticed. The question was finally taken, and the Senate decided to admit New Mexico as a State. We sincerely regret this action, for the welfare of the country requires great hesitation and the most careful deliberation upon every proposition to admit a new State, and in this instance the question of Territory or State is the question of progress against retrogression, of knowledge against ignorance, of liberty against slavery.

5–12b | Excerpts from the constitution for the state of New Mexico, 1912

Article II

Sec. 5. The rights, privileges and immunities, civil, political and religious, guaranteed to the people of New Mexico by the treaty of Guadalupe Hidalgo shall be preserved inviolate.

Article VII

Sec. 3. The right of any citizen of the state to vote, hold office, or sit upon juries, shall never be restricted, abridged or impaired on account of religion, race, language or color, or inability to speak, read or write the English or Spanish languages except as may be otherwise provided in this constitution; and the provisions of this section and of section one of this article shall never be amended except upon a vote of the people of this state in an election at which at least three-fourths of the electors voting in the whole state, and at least two-thirds of those voting in each county of the state, shall vote for such amendment.

Article XII

Sec. 8. The legislature shall provide for the training of teachers in the normal schools or otherwise so that they may become proficient in both the English and Spanish languages, to qualify them to teach Spanish-speaking pupils and students in the public schools and educational institutions of the state, and shall provide proper means and methods to facilitate the teaching of the English language and other branches of learning to such pupils and students.

Sec. 10. Children of Spanish descent in the State of New Mexico shall never be denied the right and privilege of admission and attendance in the public schools or other public educational institutions of the state, and they shall never be classed in separate schools, but shall forever enjoy perfect equality with other children in all public schools and educational institutions of the state, and the legislature shall provide penalties for the violation of this section. This section shall never be amended except upon a vote of the people of this state, in an election at which at least three-fourths of the electors voting in the whole state and at least two-thirds of those voting in each county in the state shall vote for such amendment.

DISCUSSION QUESTIONS

1 How did the writer of the *Harper's Weekly* piece react to the idea of admitting New Mexico as a state? On what information did they base their opinion?

2 Why might the framers of the New Mexico Constitution want to protect the diversity present within the state?

3 How did each of these sources define the grounds for statehood and citizenship?

6

Western Expansion and Empire

MOTIVES FOR EMPIRE

The nineteenth and early twentieth centuries saw the growth of enormous global empires built by nation-states empowered by industrialization to conquer and outproduce non-industrialized societies. The British had the largest reach, but nearly all European states, the United States, and Japan participated in what is usually referred to as New Imperialism. These empires accelerated the process of globalization, spreading ideas, exchanging goods, and encouraging migration. The success of the West in building empires fed an unhealthy sense of cultural superiority, often resulting in a disregard for and even destruction of traditions, laws, language, and institutions of conquered peoples. The sources included here are examples of the ways in which states attempted to justify their imperial ambitions.

Jules Ferry, excerpts of speech before the French Chamber of Deputies, France, 1884

Mr. Jules Ferry: Gentlemen, I am embarrassed at making such an extended demand on the kind attention of the Chamber, but I do not believe I am fulfilling a pointless task in this forum. It is as arduous for me as it is for you, but there is, I believe, some utility in summarizing and condensing, in the form of arguments, the principles, motives, [and] diverse interests that justify the policy of colonial expansion—[being] of course wise, moderate, and never losing sight of the great continental interests that are the primary concerns of this country.

I was saying, in support of this proposal, that in fact, as we say, the policy of colonial expansion is a political and economic system, [and] I said that this system could be linked to three kinds of ideas: economic ideas, ideas of civilization in its highest sense, and ideas of a political and patriotic nature.

On the matter of economics, I have allowed myself to place before you, support-ed by a few figures, the considerations that justify the policy of colonial expansion from the point of view of this need—more and more urgently felt by the industrial populations of Europe—and particularly [from the point of view] of our wealthy and hard-working country of France, the need for markets. . . . Why? Because right next door to us, Germany has wrapped itself in barriers, because beyond the ocean the United States of America has become extremely protectionist; because not only are these large markets, I will not say closed, but shrinking, becoming more and more difficult for our industrial products to reach; [but also] because these great states are beginning to pour into our own markets products we have not seen here before. . . .

Gentlemen, there is a second point, a second order of ideas that I must equally address, as quickly as possible, believe it: that is the humanitarian and civilizing side of the question. On this point, the honorable Mr. Camille Pelletan has ridiculed extensively, with his usual spirit and finesse; he mocks, he condemns, he says, "What is this civilization imposed with cannon fire? What is it but another form of barbarism? Do not these populations of inferior race have the same rights as you? Are they not masters of their own homes? Did they call on you? You go to them against their will; you assault them, but you do not civilize them."

There, gentlemen, is the thesis; I do not hesitate to say that it is not about policy, nor about history: it is about political metaphysics. ["Ah! Ah!" from the far left]. . . .

Gentlemen, it is necessary to speak louder and more truthfully! It is necessary to say openly that, in effect, superior races have rights regarding inferior races. . . . [Murmurs from several benches on the far left.]

Mr. Jules Maigne: Oh—you dare to say that in the country in which the rights of man have been proclaimed!

Mr. de Guilloutet: This is the justification of slavery and the black slave trade!

Mr. Jules Ferry: If the honorable Mr. Maigne is correct, if the declaration of the rights of man has been written for the blacks of equatorial Africa, then by what right do you impose trade on them? They did not call on you! [Interruptions from the extreme left and the right. "Hear, hear!" from several benches on the left.]

Mr. Raoul Duval: We do not want to impose [trade] on them! It is you who imposes [it] on them!

Mr. Jules Maigne: To propose and to impose are vastly different things!

Mr. Georges Périn: You cannot, however, force trade!

Mr. Jules Ferry: I repeat that superior races have a right, because they have a duty. They have a duty to civilize inferior races. . . . [Approval again from the benches on the left—new interruptions from the extreme left and the right.] . . .

Mr. Jules Ferry: Gentlemen, there are considerations that deserve patriots' full attention. The conditions of maritime warfare are profoundly changed. ["Hear, hear!"]

Currently, as you know, a warship cannot carry, however perfectly it is organized, more than fourteen days' worth of coal, and a ship that is out of coal is flotsam on the surface of the sea, abandoned to whoever comes along. Thence [comes] the need to have at sea supply bays, shelters, ports for defense and provisioning. [Applause from the center and the left. Various interruptions.] And that is why we need Tunisia; that is why we need Saigon and Cochinchina; this is why we need Madagascar, and why we're at Diego Suarez and Vohemar, and we'll never leave them! . . . [Applause from many benches.] Gentlemen, in Europe at the moment, in this competition of so many rivals that we see growing around us, some by military or maritime improvements, others by the prodigious development of an incessantly growing population; in a Europe, or rather in a universe, of this sort, the policy of quiet contemplation or abstention is simply a highway to decadence! Nations, in our time, are great only by virtue of the activity they develop; it is not "through the peaceful influence of institutions" [Interruptions from the extreme left and the right] that they are great in this day and age. . . .

France needs something else: to be not just a free country, but also a great country, exercising over Europe's destinies all the influence that that is properly hers; she must spread this influence across the world, and carry wherever she can her language, her customs, her flag, her arms, her genius. [Applause from the center and from the left.]

John Paton on the New Hebrides Mission, UK, 1883

Sir,

For the following reasons we think the British Government ought now to take possession of the New Hebrides group of the South Sea Islands, of the Solomon group, and of all the intervening chain of islands from Fiji to New Guinea.

1. Because she has already taken possession of Fiji in the east, and we hope it will soon be known authoritatively that she has taken possession of New Guinea at the north-west, adjoining her Australian possessions, and the islands between complete this chain of islands lying along the Australian coast. . . .

2. The sympathy of the New Hebrides natives are all with Great Britain, hence they long for British protection, while they fear and hate the French, who appear eager to annex the group, because they have seen the way the French have treated the native races in New Caledonia, the Loyalty Islands, and other South Sea islands.

3. Till within the past few months almost all the Europeans on the New Hebrides were British subjects, who long for British protection.

4. All the men and all the money (over 140,000*l.*) used in civilising and Christianising the New Hebrides, have been British. Now 14 missionaries and the Dayspring mission ship, and about 150 native evangelists and teachers are employed in the above work on this group, in which over 6000*l.* yearly of British and British-Colonial money is expended; and certainly it would be unwise to let any other power now take possession and reap the fruits of all this British outlay.

5. Because the New Hebrides are already a British dependency in this sense—all its imports are from Sydney and Melbourne and British Colonies, and all its exports are also to British Colonies.

6. The islands on this group are generally very rich in soil and in tropical products so that if a possession of Great Britain, and the labour traffic stopped, so as to retain what remains of the native populations on them, they would soon, and for ages to come, become rich sources of tropical wealth to these Colonies, as sugar-cane is extensively cultivated on them by every native of the group, even in his heathen state. . . . The islands also grow maize, cotton, coffee, arrowroot, and spices, &c., and all tropical products could be largely produced on them.

7. Because if any other nation takes possession of them, their excellent and spacious harbours, as on Efate, so well supplied with the best fresh water, and their near

proximity to Great Britain's Australasian Colonies, would in time of war make them dangerous to British interests and commerce in the South Seas and her Colonies.

8. The 13 islands of this group on which life and property are now comparatively safe, the 8,000 professed Christians on the group, and all the churches formed among them, are by God's blessing the fruits of the labours of British missionaries, who, at great toil, expense, and loss of life, have translated, got printed, and taught the natives to read the Bible in part or in whole in nine different languages of this group, while 70,000 at least are longing and ready for the gospel. On this group 21 members of the mission families died or were murdered by the savages in beginning God's work among them, not including good Bishop Paterson, of the Melanesian Mission, and we fear all this good work would be lost if the New Hebrides fall into other than British hands.

9. Because we see no other way of suppressing the labour traffic in Polynesia, with all its many evils, as it rapidly depopulates the islands, being attended by much bloodshed, misery, and loss of life. It is an unmitigated evil to the natives, and ruinous to all engaged in it, and to the work of civilising and Christianising the islanders, while all experience proves that all labour laws and regulations, with Government agents and gunboats, cannot prevent such evils, which have always been the sad accompaniments of all such traffic in men and women in every land, and because this traffic and its evils are a sad stain on our British glory and Australasian honour, seeing Britain has done so much to free the slave and suppress slavery in other lands.

For the above reasons, and others that might be given, we sincerely hope and pray that you will do all possible to get Victoria and the other Colonial Governments to help and unite in urging Great Britain at once to take possession of the New Hebrides group. Whether looked at in the interests of humanity, or of Christianity, or commercially, or politically, surely it is most desirable that they should at once be British possessions; hence we plead for your judicious and able help, and remain, your humble servant,

John G. Paton,
Senior Missionary,
New Hebrides Mission.

Image of certificate for the American Board of Commissioners for Foreign Missions, Missionary House, Boston, Mass., 1857

SEE COLOR INSERT

Kaiser Wilhelm II's speech to the North German Regatta Association, Germany, 1901

In spite of the fact that we have no such fleet as we should have, we have conquered for ourselves a place in the sun. It will now be my task to see to it that this place in the sun shall remain our undisputed possession, in order that the sun's rays may fall fruitfully upon our activity and trade in foreign parts, that our industry and agriculture may develop within the state and our sailing sports upon the water, for our future lies upon the water. The more Germans go out upon the waters, whether it be in races of regattas, whether it be in journeys across the ocean, or in the service of the battle-flag, so much the better will it be for us. For when the German has once learned to direct his glance upon what is distant and great, the pettiness which surrounds him in daily life on all sides will disappear. Whoever wishes to have this larger and freer outlook can find no better place than one of the Hanseatic cities . . . we are now making our efforts to do what, in the old time, the Hanseatic cities could not accomplish, because they lacked the vivifying and protecting power of the empire. May it be the function of my Hansa during many years of peace to protect and advance commerce and trade!

. . . I see the indication that European peace is assured for many years to come; for the achievements of the particular contingents have brought about a mutual respect and feeling of comradeship that can only serve the furtherance of peace. But in this period of peace I hope that our Hanseatic cities will flourish. Our new Hansa will open new paths and create and conquer new markets for them.

As head of the empire I therefore rejoice over every citizen, whether from Hamburg, Bremen, or Lübeck, who goes forth with this large outlook and seeks new points where we can drive in the nail on which to hang our armor . . . in order to make for us friendly conquests whose fruits will be gathered by our descendants.

Okuma Shigenobu, excerpts from *Fifty Years of New Japan*, Japan, 1910

By comparing the Japan of fifty years ago with the Japan of to-day, it will be seen that she has gained considerably in the extent of her territory, as well as in her population, which now numbers nearly fifty millions. Her Government has become constitutional not only in name, but in fact, and her national education has attained to a high degree of excellence. In commerce and industry, the emblems of peace, she has also made rapid strides, until her import and export trades together amounted in 1907 to the enormous sum of 926,000,000 *yen*. . . . Her general progress, during the short space of half a century, has been so sudden and swift that it presents a spectacle rare in the history of the world. This leap forward is the result of the stimulus which the country received on coming into contact with the civilization of Europe and America, and may well, in its broad sense, be regarded as a boon conferred by foreign intercourse. Foreign intercourse it was that animated the national consciousness of our people, who under the feudal system lived localized and disunited, and foreign intercourse it is that has enabled Japan to stand up as a world-Power. We possess to-day a powerful army and navy, but it was after Western models that we laid their foundations by establishing a system of conscription, in pursuance of the principle "all our sons are soldiers," by promoting military education, and by encouraging the manufacture of arms and the art of shipbuilding. We have reorganized the systems of central and local administration, and effected reforms in the educational system of the empire. All this is nothing but the result of adopting the superior features of Western institutions. That Japan has been enabled to do so is a boon conferred on her by foreign intercourse, and it may be said that the nation has succeeded in this grand metamorphosis through the promptings and the influence of foreign civilization. . . .

In the foregoing pages frequent references have been made to the susceptibility of the Japanese to the influences of foreign civilization. If Japan has been endowed from the earliest days with this peculiarly sensitive faculty, she is gifted also with a strong retentive power which enables her to preserve and retain all that is good in and about herself. For twenty centuries the nation has drunk freely of the civilizations of Korea, China, and India, being always open to the different influences impressed on her in succession. Yet we remain to-day politically unaltered under one Imperial House and Sovereign, that has descended in an unbroken line for a length of time absolutely unexampled in the world. This fact furnishes at least an incontestable proof that the Japanese are not a race of people who, inconstant and capricious, are given to loving all that is new and curious, always running after passing fashions. They have welcomed Occidental civilization while preserving their old Oriental civilization. They have attached great importance to *Bushidō*, and at the same time held in the highest respect the spirit of charity and humanity. They have ever made a point of choosing the middle course in everything, and have aimed at being always well-balanced. . . . We are conservative simultaneously with being progressive; we are aristocratic and at the same time democratic; we are individualistic while being also socialistic. In these respects we may be said to somewhat resemble the Anglo-Saxon race. . . .

. . . [T]he Japanese should grow in the belief that on them alone devolves the mission of harmonizing the civilizations of the East and West, so as to lead the world as a whole to a higher plane. Should our people, fully appreciating this their heaven-ordained office, resolve to accomplish the mission, the effect will be far—if not world—reaching . . . I do not believe there is a nation on the face of the earth better fitted than the Japanese to achieve this grand mission, for we are a nation which represents the civilization of the Orient and has assimilated the civilization of the Occident.

360 DISCUSSION QUESTIONS

1   In what ways were politics and nationalism related to empire?

2   In what ways were religion and culture related to empire?

3   Imperialism often seems the business of states and corporations. In what ways do these sources demonstrate the reach of empire and imperialism to "ordinary people"?

TO THE WEST

6-1a | Harriet Martineau, on land lust in America, UK, 1837

Harriet Martineau (1802–1876) is often cited as the first female sociologist. This British social theorist and reformer wrote many books and essays that drew on her diverse research interests, including classical economics, evolution of religion, and English history. After an extended visit to the United States (1834–1836), she wrote two sociological studies, *Society in America* (1837) and *How to Observe Morals and Manners* (1838). Here, in an excerpt from the first title, Martineau shared her observations on the meaning of land to Americans in an age rife with forces pushing expansionism.

The pride and delight of Americans is in their quantity of land. I do not remember meeting with one to whom it had occurred that they had too much. Among the many complaints of the minority, this was never one. I saw a gentleman strike his fist on the table in an agony at the country being so "confoundedly prosperous": I heard lamentations over the spirit of speculation; the migration of young men to the back country; the fluctuating state of society from the incessant movement westwards; the immigration of labourers from Europe; and the ignorance of the sparse population. All these grievances I heard perpetually complained of; but in the same breath I was told in triumph of the rapid sales of land; of the glorious additions which had been made by the acquisition of Louisiana and Florida, and of the probable gain of Texas. Land was spoken of as the unfailing resource against over manufacture; the great wealth of the nation; the grand security of every man in it. . . .

The possession of land is the aim of all action, generally speaking, and the cure for all social evils, among men in the United States. If a man is disappointed in politics or love, he goes and buys land. If he disgraces himself, he betakes himself to a lot in the west. If the demand for any article of manufacture slackens, the operatives drop into the unsettled lands. If a citizen's neighbours rise above him in the towns, he betakes himself where he can be monarch of all he surveys. An artisan works, that he may die on land of his own. He is frugal, that he may enable his son to be a landowner. Farmers' daughters go into factories that they may clear off the mortgage from their fathers' farms; that they may be independent landowners again. All this is natural enough in a country colonised from an old one, where land is so restricted in quantity as to be apparently the same thing as wealth. It is natural enough in a young republic, where independence is of the highest political value.

6–1b | Kiowa, ledger art, perhaps depicting Buffalo Wallow Battle of the Red River Wars in 1874

Composed on paper or cloth, ledger art was a form of Plains Indian narrative drawing, popular from the 1860s to 1920s. New materials, such as accounting ledger books and modern drawing instruments, became available to tribal groups in the nineteenth century, often because groups were forced onto reservations. These new tools allowed for added detail and experimentation in a pictorial form that drew on a Plains Indian tradition of hide painting. Below is Kiowa ledger art from the Red River War (1874–1875) that possibly depicts the Buffalo Wallow Fight of 1874, a battle between southern Plains Indians and the U.S. Army in the Texas panhandle. The image depicts soldiers barricaded in a hole or depression with Indian warriors surrounding.

SEE COLOR INSERT

DISCUSSION QUESTIONS

1   In what ways did Martineau describe the desire for land to be a particularly American phenomenon?

2   How were the quest for land in the West and the conflicts between white Americans and Indian tribal groups connected?

3   What do you notice about the depiction of the battle in the Kiowa ledger art?

6–2 | Description of San Francisco as a Gold Rush city, *New York Herald*, 1849

San Francisco, founded as a Spanish mission and pueblo, came under new rule with the end of the successful Mexican War for Independence in 1821. Control of the small settlement changed again with U.S. control established in 1846. Although there had been knowledge of gold deposits in the northern California region for years, James W. Marshall's discovery in Sutter Creek near Coloma, California, in January 1848 set off a frenzy. San Francisco became the primary port for the Gold Rush booming from a small settlement of about 200 in 1846 to 25,000 in 1849. The activity also placed the territory on the fast track to statehood, which occurred in September 1850. The description below, written by a emigrant to California, captured the cosmopolitan character of the age.

A "bee hive" is the best comparison for the town of "San Francisco." To define who is "king bee" would puzzle a smarter fellow than ever emanated from the "Philadelphia bar." . . . What is strange medley is the composition of the population located here—by far the largest portion are the citizens of the "old States," but every part of Europe is represented, as well as Africa and Asia—all classes and conditions. I meet every day men who, at home, were esteemed wealthy, and many that I know have been—those who have led the fashions, gave morning concerts at gilded salons, and first Dilettanti at the opera, active merchants, etc.—now bustling about in all eagerness of trade, leaving behind them the enjoyments of the social circle, family, friends and comfortable quarters to carry on business in a shanty or canvas house, enduring all sorts of privations, and in many instances, forced to do their own "pulling and hauling"; then there are hosts in speculators in real estate, brokers in gold dust, "black legs," [swindlers] and broken down gentlemen—all bent upon one sole subject—"gold." "But where the honey is there you will find the bees."—and, by the way, judging from the number of gambling establishments about town, and the high rates they pay for room hire, they are the ones who will pocket all the loose gold.

DISCUSSION QUESTIONS

1   How did the author describe the population of San Francisco in the mid-nineteenth century?

2   Based on this description, how might San Francisco have differed from other U.S. cities in the nineteenth century? How might it have been the same?

3   What sort of challenges would such rapid growth present to a new state?

6–3a | Samuel Bowles, description of the West's changing landscape, 1869

Samuel Bowles (1826–1878), longtime publisher and editor of the *Springfield Republican*, journeyed west from Massachusetts in 1865, 1868, and 1869, making extensive observations of the areas he visited. He published his encyclopedic observations of the features of life in the American West in his *Our New West* (1869). Below, he describes the emerging industrial landscape he witnessed.

So completely is the Pacific Railroad henceforth the key to all our New West; so thoroughly must all knowledge of the characteristics of the latter radiate out of the former as a central line, that its story should be told almost at the outset, even to the anticipation of earlier experiences. Marked, indeed, was the contrast between the stage ride of 1865 and the Railroad ride of 1868 across the Plains. The then long-drawn, tedious endurance of six days and nights, running the gauntlet of hostile Indians, was now accomplished in a single twenty-four hours, safe in a swiftly-moving train, and in a car that was an elegant drawing-room by day and a luxurious bedroom at night.

The long lines of travel in our wide and fresh West have given birth to more luxurious accommodations for passengers than exist in Europe or the Atlantic States. With the organization of travel over the Pacific Railroad come cars that will carry their occupants through from New York to San Francisco, without stop or change, and with excellent bed and board within them. Only America could have demanded, conceived and organized for popular use such accommodations as the Pullman Palace and Sleeping Cars of the West. To some, as to ours, are added the special luxury of a house organ; and the passengers while away the tedious hours of long rides over unvarying prairies with music and song.

Omaha, in 1865, a feeble rival of Atchison, Leavenworth, and Nebraska City in outfitting emigrant and merchandise wagons for Colorado and Utah, and without a single mile of railroad within one hundred miles, has already become the greatest railroad center of the Missouri and Mississippi Valleys. It is the starting point of the Pacific Railroad, which stretches a completed line of eighteen hundred miles west to the Pacific Ocean; to the east are two or three completed lines of five hundred miles across Iowa and Illinois to Chicago, and others are in progress; to the south are open roads to St. Louis across the Missouri; and to the north is a finished road to Sioux City, and fast stretching on to St. Paul. The three great states of the Mississippi Valley, Illinois, Iowa and Missouri, the garden and granary of the nation, and the seat of its middle empire, are slashed in all directions by railroad lines, completed or rapidly constructing, meeting as a western focus at Omaha and Council Bluffs, sister towns on either bank of the Missouri, and converging on the east into either Chicago or St. Louis. Their consequent development, in population and wealth, is perhaps the most wonderful illustration of modern American growth. It is within this area that New England is pouring the best of her emigration, and reproducing herself, in energy and industry and intelligence, on a broader, more generous and more national basis.

Out now upon the continental Railroad. For five hundred miles, a straight, level line, across the broad Plains, along the valley of the Platte. It was but a play to build a railroad here. Yet there is a steady ascent of ten feet to the mile; and for the first two hundred miles the country has the exquisite roll and the active fertility of the Iowa and Illinois prairies. Through this region the growth of Nebraska shares that of those two states; and she has the advantage of them, generally, in climate, in water, and in wood. But beyond this limit,—out upon the real Plains,—the first results of the Railroad are to kill what settlement and cultivation they had reached under the patronage of slow-moving emigration, stage-travel, and prairie-schooner freightage. The ranches which these supported are now deserted; the rails carry everybody and everything; the old roads are substantially abandoned; the old settlers, losing all their improvements and opportunities, gather in at the railway stations, or move backwards or forwards to greater local developments. They are the victims, in turn, of a higher civilization; they drove out the Indian, the wolf, and the buffalo; the locomotive whistles their occupation away; and invites back for the time the original occupants.

The day's ride grows monotonous. The road is as straight as an arrow. Every dozen or fifteen miles is a station,—two or three sheds, a water-spout and wood pile; every one hundred miles or so a home or division depot, with shops, eating-house, "saloons" uncounted, a store or two, a few cultivated acres, and the invariable half-a-dozen seedy, staring loafers, that are a sort of fungi indigenous to American railways. We yawn over the unchanging landscape and the unvarying model of the stations, and lounge and read by day, and go to bed early at night. But the clear, dry air charms; the half dozen soldiers hurriedly marshalled into line at each station, as the train comes up, suggest that the Indian question is not disposed of yet; we catch a glimpse of antelopes in the distance; and we watch the holes of the prairie dogs for their piquant little owners and their traditional companions of owls and snakes,—but never see the snakes.

6–3b | Advertisement, "The Great American Panorama," 1900

The coming of the transcontinental railway dramatically changed the economic, political, social, and cultural landscape of the United States. Since the opening of first section of the Baltimore and Ohio Railroad (or B&O) on the East Coast in 1830, the network had slowly grown as a loosely organized network. The second half of the nineteenth century was the great age of railway building; miles of railroad track increased from 9,000 in 1850 to almost 130,000 in 1890. With revolutionized transport from coast to coast, people, goods, ideas, and information now moved quickly. Promotion went hand in hand with expansion. Here, the Pacific Railway entices travelers to "Go and See" what the West has to offer.

SNOW SHEDS ON THE CENTRAL PACIFIC RAILWAY, CALIFORNIA.

SEE COLOR INSERT

DISCUSSION QUESTIONS

1   How did Bowles describe the expansion of the railroad system in the United States?

2   Why might the artist's choice of spectators of the Pacific Railway in the panorama be significant?

3   Based on these sources, how would the expansion of railroads in industrialized countries affect development? What aspects were particularly true for the United States?

6-4 | Walt Whitman, excerpt from poem "Passage to India," 1870

Walt Whitman (1819–1892), essayist, journalist, and groundbreaking poet, published what many consider to be his last major poem, "Passage to India," in 1871. It extols three modern achievements: the transatlantic cable (1866), the Suez Canal (1869), and the Union and Central Pacific transcontinental railroad (1869). Although Whitman's poem celebrates these accomplishments and the imperialist impulse, the piece also speaks of the striving for the transcendental state, beyond notions of progress and materialism.

1

Singing my days,
Singing the great achievements of the present,
Singing the strong light works of engineers,
Our modern wonders, (the antique ponderous Seven outvied,)
In the Old World the east the Suez canal,
The New by its mighty railroad spann'd,
The seas inlaid with eloquent gentle wires;
Yet first to sound, and ever sound, the cry with thee O soul,
The Past! the Past! the Past!

The Past—the dark unfathom'd retrospect!
The teeming gulf—the sleepers and the shadows!
The past—the infinite greatness of the past!
For what is the present after all but a growth out of the past?
(As a projectile, form'd, impell'd, passing a certain line, still keeps on,
So the present, utterly form'd, impell'd by the past.)

. . .

3

Passage to India!
Lo soul for thee of tableaus twain,
I see in one the Suez canal initiated, open'd,
I see the procession of steamships, the Empress Eugenie's leading the van,
I mark, from on deck the strange landscape, the pure sky, the level sand in the distance,
I pass swiftly the picturesque groups, the workmen gather'd,
The gigantic dredging machines.

In one again, different, (yet thine, all thine, O soul, the same,)
I see over my own continent the Pacific Railroad, surmounting every barrier,
I see continual trains of cars winding along the Platte, carrying freight and passengers,
I hear the locomotives rushing and roaring, and the shrill steam-whistle,
I hear the echoes reverberate through the grandest scenery in the world,
I cross the Laramie plains, I note the rocks in grotesque shapes, the buttes,
I see the plentiful larkspur and wild onions, the barren, colorless, sage-deserts,
I see in glimpses afar or towering immediately above me the great mountains, I see the
Wind River and the Wahsatch mountains,
I see the Monument mountain and the Eagle's Nest, I pass the Promontory, I ascend the
Nevadas,
I scan the noble Elk mountain and wind around its base,
I see the Humboldt range, I thread the valley and cross the river,
I see the clear waters of Lake Tahoe, I see forests of majestic pines,
Or crossing the great desert, the alkaline plains, I behold enchanting mirages of waters
and meadows,
Marking through these and after all, in duplicate slender lines,
Bridging the three or four thousand miles of land travel,

Tying the Eastern to the Western sea,
The road between Europe and Asia.

(Ah Genoese thy dream! thy dream!
Centuries after thou art laid in thy grave,
The shore thou foundest verifies thy dream.)

4

Passage to India!
Struggles of many a captain, tales of many a sailor dead,
Over my mood stealing and spreading they come,
Like clouds and cloudlets in the unreach'd sky.

Along all history, down the slopes,
As a rivulet running, sinking now, and now again to the surface rising,
A ceaseless thought, a varied train—lo, soul, to thee, thy sight, they rise,
The plans, the voyages again, the expeditions;
Again Vasco de Gama sails forth,
Again the knowledge gain'd, the mariner's compass,
Lands found and nations born, thou born America,
For purpose vast, man's long probation fill'd,
Thou, rondure of the world at last accomplish'd.

DISCUSSION QUESTIONS

1   Why do you think Whitman saw these specific technological achievements as most notable?

2   Why do you think Whitman titled his poem "Passage to India"? What connections was he drawing to earlier historical events?

3   How did the idea of progress shape America in the nineteenth century?

6–5 | Posters, Nebraska Land Sale, written in Czech and Danish, 1879

The expansion of the railroad network, and the accompanying federal land grants to support their efforts, opened millions of acres of land for settlement across the U.S. West. The Chicago, Burlington and Quincy Railroad (CB&Q) aggressively promoted the sale of their large land holdings in Nebraska and Iowa in the 1870s though hundreds of thousands of advertising pamphlets printed in English, German, French, Welsh, Norwegian, Swedish, Czech (first image below), and Danish (second image below) and distributed throughout North America and Europe. Land offices were also opened in England, Scotland, Germany, and Sweden.

Czech Poster Translation

The poster reads "One million acres/B. & M. Railway/Plots/in Iowa and Nebraska/For Sale/For reasonable prices and with easy terms/The best plots in the West for farmers and stockbreeders. Longest terms, lowest interest, most liberal conditions, what, when, from whom—Kolín SPD/Read the contents."

Danish Poster Translation

The poster reads "One million acres/Nebraska land/By B. &. M. Railroad/For Sale/ Low prices and good conditions/It is the best land in the West for grain cultivation and animal grazing./The longest pay period, the lowest rents, and the best conditions that are offered by any company./See on next page."

DISCUSSION QUESTIONS

1   Why would the railroad company target these particular audiences?

2   What significant trends in U.S. history can be connected to the extensive availability of inexpensive land in the West?

THE UNITED STATES IN THE AGE OF IMPERIALISM

6–6a | Millard Fillmore, letter to the emperor of Japan presented by Commodore Perry, 1853

Millard Filmore (1800–1874) was an active U.S. President in foreign affairs, particularly in Asia and the Pacific. There were varied reasons to press to "open up" Japan to a formal relationship. In 1850, planning began for the expedition, which did not leave until November 1852. Commodore Matthew C. Perry led the expedition, choosing the black-hulled paddle-wheeled *Mississippi* as his flagship. The venture made several port-of-calls on their long journey, not reaching Japan until July 1853, months after Fillmore left office.

MILLARD FILLMORE,
President of the United States of America
to his Imperial Majesty,

THE EMPEROR OF JAPAN

Great and Good Friend: I send you this public letter by Commodore Matthew C. Perry, an officer of the highest rank in the navy of the United States, and commander of the squadron now visiting your imperial majesty's dominions.

I have directed Commodore Perry to assure your imperial majesty that I entertain the kindest feelings toward your majesty's person and government, and that I have no other object in sending him to Japan but to propose to your imperial majesty that the United States and Japan should live in friendship and have commercial intercourse with each other.

The Constitution and laws of the United States forbid all interference with the religious or political concerns of other nations. I have particularly charged Commodore Perry to abstain from every act which could possibly disturb the tranquility of your imperial majesty's dominions.

The United States of America reach from ocean to ocean, and our Territory of Oregon and State of California lie directly opposite to the dominions of your imperial majesty. Our steamships can go from California to Japan in eighteen days.

Our great State of California produces about sixty millions of dollars in gold every year, besides silver, quicksilver, precious stones, and many other valuable articles. Japan is also a rich and fertile country, and produces many very valuable articles. Your imperial majesty's subjects are skilled in many of the arts. I am desirous that our two countries should trade with each other, for the benefit both of Japan and the United States.

We know that the ancient laws of your imperial majesty's government do not allow of foreign trade, except with the Chinese and the Dutch; but as the state of the world changes and new governments are formed, it seems to be wise, from time to time, to make new laws. There was a time when the ancient laws of your imperial majesty's government were first made.

About the same time America, which is sometimes called the New World, was first discovered and settled by the Europeans. For a long time there were but a few people, and they were poor. They have now become quite numerous; their commerce is very extensive; and they think that if your imperial majesty were so far to change the ancient laws as to allow a free trade between the two countries it would be extremely beneficial to both.

If your imperial majesty is not satisfied that it would be safe altogether to abrogate the ancient laws which forbid foreign trade, they might be suspended for five or ten years, so as to try the experiment. If it does not prove as beneficial as was hoped, the ancient laws can be restored. The United States often limit their treaties with foreign States to a few years, and then renew them or not, as they please.

I have directed Commodore Perry to mention another thing to your imperial majesty. Many of our ships pass every year from California to China; and great numbers of our people pursue the whale fishery near the shores of Japan. It sometimes happens, in stormy weather, that one of our ships is wrecked on your imperial majesty's shores. In all such cases we ask, and expect, that our unfortunate people should be treated with kindness, and that their property should be protected, till we can send a vessel and bring them away. We are very much in earnest in this.

Commodore Perry is also directed by me to represent to your imperial majesty that we understand there is a great abundance of coal and provisions in the Empire of Japan. Our steamships, in crossing the great ocean, burn a great deal of coal, and it is not convenient to bring it all the way from America. We wish that our steamships and other vessels should be allowed to stop in Japan and supply themselves with coal, provisions, and water. They will pay for them in money, or anything else your imperial majesty's subjects may prefer; and we request your imperial majesty to appoint a convenient port, in the southern part of the Empire, where our vessels may stop for this purpose. We are very desirous of this.

These are the only objects for which I have sent Commodore Perry, with a powerful squadron, to pay a visit to your imperial majesty's renowned city of Yedo: friendship, commerce, a supply of coal and provisions, and protection for our shipwrecked people.

We have directed Commodore Perry to beg your imperial majesty's acceptance of a few presents. They are of no great value in themselves; but some of them may serve as specimens of the articles manufactured in the United States, and they are intended as tokens of our sincere and respectful friendship.

May the Almighty have your imperial majesty in His great and holy keeping!

In witness whereof, I have caused the great seal of the United States to be hereunto affixed, and have subscribed the same with my name, at the city of Washington, in America, the seat of my government, on the thirteenth day of the month of November, in the year one thousand eight hundred and fifty-two.

Your good friend,
MILLARD FILLMORE, President

6–6b | Depictions of Perry's black ships entering Japan, 1853–1854

As Commodore Perry's ships arrived in Edo (Tokyo), they met one of the largest urban centers in the world, with a population of approximately one million. Initial negotiations, however, took place in smaller seaside enclaves. These were not the first Americans to arrive, but their well-armed, steam-driven warships convinced the Japanese to receive them for discussions. Perry's initial visit in 1853 was brief; he presented Fillmore's letter and announced he would return, with a larger contingent, to receive the Japanese response. In March 1854, he arrived with nine vessels, over one hundred mounted guns, and a crew of approximately 1,800. Greater interaction accompanied this second trip, which culminated in the Treaty of Kanagawa, which opened two Japanese ports for provision and refuge and laid the groundwork for future diplomatic exchanges. Below are two dramatically different representations of Perry's black ships from the period, one, U.S. in origin and, the other, from Japan.

SEE COLOR INSERT

U.S. JAPAN FLEET, C— PERRY carrying the "GOSPEL o GOD" to the HEATHEN, 1853.

SEE COLOR INSERT

DISCUSSION QUESTIONS

1   What was the main request President Fillmore made of the Japanese emperor, and what was the tone of his request?

2   Contrast Japanese and U.S. perceptions of Perry's fleet in Japan. Give evidence from each image to support your answer.

3   What might be the international implications of the U.S.-Japanese interaction?

6–7a | C. G. Bush, political cartoon, "Spain's Sense of Justice," 1898

For decades, Cuban rebels had waged an irregular resistance to Spanish rule of the island colony. By 1895, this conflict had expanded into a war for Cuban independence. American public opinion favored the Cubans in the fight. As the situation deteriorated, the U.S. interceded to initially try to negotiate a settlement, but when new riots broke out in January 1898, President William McKinley sent the battleship USS *Maine* to the region. Just a month later it exploded in Havana Harbor. On March 20, an American court of inquiry concluded an underwater mine was the culprit, and Spain was blamed. Published the same day that President William McKinley issued an ultimatum to Spain demanding Cuban independence (March 29, 1898), "Spain's Sense of Justice" by Charles G. Bush expressed outrage at the European power's treatment of the insurgent territory, depicting the U.S. as redeemer. On April 20, Congress declared war on Spain.

6–7b | M. Moliné, political cartoon, "La Fatlera del Oncle Sam," Spain, 1896

Although Spanish contact with the island dated back to 1492, the first permanent Spanish settlement in Cuba was Baracoa (1511). Cuba served as a central feature of New Spain, first, as a launching point for exploration of the continent, and, later, for its production of sugarcane. Cuban sugar, planted and cultivated by enslaved labor, developed a global market. The decline of the Spanish Empire in the nineteenth century fueled the push for independence in Cuba. As can be seen from the Catalan cartoon below, however, some of those in Spain blamed the U.S., who had long had economic relations with the island. The image is titled "Uncle Sam's craving," with the lower reading "Saving the island so it won't get lost."

LA FATLERA DEL ONCLE SAM (per M. MOLINÉ).

Guardarse l' isla perque no 's perdi.

DISCUSSION QUESTIONS

1   How are the main figures portrayed in the first cartoon?

2   How are the main figures portrayed in the second cartoon?

3   What motivations might the two countries have had for portraying the situation in this manner? What emotions or sympathies might each have been trying to evoke?

6–8a | Rudyard Kipling, poem, excerpts from "The White Man's Burden," UK, 1899

Written in response to the Spanish-American War (1898), the subtitle of English writer Rudyard Kipling's poem is "The United States and The Philippine Islands." In verse, Kipling encourages the United States to take up the mantle of empire, as Britain and other European nations before them. The poem coincided with the beginning of the Philippine-American War and the U.S. Senate ratification of the treaty that placed Puerto Rico, Guam, Cuba, and the Philippines under American control. The racialized "white man's burden" became synonymous with imperialism, hailed by groups that sponsored it and criticized by anti-imperialists.

Take up the White Man's burden—
Send forth the best ye breed—
Go, bind your sons to exile
To serve your captives' need;
To wait, in heavy harness,
On fluttered folk and wild—
Your new-caught, sullen peoples,
Half devil and half child.

Take up the White Man's burden—
In patience to abide,
To veil the threat of terror
And check the show of pride;
By open speech and simple,
An hundred times made plain
To seek another's profit,
And work another's gain.

Take up the White Man's burden—
The savage wars of peace—
Fill full the mouth of Famine,
And bid the sickness cease;
And when your goal is nearest
(The end for others sought)
Watch sloth and heathen folly
Bring all your hopes to nought.

Take up the White Man's burden—
No iron rule of kings,
But toil of serf and sweeper—
The tale of common things.
The ports ye shall not enter,
The roads ye shall not tread,
Go, make them with your living
And mark them with your dead.

Take up the White Man's burden,
And reap his old reward—
The blame of those ye better,
The hate of those ye guard—
The cry of hosts ye humour
(Ah, slowly!) toward the light:—
"Why brought ye us from bondage,
Our loved Egyptian night?"

Take up the White Man's burden—
Ye dare not stoop to less—

Nor call too loud on Freedom
To cloke your weariness.
By all ye will or whisper,
By all ye leave or do,
The silent sullen peoples
Shall weigh your God and you.

Take up the White Man's burden!
Have done with childish days—
The lightly-proffered laurel,
The easy ungrudged praise:
Comes now, to search your manhood
Through all the thankless years,
Cold, edged with dear-bought wisdom,
The judgment of your peers.

6–8b | Victor Gillam, political cartoon, "The White Man's Burden," 1899

Victor Gillam (ca. 1858–1920) took Rudyard Kipling's poem and created a visual depiction of it in this 1899 cartoon from the popular U.S. satirical magazine *Judge*. Here, a bedraggled Uncle Sam follows John Bull (UK) in step, up the mountain of obstacles towards civilization, holding out "education" and "liberty." Reinforcing the heavily racialized stanzas of Kipling's verse are caricatures of the peoples in each nation's sphere of influence, including Great Britain bearing India and China ahead of the United States hauling Cuba, Hawaii, and Puerto Rico.

"THE WHITE MAN'S BURDEN."

SEE COLOR INSERT

6–8c | Udo Keppler, political cartoon, "A Trifle Embarrassed," 1898

Udo Keppler (1872–1956) composed this political cartoon as the Spanish-American War moved toward its resolution. Although the American war declaration in the conflict included the Teller Amendment, which prohibited annexation of Cuba, it was clear that the U.S. would have an expanded authority on the island after the conflict. In this image, Cuba, Puerto Rico, Hawaii, and the Philippines arrive as infants, welcomed by Lady Liberty, to join the U.S. Foundling Asylum. On the lawn, adolescent children in the asylum—California, Texas, New Mexico—play on the lawn. At the gate stands a bewildered Uncle Sam who states "Gosh! I wish they wouldn't come quite so many in a bunch; but, if I've got to take them, I guess I can do as well by them as I've done by the others!"

SEE COLOR INSERT

DISCUSSION QUESTIONS

1   In your own words, describe the "White Man's Burden" according to these sources.

2   What racial and ethnic devices are used by the artists to reinforce the idea of Anglo superiority?

3   How does the third image extend and expand the themes presented in "The White Man's Burden"?

6–9a | Henri Meyer, political cartoon, "En Chine: Le gâteau des Rois et . . . des Empereurs," France, 1898

Imperial powers turned their attention toward China in the wake of Japan's surprise victory in the First Sino-Japanese War (1894–1895), in order to safeguard economic interests by establishing spheres of influence in the Chinese Empire. Meyer (1841–1899), a prolific French cartoonist and illustrator, used symbols and stereotypes to depict both the competitors and the prize in this cartoon for the *Illustrated Supplement* to France's *Petit Journal*, a full-color weekly that had a circulation of over one million copies. The title, when translated, reads, "China: The Cake of Kings and Emperors," and the words on the pizza-like cake refer to locations in the Qing Empire claimed by imperial powers.

EN CHINE
Le gâteau des Rois et... des Empereurs

SEE COLOR INSERT

6–9b | J. S. Pughe, political cartoon, "Putting His Foot Down," 1899

U.S. Secretary of State John Hay issued the Open Door Note in the fall of 1899 to the imperial powers competing in China, proclaiming open and equal trade in China for all nations. U.S. business interests applauded the move, as did anti-imperialists, yet the policy lacked enforcement power and ended up benefitting imperialist powers rather than China. In this 1899 cartoon by John Samuel Pughe for *Puck*, the first color-illustrated humor magazine in the U.S., Uncle Sam appears to dictate terms of a "trade treaty"—the Open Door—to foreign powers.

SEE COLOR INSERT

DISCUSSION QUESTIONS

1   Which nations are depicted in the cartoons? What function does position play in each?

2   Contrast the actions of the imperialist powers with that of Uncle Sam in the *Puck* cartoon. Why wouldn't Uncle Sam be included in the first cartoon, and what does that suggest about the second cartoon?

3   How might these developments in China influence views of Asia, Asian immigrants, and imperialism in the U.S.?

6–10a | Homer Davenport, political cartoon, "John Bull Presents the Western Hemisphere to Uncle Sam," 1902

This political cartoon appeared as the full-page frontispiece of the first issue of *The American Review of Reviews*, a progressive reform monthly journal, in January 1902. Drawn by Homer Davenport, the highest-paid cartoonist of his time, the illustration precedes a full-throated textual defense of the Monroe Doctrine (see chapter 3, item 6) buried among critiques of the Boer War, praise for recent technological progress, concerns about instability in South America, and a discussion of a proposed canal in Central America.

ACCEPTING THE MONROE DOCTRINE.

JOHN BULL GRATEFULLY ADMITS THAT UNCLE SAM IS THE PROPER CUSTODIAN OF THE WESTERN HEMISPHERE.

From a cartoon by Homer Davenport.

6–10b | Theodore Roosevelt, excerpt from speech announcing the Roosevelt Corollary to the Monroe Doctrine, 1904

President Theodore Roosevelt (1858–1919) announced what became known as the Roosevelt Corollary to the Monroe Doctrine in his 1904 State of the Union Address. While

Monroe intended to prevent European intervention in the western hemisphere, Roosevelt went a step further and pledged U.S. intervention—as a "last resort"—in troubled states of the western hemisphere. Roosevelt's words helped to justify and explain U.S. actions in the Venezuela Crisis (1902–1903), when his willingness to activate the U.S. Navy forced Britain and Germany into arbitration with Venezuela over unpaid debts, and gave teeth to the Monroe Doctrine. It also set up the U.S. as the self-proclaimed policeman of the western hemisphere, exacerbating an already-complicated relationship with nation-states in the Americas (see chapter 6, item 14).

In treating of our foreign policy and of the attitude that this great Nation should assume in the world at large, it is absolutely necessary to consider the Army and the Navy, and the Congress, through which the thought of the Nation finds its expression, should keep ever vividly in mind the fundamental fact that it is impossible to treat our foreign policy, whether this policy takes shape in the effort to secure justice for others or justice for ourselves, save as conditioned upon the attitude we are willing to take toward our Army, and especially toward our Navy. It is not merely unwise, it is contemptible, for a nation, as for an individual, to use high-sounding language to proclaim its purposes, or to take positions which are ridiculous if unsupported by potential force, and then to refuse to provide this force. If there is no intention of providing and keeping the force necessary to back up a strong attitude, then it is far better not to assume such an attitude.

The steady aim of this Nation, as of all enlightened nations, should be to strive to bring ever nearer the day when there shall prevail throughout the world the peace of justice. There are kinds of peace which are highly undesirable, which are in the long run as destructive as any war. Tyrants and oppressors have many times made a wilderness and called it peace. Many times peoples who were slothful or timid or shortsighted, who had been enervated by ease or by luxury, or misled by false teachings, have shrunk in unmanly fashion from doing duty that was stern and that needed self-sacrifice, and have sought to hide from their own minds their shortcomings, their ignoble motives, by calling them love of peace. The peace of tyrannous terror, the peace of craven weakness, the peace of injustice, all these should be shunned as we shun unrighteous war. The goal to set before us as a nation, the goal which should be set before all mankind, is the attainment of the peace of justice, of the peace which comes when each nation is not merely safe-guarded in its own rights, but scrupulously recognizes and performs its duty toward others. Generally peace tells for righteousness; but if there is conflict between the two, then our fealty is due first to the cause of righteousness. Unrighteous wars are common, and unrighteous peace is rare; but both should be shunned. The right of freedom and the responsibility for the exercise of that right can not be divorced. One of our great poets has well and finely said that freedom is not a gift that tarries long in the hands of cowards. Neither does it tarry long in the hands of those too slothful, too dishonest, or too unintelligent to exercise it. The eternal vigilance which is the price of liberty must be exercised, sometimes to guard against outside foes; although of course far more often to guard against our own selfish or thoughtless shortcomings.

If these self-evident truths are kept before us, and only if they are so kept before us, we shall have a clear idea of what our foreign policy in its larger aspects should be. It is our duty to remember that a nation has no more right to do injustice to another nation, strong or weak, than an individual has to do injustice to another individual; that the same moral law applies in one case as in the other. But we must also remember that it is as much the duty of the Nation to guard its own rights and its own interests as it is the duty of the individual so to do. Within the Nation the individual has now delegated this right to the State, that is, to the representative of all the individuals, and it is a maxim of the law that for every wrong there is a remedy. But in international law we have not advanced by any means as far as we have advanced in municipal law. There is as yet no judicial way of enforcing a right in international law. When one nation wrongs another or wrongs many others, there is no tribunal before which the wrongdoer can be brought. Either it is necessary supinely to acquiesce in the wrong, and thus put a premium upon brutality and aggression, or else it is necessary for the aggrieved nation valiantly to stand up for its rights. Until some method is devised by which there shall be a degree of international control over offending nations, it would be a wicked thing for the most civilized powers, for those with most sense of international obligations and with keenest and most generous appreciation of the difference between right and wrong, to disarm. If the great civilized nations of the present day should completely disarm, the result would mean an immediate recrudescence of barbarism in one form or another. Under any circumstances a sufficient armament would have to be kept up to serve the purposes of international police; and until international cohesion and the sense of international duties and rights are far more advanced than at present, a nation desirous both of securing respect for itself and of doing good to others must have a force adequate for the work which it feels is allotted to it as its part of the general world duty. Therefore it follows that a self-respecting, just, and far-seeing nation should on the one hand endeavor by every means to aid in the development of the various movements which tend to provide substitutes for war, which tend to render nations in their actions toward one another, and indeed toward their own peoples, more responsive to the general sentiment of humane and civilized mankind; and on the other hand that it should keep prepared, while scrupulously avoiding wrongdoing itself, to repel any wrong, and in exceptional cases to take action which in a more advanced stage of international relations would come under the head of the exercise of the international police. A great free people owes it to itself and to all mankind not to sink into helplessness before the powers of evil.

We are in every way endeavoring to help on, with cordial good will, every movement which will tend to bring us into more friendly relations with the rest of mankind. In pursuance of this policy I shall shortly lay before the Senate treaties of arbitration with all powers which are willing to enter into these treaties with us. It is not possible at this period of the world's development to agree to arbitrate all matters, but there are many matters of possible difference between us and other nations which can be thus arbitrated. Furthermore, at the request of the Interparliamentary Union, an eminent body composed of practical statesmen from all countries, I have asked the Powers to join with this Government in a second Hague conference, at which it is hoped that the work already so happily begun at The Hague may be carried some steps further toward completion. This carries out the desire expressed by the first Hague conference itself.

It is not true that the United States feels any land hunger or entertains any projects as regards the other nations of the Western Hemisphere save such as are for their welfare. All that this country desires is to see the neighboring countries stable, orderly, and prosperous. Any country whose people conduct themselves well can count upon our hearty friendship. If a nation shows that it knows how to act with reasonable efficiency and decency in social and political matters, if it keeps order and pays its obligations, it need fear no interference from the United States. Chronic wrongdoing, or an impotence which results in a general loosening of the ties of civilized society, may in America, as elsewhere, ultimately require intervention by some civilized nation, and in the Western Hemisphere the adherence of the United States to the Monroe Doctrine may force the United States, however reluctantly, in flagrant cases of such wrongdoing or impotence, to the exercise of an international police power. If every country washed by the Caribbean Sea would show the progress in stable and just civilization which with the aid of the Platt Amendment Cuba has shown since our troops left the island, and which so many of the republics in both Americas are constantly and brilliantly showing, all question of interference by this Nation with their affairs would be at an end. Our interests and those of our southern neighbors are in reality identical. They have great natural riches, and if within their borders the reign of law and justice obtains, prosperity is sure to come to them. While they thus obey the primary laws of civilized society they may rest assured that they will be treated by us in a spirit of cordial and helpful sympathy. We would interfere with them only in the last resort, and then only if it became evident that their inability or unwillingness to do justice at home and abroad had violated the rights of the United States or had invited foreign aggression to the detriment of the entire body of American nations. It is a mere truism to say that every nation, whether in America or anywhere else, which desires to maintain its freedom, its independence, must ultimately realize that the right of such independence can not be separated from the responsibility of making good use of it.

In asserting the Monroe Doctrine, in taking such steps as we have taken in regard to Cuba, Venezuela, and Panama, and in endeavoring to circumscribe the theater of war in the Far East, and to secure the open door in China, we have acted in our own interest as well as in the interest of humanity at large. There are, however, cases in which, while our own interests are not greatly involved, strong appeal is made to our sympathies. Ordinarily it is very much wiser and more useful for us to concern ourselves with striving for our own moral and material betterment here at home than to concern ourselves with trying to better the condition of things in other nations. We have plenty of sins of our own to war against, and under ordinary circumstances we can do more for the general uplifting of humanity by striving with heart and soul to put a stop to civic corruption, to brutal lawlessness and violent race prejudices here at home than by passing resolutions about wrongdoing elsewhere. Nevertheless there are occasional crimes committed on so vast a scale and of such peculiar horror as to make us doubt whether it is not our manifest duty to endeavor at least to show our disapproval of the deed and our sympathy with those who have suffered by it. The cases must be extreme in which such a course is justifiable. There must be no effort made to remove the mote from our brother's eye if we refuse to remove the beam from our own. But in extreme cases action may be justifiable and proper. What form the action shall take must depend upon the circumstances of the case; that is, upon the degree of the atrocity and upon our power to remedy it. The cases in which we could interfere by force of arms as we interfered to put a stop to intolerable conditions in Cuba are necessarily very few. Yet it is not to be expected that a people like ours, which in spite of certain very obvious shortcomings, nevertheless as a whole shows by its consistent practice its belief in the principles of civil and religious liberty and of orderly freedom, a people among whom even the worst crime, like the crime of lynching, is never more than sporadic, so that individuals and not classes are molested in their fundamental rights—it is inevitable that such a nation should desire eagerly to give expression to its horror on an occasion like that of the massacre of the Jews in Kishenef, or when it witnesses such systematic and long-extended cruelty and oppression as the cruelty and oppression of which the Armenians have been the victims, and which have won for them the indignant pity of the civilized world.

DISCUSSION QUESTIONS

1   How do you interpret the cartoon? In what ways does it reflect a U.S. perspective on late nineteenth-century events?

2   Explain Roosevelt's conditions for U.S. intervention in Latin American states. What might be problematic about his conditions?

3   How did shifting ideas about imperial power influence the United States' relationship with the world in the early twentieth century?

RESPONSES TO IMPERIALISM

6–11 | Anti-imperialist sentiments

As in every imperial power, the United States' imperial project was always contested—most obviously by those who experienced oppression abroad, but also domestically, by an array of Americans who refused to support imperialism for varying reasons. Below are two examples of such opposition.

The first, from an article written by Scots-American industrialist and millionaire philanthropist Andrew Carnegie (1835–1919), lists a number of arguments against the extension of U.S. power abroad. It appeared in the *North American Review*, the U.S.' oldest literary journal, just about the time the brief Spanish-American War was ending in August 1898.

The second piece is excerpted from a three-hour speech given in the U.S. Senate by Senator George Frisbie Hoar (R-Massachusetts), in which he railed against the United

States' war in the Philippines (1899–1902) and called for official recognition of Filipino independence. Hoar, who served as a member of Congress from 1869 until his death in 1904, stood against imperialism throughout his long career, denouncing the annexation of Hawai'i, the war in Cuba, and intervention in Panama.

6-11a | Andrew Carnegie, arguments against imperialism, 1898

Is the Republic, the apostle of Triumphant Democracy, of the rule of the people, to abandon her political creed and endeavor to establish in other lands the rule of the foreigner over the people, the Triumphant Despotism?

Is the Republic to remain one homogenous whole, one united people, or to become a scattered and disjointed aggregate of widely separated and alien races?

Is she to continue the task of developing her vast continent until it holds a population as great as that of Europe, all Americans, or to abandon that destiny to annex, and to attempt to govern, other far distant parts of the world as outlying possessions, which can never be integral parts of the Republic? . . .

Some of the organs of manufacturing interests, we observe, favor foreign possessions as necessary or helpful markets for our products. But the exports of the United States this year are greater than those of any other nation in the world. Even Britain's exports are less, yet Britain "possesses," it is said, a hundred "colonies" and "dependencies" scattered all over the world. . . .

If we could establish colonies of Americans, and grow Americans in any part of the world now unpopulated and unclaimed by any of the great powers, and thus follow the example of Britain, heart and mind might tell us that we should have to think twice, yea, thrice, before deciding adversely. . . . What we have to face is the question whether we should embark upon the difficult and dangerous policy of undertaking the government of alien races in lands where it is impossible for our own race to be produced. . . .

The Philippines have about seven and a half millions of people, composed of races bitterly hostile to one another, alien races, ignorant of our language and institutions. Americans cannot be grown there. . . . With what face shall we hang in the schoolhouses of the Philippines the Declaration of our own Independence, and yet deny independence to them? What response will the heart of the Philippine Islander make, as he reads of Lincoln's Emancipation Proclamation? Are we to practice independence and preach subordination, to teach rebellion in our books, yet to stamp it out with our swords, to sow the seed of revolt and expect the harvest of loyalty? . . .

To be more powerful at home is the surest way to be more powerful abroad. To-day the Republic stands the friend of all nations, the ally of none; she has no ambitious designs upon the territory of any power upon another continent; she crosses none of their ambitious designs, evokes no jealousy of the bitter sort, inspires no fears; she is not one of them, scrambling for "possessions;" she stands apart, pursuing her own great mission, and teaching all nations by example. Let her become a power annexing foreign territory, and all is changed in a moment.

6–11b | Excerpts from Senator George Frisbie Hoar, anti-imperialist speech, 1902

We have to deal with a territory ten thousand miles away, twelve hundred miles in extent, containing ten million people. A majority of the Senate think that people are under the American flag and lawfully subject to our authority. We are not at war with them or with anybody. The country is in a condition of profound peace as well as of unexampled prosperity. The world is in a profound peace, except in one quarter, in South Africa, where a handful of republicans are fighting for their independence, and have been doing better fighting than has been done on the face of the earth since Thermopylæ, or certainly since Bannockburn.

You are fighting for sovereignty. You are fighting for the principle of eternal dominion over that people, and that is the only question in issue in the conflict. We said in the case of Cuba that she had a right to be free and independent. We affirmed in the Teller resolution, I think without a negative voice, that we would not invade that right and would not meddle with her territory or anything that belonged to her. That declaration was a declaration of peace as well as of righteousness; and we made the treaty, so far as concerned Cuba, and conducted the war and have conducted ourselves ever since on that theory—that we had no right to interfere with her independence; that we had no right to her territory or to anything that was Cuba's. So we only demanded in the treaty that Spain should hereafter let her alone. If you had done to Cuba as you have done to the Philippine Islands, who had exactly the same right, you would be at this moment, in Cuba, just where Spain was when she excited the indignation of the civilized world and we compelled her to let go. And if you had done in the Philippines as you did in Cuba, you would be to-day or would soon be in those islands as you are in Cuba.

But you made a totally different declaration about the Philippine Islands. You undertook in the treaty to acquire sovereignty over her for yourself, which that people denied. You declared not only in the treaty, but in many public utterances in this Chamber and elsewhere, that you had a right to buy sovereignty with money, or to treat it as the spoils of war or the booty of battle. The moment you made that declaration the Filipino people gave you notice that they treated it as a declaration of war. So your generals reported, and so Aguinaldo expressly declared. In stating this account of profit and loss I hardly know which to take up first, principles and honor, or material interests—I should have known very well which to have taken up first down to three years ago—what you call the sentimental, the ideal, the historical on the right side of the column; the cost or the profit in honor or shame and in character and in principle and moral influence, in true national glory; or the practical side, the cost in money and gain, in life and health, in wasted labor, in diminished national strength, or in prospects of trade and money getting.

What has been the practical statesmanship which comes from your ideals and your sentimentalities. You have wasted nearly six hundred millions of treasure. You have sacrificed nearly ten thousand American lives—the flower of our youth. You have devastated provinces. You have slain uncounted thousands of the people you desire to benefit. You have established reconcentration camps. Your generals are coming home from their harvest bringing sheaves with them, in the shape of other thousands of sick and wounded and insane to drag out miserable lives, wrecked in body and mind. You make the American flag in the eyes of a numerous people the emblem of sacrilege in Christian churches, and of the burning of human dwellings, and of the horror of the water torture. Your practical statesmanship which disdains to take George Washington and Abraham Lincoln or the soldiers of the Revolution or of the Civil War as models, has looked in some cases to Spain for your example. I believe—nay, I know—that in general our officers and soldiers are humane. But in some cases they have carried on your warfare with a mixture of American ingenuity and Castilian cruelty.

Your practical statesmanship has succeeded in converting a people who three years ago were ready to kiss the hem of the garment of the American and to welcome him as a liberator, who thronged after your men when they landed on those islands with benediction and gratitude, into sullen and irreconcilable enemies, possessed of a hatred which centuries can not eradicate.

The practical statesmanship of the Declaration of Independence and the Golden Rule would have cost nothing but a few kind words. They would have bought for you the great title of liberator and benefactor, which your fathers won for your country in the South American Republics and in Japan, and which you have won in Cuba. They would have bought for you undying gratitude of a great and free people and the undying glory which belongs to the name of liberator. That people would have felt for you as Japan felt for you when she declared last summer that she owed everything to the United States of America.

What have your ideals cost you, and what have they bought for you?

1. For the Philippine Islands you have had to repeal the Declaration of Independence. For Cuba you had to reaffirm it and give it new luster.

2. For the Philippine Islands you have had to convert the Monroe Doctrine into a doctrine of mere selfishness. For Cuba you have acted on it and vindicated it.

3. In Cuba you have got the eternal gratitude of a free people. In the Philippine Islands you have got the hatred and sullen submission of a subjugated people.

4. From Cuba you have brought home nothing but glory. From the Philippines you have brought home nothing of glory.

5. In Cuba no man thinks of counting the cost. The few soldiers who came home from Cuba wounded or sick carry about their wounds and their pale faces as if they were medals of honor. What soldier glories in a wound or an empty sleeve which he got in the Philippines?

6. The conflict in the Philippines has cost you six hundred million dollars, thousands of American soldiers—the flower of your youth—the health and sanity of thousands more, and hundreds of thousands of Filipinos slain.

Another price we have paid as the result of your practical statesmanship. We have sold out the right, the old American right, to speak out the sympathy which is in our hearts for people who are desolate and oppressed everywhere on the face of the earth.

This war, if you call it war, has gone on for three years. It will go on in some form for three hundred years, unless this policy be abandoned. You will undoubtedly have times of peace and quiet, or pretended submission. You will buy men with titles, or office, or salaries. You will intimidate cowards. You will get pretended and fawning submission. The land will smile and seem at peace. But the volcano will be there. The lava will break out again. You can never settle this thing until you settle it right.

Gentlemen tell us that the Filipinos are savages, that they have inflicted torture, that they have dishonored our dead and outraged the living. That very likely may be true. Spain said the same thing of the Cubans. We have made the same charges against our own countrymen in the disturbed days after the war. The reports of committees and the evidence in the documents in our library are full of them. But who ever heard before of an American gentleman, or an American, who took as a rule for his own conduct the conduct of his antagonist, or who claimed that the Republic should act as savages because she had savages to deal with? I had supposed, Mr. President, that the question, whether a gentleman shall lie or murder or torture, depended on his sense of his own character, and not on his opinion of his victim. Of all the miserable sophistical shifts which have attended this wretched business from the beginning, there is none more miserable than this.

Mr. President, this is the eternal law of human nature. You may struggle against it, you may try to escape it, you may persuade yourself that your intentions are be-nevolent, that your yoke will be easy and your burden will be light, but it will assert itself again. Government without the consent of the government—an authority which heaven never gave—can only be supported by means which heaven never can sanction.

The American people have got this one question to answer. They may answer it now; they can take ten years, or twenty years, or a generation, or a century to think of it. But it will not down. They must answer it in the end: Can you lawfully buy with money, or get by brute force of arms, the right to hold in subjugation an unwilling people, and to impose on them such constitution as you, and not they, think best for them.

We have answered this question a good many times in the past. The fathers an-swered it in 1776, and founded the Republic upon their answer, which has been the corner-stone. John Quincy Adams and James Monroe answered it again in the Monroe doctrine, which John Quincy Adams declared was only the doctrine of the consent of the governed. The Republican party answered it when it took possession of the force of government at the beginning of the most brilliant period in all legislative history. Abraham Lincoln answered it when, on that fatal journey to Washington in 1861, he announced that the doctrine of his political creed, and declared, with prophetic vision, that he was ready to be assassinated for it if need be. You answered it again yourselves when you said that Cuba, who had no more title than the people of the Philippine Is-lands had to their independence, of right ought to be free and independent.

The question will be answered again hereafter. It will be answered soberly and de-liberately and quietly as the American people are wont to answer great questions of duty. It will be answered, not in any turbulent assembly, amid shouting and clapping of hands and stamping of feet, where men do their thinking with their heels and not with their brains. It will be answered in the churches and in the schools and in the colleges; and it will be answered in fifteen million American homes; and it will be answered as it has always been answered. It will be answered right.

DISCUSSION QUESTIONS

1   Compare and contrast arguments against U.S. imperialism made by Carnegie and Hoar in the above excerpts.

2   How might pro-expansionist Americans have responded to these arguments?

3   Considering the arguments above, what other arguments against imperialism may have been posed by voices at home and abroad?

6–12 | African American resolution from Boston protesting the American possession of the Philippine Islands, 1899

The issues of race and imperialism intertwined in a number of ways. For the United States, a nation that had ended slavery yet still experienced the violent legacies of centuries of slavery and white dominance, the question of U.S. expansion into the lands of "brown people" became bound up with the inability to conquer racism and inequality at home. A number of African Americans became prominent members of the Anti-Imperialist League. These resolutions, published in a Boston newspaper, resulted from a meeting of African Americans in that city organized by anti-imperialists decrying the actions of the Republican McKinley administration.

Resolved. That the colored people of Boston in meeting assembled desire to enter their solemn protest against the present unjustified invasion by American soldiers in the Philippine Islands.

Resolved. That, while the rights of the colored citizens in the south, sacredly guaranteed them by the amendment of the Constitution, are shamefully disregarded; and, while the frequent lynchings of negroes who are denied a civilized trial are a reproach to republican government, the duty of the president and country is to reform these crying domestic wrongs and not to attempt the civilization of alien peoples by powder and shot.

Resolved. That a copy of these resolutions be sent to the president of the United States and to the press.

DISCUSSION QUESTIONS

1   How did the supporters of this protest compare experiences of African Americans in the United States with the treatment of Filipinos?

2   What can a document like this tell us about race, nationalism, and imperialism?

6–13 | Clemencia López, address at the annual meeting of the New England Woman Suffrage Association, Philippines, 1902

Twenty-six-year-old Filipino Clemencia López (1876–1963) embarked upon a remarkable nineteen-month journey to the United States in 1901, intent upon personally petitioning President Theodore Roosevelt for her brothers' freedom. Three of her brothers had been arrested by U.S. troops for suspected involvement in the Filipino "insurgency" in the Philippine-American War (1899–1902). López won over audiences across the U.S., challenging the racist and sexist stereotyping of Filipinos made by pro-expansionists. This speech, delivered in Spanish, was translated and published in English in *The Woman's Journal* as well as several newspapers. Lopez returned to the Philippines and helped found the first women's rights organization there in 1905.

It gives me very great pleasure to greet the Massachusetts Woman Suffrage Association on behalf of the women of my country. . . . I believe that we are both striving for much the same object—you for the right to take part in national life; we for the right to have a national life to take part in. And I am sure that, if we understood each other better, the differences which now exist between your country and mind would soon disappear.

You will no doubt be surprised and pleased to learn that the condition of women in the Philippines is very different from that of the women of any country in the East, and that it differs very little from the general condition of the women of this country. Mentally, socially, and in almost all the relations of life, our women are regarded as the equals of our men. You will also be surprised to know that this equality of women in the Philippines is not a new thing. It was not introduced from Europe, but was innate, and the natural expression of the love and respect which a man ought to feel toward his mother, his wife and his daughters. And I believe there is no country in the world where family life is held in higher esteem, or where there is more respect for family relations than in the Philippine Islands. . . . All this . . . is in striking contrast with the condition of women in India and China, and the East in general.

But perhaps it will be more interesting to you if I tell you something about Philippine women at the present time. I know that the Philippine women are not as highly educated as the majority of American women: they have never had the same opportunities; but they are in general very devoted to their families. A mother, there as here, is willing to make every sacrifice for her children. . . . The wife is very faithful to her husband, and assists him in every way . . . assist[ing] in the management of the business, acting as cashier and book-keeper . . . [or] assisting to harvest the rice, corn and other grains. . . . The Philippine women are also devoted to their parents. . . .

Before closing, I should like to say a word about the patriotism of the women. This is a delicate subject, for to be patriotic to our country means that we must oppose the policy of yours. But patriotism is a quality which we all ought to be able to admire, even in an opponent. I should indeed have reason to be ashamed if I had to come before this

Association with the admission that our women were indifferent to the cause of their country's independence. You would have a right to despise me and my countrywomen if we had so little love for our native land as to consent that our country should be governed by foreign hands. . . .

For this reason it would seem to me an excellent idea that American women should take part in any investigation that may be made in the Philippine Islands. . . . Would it not also seem to you an excellent idea, since representation by our leading men has been refused us, that a number of representative Philippine women should come to this country to that you might become better acquainted with us?

In conclusion, in the name of the Philippine women, I pray the Massachusetts Woman Suffrage Association to do what it can to remedy all this misery and misfortune in my unhappy country. You can do much to bring about the cessation of these horrors and cruelties which are to-day taking place in the Philippines, and to insist upon a more humane course. I do not believe that you can understand or imagine the miserable condition of the women of my country, or how real is their suffering. Thousands have been widowed, orphaned, left alone and homeless, exposed and in the greatest misery. It is, then, not a surprising fact that the diseases born of hunger are increasing, and that to-day immorality prevails in the Philippines to an extent never before known. After all, you ought to understand that we are only contending for the liberty of our country, just as you once fought for the same liberty for yours.

DISCUSSION QUESTIONS

1   What initial clarification did López make, in describing the status of women in the Philippines?

2   In what ways did López attempt to make connections between the people of the Philippines and her audience? Why?

3   What connections did López make between the struggle for women's suffrage and the conflict in the Philippines?

6–14 | Rubén Darío, poem, "To Roosevelt," Nicaragua, 1904

Best known as a poet and founder of Spanish-American *modernismo* writing under the name Rubén Darío, Nicaraguan Félix Rubén García y Sarmiento (1867–1916) traveled extensively in Latin America and Europe, wrote for several newspapers, and served as diplomat to several countries. Darío also covered the Spanish-American War from Spain, publishing stories in an Argentine paper. This poem, written in 1904 and addressed to President Theodore Roosevelt, was inspired by the U.S. involvement in Colombian affairs that resulted in exclusive U.S. control of the Panama Canal Zone.

One needs the Bible's voice or Walt Whitman's verse,
to reach you, Hunter!
Primitive and modern, simple and complex,
with a bit of Washington and a bit more of Nimrod.
You are the United States;
you are the future invader
of the naive America that has native blood,
that still prays to Jesus Christ and still speaks Spanish.

You are the proud and strong exemplar of your race;
you are cultured, you are skillful; you oppose Tolstoy.
Whether taming horses or killing tigers,
you are an Alexander-Nebuchadnezzar.
(You are Professor of Energy,
as the madmen of today say.)
You believe life is fire,
that progress is eruption,
and where you place the bullet
you place the future.

No.

The United States are powerful and great.
When they tremble there is a deep tremor
that passes through the enormous spine of the Andes.
If you shout, it is heard as the roaring of the lion.
Hugo told Grant: "The stars are yours."
(The rising Argentine sun hardly shines
before the Chilean star rises . . .) You are rich.
You join the cult of Mammon to the cult of Hercules.
Illuminating the path of easy conquest,
Freedom raises her torch in New York.

But our America, which has had poets
from the ancient times of Netzahualcoyotl,
which has preserved the footprints of the great Bacchus,
who learned Pan's alphabet all at once;
which consulted the stars, which knew Atlantis,
whose name echoes down to us from Plato,
who since the distant moments of her life
lives on light, on fire, on perfume, on love,
the America of the great Montezuma, of the Inca,
the fragrant America of Christopher Columbus,
Catholic America, Spanish America,
the America in which the noble Cuauhtémoc said,
"I lie not on a bed of roses." That America,
which trembles with hurricanes and lives on Love;
men of Saxon eyes and savage soul, she lives.

She dreams. She loves, and she trembles; she is the daughter of the Sun.
Be on your guard. Spanish America lives!
There are a thousand cubs loosed from the Spanish Lion.
Roosevelt, one would need to be, by God Himself,
the tremendous Marksman and strong Hunter,
to be able to catch us in your iron claws.

And, although you assume you have everything, one thing is missing: God!

DISCUSSION QUESTIONS

1   How did Darío depict Roosevelt, the United States, and Latin America in his poem?
2   For what purposes might he have used historical allusions? (Look up any names or events that are unfamiliar to you.)
3   This poem was published the same year as Roosevelt announced his addition to the Monroe Doctrine (see chapter 6, item 10b). Based on the poem, what was Darío's fear about the future of the relationship between Latin America and the United States? Were his fears founded?

6-15 | Louis S. Meikle, discussion of Panama, United States annexations, and race, Jamaica, 1912

Jamaican Dr. Louis Sancroft Meikle (1874–1937) was a dentist and physician who worked for the U.S. Public Health Service during the building of the Panama Canal. He authored the 1912 book *Confederation of the British West Indies versus Annexation to the United States of America: A Political Discourse on the West Indies*, in which he laid out arguments against the annexation of the British West Indies—nearly two dozen territories of the Anglo-Caribbean, including Jamaica, the Bahamas, Belize, Turks and Caicos, Grenada, and Barbados—to the U.S. or Canada. This excerpt from his polemic draws on Meikle's observations of Americans while in Panama.

There are so many objections to advance against the annexation of the British West Indian possessions to the United States that the commercial benefits which would be derived from such a union are completely overshadowed.

One of the main points at issue is the standard of inequality (set up by the Americans with respect to other persons) based on colour, creed, and race, irrespective of qualifications.

With the Americans you must be White! White!! White!!! You must be white to be truthful and honest. You must be white to hold any position of trust outside of the political realm; and more than all, the American white man is rated, in the United States, at a higher premium than any other member of the Caucasian race, and so it is wherever the Stars and Stripes float as the controlling power.

In this connection, with reference to race hatred, it is not the negro alone that is singled out for attack. The Jews, the Chinese, and the Japanese come in for their proportionate share of ostracism, with the exception that it is administered to these in a much milder form. . . .

Let the annexationists take a trip to Puerto Rico, Cuba, or the Philippines, and last, but not least, the Republic of Panama, and see for themselves how these people are being treated by the Americans, before attempting to barter their birthright for a mere shadow.

It is safe to say that the experience of the inquirer would be of such an astounding nature as to compel him to abandon his unrighteous cause for all time.

On the Isthmus of Panama, where, like the West Indies, the larger portion of the population is either mixed with negro or Indian blood, the expected has happened. Americans from the Canal Zone who go over to the cities of Panama and Colon, on the territory of Panama, to make small purchases (the large purchases being procured from the U.S. Commissary) are now refusing to be attended to by coloured clerks, and as a result, managers and owners of these establishments have been contemplating whether, for the benefit of their business, they should not dispense with coloured helps altogether.

There is great and widespread unrest in Cuba and Panama over the extreme position taken up by the Americans, who have assumed the position of official masters.

These people have made themselves overbearing in their manner to such an extent towards every one with whom they come in contact, that they foster hatred rather than love, to their discredit as juvenile colonizers.

The Republic of Panama, having practically surrendered their sovereignty to the United States in a most extraordinary document called the "Panama Canal Treaty," which gives the latter *the power of eminent domain in* perpetuity, are now in a quandary what to do with the Americans who have unblushingly taken unto themselves the rôle of dictators over their country. . . .

No sooner had the United States implanted herself on the Isthmus of Panama, than the Americans began to set up their *religion*, that the superiority of one man over the other was not dependent upon education, achievement, or wealth, but upon the hue of the skin.

At the restaurants and boarding-houses a screen would be put before the table of a previously welcomed coloured patron, and *that table* removed to the rear of the dining-room: then he would be asked to use the side entrance there-after.

Since the advent of the Americans on the Isthmus, bar-rooms, ice-cream parlours, billiard parlours, and other places of refreshment and amusement which were opened to every one, now admit only white persons.

Those who travelled in Cuba returned with a tale of woe, that the same intolerable conditions exist there which were unknown in the darkest days of Spain's regime; and the reason for this state of affairs is attributed to Yankee invasion.

It has been argued that the American Constitution does not follow the flag: that may be so, but it is a certainty that the feeling of race-hatred follows the people wherever they go. . . .

The inhabitants of Puerto Rico, Cuba, and Panama, would gladly return to their former control, rather than tolerate for another day the dictates which come with American rule, but it is *too late! too late!!*

DISCUSSION QUESTIONS

1   In your own words, describe Meikle's critique of the United States.

2   According to Meikle, what was the meaning of "white" and what privileges did white Americans have?

7

Constructing the Urban Landscape

360 | International Views of Cities in the United States

Challenges and Promises of the City

Reform

INTERNATIONAL VIEWS OF CITIES IN THE UNITED STATES

The end of the nineteenth century and the beginning of the twentieth was an age of rapid urbanization of the United States—as it was in every industrializing state. In 1869, just nine cities had populations over 100,000, but in 1890 twenty-eight had reached that number. These population centers, led by New York, Chicago, Philadelphia, St. Louis, Boston, and Baltimore, teemed with new immigrants and rural Americans who came seeking opportunities, employment, entertainment, and community. Many of these centers became overwhelmed by the rate of growth. Efforts at social, economic, political, and labor reform lagged far behind the pace of growth. Throughout the nineteenth century and into the next, visitors from abroad commented on the character of the American metropolis, as seen in these excerpts below.

Michel Chevalier's impressions of early Cincinnati, France, ca. 1833

Cincinnati has been made famous by Mrs Trollope, whose aristocratic feelings were offended by the pork-trade which is here carried on on a great scale. From her accounts many persons have thought that everybody in Cincinnati was a pork merchant, and the city a mere slaughter-house. The fact is that Cincinnati is a large and beautiful town, charmingly situated in one of those bends which the Ohio makes, as if unwilling to leave the spot. . . .

The architectural appearance of Cincinnati is very nearly the same with that of the new quarters of the English towns. The houses are generally of brick, most commonly three stories high, with the windows shining with cleanliness, calculated each for a single family, and regularly placed along well paved and spacious streets, sixty feet in width. Here and there the prevailing uniformity is interrupted by some more imposing edifice, and there are some houses of hewn stone in very good taste, real palaces in miniature, with neat porticoes, inhabited by the aristocratical portion of

Mrs Trollope's hog-merchants, and several very pretty mansions surrounded with gardens and terraces. . . .

In Cincinnati, as everywhere else in the United States, there is a great number of churches; each sect has its own, from Anglican Episcopalianism, which enlists under its banner the wealth of the country, to the Baptist and Methodist sects, the religion of the labourers and negroes. On another side, stands a huge hotel, which from its exterior you would take for a royal residence, but in which, as I can testify, you will not experience a princely hospitality; or a museum, which is merely a private specu-lation, as all American museums are, and which consists of some few crystals, some mammoth-bones, which are very abundant in the United States, an Egyptian mummy, some Indian weapons and dresses, and a halfdozen wax figures, representing, for in-stance, Washington, General Jackson, and the Indian Chiefs, Black Hawk and Tecum-seh, a figure of Napoleon afoot or on horseback, a French cuirass from Waterloo, a collection of portraits of distinguished Americans, comprising Lafayette and some of the leading men of the town, another of stuffed birds, snakes preserved in spirits, and particularly a large living snake, a boa constrictor or an anaconda. . . .

The foundries for casting steam-engines, the yards for building steamboats, the noisy, unwholesome, or unpleasant work-shops, are in the adjoining village of Ful-ton, in Covington or Newport on the Kentucky bank of the river, or in the country. As to the enormous slaughter of hogs, about 150,000 annually, and the preparation of the lard, which follows, the town is not in the least incommoded by it; the whole process takes place on the banks of a little stream called Deer Creek, which has re-ceived the nickname of the Bloody Run, from the colour of its waters during the season of the massacre, or near the basins of the great canal, which extends from Cincinnati towards the Maumee of Lake Erie. Cincinnati has, however, no squares planted with trees in the English taste, no parks nor walks, no fountains, although it would be very easy to have them. It is necessary to wait for the ornamental, until the taste for it prevails among the inhabitants; at present the useful occupies all thoughts. Besides, all improvements require an increase of taxes, and in the United States it is not easy to persuade the people to submit to this. Cincinnati also stands in need of some public provision for lighting the streets, which this repugnance to taxes has hitherto prevented. . . .

Cincinnati contains about 40,000 inhabitants, inclusive of the adjoining villages; al-though founded 40 years ago, its rapid growth dates only about 30 years back. It seems to be the rendezvous of all nations; the Germans and Irish are very numerous, and there are some Alsacians; I have often heard the harsh accents of the Rhenish French in the streets. But the bulk of the population, which gives its tone to all the rest, is of New England origin. What makes the progress of Cincinnati more surprising is, that the city is the daughter of its own works. Other towns, which have sprung up in the United States in the same rapid manner, have been built on shares, so to speak. Lowell, for example, is an enterprise of Boston merchants, who, after having raised the necessary funds, have collected workmen and told them, "Build us a town." Cincinnati has been gradually extended and embellished, almost wholly without foreign aid, by its inhabi-tants, who have for the most part arrived on the spot poor. . . .

I have said that Cincinnati was admirably situated; this is true in respect of its geographical position, but, if you follow the courses of the rivers on the map, and consider the natural resources of the district, you will find that there are several points on the long line of the rivers of the West as advantageously placed, both for trade and manufactures, and that there are some even more favored in these respects. Pittsburg, which has within reach both coal and iron, that is to say, the daily bread of industry, which stands at the head of the Ohio, at the starting point of steam-navigation, at the confluence of the Monongahela and the Allegheny, coming the one from the south and the other from the north; Pittsburg, which is near a great chain of lakes, appears as the pivot of a vast system of roads, railroads, and canals, several of which are already completed. Pittsburg was marked out by nature at once for a great manufacturing centre and a great mart of trade. Louisville, built at the falls of the Ohio, at the head of navigation for the largest class of boats, is a natural medium between the commerce of the upper Ohio and that of the Mississippi and its tributaries. In respect to manufacturing resources, Louisville is as well provided as Cincinnati, and the latter, setting aside its enchanting situation, seemed destined merely to become the market of the fertile strip between the Great and Little Miami.

But the power of men, when they agree in willing anything and in willing it perseveringly, is sufficient to overbear and conquer that of nature. In spite of the superior advantages of Louisville as an *entrepôt*, in spite of the manufacturing resources of Pittsburg, Cincinnati is able to maintain a population twice that of Louisville and half as large again as that of Pittsburg in a state of competence, which equals, if it does not surpass, the average condition of that of each of the others. The inhabitants of Cincinnati have fixed this prosperity among them, by one of those instinctive views with which the sons of New England are inspired by their eminently practical and calculating genius. . . .

The Cincinnatians make a variety of household furniture and utensils, agricultural and mechanical implements and machines, wooden clocks, and a thousand objects of daily use and consumption, soap, candles, paper, leather, &c., for which there is an indefinite demand throughout the flourishing and rapidly growing States of the West, and also in the new States of the Southwest, which are wholly devoted to agriculture, and in which, on account of the existence of slavery, manufactures cannot be carried on. Most of these articles are of ordinary quality; the furniture, for instance, is rarely such as would be approved by Parisian taste, but it is cheap and neat, just what is wanted in a new country, where, with the exception of a part of the South, there is general ease and but little wealth, and where plenty and comfort are more generally known than the little luxuries of a more refined society. The prosperity of Cincinnati, therefore, rests upon the sure basis of the prosperity of the West, upon the supply of articles of the first necessity to the bulk of the community; a much more solid foundation than the caprice of fashion, upon which, nevertheless, the branches of industry most in favor with us, depend. The intellectual also receives a share of attention; in the first place, there is a large type-foundry in Cincinnati, which supplies the demand of the whole West, and that army of newspapers that is printed in it. . . . The country trader, who keeps an assortment of everything vendible, is sure to find almost everything he wants in Cincinnati, and he, therefore goes thither in preference to any other place in order to lay in his stock of goods. Cincinnati is this in fact the great central mart of the West; a great quantity and variety of produce and manufactured articles find a vent here, notwithstanding the natural superiority of several other sites, either in regard to the extent of water communications or mineral resources. . . .

. . . [In] Cincinnati, there are no great factories or work-shops. Mechanical industry is subdivided there, pretty much as the soil is amongst us; each head of a family, with his sons and some newly arrived emigrants as assistants and servants, has his domain in this great field. Cincinnati is, therefore, as republican in its industrial organization, as in its political. This subdivision of manufactures has hitherto been attended with no inconvenience, because in the vast West, whose growth is visible to the eye, the production cannot at present keep pace with the consumption. . . .

The moral aspect of Cincinnati is delightful in the eyes of him who prefers work to every thing else, and with whom work can take the place of every thing else. But whoever has a taste for pleasure and display, whoever needs occasional relaxation from business, in gaiety and amusement, would find this beautiful city, with it picturesque environs, an insupportable residence. . . . [H]e would find himself denounced from political considerations, because men of leisure are looked upon in the United States as so many stepping-stones to aristocracy, and anathematized by religion, for the various sects, however much they may differ on other points, all agree in condemning pleasure, luxury, gallantry, the fine arts themselves. . . . There is, therefore, no such thing in Cincinnati as a class of men of leisure, living without any regular profession on their patrimony, or on the wealth acquired by their own enterprise in early life, although there are many persons of opulence, having one hundred thousand dollars and upwards. . . .

Alexis de Tocqueville on the American city, France, 1839

America has no great capital* city, whose influence is directly or indirectly felt over the whole extent of country, which I hold to be one of the first causes of the maintenance of republican institutions in the United States. In cities, men cannot be prevented from concerting together, and from awakening a mutual excitement which prompts sudden and passionate resolutions. Cities may be looked upon as large assemblies, of which all the inhabitants are members; their populace exercises a prodigious influence upon the magistrates, and frequently executes its own wishes without their intervention.

To subject the provinces to the metropolis, is therefore not only to place the destiny of the empire in the hands of a portion of the community, which may be reprobated as unjust, but to place it in the hands of a populace acting under on its own impulses, which must be avoided as dangerous. The preponderance of capital cities is therefore a serious blow upon the representative system; and it exposes modern republics to the same defect as the republics of antiquity, which all perished from not having been acquainted with that form of government.

[*Footnote text: The United States have no metropolis, but they already contain several very large cities. Philadelphia reckoned 161,000 inhabitants, and New-York

202,000, in the year 1830. The lower orders which inhabit these cities constitute a rabble even more formidable than the populace of European towns. They consist of freed Blacks in the first place, who are condemned by the laws and by public opinion, to an hereditary state of misery and degradation. They also contain a multitude of Europeans who have been driven to the shores of the New World by their misfortunes or their misconduct; and these men inoculate the United States with all our vices, without bringing with them any of those interests which counteract their baneful influence. As inhabitants of a country where they have no civil rights, they are ready to turn all the passions which agitate the community to their own advantage; thus, within the last few months serious riots have broken out in Philadelphia and in New York. Disturbances of this kind are unknown in the rest of the country, which is nowise alarmed by them, because the population of the cities has hitherto exercised neither power nor influence over the rural districts.

Nevertheless, I look upon the size of certain American cities, and especially on the nature of their population, as a real danger which threatens the future security of the democratic republics of the New World; and I venture to predict that they will perish from this circumstance, unless the Government succeeds in creating an armed force, which, whilst it remains under the control of the majority of the nation, will be independent of the town population, and able to repress its excesses.]

William Kelly on San Francisco, UK, 1851

There are numerous houses of worship in the city, but none of them externally distinguishable as such save the Roman Catholic chapel—a new frame building of capacious dimensions—erected on an eminence, which makes it quite a feature of the city. It is to be regretted, however, that their influence is exceedingly circumscribed, if any inference can be deduced from the limited attendance; for while their congregations are so lamentably thin, the dens of iniquity, the gaming-houses, are crammed to suffocation; the sacrilegious din of their crashing bands rending the solemn stillness of the Sabbath, penetrating to the shrine of worship even during the hour of prayer—the rampant bleatings of the golden calf drowning the mild tones of Christian piety.

The world's progress furnishes no parallel for the precocious depravity of San Francisco. The virgin soil of a new settlement did not use to be a garden for vice and evil. There it was the kindly philanthropist looked to find the ruddy virtues blooming in a kindred clay in an uncontaminated atmosphere, fading and sickening only in the tedious revolution of time, as moral culture degenerated into voluptuous lethargy, accumulated wealth morbidly craving the incentives of luxury, and enervating enjoyments supplanting the healthy exercise of enterprise, when, with drooping heads and shrivelled stems, they shrank into decay, choked by the rank weeds of artificial society. But in Francisco a new and anomalous phase has arisen; the infant phenomenon exhibiting the tokens of senility in its cradle, with the gangrene of vicious indulgence staining its soft cheek before it is well emancipated from its swaddling-clothes—symptoms altogether incompatible with the sanguine anticipations which predicate for it the proudest position amongst all the cities within the vast bay of oceans between the Capes of Horn and Good Hope.

In Francisco nothing is natural—everything is forced; it is a hotbed where all pursuits are stimulated by the fierce fire of one predominant lust. Trade or business is not embarked in there to be the honourable occupation of a lifetime; professions are not solely followed to secure a permanent practice and social elevation; men engage in both the one and the other to build up fortunes in a hurry with whatever materials they can grasp, to win a large stake by any means and then withdraw, confounding the tactics of the gambler with the zealous integrity of the merchant, until conscience is left without a corner to hide in, and even common decency is obliged to pick her steps through the mire. . . .

Lot property, in and about Francisco, is, and will continue for some time, to be valuable and in demand, from the unceasing stream of emigration, both by sea and land, one-fourth of whom either stay in or return to the city; and as there are no such things as empty houses or untenanted stores, those who come with an intention of starting in business have no alternative but to purchase a lot and erect a tenement; so that, I repeat, lot property contiguous to the city is for the present an improving investment; but I wish to emphasize contiguous, because surveys and allotments have been made out to ridiculously remote points, that cannot possibly come into occupation if ever, for a number of years; for you will meet, as you travel towards the city, miles from its turmoil, posts surmounted with boards, that wayfarers approach to learn the distance, but find them headed with the names of streets, and notifications "that the adjoining valuable lots are for sale"—causing the bewildered stranger to strain his optics in search of the outlines of a town, impressed, as he proceeds, with amazement, and vague notions of earthquakes and such like vagaries of nature.

But I cannot refrain from expressing my opinion—the question of title apart—that the present extravagant value of property in Francisco cannot continue to be long sustained, because commerce and business, which are its life and soul, are on an unsound and fictitious basis, that must be revolutionised to become stable and permanent. The standard of property is relatively regulated by the profits of trade, and as those profits become necessarily depressed as the vast appliances of steam open fresh facilities for intercourse and transit, its value must subside in like ratio. No sane man could put faith in the continuance of a system having to bear up against the feverish pulse of a money-market beating at an average of eight per cent. per month, against rents five hundred per cent. above those of New York or London, against wages and salaries equally exorbitant, with an exhausting domestic expenditure, despite of the most self-denying economy, and without the guarantee of insurance to cover the ruinous risks of the place from fire.

Besides, regarding it in another light, how is it possible that a city, claiming to contain 50,000 inhabitants, can be supported that in its present career by so scant a population as that California is said to contain, which, according to an average of the very best estimates, does not exceed 200,000, cities, diggings, ranches, and all; an amount, too, that is gradually on the decrease, as the placer diggings—which alone can be worked by individual energy and labour—are giving evidences of exhaustion; results that will steadily progress until the mining operations of the country are concentrated in a few large associated companies, constrainedly employing machinery instead of manual labor in stamping and grinding the quartz, amalgamations, &c., &c., to the consequent diminution of the population, who have not the attraction of agricultural resources to induce them to settle in the country; for it is a notorious fact, borne out by experience, that not one out of every hundred emigrants either start with the intention of permanent settlement, or see reason to change their minds after a season's resident in the country.

There is constantly shifting population, the one coming with the determination of working hard, and saving rapidly for home enjoyment, the other returning with the fruits of their labour and economy. At first the flood was the stronger, but latterly the ebb tide is the more impetuous, carrying along with each receding wave a portion of the sandy foundation on which this marvellous city has been built.

San Francisco, to be upheld in its present overweening pretensions, would require a thriving population of at least a couple of million at its back.

Lord (James) Bryce comments on inefficiency in New York, UK, 1912

In the great city there is a deplorable amount of economic waste. In the city the manufactories, offices, warehouses and shops, all the large places in which people are employed, whether in distributing commodities or purchasing, are in the central parts of the city. The people want to live in the outer parts of the city, and as the city grows the people are driven more and more into the outskirts. If you will consider the amount of time that is taken from work to be given to mere transportation from the residence of the workingman to his working place in the city, you will see how great the loss is.

I used to make computations of that in London. In London a large part of our working people live on the eastern side of London, the northern side and the southwest, and come in ten, twelve or fourteen miles every day to work. The man walks ten minutes to the railway station from the place where he lives, and then walks another ten minutes from the station to his work in the city, and he spends from three-quarters of an hour to fifty minutes, sometimes perhaps as much as sixty minutes, on the railroad. In other words he wastes from fifty to seventy minutes in the morning, and as much in the evening, which might be given to work, or if not to work, then to mental recreation or improvement.

Think what that means in a year. Think what is the waste that is involved in a great city like London or New York in people spending an hour or more in the morning and another hour or more in the evening in going to and fro to their work, when if they were near their work they might either be working or enjoying themselves or having wholesome rest. It is an economic waste which is really an insult to our civilization; it ought to appeal to us on the mere business side, the need for saving the productive capacity of our people from such waste.

Now, what can you do about it? I am told that there are obvious advantages in great cities. No doubt there is an advantage in that you can have a certain amount of pleasure. You can have better libraries, finer museums and zöological and botanical gardens on a larger scale. You can have larger and more varied commercial interests and a fuller social life, and you can have a far greater choice of amusements, more music, more plays in the theater.

The business man says he must be where the greatest facilities for transportation exist, namely, where the largest number of railroads converge, and the place where he can have the largest supply of labor at short notice, and where he can get any kind of labor that he wants because there is a large floating population.

I do not deny that there is force in all this. But at the same time even the business man will surely admit that it ought to be a great advantage to him in the smaller place to be able to get land very much cheaper. There he can lay out his factory building on approved lines and provide not only larger spaces for his works but also larger and more convenient dwellings for his workingmen.

Of course we all believe that business looks after itself, that men know better their own business than anybody else could tell them. At the same time I do believe that there are cases where men go by rule of thumb, merely doing as other people have done, merely following in a trodden path, without stopping to think that it is worth while to give attention to those considerations which sometimes occur to us who look at things in a theoretical as well as a practical way. You all know that in matters of shop management suggestions of great value have been recently put forward by Mr. Frederick Taylor, which have attracted much attention, and I believe are being taken advantage of, which will effect a great saving of economic waste. These suggestions might have occurred to many other business men, but it was left to Mr. Taylor to think out the matter and show its importance. So, I am sure, there are many particulars of social mechanism in which it will be possible to remove waste if people would only begin to stop and think about it instead of blindly following in the pathways they have become accustomed to tread.

Liang Qichao on New York and poverty, China, 1903

New York

The uncivilized live underground. The somewhat civilized live on the ground, while the civilized live above the ground. Those on the ground usually live in one- to two-story homes. Those below live in what look like holes in the ground, which get flooded whenever it rains. Homes in Beijing also always have several stone steps at the entrance, descending as if into the ground. In New York, on the other hand, it is not uncommon to see towers of ten to twenty stories high—the tallest is thirty-three stories. This can truly be called above the ground. That said, many American homes have both a basement and one or two stories above ground, so they can be considered as both above and below ground.

Everywhere in New York one's eye finds homes that look like pigeon coops, power lines like spider webs, and electric street cars like centipedes.

New York's Central Park stretches from 71st Street to 123rd Street. It's roughly as large as the entire International Concession in Shanghai. On every day of rest, the park becomes crowded with carriages and people jostling together. It's located directly in the center of the city; if the land were sold, it would be worth three or four times more than the Chinese government's entire annual revenue. Chinese people would say that it is a shameful waste of money on a useless piece of land. It covers an area of 7,000 square [Chinese] acres, making it the largest park of any city in the world. London has the next largest park of 6,500 acres. City policy makers all agree that in a bustling city like this, to not have such a park would be morally detrimental. After arriving in New York, I now believe that if I went a day without visiting the park, my spirits would dampen and my thoughts would become muddled.

The city is filled with vehicles. All day every day aerial cars, subways, carriages, electric cars and automobiles are thundering above, clattering below, rumbling to the left and right, banging and ringing in front and behind. It darkens the spirit and leaves one's soul shaking. People say that those who have lived in New York for a long time must have quicker eyes than normal people, otherwise they would stand at a single intersection all day, never daring to cross.

Poverty

There is no place in the world more prosperous than New York. Yet neither is there any place in the world that is bleaker than New York. Let me take a moment to describe New York's darker side. Anti-orientalists insult the Chinese as being unclean. From what I've seen, the Chinese people of New York are not the unclean ones. In summer, the Italian and Jewish streets will be filled with old and younger women, as well as children sitting on the ground with little tables. The streets become clogged. Everyone's clothes are ragged and their appearance wretched. Street cars do not go there, nor do many carriages either, though tourists constantly go to see the scene for themselves. From the outside one sees buildings and buildings stacked up against each other, yet a single building holds several dozen families. Half of the dwellings have no natural light or airflow, and gas burns day and night. Upon entering these buildings, a foul odor assails your nostrils. Roughly 230,000 New Yorkers live in such conditions.

According to statistics from 1888, on Houston and Mulberry Streets (where more than half the residents are Italian, with some Germans, Chinese, and Jews) the death rate is 35 per thousand. For children under 5 years old, it's 139 per thousand. This is compared with New York's overall statistics, where the death rate is 26 per thousand. One can imagine then the hardships of New York's poor. This death rate can be attributed to their dwellings' lack of air or light. Another statistician says that there are 37,000 rented apartments in New York, housing 1,200,000 people. This kind of living situation is not only harmful to one's health, but also to morality. Yet another statistician has said that in one building somewhere housing 483 people, 102 people committed crimes in one year. One can see the profound effect this kind of living has on people.

There is a poem by Du Fu [Tang dynasty, 712–770 AD] that says, "The villas of the rich reek of wine and meat, while the frozen bones of the dead lie on the street. The rich and poor are but steps apart, a sorrow too grim to retell." I have seen this with my own eyes in New York. According to socialists' statistics, 70% of America's wealth belongs to 200,000 wealthy people. The other 30% belongs to the remaining 79,800,000 poor people. The wealthy of America truly are wealthy then, and this so-called wealthy class constitutes no more than a mere one four-hundredth of the total population. This is akin to having one hundred dollars and dividing it among four hundred people, where one person gets seventy dollars and the remaining thirty are divided among three hundred ninety-nine people. Each person wouldn't even receive ten cents, but a mere seven. How strange is this? How bizarre is this? There is no civilized country that does not have this phenomenon, though it is particularly pronounced in large cities, and it is worst in New York and London. For uneven distribution of wealth to reach this level, to see for myself the slums of New York's poor, I sigh deeply and think that socialism absolutely must not be stopped.

Chinese American Dong Tong, confronted by racial zoning in Baltimore, 1911

Is a Chinaman a white man or is he a colored man? Whichever he is, he is man enough to get the application of the West segregation ordinance tangled.

D. Tong, a Chinese laundryman, recently purchased the house at 640 North Fremont avenue. His neighbors resented the presence of the Celestial and took their grievance to the Harlem Improvement Association, on the ground that the West segregation ordinance might apply to all persons of any color.

According to the ordinance all persons are separated into two classes, "white" and "negroes or colored people." If the Chinaman is not in the white class, then, it is claimed, he is in the other class. But others say that inasmuch as he is not black he cannot be a negro. Several agitators declare the ordinance says "colored people" and that as a Chinaman is not white, he must be colored.

The supporters of the ordinance admit that only two races were considered in the drafting of the ordinance, the white and black, and that the Chinaman received no consideration.

On this ground, others interested in the discussion say that the Chinaman has both of the other races at a disadvantage, for he is free to move whither his desire directs him. Others are wondering what will happen in a case where a Chinaman shall decide whether a block is "white" or "colored."

Chart showing global urban and rural population, 1960–2017

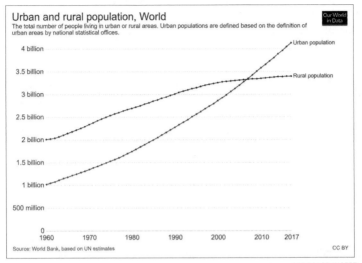

SEE COLOR INSERT

Chart showing share of population living in urbanized areas, 1800–2000

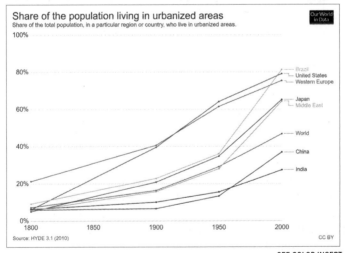

SEE COLOR INSERT

360

360 DISCUSSION QUESTIONS

1   On which topics did foreign visitors to U.S. cities most often comment? Did this differ based on their country of origin? Why? Why not?

2   Do you notice a difference in descriptions of cities in the early part of the century (1830s) from those that were offered later (1900s)?

3   Considering the chart on total urban and rural population, what is the trend since 1960? What challenges or opportunities might that reality present for cities in the U.S. as well as around the globe?

4   How might comparative rates of urbanized peoples in the countries on the final chart inform different issues these countries face? Draw out specific examples.

CHALLENGES AND PROMISES OF THE CITY

7–1a | George E. Waring, comments on modern sewage disposal, 1891

George E. Waring Jr. (1833–1898), prominent American sanitation engineer and civic reformer, gained his national reputation when he was sent by the newly created National Board of Health to modernize the sewer drainage system in Memphis, Tennessee, after a yellow fever outbreak in 1878. The belief, incorrect it turns out, was that yellow fever was caused by inadequate sanitation, but it resulted in a drive to separate sewage from other water sources, which did improve health. As cities grew rapidly in the late nineteenth century outdated systems made for smaller settlements were overwhelmed by the demand of the new urban centers (see 1840s discussion of similar concerns in England in chapter 7, item 7). Here, in an 1891 publication, this engineer and Civil War veteran comments on the international and national state of sewerage at the end of the nineteenth century.

The life of man involves both the production of food, directly or indirectly by the growth of plants, and the consumption and destruction of the organized products of such growth. The production and the destruction are constant. Between consumption and renewed growth there intervenes a process which prepares what we reject for the use of plants.

It is this intervening process that we have to consider in applying the comparatively new art of sewage disposal. The process itself has gone on from the beginning of the world, but it has been left to unguided natural action, which takes no account of the needs and conditions of modern communities.

In the primitive life of sparse populations, it was comparatively safe to disregard it; but, as population became more dense, and especially as men gathered into communities, it became increasingly important to bring it under control, for it then involved a serious menace to the safety of the people. So long as our offscourings could be scattered broadcast over the ground, their destruction was attended with little danger; but when it became necessary to concentrate them in underground receptacles, a capacity for real mischief was developed. As these receptacles increased, with the growth of communities, the menace increased, until, in the light of modern knowledge as to the conditions of healthful living, the need for radical measures of relief became obvious. It is the application of these measures that we are now to consider.

The sewerage of towns, and the drainage of important buildings, are now controlled by expert engineers, and they rarely fail to be reasonably well done. The economy of good plans is understood, and especially the vital necessity for good construction. In fact, it may be said that the adoption of excellent methods and appliances for removing liquid wastes from houses and towns is becoming general. It will in time become universal.

This, however, is only the first step in sanitary improvement. It is only the step of removal. It gets our wastes out of our immediate neighborhoods; it does not destroy them. It is now recognized that quick and complete removal is only the beginning of the necessary service, and that proper ultimate disposal is no less important to health, to decency, and to public comfort. The organic wastes of human life must be finally and completely consumed. It is not enough to get them out of the house and out of the town; until they are resolved into their elements, their capacity for harm and for offense is not ended. It does not suffice to discharge them into a cesspool, nor does it always suffice to discharge them into a harbor, or into a water-course, leaving them there to the slow process of putrefaction.

The need for improving the conditions of sewage disposal has long been recognized, and, especially in connection with large foreign towns, efforts of the most costly character have been made to obviate accumulations due to the discharge of sewers. The floods made foul with the wastes of the huge population of London have been poured into the Thames, until, in spite of years of efforts to relieve that river, its condition has become, in the language of Lord Bramwell, "a disgrace to the Metropolis and to civilization." The millions expended since 1850 on the still unsolved problem have not thus far effected more than a mitigation of the evil. London is to-day, apparently, as far as ever from its ultimate solution, though of course the former direct discharge of sewage all along the river front, and the resulting local stench, have been suppressed. The case grows in gravity with the growth of the population, and measures which promise success when adopted are not able to cope with the greater volumes produced later. . . .

In our country, New York City and the towns on the Mississippi, and on other very large rivers, have such tidal and flood conditions as to secure satisfactory disposal by dilution and removal. At Boston, Philadelphia, and Chicago, the needed relief can, under the methods adopted, be secured only by works of the greatest magnitude and cost, while the smaller towns have, as a rule, yet to devise methods by which, unless they are exceptionally well placed, they can destroy their wastes at a practicable cost. The importance of relief is being more and more realized, but the means of relief are little understood by the people. A wider appreciation of the efficiency of these means is a necessary condition precedent to general improvement.

Systematic works, chiefly by removal through intercepting sewers, have, until recently, been confined to cities. Smaller towns are now perfecting their methods of removal, and there is a growing desire to find means for purifying the outflow which will not cost more than can be afforded. Interest is also growing among householders, who are becoming convinced of the dangers of cesspools, with their retention of putrefying wastes within contaminating reach of houses and of their sources of water-supply.

In its progress thus far, the art of disposal has worked itself out mainly by progressive practice. It began in the instinctive desire to get offensive matters out of sight. As new difficulties presented themselves, and as the requirements of a better civilization arose, new methods were devised for better concealment in the ground, or better removal by sewers. . . . It is hardly half a century since the dangers of incomplete sewage removal were appreciated and radical measures of relief were attempted. . . .

Then, too, it was long thought that if sewage could be purged of its suspended matter,—of that which clouds it and colors it,—purification would be effected. An imperfect clarification by mechanical or chemical processes is still applied in some cases where a high degree of purification is really needed, although it is now well known that such clarification does not and cannot remove from sewage its most putrescible matters, nor its minute living organisms. Imperfect results, which have satisfied legal requirements in Europe, are in such cases accepted as sufficient, in spite of a recognition of their incompleteness.

The purification of sewage is surely on the eve of great extension in this country, and it is necessary to its success that the importance of making it as thorough as possible be made known, as well as its conditions and requirements. If the work is to be done at all, it is surely worth while to do it well. Half-way measures, like chemical precipitation, may satisfy present legal demands, and they may, in exceptional cases, be advisable, but they will not meet the requirements of the better-informed public opinion that is now growing up. The means for entire purification are within reach, and imperfect results will not long be acceptable as sufficient.

In practical work, two cardinal principles should be kept in view, and should control our action:—

(a) *Organic wastes must be discharged at the sewer outlet in their fresh condition,—before putrefaction has set in;* and

(b) *They must be reduced to a state of complete oxidation without the intervention of dangerous or offensive decomposition.*

7–1b | George E. Waring, photographs, before-and-after images of Morton Street in New York City, 1893 and 1895

In 1895, George E. Waring Jr. was appointed sanitation commissioner of New York. Although his tenure would be brief, he laid the foundations for recycling, street sweeping, and garbage collection. He began the cleanup by securing a law that required horses and carts to be stabled overnight, instead of remaining on the streets. The most striking feature of his reforms was the corps of street cleaners he created, each dressed daily in all-white uniforms. His reform efforts were successful immediately—so much so that a grand parade was held for the sanitation works in 1896.

MORTON STREET, CORNER OF BEDFORD, LOOKING TOWARD BLEECKER STREET,
MARCH 17, 1893.

THE SAME STREET, MAY 29, 1895.

DISCUSSION QUESTIONS

1   What were the major problems outlined by Waring? What were his solutions?

2   Besides the aesthetic improvement, what aspects of urban life would be affected by changes seen in the 1895 photograph?

3   What do these sources tell us about some of the chief concerns of urbanization, and how might they have differed from rural concerns?

7–2a | Charles J. Bushnell, map, Chicago, showing the locale of largest industries, 1901

Charles Joseph Bushnell (1875–1950), American sociologist, included this map in a 1901 *American Journal of Sociology* study on the neighborhoods near the Union Stock Yard in Chicago. As noted by Bushnell, he based the map on official drawings from city election commissioners and the commissioner of health. The shaded portion indicated the districts where, he argued, these abnormal conditions most generally existed. For Bushnell, "this district has all the characteristic traits of the industrial community."

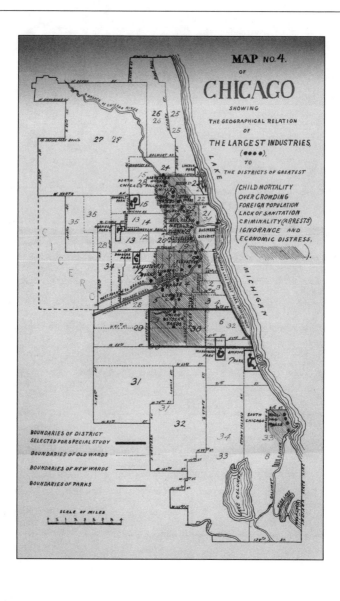

7–2b | Florence Kelley et al., map, nationalities in neighborhood near Chicago's Hull House, 1895

Inspired by the work of social researcher and reformer Charles Booth (1840–1916), who documented the poor of London, activist Jane Addams, Florence Kelley, and other Hull House settlement workers and residents published five years of research in *Hull House Maps and Papers* (1895). The publication included detailed maps highlighting the conditions within which Chicago's poor lived and worked. Below is Nationality Map No. 1, which depicts the diverse makeup of even this small area from W. Polk Street to W. Twelfth Street, north to south, and S. Jefferson to S. Halsted, east to west.

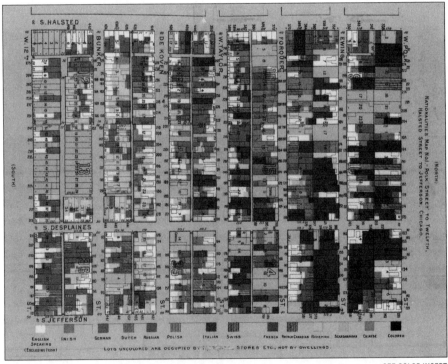

SEE COLOR INSERT

7–2c | Jane Addams, on the work of Hull House with immigrant populations, 1911

Jane Addams (1860–1935) was a leading American progressive social reformer and activist. In 1889, Jane Addams and Ellen Gates Starr (1859–1940) founded the nation's first settlement house, Hull House, in Chicago's impoverished and industrial west side. The year before, they found a model for their vision in Toynbee Hall, a settlement house serving the needy in London's East End. Addams and Starr drew volunteers to assist them as they offered a variety of social services to the urban poor, including English language education, job training, day care, cooking classes, job-placement services, and a community center. Addams' long career and international respect for her peace activism contributed to her receiving the Nobel Peace Prize in 1931, the first American women to receive this honor.

We have in America a fast-growing number of cultivated young people who have no recognized outlet for their active faculties. They hear constantly of the great social maladjustment, but no way is provided for them to change it, and their uselessness hangs about them heavily. Huxley declares that the sense of uselessness is the severest shock which the human system can sustain, and that if persistently sustained, it results in atrophy of function. These young people have had advantages of college, of European travel, and of economic study, but they are sustaining this shock of inaction. . . . Many of them dissipate their energies in so-called enjoyment. Others not content with that, go on studying and go back to college for their second degrees; not that they are especially fond of study, but because they want something definite to do, and their powers have been trained in the direction of mental accumulation. Many are buried beneath this mental accumulation with lowered vitality and discontent. . . .

This young life, so sincere in its emotion and good phrases and yet so undirected, seems to me as pitiful as the other great mass of destitute lives. One is supplementary to the other, and some method of communication can surely be devised. Mr. Barnett, who urged the first Settlement,—Toynbee Hall, in East London,—recognized this need of outlet for the young men of Oxford and Cambridge, and hoped that the Settlement would supply the communication. It is easy to see why the Settlement movement originated in England, where the years of education are more constrained and definite than they are here, where class distinctions are more rigid. The necessity of it was greater there, but we are fast feeling the pressure of the need and meeting the necessity for Settlements in America. Our young people feel nervously the need of putting theory into action, and respond quickly to the Settlement form of activity.

Other motives which I believe make toward the Settlement are the result of a certain renaissance going forward in Christianity. The impulse to share the lives of the poor, the desire to make social service, irrespective of propaganda, express the spirit of Christ, is as old as Christianity itself. . . .

That Christianity has to be revealed and embodied in the line of social progress is a corollary to the simple proposition, that man's action is found in his social relationships in the way in which he connects with his fellows; that his motives for action are the zeal and affection with which he regards his fellows. By this simple process was created a deep enthusiasm for humanity, which regarded man as at once the organ and the object of revelation; and by this process came about the wonderful fellowship, the true democracy of the early Church, that so captivates the imagination. The early Christians were preëminently nonresistant. They believed in love as a cosmic force. There was no iconoclasm during the minor peace of the Church. They did not yet denounce nor tear down temples, nor preach the end of the world. They grew to a mighty number, but it never occurred to them, either in their weakness or in their strength, to regard other men for an instant as their foes or as aliens. The spectacle of the Christians loving all men was the most astounding Rome had ever seen. They were eager to sacrifice themselves for the weak, for children, and for the aged; they identified themselves with slaves and did not avoid the plague; they longed to share the common lot that they might receive the constant revelation. It was a new treasure which the early Christians added to the sum of all treasures, a joy hitherto unknown in the world—the joy of finding the Christ which lieth in each man, but which no man can unfold save in fellowship. . . .

I believe that there is a distinct turning among many young men and women toward this simple acceptance of Christ's message. They resent the assumption that Christianity is a set of ideas which belong to the religious consciousness, whatever that may be. They insist that it cannot be proclaimed and instituted apart from the social life of the community and that it must seek a simple and natural expression in the social organism itself. The Settlement movement is only one manifestation of that wider humanitarian movement which throughout Christendom, but pre-eminently in England, is endeavoring to embody itself, not in a sect, but in society itself.

I believe that this turning, this renaissance of the early Christian humanitarianism, is going on in America, in Chicago, if you please, without leaders who write or philosophize, without much speaking, but with a bent to express in social service and in terms of action the spirit of Christ. Certain it is that spiritual force is found in the Settlement movement, and it is also true that this force must be evoked and must be called into play before the success of any Settlement is assured. There must be the overmastering belief that all that is noblest in life is common to men as men, in order to accentuate the likenesses and ignore the differences which are found among the people whom the Settlement constantly brings into juxtaposition. . . .

In a thousand voices singing the Hallelujah Chorus in Handel's "Messiah," it is possible to distinguish the leading voices, but the differences of training and cultivation between them and the voices in the chorus, are lost in the unity of purpose and in the fact that they are all human voices lifted by a high motive. This is a weak illustration of what a Settlement attempts to do. It aims, in a measure, to develop whatever of social life its neighborhood may afford, to focus and give form to that life, to bring to bear upon it the results of cultivation and training; but it receives in exchange for the music of isolated voices the volume and strength of the chorus. It is quite impossible for me to say in what proportion or degree the subjective necessity which led to the opening of Hull-House combined the three trends: first, the desire to interpret democracy in social terms; secondly, the impulse beating at the very source of our lives, urging us to aid in the race progress; and, thirdly, the Christian movement toward humanitarianism. It is difficult to analyze a living thing; the analysis is at best imperfect. Many more motives may blend with the three trends; possibly the desire for a new form of social success due to the nicety of imagination, which refuses worldly pleasures unmixed with the joys of self-sacrifice; possibly a love of approbation, so vast that it is not content with the treble clapping of delicate hands, but wishes also to hear the bass notes from toughened palms, may mingle with these.

The Settlement, then, is an experimental effort to aid in the solution of the social and industrial problems which are engendered by the modern conditions of life in a great city. It insists that these problems are not confined to any one portion of a city. It is an attempt to relieve, at the same time, the overaccumulation at one end of society and the destitution at the other; but it assumes that this overaccumulation and the destitution is most sorely felt in the things that pertain to social and educational privileges. From its very nature it can stand for no political or social propaganda. It must, in a sense, give the warm welcome of an inn to all such propaganda, if perchance one of them be found an angel. The only thing to be dreaded in the Settlement is that it lose its flexibility, its power of quick adaptation, its readiness to change its methods as its environment may demand. It must be open to conviction and must have a deep and abiding sense of tolerance. It must be hospitable and ready for experiment. It should demand from its residents a scientific patience in the accumulation of facts and the steady holding of their sympathies as one of the best instruments for that accumulation. It must be grounded in a philosophy whose foundation is on the solidarity of the human race, a philosophy which will not waver when the race happens to be represented by a drunken woman or an idiot boy. Its residents must be emptied of all conceit of opinion and all self-assertion, and ready to arouse and interpret the public opinion of their neighborhood. They must be content to live quietly side by side with their neighbors, until they grow into a sense of relationship and mutual interests. Their neighbors are held apart by differences of race and language which the residents can more easily overcome. They are bound to see the needs of their neighborhood as a whole, to furnish data for legislation, and to use their influence to secure it. In short, residents are pledged to devote themselves to the duties of good citizenship and to the arousing of the social energies which too largely lie dormant in every neighborhood given over to industrialism. They are bound to regard the entire life of their city as organic, to make an effort to unify it, and to protest against its over-differentiation.

DISCUSSION QUESTIONS

1   What do the two maps tell us about the population and conditions of Chicago in an era of rapid urbanization and industrialization?

2   According to Addams, what was the purpose of settlement houses, particularly Hull House? What impulses informed the movement?

3   Based on these sources, discuss the relationships between disparate groups in an urban environment.

7-3 | Irish immigrant trading cards, 1882

The composition of the Boston, Massachusetts, population changed rapidly in the nineteenth century. Although the Irish had been in the settlement since colonial times, a new wave of immigration to Boston began in the 1820s and accelerated during the Great Irish Famine (1845–1852). By 1850, the Irish comprised the largest ethnic group in Boston. Most of this wave of new immigration were poor, unskilled laborers from a rural background. The large number of Irish gave rise to both powerful political machines and elements concerned about Irish acculturation.

SEE COLOR INSERT

DISCUSSION QUESTIONS

1   How would you describe this Irish immigrant's transition over the ten-year period?

2   What do these trading cards tell us about assumptions made of new immigrants to the United States?

3   Do you think immigrants from other places would be viewed the same way? Why or why not?

7-4a | Cover, *Spalding's Official Baseball Guide*, 1889

Although the early nineteenth-century origins of baseball are unclear, by the 1880s the rapid urbanization of the United States and the increased availability of leisure time had created a climate for the organization and professionalization of the sport. The rise corresponded with the creation of the modern press, which had a customer base interested in regular and reliable information on their favorite team. Albert Spalding (1849–1915) was a pitcher, manager, and executive in professional baseball and co-founded A.G. Spalding sporting goods company (1876). Spalding published the first official rules guide for baseball, and *Spalding's Official Baseball Guide* was the most widely read baseball publication.

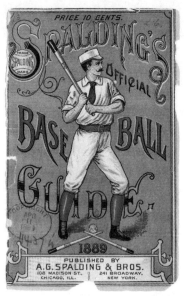

SEE COLOR INSERT

7-4b | Film poster, "Cinématographe Lumière," France, 1896

The Lumière brothers, Auguste Marie Louis Nicolas (1862–1954) and Louis Jean (1864–1948), were among the world's first filmmakers. They patented an improved motion picture film camera and projector, the cinematograph, showcased in the advertisement below. In this poster, the French short film *L'Arroseur Arrosé* (1895) is being shown. The Lumières directed and produced this 45-second piece of slapstick comedy. The novelty of pieces such as these delighted international audiences, finding a mass market in urban settings.

SEE COLOR INSERT

DISCUSSION QUESTIONS

1   How was the rise and popularity of each of these activities related to urbanization?

2   In what ways were these activities depicted as gendered?

3   What historical factors in the late eighteenth and early nineteenth centuries would have led to more focus on leisure activities?

7–5a | Ernesto Galarza, excerpts of *Barrio Boy*, 1910s

Dr. Ernesto Galarza (1905–1984), Mexican-American activist, professor, and writer, was born in Jalcocotán, Nayarit, Mexico. He immigrated to California at age six with his mother and two uncles after the Mexican Revolution began. Here, in a memoir written in 1972, he describes his experiences of the *barrio* and in the state's public school system. Galarza would later attend Occidental College and receive two advanced degrees, an MA in history and political science from Stanford University (1929) and a PhD in those disciplines from Columbia University (1947). He is considered a leading Chicano scholar of the twentieth century.

The older people of the *barrio*, except in those things which they had to do like the Americans because they had no choice, remained Mexican. Their language at home was Spanish. They were continuously taking up collections to pay somebody's funeral expenses or to help someone who had had a serious accident. Cards were sent to you to attend a burial where you would throw a handful of dirt on top of the coffin and listen to tearful speeches at the graveside. At every baptism a new *compadre* and a new *comadre* joined the family circle. New Year greeting cards were exchanged, showing angels and cherubs in bright colors sprinkled with grains of mica so that they glistened like gold dust. At the family parties the huge pot of steaming tamales was still the center of attention, the *atole* served on the side with chunks of brown sugar for sucking and crunching. If the party lasted long enough, someone produced a guitar, the men took over and the singing of *corridos* began.

In the *barrio* there were no individuals who had official titles or who were otherwise recognized by everybody as important people. The reason must have been that there was no place in the public business of the city of Sacramento for the Mexican immigrants. We only rented a corner of the city and as long as we paid the rent on time everything else was decided at City Hall or the County Court House, where Mexicans went only when they were in trouble. Nobody from the *barrio* ever ran for mayor or city councilman. For us the most important public officials were the policemen who walked their beats, stopped fights, and hauled drunks to jail in a paddy wagon we called *La Julia*.

The one institution we had that gave the *colonia* some kind of image was the *Comisión Honorífica*, a committee picked by the Mexican Consul in San Francisco to organize the celebration of the *Cinco de Mayo* and the Sixteenth of September, the anniversaries of the battle of Puebla and the beginning of our War of Independence. These were the two events which stirred everyone in the *barrio*, for what we were celebrating was not only the heroes of Mexico but also the feeling that we were still Mexicans ourselves. On these occasions there was a dance preceded by speeches and a concert. For both the *cinco* and the sixteenth queens were elected to preside over the ceremonies.

Between celebrations neither the politicians uptown nor the *Comisión Honorífica* attended to the daily needs of the *barrio*. This was done by volunteers—the ones who knew enough English to interpret in court, on a visit to the doctor, a call at the county hospital, and who could help make out a postal money order. By the time I had finished the third grade at the Lincoln School I was one of these volunteers. My services were not professional but they were free, except for the IOU's accumulated from families who always thanked me with, "God will pay you for it."

My clients were not *pochos*, Mexicans who had grown up in California, probably had even been born in the United States. They had learned to speak English of sorts and could still speak Spanish, also of sorts. They knew much more about the Americans than we did, and much less about us. The *chicanos* and the *pochos* had certain feelings about one another. Concerning the *pochos*, the *chicanos* suspected that they considered themselves too good for the *barrio* but were not, for some reason, good enough for the Americans. Toward the *chicanos*, the *pochos* acted superior, amused at our confusions but not especially interested in explaining them to us. In our family when I forgot my manners, my mother would ask me if I was turning *pochito*.

Turning *pocho* was a half-step toward turning American. And America was all around us, in and out of the *barrio*. Abruptly we had to forget the ways of shopping in a *mercado* and learn those of shopping in a corner grocery or in a department store. The Americans paid no attention to the Sixteenth of September, but they made a great commotion about the Fourth of July. In Mazatlán Don Salvador had told us, saluting and marching as he talked to our class, that the *Cinco de Mayo* was the most glorious date in history. The Americans had not even heard about it. . . . We were by now settled at 418 L Street and the time had come for me to exchange a revolution for an American education. . . .

During the next few weeks Miss Ryan overcame my fears of tall, energetic teachers as she bent over my desk to help me with a word in the pre-primer. Step by step, she loosened me and my classmates from the safe anchorage of the desks for recitations at the blackboard and consultations at her desk. Frequently she burst into happy announcements to the whole class. "Ito can read a sentence," and small Japanese Ito, squint-eyed and shy, slowly read aloud while the class listened in wonder: "Come, Skipper, come. Come and run." The Korean, Portuguese, Italian, and Polish first graders had similar moments of glory, no less shining than mine the day I conquered "butterfly," which I had been persistently pronouncing in standard Spanish as boo-ter-flee. "Children," Miss Ryan called for attention. "Ernesto has learned how to pronounce *butterfly*!" And I proved it with a perfect imitation of Miss Ryan. From that celebrated success, I was soon able to match Ito's progress as a sentence reader with "Come, butterfly, come fly with me." . . .

Like the first grade, the rest of the Lincoln School was a sampling of the lower part of town where many races made their home. My pals in the second grade were Kazushi, whose parents spoke only Japanese; Matti, a skinny Italian boy; and Manuel, a fat Portuguese who would never get into a fight but wrestled you to the ground and just sat on you. Our assortment of nationalities included Koreans, Yugoslavs, Poles, Irish, and home-grown Americans.

Miss Hopley and her teachers never let us forget why were were at Lincoln: for those who were alien, to become good Americans; for those who were so born, to accept the rest of us. Off the school grounds we traded the same insults were heard from our elders. On the playground we were sure to be marched up to the principal's office for calling someone a wop, a chink, a dago, or a greaser. The school was not so much a melting pot as a griddle where Miss Hopley and her helpers warmed knowledge into us and roasted racial hatreds out of us.

At Lincoln, making us into Americans did not mean scrubbing away what made us originally foreign. The teachers called us as our parents did, or as close as they could pronounce our names in Spanish or Japanese. No one was ever scolded or punished for speaking in his native tongue on the playground. Matti told the class about his mother's down quilt, which she had made in Italy with the fine feathers of a thousand geese. Encarnación acted out how boys learned to fish in Philippines. I astounded the third grade with the story of my travels on a stagecoach, which nobody else in the class had seen except in the museum at Sutter's Fort. After a visit to the Crocker Art Gallery and its collection of heroic paintings of the golden age of California, someone showed a silk scroll with a Chinese painting. Miss Hopley herself had a way of expressing wonder over these matters before a class, her eyes wide open until they popped slightly. It was easy for me to feel that becoming a proud American, as she said we should, did not mean feeling ashamed of being a Mexican.

The Americanization of Mexican me was no smooth matter. I had to fight one lout who made fun of my travels on the *diligencia*, and my barbaric translation of the word into "diligence." He doubled up with laughter over the word until I straightened him out with a kick. In class I made points explaining that in Mexico roosters said "qui-qui-ri-qui" and not "cock-a-doodle-doo," but after school I had to put up with the taunts of a big Yugoslav who said Mexican roosters were crazy.

But it was Homer who gave me the most lasting lesson for a future American.

Homer was a chunky Irishman who dressed as if every day was Sunday. He slicked his hair between a crew cut and a pompadour. And Homer was smart, as he clearly showed when he and I ran for president of the third grade.

Everyone understood that this was to be a demonstration of how the American people vote for president. In an election, the teacher explained, the candidates could be generous and vote for each other. We cast our ballots in a shoe box and Homer won by two votes. I polled my supporters and came to the conclusion that I had voted for Homer and so had he. After class he didn't deny it, reminding me of what the teacher had said—we could vote for each other but didn't have to.

7–5b | Excerpts of immigrant testimonies, ca. 1900

Hamilton Holt (1872–1951) worked as publisher and editor of the liberal weekly New York magazine *The Independent* from 1897 to 1921. As an outspoken reform advocate on many issues, including immigrant rights, he published *The Life Stories of Undistinguished Americans As Told By Themselves* in 1906. This publication was a compilation of sixteen of the more than seventy-five immigrant stories that had already appeared in pages of his weekly periodical. According to Holt, the "aim of each autobiography was to typify the life of the average worker in some particular vocation, and to make each story the genuine experience of a real person."

Story of a Lithuanian

[After I arrived in the United States] Everything got quicker—worse and worse—till then at last I was in a boarding house by the stockyards in Chicago with three Lithuanians, who knew my father's sisters at home.

That first night we sat around in the house and they asked me, "Well, why did you come?" I told them about that first night and what the ugly shoemaker said about "life, liberty and the getting of happiness." They all leaned back and laughed. "What you need is money," they said. "It was all right at home. You wanted nothing. You ate your own meat and your own things on the farm. You made your own clothes and had your own leather. The other things you got at the Jew man's store and paid him with sacks of rye. But here you want a hundred things.

Whenever you walk out you see new things you want, and you must have money to buy everything."

Then one asked me, "How much have you?" and I told him $30. "You must buy clothes to look rich, even if you are not rich," he said, "With good clothes you will have friends."

The next morning three of these men took me to a store near the stockyards to buy a coat and pants. . . . "You stand still. That is all you have to do," they said. So the Jew man kept putting on coats and I moved my arms and back and sides when they told me. We stayed there till it was time for dinner. Then we bought a suit. I paid $5 and then I was to pay $1 a week for five weeks. . . .

The next night they took me for a walk down town. We would not pay to ride, so we walked so long that I wanted to take my shoes off, but I did not tell them this. When we came there I forgot my feet. We stood by one theater and watched for half an hour. Then we walked all around a store that filled one whole block and had walls of glass. Then we had a drink of whiskey, and this is better than vodka. We felt happier and looked into *cafés*. We saw shiny carriages and automobiles. I saw men with dress suits, I saw women with such clothes that I could not think at all. Then my friends punched me and I turned around and saw one of these women, and with her was a gentleman in a fine dress suit. I began looking harder. It was the Jew man that sold me my suit. . . . Then we walked home and I felt poor and my shoes got very bad. . . .

The next morning my friends woke me up at five o'clock and said, "Now, if you want life, liberty and happiness," they laughed, "you must push for yourself. You must get a job. Come with us." And we went to the yards. Men and women were walking in by thousands as far as we could see. We went to the doors of one big slaughter house. There was a crowd of about 200 men waiting there for a job. They looked hungry and kept watching the door. At last a special policeman came out and began pointing to men, one by one. Each one jumped forward. Twenty-three were taken. Then they all went inside, and all the others turned their faces away and looked tired. I remember one boy sat down and cried, just next to me, on a pile of boards. Some policemen waved their clubs and we all walked on. I found some Lithuanians to talk with, who told me they had come every morning for three weeks. Soon we met other crowds coming away from other slaughter houses, and we all walked around and felt bad and tired and hungry.

That night I told my friends that I would not do this many days, but would go some place else. "Where?" they asked me, and I began to see then that I was in bad trouble, because I spoke no English. Then one man told me to give him $5 to give the special policeman. I did this and the next morning the policeman pointed me out, so I had a job. I have heard some big talk since then about my American freedom of contract, but I do not think I had much freedom in bargaining for this job with the Meat Trust. My job was in the cattle killing room. I pushed the blood along the gutter. . . . One Lithuanian who worked with me, said, "They get all the blood out of those cattle and all the work out of us men." This was true, for we worked that first day from six in the morning till seven at night. The next day we worked from six in the morning till eight at night.

The next day we had no work. So we had no good, regular hours. It was hot in the room that summer, and the hot blood made it worse. . . .

The Republican boss in our district, Jonidas, was a saloon keeper. A friend took me there. Jonidas shook hands and treated me fine. He taught me to sign my name, and the next week I went with him to an office and signed some paper, and then I could vote. I voted as I was told, and then they got me back into the yards to work, because one big politician owns stock in one of the houses. Then I felt that was getting in beside the game. I was in a combine like other sharp men. Even when work was slack I was all right, because they got me a job in the street cleaning department. I felt proud, and I went to the back room in Jonidas's saloon and got him to write a letter to Alexandrìa to tell her she must come soon and be my wife.

But this was just the trouble. All of us were telling our friends to come soon. Soon they came—even thousands. The employers in the yard liked this, because those sharp foremen are inventing new machines and the work is easier to learn, and so these slow Lithuanians and even green girls can learn to do it, and then the Americans and Germans and Irish are put out and the employer saves money, because the Lithuanians work cheaper. This was why the American labor unions began to organize us all just the same as they had organized the Bohemians and Poles before us. . . .

With more time and more money I live much better and I am very happy. So is Alexandrìa. She came a year ago and has learned to speak English already. Some of the women go to the big store the day they get here, when they have not enough sense to pick out the clothes that look right, but Alexandrìa waited three weeks till she knew, and so now she looks the finest of any woman in the district. We have four nice rooms, which she keeps very clean, and she has flowers growing in boxes in the two front windows. We do not go much to church, because the church seems to be too slow. But we belong to a Lithuanian society that gives two picnics in summer and two big balls in winter, where we have a fine time. I go one night a week to the Lithuanian Concertina Club. On Sundays we go on the trolley out into the country.

But we like to stay at home more now because we have a baby. When he grows up I will not send him to the Lithuanian Catholic school. They have only two bad rooms and two priests who teach only in Lithuanian from prayer books. I will send him to the American school, which is very big and good. The teachers there are Americans and they belong to the Teachers' Labor Union, which has three thousand teachers and belongs to our Chicago Federation of Labor. I am sure that such teachers will give him a good chance.

Story of a Polish Sweatshop Girl

I lived at this time with a girl named Ella, who worked in the same factory and made $5 a week. We had the room all to ourselves, paying $1.50 a week for it, and doing light housekeeping. It was in Allen street, and the window looked out of the back, which was good, because there was an elevated railroad in front, and in summer time a great deal of dust and dirt came in at the front windows. We were on the fourth story and could see all that was going on in the back rooms of the houses behind us, and early in the morning the sun used to come in our window.

We did our cooking on an oil stove, and lived well, as this list of our expenses for one week will show:

Ella and Sadie for Food	(one week)
Tea	$0.06
Cocoa	.10
Bread and rolls	.40
Canned vegetables	.20
Potatoes	.10
Milk	.21
Fruit	.20
Butter	.15
Meat	.60
Fish	.15
Laundry	.25
	————
Total	$2.42
Add rent	1.50
	————
Grand Total	$3.92

Of course, we could have lived cheaper, but we are both fond of good things and felt that we could afford them.

We paid 18 cents for a half pound of tea so as to get it good, and it lasted us three weeks, because we had cocoa for breakfast. We paid 5 cents for six rolls and 5 cents a loaf for bread, which was the best quality. Oatmeal cost us 10 cents for three and one-half pounds, and we often had it in the morning, or Indian meal porridge in the place of it, costing about the same. Half a dozen eggs cost about 13 cents on an average, and we could get all the meat we wanted for a good hearty meal for 20 cents—two pounds of chops, or a steak, or a bit of veal, or a neck of lamb—something like that. Fish included butter fish, porgies, codfish and smelts, averaging about 8 cents a pound.

Some people who buy at the last of the market, when the men with the carts want to go home, can get things very cheap, but they are likely to be stale, and we did not often do that with fish, fresh vegetables, fruit, milk or meat. Things that kept well we did buy that way and got good bargains. I got thirty potatoes for 10 cents one time, though generally I could not get more than fifteen of them for that amount. Tomatoes, onions and cabbages, too, we bought that way and did well, and we found a factory where we could buy the finest broken crackers for 3 cents a pound, and another place where we got broken candy for 10 cents a pound. Our cooking was done on an oil stove, and the oil for the stove and the lamp cost us 10 cents a week.

It cost me $2 a week to live, and I had a dollar a week to spend on clothing and pleasure, and saved the other dollar. I went to night school, but it was hard work learning at first as I did not know much English.

Story of a Japanese Servant

The desire to see America was burning at my boyish heart. The land of freedom and civilization of which I heard so much from missionaries and the wonderful story of America I heard of those of my race who returned from here made my longing ungovernable. Meantime I have been reading a popular novel among the boys, "The Adventurous Life of Tsurukichi Tanaka, Japanese Robinson Crusoe." How he acquired new knowledge from America and how he is honored and favored by the capitalists in Japan. How willingly he has endured the hardships in order to achieve the success. The story made a strong impression on my mind. Finally I made up my mind to come to this country to receive an American education.

I was an orphan and the first great trouble was who will help me the expense? I have some property my father left for me. But a minor has not legally inherited, hence no power to dispossess them. There must be at least 200 yen for the fare and equipment. While 200 yen has only exchange value to $100 of American gold. the sum is really a considerable amount for a boy. Two hundred yen will be a sufficient capital to start a small grocery store in the country town or to start a prospective fish market in the city. Of course, my uncle shook his head and would not allow me to go to America. After a great deal of difficulty and delay I have prevailed over his objection. My heart swelled joy when I got a passport, Government permission to leave the country, after waiting thirty days investigated if really I am a student and who are the guardians to pay money in case of necessity. A few days later I found myself on board the *Empress of Japan*, of the Canadian Pacific Line. The moment steamer commence to leave Yokohama I wished to jump back to shore, but was too late and I was too old and ashamed to cry.

After the thirteen days' weary voyage we reached Victoria, B.C. When I have landed there I have disappointed as there not any wonderful sight to be seen not much different that of foreign settlement in Yokohama. My destination was Portland, Ore., where my cousin is studying. Before I took a boat in Puget Sound to Tacoma, Wash., we have to be examined by the immigration officer. To my surprise these officers looked to me like a plain citizen—no extravagant dignity, no authoritative air. I felt so envious, I said to myself, "Ah! Indeed this is the characteristic of democracy, equality of personal right so well shown." I respect the officers more on this account. They asked me several questions. I answered with my broken English I have learned at Yokohama Commercial School. Finally they said: "So you are a student? How much money have you at hand?" I showed them $50. The law requires $30. The officers gave me a piece of stamped paper—certificate—to permit me go into the United States. I left Victoria 8 p.m. and arrived Tacoma, Wash., 6 a.m. Again I have surprised with the muddy streets and the dirty wharf. I thought the wharf of Yokohama is hundred times better. Next morning I left for Portland, Ore.

Great disappointment and regret I have experienced when I was told that I, the boy of 17 years old, smaller in stature indeed than an ordinary 14 years old American boy, imperfect in English knowledge, I can be any use here, but become a domestic servant, as the field for Japanese very narrow and limited. Thus reluctantly I have submitted to be a recruit of the army of domestic servants of which I ever dreamed up to this time. The place where I got to work in the first time was a boarding house. My duties were to peel potatoes, wash the dishes, a few laundry work, and also I was expected to do whatever mistress, waitress and cook has told me.

When I first entered the kitchen wearing a white apron what an uncomfortable and mortifying feeling I experienced. I thought I shall never be able to proceed the work. I felt as if I am pressed down on my shoulder with loaded tons of weight. My heart palpitates. I did not know what I am and what to say. I stood by the door of kitchen motionless like a stone, with a dumfounded silence. The cook gave me a scornful look and said nothing. Perhaps at her first glance she perceived me entirely unfit to be her help. A kindly looking waitress, slender, alert Swedish girl, sympathetically put the question to me if I am first time to work. She said, "Oh! well, you will get learn and soon be used to it!" as if she has fully understand the situation. Indeed, this ordinary remarks were such a encouragement. She and cook soon opened the conference how to rescue me. In a moment I was to the mercy of Diana of the kitchen like Arethusa. Whistling up the courage I started to work. The work being entirely new and also such an unaccustomed one, I felt exceedingly unpleasant and hard. . . .

After I stay there about ten days I asked the old lady that I should be discharged. She wanted me to state the reason. My real objection was that the work was indeed too hard and unpleasant for me to bear and also there were no time even to read a book. But I thought it rather impolite to say so and partly my strange pride hated to confess my weakness, fearing the reflection as a lazy boy. Really I could not think how smoothly I should tell my reasons. So I kept silent rather with a stupefied look. She suggested me if the work were not too hard. It was just the point, but how foolish I was; I did positively denied. "Then why can you not stay here?" she went on. I said, childishly, "I have nothing to complain; simply I wants to go back to New York. My passion wants to." Then she smiled and said, "Poor boy; you better think over; I shall speak to you to-morrow." Next day she told me how she shall be sorry to lose me just when I have began to be handy to her after the hard task to taught me work how. Tactfully she persuaded me to stay. At the end of second week I asked my wages, but she refused on the ground that if she does I might leave her. Day by day my sorrow and regret grew stronger. My heavy heart made me feel so hard to work. At that moment I felt as if I am in the prison assigned to the hard labor. My coveted desire was to be freed from the yoke of this old lady. Believing the impossibility to obtain her sanction, early in the next morning while everybody still in the bed, I hide my satchel under the bush in the back yard. When mistress went on market afternoon, while everybody is busy, I have jumped out from the window and climbed up the fence to next door and slip away. Leaving the note and wages behind me, I hurried back to Japanese Christian Home.

Since then I have tried a few other places with a better success at each trial and in course of time I have quite accustomed to it and gradually become indifferent as the humiliation melted down. Though I never felt proud of this vocation, in several cases I have commenced to manifest the interest of my avocation as a professor of Dust and Ashes. . . .

DISCUSSION QUESTIONS

1   How did these immigrants describe their reasons for coming to the United States?

2   What were their experiences when they arrived? How were they different or similar based on age, nationality, and sex?

3   Did these testimonies change your understanding of immigrant experiences? Why or why not?

7–6a | *Le Petit Journal*, cover, "Les 'lynchages' aux États-Unis," France, 1906

In the Atlanta Race Riot of 1906 (September 22–24), white mobs killed dozens of African Americans and wounded scores more. The causes, which were complex, included strict Jim Crow segregation, economic competition, strains between the black upper and working class of Atlanta, prohibition efforts, rising crime rates, and sensationalized newspaper reports. On September 22, 1906, news broke of four alleged assaults, none of which were ever substantiated, upon local white women. A white crowd gathered in downtown Atlanta turned into a mob and began attacking black-owned businesses. The white vigilante groups expanded the violence into the city's black neighborhoods until the riot ended two days later. The events in Atlanta made international news, including the French example below. *Le Petit Journal* was a conservative Parisian newspaper, published daily.

SEE COLOR INSERT

7–6b | Liang Qichao, on lynching in America, China, 1903

Liang Qichao (1873–1929), often considered one of the leading Chinese intellects of the early twentieth century, was a disciple of scholar Kang Youwei, who reinterpreted the classical writings of Confucius to justify widespread innovations he prescribed for Chinese culture. When the Empress Dowager Cixi (1835–1908) ended reforms, he narrowly escaped his home country to settle in Japan in 1898. He lived there in exile for the next fourteen years. It was during this period that he embarked on an eight-month lecture tour of the United States, subsequently publishing his travel memoir.

Americans have an unofficial form of punishment known as "lynching" with which to treat blacks. Such a phenomenon is unimaginable among civilized countries. It started with a farmer named Lynch. Because he had been offended by a black, he suspended him from a tree to wait for the police officers to arrive, but the black man died before they came. So his name has been used for this ever since. Recently the common practice is burning people to death. Whenever a black has committed an offense a mob will be directly gathered and burn him without going through the courts.

Had I only been told about this and not been to America myself I would not have believed that such cruel and inhuman acts could be performed in broad daylight in the twentieth century. During the ten months I was in America I counted no less than ten-odd accounts of this strange business in the newspapers. At first I was shocked, but have become accustomed to reading about it and no longer consider it strange. Checking the statistics on it, there have been an average of 157 such private punishments each year since 1884. Hah! When Russia killed a hundred and some score Jews, the whole world considered it savage. But I do not know how to decide which is worse, America or Russia.

. . . Why does the government allow wanton lynchings to go unpunished even though there is a judiciary? The reason is none other than preconceived opinions about race. The American Declaration of Independence says that people are all born free and equal. Are blacks alone not people? Alas, I now understand what it is that is called "civilization" these days!

DISCUSSION QUESTIONS

1 What is the main argument of each of these sources?
2 What do these sources tell you about non-U.S. perspectives on the United States' treatment of black citizens?

REFORM

7–7a | Poor Law Commissioners, excerpts from the inquiry into the sanitary conditions of the laboring population of Great Britain, UK, 1842

Edwin Chadwick (1800–1890) was an English lawyer and member of the Poor Law Commission in the mid-nineteenth century, called to reconsider social welfare laws in Great Britain. Chadwick financed a three-year investigation into sanitation and its role in the spread of disease in cities, utilizing doctors to document illnesses and personally surveying all sorts of public officials, builders, and engineers to detail the living conditions of poor people. His 1842 report, excerpted here, resulted in the Public Health Act of 1848, which set precedents for the role of the state in public health maintenance. It is worth noting that Chadwick's report predates scientific proof or widespread acceptance of germ theory.

After as careful an examination of the evidence collected as I have been enabled to make, I beg leave to recapitulate the chief conclusions which that evidence appears to me to establish.

First, as to the extent and operation of the evils which are the subject of this inquiry:—

That the various forms of epidemic, endemic, and other disease caused, or aggravated, or propagated chiefly amongst the labouring classes by atmospheric impurities produced by decomposing animal and vegetable substances, by damp and filth, and close and over-crowded dwellings prevail amongst the population in every part of the kingdom, whether dwelling in separate houses, in rural villages, in small towns, in the larger towns—as they have been found to prevail in the lowest districts of the metropolis.

That such disease, wherever its attacks are frequent, is always found in connexion with the physical circumstances above specified, and that where those circumstances are removed by drainage, proper cleansing, better ventilation, and other means of diminishing atmospheric impurity, the frequency and intensity of such disease is abated; and where the removal of the noxious agencies appears to be complete, such disease almost entirely disappears.

The high prosperity in respect to employment and wages, and various and abundant food, have afforded to the labouring classes no exemptions from attacks of epidemic disease, which have been as frequent and as fatal in periods of commercial and manufacturing prosperity as in any others.

That the formation of all habits of cleanliness is obstructed by defective supplies of water.

That the annual loss of life from filth and bad ventilation are greater than the loss from death or wounds in any wars in which the country has been engaged in modern times.

That of the 43,000 cases of widowhood, and 112,000 cases of destitute orphanage relieved from the poor's rates in England and Wales alone, it appears that the greatest proportion of deaths of the heads of families occurred from the above specified and other removable causes; that their ages were under 45 years; that is to say, 13 years below the natural probabilities of life as shown by the experience of the whole population of Sweden.

That the public loss from the premature deaths of the heads of families is greater than can be represented by any enumeration of the pecuniary burdens consequent upon their sickness and death.

That, measuring the loss of working ability amongst large classes by the instances of gain, even from incomplete arrangements for the removal of noxious influences from places of work or from abodes, that this loss cannot be less than eight or ten years.

That the ravages of epidemics and other diseases do not diminish but tend to increase the pressure of population.

That in the districts where the mortality is greatest the births are not only sufficient to replace the numbers removed by death, but to add to the population.

That the younger population, bred up under noxious physical agencies, is inferior in physical organization and general health to a population preserved from the presence of such agencies.

That the population so exposed is less susceptible of moral influences, and the effects of education are more transient than with a healthy population.

That these adverse circumstances tend to produce an adult population short-lived, improvident, reckless, and intemperate, and with habitual avidity for sensual gratifications.

That these habits lead to the abandonment of all the conveniences and decencies of life, and especially lead to the overcrowding of their homes, which is destructive to the morality as well as the health of large classes of both sexes.

That defective town cleansing fosters habits of the most abject degradation and tends to the demoralization of large numbers of human beings, who subsist by means of what they find amidst the noxious filth accumulated in neglected streets and bye-places.

That the expenses of local public works are in general unequally and unfairly assessed, oppressively and uneconomically collected, by separate collections, wastefully expended in separate and inefficient operations by unskilled and practically irresponsible officers.

That the existing law for the protection of the public health and the constitutional machinery for reclaiming its execution, such as the Courts Leet, have fallen into desuetude, and are in the state indicated by the prevalence of the evils they were intended to prevent.

Secondly. As to the means by which the present sanitary condition of the labouring classes may be improved:—

The primary and most important measures, and at the same time the most practicable, and within the recognized province of public administration, are drainage, the removal of all refuse of habitations, streets, and roads, and the improvement of the supplies of water.

That the chief obstacles to the immediate removal of decomposing refuse of towns and habitations have been the expense and annoyance of the hand labour and cartage requisite for the purpose.

That this expense may be reduced to one-twentieth or to one-thirtieth, or rendered inconsiderable, by the use of water and self-acting means of removal by improved and cheaper sewers and drains.

That refuse when thus held in suspension in water may be most cheaply and innoxiously conveyed to any distance out of towns, and also in the best form for productive use, and that the loss and injury by the pollution of natural streams may be avoided.

That for all these purposes, as well as for domestic use, better supplies of water are absolutely necessary.

That for successful and economical drainage the adoption of geological areas as the basis of operations is requisite.

That appropriate scientific arrangements for public drainage would afford important facilities for private land-drainage, which is important for the health as well as sustenance of the labouring classes.

That the expense of public drainage, of supplies of water laid on in houses, and of means of improved cleansing would be a pecuniary gain, by diminishing the existing charges attendant on sickness and premature mortality.

That for the protection of the labouring classes and of the ratepayers against inefficiency and waste in all new structural arrangements for the protection of the public health, and to ensure public confidence that the expenditure will be beneficial, securities should be taken that all new local public works are devised and conducted by responsible officers qualified by the possession of the science and skill of civil engineers.

That the oppressiveness and injustice of levies for the whole immediate outlay on such works upon persons who have only short interests in the benefits may be avoided by care in spreading the expense over periods coincident with the benefits.

That by appropriate arrangements, 10 or 15 per cent. on the ordinary outlay for drainage might be saved, which on an estimate of the expense of the necessary structural alterations of one-third only of the existing tenements would be a saving of one million and a half sterling, besides the reduction of the future expenses of management.

That for the prevention of the disease occasioned by defective ventilation, and other causes of impurity in places of work and other places where large numbers are assembled, and for the general promotion of the means necessary to prevent disease, that it would be good economy to appoint a district medical officer independent of private practice, and with the securities of special qualifications and responsibilities to initiate sanitary measures and reclaim the execution of the law.

That by the combinations of all these arrangements, it is probable that the full ensurable period of life indicated by the Swedish tables; that is, an increase of 13 years at least, may be extended to the whole of the labouring classes.

That the attainment of these and the other collateral advantages of reducing existing charges and expenditure are within the power of the legislature, and are dependent mainly on the securities taken for the application of practical science, skill, and economy in the direction of local public works.

And that the removal of noxious physical circumstances, and the promotion of civic, household, and personal cleanliness, are necessary to the improvement of the moral condition of the population; for that sound morality and refinement in manners and health are not long found co-existent with filthy habits amongst any class of the community.

7–7b | Sarah Friedman Dworetz, testimony of survivor of the Triangle Shirtwaist Factory Fire, 1958

Sarah Friedman Dworetz survived the 1911 Triangle Shirtwaist Fire in New York City's Greenwich Village, a horrific industrial "accident" in which a fire swept through the upper floors of a garment factory. Panicked workers were only able to escape via one fire escape—which collapsed—and one elevator, trapped by locked or inward-swinging doors and beyond the reach of contemporary fire ladders, resulting in the death of 146 workers, mostly immigrant women and teenagers. An excerpt of Dworetz's testimony, recorded in 1958, follows. After the disaster, despite the owners of the company being found not guilty of manslaughter, state officials passed dozens of labor laws and a Department of Labor to improve working conditions in New York.

Sarah Friedman Dworetz

Job: unknown

9th floor

Interviewed: June 12, 1958

On the day of the fire I was working on the 9th floor, I had gotten my pay and we were all ready to leave and all dressed.

The fire must have been burning on the 8th floor for some time when we went to the freight elevator exit to go home. We had to leave that way because that is the way the watchman was able to look in our bags and where he stayed.

There was a narrow vestibule leading to the freight elevator. I was waiting in that vestibule when all of a sudden the smoke, and then the fire, began to come up the elevator shaft. I turned to run back to the other end of the shop where the freight elevator was. I took one look into the shop as I ran and I saw the flames coming in from all sides.

The elevators were going up and down. On the front side the door to the staircase was closed. I had to fight and push my way across the shop. There was screaming and shoving and many girls tried to climb over the machine tables.

The elevator had made several trips. I knew this was the last one but it was so loaded that the car started to go down. The door was not closed. Suddenly I was holding to the sides of the door looking down the elevator shaft with girls screaming and pushing behind me.

It was the old style elevator—cable elevator—to make it go down, you pulled the cable from the floor up. That cable was at the side of the elevator shaft. I reached out and grabbed it. I remember sliding all the way down. I was the first one to slide down the shaft. I ended up on top of the elevator and then I lost consciousness. Others must have landed on top of me. When the rescue workers came to the shaft they pulled me out and laid me out on the street. I had a broken leg, broken arm. My skull had been injured. One of my hands had been burned by friction.

NOTE: (apparently this is a case in which the victim, taken for dead, was removed with the other bodies but separated from them when life was detected in time.)

They moved me into the book store. My only worry was that I did not want to go to a hospital. We lived on 170 Henry St. I was only afraid of the shock to my mother. I lived on the 4th floor.

I was sick for 6 months.

I never heard from the company after.

At the trial, the lawyer asked me over and over again but I refused to say that the door was open.

We got a $1.50 for being witnesses.

I must have worked there about a year at the time of the fire but the day of the fire was the first time I tried to use the front elevator.

NOTE: Mrs. Dworetz learned in this interview for the first time that there was a fire escape.

While we were on the freight side I saw flames in the shop. The flames were all around us as we ran across the floor.

When I got home I still had my pay envelope still clutched in my hand.

NOTE: Mrs. Dworetz volunteered the information that every time March 25th rolls around many of these event[s] seize her.

She said that some people are amused by her practice of not locking her door when she is at summer resorts but she says they just don't understand.

DISCUSSION QUESTIONS

1   What factors help explain the living and working conditions of the working class?

2   Describe the connections that were being made between these conditions and morality.

3   One of these reform efforts was caused by disease, the other by a deadly fire. What might that suggest about the relationship between catastrophe and reform? Explain.

7–8a | Preface to the General Rules of The International Workingmen's Association, UK, 1864

Labor unions, or trade unions, emerged with industrialization and the creation of a working class. The purpose of a union was—and is—to represent its members, whether a particular group of people with specific skills, a national group of unskilled laborers, or an international group of professionals, through collective bargaining and agreements with employers. The first unions began in Great Britain in the eighteenth century, though only in 1871 were they legalized, and spread to other industrializing countries in the mid- to late nineteenth century. The International Workingmen's Association (IWA), founded in 1864 in London, was the first attempt at bringing unions and workers of varying leftist political persuasions around the world under an international umbrella organization. Sometimes called the First International, the IWA gained millions of members and exercised considerable influence until its demise in 1881. Below is the preamble to its list of organizational rules.

Considering,

That the emancipation of the working classes must be conquered by the working classes themselves; that the struggle for the emancipation of the working classes means not a struggle for class privileges and monopolies, but for equal rights and duties, and the abolition of all class rule;

That the economical subjection of the man of labour to the monopoliser of the means of labour, that is the sources of life, lies at the bottom of servitude in all its forms, of all social misery, mental degradation, and political dependence;

That the economical emancipation of the working classes is therefore the great end to which every political movement ought to be subordinate as a means;

That all efforts aiming at the great end hitherto failed from the want of solidarity between the manifold divisions of labour in each country, and from the absence of a fraternal bond of union between the working classes of different countries;

That the emancipation of labour is neither a local, nor a national, but a social prob- lem, embracing all countries in which modern society exists, and depending for its solution on the concurrence, practical and theoretical, of the most advanced countries;

That the present revival of the working classes in the most industrious countries of Europe, while it raises a new hope, gives solemn warning against a relapse into the old errors, and calls for the immediate combination of the still disconnected movements;

For these reasons:–

> The first International Working Men's Association declares that this
> International Association and all societies and individuals adhering
> to it will acknowledge truth, justice, and morality, as the basis of their
> conduct towards each other, and towards all men, without regard to
> colour, creed or nationality;

This Congress considers it the duty of a man to claim the rights of a man and of a citizen, not only for himself, but for every man who does his duty. No rights without duties, no duties without rights;

7-8b | Walter Crane, woodcut, *Solidarity of Labor,* UK, 1889

English artist-illustrator Walter Crane (1845–1915), while best known for his influential and striking illustrations in children's books, enjoyed another title: "the artist of socialism." Crane, a committed socialist, contributed designs for book illustrations, posters, ads, invitation cards, magazine covers, insignias, and even firework displays, "for the cause." This 1889 woodcut, after a picture by Crane, celebrates the creation of the first Labor Day—or First of May—as an international holiday of the working class movement. The German words on the banner near the top read "Equality," "Freedom," and "Brotherhood," while the banner across the globe reads "Workers of the World Unite! Karl Marx." Place-names can be found on other banners.

SEE COLOR INSERT

DISCUSSION QUESTIONS

1   How did the International Workingmen's Association explain the need for solidarity among laborers all over the world?

2   Describe the illustration. What does it depict?

3   What is the historical significance of the quotation on the illustration? How might that connect to other events in the twentieth century?

7–9a | Lewis Hine, photograph, "Manuel, the Young Shrimp Picker," 1911

The title of this 1911 photograph reads, "Manuel, the young shrimp-picker, five years old, and a mountain of child-labor oyster shells behind him. He worked last year. Understands not a word of English." Famed photographer and reformer Lewis Hine (1874–1940) took this picture in Biloxi, Mississippi, at the Dunbar, Lopez, Dukate Company while freelancing for the National Child Labor Committee (NCLC). The NCLC was a private non-profit agency advocating child labor reform in the United States. Hine took over five thousand photographs between 1908 and 1924, documenting working and living conditions for U.S. workers—including children—many of which were published in publications, newspapers, and presentations by the NCLC.

7–9b | Poster, "Some Questions Answered—National Child Labor Committee," 1914

According to the 1900 U.S. census, over 20 percent of children between the ages of ten and fifteen were employed, mostly in agriculture, but also in industry. The National Child Labor Committee, founded in 1904, sought to both end child labor and establish free, mandatory public education for all children. It eventually became the largest and most significant national child welfare organization. Below is an example of an NCLC exhibit panel, probably from about 1914, featuring two more of Hine's photographs in an effort to counter arguments made by those resistant to child labor laws. Though the NCLC successfully guided a number of state laws prohibiting child labor through to adoption in the early twentieth century, Congress passed no federal law affecting child labor until the 1938 Fair Labor Standards Act. A 1924 Child Labor Amendment to the Constitution passed, but was never ratified.

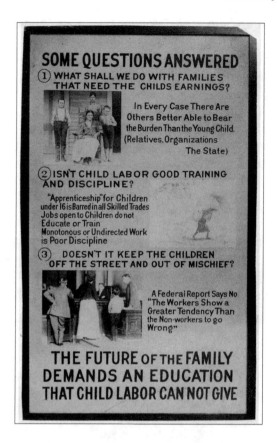

DISCUSSION QUESTIONS

1   How would you describe the boy in the photo? What about the work he is doing?

2   Consider the poster. Why do you think those particular questions are being addressed? What evidence was provided in response to the questions?

3   What historical factors led to such widespread child labor?

7–10a | H. D. Lloyd, excerpt from
"The Story of a Great Monopoly," *The Atlantic Monthly*, 1881

The excerpt here, from an 1881 article in *The Atlantic Monthly* by muckraker-journalist Henry Demarest Lloyd (1847–1903), was one of the first investigative exposés by progressives determined to reveal corruption in U.S. institutions. In so doing, Lloyd took on the Standard Oil Company (est. 1870), an enormously powerful monopoly headed by millionaire John D. Rockefeller, and Cornelius Vanderbilt, the wealthiest man in the United States. Though Lloyd's controversial essay has been shown to have included some false evidence, his charges and moral argument against corruption struck a chord with readers. *The Atlantic Monthly* reported that the issue sold out seven times and initiated serious discussions about antitrust legislation.

When Commodore Vanderbilt began the world he had nothing, and there were no steamboats or railroads. He was thirty-five years old when the first locomotive was put into use in America. When he died, railroads had become the greatest force in modern industry, and Vanderbilt was the richest man in Europe or America, and the largest owner of railroads in the world. He used the finest business brain of his day and the franchise of the state to build up a kingdom within the republic, and like a king he bequeathed his wealth and power to his eldest son. Bancroft's History of the United States and our railroad system were begun at the same time.

The history is not yet finished, but the railroads owe on stocks and bonds $4,600,000,000, more than twice our national debt of $2,220,000,000, and tax the people annually $490,000,000, one and a half times more than the government's revenue last year of $274,000,000. More than any other class, our railroad men have developed the country, and tried its institutions. The evasion of almost all taxes by the New York Central Railroad has thrown upon the people of New York State more than a fair share of the cost of government, and illustrates some of the methods by which the rich are making the poor poorer. Violations of trust by Credit Mobiliers, Jay Gould's wealth and the poverty of Erie stockholders, such corruption of legislatures as gave the Pacific Mail its subsidies, and nicknamed New Jersey "The State of Camden and Amboy," are sins against the public and private faith on a scale impossible in the early days of republics and corporations.

A lawsuit still pending, though begun ten years ago by a citizen of Chicago, to recover the value of baggage destroyed by the Pennsylvania Railroad; Judge Barnard's midnight orders for the Erie ring; the surrender of its judicial integrity by the supreme court of Pennsylvania at the bidding of the Pennsylvania Railroad, as charged before Congress by President Gowen, of the Reading Railroad; the veto by the Standard Oil Company of the enactment of a law by the Pennsylvania legislature to carry out the provision of the constitution of the State that every one should have equal rights on the railroads,—these are a few of the many things that have happened to kill the confidence of our citizens in the laws and the administration of justice. No other system of taxation has borne as heavily on the people as those extortions and inequalities of railroad charges which caused the granger outburst in the West, and the recent uprising in New York. In the actual physical violence with which railroads have taken their rights of way through more than one American city, and in the railroad strikes of 1876 and 1877 with the anarchy that came with them, there are social disorders we hoped never to see in America. These incidents in railroad history show most of the points where we fail, as between man and man, employer and employed, the public and the corporation, the state and the citizen, to maintain the equities of "government"—and employment—"of the people, by the people, for the people."

Our treatment of "the railroad problem" will show the quality and calibre of our political sense. It will go far in foreshadowing the future lines of our social and political growth. It may indicate whether the American democracy, like all the democratic experiments which have preceded it, is to become extinct because the people had not wit enough or virtue enough to make the common good supreme.

. . .

[Standard Oil]

Its genius for monopoly has given the Standard control of more than the product of oil and its manufacture. Wholesale merchants in all the cities of the country, except New York, have to buy and sell at the prices it makes. Merchants who buy oil of the Standard are not allowed to sell to dealers who buy of its few competitors. Some who have done so have been warned not to repeat the offense, and have been informed that, if they did so, the Standard, though under contract to supply them with oil, would cut them off, and would fight any suit they might bring through all the courts without regard to expense. At least one case is known where the deputy oil inspector, in a city to which oil had been shipped by an outside dealer, received from the state inspector peremptory orders by telegraph, before the oil had arrived, to condemn it. In the South, the Standard's control is absolute. It has now stretched out its hands to grasp the turpentine trade, and its peculiar tactics have already been disastrously felt in the turpentine market.

These oil producers and refiners whom the Standard was robbing with and without forms of law fought with every weapon they could command. The struggle has been going on continuously for nine years. All that men could do who were fighting for self-preservation was done. They caused to be introduced into Congress the first original bill to regulate railroads in interstate commerce. The outrages done by the roads and the Standard were proved before an investigating committee of Congress, but Congress did nothing. The legislature of Pennsylvania was besought to pass laws to enforce the constitutional provision for equal rights on the railroads of the State, but the money of the Standard was more powerful than the petition of business men who asked only for a fair chance. Numbers of suits were brought, by individuals and nominally by the State, but by the harmonious efforts of the governor, the attorney-general, the courts, and the defendants they were prevented from coming to any conclusion. Indictments for criminal conspiracy were found by a grand jury, but when Governor Hoyt, of Pennsylvania, in due course of law, was called upon to issue requisitions for the extradition of the two Rockefellers and their accomplices, he refused to do so. Worst failure of all, the supreme court of Pennsylvania stayed the trial of the most important of the cases in progress in a lower court, and so brought the legal proceedings against the Standard and the railroads to an end, in striking agreement with the prediction of one of the defendants that "the case would never be tried." In short, the plundered found that the courts, the governor, and the legislature of their State, and the Congress of the United States were the tools of the plunderers, and were forced to compromise. This compromise, signed February 5, 1880, was a victory in forcing a pledge from the Standard and the railroads of the abandonment of the worst of their practices, but there lies in it, as in most compromises, a germ of disaster. It permits the Standard to receive any rebate the railroads have a right to grant, and allows the railroad to give rebates to large shippers, of whom there is but one,—the Standard. This is the relative position of the parties today. The Standard holds it vantage-ground, and America has the proud satisfaction of having furnished the world with the greatest, wisest, and meanest monopoly known to history.

7–10b | Udo Keppler, political cartoon, "Next!" (the Standard Oil Octopus), 1904

More than two decades after Lloyd's article, Udo Keppler's 1904 cartoon "Next!" took on Standard Oil in the U.S. magazine *Puck*, a heavily illustrated journal of political satire and humor.

SEE COLOR INSERT

DISCUSSION QUESTIONS

1   How did Lloyd describe monopolies and their leaders? How did he describe their influence on the U.S. economy?

2   How did Keppler depict monopolies in his cartoon?

3   What forces were working for and against monopoly in the context of industrial capitalism?

7-11 | Qiu Jin, excerpts of "An Address to Two Hundred Million Fellow Countrywomen," China, ca. 1903–1906

Qiu Jin (1875–1907) was born into an era of great change in the Qing Empire in China. Foreign influencers threatened China's sovereignty (see chapter 6, item 9), while Chinese nationalists rued the rule of the non-Han Qing dynasty. Western-educated literati challenged Chinese traditions and values. Qiu Jin, though raised in a traditional Chinese family, embraced feminism and Western political ideals, pursued a Western-style education in Japan, and joined several anti-Qing revolutionary societies. Informed by these influences and ideas, Qiu Jin issued a call to action to her fellow countrywomen, excerpted below. Arrested in a failed uprising in 1907, Qiu Jin was beheaded by the state; now she is considered a national hero.

Alas, the greatest injustice in the world is that suffered by our two hundred million fellow countrywomen! If a girl is lucky enough to have a good father, at least she'll be able to tolerate her life. If her father is ill-tempered and unreasonable, he'll say remorselessly, "Such bad luck, another useless thing," itching simply to toss her away to her death. He looks at her coldly, knowing that she'll simply be given away to another family in the future. At just a few years old, without asking if it's right or wrong, he binds her soft and tender feet with white cloth, not even allowing her respite in sleep until her flesh has rotted and her bones have broken. Then when it comes time for marriage, friends and neighbors will merely say, "Your daughter has such nice small feet." That's not even to mention how when it comes time to find a husband, the parents lean on the words of two shameless matchmakers and only consider whether the man is rich and powerful, never asking whether he comes from a respectable family or whether he is kind or educated. When it comes time for the wedding, the daughter is carted off in a red and green sedan chair, unable to voice any kind of protest. After arriving at her husband's home, if he at least behaves peacefully she's considered as being rewarded for good deeds in her past life. If he is bad, people will say that she is being punished for sinning in a past life, or simply that she is unlucky. If she complains or talks back to her husband at all, she'll be beaten and reprimanded while others look on and say that she is a bad woman who doesn't know how to be a proper wife. Listen now, is this not a grave injustice? But what can we do? That's not all though. When a man dies, his wife must mourn for three years and can never remarry. Yet when a woman dies, her husband need only tie his queue with a few blue threads. Some men complain that it looks ugly and don't even tie it at all. Within not even three days he may go out for some philandering, and within seven a new bride will be at his door. When Heaven created humans, there was no difference between men and women. I ask you, where would these people be without women? How is this not unfair? Those men constantly say, "The mind is just, and we must treat everyone with kindness." So why then do they treat us like black slaves from Africa? How did this injustice reach this point?

Everyone, you must know that you can never rely on others, only on yourselves. We women must stand resolute, together as comrades to denounce those so-called scholars when they quote such nonsense as "Males are superior to females," "A talentless woman is a woman of virtue," or "The wife must follow the husband." To bring back the example of foot binding, if we feel shame over this, we should vehemently criticize it. If we don't, and we wait until even our legs are bound, then we'll never be able to resist. Men are afraid that if we were educated we would outdo them, so they don't allow us to study. How then could we ever argue for ourselves rather than simply agree with them? This is a duty that we women have abandoned ourselves—if we see a man do something, we are happy to let him do it rather than do it ourselves. When a man says we're useless, we become useless. When he says we're incapable, then as long as we're comfortable, we content ourselves to being his slave. Meanwhile we become insecure that this comfort might not last, having done nothing to earn it. So when we hear that the man likes small feet, we rush to bind them, doing anything to keep him happy so that we can continue having free meals. When they disallowed us an education, isn't that exactly what we'd want? Think about it, has there ever been any great thing given to you for free? It's only natural that power would be given to the educated, insightful, capable men, and that we would be their slaves. As their slaves, how could we break this oppression? How can we complain when we brought it upon ourselves? It pains me to bring up these things. You are all victims yourselves and do not need me to explain in detail.

I hope that from here on, we sisters can put all of this in the past and start anew, that we can focus our energies on new achievements, and let the past die off so that we may be reborn. For those who are older, do not say you are "old and useless." If you have a good husband who wants to open a school, don't stop him. If you have a good son who wants to study abroad, don't stop him. For those younger women who are now wives, do not be a burden on your husbands; do not discourage him and hinder his success. If you have a son, you should send him to school, as you should for your daughter too, and I urge you, I beg of you, do not bind her feet. For little girls it is best to go to school, but if not, you must let her learn how to read and write at home. For the wealthier among you in government, urge your husbands to do things for the good of the people, like opening a school or a factory. If you're not so wealthy, help your husband through his struggles, do not be idle. These are my dreams. We all know that our country is dying, and if the men cannot protect it themselves, how can we still rely on them? If we do not stand up until our country has already perished, it will be too late. Everyone! Everyone! We must make these dreams reality!

DISCUSSION QUESTIONS

1   What evidence did Qiu Jin give for the oppression of women in China?

2   Who or what did she blame for this situation and what solutions did she offer?

3   How might this document serve as evidence of the globalization of the women's movement?

7-12a | Ida B. Wells-Barnett, excerpts from "History of the East St. Louis, Illinois, Riot," 1917

Journalist and reformer Ida B. Wells (1862–1931) took on segregated schooling, unfair discrimination against African Americans by businesses, indifference to African American suffering by women's suffrage organizations, and mob violence—specifically, lynching—at the risk of her own life. She traveled internationally, speaking on racial oppression and women's rights in the U.S. In 1917, she went to East St. Louis, Illinois, to collect testimonies of the race riots that occurred in July. A spate of attacks by white working men on black men, women, and children rocked the city over a two-day period. Tensions in the community had risen dramatically during World War I, when employers used African American strikebreakers—many of whom had been recruited by employers from the South—to replace white unionized workers. National outrage over the inaction by police and local officials became particularly acute in the context of a war being fought to make the world "safe for democracy."

Mrs. Willie Flake's Story

Mrs. Flake is a widow with three children, 11, 8 and 6 years old. She is a laundress who came to East St. Louis four year ago from Jackson, Tenn. She took care of her little family by taking in washing, and she worked from Monday morning until Saturday night at the ironing board. She too had three rooms full of nice furniture. Both of the two front rooms having nice rugs on the floor, a brass bedstead and other furniture to correspond. She had about a hundred dollars worth of furniture ruined, fifty dollars worth of clothing and about fifty dollars more of bedding, mattresses, etc. The mob had taken a phonograph for which she had paid $15.00 and twenty-five records for which she had paid 75 cents and $1.00 each. She got away with her children before the mob reached her house and she too came back that morning to get some clothes for herself and children. The mob hadn't left much, but out of the debris, she was able to pack one trunk with some clothing and quilts for herself and children. It was in this house that I picked up one child's new shoe and although we looked the house over, we couldn't find the other. In its spasm of wanton destruction, the mob had doubtless carried it away. Mrs. Flake also had life insurance policies for herself and children, but she couldn't find any of the books. She too had already found a flat in St. Louis and was only too anxious to get away from the town where such awful things were transpiring, and where not even widows and children were safe from the fury of the mob bent on killing everything with black skins. . . .

Clarrissa Lockett's Story

Mrs. Lockett lived in the house with her brother where she had been ever since both he and she came from Mississippi. Her brother worked nights, so that all during the rioting Monday night she was alone. They didn't get to set fire to her house that night, but she sat up all night long waiting. She was unwilling to leave her household goods until she had to. She went to work at the packing house Tuesday morning early, but quit at 9 A. M. The soldiers who were guarding the plant took her and the other colored women home. Tuesday night the mob came to her number, 48 Third street, rear. After they had set fire to it and run her out, she ran into a Polish saloon not far away and the saloonkeeper and his wife agreed to let her stay there that night, although they knew the risk they ran in so doing. They told her to crouch down behind the piano and to stay there quietly all night. This she did, glad of the chance. She had been able only to bring her dog and her gun when she ran out of her home. After the saloonkeeper and his wife had gone upstairs to bed about 1 o'clock in the morning, the barkeeper and a man friend of his came back behind the piano and attempted to assault her. She drew her pistol and drove them off. When they found she had a gun, they left her in peace until morning. Early Wednesday morning, the day of our national independence, she found a man who hauled her trunk containing her own and her brother's clothes over into St. Louis, Missouri. She left two rooms filled with new furniture. She saw soldiers take guns and knives from colored men, and then the mob would set on them and beat or murder them.

When I saw her at St. Louis, Missouri, she had not yet recovered from the shock. Her brother had come straight out of the packing plant for which he was working and went straight to the train in his working clothes and went to Meridan, Mississippi, his former home. She was very anxious until she got a card letting her know where he was. . . .

[quoting from *St. Louis Dispatch* story by Carlos Hurd] What I saw, in the 90 minutes between 6:30 P. M. and the lurid coming of darkness, was but one local scene of the drama of death. I am satisfied that, in spirit and method, it typified the whole. And I cannot somehow speak of what I saw as mob violence. It was not my idea of a mob.

A mob is passionate, a mob follows one man or a few men blindly; a mob sometimes take chances. The East St. Louis affair, as I saw it, was a man hunt, conducted on a sporting basis, though with anything but the fair play which is the principle of the sport. The East St. Louis men took no chances, except the chance from stray shots, which every spectator of their acts took. They went in small groups, there was little leadership, and there was a horribly cool deliberateness and a spirit of fun about it. I cannot allow even the doubtful excuse of drink. No man whom I saw showed the effect of liquor. It was no crowd of hot-headed youths. Young men were in the greater number, but there were the middle-aged, no less active in the task of destroying the life of every discoverable black man. It was a shirtsleeve gathering, and the men were mostly workingmen, except for some who had the aspect of mere loafers. I have mentioned the peculiarly brutal crime committed by the only man there who had the appearance of being a business or professional man of any standing.

I would be more pessimistic about my fellow-Americans than I am today, if I could not say that there were other workingmen who protested against the senseless slaughter. I would be ashamed of myself if I could not say that I forgot my place as a professional observer and joined in such protests. But I do not think any verbal objection had the slightest effect. Only a volley of lead would have stopped those murderers.

"Get a nigger," was the slogan, and it was varied by the recurrent cry, "Get another!" It was like nothing so much as the holiday crowd, with thumbs turned down, in the Roman Coliseum, except that here the shouters were their own gladiators, and their own wild beasts. . . .

Story of James Taylor

The mob started at 2:05 A. M. At 4:15 they hanged two Negroes who were coming from work, to a telegraph pole and shot them to pieces. Saw them rush to cars and pull women off and beat them to death, and before they were quite dead, stalwart men jumped on their stomachs and finished them by tramping them to death. This was at the corner of Broadway and Collinville. The cars were crowded and moving, yet they jumped on and pulled them off. Others they stuck to death with hat pins, sometimes picking out their eyes with them before they were quite dead.

An old woman between 70 and 80 years old, who had returned to her house to get some things, was struck almost to death by women, then men stamped her to death.

A colored store keeper at 8th and Broadway with his family was shot and wounded. The store was set on fire and they burned to death.

George Launders and Robert Mosely were burned to death at the Library Flats at 8th and Walnut.

Rev. James Taylor's wife fled to the Broadway theatre with her five children, but left there in safety before it was burned. She said when she left there were about twenty-five white women in the basement of the theatre where they had sought safety.

There were 10 or 12 men with Rev. Taylor when he made a dash for safety, several of them armed. Doesn't know if any of them escaped.

He saw a soldier hand his gun to one of the mob.

Had narrow escape as there were men in autos and on motor cycles who shot into the grass and bushes everywhere they thought anyone might be hiding. Came across woman also hiding, who were frightened almost to death. Swam the Cahokia River with her.

Men had fingers cut off by mob, then heads split open with axes.

Colored people acted bravely in spite of handicaps.

Mr. Taylor said, he was searched 29 times for fire arms.

Colored men were frequently beaten while enroute [sic] to and from packing houses, with no protest from companies or police.

"The first and last shot fired at me was by a soldier in uniform."

7–12b | Photograph, silent protest parade in New York City, 1917

The violence in East St. Louis in 1917 and two lynchings in Waco, Texas, and Memphis, Tennessee, the previous year drew international attention and kindled deep anger over injustice, particularly in the black community. The newly formed National Association for the Advancement of Colored People (NAACP) organized a massive peaceful protest in New York City to be held in late July. Nearly ten thousand black participants, foreign and native, were organized into blocks of children, women, and men, with white-clad children leading the way. They marched through the business district of New York City silently, accompanied only by drumbeats. As they walked, they carried the flags of the U.S., England, Liberia, and Haiti and signs, some of which can be seen in the photograph.

Children in the "Silent Protest" Parade, New York City   *Underwood & Underwood.*

DISCUSSION QUESTIONS

1   Summarize the events Ida B. Wells described: what might be significant about the victims, the perpetrators, and the location?

2   What does this say about race and the urban landscape? Was this uniquely American?

3   Are there some general themes that emerge from the mottoes used in the silent protest parade?

8

The Great War

GREAT WAR PROPAGANDA POSTERS

Posters, as a modern medium, became a popular means of mass communication with revolutions in color printing and reproduction in the late nineteenth century. Though most posters had been artistic or commercial in nature, the onset of the Great War provided a new purpose: propaganda. Total war demanded the mobilization of entire populations. State authorities in all countries recognized the potential of mass, image-based messaging to reach and influence citizen audiences. State agencies and, to a lesser extent, private publishers produced posters to encourage patriotic behaviors, donations, increased production, enlistment, and hatred for the enemy, to raise morale, and to inform the public about war aims. Inexpensively printed and easily transported and displayed, the poster became ubiquitous. Every belligerent produced propaganda posters; the U.S., for example, produced 20 million posters in its eighteen months of participation in the Great War. The following are examples from both the Allied and Central Powers.

"Destroy This Mad Brute," United States, 1918

SEE COLOR INSERT

"Daddy, what did *YOU* do in the Great War?" UK, 1915

SEE COLOR INSERT

**"Pour la Liberté du Monde.
Souscrivez à l'Emprunt National à
la Banque Nationale de Crédit" ("For
the freedom of the world. Subscribe
to the National Loan at the Banque
Nationale de Crédit"), France, 1917**

**"They serve France. How can I
serve Canada?" Canada, 1915**

SEE COLOR INSERT   SEE COLOR INSERT

**"Landes-Kriedsfürsorge-Ausstellung"
(National War Relief Exhibition in Pozsony), Austria, 1917**

SEE COLOR INSERT

360

360 DISCUSSION QUESTIONS

1   Describe the visual messages imparted by these posters. Compare and contrast by country.

2   What symbols or imagery strike you most powerfully? Why? What would be the propagandists' purpose in using these symbols and images?

3   If we look at these pieces as calls to action? What are viewers encouraged to do? Discuss the range of potential responses.

ROAD TO WAR

8–1 | Map, *Humoristische Karte von Europa in Jahre 1914*, Germany, 1914

The map below is a piece of German propaganda published around the outbreak of the Great War. Here, geographic areas are reduced to ethnic or national stereotypes through caricature. Before the twentieth century, caricatures were commonly used to satirize a subject and maps such as this were popular in Europe. It contains many symbols and narratives, ones that would have resonated with viewers of it at the time of its publication.

SEE COLOR INSERT

DISCUSSION QUESTIONS

1   Provide at least three examples of cultural stereotypes present in the map's caricatures. What was the cartographer trying to communicate by employing this technique?

2   Which nations were presented positively? Negatively? Why?

3   How does this map illustrate tensions and alliances in Europe on the eve of World War I?

8–2a | Zimmermann telegram, image of telegram, coded message, 1916

Below is the coded original message from German Foreign Minister Arthur Zimmermann (1864–1940) in Washington, D.C., to Ambassador Heinrich von Eckardt (1861–1944) in Mexico on January 16, 1917. Zimmermann instructed von Eckardt to approach Mexican President Venustiano Carranza (1859–1920) with a two-part proposal: (1) form an alliance with Germany, (2) if Germany dropped its neutrality against the United States, join Germany in an attack on the U.S. and work to persuade Japan to partner as well. In return, with the defeat of the enemy, Mexico would acquire areas lost to the United States, principally Texas, New Mexico, and Arizona.

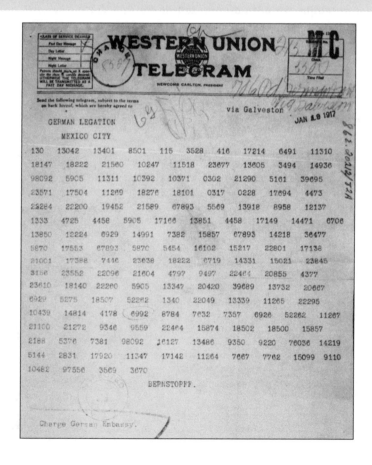

8-2b | Zimmermann telegram, transcript, 1916

The Zimmermann telegram was sent, via the transatlantic cable, from Germany, through Washington, D.C., to be routed to Mexico City. The telegram was intercepted and decoded by British intelligence. On February 19, the decoded message was provided to the U.S. Embassy in London, the information made its way back to Washington, and on February 28, President Woodrow Wilson released the full text of the message to the media. The telegram was initially widely believed to be a forgery by British intelligence, but Arthur Zimmermann admitted it was true in March 1917. The telegram and the resumption of unrestricted submarine warfare on the part of Germany on February 1, 1917, made U.S. public opinion hawkish.

FROM 2nd from London # 5747.

We intend to begin on the first of February unrestricted submarine warfare. We shall endeavor in spite of this to keep the United States of America neutral. In the event of this not succeeding, we make Mexico a proposal of alliance on the following basis: make war together, make peace together, generous financial support and an understanding on our part that Mexico is to reconquer the lost territory in Texas, New Mexico, and Arizona. The settlement in detail is left to you. You will inform the President of the above most secretly as soon as the outbreak of war with the United States of America is certain and add the suggestion that he should, on his own initiative, invite Japan to immediate adherence and at the same time mediate between Japan and ourselves. Please call the President's attention to the fact that the ruthless employment of our submarines now offers the prospect of compelling England in a few months to make peace. Signed, ZIMMERMANN

DISCUSSION QUESTIONS

1   Why would Mexico be a valuable nation with which to form an alliance against the United States?

2   What fears would this offer by Germany trigger in the American public?

3   How might routes of international information shape U.S. views of the ongoing war?

8-3a | Postcard depicting U-Boat *UC-5*, 1916

SM *UC-5* was a U-Boat or Type UC I minelayer submarine in the German Imperial Navy, ordered in November 1914 and launched June 1915. Over the life of its operation, *UC-5* sank twenty-nine ships on twenty-nine patrols. It was the first submarine minelayer to infiltrate the English Channel, laying twelve mines. On April 27, 1916, the submarine ran aground. It was captured and disarmed by the British, then displayed at Temple Pier on the Thames River and later, as can be seen below, in New York. At the beginning of the

Great War, Germany had forty-eight submarines in service or under construction. The instrument of war proved highly effective, targeting their efforts primarily at merchant convoys brings supplies to the Allies.

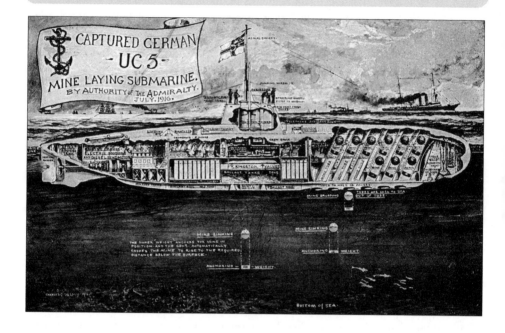

8–3b | Woodrow Wilson, excerpts from war message, 1917

After a March 1916 German U-boat attack on the SS *Sussex*, a British ferry, American opinion became enraged against Germany. The fear of U.S. entry into the war led Germany to declare what became known as the Sussex pledge, a promise to restrict use of the U-boat. British control of the sea ultimately led Germany to renounce that pledge and on February 1, 1917, Germany declared unrestricted submarine warfare. On March 17, German sank three American merchant vessels. This combined with other elements, such as the Zimmermann telegram (see chapter 8, item 2), led the U.S. to declare war on Germany. Here, in excerpts from his war message delivered to Congress, President Woodrow Wilson explained both the rationales for war and the hopes for peace.

Gentlemen of the Congress:

I have called the Congress into extraordinary session because there are serious, very serious, choices of policy to be made, and made immediately, which it was neither right nor constitutionally permissible that I should assume the responsibility of making.

On the third of February last I officially laid before you the extraordinary announcement of the Imperial German Government that on and after the first day of February it was its purpose to put aside all restraints of law or of humanity and use its submarines to sink every vessel that sought to approach either the ports of Great Britain and Ireland or the western coasts of Europe or any of the ports controlled by the enemies of Germany within the Mediterranean.

That had seemed to be the object of the German submarine warfare earlier in the war, but since April of last year the Imperial Government had somewhat restrained the commanders of its undersea craft in conformity with its promise then given to us that passenger boats should not be sunk and that due warning would be given to all other vessels which its submarines might seek to destroy, when no resistance was offered or escape attempted, and care taken that their crews were given at least a fair chance to save their lives in their open boats.

The precautions taken were meager and haphazard enough, as was proved in distressing instance after instance in the progress of the cruel and unmanly business, but a certain degree of restraint was observed. The new policy has swept every restriction aside.

Vessels of every kind, whatever their flag, their character, their cargo, their destination, their errand, have been ruthlessly sent to the bottom without warning and without thought of help or mercy for those on board, the vessels of friendly neutrals along with those of belligerents. Even hospital ships and ships carrying relief to the sorely bereaved and stricken people of Belgium, though the latter were provided with safe conduct through the proscribed areas by the German Government itself and were distinguished by unmistakable marks of identity, haven been sunk with the same reckless lack of compassion or of principle.

I was for a little while unable to believe that such things would in fact be done by any government that hitherto subscribed to the humane practices of civilized nations. International law had its origin in the attempt to set up some law which would be respected and observed upon the seas, where no nation had right of dominion and where lay the free highways of the world. By painful stage after stage has that law been built up, with meager enough results, indeed, after all was accomplished that could be accomplished, but always with a clear view, at least, of what the heart and conscience of mankind demanded.

This minimum of right the German Government has swept aside under the plea of retaliation and necessity and because it had no weapons which it could use at sea except these which it is impossible to employ as it is employing them without throwing to the winds all scruples of humanity or of respect for the understandings that were supposed to underlie the intercourse of the world.

I am not now thinking of the loss of property involved, immense and serious as that is, but only of the wanton and wholesale destruction of the lives of non-combatants, men, women, and children, engaged in pursuits which have always, even in the darkest periods of modern history, been deemed innocent and legitimate. Property can be paid for; the lives of peaceful and innocent people cannot be.

The present German submarine warfare against commerce is a warfare against mankind.

It is war against all nations.

American ships have been sunk, American lives taken, in ways which it has stirred us very deeply to learn of, but the ships and people of other neutral and friendly nations have been sunk and overwhelmed in the waters in the same way. There has been no discrimination. The challenge is to all mankind.

Each nation must decide for itself how it will meet it. The choice we make for ourselves must be made with a moderation of counsel and temperateness of judgment befitting our character and our motives as a nation. We must put excited feeling away. Our motive will not be revenge or the victorious assertion of the physical might of the nation, but only the vindication of right, of human right, of which we are only a single champion. . . .

While we do these things, these deeply momentous things, let us be very clear, and make very clear to all the world what our motives and our objects are. My own thought has not been driven from its habitual and normal course by the unhappy events of the last two months, and I do not believe that the thought of the nation has been altered or clouded by them. I have exactly the same things in mind now that I had in mind when I addressed the Senate on the twenty-second of January last; the same that I had in mind when I addressed the Congress on the third day of February and on the twenty-sixth of February. Our object now, as then, is to vindicate the principles of peace and justice in the life of the world as against selfish and autocratic power and to set up amongst the really free and self-governed peoples of the world such a concert of purpose and of action as will henceforth ensure the observance of those principles.

Neutrality is no longer feasible or desirable where the peace of the world is involved and the freedom of its peoples, and the menace to that peace and freedom lies in the existence of autocratic governments backed by organized force which is controlled wholly by their will, not by the will of their people. We have seen the last of neutrality in such circumstances. We are at the beginning of an age in which it will be insisted that the same standards of conduct and responsibility for wrong done shall be observed among nations and their governments that are observed among the individual citizens of civilized states.

We have no quarrel with the German people. We have no feeling towards them but one of sympathy and friendship. It was not upon their impulse that their government acted in entering this war. It was not with their previous knowledge or approval. It was a war determined upon as wars used to be determined upon in the old, unhappy days when peoples were nowhere consulted by their rulers and wars were provoked and waged in the interest of dynasties or of little groups of ambitious men who were accustomed to use their fellow men as pawns and tools.

Self-governed nations do not fill their neighbor states with spies or set the course of intrigue to bring about some critical posture of affairs which will give them an opportunity to strike and make conquest. Such designs can be successfully worked out only under cover and where no one has the right to ask questions. Cunningly contrived plans of deception or aggression, carried, it may be, from generation to generation, can be worked out and kept from the light only within the privacy of courts or behind carefully guarded confidences of a narrow and privileged class. They are happily impossible where public opinion commands and insists upon full information concerning all the nation's affairs.

A steadfast concert for peace can never be maintained except by a partnership of democratic nations. No autocratic government could be trusted to keep faith within it or observe its covenants. It must be a league of honor, a partnership of opinion. Intrigue would eat its vitals away; the plottings of inner circles who could plan what they would and render account to no one would be a corruption seated at its very heart. Only free peoples can hold their purpose and their honor steady to a common end and prefer the interests of mankind to any narrow interest of their own. . . .

We are glad, now that we see the facts with no veil of false pretense about them, to fight thus for the ultimate peace of the world and for the liberation of its peoples, the German peoples included: for the rights of nations great and small and the privilege of men everywhere to choose their way of life and of obedience. The world must be made safe for democracy. Its peace must be planted upon the tested foundations of political liberty. We have no selfish ends to serve.

We desire no conquest, no dominion. We seek no indemnities for ourselves, no material compensation for the sacrifices we shall cheerfully make. We are but one of the champions of the rights of mankind. We shall be satisfied when those rights have been made as secure as the faith and the freedom of nations can make them.

Just because we fight without rancor and without selfish object, seeking nothing for ourselves but what we shall wish to share with all free peoples, we shall, I feel confident, conduct our operations as belligerents without passion and ourselves observe with proud punctilio the principles of right and fair play we profess to be fighting for. . . .

We shall, happily, still have an opportunity to prove that friendship in our daily attitude and actions towards the millions of men and women of German birth and native sympathy who live amongst us and share our life, and we shall be proud to prove it towards all who are in fact loyal to their neighbors and to the Government in the hour of test. They are, most of them, as true and loyal Americans as if they had never known any other fealty or allegiance. They will be prompt to stand with us in rebuking and restraining the few who may be of a different mind and purpose. If there should be disloyalty, it will be dealt with a firm hand of stern repression; but, if it lifts its head at all, it will lift it only here and there and without countenance except from a lawless and malignant few.

It is a distressing and oppressive duty, Gentlemen of the Congress, which I have performed in thus addressing you. There are, it may be, many months of fiery trial and sacrifice ahead of us. It is a fearful thing to lead this great peaceful people into war, into the most terrible and disastrous of all wars, civilization itself seeming to be in the balance.

But the right is more precious than peace, and we shall fight for the things which we have always carried nearest our hearts, for democracy, for the right of those who submit to authority to have a voice in their own governments, for the rights and liberties of small nations, for a universal dominion of right by such a concert of free peoples as shall bring peace and safety to all nations and make the world at last free.

To such a task we can dedicate our lives and our fortunes, everything that we are and everything that we have, with the pride of those who know that the day has come when America is privileged to spend her blood and her might for the principles that gave her birth and happiness and the peace which she has treasured. God helping her, she can do no other.

DISCUSSION QUESTIONS

1   Why might Britain produce and share an internal drawing of the *UC-5*?

2   What about Germany's use of submarines influenced Wilson's reasons for asking Congress to declare war?

3   Discuss Wilson's rationale for entering the Great War. In what ways did he articulate a war aim broader than the defeat of Germany?

8–4a | Ed Morton, sheet music, selected lyrics of "I Didn't Raise My Boy to Be a Soldier," 1915

In 1915, the U.S. pursued an official position of neutrality in the ongoing conflict overseas. This, despite greater popular and economic support for the Allies in the United States. Popular sentiment against noninvolvement in the conflict had been ongoing since July 1914. In fact, President Woodrow Wilson's reelection campaign in 1916 trumpeted the fact that "He Kept Us Out of War." Below are the lyrics to one of the first antiwar songs that was influential with the prewar pacifist movement. The recording, made in December 1914, was a hit song the next year, selling 650,000 copies.

Verse 1
Ten million soldiers to the war have gone,
Who may never return again.
Ten million mothers' hearts must break
For the ones who died in vain.
Head bowed down in sorrow
In her lonely years,
I heard a mother murmur thru' her tears:

Chorus
I didn't raise my boy to be a soldier,
I brought him up to be my pride and joy.
Who dares to place a musket on his shoulder,
To shoot some other mother's darling boy?
Let nations arbitrate their future troubles,
It's time to lay the sword and gun away.
There'd be no war today,

If mothers all would say,
"I didn't raise my boy to be a soldier."

Verse 2

What victory can cheer a mother's heart,
When she looks at her blighted home?
What victory can bring her back
All she cared to call her own?
Let each mother answer
In the years to be,
Remember that my boy belongs to me!

Repeat Chorus 2x

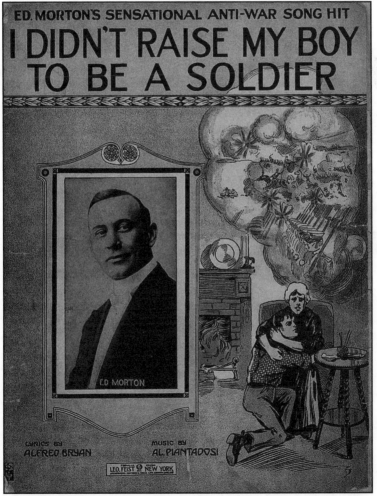

SEE COLOR INSERT

8–4b | Theodore Baker, sheet music, selected lyrics of "I Didn't Raise My Boy to Be a Slacker," 1917

The message of the 1915 Ed Morton hit above was parodied by many other songs that were produced, such as "I Did Not Raise My Boy to Be a Coward," and "I Didn't Raise My Boy to Be a Soldier, But I'll Send My Girl to Be a Nurse." The biggest change in attitude, however, came with the growth of popular support for the war in early 1917. Although public debate on the subject ended with the U.S. declaration of war against Germany on April 6, 1917, approximately 300,000 American men evaded or refused conscription during the Great War.

Verse 1

I didn't raise my boy to be a slacker,
I'd never own a shirk for son of mine!
There are things that must be done
by every mother's son,
And it's not for him to lag behind the line;
Some day our Uncle Sam may have to call him,
And where's the man who will not heed the call?
But if you are not prepared
to do as you have dared,
It's ten to one you're riding for a fall.

Refrain

So, whether you're a boy or a full-grown man,
Keep as hearty and as hardy and as husky as you can;
Play a manly part in the nation's plan,
One and all, and all as one!

Verse 2

They whimper "Don't you care!" on every corner,
They bluster "Don't you dare!" with tongue and pen;
Let the craven's dismal cry,
the traitor's loudest lie,
Find their answer in the hearts of loyal men!
I love my boy as only mothers can love,
His life to me is dearer than my own,
But I'd rather he were dead,
than see him hang his head
When our men go out across the danger zone.

Refrain

So, whether you're a boy or a full-grown man,
Keep as hearty and as hardy and as husky as you can;
Play a manly part in the nation's plan,
One and all, and all as one!

Verse 3

Who falters when the signs are in the heavens?
Who wavers for his love for home and wife?
Is there one so poor and small
he will not give his all,
Who in freedom's cause will not lay down his life?
Columbia now is watching you, her children,
She's arming for the awful hour of war;
While for faith and right we stand,
our firm, united land
Will show the world we're men like those of yore!

Refrain

So, whether you're a boy or a full-grown man,
Keep as hearty and as hardy and as husky as you can;
Play a manly part in the nation's plan,
One and all, and all as one!

SEE COLOR INSERT

DISCUSSION QUESTIONS

1   How does each song frame the image of the soldier himself? How does that make a difference?

2   How does each piece reveal the connection between pop culture and politics? Consider the date of publication.

3   Compare and contrast the portrayals of motherhood in each of the songs. Why are mothers central to the songs' respective meanings?

WAR AND AFTERMATH

8–5a | Photograph, soldiers in the German Colonial Forces, West Africa, 1914

With the intense warfare of the European theater, the global nature of World War I can often be overlooked. At the start of the conflict, all of Africa, outside of Ethiopia and Liberia, was under European rule. That fact both brought war to the continent and took Africans abroad as belligerents. This was especially true for the UK, Germany, France, and Belgium. In West and East Africa, all these European powers relied on locally recruited soldiers and workers to sustain their war efforts. Even with conservative estimates, European and American armies mobilized well over 4 million non-white men into combat and non-combat roles during the Great War.

8–5b | Indian Corps member Mohammed Agim, excerpt of letter to Subedar Major Firoz Khan describing the war, France, 1915

Subedar Mohammed Agim fought with the 57th Wilde's Rifles on the Western Front in France and Belgium during the Great War. Here, he writes of his views of the enemy and his concern that Italy might join the Central Powers. In 1914, the Indian Army was one of the two largest volunteer armies in the world. Over the course of the Great War, over one million Indian troops served in the European, Mediterranean, and Middle Eastern theaters.

From Muhamed Agim, Subedar, 57th Rifles, Indian General Hospital Brighton, to Subedar Major Firoz Khan, 56th Rifles, P.Force, Egypt.

28/5/15). "I am telling you the trouble. What can I say of the war? It is a manifestation of divine wrath. There is no counting the number of lives lost. We have to deal with a terrible and powerful enemy, who is completely equipped with every sort of contrivance. Out of the 64th Regiment which arrived in full strength, only about 10 men are left. In my regiment the 57th absolutely none are left, with the exception of Jamadar Isam Ali now appointed Subedar, and one newly joined Lieutenant. Not a single British or native officer of the old regiment is left and not a sepoy. It is just like the grinding of corn in a mill. The enemy is one completely equipped with all contrivances. . . . There remains to be seen what effect the joining of Italy will have on the war. It is possible that the war may end soon, as Italy has an army of 3 millions."

DISCUSSION QUESTIONS

1   What elements of the photo and letter show World War I as a conflict between global empires?
2   What might be some of the implications of involving so many colonial troops in service during the Great War?

8–6 | Excerpts from *A War Nurse's Diary: Sketches from a Belgian Field Hospital*, Belgium, 1918

Written by an anonymous British woman who volunteered as a nurse in 1914, this firsthand account describes the sights and sounds of war on the European continent. Serving in a mobile hospital unit in Belgium, the author records her day-to-day observations. The excerpt below details the chaotic evacuation of wounded troops from a besieged Antwerp to Ghent.

At 11.00 A.M. the old cook ran out wringing her hands. "The gas has gone out," she said, for a shell had struck the gas works. This was a grave difficulty, as we had no other form of fuel. Not only could we cook no food, but the theatre, which at that moment had two tables occupied all the time, had no means of sterilizing instruments. One of our medical students had an uncle with Winston Churchill, so he just went round to Headquarters and borrowed three London Motor Omnibuses. These lumbering vehicles looked so incongruous still pasted with the latest music hall advertisements, such as "The Glad Eye," the familiar London "Elephant & Castle" marking their original destination.

It was represented to us that it was a most dangerous adventure to try to escape, but that we must save some of the more seriously wounded. Who would volunteer to attend the patients? My friend and I were standing near, so we offered. Quickly the men were packed in, as the shells fell thicker and nearer. . . .

It was now twelve noon; the Germans had cleared the town of civilians, they supposed, so they started in with howitzer shells and bombs from siege-guns. The shrapnel was child's play beside these. Instead of one house, it was now a block of buildings that went high into the air in a thick cloud of black dust and debris; when this settled down, all that remained was a mass of broken brick and dust. The whole earth shook and it was impossible to hear people shouting. Our Chief immediately went round to that omnibus garage and commandeered five more London buses. . . .

We felt in taking these buses that we were no longer robbing the Marines. Many of them were with us; many more were dead and had no use for them. It was now 3 P.M. on Thursday. As soon as the five buses arrived we commenced loading them up with our wounded. Those who could sit up were placed on top and the stretcher cases lay across from seat to seat inside. We formed a long procession, for there were five private cars as well. My car was the first to get loaded, and I was put in charge of the inside passengers. Shall we ever forget the loading up of those cars? They tried to save all the theatre instruments. What an eternity it seemed! Just sitting still, with the guns at last trained on to our locality. . . .

Even to the last minute patients arrived, chiefly British. Just before we started a tall Marine in a navy jersey and sailor's cap was helped in. He sat in the corner next to me. All his ribs were broken down one side, and he had no plaster or support. Opposite me were two Tommies with compound fractures of the leg. I placed both legs on my knees to lessen the jolting.

The Marine suffered in silent agony, his lips pressed tightly together, and his white face set. I looked at him helplessly, and he said "Never mind me, Sister; if I swear don't take any notice." Fortunately, they had pushed in two bottles of whiskey and some soda-syphons; I just dosed them all around until it was finished. Placing the Marine's arm around my shoulders, I used my right arm as a splint to support his ribs, and so we sat for seven and a half hours without moving. Then another nurse took my place and I went up top. During the first part of the ride I bethought me of that tube of morphia, and it came in very useful, as I gave each of those poor sufferers one or two tablets to swallow.

How can I ever describe that journey to Ghent of fourteen and a half hours? No one but those who went through it can realize it. Have you ever ridden in a London motor bus? If not, I can give little idea of what our poor men suffered. To begin with, even traversing the smooth London streets these vehicles jolt you to bits, whilst inside the smell of burnt gasoline is often stifling, so just imagine unwieldy things bumping along over cobblestones and the loose sandy ruts of rough tracks among the sand-dunes, which constantly necessitated every one who could, dismounting and pushing behind and pulling by ropes in front, to get the vehicle into an upright position again, out of the ruts. When you have the picture of this before you, just think of the passengers—not healthy people on a penny bus ride, but wounded soldiers and sailors. Upon the brow of many Death had set his seal. All those inside passengers were either wounded in the abdomen, shot through the lungs, or pierced through the skull, often with their brains running out through the wound, whilst we had more than one case of men with broken backs. Many of these had just been operated upon. . . . Now that you understand the circumstances, I will ask you to accompany me on that journey.

Leaving our own shell-swept street which seemed like hell let loose, we turned down a long boulevard. From one end to the other the houses were a sheet of flames. We literally travelled through a valley with walls of fire. Keeping well in the middle of the street we constantly had to make detours to avoid large shell holes. . . .

From Antwerp to St. Nicolas is about twenty miles. It was the Highway of Sorrow. Some people escaped in carriages and carts, but by far the greater number plodded on foot. It was now 5 P. M. on an October evening; there was a fine drizzling rain; it was cold and soon it was dark. Along that road streamed thousands, panic-stricken, cold, hungry, weary, homeless. Where were they going? Where would they spend the night? Here was a mother carrying her baby, around her skirts clung four of five children, small sisters of five or six carried baby-brothers of two years old. There was a donkey cart piled high with mattresses and bundles and swarming on it were bedridden old men and women and babies. Here was a little girl wheeling an old fashioned cot-perambulator, with an old grey-bearded man in it, his legs dangling over the edge. Suddenly a girl's voice called out of the darkness, "Oh Mees, Mees, take me and my leetle dog with you. I have lost my father and he has our money." So we gave her a seat on the spiral stairs outside.

Very soon all the ills that could happen to sick men came upon us. The jolting and agony made them violently sick. Seizing any utensil which had been saved from the theatre I gave it to them, and we kept that mademoiselle busy outside. All along the road we saw little groups, weary mothers sitting on the muddy banks of a ditch sharing the last loaf among the family. . . . We passed very few houses, as we avoided towns and villages; any habitations we saw were shuttered and barred, for the people hid in terror expecting every one who passed to be the dreaded enemy. All this time our men were in torture, constantly they asked "Are we nearly there, Sister? How much longer?" I, who was strong, felt dead beat, so what must they have felt? One weary soul gave up the battle and just died. We could not even reach him to cover his face as he lay there among his companions.

From St. Nicolas I was faced with new anxiety. Where were our friends who went to Ghent with the first convoy of wounded? Had they taken the main road and fallen into the hands of the Germans? I thought of all the tales I had heard of the treatment of Englishwomen received at their hands. At any place where people were visible we anxiously inquired if three buses had passed that way earlier. We could get no satisfactory answer.

Soon we began to meet the first detachments of the Expeditionary Force. In a narrow lane with a ditch on one side lay an overturned cannon whilst a plump English Major cursed and swore in the darkness. Then a heavy motor lorry confronted us; one of us had to back till a suitable place came in the narrow lane where we could pass. Later on we met small companies of weary Tommies, wet and footsore, who had lost their way. Our Scout Captain warned them to turn back, telling them the Germans had by now entered Antwerp, but they did not believe us. Even had they believed us, they had their orders to relieve Antwerp, so to Antwerp they went, never to return.

At last that weary night came to an end. For some hours I had been relieved by another nurse, and sat on top in the rain and cold. The medical students were so worn out that they lay down in the narrow passage between the seats and slept, oblivious of our trampling over them. Before dawn we entered the suburbs of Ghent. . . .

DISCUSSION QUESTIONS

1   Discuss the ways twentieth-century technology was changing the battlefield. Why might improvisation still be a helpful skill in field medicine? Provide three examples of this from the text.

2   What types of injuries did this nurse and her colleagues encounter? How did they treat them?

3   In what ways does a nurse's perspective add to accounts of the realities of World War I?

8–7 | Wilfred Owen, poem, "Dulce et Decorum Est," UK, 1920

The Great War pitted the world's most heavily industrialized and militarized nations against each other. In just over four years of unprecedented slaughter, nearly 10 million soldiers lost their lives and millions more were wounded. The Western Front's trench warfare, confined to a 440-mile by 90-mile space, subjected troops not only to modern firepower and artillery attacks, but also poison gas. Wilfred Owen (1893–1918), one of the best-known of Britain's war poets, experienced the horrors of the frontline and captured it in verse. At the age of twenty-five, Owen was killed in action one week before war's end, in November 1918.

Bent double, like old beggars under sacks,
Knock-kneed, coughing like hags, we cursed through sludge,
Till on the haunting flares we turned our backs,
And towards our distant rest began to trudge.
Men marched asleep. Many had lost their boots,
But limped on, blood-shod. All went lame; all blind;
Drunk with fatigue; deaf even to the hoots
Of gas-shells dropping softly behind.

Gas! GAS! Quick, boys!—An ecstasy of fumbling
Fitting the clumsy helmets just in time,
But someone still was yelling out and stumbling
And flound'ring like a man in fire or lime.—
Dim through the misty panes and thick green light,
As under a green sea, I saw him drowning.

In all my dreams before my helpless sight,
He plunges at me, guttering, choking, drowning.

If in some smothering dreams, you too could pace
Behind the wagon that we flung him in,
And watch the white eyes writhing in his face,
His hanging face, like a devil's sick of sin;
If you could hear, at every jolt, the blood
Come gargling from the froth-corrupted lungs,
Obscene as cancer, bitter as the cud
Of vile, incurable sores on innocent tongues,—
My friend, you would not tell with such high zest
To children ardent for some desperate glory,
The old Lie: *Dulce et decorum est*
Pro patria mori.

DISCUSSION QUESTIONS

1   Describe the effects of a gas attack. How might this technology alter warfare?

2   How does this poem expose the "Lie": *Dulce et decorum est pro patria mori* [It is sweet and fitting to die for one's country]?

3   What imagery does Owen use to convey the realities of trench warfare?

8–8a | William W. Cadbury, description of the 1918 pandemic of influenza in Canton, China, 1920

Adding to the general misery of the Great War, waves of "Spanish" flu swept around the world in 1918–1919 with devastating results. The origins of this strain of influenza—an H1N1 virus—remain unknown, but one-third of the world's population (500 million people) became infected and an estimated 50 million people died from this pandemic. In the U.S., doctors first noted the flu in military personnel in spring 1918; eventually 675,000 Americans would perish. As vaccines and antibiotics did not exist, treatment measures included improved hygiene, quarantine, and disinfectants. In the excerpt below, Dr. William Cadbury contextualizes flu in Canton (Guangzhou), China.

It is estimated that in September, October, and November [1918], there were more than 400,000 deaths from the disease in America. Among the troops, from September 20 to November 1 there were reported 725 cases of influenza, and 18,704 from pneumonia. In the cities of America the death rate ranged from 1.8 per thousand in Milwaukee, to 7.4 per thousand in Philadelphia for a period of ten weeks. At the Christian College [in Canton] only one death occurred between June and January, or a rate of 1 per thousand for the three epidemics. Elsewhere in Canton the disease seems to have been very much less malignant than in the United States, although there are rumors of entire families being wiped out, and of 500 deaths having occurred in one block of a city street. At the Canton Hospital there were no deaths in June, and only four among 27 cases in October.

Rumors indicate that the disease was much more fatal in certain outlying districts of Canton, but the reports from Hongkong and Shanghai agree with our observations that the death rate was extremely low in China. That tropical countries did suffer severely from the disease is shown by [reports from] the Philippines and by recent dispatches from India stating that the deaths there ran up into the millions. As Christian emphasizes, it is a misnomer to speak of some deaths as being due to influenza and others due to pneumonia, since death is practically always caused by pneumonia.

8–8b | Gresham Life Assurance Society, report on influenza claims exceeding war claims, UK, 1919

The July 1, 1919, issue of *The Times* carried a lengthy summary of the seventeenth ordinary general meeting of the Gresham Life Assurance Society, Limited, at their offices in St. Mildred's House, The Poultry, London. The Gresham Life Assurance Society was an international firm providing life insurance via branches in Spain, South Africa, Canada, Austria, Belgium, Egypt, and the Balkans. Notable in 1919 were observations about the war and the flu pandemic, excerpted below.

[The] death claims brought into account during the year [1918] amo
mally large sum and show an exceptionally large increase upon the figu
The total war claims from 1914 to 1918 inclusive . . . amount to no less th

It may interest you to know that the death claims from the fatal scou
which last year so rapidly spread over all parts of the world, have, in our experience at
any rate, exceeded considerably the war claims of the year. These, likewise, are obviously included. But, gentlemen, it affords myself and my colleagues great pleasure to be
able to state to you that, large as are the death claims reported, it is our duty and pleasure now to report that they are nevertheless, as we are advised by the actuary, within
the actuarial expectation. (Hear, hear.) Obviously the margin cannot be a great one, but
it is gratifying to know that, notwithstanding the exceptional conditions of the year—
the accumulation of the past and the influenza—we are on the safety side of the line.

DISCUSSION QUESTIONS

1 Did Cadbury observe similarities between the areas that share high mortality rates?
   What does that suggest?

2 What does looking at an insurance company's report contribute to our knowledge
   about this pandemic?

3 What do these sources say about the transmission and impact of influenza?

8–9 | General Syrian Congress, objections to Zionism and Western imperialism, Syria, 1919

U.S. President Woodrow Wilson's statement of principles, the Fourteen Points (1918),
electrified nationalist movements around the world with its condemnation of imperialism
and advocacy of national self-determination and democracy. Among other things, it
also called for an international League of Nations and an end to secret treaties. The
General Syrian Congress relied on Wilson's idealistic principles to make an argument for
their own postwar independence and against the imposition of a Jewish homeland in
Palestine. Though Zionists had argued for a Jewish state since 1897, its establishment
in the Middle East gained traction with a pledge of British support in the wartime Balfour
Declaration (1917).

The General Syrian Congress, Our Objections to Zionism and Western Imperialism

1. We ask . . . [for] complete political independence for [Greater] Syria . . .
   [encompassing Lebanon and Palestine].

2. We ask that the Government of this Syrian country should be a democratic
   civil constitutional Monarchy . . . safeguarding the rights of minorities, and

that the King be the Emir Feisal, who carried on a glorious struggle in the cause of our liberation and merited our full confidence and entire reliance.

3. Considering the fact that the Arabs inhabiting the Syrian area are not naturally less gifted than other more advanced races and that they are by no means less developed than the Bulgarians, Serbians, Greeks, and Romanians at the beginning of their independence, we protest against Article 22 of the Covenant of the League of Nations, placing us among the nations in their middle stage of development which stand in need of a mandatory power.

4. In the event of the rejection by the Peace Conference of this just protest for certain considerations that we may not understand, we, relying on the declarations of President Wilson, that his object in waging war was to put an end to the ambition of conquest and colonization, can only regard the mandate mentioned in the Covenant of the League of Nations as equivalent to the rendering of economical and technical assistance that does not prejudice our complete independence. And desiring that our country should not fall prey to colonization and believing that the American Nation is farthest from any thought of colonization and has no political ambition in our country, we will seek the technical and economical assistance from the United States of America, provided that such assistance does not exceed twenty years.

5. In the event of America not finding herself in a position to accept our desire for assistance, we will seek this assistance from Great Britain, also provided that this assistance does not infringe on the complete independence and unity of our country and that the duration of such assistance does not exceed that mentioned in the previous article.

6. We do not acknowledge any right claimed by the French Government in any part whatsoever of our Syrian country and refuse that she should assist us or have a hand in our country under any circumstances and in any place.

7. We oppose the pretensions of the Zionists to create a Jewish commonwealth in the southern part of Syria, known as Palestine, and oppose Zionist migration to any part of our country; for we do not acknowledge their title but consider them a grave peril for our people from the national, economical, and political points of view. Our Jewish compatriots shall enjoy our common rights and assume the common responsibilities.

8. We ask that there be no separation of the southern part of Syria, known as Palestine, nor of the littoral western zone, which includes Lebanon, from the Syrian country. We desire that the unity of the country should be guaranteed against partition under whatever circumstances.

9. We ask for complete independence for emancipated Mesopotamia [Iraq] and that there should be no economical barriers between the two countries.

10. The fundamental principles laid down by President Wilson in condemnation of secret treaties impel us to protest most emphatically against any treaty that stipulates the partition of our Syrian country and against any private engagement aiming at the establishment of Zionism in the southern part of Syria; therefore we ask the annulment of these conventions and agreements.

The noble principles enunciated by President Wilson strengthen our confidence that our desires emanating from the depths of our hearts shall be the decisive factor in determining our future; and that President Wilson and the free American people will be our supporters for the realization of our hopes, thereby proving their sincerity and noble sympathy with the aspiration of the weaker nations in general and the Arab people in particular.

We also have the fullest confidence that the Peace Conference will realize that we would not have risen against the Turks, with whom we had participated in all civil, political, and representative privileges, but for the violation of our national rights, and so will grant us our desires in full in order that our political rights may not be less after the war than they were before, since we have shed so much blood in the cause of our liberty and independence.

We request to be allowed to send a delegation to represent us at the Peace Conference to defend our rights and secure the realization of our aspirations.

DISCUSSION QUESTIONS

1   What are the demands of the Syrian Congress?

2   What view did this document take toward the United States and President Wilson? How did the Syrian Congress connect its claims of independence to the U.S. and Wilson?

3   What are their arguments against Zionist claims in the Middle East?

8–10a | John T. McCutcheon, political cartoon, "Interrupting the Ceremony," 1918

The centerpiece of President Woodrow Wilson's Fourteen Points (1918) was the establishment of a League of Nations, an international body where the rights and voices of all states, large and small, could be protected and heard in the interests of peace and progress. Wilson insisted that the League's charter be attached to the Treaty of Versailles, the peace settlement of the Great War. Some members of the U.S. Congress, however, were less enthused about continuing national involvement with the world and its ills. Wilson faced serious opposition to his proposed League when he returned from the peace talks. This political cartoon by Pulitzer Prize winner John T. McCutcheon (1870–1949) illustrates some of the concerns of Wilson's opposition.

INTERRUPTING THE CEREMONY

8–10b | Henry Cabot Lodge, excerpts from a speech on the League of Nations, 1919

Sen. Henry Cabot Lodge (1850–1924), longtime Republican congressman representing Massachusetts, led the opposition to both the treaty and President Wilson's League of Nations. Below is an excerpt of one of Lodge's most famous speeches against Wilson's proposed agreements. It reflects the return of isolationist sentiment in the U.S., a powerful element in the interwar period. Though the Treaty of Versailles went into effect, the U.S. made its own separate settlements with the former Central Powers, and never became a member of the League of Nations.

Mr. President:

. . .

The independence of the United States is not only more precious to ourselves but to the world than any single possession. Look at the United States to-day. We have made mistakes in the past. We have had shortcomings. We shall make mistakes in the future and fall short of our own best hopes. But none the less is there any country to-day on the face of the earth which can compare with this in ordered liberty, in peace, and in the largest freedom? I feel that I can say this without being accused of undue boastfulness, for it is the simple fact, and in making this treaty and taking on these obligations all that we do is in a spirit of unselfishness and in a desire for the good of mankind. But it is well to remember that we are dealing with nations every one of which has a direct individual interest to serve, and there is grave danger in an unshared idealism.

Contrast the United States with any country on the face of the earth to-day and ask yourself whether the situation of the United States is not the best to be found. I will go as far as anyone in world service, but the first step to world service is the maintenance of the United States. You may call me selfish if you will, conservative or reactionary, or use any other harsh adjective you see fit to apply, but an American I was born, an American I have remained all my life. I can never be anything else but an American, and I must think of the United States first, and when I think of the United States first in an arrangement like this I am thinking of what is best for the world, for if the United States fails, the best hopes of mankind fail with it. I have never had but one allegiance—I cannot divide it now. I have loved but one flag and I cannot share that devotion and give affection to the mongrel banner invented for a league. Internationalism, illustrated by the Bolshevik and by the men to whom all countries are alike provided they can make money out of them, is to me repulsive. National I must remain, and in that way I like all other Americans can render the amplest service to the world. The United States is the world's best hope, but if you fetter her in the interests and quarrels of other nations, if you tangle her in the intrigues of Europe, you will destroy her power for good and endanger her very existence. Leave her to march freely through the centuries to come as in the years that have gone. Strong, generous, and confident, she has nobly served mankind. Beware how you trifle with your marvelous inheritance, this great land of ordered liberty, for if we stumble and fall freedom and civilization everywhere will go down in ruin.

We are told that we shall 'break the heart of the world' if we do not take this league just as it stands. I fear that the hearts of the vast majority of mankind would beat on strongly and steadily and without any quickening if the league were to perish altogether. If it should be effectively and beneficently changed the people who would lie awake in sorrow for a single night could be easily gathered in one not very large room but those who would draw a long breath of relief would reach to millions.

We hear much of visions and I trust we shall continue to have visions and dream dreams of a fairer future for the race. But visions are one thing and visionaries are another, and the mechanical appliances of the rhetorician designed to give a picture of a present which does not exist and of a future which no man can predict are as unreal and shortlived as the steam or canvas clouds, the angels suspended on wires and the artificial lights of the stage. They pass with the moment of effect and are shabby and tawdry in the daylight. Let us at least be real. Washington's entire honesty of mind and his fearless look into the face of all facts are qualities which can never go out of fashion and which we should all do well to imitate.

Ideals have been thrust upon us as an argument for the league until the healthy mind, which rejects cant, revolts from them. Are ideals confined to this deformed experiment upon a noble purpose, tainted as it is with bargains, and tied to a peace treaty which might have been disposed of long ago to the great benefit of the world if it had not been compelled to carry this rider on its back? "*Post equitem sedet atra cura,*" Horace tells us, but no blacker care ever sat behind any rider than we shall find in this covenant of doubtful and disputed interpretation as it now perches upon the treaty of peace.

No doubt many excellent and patriotic people see a coming fulfillment of noble ideals in the words "league for peace." We all respect and share these aspirations and desires, but some of us see no hope, but rather defeat, for them in this murky covenant. For we, too, have our ideals, even if we differ from those who have tried to establish a monopoly of idealism. Our first ideal is our country, and we see her in the future, as in the past, giving service to all her people and to the world. Our ideal of the future is that she should continue to render that service of her own free will. She has great problems of her own to solve, very grim and perilous problems, and a right solution, if we can attain to it, would largely benefit mankind. We would have our country strong to resist a peril from the West, as she has flung back the German menace from the East. We would not have our politics distracted and embittered by the dissensions of other lands. We would not have our country's vigor exhausted or her moral force abated, by everlasting meddling and muddling in every quarrel, great and small, which afflicts the world. Our ideal is to make her ever stronger and better and finer, because in that way alone, as we believe, can she be of the greatest service to the world's peace and to the welfare of mankind.

DISCUSSION QUESTIONS

1   How did "Interrupting the Ceremony" present U.S. concerns about the League of Nations?

2   What were Cabot Lodge's arguments against U.S. participation in the League of Nations?

3   What might reinforce the allure of isolationism at this time?

9

Wrestling with the Modern Age

THE MODERN WOMAN

By the 1920s, the idea of women's civic equality had been global for several decades, and barriers to public life and independence long established in many societies began to erode, albeit slowly. Some women expressed this newfound freedom through fashion choices and purchasing power, leisure activities, and careers. Many others felt more ambivalent about—or even resisted—changes in traditional roles for men and women, educational or career opportunities, and political participation. Contemporaries noted the 1920s as a time when the definition of womanhood appeared to be in flux, as societies around the world sought to define the proper place of woman in the modern age.

**World map by country with the decade women
obtained the right to vote, 1893–2011**

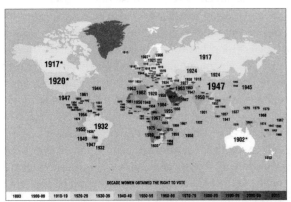

SEE COLOR INSERT

Margaret Sanger's "No Healthy Race without Birth Control," excerpt, 1921

Our girls must be brought up to realize that Motherhood is the most sacred profession in the world, and that it is a profession that requires more preparation than any other open to women. This preparation must be begun in infancy; but unlike much of the dull routine of what passes for preliminary "education" to-day, the "prerequisites" for motherhood should be made, and luckily for us, are being made more and more interesting for girls and young women. The first requisite is, of course, sound healthy bodies—and incidentally sound healthy minds—built up by play and sport and work of the right kind.

One of the most encouraging signs to-day is that more and more girls and women are entering into sports that build up strong bodies—swimming, diving, skating, tennis and many others—and that the old ideals and fashions of the all-too-ladylike are disappearing. The old-time fashion of fainting or swooning we read about in the novels of the nineteenth century is dead. The "wasp" waist is gone; and if the corset has not completely gone, it is going rapidly, with the long skirts that hampered the limbs, and the high heels that make walking a caricature. Once freed of these silly impediments women can never again give up their freedom. And if these styles are fatal to the flaws of obesity and thinness, those defects will somehow also disappear.

I place this stress upon healthy bodies for the future mothers of the race, because I am firmly convinced that strong healthy women will not choose as the fathers of their children puny, anemic men; and thus if our girls become more and more gloriously healthy, the boys will likewise have to be. The day is passing when any puny, underdeveloped male can "choose the mother of his children." The new, strong young woman will only be attracted to the physically fit young man. In this matter, we may trust the girl more than the young man.

Beauty is no longer skin deep. Nothing could be more false than that silly adage. Beauty, as we are more and more coming to recognize, is not a matter of a pair of blue eyes or brown, of Mary Pickford curls, or a skilfully imposed mask of make-up. Beauty is bone deep. Beauty is health and strength and soundness of limb and body. Take care of the body and the complexion will take care of itself. Develop your body and beauty, the real beauty, not the conventional and artificial, will inevitably result.

The well-developed, strong, healthy body is the first requisite for motherhood. And that includes brain development, intelligence and spirituality as well. These latter qualities are needed in the choosing of the husband. But once these problems are satisfactorily solved, the young woman may yet be unprepared for motherhood. If she has been a working woman, she will probably need rest and relaxation before undertaking the supreme task of maternity. . . . Under such conditions, while it may be most advisable for the young couple to marry, it may be financially impossible or impractical to bring children into the world the first years of marriage. This is especially true of city dwellers, where high rents and the high cost of living must first be met and mastered. Birth control, in one form or another, is then the most practical solution of this difficulty, and intelligent and irreproachable young married people are, more and more, in the interest of their children and the proper "spacing" of their families, becoming adherents of this doctrine. . . .

Physical fitness being the first great requirement for parenthood, the young married woman cannot be too selfish regarding her own health. She must guard it jealously; and she is always justified in refusing to sacrifice this health for sentimental reasons. It is her own most precious treasure as well as that of the whole race. With the physical exercises and sports I mentioned above, there is an equal and no less important complementary need of complete relaxation and rest. Too much importance cannot be put on the value of deep untroubled sleep as the completest and sweetest restorer of tired nerves and muscles.

Only secondary to the menace of the great racial diseases is the danger of fatigue to potential motherhood. . . .

Every mother and mother-to-be should protect the fundamental rights of her babies and in fact of all babies. . . .

An awakened and enlightened public opinion, particularly of a mobilized and militant motherhood, might accomplish in this field invaluable benefits and put us on the surest and straightest road to radiant racial health.

Tamara de Lempicka image of the modern woman in *Die Dame* magazine, Germany, 1929

Kiyoshi Kobayakawa art piece on the modern female, Japan, 1930

SEE COLOR INSERT

Deng Yingchao's experiences in the May Fourth Movement, China, 1919

The May Fourth Movement was also the catalyst for the women's liberation movement in China. Women's liberation was an important part of the democratic ideals behind the May Fourth Movement, and brought forth slogans such as "equality between men and women" and "oppose arranged marriage," while demanding such ideals as "open social interaction," "freedom of love," "freedom of marriage," "lift restrictions on women's education," "open employment for women in every sphere," and more. The first step towards this in Tianjin was for the male and female student unions to merge and work together. This also faced some opposition at first. Not all female students agreed with it. Some worried that public opinion was not on their side, while others were afraid that people would say integration would lead to both men and women making fools of themselves. The progressive activist students, both male and female, broke through these obstacles and integrated with great results. Male and female students worked together in a spirit of candor, respect, and equality. Everyone put all their efforts into the struggle to save their country. In any kind of working competition, the women never gave way. The female activists understood that they must blaze a trail for future generations. They had to serve as a model, never drawing ridicule from society, so that the next generation could carry on their legacy. The male activists of the time were well influenced by the new tide of thinking and had broken away from old ideals that value men over women, treating all their female peers with respect. Working duties were almost entirely equal. For every department in the student union, where there was a male in charge there also had to be a female counterpart.

Hu Huaichen article on freeing slave girls, China, 1920

Why did I want to write this essay? Because I see that the Chinese system of keeping slave girls is wrong. Their masters don't treat slave girls as people, and abuse them as they would cattle or horses. Some cattle and horses even receive better treatment than the slave girls do, yet there is nothing the girls can do about it. This is certainly wrong from a humanist perspective. Furthermore, since their masters do not treat them as people, they themselves do not know how to act as such. They always have intentions to cheat their masters; when shopping, they lose money. When doing chores, they slack off, not caring if they cause inconvenience to others. When cooking, they waste oil, fuel, and ingredients. In the end, this is detrimental to their masters. When looking at it this way, we see that the slave girl system should be abolished. Those who have embraced the new thinking of this time understand this, so I won't speak of these factors much. The problem is that they speak of this problem too loftily and broadly, and not in terms of practicality. They speak the truth, yet their ideas cannot necessarily be put into action. The purpose of this essay is to not only speak of the problem but provide practical solutions, rather than preach empty words.

Why do I say that their ideas are too lofty, or too broad? With the new wave of thinking, when people discuss women's liberation, it includes nearly all kinds of women. Isn't this too broad? For example, women who are already able to live independently of course do not need liberation. Women who are not well-educated and require assistance before they can live independently also do not fall into the range of women who need liberation. There are roughly three types of women who do need liberation: prostitutes, concubines, and slave girls. These three kinds of women have truly been bound by others, their freedoms seized and discarded. They live in terrible conditions. When discussing humanism, why is it that we do not discuss these people, who are bound in a living hell? Furthermore, if they are not liberated, not only will they come to harm, so too will others. If we are to change our society, it is imperative that we free these people.

That said, these three kinds of people are quite different, and the methods by which our movement must liberate them are also different. It will be more difficult to free the prostitutes and concubines than to free the slave girls. Therefore, for now I will first discuss only how to free the slave girls. This is not to say that we should not free prostitutes or concubines, nor is it to say that their liberation should be any slower than that of slave girls. Rather, this essay is specifically for those women who have embraced the new thinking of our time. My hope is that this task will be carried out by women, without the need of additional help from men. Given the current situation, it will be much easier for women to liberate slave girls than to liberate the prostitutes and concubines. Therefore, why not start from this easier task? . . .

Why do I want women to do this themselves? Educated women with new ideas are women, yet so too are slave girls. Women have a closer stake in this matter than men do. Furthermore, most slave girls work for women, not men. Therefore, the power to free slave girls is in the hands of women, and must be completed by them rather than men. It is for this reason that I say this is a task that women must carry out themselves. How then, should this liberation happen? The way I see it, there are two layers to this issue. The first is that those who do not have slave girls must never claim one. The second is that those who do have slave girls must release them immediately.

There are two methods for liberation. The first is for those who have the power to release their slave girls to release them immediately. The second is for those who do not have the power to release a slave girl to urge those who do have that power to do so. For example, if my mother, sister, other relative, or neighbor keeps a slave girl, I do not have the power to release that slave girl. I must persuade my mother, sister, or neighbor to release them. If they don't listen the first time, try a second time. If they don't listen the second time, try a third time, and again and again until the day you finally reach your goal. These are the only two methods of freeing slave girls, and anyone can do them.

A big problem then is what these girls shall do after being freed. The way I see it, the only thing one can do is to treat them as one's own daughter. If she is young, she can be sent to school. When she comes home, she can be taught how to help around the house, only being told to do those things that she can do, should do, that are beneficial to the household, and will not harm her. If she is older, she can be married or kept in the family, where you can teach her good human behavior yourself and how to contribute to the household. When it comes time for her to be married however, do so with care; do not simply sell her off for the money. If you treat her well like this, she will naturally come to see you as her own mother. She will not want to deceive you anymore. Though such habits are hard to break overnight, so you must teach her slowly and patiently.

While she may be disciplined for misbehavior, only do so as you would your own family member. One's own children also misbehave sometimes, yet a one-time misbehavior does not change your unending love for them. This must also be how we treat these slave girls. In short, they must be treated as one's own family.

Some people say that slave girls are also daughters to their own families. It was only because their families had no money that they sold them into slavery. Therefore, pitying the girls would not be as good as returning them to their families without demanding any money in return. In rare cases, this can be done. There are several difficulties in this however. For starters, most slave girls don't know where their real parents are, and wouldn't be able to find them. Secondly, their parents were able to sell them off once before. If you return the girl to them, there is no guarantee that they would not do so again. This kind of liberation is no liberation at all. This is why I say that while occasionally this method can be done, it must be done with great care. One must understand completely the responsibility on one's shoulders for freeing slave girls.

These are the only methods for freeing slave girls. As for what to do with the slave girls after they are freed, I have one more thing to say. I wish to say to everyone that no matter the issue, when only one person does it, everyone else will think it is strange. There will be many who oppose it, so it will become more difficult to be carried out to completion. Yet if many people do it, others will see it and think that they should do it too, and there will be less opposition, making the task easier to complete. Therefore, if women wish to do this, they should first form an association for freeing slave girls, where they can achieve much more by combining their energies. The guiding principles for this association would roughly be as such:

First, this association's name shall be The Association for the Liberation of Slave Girls.

Second, all association members shall be women.

Third, the duties of association members shall be that those who have slave girls release them, those that don't persuade those who do to release their slave girls.

Fourth, there are no duties beyond these.

By following these few steps, creating this association should be relatively easy. There need not be any special procedures; members need only quietly carry out their duties. This method of liberation only involves freeing one or two people at a time, rather than many all at once. And finally, the girls would still stay in their masters' homes, the only difference would be their treatment. This is easy to do.

Some will say that this sounds great, but are afraid that there are many people who will not understand. They might listen to you and say that they will free their slave girls, but continue to abuse them the moment you turn your back, so why do you waste your breath? To that I say that there certainly will be people like this. But if out of ten people, four or five listen to me and free their slave girls, then we could say that we have nearly a 50% success rate. For those who said they would free their slave girls but didn't, we can continue to persuade at least one or two of them, increasing our success rate 10 or 20%. Those remaining who still don't listen may be ostracized. They will lose face and have no choice but to change. Furthermore, a system should be established to monitor the treatment of these freed girls, as well as a system to teach these girls how to become aware themselves. If these three things are all done at once, how will it not succeed?

My wish in writing this essay is that others will take its ideas to fruition. Originally, I had hoped to start this organization myself. However, I hope that it will be women who create this association for freeing slave girls, so I do not wish to interfere. I do not have any slave girls myself to free either, so I see my duty as nothing more than writing this essay. I hope that the ideas within will be carried out by the women who have embraced new thinking.

Queen Soraya on the liberation of Afghan women, Afghanistan, 1922

To my dear sisters, the inhabitants of Kabul and its vicinity:

The following provisions have been ratified for your welfare and that of your daughters and are herewith announced for your information.

Every one knows that mankind originated from one man and one woman. Had there been only one man and not a woman or vice versa the human race would have been quickly extinguished from the surface of the earth. Therefore, by strict definition, neither a man nor a woman alone can be regarded as a complete human. A man and a woman together form the complete human being, as the survival of both is essential for the continuation of the human race. Thus, the responsibilities of life have been divided between men and women. Women are in charge of raising children, preparing food and managing the household, and men are responsible for earning a living and providing for the family. If we examine their respective roles carefully, we see that the responsibilities of women are even more difficult than those of men, particularly in the area of child care, which means that without acquiring proper education herself, it is virtually impossible for a woman to properly fulfill this most important responsibility in life. Women are in charge of bringing up the future generation, the most important responsibility in life. If we deprive women of education, we have, in effect, incapacitated half of our body and have destroyed our subsistence with our own hands.

It was not in vain that Hazrat Mohammad (may peace be upon him) made the acquisition of knowledge obligatory for both men and women without ascribing any special privilege [to men] when he said, "to gain knowledge is the religious duty of all Muslim men and women." The Mohammadan law (*shar`-imostafawi*) allows a woman to become a *qazi*, and it is obvious that in order to reach that rank one has to go through years of study with a great master and acquire a great deal of knowledge. This proves that [in Islam] education is considered equally important for women. In the days when literacy had become common among Muslims and educational centers were established throughout the Muslim world, many women like men became famous scholars, *mohadithas* (specialists of *hadith*), literary persons, and artists. We all know that the *sahaba* and *tabe`in* consulted the Hazrats Om al-Momenin `Ayisha Seddiqa, Om Salma and Hafasa and sought their *fatwa* on difficult matters. Asiya bint Jar al-Allah was one of the great scholars of *hadith*. Jalal al-Din Saiyuti, the great Muslim scholar, took lessons from her. Ay Malak, the sister of Sheikh Jamal-al-Din Shara`i, was a contemporary of lbn `Ajaz `Asqalan, the great scholar of *mohadith*, with whom she had many scholarly debates. Asma' bint Mohammad, the sister of Qazi al-Qozat Najm al-Din, was acclaimed as a pious woman and a scholar of *hadith*. She studied and taught many books on the *hadith* of Makki. Imam Saiyuti studied the *Thalathiyat-i-Mosnad* under Alef bint al-Jamal. There are many examples of highly educated and famous women scholars, teachers, and saints in Islamic history, and there are many examples of women who demonstrated great bravery in war. In short, it is rational and legally proper for women to acquire knowledge.

In response to an urgent need, two girls schools, Maktab-i-Masturat and Maktab-i-`Asmat, were established last year in Sara-i-`Olya and Qal`a-i-Baqer Khan in Kabul. However, since neither of these schools could accommodate more students, and the first one was a little too far from the city, both schools were merged in Golistan Saray, which has superior rooms and can house 800 students. In this way all female students will be able to meet in one place, where their expenses for clothing, food, veils, and books will be paid by the government on an equal basis. A number of skilled teachers will be recruited from inside the country and from abroad to teach classes in home economics, child development, sewing, knitting, and cooking. Since the regular girls' school will recruit only young girls between the ages of six and ten, a vocational school has been established for adult women to provide professional training in sewing, cooking, and making artificial flowers. The purpose of this school is to help women learn new skills and become financially independent in order to release themselves from total financial dependence on their husbands or their families. By the end of the year 1301 [1922], the students who graduate with the first, second or third rank in any of the above professions will receive awards of 1000, 700, and 400 rupees, respectfully. If a student ranks first in all three, she will receive 1,500, and if she ranks second in all three, she will receive 1000 rupees. In addition, by learning a skill that will help them earn money, women will become assets to their husbands. The vocational women's school (Maktab-iSanayi`-i-Onathia) is also housed in Golistan Saray and is awaiting the attendance of ambitious and high-minded sisters.

Qualified teachers will receive good salaries and, in addition, will render a service to the educational program of our beloved country.

By means of his proclamation, I inform you that whosoever wants to register in Maktab-i-Masturat or Sanayi`-i-Onathia or would like to apply for a teaching position should send her resume to the director of Maktab-i-Masturat for permission and benefit from sources of knowledge and information. At this stage, students will be placed in different classes according to the level of their achievement.

> The supervisor of women's schools
> Seal of Queen Soraya
> (signed) Shahzada Khanom

360 DISCUSSION QUESTIONS

1   During this period, what were some women in the U.S. doing to demonstrate their modernity? Compare and contrast to other examples above.

2   What was the role of consumerism in the persona of the modern woman?

3   According to the sources here, how did different individuals and societies define "freedom" for women?

4   What appears to have been the connection between being "modern" and being "Western"?

POSTWAR UNREST

9-1 | Selection from the application for membership in the Communist International on behalf of the Communist Party of America, 1919

The 1917 revolutions in Russia first raised, then dashed U.S. hopes for a democratic ally in Eurasia. The abdication of Tsar Nicholas II in February 1917, the promise of elections, and the willingness of the provisional government to continue fighting the Great War seemed to portend increased cooperation between the United States and Russia. The unexpected Bolshevik Revolution in October 1917, however, established a communist government for the first time, elevating to power Vladimir Lenin (1870–1924) and the Bolshevik Party. The new regime withdrew from the Great War and lobbied workers around the world to join in international revolution. Lenin made a personal, public appeal to American workers in 1918. The Third International, or Comintern, was the proselytizing arm of the Bolsheviks. U.S. fears about the spread of communism, the radicalization of labor and other oppressed peoples, and domestic unrest led to the First Red Scare (1919–1920). Below is the closing section of the Communist Party of America's application for membership in Comintern.

6. The General Situation

The Communist Party appears at a moment of profound proletarian unrest. There has been strike after strike, developing larger and more aggressive character. There is now a strike of more than 300,000 workers in the steel industry, a really terrific portent to American Capitalism.

There is a revolutionary upsurge in the old unions; the longshoremen of Seattle have just refused to allow munitions for Kolchak & Co. to be transported. There is a strong sentiment in favor of the Russian Soviet Republic. In the unions the workers are becoming conscious of the reactionary character of their officials, and movements of protest and a sentiment for industrial unionism are developing.

But the American Federation of Labor, as a whole, is hopelessly reactionary. At its recent convention the A.F. of L. approved the Versailles Peace Treaty and the League of Nations, and refused to declare its solidarity with Soviet Russia. It did not even protest the blockade of Russia and Hungary! This convention, moreover, did all in its power to break radical unions. The A.F. of L. is united with the government, securing a privileged status in the governing system of State Capitalism. A Labor Party is being organized—much more conservative than the British Labor Party.

The Industrial Workers of the World is waging an aggressive campaign of organization. It has decided to affiliate with the Communist International; but its press and spokesmen show no understanding of Communist tactics. The I.W.W. still clings to its old concepts of organizing all the workers industrially, gradually "growing into" the new society, as the only means of achieving the revolution; a conception as utopian as that of the moderate socialist, who proposes to "grow into" socialism by transforming the bourgeois state. The Communist Party endorses the I.W.W. as a revolutionary mass movement, while criticising its theoretical shortcomings.

Imperialism is now consciously dominant in the United States. In his recent tour for the League of Nations, President Wilson threw off the mask and spoke in plain imperialistic terms, emphasizing the absolute necessity of crushing Soviet Russia. Congress drifts, and is impotent. The government, federal and local, is adopting the most repressive measures against the proletariat. Armed force, martial law, and military invasion are used against strikes. State after state has adopted "Criminal Syndicalism" measures, making almost any advocacy of militant proletarian tactics a crime. On the least pretext agitators are arrested. Deportations occur almost daily; one of our International Delegates, A. Stoklitsky, is now under trial for deportation.

American imperialism is usurping world power, constituting the very heart of international reaction. Reaction in Europe and the campaign against Soviet Russia are supported morally and financially by "our" government. An enormous agitation is being waged for military intervention in Mexico. The American capitalist class is brutal, unscrupulous, powerful; it controls enormous reserves of financial, industrial, and military power; it is determined to use this power to conquer world supremacy and to crush the revolutionary proletariat.

The Communist Party realizes the immensity of the task; it realizes that the final struggle of the Communist proletariat will be waged in the United States, our conquest of power alone assuring the world Soviet Republic. Realizing all this, the Communist Party prepares for the struggle.

Long live the Communist International! Long live the world revolution!

> Fraternally Yours,
> Louis C. Fraina
> International Secretary

Attest:
C. Ruthenberg
Executive Secretary

DISCUSSION QUESTIONS

1 How did Fraina characterize the relationships between workers, employers, and
   authorities in the U.S.?

2 How did Fraina distinguish the approaches of the American Federation of Labor and
   the Industrial Workers of the World?

3 Why, according to Fraina, was the Communist Party necessary in the United States?

9–2 | Carey Orr, political cartoon, "Close the Gate," 1919

Carey Orr (1890–1967) was a Pulitzer Prize–winning American editorial cartoonist.
Here, in "Close the Gate," the sentiments of the First Red Scare (1919–1920) in the
United States are expressed. This fear of anarchism and Bolshevism came both from the
hyper-nationalism of World War I and the outcome of the October Revolution in Russia.
Both real and imagined events drove a breakdown in social order that led to unwarranted
arrests and detentions, deportations, illegal search and seizures, and violence.

CLOSE THE GATE.
—Orr in the Chicago *Tribune.*

DISCUSSION QUESTIONS

1 Describe how the artist portrayed both immigrants and the United States. What visual
   clues did he provide?

2 How might an opponent of immigration restriction respond?

9–3a | Photograph, two soldiers facing off during
Red Summer riots in Chicago, 1919

Demobilization combined with racial tensions and the Red Scare (see chapter 9, item 1) to create conditions ripe for social unrest in the United States. In 1919, a series of violent and deadly race riots wracked cities and communities across the country, resulting in the deaths of hundreds. Three of the worst occurred in Washington, D.C., Phillips County, Arkansas, and Chicago, the setting of the photograph below. For thirteen days, white mobs rampaged through black homes and businesses on Chicago's South Side, attacking black people as they went. Notable about the Red Summer confrontations, however, was the presence and role of black veterans of the Great War, empowered by their military service abroad to confront injustice at home. They defended themselves, and, in conjunction with the National Guard, were able to bring the rioting to an end.

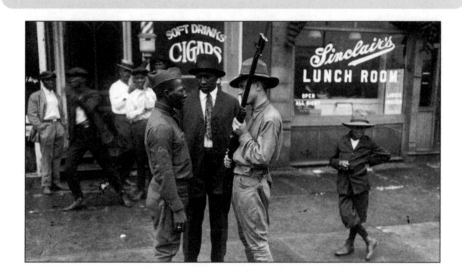

9–3b | The African Christian Association, petition to the Lord Mayor
regarding the plight of West Indians and Africans in Liverpool, UK, 1920

Although it was not as widespread as in the United States, Great Britain dealt with unrest related to demobilization of troops, competition for jobs, imperial immigration, and racial tension. Black defense workers, sailors, and troops played a key role in sustaining the British war effort in the Great War. Labor unions blamed black men for the lack of jobs at war's end and imposed rules against hiring black laborers. As in the U.S. case, demobilized black veterans of the war and war workers asserted their rights, protesting against racist hiring practices. Violence broke out in the seaport of Liverpool in the summer of 1919, as mobs of white men ransacked black homes and attacked their inhabitants, and continued into the 1920s. The petition below, from the African Christian

Association, appealed to the Mayor of Liverpool on behalf of the black community. As a solution, authorities first suggested repatriation of black people, then proceeded to legalize discrimination against hiring anyone born in the colonies.

A Petition to the Lord Mayor of Liverpool from the African Christian Association

To:-

His Honour The Lord Mayor,

LIVERPOOL.

May it please your Lordship. The petition of your humble servants showeth:-

That in the City of Liverpool and districts there are several hundred coloured men; Africans, West Indians etc, and that the African Christian Association, an organisation founded for the welfare of the coloured people of Liverpool, have deputised us to lay before your Lordship the following facts on their behalf:—

That the majority of these men are British subjects and saw service during the War either as soldiers or sailors in the Mercantile Marine or else were engaged in factories on essential products and very many of them served with distinction in the firing line on all fronts.

Many of the men during the Submarine menace, were employed in plying the seas, bringing food and material into England, and we particularly want to emphasise that during the period of England's greatest danger, every inducement was given to these men to come into England and they were led to believe that they were very welcome in this country.

This belief was first shattered in the riots of June 1919. Since then, coloured men in Liverpool have found themselves opposed to a very unfavourable public sentiment through no fault of their own.

To be specific:—

(1). The coloured people of this City are daily insulted in the streets and their presence barely tolerated in many places.

(2). They are attacked and assaulted without the slightest provocation and,

(3). As a result of an economic boycott, hundreds of our men have been ejected from their employment and left completely stranded in the City to-day.

It is superfluous to remind your Lordship that such a state of things cannot long continue without leading to serious trouble; also, as it is almost impossible for the men to obtain employment, and any scheme that may be launched for their repatriation must necessarily occupy a considerable time, your Lordship must see that there is only the Workhouse or crime left open to the men.

It is because we are anxious therefore to prevent our men from being involved in any trouble, that your petitioners have approached your Lordship and pray for a release from this dire predicament.

We ask it all the more because we feel that the present treatment to which the men are subjected is:—

(1). Incompatible with the traditional British sense of justice and fair-play.

(2). As British subjects, the men feel themselves entitled to better consideration from the public for whom they fought and died.

(3). The coloured man has never spared himself to ensure the integrity and solidarity of the Empire.

(4). And particularly do we appeal to your Lordship because the welfare of this City is, to a considerable degree, dependent on the exertions of our "kith and kin" in Africa, and it is easy to imagine what an economic boycott on the other end would mean.

(5). And surely your Lordship must agree with your petitioners that it is not the soundest policy to allow these men to return to their homes and tribes with any bitterness in their hearts from the result of maltreatment in England.

We venture to hope that your Lordship will give us your sympathetic consideration, for which we are ever bound to pray, and afford us the benefit of your advice and a solution out of the present dilemma.

We remain, with sentiments of the highest esteem and consideration, on behalf of the A.C.A.

> J. A. Dewitt Martyn
> Secretary A.C.A.
> August 17th 1920.

DISCUSSION QUESTIONS

1   Consider the photograph and its date. Describe what might be happening in the photo.

2   What were the ACA leaders trying to accomplish by contacting the Lord Mayor?

3   How did demobilization alter the lives of soldiers and workers?

9–4 | Illustration, graphing of foreign-born population in United States in 1920, 1921

The illustration below appeared in the May 2, 1921, issue of *The Literary Digest*, a well-regarded U.S. general interest magazine published by Funk & Wagnalls. It features an array of the "foreign-born" presumably clad in some mishmash of national costume and immigrant-wear, along with U.S. population statistics for 1920. The illustrated chart accompanied an article titled "An Alien Antidumping Bill," a lengthy piece detailing arguments for and against what would later be known as the Emergency Quota Act of 1921—the first act in U.S. history to employ numerical limits to immigration via a quota system based on national origins. A product of postwar anxieties, xenophobia, and isolationist sentiment, the Emergency Quota Act limited immigration to 3 percent of the total of each nationality in the 1910 U.S. census. Although it was intended as an "emergency measure" of limited duration—fourteen months—the act opened the door for future policymakers.

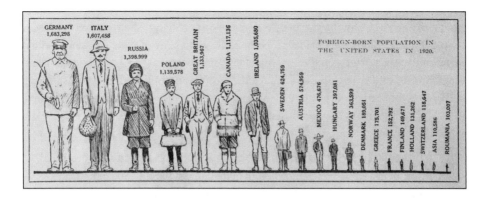

DISCUSSION QUESTIONS

1   Why would immigration be such an issue during this period? Would any of these immigrant population numbers have caused a particular concern? Why?

2   What might have been arguments for and against using a quota system to regulate immigration?

3   From what countries were immigrants coming? How would you characterize immigration patterns according to the 1920 census?

CULTURE AND SOCIETY IN THE INTERWAR PERIOD

9–5a | Marcus Garvey and the Universal Negro Improvement Association (UNIA), excerpts from the "Declaration of the Rights of the Negro Peoples of the World," 1920

Marcus Garvey (1887–1940), a Jamaican activist and writer, founded the Universal Negro Improvement Association and African Communities League (UNIA) in July 1914. Capitalizing on postwar dissatisfaction among black veterans, the UNIA expanded to include branches in at least thirty-eight states of the U.S., the West Indies, Central America, and West Africa by the 1920s. Founded as a black nationalist organization for Africans and the African diaspora, the UNIA proposed racial separatism—specifically, an autonomous black state in Africa—as the solution to the inequalities faced by the black community worldwide. A controversial figure, Garvey supported the Back to Africa movement, expressed approval of Ku Klux Klan principles, and proposed he rule a united African state, for which he was reviled as a dangerous demagogue by many African American leaders, such as W. E. B. Du Bois. Nevertheless, Garvey's Declaration of the Rights of the Negro Peoples of the World is regarded as a seminal statement of black pride and human rights, and the influence of the UNIA can be seen in the Nation of Islam and Rastafarianism.

Be it Resolved, That the Negro people of the world, through their chosen representatives in convention assembled in Liberty Hall, in the City of New York and United States of America, from August 1 to August 31, in the year of our Lord, one thousand nine hundred and twenty, protest against the wrongs and injustices they are suffering at the hands of their white brethren, and state what they deem their fair and just rights, as well as the treatment they propose to demand of all men in the future.

We complain:

I.   That nowhere in the world, with few exceptions, are black men accorded equal treatment with white men, although in the same situation and circumstances, but, on the contrary, are discriminated against and denied the common rights due to human beings for no other reason than their race and color.

     We are not willingly accepted as guests in the public hotels and inns of the world for no other reason than our race and color.

II.   In certain parts of the United States of America our race is denied the right of public trial accorded to other races when accused of crime, but are lynched and burned by mobs, and such brutal and inhuman treatment is even practiced upon our women.

III.   That European nations have parcelled out among them and taken possession of nearly all of the continent of Africa, and the natives are compelled to surrender their lands to aliens and are treated in most instances like slaves.

IV.   In the southern portion of the United States of America, although citizens under the Federal Constitution, and in some states almost equal to the whites in population and are qualified land owners and taxpayers, we are nevertheless, denied all voice in the making and administration of the laws and are taxed without representation by the State governments, and at the same time compelled to do military service in defense of the country.

V.   On the public conveyances and common carriers in the Southern portion of the United States we are jim-crowed and compelled to accept separate and inferior accommodations and made to pay the same fare charged for first-class accommodations, and our families are often humiliated and insulted by drunken white men who habitually pass through the jim-crow cars going to the smoking car.

VI.   The physicians of our race are denied the right to attend their patients while in the public hospitals of the cities and States where they reside in certain parts of the United States.

     Our children are forced to attend inferior separate schools for shorter terms than white children, and the public school funds are unequally divided between the white and colored schools.

VII. We are discriminated against and denied an equal chance to earn wages for the support of our families, and in many instances are refused admission into labor unions, and nearly everywhere are paid smaller wages than white men.

VIII. In Civil Service and departmental offices we are everywhere discriminated against and made to feel that to be a black man in Europe, America and the West Indies is equivalent to being an outcast and a leper among the races of men, no matter what the character attainments of the black man may be.

IX. In the British and other West Indian Islands and colonies, Negroes are secretly and cunningly discriminated against, and denied those fuller rights of government to which white citizens are appointed, nominated and elected.

X. That our people in those parts are forced to work for lower wages than the average standard of white men and are kept in conditions repugnant to good civilized tastes and customs.

XI. That the many acts of injustice against members of our race before the courts of law in the respective islands and colonies are of such nature as to create disgust and disrespect for the white man's sense of justice.

XII. Against all such inhuman, unchristian and uncivilized treatment we here and now emphatically protest, and invoke the condemnation of all mankind.

In order to encourage our race all over the world and to stimulate it to a higher and grander destiny, we demand and insist on the following Declaration of Rights:

1. Be it known to all men that whereas, all men are created equal and entitled to the rights of life, liberty and the pursuit of happiness, and because of this we, the duly elected representatives of the Negro peoples of the world, invoking the aid of the just and Almighty God to declare all men, women and children of our blood throughout the world free citizens, and do claim them as free citizens of Africa, the Motherland of all Negroes.

2. That we believe in the supreme authority of our race in all things racial: that all things are created and given to man as a common possession: that there should be an equitable distribution and apportionment of all such things, and in consideration of the fact that as a race we are now deprived of those things that are morally and legally ours, we believed it right that all such things should be acquired and held by whatsoever means possible.

3. That we believe the Negro, like any other race, should be governed by the ethics of civilization, and therefore should not be deprived of any of those rights or privileges common to other human beings.

4. We declare that Negroes, wheresoever they form a community among themselves should be given the right to elect their own representatives to represent them in Legislatures, courts of law, or such institutions as may exercise control over that particular community.

5. We assert that the Negro is entitled to even-handed justice before all courts of law and equity in whatever country he may be found, and when this is denied him on account of his race or color such denial is an insult to the race as a whole and should be resented by the entire body of Negroes.

6. We declare it unfair and prejudicial to the rights of Negroes in communities where they exist in considerable numbers to be tried by a judge and jury composed entirely of an alien race, but in all such cases members of our race are entitled to representation on the jury.

7. We believe that any law or practice that tends to deprive any African of his land or the privileges of free citizenship within his country injust and immoral, and no native should respect any such law or practice.

8. We declare taxation without representation unjust and tyrranous [sic], and there should be no obligation on the part of the Negro to obey the levy of a tax by any law-making body from which he is excluded and denied representation on account of his race and color.

9. We believe that any law especially directed against the Negro to his detriment and singling him out because of his race or color is unfair and immoral, and should not be respected.

10. We believe all men entitled to common human respect, and that our race should in no way tolerate any insults that may be interpreted to mean disrespect to our color.

11. We deprecate the use of the term "nigger" as applied to Negroes, and demand that the word "Negro" be written with a capital "N."

12. We believe that the Negro should adopt every means to protect himself against barbarous practices inflicted upon him because of color.

13. We believe in the freedom of Africa for the Negro people of the world, and by the principle of Europe for the Europeans and Asia for the Asiatics, we also demand Africa for the Africans at home and abroad.

14. We believe in the inherent right of the Negro to possess himself of Africa, and that his possession of same shall not be regarded as an infringement of any claim or purchase made by any race or nation.

15. We strongly condemn the cupidity of those nations of the world who, by open aggression or secret schemes, have seized the territories and inexhaustible natural wealth of Africa, and we place on record our most solemn determination to reclaim the treasures and possession of the vast continent of our forefathers.

16. We believe all men should live in peace one with the other, but when races and nations provoke the ire of other races and nations by attempting to

infringe upon their rights, war becomes inevitable, and the attempt in any way to free one's self or protect one's rights or heritage becomes justifiable.

17. Whereas, the lynching, by burning, hanging or any other means, of human beings is a barbarous practice and a shame and disgrace to civilization, we therefore declare any country guilty of such atrocities outside the pale of civilization.

18. We protest against the atrocious crime of whipping, flogging and overworking of the native tribes of Africa and Negroes everywhere. These are methods that should be abolished, and all means should be taken to prevent a continuance of such brutal practices.

19. We protest against the atrocious practice of shaving the heads of Africans, especially of African women or individuals of Negro blood, when placed in prison as a punishment for crime by an alien race.

20. We protest against segregated districts, separate public conveyances, industrial discrimination, lynchings and limitations of political privileges of any Negro citizen in any part of the world on account of race, color or creed, and will exert our full influence and power against all such. . . .

9–5b | W. E. B. Du Bois, excerpts from "Credo" and "The Souls of White Folk," 1920

William Edward Burghardt Du Bois (1868–1963), Harvard PhD, historian and sociologist, professor, activist, public intellectual, and writer, was the foremost spokesperson in the African American civil rights movement in the first half of the twentieth century. Like Garvey, Du Bois conceived of the black community as global. As illustrated in the selections below, he railed against imperialism and its attitudes, while praising black pride; he deplored Jim Crow and discrimination, while hailing black unity across borders. Unlike Garvey, Du Bois sought racial integration, not separatism. As a co-founder of the multiracial National Association for the Advancement of Colored People (NAACP), he publicized and supported its campaigns against segregation, disenfranchisement, and lynching.

Credo

I believe in God, who made of one blood all nations that on earth do dwell. I believe that all men, black and brown and white, are brothers, varying through Time and Opportunity, in form and gift and feature, but differing in no essential particular, and alike in soul and the possibility of infinite development.

Especially do I believe in the Negro Race; in the beauty of its genius, the sweetness of its soul, and its strength in that meekness which shall yet inherit this turbulent earth.

I believe in pride of race and lineage and self; in pride of self so deep as to scorn injustice to other selves; in pride of lineage so great as to despise no man's father; in pride of race so chivalrous as neither to offer bastardy to the weak nor beg wedlock of the strong, knowing that men may be brothers in Christ, even tho they be not brothers-in-law.

I believe in Service—humble reverent service, from the blackening of boots to the whitening of souls; for Work is Heaven, Idleness Hell, and Wage is the "Well done!" of the Master who summoned all them that labor and are heavy laden, making no distinction between the black sweating cotton hands of Georgia and the First Families of Virginia, since all distinction not based on deed is devilish and not divine.

I believe in the Devil and his angels, who wantonly work to narrow the opportunity of struggling human beings, especially if they be black; who spit in the faces of the fallen, strike them that cannot strike again, believe the worst and work to prove it, hating the image which their Maker stamped on a brother's soul.

I believe in the Prince of Peace. I believe that War is Murder. I believe that armies and navies are at bottom the tinsel and braggadocio of oppression and wrong; and I believe that the wicked conquest of weaker and darker nations by nations whiter and stronger but foreshadows the death of that strength.

I believe in Liberty for all men: the space to stretch their arms and their souls; the right to breathe and the right to vote, the freedom to choose their friends, enjoy the sunshine and ride on the railroads, uncursed by color; thinking, dreaming, working as they will in a kingdom of God and love.

I believe in the training of children black even as white; the leading out of little souls into the green pastures and beside the still waters, not for pelf or peace, but for Life lit by some large vision of beauty and goodness and truth: lest we forget and the sons of the fathers, like Esau, for mere meat barter their birthright in a mighty nation.

Finally, I believe in Patience—patience with the weakness of the Weak and the strength of the Strong, the prejudice of the Ignorant and the ignorance of the Blind; patience with the tardy triumph of Joy and the mad chastening of Sorrow—patience with God!

The Souls of the White Folk

Whither is this expansion? What is that breath of life, thought to be so indispensable to a great European nation? Manifestly it is expansion overseas; it is colonial aggrandizement which explains, and alone adequately explains, the World War. How many of us today fully realize the current theory of colonial expansion, of the relation of Europe which is white, to the world which is black and brown and yellow? Bluntly put, that theory is this: It is the duty of white Europe to divide up the darker world and administer it for Europe's good.

This Europe has largely done. The European world is using black and brown men for all the uses which men know. Slowly but surely white culture is evolving the theory that "darkies" are born beasts of burden for white folk. It were silly to think otherwise, cries the cultured world, with stronger and shriller accord. The supporting arguments grow and twist themselves in the mouths of merchant, scientist, soldier, traveler, writer, and missionary: Darker peoples are dark in mind as well as in body; of dark, uncertain, and imperfect descent; of frailer, cheaper stuff; they are cowards in the face of mausers and maxims; they have no feelings, aspirations, and loves; they are fools, illogical idiots,—"half-devil and half-child."

. . .

This theory of human culture and its aims has worked itself through warp and woof of our daily thought with a thoroughness that few realize. Everything great, good, efficient, fair, and honorable is "white"; everything mean, bad, blundering, cheating, and dishonorable is "yellow"; a bad taste is "brown"; and the devil is "black." The changes of this theme are continually rung in picture and story, in newspaper heading and moving-picture, in sermon and school book, until, of course, the King can do no wrong,—a White Man is always right and a Black Man has no rights which a white man is bound to respect.

. . .

Let me say this again and emphasize it and leave no room for mistaken meaning: The World War was primarily the jealous and avaricious struggle for the largest share in exploiting darker races. As such it is and must be but the prelude to the armed and indignant protest of these despised and raped peoples. Today Japan is hammering on the door of justice, China is raising her half-manacled hands to knock next, India is writhing for the freedom to knock, Egypt is sullenly muttering, the Negroes of South and West Africa, of the West Indies, and of the United States are just awakening to their shameful slavery. Is, then, this war the end of wars? Can it be the end, so long as sits enthroned, even in the souls of those who cry peace, the despising and robbing of darker peoples? If Europe hugs this delusion, then this is not the end of world war,—it is but the beginning!

We see Europe's greatest sin precisely where we found Africa's and Asia's,—in human hatred, the despising of men; with this difference, however: Europe has the awful lesson of the past before her, has the splendid results of widened areas of tolerance, sympathy, and love among men, and she faces a greater, an infinitely greater, world of men than any preceding civilization ever faced.

It is curious to see America, the United States, looking on herself, first, as a sort of natural peacemaker, then as a moral protagonist in this terrible time. No nation is less fitted for this rôle. For two or more centuries America has marched proudly in the van of human hatred,—making bonfires of human flesh and laughing at them hideously, and making the insulting of millions more than a matter of dislike,—rather a great religion, a world war-cry: Up white, down black; to your tents, O white folk, and world war with black and parti-colored mongrel beasts!

DISCUSSION QUESTIONS

1   Categorize the complaints and demands in Garvey's Declaration.

2   What methods and systems, according to Du Bois, perpetuated the myth of black inferiority?

3   How were the solutions to racial discrimination offered by Garvey and the UNIA different from the one offered by Du Bois?

9–6a | Cover, *Dearborn Independent's*
"The International Jew: The World's Problem," 1920

Henry Ford (1863–1947) was an inventor and businessman who launched the Ford Motor Company (1903) and, in 1908, its mass-produced, affordable Model T automobile. He was also an avowed anti-Semite. Hostility toward Jews pervaded Europe; in the United States, an upsurge in anti-Semitism accompanied increased Jewish immigration to the U.S. in the late nineteenth and early twentieth centuries. In 1918, Ford bought *The Dearborn Independent,* a Michigan newspaper, and by 1919, unleashed a ninety-one issue series titled "The International Jew." It repeated themes common to European anti-Semitic publications, writing of a global Jewish conspiracy aiming at world domination and blaming Jews for a variety of problems in the U.S. Ford's *Dearborn Independent* was available in every Ford dealership across America, thus legitimizing and guaranteeing widespread distribution of outrageous forgeries such as *The Protocols of the Elders of Zion*.

The Ford International Weekly

THE DEARBORN
INDEPENDENT

One Dollar   Dearborn, Michigan, May 22, 1920   Five Cents

The International Jew:
The World's Problem

"Among the distinguishing mental and moral traits of the Jews may be mentioned: distaste for hard or violent physical labor; a strong family sense and philoprogenitiveness; a marked religious instinct; the courage of the prophet and martyr rather than of the pioneer and soldier; remarkable power to survive in adverse environments, combined with great ability to retain racial solidarity; capacity for exploitation, both individual and social; shrewdness and astuteness in speculation and money matters generally; an Oriental love of display and a full appreciation of the power and pleasure of social position; a very high average of intellectual ability."

—*The New International Encyclopedia.*

9–6b | Selected Jewish exclusion laws, Germany, 1930s

Emerging in the 1920s, the National Socialist German Workers Party, or Nazi Party, made anti-Semitism a central plank in its platform. Fueled by anti-Semitic rumor and literature—including Henry Ford's writings—many among the German elite blamed Jews for the German defeat in the Great War and for the "Judeo-Bolshevik" communist movement. A weak hyper-democracy in Germany, combined with economic pressures of war debts and worldwide depression, catapulted the Nazis—and party leader Adolf Hitler (1889–1945)—to power, with Hitler gaining the chancellorship in 1933. After eliminating all remaining political competition, the Nazi regime began creating a nation after its own image. Below are German citizenship laws enacted in 1935.

1935 REICHSGESETZBLATT, PART I, PAGE 1146

The Reich Citizenship Law of 15 Sept 1935

The Reichstag has adopted unanimously, the following law, which is herewith promulgated.

Article 1

1. A subject of the State is a person, who belongs to the protective union of the German Reich, and who, therefore, has particular obligations towards the Reich.

2. The status of the subject is acquired in accordance with the provisions of the Reich and State Law of Citizenship.

Article 2

1. A citizen of the Reich is only that subject, who is of German or kindred blood and who, through his conduct, shows that he is both desirous and fit to serve faithfully the German people and Reich.

2. The right to citizenship is acquired by the granting of Reich citizenship papers.

3. Only the citizen of the Reich enjoys full political rights in accordance with the provision of the laws.

Article 3

The Reich Minister of the Interior in conjunction with the Deputy of the Fuehrer will issue the necessary legal and administrative decree for the carrying out and supplementing of this law.

1935 REICHSGESETZBLATT, PART I, PAGE 1333

First Regulation to the Reichs Citizenship Law of 14 Nov. 1935

On the basis of Article 3, Reichs Citizenship Law, of 15 Sept. 1935 (RGB1 I, page 146) the following is ordered:

Article 1

1. Until further issue of regulations regarding citizenship papers, all subjects of German or kindred blood, who possessed the right to vote in the Reichstag elections, at the time the Citizenship Law came into effect, shall, for the time being, possess the rights of Reich citizens. The same shall be true of those whom the Reich Minister of the Interior, in conjunction with the Deputy of the Fuehrer, has given the preliminary citizenship.

2. The Reich Minister of the Interior, in conjunction with the Deputy of the Fuehrer, can withdraw the preliminary citizenship.

Article 2

1. The regulations in Article 1 are also valid for Reichs subjects of mixed, Jewish blood.

2. An individual of mixed Jewish blood, is one who descended from one or two grandparents who were racially full Jews, insofar as does not count as a Jew according to Article 5, paragraph 2. One grandparent shall be considered as fullblooded if he or she belonged to the Jewish religious community.

Article 3

Only the Reich citizen, as bearer of full political rights, exercises the right to vote in political affairs, and can hold a public office. The Reich Minister of the Interior, or any agency empowered by him, can make exceptions during the transition period, with regard to occupying public offices. The affairs of religious organizations will not be touched upon.

Article 4

1. A Jew cannot be a citizen of the Reich. He has no right to vote in political affairs, he cannot occupy a public office.

2. Jewish officials will retire as of 31 December 1935. If these officials served at the front in the World War, either for Germany or her allies, they will receive in full, until they reach the age limit, the pension to which they were entitled according to last received wages; they will, however, not advance in seniority. After reaching the age limit, their pension will be calculated anew, according to the last received salary, on the basis of which their pension was computed.

3. The affairs of religious organizations will not be touched upon.

4. The conditions of service of teachers in Jewish public schools remain unchanged, until new regulations of the Jewish school systems are issued.

Article 5

1. A Jew is anyone who descended from at least three grandparents who were racially full Jews. Article 2, par. 2, second sentence will apply.

2. A Jew is also one who descended from two full Jewish parents, if: (a) he belonged to the Jewish religious community at the time this law was issued, or who joined the community later; (b) he was married to a Jewish person, at the time the law was issued, or married one subsequently; (c) he is the offspring from a marriage with a Jew, in the sense of Section 1, which was contracted after the Law for the protection of German blood and German honor became effective (RGB 1. I, page 1146 of 15 Sept 1935); (d) he is the offspring of an extramarital relationship, with a Jew, according to Section 1, and will be born out of wedlock after July 31, 1936.

Article 6

1. As far as demands are concerned for the pureness of blood as laid down in Reichs law or in orders of the NSDAP and its echelons—not covered in Article 5—they will not be touched upon.

2. Any other demands on pureness of blood, not covered in Article 5, can only be made with permission from the Reich Minister of the Interior and the Deputy of the Fuehrer. If any such demands have been made, they will be void as of 1 Jan 1936, if they have not been requested from the Reich Minister of the Interior in agreement with the Deputy of the Fuehrer. These requests must be made from the Reich Minister of the Interior.

Article 7

The Fuehrer and Reichs Chancellor can grant exemptions from the regulations laid down in the law.

1935 REICHGESETZBLATT, PART I, PAGE 1146
Law for the Protection of the German Blood and of the
German Honor of 15 September, 1935

Permeated by the knowledge that the purity of the German blood is the hypothesis for the permanence of the German people and animated by the inflexible determination to safeguard the German nation for all time, the Reichstag has unanimously decreed the following law which is hereby published:

1.

(1) Marriages between Jews and citizens of German or similar blood are forbidden. Contracted marriages are invalid even if they are contracted abroad within the scope of this law.

(2) The proceedings for annulment can only be brought by the Public Prosecutors.

2.

Extra marital intercourse between Jews and citizens of German and similar blood is forbidden.

3.

Jews may not employ female citizens of German and similar blood under 45 years of age in their households.

4.

(1) Jews are forbidden to hoist the Reich and national flag and to display the colors of the Reich.

(2) On the other hand, the display of Jewish colors is permissible. The practice of this authorization is under State protection.

5.

(1) Whoever acts contrary to the prohibition of 1 will be punished by penitentiary.

(2) The man who acts contrary to the prohibition of 2 will be punished by imprisonment or penitentiary.

(3) Whoever acts contrary to the terms of 3 or 4 will be punished by imprisonment up to 1 year and by fine or by one of these penalties.

6.

The Reich Minister of the Interior issues in agreement with the Fuehrer's Deputy and the Reich Minister of Justice the legal and administrative regulations necessary for the execution and supplementing of the law.

7.

The law comes into force on the day of publication.
"3" however only on 1 January 1936.

DISCUSSION QUESTIONS

1   What do these sources tell you about the institutionalization of anti-Semitism in the interwar period?

2   How were the Nazis redefining citizenship in Germany in the 1930s?

3   How did these sources define a Jew? What made the American and German definitions similar and different?

9–7a | Representative John Box, comments on Mexican immigration restriction, 1928

Texan John Calvin Box (1871–1941) served as a Democratic representative to the U.S. Congress from 1919 to 1931. He garnered national attention for his efforts to uphold the national origins quota system established in the Immigration Act of 1924 (Johnson-Reed Act). Along with preventing immigration from Asia, this highly restrictive legislation limited other immigrants to 2 percent of the U.S. population from that country, as recorded in the 1890 census. These quotas severely cut arrivals from groups with low populations in 1890, including Italians, Jews, Greeks, Poles, and Slavs. In total, it realized an 80 percent reduction in immigration from pre–Great War averages.

Every reason which calls for the exclusion of the most wretched, ignorant, dirty, diseased, and degraded people of Europe or Asia demands that the illiterate, unclean, peonized masses moving this way from Mexico be stopped at the border. . . .

The admission of a large and increasing number of Mexican peons to engage in all kinds of work is at variance with the American purpose to protect the wages of its working people and maintain their standard of living. Mexican labor is not free; it is not well paid; its standard of living is low. The yearly admission of several scores of thousands from just across the Mexican border tends constantly to lower the wages and conditions of men and women of America who labor with their hands in industry, in transportation, and in agriculture. One who has been in Mexico or in Mexican sections of cities and towns of the southwestern United States enough to make general observation needs no evidence or argument to convince him of the truth of the statement that Mexican peon labor is poorly paid and lives miserably in the midst of want, dirt, and disease.

In industry and transportation they displace great numbers of Americans who are left without employment and drift into poverty, even vagrancy, unable to maintain families or to help sustain American communities. . . .

The importers of such Mexican laborers as go to farms all want them to increase farm production, not by the labor of American farmers, for the sustenance of families and the support of American farm life, but by serf labor working mainly for absentee landlords on millions of acres of semiarid lands. Many of these lands have heretofore been profitably used for grazing cattle, sheep, and goats. Many of them are held by speculative owners.

A great part of these areas can not be cultivated until the Government has spent vast sums in reclaiming them. . . . Their occupation and cultivation by serfs should not be encouraged. . . .

Another purpose of the immigration laws is the protection of American racial stock from further degradation or change through mongrelization. The Mexican peon is a mixture of Mediterranean-blooded Spanish peasant with low-grade Indians who did not fight to extinction but submitted and multiplied as serfs. Into that was fused much Negro slave blood. This blend of low-grade Spaniard, peonized Indian, and negro slave mixes with Negroes, mulattoes, and other mongrels, and some sorry whites, already here. The prevention of such mongrelization and the degradation it causes is one of the purposes of our laws which the admission of these people will tend to defeat. . . .

To keep out the illiterate and the diseased is another essential part of the Nation's immigration policy. The Mexican peons are illiterate and ignorant. Because of their unsanitary habits and living conditions and their vices they are especially subject to smallpox, venereal diseases, tuberculosis, and other dangerous contagions. Their admission is inconsistent with this phase of our policy.

The protection of American society against the importation of crime and pauperism is yet another object of these laws. Few, if any, other immigrants have brought us so large a proportion of criminals and paupers as have the Mexican peons.

9–7b | Ernesto Galarza, remarks defending immigration from Mexico, 1929

Ernesto Galarza (1905–1984) gave this address at the National Conference of Social Work in 1929. Throughout U.S. history, immigration laws had generally provided for exemptions for entrants from Mexico, focused instead on controlling arrivals from overseas. The key motive for this was the vital role Mexican labor served in sectors of the United States economy. The economic slowdown and joblessness of the Great Depression, however, led to a rise in anti-immigration sentiment aimed at Mexico. From 1929 to 1931, legal Mexican immigration fell by 95 percent and, throughout the 1930s, as many as 400,000 Mexican citizens were deported.

. . . [S]omething must be done in the way of social and economic amelioration for those Mexicans who have already settled in the United States and whose problem is that of finding adjustment. Thus far in the discussion the Mexicans who have settled more or less permanently here have been taken into account negatively. . . .

For the moment . . . everyone has presented his side of the case except the Mexican worker himself. . . . I speak to you today as one of these immigrants. . . .

First, as to unemployment. The Mexican is the first to suffer from depression in industrial and agricultural enterprises. . . . I flatly disagree with those who maintain that there is enough work for these people but that they refuse to work, preferring to live on charity. On the contrary, it is widely felt by the Mexicans that there are more men than there are jobs. . . . [T]he precariousness of the job in the face of so much competition has brought home to the Mexican time and again his absolute weakness as a bargainer for employment. . . .

He has also something to say as to the wage scale. . . . The Mexican . . . recognizes his absolute inability to force his wage upward and by dint of necessity he shuffles along with a standard of living which the American worker regards with contempt and alarm. . . .

The distribution of the labor supply is felt by the Mexican to be inadequate. At present he has to rely mainly on hearsay or on the information of unscrupulous contractors who overcharge him for transportation. . . .

[T]he Mexican immigrant still feels the burden of old prejudices. Only when there are threats to limit immigration from Mexico is it that a few in America sing the praises of the peon. . . . At other times the sentiments which seem to be deeply rooted in the American mind are that he is unclean, improvident, indolent, and innately dull. Add to this the suspicion that he constitutes a peril to the American worker's wage scale and you have a situation with which no average Mexican can cope. . . .

I would ask for recognition of the Mexican's contribution to the agricultural and industrial expansion of the western United States. . . . From Denver to Los Angeles and from the Imperial Valley to Portland, it is said, an empire has been created largely by the brawn of the humble Mexican, who laid the rails and topped the beets and poured the cubic miles of cement. . . . If it is true that the Mexican has brought to you arms that have fastened a civilization on the Pacific slope, then give him his due. If you give him his earned wage and he proves improvident, teach him otherwise; if he is tuberculous, cure him; if he falls into indigence, raise him. He has built you an empire!

DISCUSSION QUESTIONS

1   What were Congressman Box's justifications against Mexican immigration to the United States?

2   What voice did Galarza add to the conversation about Mexican immigration to the United States? How does that change the discussion?

3   What lens does each of these pieces use in assessing the value of immigrants to America? Describe the tension between these perspectives.

1-360 | Painting by Giuseppe Arcimboldo, *Vertumnus* (Rudolf II as Vertumnus), Milan, 1590
Text page 3

1-360 | Ottoman men smoking hookah at a Turkish café, Ottoman Empire, between 1880 and 1900
Text page 4

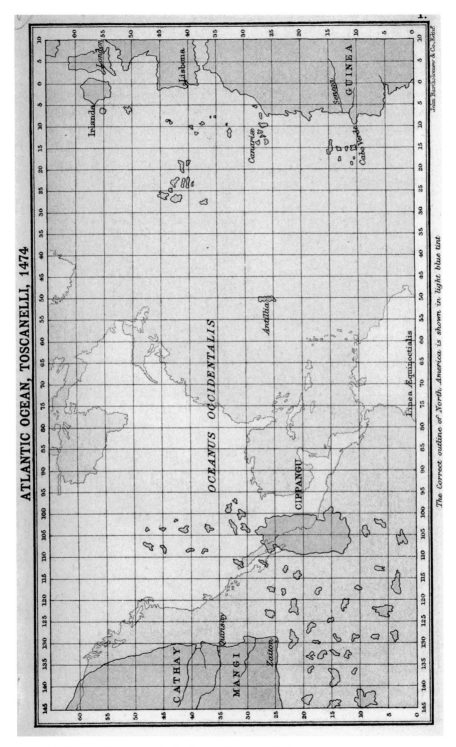

1–1 | Paolo Toscanelli, map of Atlantic Ocean, Florence, 1474

Text page 7

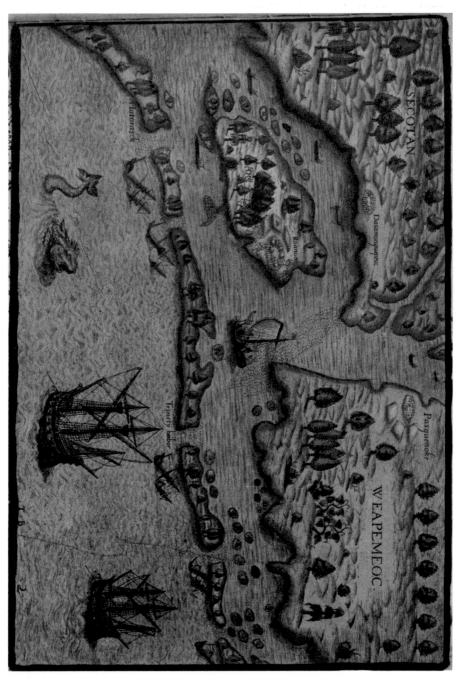

1–4a | Engraving by Theodor de Bry of a watercolor by John White, *The arriual of the Englishemen in Virginia,* England and Germany, 1590

Text page 12

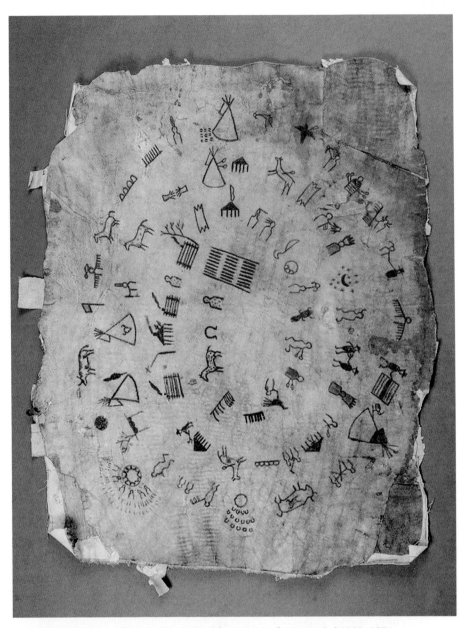

1–5 | *Waniyetu Wowapi* (Nakota Winter Count), Lone Dog, first recorded 1800–1871
Text page 14

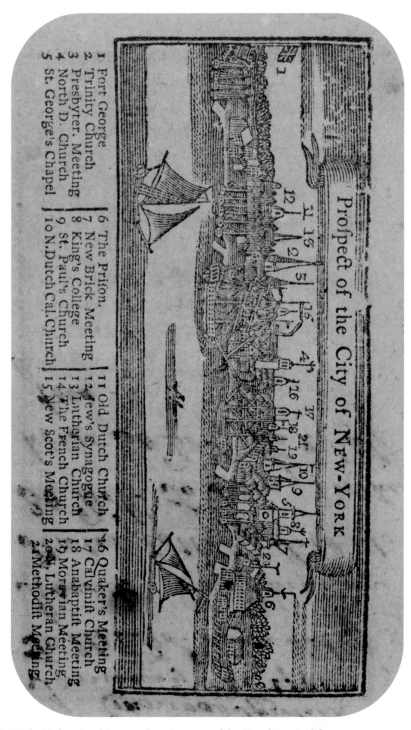

1−7a | John Nathan Hutchins, woodcut, *Prospect of the City of New-York* from
New York Almanac, 1771

Text page 18

Incendie du Cap.

Révolte générale des Négres. Massacre des Blancs.

2–10 | Illustrated frontispiece, *Incendie du Cap* (Burning of Cap-Français, Haiti), France, 1815
Text page 63

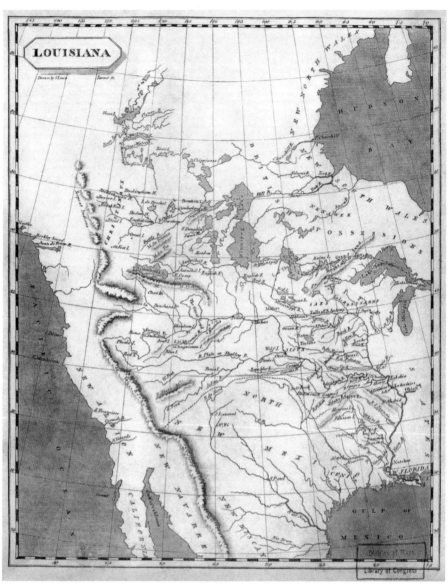

3–2b | Samuel Lewis, map of Louisiana, 1804
Text page 83

3–4 | James Gillray, political cartoon, "The Plumb-pudding in danger;—or—State Epicures taking un Petit Souper," England, 1805

Text page 85

3–8b | Lam Qua, paintings for Dr. Peter Parker, China, 1830s
Text page 96

4–360 | Woodblock print by Inoue Tankei, *Famous Places in Tokyo: Picture of Azuma Bridge and a Distant View of a Torpedo Explosion*, Japan, 1888

Text page 107

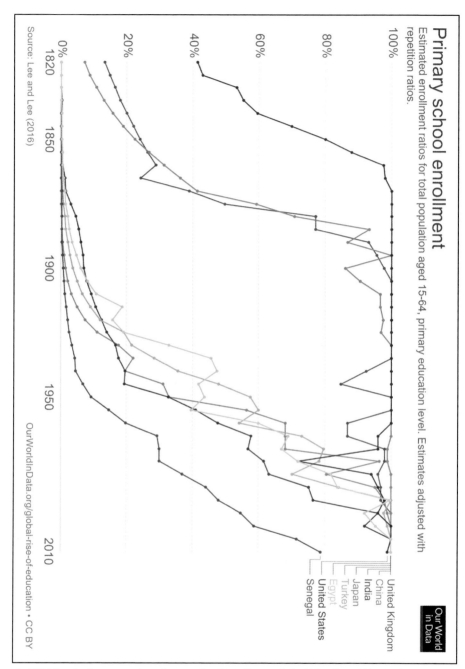

Primary school enrollment

Estimated enrollment ratios for total population aged 15-64, primary education level. Estimates adjusted with repetition ratios.

100%

80%

60%

40%

20%

0%

1820   1850   1900   1950   2010

United Kingdom
China
India
Japan
Turkey
Egypt
United States
Senegal

Source: Lee and Lee (2016)

OurWorldInData.org/global-rise-of-education • CC BY

4-360 | Graph of comparative primary school enrollment, United Kingdom, China, India, Japan, Turkey, Egypt, United States, and Senegal, 1820 to 2010

Text page 109

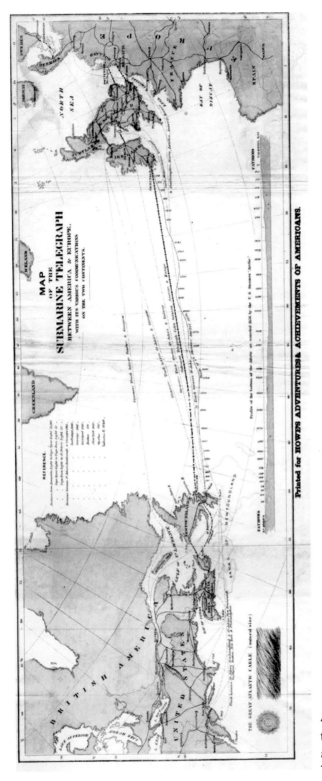

4–12a | Map of the submarine telegraph between America and Europe, 1858

Text page 133

4–13 | Advertisement, "All nations use Singer sewing machines," ca. 1892
Text page 135

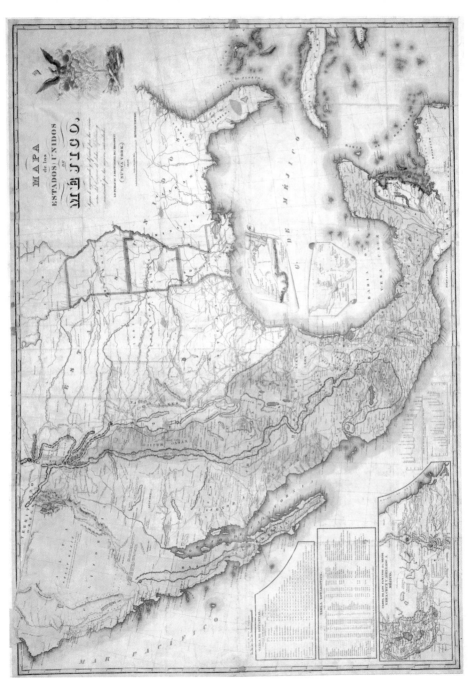

5-3b | Map, *Mapa de los Estados Unidos Méjico*, 1847
Text page 152

5-11c | George Frederick Keller, political cartoon, "A Statue for *Our* Harbor," 1881
Text page 182

6 | Western Expansion and Empire

6–360 | Image of certificate for the American Board of Commissioners for Foreign Missions, Missionary House, Boston, Mass., 1857
Text page 192

6–1b | Kiowa, ledger art, perhaps depicting Buffalo Wallow Battle of the Red River Wars in 1874
Text page 196

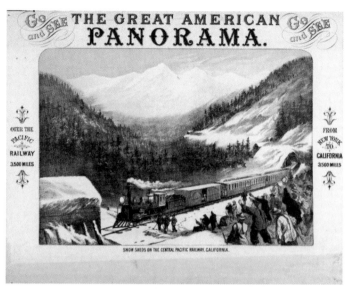

6–3b | Advertisement, "The Great American Panorama," 1900
Text page 199

6–6b | Depictions of Perry's black ships entering Japan, 1853–1854
Text page 206

6–6b | Depictions of Perry's black ships entering Japan, 1853–1854

Text page 206

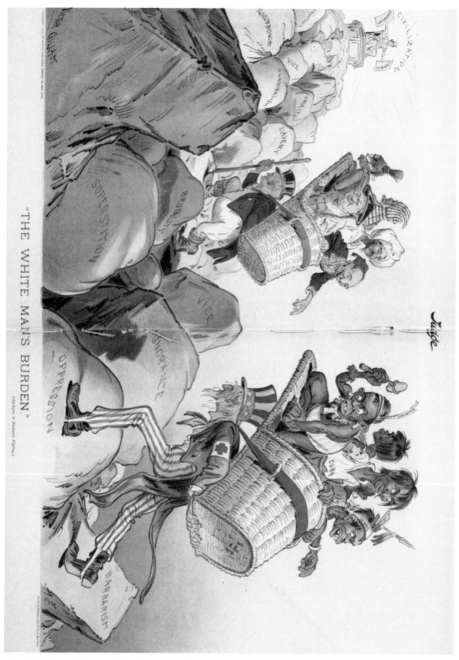

6–8b | Victor Gillam, political cartoon, "The White Man's Burden," 1899
Text page 211

6–8c | Udo Keppler, political cartoon, "A Trifle Embarrassed," 1898
Text page 212

6-9a | Henri Meyer, political cartoon, "En Chine: Le gâteau des Rois et . . .
des Empereurs," France, 1898
Text page 213

6-9b | J. S. Pughe, political cartoon, "Putting His Foot Down," 1899
Text page 214

7 | Constructing the Urban Landscape

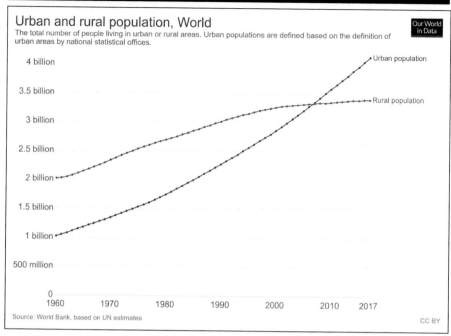

Urban and rural population, World
The total number of people living in urban or rural areas. Urban populations are defined based on the definition of urban areas by national statistical offices.

Source: World Bank, based on UN estimates

CC BY

7-360 | Chart showing global urban and rural population, 1960–2017
Text page 243

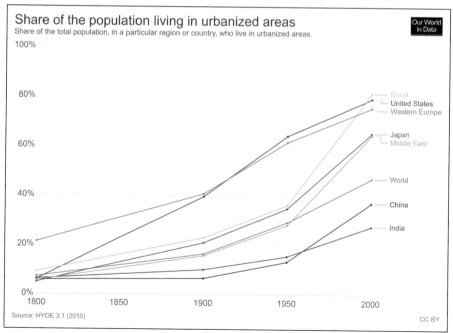

Share of the population living in urbanized areas
Share of the total population, in a particular region or country, who live in urbanized areas.

Source: HYDE 3.1 (2010)

CC BY

7-360 | Chart showing share of population living in urbanized areas, 1800–2000
Text page 243

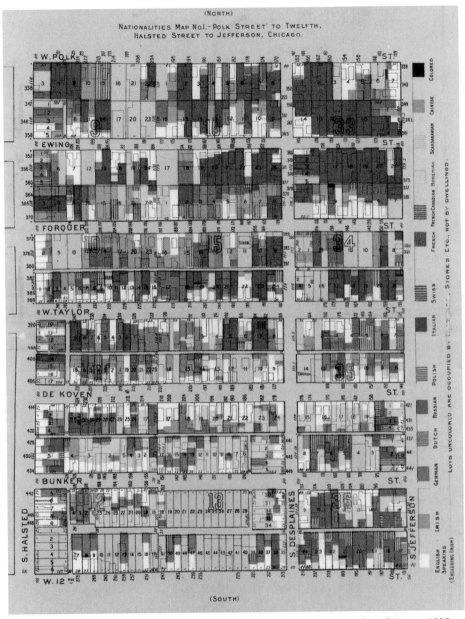

7-2b | Florence Kelley et al., map, nationalities in neighborhood near Chicago's Hull House, 1895
Text page 249

7–3 | Irish immigrant trading cards, 1882
Text page 253

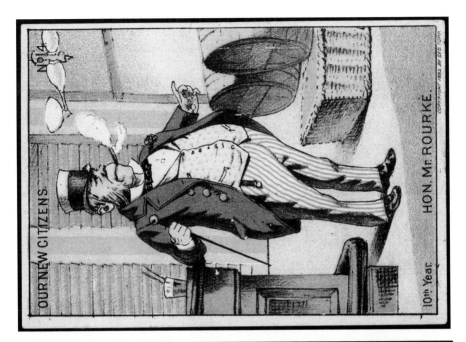

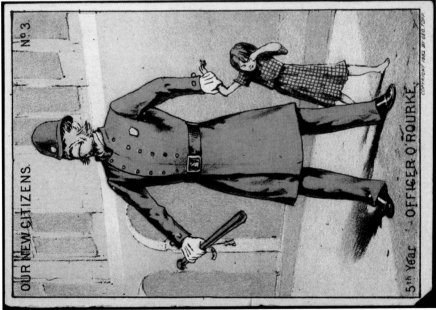

7–3 | Irish immigrant trading cards, 1882

Text page 253

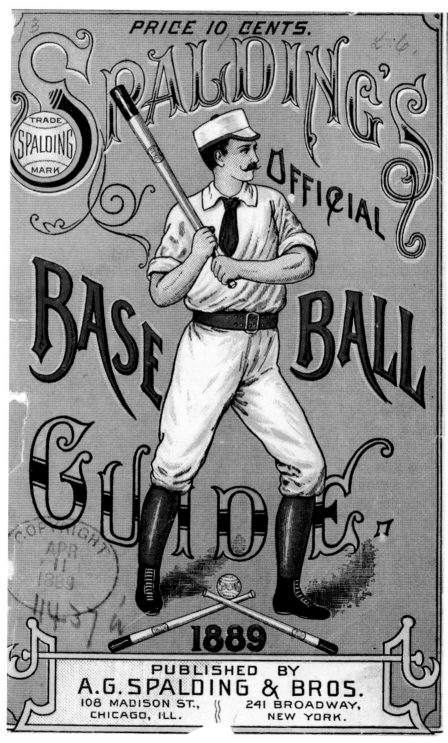

7-4a | Cover, *Spalding's Official Baseball Guide*, 1889
Text page 254

7–4b | Film poster, "Cinématographe Lumière," France, 1896

Text page 254

Le Petit Journal

Le Petit Journal
CHAQUE JOUR — 6 PAGES — 5 CENTIMES
Administration : 61, rue Lafayette

5 Centimes

SUPPLÉMENT ILLUSTRÉ

5 Centimes

ABONNEMENTS

Le Supplément illustré
CHAQUE SEMAINE 5 CENTIMES

Le Petit Journal Militaire, Maritime, Colonial.... 10 cent.
Le Petit Journal agricole, 5 cent. ✳ LA MODE du Petit Journal, 10 cent.
Le Petit Journal illustré de La Jeunesse.... 10 cent.
On s'abonne sans frais dans tous les bureaux de poste

	SIX MOIS	UN AN
SEINE ET SEINE-ET-OISE	2 fr.	3 fr. 50
DÉPARTEMENTS	2 fr.	4 fr. »
ÉTRANGER	2.50	5 fr. »

Les manuscrits ne sont pas rendus

Dix-septième année — **DIMANCHE 7 OCTOBRE 1906** — Numéro 829

LES « LYNCHAGES » AUX ÉTATS-UNIS
Massacre de nègres à Atlanta (Georgie)

7–6a | *Le Petit Journal,* cover, "Les 'lynchages' aux États-Unis," France, 1906
Text page 264

7–8b | Walter Crane, woodcut, *Solidarity of Labor,* UK, 1889
Text page 272

7–10b | Udo Keppler, political cartoon, "Next!" (the Standard Oil Octopus), 1904
Text page 277

8–360 | "Destroy This Mad Brute," United States, 1918
Text page 287

8–360 | "Daddy, what did *YOU* do in the Great War?" UK, 1915
Text page 287

8–360 | "Pour la Liberté du Monde. Souscrivez à l'Emprunt National à la Banque Nationale de Crédit" ("For the freedom of the world. Subscribe to the National Loan at the Banque Nationale de Crédit"), France, 1917

Text page 288

8–360 | "They serve France. How can I serve Canada?" Canada, 1915
Text page 288

8–360 | "Landes-Kriedsfürsorge-Ausstellung" (National War Relief Exhibition in Pozsony), Austria, 1917

Text page 288

8–1 | Map, *Humoristische Karte von Europa in Jahre 1914*, Germany, 1914
Text page 289

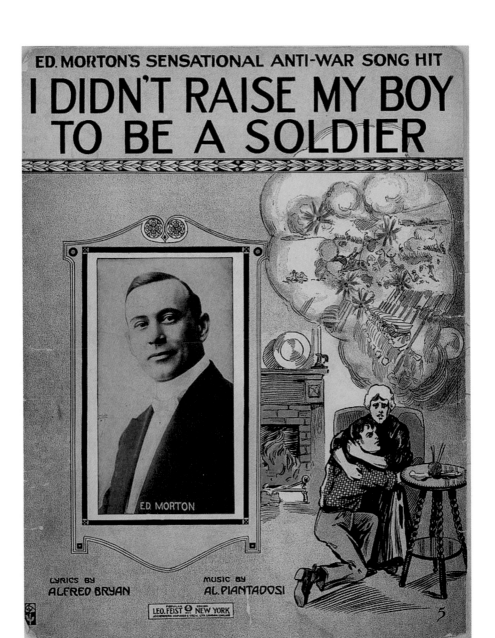

8–4a | Ed Morton, sheet music, selected lyrics of "I Didn't Raise My Boy to Be a Soldier," 1915
Text page 296

8−4b | Theodore Baker, sheet music, selected lyrics of "I Didn't Raise My Boy to Be a Slacker," 1917
Text page 298

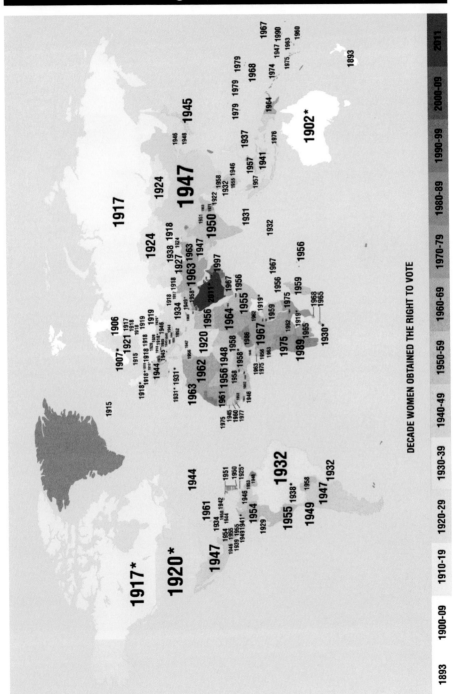

DECADE WOMEN OBTAINED THE RIGHT TO VOTE

| 1893 | 1900-09 | 1910-19 | 1920-29 | 1930-39 | 1940-49 | 1950-59 | 1960-69 | 1970-79 | 1980-89 | 1990-99 | 2000-09 | 2011 |

9-360 | World map by country with the decade women obtained the right to vote, 1893-2011
Text page 317

9–360 | Tamara de Lempicka, cover art, *Die Dame*, Germany, 1929
Text page 319

9–360 | Kiyoshi Kobayakawa, woodblock print, *Tipsy*, Japan, 1930
Text page 319

10–7b | Aurelio Bertiglia, postcard, on Italian conquest of Ethiopia, Italy, ca. 1936
Text page 383

11–2b | Jack Kirby, cover of *Captain America* #1, 1941
Text page 413

11–4b | Leon Helguera, poster, "Americanos todos: luchamos por la victoria" (Americans All: Let's Fight for Victory), 1943
Text page 419

11-5 | *LIFE* magazine, advertisement, Schenley Laboratories penicillin production, 1944

Text page 420

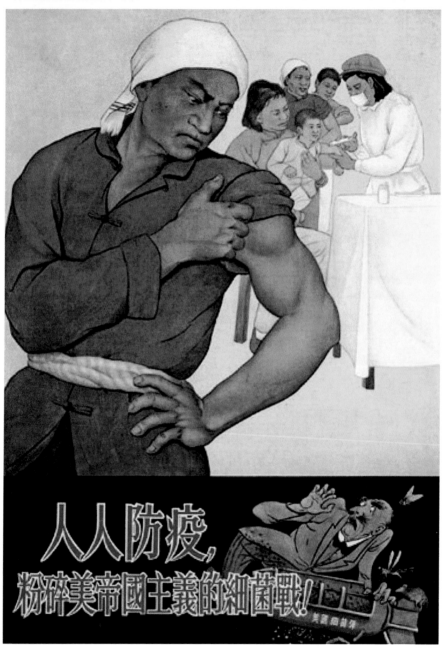

12–5b | Ye Shanlu, poster, "Everybody must take precautions against epidemics to smash the germ warfare of American imperialism!" 1952
Text page 468

12–6a | Poster, U.S. Information Agency, Operation Passage to Freedom, South Vietnam, 1954
Text page 470

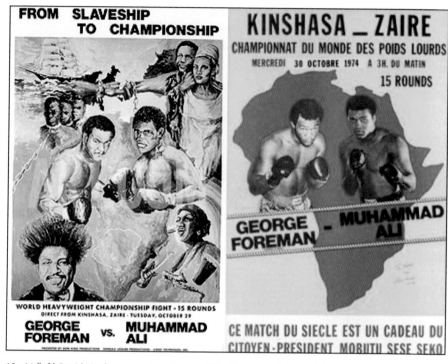

13–4 | (left) David Mosley, promotional poster, "The Rumble in the Jungle," Zaire, 1974
Text page 503

13–6b | Wen Bing, poster, "Awakened Peoples You Will Surely Attain Ultimate Victory!" China, 1963
Text page 508

13–10a | Photograph, "The Blue Marble," space, 1972
Text page 522

13–10c | Photograph, the Apollo-Soyuz Test
Project patch, space, 1975
Text page 523

14–360 | Tomasz Sarnecki, poster, "High Noon," Poland, 1989
Text page 533

14–1b | Photograph, anti–arms race protest, West Germany, 1983
Text page 535

NONE OF THESE WILL GIVE YOU AIDS

WORKING TOGETHER

GOING TO LUNCH

SHARING A HUG

USING A RESTROOM

SWIMMING IN PUBLIC POOLS

TOUCHING A DOORNOB

The American Hospital Association states: "There has been no evidence of person-to-person transmission (of AIDS) through ordinary social or occupational contact; likewise, there has been no evidence of airborne or foodborne transmission of this illness." The AIDS virus is transmitted by intimate sexual contact, contaminated blood products, or by sharing needles.

FOR MORE INFORMATION

UNIVERSITY OF CALIFORNIA

14–9a | University of California System, poster, "None of These Will Give You AIDS," 1985
Text page 562

14–9b | UNESCO/Aidthi Workshop, poster, AIDS information, India, 1995
Text page 563

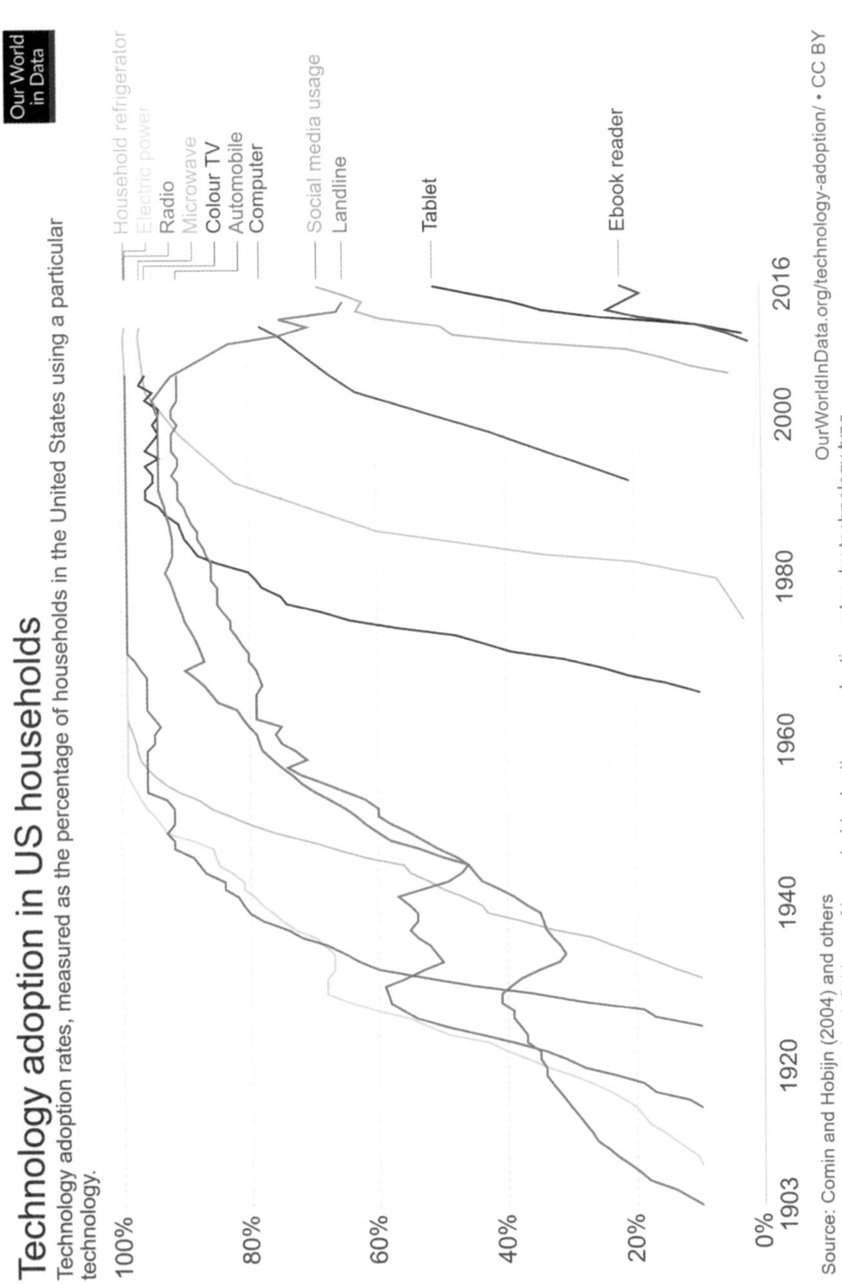

Technology adoption in US households
Technology adoption rates, measured as the percentage of households in the United States using a particular technology.
Our World in Data
100%
80%
60%
40%
20%
0%
1903
1920
1940
1960
1980
2000
2016
Household refrigerator
Electric power
Radio
Microwave
Colour TV
Automobile
Computer
Social media usage
Landline
Tablet
Ebook reader
Source: Comin and Hobijn (2004) and others
Note: See the sources tab for definitions of household adoption, or adoption rates, by technology type.
OurWorldInData.org/technology-adoption/ • CC BY

15–360 | Chart, technology adoption in U.S. households, 1903–2016

Text page 573

Share of individuals using the internet, 2017

Share of individuals using the internet, measured as the percentage of the population. Internet users are individuals who have used the Internet (from any location) in the last 3 months. The Internet can be used via a computer, mobile phone, personal digital assistant, games machine, digital TV etc.

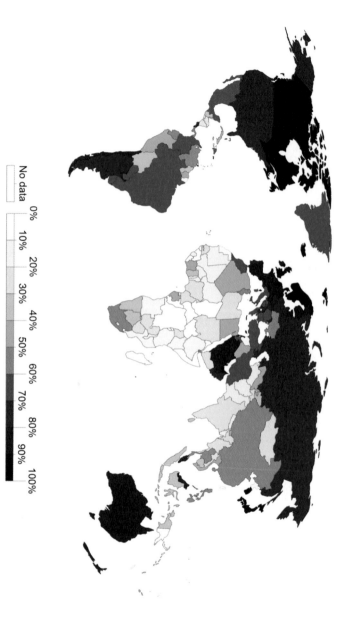

No data

0% 10% 20% 30% 40% 50% 60% 70% 80% 90% 100%

Source: World Bank

15–360 | Share of the population using the Internet, 2017
Text page 574

15–360 | Manoocher Deghati, photograph, art student from the University of Helwan paints the Facebook logo on a mural, Egypt, 2011
Text page 577

15-1a | Erik Junberger, photograph, National September 11 Memorial
Text page 578

Number of fatalities from terrorist attacks

Total number of fatalities per year from terrorist attacks. This represents the number of total confirmed fatalities for the incident. This includes all victims and attackers who died as a direct result of the incident.

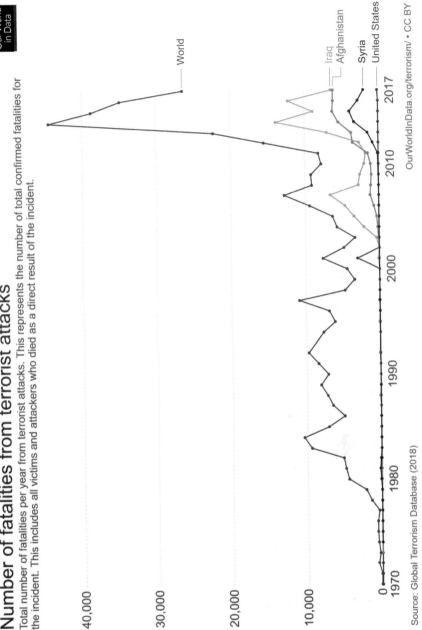

Source: Global Terrorism Database (2018)

15–3b | Chart, numbers of deaths from terrorist attacks globally, 1970–2017

Text page 584

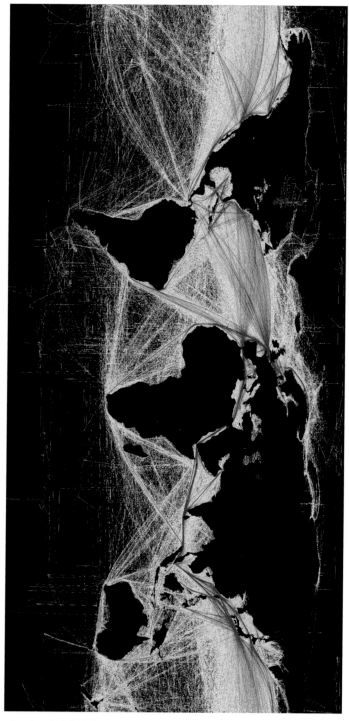

15–8 | Map, density of global shipping routes in the world's oceans, 2012
Text page 594

Number of Immigrants and Their Share of the Total U.S. Population, 1850-2018

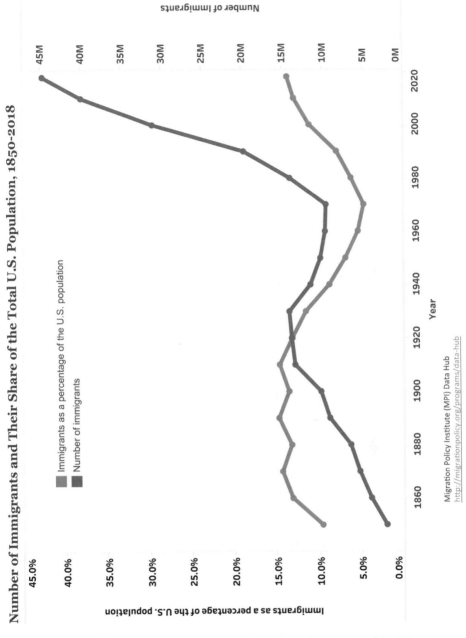

Migration Policy Institute (MPI) Data Hub
http://migrationpolicy.org/programs/data-hub

15-10a | Graph, number of immigrants and their share of the total population of the United States, 1850-2018

Text page 597

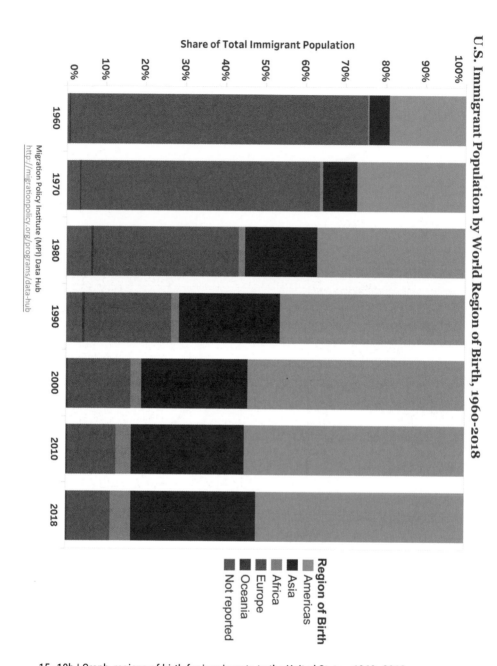

U.S. Immigrant Population by World Region of Birth, 1960-2018

Share of Total Immigrant Population

0% 10% 20% 30% 40% 50% 60% 70% 80% 90% 100%

1960
1970
1980
1990
2000
2010
2018

Migration Policy Institute (MPI) Data Hub
http://migrationpolicy.org/programs/data-hub

Region of Birth
Americas
Asia
Africa
Europe
Oceania
Not reported

15–10b | Graph, regions of birth for immigrants to the United States, 1960–2018
Text page 597

9-8 | Photograph, rural family listening to the radio, 1930s

Central in the new technologies that shaped American life in the 1920s and 1930s was radio. The first electronic mass medium technology, radio distributed news and entertainment to both urban and rural audiences and had dramatic cultural and economic effects. By 1930, more than 40 percent of U.S. households owned a radio; by 1940, that number had more than doubled, growing to 83 percent. The broadcast of live music was popular in the early radio age, but programming soon diversified to include drama, comedy, talk, and educational programs. With rural electrification under New Deal programs of the 1930s, families such as the one from Kentucky pictured below joined in on the popular craze.

DISCUSSION QUESTIONS

1   Describe the relationship between the radio and family life in this image.

2   Why might persons in rural communities find owning radios especially valuable?

AMERICAN CULTURE ABROAD

9–9a | Photograph, King Oliver's Jazz Band, 1923

Joseph Nathan "King" Oliver (1881–1938), cornet player and band leader, was a pioneering jazz musician, including his mentorship of Louis Armstrong. From 1908 to 1917 he played in New Orleans brass bands in Storyville, and in 1918, when the red-light district closed, he relocated to Chicago. It was there his ensemble began performing as King Oliver's Jazz Band. Jazz, with its roots in African American music traditions such as blues and ragtime, is recognized as an original American art form. Noted for its improvisational style, the genre became a worldwide phenomenon that drew on national, regional, and local cultures wherever it went.

9–9b | Photograph, Crickett Smith's Indian Band, India, mid-1930s

In the 1920s, jazz came to India when African American musicians performed shows in Bombay (Mumbai) and Calcutta (Kolkata). Jazz musicians toured the country throughout what was known as the golden age for jazz in India in the 1930s to the 1950s. In India, these African American musicians, including cornetist and trumpeter Crickett Smith (1881–1947), worked with freedom from segregation that they still experienced back in the U.S. The Indian embrace of jazz corresponded with the rising freedom struggle against British rule, an impulse for political freedom that was seen in artistic expressions of the era as well.

DISCUSSION QUESTIONS

1   How do the musicians' poses in the picture of King Oliver's Creole Jazz Band illustrate the characteristics of the genre of jazz music?

2   What similarities and differences do you observe between the two jazz bands? What does that tell you about jazz and globalization?

9–10 | Photograph, Babe Ruth with youth baseball players on his Japanese tour, Japan, 1934

George Herman "Babe" Ruth Jr. (1895–1948) came into Major League Baseball as a star left-handed pitcher for the Boston Red Sox in 1914. His desire to play every day led to a switch of positions, and as an outfielder he hit an MLB record twenty-nine home runs in 1919. After a controversial sale of Ruth's contract to the New York Yankees, Babe went on to win seven American League pennants and four World Series, setting MLB records for career home runs, runs batted in (RBIs), and slugging percentage. In Japan, baseball had grown in popularity since its introduction in the 1870s. American all-star teams began traveling to Japan for exhibition games in 1908, and tours happened throughout the 1910s and 1920s. In 1934, a team of the best MLB players, headlined by the Babe, came for an eighteen-game competition with the Big-Six University League, the highest level of Japanese baseball at the time. More than 500,000 greeted their arrival, and the mass popularity of the tour contributed to the creation of professional baseball in Japan.

DISCUSSION QUESTIONS

1   Explain how this image documents the influence of American culture.

2   Can sports and athletes serve a diplomatic function? Why or why not?

10

The Search for Solutions

RISE OF FASCISM

Many people responded to the horrific slaughter of the Great War by questioning the legitimacy of existing systems of thought, governance, economics, and social organization. Fascism first emerged as a "third way" alternative to liberal democracy and leftist socialism in Italy during the war, spread to the rest of Europe, and then beyond in the 1920s. As an ultra-right-wing, ultra-nationalist ideology, fascism opposed both democratic and communist systems, glorifying instead the State, its embodiment in an authoritarian ruler, and its future glory as envisioned by said ruler. Citizens were to find their value in their loyalty and usefulness to the state, but racism or ethnocentrism often excluded segments of the population. Sustained by modern surveillance, communication, and media technologies, fascist states sought to exert total control over the individual. Rejecting the laissez-faire attitude of the liberal democratic states, fascist authorities instead attempted to dictate norms in public and private behaviors. Glorifying violence against opponents and celebrating the (proper) young, fascists appealed to many as dynamic visionaries preaching national unification in a time of great global uncertainty and depression. Although Mussolini's Italy and Hitler's Germany were perhaps the most recognized examples in the 1930s, many other fascist states, fascist political parties, or admirers of fascism emerged in the interwar period. The selections below reflect this.

Giovanni Gentile's "What Is Fascism?" Italy, 1925

We see two Italys before us: an old one and a new one. The Italy of centuries past, which is our glory but also our sad legacy, which weighs upon our shoulders and is a burden on the soul. And, let us say it plainly, there is also the shame of which we wish to cleanse ourselves, for which we must make amends. And it is exactly that great Italy that has, as I was saying, so grand a place in the history of the world. The only Italy, one might say, that is known, studied, and investigated by all the civilized people of the world and whose history is not a particular history but a period of universal history:

the Renaissance. . . . Therefore it is the Italy of foreigners and not of Italians. Italians without faith and therefore absent. Is this not the old Italy of decadence? . . .

And, if it pleases to do so, let us also add some new monuments. Let us raise them in our piazzas to temper ourselves, to honor the living more than the dead in the consecration of recent memories, which truly are more glorious than those in Italian history, and to elevate our consciousness of free citizens of a grand nation in the admonishment of generous memories. Because, where one means a nation in this way, even liberty more than a right is an obligation: a lofty achievement that one does not obtain unless through the self-denial of the citizen who is ready to give everything to his fatherland without asking for anything.

Even this concept of the nation, on which we insist today, is not a fascist invention. It is the spirit of that new Italy that little by little must overcome the old. Fascism, with its vigorous sentiment of the national surge that drew the Italians into the fire of the Great War and made them endure victoriously the tragic test, with its energetic reaction to the materialists of yesterday who tried to nullify the valor of that test. . . . Fascism waves before the eyes of the people the grandness and beauty of the sacrifice accomplished as its greatest patrimony for the future. . . .

Through insipid malevolence hasn't fascism so often been accused of barbarity? Well, yes. You understand the just significance of this barbarity, and we will boast of it, as of healthy powers that smash false and ruinous idols and restore the safety of the nation in the power of the State aware of its sovereign rights, which are its obligations. . . .

It means that the ethical State of the fascist is no longer the agnostic State of the old liberalism. Its ethics are spirituality, its personality which is awareness, its system which is its will. . . . The State is the grand will of the nation, and therefore its intelligence. It neglects nothing and withholds itself from nothing that touches the interests of the citizen, which are its own interests, neither in terms of economics nor morality. *Nihil humani a se alienum putat* [It considers nothing human to be foreign to itself—*translator's note*]. The State is neither a grand facade nor an empty structure; it is the man himself, the house constructed, inhabited, and enlivened by the joy, grief, work, and the whole life of the human spirit. . . .

Gentlemen, fascism is a party, a political doctrine. But fascism . . . inasmuch as it is a party, a political doctrine, it is in the first place a complete concept of life. . . . Just as the Catholic, if he is Catholic, invests his religious feeling into his whole life . . . in this way the fascist . . . whether he writes in the newspapers or reads them, provides for his private life or converses with others, watches for the future or recalls his own past and that of his people, must always remember that he is a fascist!

Thus he carries out that which truly can be called the hallmark of fascism, to take life seriously. Life is tiresome—it is struggle, it is sacrifice, it is hard work; a life in which we know well there is no fun, there is no time to have fun. . . .

There stands before us, always, an ideal to be realized; an ideal that does not give us rest. We cannot waste time.

Franz Pfeffer von Salomon's internal National Socialist German Workers Party (NSDAP) memo on breeding, Germany, 1925

First of all I share with Strasser and all revolutionaries the view that property in Germany is wrongly distributed: property, power, culture are in the wrong hands, misery and ruin are suffered by the wrong people, and this situation is growing and consolidating itself to such an extent that only the most drastic, ruthless intervention can force German life and culture [*Volkstum*] back into the right paths. Immediately after this common assumption, however, the thinking diverges.

There are those who take as their starting-point the equality of human beings, or rather the equality of *Germans*. This premiss leads naturally to the logical conclusion that there can be no reason why among equals a different distribution of property, state power, culture should prevail. If someone who is equal is forced to live in circumstances significantly lower than the mean, then this is naturally 'unjust', or a 'scandal' with respect to other equals. If someone who is equal is treated markedly better than the average then this is likewise 'unjust', for it can only happen 'at the expense of the share the other equals enjoy of property, power, and culture. . . .

In the last analysis I accuse Strasser's programme of being rooted in this basic mentality (and I fear I must accuse him of coming out with far too many arguments which in our camp are called "socialist"). It is the Jewish-liberal-democratic-Marxist-humanitarian mentality. As long as there is even a single minute tendril which connects our programme with this root then it is doomed to be poisoned and hence to wither away to a miserable death. . . .

All Germans are unequal. That is the starting-point. . . . The first logical conclusion to be drawn from inequality is the inequality of value. Some Germans are more valuable than others ('value' is a relative concept, which I use here naturally to refer to value measured in terms of the German, Nordic world-view, and within this measured in terms of what serves the interests of collective German well-being).

A logical consequence of this inequality must be the principle of *unequal* treatment, that is, unequal share of state power, property, culture. All these must be distributed to people on the basis of how valuable they are. . . .

A further logical consequence of inequality in what people are worth, and the continuous changes brought about by the development of the nation [*Volk*], is the duty of the state to take charge of this development, which means influencing it in every way possible. Excellence must be increased and enhanced further. Inferiority must be reduced. In plain terms this is a question of breeding. Improving the stock of the race. Breeding human beings. . . . From the above considerations I can draw up the following programmatic demands of our future state, the "Third Reich":

a. To determine the degree of higher or lower value of all inhabitants of Germany. The value will be assessed as the function of four criteria:

(1) actual performance in their professions

(2) physical attributes, according to health and racial characteristics

(3) spiritual, moral and cultural traits

(4) hereditary traits evaluated by considering parents and grandparents . . .

f. No pity is to be shown to those who occupy the lower categories of the inferior groups: cripples, epileptics, the blind, the insane, deaf and dumb, children born in sanatoria for alcoholics or in care, orphans (=children born out of wedlock), criminals, whores, the sexually disturbed, etc. Everything done for them not only means taking resources away from more deserving causes, but counteracts the breeding selection process. Nor should we mourn the dumb, the weak, the spineless, the apathetic, those with hereditary diseases, the pathological, because they go under "innocently." . . .

This bottom category means destruction and death. Weighed and found wanting. Trees which do not bear fruit should be cut down and thrown into the fire.

Paula Siber, excerpt from *The Women's Issue and Its National Socialist Solution*, Germany, 1933

Womanhood means motherhood. It means to embrace motherhood purposefully and consciously with the full thrust of one's soul and to elevate and recognize it as an overarching law of life.

The role of physical motherhood is preset by nature and therefore supported by National Socialism as a clear priority. This circumstance, however, does not imply that the responsibilities of National Socialist women within the People's Community are restricted to that of carriers of our race and our blood and as mere guarantors of the biological survival of our people.

For far above this purely generational duty of procreation to assure the preservation and continuation of our race and our people ranks for men and women the sacred task of enhancing one's deeper spiritual qualities and ensuring their further development. After all, for a woman nothing could be more ennobling than reaching the state of motherhood of the soul as the ultimate fulfillment of any woman's essence, no matter whether she is married or not.

For that reason, only such a woman may take her place beside her man who can rise above and beyond her duty to bear children, to be admired as a precious and lovely adornment, or to be able to cook and keep the house clean. Rather the woman has the sacred responsibility of becoming a partner for life, a comrade, who walks the path of womanhood proudly from the strength of her inner inspiration and the warmth of her soul. . . .

To be a woman in the most profound and most beautiful sense of the word is the best preparation for motherhood.

For the highest calling of a National Socialist woman is not merely to give birth to children to educate and raise them for her people while being consciously and totally immersed in her dedication to her motherhood and the responsibilities that spring from it. . . .

The mother is also the one who provides for her offspring the link to her people and its national traditions to which she and her child belong. For she is the guardian of this culture which she transmits to her child in the form of fairytales, sagas, games, and customs so that the child's later values and attitudes toward its people can rest on these childhood experiences. . . .

Moreover, in a National Socialist Germany women must predominate in the field of social services. For wherever there is a need for care and social work, that is where a woman has her place.

Besides her roles as the people's principal preserver, educator, and caregiver, a woman enjoys a further crucial area of responsibility—her contributions to the national economy. Women manage some seventy-five percent of the collective national income by virtue of being in charge of their households. . . .

The national economy also includes agriculture. No one could imagine these days what agriculture would be like without our women's daily struggle for existence and the hard work involved in raising the yield of crops, in breeding stronger animals, in bringing new lands into production, and in supervising and directing farm activities.

Excerpts from Antonio Vallejo-Nágera's *Eugenesis of Spanishness and Regeneration of the Race,* Spain, 1937

It has been the patriotic spirit that has raised up the peoples that fell into poverty and misfortune after the catastrophe of the Great War. The races that have known how to find themselves, the nations that have examined their own history, the peoples that have fought for the recovery of their spiritual values and revived the old traditions: these, like a phoenix, have been reborn from their ashes and been able to face up to the whole world in order to maintain their racial personality. . . .

A patriot desires for his country prosperity, respect for its rights, and its true place in the world order. Territorial patriotism is dangerous because it disregards the fact that the life of peoples must adjust to the general principles of right and morality. If one nation steals and kills another to advance itself and subjects universal morality to its own whims, it is ignoble in its conduct, and its thought will not acquire universality. . . .

The regeneration of a race requires a policy that can neutralize the harm—both physical and psychological, material and moral—that pathogenic agents can cause to the germinal plasma. We agree with the National-Socialists that each race has a particular cultural significance as well as some excellent bio-psychological characteristics worthy of praise. We Spaniards neither fear nor have feared illegitimate bonds: we have mingled casually with the most diverse races, without losing our individuality, but rather affirming it, meanwhile conserving the essence of Spanishness that nourished our psychological personality.

We do not at all intend to defend a racial policy focused on the endogamic sense of primitive societies. We will never oppose the mixture of the superior and inferior castes of our race. But we will advocate for a Hispanic supercaste: ethnically improved, morally robust, spiritually vigorous. For that, we must stimulate the fertility of the best of our kind, for in biology quantity is not opposed to quality. . . . But we need not limit ourselves to stimulating the fertility of the best. Our program tends to awaken in individuals of all social classes a desire to ascend to the best hierarchies, aristocratic in body and spirit, an ambitious program that demands the collaboration of sociologists, economists, and politicians. We are referring to the politicians of doctrine, not party politicians, because the latter exert a terrible and destructive influence upon the race.

The regeneration of the race depends necessarily on the regeneration of the family institution, because the family constituted in accordance with traditional principles of Christian morality represents a nursery of social virtues, a shield against societal corruption, a sacred depository of traditions. . . . The family becomes a kind of cell in the social body that forms the race. The vigor and health of many cells, besides lending the body vitality, defends it against infections and poisons. Many healthy and prestigious families serve to invigorate a dying race.

Culture and religion are consubstantial with the Christian family, which radiates a purifying moral influence that consolidates and maintains racial values. The Greek and Roman civilizations have survived twenty centuries thanks to the purification effected by Christianity. The Arab people, heirs also of Greek civilization, suffered after a few centuries a degenerative collapse from which they have not been able to recover. Let us reflect a few moments about the bases of the family institution as Catholicism understands it, and we will be convinced of the solid support it offers for the regeneration of the race.

Nakano Seigō, speech to the Far East Society national convention, Japan, 1939

Some people might say that neither Fascism nor Nazism would work for who we are as a nation. However, I believe there is no fundamental difference in how people frame their mind when facing challenges, whether in Italy, Germany, or Japan [*applause*]. Both Fascism and Nazism are different from the despotism of the old era. They are not the conservatism that retrogressed from democracy but rather a democratic form that has passed beyond democracy. This is just my viewpoint, not an observation by a scholar: democracy has lost its spirit and reduced itself to a mere mechanism that does not consider the quality of human beings but claims numerical superiority. In other words, only the majority matters. However, that is no good because that is exactly what brought on the present-day decadence. Totalitarianism must see beyond numbers and base itself on essentials [*applause*]. Getting the consensus of the majority of people or having people participate in elections is just not enough. Individuals must unite organically, share common ideals and sense, and work together with people around them from the beginning till the end, or they will not be regarded as a complete national organization. We must not be an individualist who does not care about others. Imagine members of the community treating other people's matters as their own, their own matters as the matters of other people, public concerns as their own, and the nation's problems as their own, having understanding with each other, and pressing forward united as one in many ways. I believe in government ruled by the majority—but only in the case of a government that is, as one might say, more essential and active than democracy. And I believe that totalitarianism can make this system more defined and sophisticated.

360 DISCUSSION QUESTIONS

1   What might have been appealing about fascism at this particular time?

2   According to these documents, how might fascism affect the individual? Families? Societies?

3   What about fascism, as described here, foreshadows events of World War II?

ECONOMIC DEPRESSION

10-1a | Photograph, the Single Men's Unemployed Association parading to Bathurst Street United Church, Canada, ca. 1930

The collapse of the international economy between 1929 and 1932 was felt severely by a broad range of social classes around the globe. In Canada, the average per capita income fell 48 percent, with professional incomes declining 36 percent between 1928 and 1933. Unemployment in the nation grew to 30 percent and one in five Canadians was dependent on government relief. Below, the protesting Single Men's Unemployed Association marches in Toronto, Ontario, early in the depression years.

10–1b | Chart, depicting peak-to-trough decline in industrial production in various countries, 1929–1939

The Great Depression began as an ordinary recession in the summer of 1929 and worsened with the U.S. stock market crash of October 1929. This four-day collapse in stock prices, the most dramatic in American history, saw the Dow Jones Industrial Average drop 25 percent. The crash accelerated economic deterioration of which it was also a symptom. Over the next few years, consumer spending and investment fell, causing sharp declines in industrial output. These reductions led to workers being laid off, which exacerbated economic conditions. Restrictive tariffs and the contraction of available credit also added to the decade-long crisis.

Peak-to-Trough Decline in Industrial Production in Various Countries (Annual Data)

Country	Decline
United States	46.8%
Great Britain	16.2%
Germany	41.8%
France	31.3%
Canada	42.4%
Czechoslovakia	40.4%
Italy	33.0%
Belgium	30.6%
Netherlands	37.4%
Sweden	10.3%
Denmark	16.5%
Poland	46.6%
Argentina	17.0%
Brazil	7.0%
Japan	8.5%

DISCUSSION QUESTIONS

1   What connection were the men in the photograph making between transience and citizenship?

2   If degree of depression is linked to the difference between the peak and trough in production, which three countries experienced the most severe depressions? The least? Why might this be the case?

3   How do these sources illustrate the connection between production and unemployment that occurred during the Depression?

10-2 | No-Yong Park, excerpts from *An Oriental View of American Civilization*, Korea, 1934

A child of Korean refugees in Manchuria during the Japanese invasion of Korea, No-Yong Park (1889–1976) pursued a Western education in the United States during the Great War. He eventually earned MA and PhD degrees in political science and international relations from Harvard University. He ended up staying in the United States, becoming a nationally known expert on China and East-West relations. Here, however, Park shares his insights on the West rather than the East, commenting on the state of American capitalism and democracy in the midst of the Great Depression.

American Democracy in Crisis

The collapse of democracy and the rise of dictatorship is one of the most alarming developments in modern times. Russia, Italy, Germany, one after another came under the sway of some form of dictatorship. Even the United States of America has come under a semi-dictatorship. Hitler, Stalin and Mussolini appear to be prophets of a new era, the era of dictatorship. It would seem almost that democracy has seen its day and is now resigning in favor of Fascism or Hitlerism.

The retreat of democracy before the onslaught of dictatorship is a product of this turbulent age. Democracy is better suited to peaceful times, but dictatorship is more appropriate for times of crisis. It is quite natural, then, that Hitler and Mussolini should have arisen in this stormy, turbulent, present-day world of ours. The dictators will probably continue to run the whole show so long as the weather is bad and the sea is rough. But no sooner will the crisis be over than these dictators will be forgotten and buried. No one can tell when the crisis will be ended. No one can tell when this violent storm created by the World War will become calm. But one thing is sure, and that is that the storm will not last forever. The present collapse of the democratic system, therefore, cannot be regarded as a defeat, although it may be regarded as a temporary resignation. With this belief, I shall review the workings of American democracy.

American democracy is a child of the seventeenth and eighteenth century political thinkers of Europe. Milton, Sydney, Harrington, Locke, Rousseau, Montesquieu are some of the men who may be called the fathers of American democracy. So far as the *theory* of democracy goes, America has contributed nothing new but in practical politics her contribution is immeasurable. America proved that democracy is applicable in large states as well as in small states; she succeeded in creating a national government in a federal state; she introduced the presidential system in contrast to a parliamentary one; she built up the doctrine of judicial supremacy; she has made the best attempt that has been made to use the principles of checks and balances and of the separation of powers; and after all she has demonstrated that democracy is not a mere ideal but an actual working principle. The fact that the Union has been preserved for one hundred and fifty years and that the people have enjoyed freedom, liberty and prosperity unprecedented in history is a great tribute to American democracy.

The success of American democracy is due to the temperament, the wisdom, and the experience, of the American people, received in England as well as in America, and, above all, it is due to the malleable character of American democratic institutions. When an institution is so rigid as to prevent orderly changes in a peaceful way, it is bound to invite war and revolution with ruin and destruction. All of the twenty-five great dynastic changes in Chinese history were executed by war and bloodshed. By this one can easily understand the expense of an absolute monarchy or dictatorship. It is easy to put up a dictatorship, but it is very expensive to get rid of one. Democratic institutions also may be made so rigid as to tolerate no peaceful changes. But the American nation has found it possible to launch one of the greatest revolutions in world history without wasting one drop of blood. The way the American people set up a temporary semidictatorship is nothing short of a miracle.

The success in America, however, is no proof that it will work elsewhere. What makes a government good or bad is not so much in the form or principles of the government as in the application of it. The best government is that government which fits best into the prevailing conditions of a country, and the worst is the opposite. Democracy may be a good political principle for some people at some times, but not good for all peoples in all times. I cannot help feeling that the leaders of the Chinese revolution made a great mistake in thinking that democracy is better than monarchy or aristocracy.

Even if it is assumed that the eclipse of democracy is only a temporary phenomenon, and that democracy has accomplished much in America and elsewhere, and that it has a greater future, no one can deny that it has many shortcomings and weaknesses. The domination of the so-called democratic government by a small minority representing vested interests is one of the inherent dangers. Looking from the outside, America seems to be a truly democratic country. The executive is elected by the people, laws are made by the people, money is raised by the people and spent for them. Every citizen of mature age has the same vote, and every one has precisely the same right to run for any government position, including the office of president. But a peek into the inside will convince any man that there is not much of democracy in democracy. It is not the people who actually rule; it is a handful of irresponsible self-appointed autocrats representing the vested interests that move the wheels of the government, dictate the affairs of state, make and unmake laws and defeat or elect the president. In reality, under a republic the people are as completely dominated by the minority as under a monarchy or a dictatorship. One difference, however, is that in the republic the people think they are controlling their leaders as the little sparrows which fly after the eagle would think the big bird is being chased away by them.

Another great danger arises from the indifference of the so-called sovereign people. When the people had no vote, they shouted and yelled for it as the child would cry out for a new toy at sight. But when the vote was given them, they forgot all about it, and fell asleep in indifference. Even those who do vote do not know how to vote intelligently. But the Americans are no exception. The same is true of all peoples in all ages. That is the reason why democracy at its best is a fiction and republicanism a delusion. . . .

Since the government is a playground of the jokers and of the crooks, the people have no respect for the government and no respect for the laws. The Americans make more laws than any other people in the world. Think of it, they make more than sixteen thousand laws every year! But they violate them more than any other people in the world. At times it seems as if they made laws just so that they could break them. The very fact that the cost of crime in America is about thirteen billions of dollars annually, and that the cases of robbery in the city of Chicago alone are twenty-four times as many in a year as in all of England and Wales, indicates the seriousness of the situation. Whatever they do, the Americans do superlatively well and even in the field of crime they make the most enviable record. We Chinese cannot laugh at America, for we have more bandits than America has. But we must give the Americans the credit of having better bandits than we. . . .

The Collapse of American Capitalism

There are curious similarities between the Chinese political chaos and the American industrial anarchy. The former may be described as political feudalism and the latter as economic feudalism. The political feudalism in China is the creation of armed bandits, and the economic feudalism in America has been the creation of gamblers and speculators. The collapse of the Chinese political machinery is largely due to failure in controlling the armed bandits, and the collapse of the American industrial system has been largely due to failure in controlling the profit-makers and exploiters. In the one country a handful of arrogant and unscrupulous militarists wages political wars, endless and interminable, and in the other a small group of selfish and irresponsible capitalists has staged industrial wars which have been no less deadly in their effects. In the one country, the armed militarists are kings and dictators, and in the other the selfish capitalists are armed with industrial machinery. But in both countries, the sufferers have been the innocent people.

The capitalists in America have been as free as the militarists in China, and the people in the one country as much subjected to them as in the other. There is no other country in the world where the militarists are so free to exploit the masses as in China. Nor is there any other country where the capitalists have been so free and so uncontrolled as in America. China is a country of free militarists and America has been a land of free capitalists, free to exploit, free to gamble, free to wage wars, free from all responsibilities. Nothing can explain the situation better than the gambling in stocks and other securities. Probably one of the most diabolical things in the world is this gambling in securities. Hanging may be too good a reward for most of these speculators, but they have been left practically uncontrolled to cheat, rob the people of millions and to put the entire nation into jeopardy. A movement towards control is now under way. This control must not be so rigid as to smother individual initiative, but the extent of the freedom which the capitalists have hitherto enjoyed in America is beyond the imagination of any reasonable man. There can be no economic security in America until the irresponsible blood-suckers have been brought under control, as there can be no political order in China unless the armed militarists are brought under rule.

The American capitalists have been as irresponsible as the Chinese militarists in dealing with their fellow men. The Chinese militarist drags the poor fellows into his service. He pays them while they risk their lives in the battlefield, but when the crisis is over, he is not responsible for the well-being of his men. They are scattered throughout the country and become the burden of the people. Precisely the same situation has prevailed in America. A few years ago when business conditions were good the workers were paid well. The thrifty and hard-working saved a few dollars every week for the rainy day that might overtake them. Some bought stocks, some deposited their money in banks, others bought bonds. It seemed for some time that the wage earners would all be financially independent, sooner or later. But when prosperity vanished, millions of men were thrown out into the streets. These jobless men had no means of living through the workless days. Unlike the practice in some European countries, there was no unemployment insurance to which they could look for help. The only hope they had was those savings they had accumulated. Look what became of their savings! Their stocks went to pieces. Their banks, many of them, closed their doors. Their bonds lost their values, some of them nearly one hundred per cent. These men were as helpless as they were hopeless. But their employers disclaimed responsibility for their welfare and these men thus without the means to live, became the burden of the public.

The greatness of a nation does not depend on the size of its territory, or the number of its population, or the strength of its army and navy; it rests on its ability to maintain justice,—justice that will insure every man what is due to him, be it reward or punishment. There is no justice in the Chinese political chaos, nor has there been justice in the American economic anarchy. There is no justice in a state where armed men, like Chinese bandits and Japanese soldiers, are kings, nor in a country where speculators and profit-makers are left uncontrolled. In the one case, a few bandits armed with machine-guns run amuck and rob and murder innocent millions, and in the other, a few unscrupulous blood-suckers armed with industrial machinery drive the helpless people into poverty, misery and extermination. Look at the suffering millions in China, the victims of robbery, banditry, war and bloodshed. Look at the thousands of jobless American workmen, who once were proud, honest, willing, efficient workers, but who were driven into darksome slums, sheltered like pigs and fed by charity. No doubt some of them were the victims of their own sins, but most of them have been the victims of the gamblers and speculators, who deserve nothing but an electric chair and a stone overcoat. No civilized state should allow its soldiers to use the instruments of war against the innocent population, nor should it allow its speculators and the reckless producers to use the machinery of industry to enslave and slaughter mankind. Both must be drastically controlled, or else civilization itself may be ruined and destroyed.

There is another striking similarity between the American industrial condition and the Chinese political situation. The Americans have gone as far with their business as the Chinese have gone with their politics. From time immemorial the Chinese have lived democracy but their democracy has never extended beyond the walls of the little villages. Since the revolution in 1912 they have tried to extend the principle to the entire state but so far they have failed. Therefore, there is turmoil and unrest in China. Similarly, the Americans demonstrated their business genius but their success has been confined only within the walls of the individual plants, and so far they have failed to extend the system, the plan and the mechanism operating within the factory to the entire state. Therefore chaos came in American industry.

There is no question that the American business man, in general, has made a great success, individually, within his own plant. He has organized billion-dollar corporations, and systematized, standardized and improved his machines, his staff and all that has to do with efficiency within his own business. But outside of his business he has done little or nothing. He has had no plans, no system, no mechanism, not a thing to protect him and his fellow men. Hence economic society became nothing but chaos and disorder. The minute he left his office, he was out in the dark, kicked, tossed, dragged and trampled down by the surging mass of unknown forces beyond his control. His success within his own plant was compromised by his failure outside of his plant. His system and his plan, which had eliminated waste and increased production within the plant, were completely lost by his lack of plan and his inability to organize and direct the forces outside of his business. A success in individual industry, he has been a failure in national economy. . . .

It seems to me that the problem of America is not one of invention or the perfection of bigger turbines, for instance, or more powerful machinery in general, but is one of control, regulation and co-ordination of the various economic forces lying outside the individual plants and industry. In the old days, when each man or household was an independent, self-sufficing economic unit, there was no necessity of control and planning, but in this machine age, when all men and all nations are dependent on one another, the question of co-ordination and regulation is a question of life and death for all. The business situation to-day is like the weather. Everybody, as Mark Twain said, talks about it but nobody does anything about it. So long as business remains like the weather, outside of human control, there will always be cold, bleak wintry nights as well as hot, sultry summer days. The great challenge to twentieth century men, therefore, seems to be the question of harnessing economic forces for the service of mankind.

Since 1929, many thoughtful men and women have been seriously considering the question of economic control and planning. The entire country was flooded with literature on the Russian experiment. Norman Thomas, exponent of Socialism, was winning an unprecedented popularity in America. Both the employed and the unemployed, the young and the old, the educated and the uneducated, street cleaners and barbers, politicians and bootleggers, all were talking about Socialism, Communism and Capitalism. While the country was literally seething with cries for economic planning and reform, Franklin D. Roosevelt walked into the White House and silenced them all. President Roosevelt not only could talk but could act, as well, and no one would listen to anybody who could do nothing but talk. Naturally, the long-winded senators and representatives had to take back seats for the moment.

Now let us get a glimpse of President Roosevelt's political philosophy and his economic programme.

DISCUSSION QUESTIONS

1   Summarize the benefits and shortcomings of American democracy as observed by Park.

2   In Park's view, what practices contributed to the Great Depression in America?

3   What comparisons did Park make between the United States and China? For what purpose(s)?

RESPONSES TO WESTERN IMPERIALISM

10–3a | The Circle for Peace & Foreign Relations, call for 1927 Pan-African Congress in New York City, 1927

The six Pan-African Congresses held between 1900 and 1945 discussed colonial control and plans for the liberation of Africa. The ideals of Pan-African unity emerged in the late nineteenth century in response to European colonization and racial discrimination. The fourth Pan-African Congress was in New York, organized by the Women's International Circle for Peace and Foreign Relations, a black women's club in the city led by Anna Hunton, Nina Du Bois, and Minnie Pickens. The opportunity to meet in New York came after the French and British governments blocked a planned meeting in Tunisia or the Caribbean.

Fourth Pan-African Congress

The Circle for Peace and Foreign Relations of the United States is hereby calling a Fourth Pan-African Congress to meet in the City of New York, U.S.A., August 21, 22, 23 and 24, 1927. The Circle and those who are united in this call believe:

1.   That Conference is the beginning of wisdom.

2.   That the three Pan-African Congresses of 1919, 1921, 1923, held in London, Paris, Brussels and Lisbon were valuable steps in bringing together widely separated groups of men and women of Negro blood and their friends to consult on the present condition and the future of the black race and to achieve mutual understanding and acquaintanceship.

3.   That such conferences undertaken in so spirit of racial exclusiveness and with no thought of agression [sic] upon the rights of others, but only with the earnest desire for light, freedom and self-expression for all men, are real steps for the social uplift of black folk, and that the day is far past when any

man or group can speak for a people who are able and willing to speak for themselves.

Therefore, the Circle for Peace and Foreign Relations, with the co-operation and consent of many persons of prominence whose names will be published later, invite you and your friends to be present at this congress and to take part in it and to induce as many others to attend as you may be able to.

Signed for the Circle for Peace and Foreign Relations.

> THE EXECUTIVE COMMITTEE
> Addie Waite Hunton, chairman
> Dorothy R. Peterson, Secretary
> Menta B. Trotman
> Nina G. Du Bois
> Lottie E. Cooper
> Lillian A. Alexander
> Sadie E. Stockton
> Eunise Hunton Carter
> Minnie McA. Pickens
> Annie M. Dingle
> Room 688 Bible House, Astor Place, New York, N.Y., U.S.A.

10–3b | Hasan al-Banna, excerpts from *Between Yesterday and Today*, Egypt, late 1930s

Egyptian schoolteacher and imam Hasan al-Banna (1906–1949) is best known for founding the Muslim Brotherhood, a transnational Sunni Islamist organization. Initially, the organization operated as a Pan-Islamic, religious, and social movement, but later became more focused on politics, specifically seeking the end of British colonial rule in Egypt. He rejected Arab nationalism and saw all Muslims as members of a single nation-community.

The Tyranny of Materialism over the Lands of Islam

The Europeans strove for a wave of this materialistic life—with its decadent appearances and lethal germs—to flood all the Islamic lands to which their hands extended. Under their control, misfortune overtook the lands, as they endeavored to seize and deprive these nations of such elements of righteousness and power as science, knowledge, and industry. The Europeans masterfully planned this social invasion, deploying their political guile and military might until they accomplished what they desired. They enticed the Muslim leaders to take on debts and do business with them, facilitating these practices such that they could acquire the right to economic intervention; flood the lands with their capital, banks, and companies; direct the gears of the economy as they wished; and monopolize, to the exclusion of the inhabitants, immense profits and formidable wealth. Afterwards, they were able to change foundational principles of rule, justice, and education and tinge political, legislative, and cultural systems with their particular, unadulterated character in even the most powerful of the lands of Islam. They brought with them to these lands their scantily clad women, their liquors, their theaters, their ballrooms, their amusements, their stories, their newspapers, their novels, their fantasy, their futility, and their impudence. They permitted crimes they did not permit in their own lands, and they embellished this frivolous and tumultuous world, teeming with sin and overflowing with debauchery, before the eyes of the gullible and simpleminded among wealthy Muslims, those in the know, and those of stature and authority. . . .

Our Mission Is One of Reawakening and Deliverance

. . . B. Our General Goals: What do we want, brothers? Do we want to amass wealth, a fleeting shadow? Or do we want amplified status, a shifting and accidental trait? Or do we want omnipotence over the earth? . . . Rather, always recall that you have two fundamental goals:

1. That the Islamic homeland be liberated of all foreign power, as this is a natural right of every human being, denied only by an unjust oppressor or vanquishing tyrant.

2. That in this homeland arise a free Islamic state operating according to the decrees of Islam, applying its social order, proclaiming its righteous values, and transmitting its wise mission to the people. For as long as this state does not arise, Muslims altogether are sinners, responsible in the hands of God, the Great and Exalted, for their failure and refraining in establishing and creating it. It is a disrespect to humanity should, in these uncertain circumstances, a state arise extolling wrongful principles and proclaiming oppressive propaganda without anyone working to establish a state of truth, justice, and peace. We want to achieve these two goals in the Nile Valley, the Arab countries, and every land made fortunate by God with the creed of Islam: a religion, a nationality, and a conviction uniting all Muslims.

C. Our Particular Goals: We have, following these two goals, some particular goals that society must achieve to become fully Islamic. Recall, brothers: that more than 60 percent of Egyptians live off less than an animal's livelihood, getting nourishment only with great effort; that Egypt is threatened by ravaging famine and exposed to many economic problems, the outcome of which only God knows; that there are more than 320 foreign companies in Egypt monopolizing all the public institutions and important facilities across the country; that the gears of commerce and industry and economic facilities altogether are in the hands of foreign usurers; that the wealth of the land is passing at lightning speed from the hands of patriots to the hands of those foreigners; that Egypt, out of all civilized countries in the world, is the most afflicted with illnesses, epidemics, and disorders; that more than 90 percent of the Egyptian people are threatened with weak constitutions, the loss of sensory faculties, and different illnesses and diseases; that Egypt is still to this day ignorant, with less than a fifth of the population educated, including over 100,000 whose education did not surpass the compulsory school level; that crime is doubling in Egypt and multiplying by such a tremendous rate that prisons graduate more than schools do; that Egypt has yet to be able to provide a single army division with full equipment; and that such signs and depictions present themselves in each and every one of the countries of the Islamic world. Thus it is among your goals to work to reform education; to fight poverty, ignorance, disease, and crime; and to constitute an exemplary society worthy of associating with the law of Islam.

D. Our General Means: How do we attain these goals? Speeches, statements, letters, lessons, lectures, the diagnosing of ills and the prescribing of remedies—all of these alone do no good, achieve no ends, and bring no advocates of our mission to any goal. However, missionary work does have means that must be taken up and worked toward. The general means for missionary activity do not change or vary, never exceeding these three matters:

1. Deep faith

2. Careful constitution

3. Continuous work

And these, brothers, are your general aims, so believe in your shared view, rally around it, work toward it, and stand by it.

E. Additional Means: Besides these general means, there are perhaps some additional means necessary to take up and follow. . . . We might be asked to break customs and conventions and go against regulations and situations with which people have become acquainted and familiar; our mission, in its true essence, is nothing other than a fight against conventions and a transformation of customs and situations. So are you prepared for this, brothers?

F. Discouragement: Many people will say, "What do these missions mean? And of what use could they possibly be in building a nation and restoring a society with such chronic issues and numerous, persistent corruptions? How do you manage the economy on a nonusurious basis? How do you act on the issue of women? And how do you achieve what you are due without the use of violence?" Know, brothers, that the devil casts his temptations in the wishes of every reformer, only for God to abrogate them, then decree His miracles, for God is omniscient and perfectly wise. Remind all these people that, through the accounts of nations past and present, history relays to us a lesson and warning. And a nation resolved to live cannot die.

DISCUSSION QUESTIONS

1   How does the idea of pan-Africanism help explain the setting and goals of the 1927 Pan-African Congress?

2   According to al-Banna, by what methods had the British gained control of Egypt?

3   What do these documents suggest about imperialism and independence movements in the interwar period?

10–4a | Platform elements for the *Alianza Popular Revolucionaria Americana*, Peru, 1926

Founded by Peruvian politician and author Víctor Raúl Haya de la Torre (1895–1979) in 1924, the American Popular Revolutionary Alliance (APRA) aspired to become a continent-wide party. Initially, the group espoused anti-imperialism, Pan-Americanism, international solidarity, and economic nationalism. The APRA was influential in a number of other Latin American political movements. It rejected both U.S. imperialism and Soviet communism. Below, de la Torre lays out the organization and early aims of the movement.

The struggle organised in Latin America against Yankee Imperialism, by means of an international united front of manual and intellectual workers with a programme of common action, that is the A.P.R.A., the four initial letters of the following words: Alianza Popular Revolucionaria Americana (Popular Revolutionary American Alliance).

Its Programme

The programme of international action of the A.P.R.A. has five general points which serve as a basis for the national sections :—

(1) Action of the countries of Latin America against Yankee Imperialism.

(2) The political unity of Latin America.

(3) The nationalisation of land and industry.

(4) The internationalisation of the Panama Canal.

(5) The solidarity of all the oppressed people and classes of the world.

Its Organisation

The A.P.R.A. is a young organisation formed by the young men of the new generation of manual and intellectual workers of Latin America. It was founded in 1924 and has organised sections in various countries in Latin America and also in Europe, where the number of anti-Imperialist Latin American students is pretty large. The principal sections of the A.P.R.A are at present working in Mexico, Buenos Aires, Central America, Paris and other places in which for political reasons the action of these sections is not publicly allowed. A Central Executive Committee directs the action of all the sections.

The United Front

The A.P.R.A. organises the great Latin American Anti-Imperialist united front and works to include in its ranks all those who in one way or another have struggled and are still struggling against the North American danger in Latin America. Until 1923 this danger was regarded as a possible struggle of races—the Saxon and the Latin races—as a "conflict of cultures" or as a question of nationalism. From the "Gonzalez Prada" Popular Universities of Peru a new conception of the problem has arisen: the economic conception. In 1924 the first Pan-American Anti-Imperialist League was formed in Mexico and also the Latin American Union in Buenos Aires. The Anti-Imperialist Leagues were the first endeavour of the international united front of workers, peasant and students against Yankee Imperialism. The Latin American Union was founded as the Anti-Imperialist *Frente Unico* of the Intellectuals. As a matter of fact, the Anti-Imperialist Leagues have no fixed political programme, but only that of resistance to Imperialism, and the Latin American Union has simply intellectual activity. The A.P.R.A. was founded in 1924, with a programme of revolutionary and political action, and it invites all the scattered forces to form themselves in a single great front.

The Class Struggle against Imperialism

The history of the political and economic relations between Latin American and the United States, especially the experience of the Mexican Revolution, lead to the following conclusions:—

(1) The governing classes of the Latin American countries—landowners, middle class or merchants—are allies of North American Imperialism.

(2) These classes have the political power in our countries, in exchange for a policy of concessions, of loans, of great operations which they—the capitalists, landowners or merchants and politicians of the Latin American dominant classes—share with Imperialism.

(3) As a result of this alliance the natural resources which form the riches of our countries are mortgaged or sold, and the working and agricultural classes are subjected to the most brutal servitude. Again, this alliance produces political events which result in the loss of national sovereignty: Panama, Nicaragua, Cuba, Santo Domingo, are really protectorates of the United States.

The International Struggle against Imperialism

As the problem is common to all the Latin American countries, in which the dominant classes are allies of Imperialism in joint exploitation of the working classes, it is not an isolated or national question, but is international among the twenty Latin American republics. But the governing classes encourage divisions among these republics, assisting the Imperialist plan which fears Latin American unity (covering eight millions of square miles and about ninety millions of inhabitants). The governing classes stir up national feeling and national conflicts, as in the case of Peru against Chile, Brazil against Argentina, Ecuador and Colombia against Peru, &c. Every time that the United States intervenes as an "amicable mediator" they arrange matters purposely so that no definite settlement can be arrived at which might produce a principle of unification. The recent question of Tacna and Arica between Peru and Chile is the clearest demonstration of this policy of Imperialism.

Imperialism cannot be Overthrown without the Political Unity of Latin America

The experience of history, especially that of Mexico, shows that the immense power of American Imperialism cannot be overthrown without the unity of the Latin American countries. Against this unity the national dominant classes, middle class, landowners, &c., whose political power is almost always buttressed by the agitation of nationalism or patriotism of countries hostile to their neighbours, are ranged. Consequently the overthrow of the governing classes is indispensable, political power must be captured by the workers, and Latin America must be united in a Federation of States. This is one of the great political objects of the A.P.R.A.

The Nationalisation of Land and Industries as the Sole Means of Combating Imperialism

Within the capitalist system, and in accordance with the dialectics of its historical process, Latin America would infallibly become a North American colony. The United States holdings of values in the world (The *New York Times*, June 27, 1926) are shown in the following table; exclusive of the war debts:—

The United States holdings in Asia	$1,000,000,000
The United States holdings in Europe	$2,000,000,000
The United States holdings in Australia	$1,000,000,000
The United States holdings in Canada	$2,500,000,000
The United States holdings in Latin America	$4,100,000,000

This introduction of capital into Latin America increases almost daily. From June to October, Imperialism has invested over $50,000,000. The conflict between the United States and Mexico shows us that Mexico has not been able to nationalise the petroleum industry, which to-day is still dominated by the menace of a North American invasion in defence of the interests of the Standard Oil Company (North American capital in Mexico petroleum $614,487,263). The "Enmienda Platt" of the Cuban Constitution and the cases of Santo Domingo, Panama, Nicaragua, Honduras, and Hayti prove to us that national authority is lost in proportion as investments by Imperialism are accepted. The nationalisation of land and industry under the direction of the producing classes is the sole means of maintaining the country's power, and is the correct policy for the countries of Latin America.

Latin American Political Unity pre-supposes the
Internationalisation of the Panama Canal

The Panama Canal in the power of the United States Government is one danger more to the sovereignty of Latin America. The programme of the A.P.R.A. frankly proclaims the "internationalisation of Panama." Dr. Alberto Ulloa, Professor of International Law in the University of St. Marcos, Lima, Peru writes in support of the thesis: "The Panama Canal must be internationalised. . . . It is not possible to allow to the United States the exercise of supreme rule in Panama." (Open letter to the President of the Federation of Students of Panama, June, 1926.)

Conclusion

The A.P.R.A. represents, therefore, a political organisation struggling against Imperialism and against the national governing classes which are its auxiliaries and its allies in Latin America. The A.P.R.A. is the united front of the toiling classes (workers, peasants, natives of the soil) united with students, intellectual revolutionaries, &c. The A.P.R.A. is an autonomous movement, completely Latin American, without foreign interventions or influences. It is the result of a spontaneous movement in defence of our countries in view of the experiences of Mexico, Central America, Panama and the Antilles, and the present position of Peru, Bolivia, and Venezuela, where the policy of "penetration" by Imperialism is already keenly felt. For this our watchword is to be the following: "Against Yankee Imperialism, for the unity of the peoples of Latin America, for the realisation of social justice."

(Paris, *October*, 1926)

10–4b | Carleton Beals, excerpts from "With Sandino in Nicaragua," 1928

Carleton Beals (1893–1979), American journalist and political activist, traveled around the world and wrote on a variety of contemporary and historical topics. A high point of his career came in February 1928 when *The Nation* sent Beals to Nicaragua, where he became the only foreign correspondent to interview General Augusto César Sandino (1895–1934) as he led the rebellion against the U.S. occupation of Nicaragua. Labeled a "bandit" by the U.S. government, Sandino was considered a hero throughout much of Latin America for his guerilla war against the U.S. Marine Corps.

Several days ago I rode out of the camp of General Augusto C. Sandino, the terrible "bandit" of Nicaragua who is holding the marines at bay. Not a single hair of my blond, Anglo-Saxon head had been injured. On the contrary, I had been shown every possible kindness. I went, free to take any route I might choose, with permission to relate to anybody I encountered any and every thing I had seen and heard. Perhaps my case is unique. I am the first and only American since Sandino began fighting the marines who has been granted an official interview, and I am the first bona fide correspondent of any nationality to talk to him face to face.

"Do you still think us bandits?" was his last query as I bade him goodby.

"You are as much a bandit as Mr. Coolidge is a bolshevik;" was my reply.

"Tell your people;" he returned, "there may be bandits in Nicaragua, but they are not necessarily Nicaraguans." . . .

[Beals goes on to recount his quest to interview Sandino.] Our Odyssey had begun. From the San Pedro ranch, the point where our connections with the next Sandino outpost were broken and we lost track of the route taken by General Sandino after his evacuation of El Chipote, our way led us even deeper into the mountains in an ever-widening inland circle about the scene of operations of the American marines. On every hand loomed height after height, crags and ridges, profound valleys, enormous precipices, all blanketed with the most dense tropical vegetation. On some days the earth simmered under a hot, tropical sky; at other times it was almost invisible while tropical storms deluged it. These would have been difficult mountains to cross even if we had known the exact direction of the trail we had to follow in order to reach Sandino. . . .

The few people we met were all loyal Sandinistas, fleeing ever deeper into the wilderness in order to escape the dreaded *macho*, the hated American marine. Their homes were burned, their crops destroyed, their possessions smashed, but one and all vowed never to give up the struggle. . . .

We dropped into a clearing where there were barracks harboring about thirty soldiers and a dozen camp *juana*, women who had attended to the cooking and washing at El Chipote. One of them, Theresa, a vivacious, slender girl with a little boy about five, was also bound for the camp and promptly offered me two packs of Camel cigarettes which she had taken from the body of a marine—rather a gruesome gift. She had been wounded in the forehead by shrapnel during an American airplane bombardment on January 14, and lifted the towel from her head to show me an ugly star-shaped scar over her left eye. She declared that Sandino in that attack had lost one man killed and another and herself wounded—a decidedly different story from the marines' report. . . .

From the depths of the forest, mountain lions roar. Huge macaws wing across the sky, crying hoarsely and flashing crimson. We ford and reford the north-flowing tributary, for endless hours we toil across the Yali range, and finally drop down near Jinotega in another night of driving rain over a road where the horses roll pitifully, up to their bellies in mud.

A few miles from Jinotega, where a hundred marines were stationed, our little group of thirty men swung boldly, in broad daylight, out through the smiling open country of farms and meadows filled with cattle and wild horses; but occasionally the men scanned the sky apprehensively for airplanes. Here the soldiers singled out the farms of *Cachurecos* (Conservatives) and confiscated horses and saddles. This was the only instance of forced requisitioning I observed on the entire trip. . . .

Soon we were at the first sentry outpost.

"*Quien viva?*"

"*Viva Nicaragua!*"

"Give the countersign."

"Don't sell out the fatherland."

"Advance one by one to be recognized."

A short, youngish soldier with a dark-green uniform and smoked glasses took me in tow, saying in perfect English, "You are the American," and "A warm welcome, sir." . . .

After describing the manner in which several American airplanes were brought down, Sandino in rapid fire gave me the basis of his demands in the present struggle: first, evacuation of Nicaraguan territory by the marines; second, the appointment of an impartial civilian President chosen by the notables of the three parties—one who has never been President and never a candidate for the Presidency; third, supervision of the elections by Latin America.

"The day these conditions are carried out," declared Sandino, "I will immediately cease all hostilities and disband my forces. In addition I shall never accept a government position, elective or otherwise. . . . No position, no salary—this I swear. I will not accept any personal reward either today or tomorrow, or at any time in the future."

He left his chair and paced to and fro to emphasize this point. He stated vehemently: "Never, never will I accept public office. I am fully capable of gaining a livelihood for myself and my wife in some humble, happy pursuit. By trade I am a mechanic and if necessary I will return to my trade. Nor will I ever take up arms again in any struggle between the Liberals and the Conservatives, nor, indeed, in any other domestic struggle—only in case of a new foreign invasion. We have taken up arms from the love of our country because all other leaders have betrayed it and have sold themselves out to the foreigner or have bent the neck in cowardice. We, in our own house, are fighting for our inalienable rights. What right have foreign troops to call us outlaws and bandits, and to say that we are the aggressors? I repeat that we are in our own house. We declare that we will never live in cowardly peace under a government installed by a foreign Power. Is this patriotism or is it not? And when the invader is vanquished, as some day he must be, my men will be content with their plots of ground, their tools, their mules, and their families."

DISCUSSION QUESTIONS

1   According to the APRA, what were the effects of U.S. imperialism on life in Latin America?

2   Why might Beals' article have garnered support for Sandino, especially in the U.S.?

3   How had conflict between Latin America and the United States previously been interpreted? How do Beals' account and the APRA challenge that interpretation?

10-5 | Franklin D. Roosevelt, excerpts from Good Neighbor Policy, 1933

The election of Franklin Delano Roosevelt (1882–1945) ushered in the longest tenure for a U.S. President in history. Coming into office focused on improving an economy mired in depression, FDR also sought to remake foreign affairs, especially in the U.S. relationship with countries in Central and South America. Rather than intervention and interference, common in the past, Roosevelt stressed cooperation and trade with Latin America. Although other presidents had used the term "Good Neighbor" towards Latin America, none expressed it in policy more than Roosevelt.

I rejoice in this opportunity to participate in the celebration of "Pan-American Day" and to extend on behalf of the people of the United States a fraternal greeting to our sister American Republics. . . .

This celebration commemorates a movement based upon the policy of fraternal cooperation. In my Inaugural Address I stated that I would "dedicate this Nation to the policy of the good neighbor—the neighbor who resolutely respects himself and, because he does so, respects the rights of others—the neighbor who respects his obligations and respects the sanctity of his agreements in and with a world of neighbors." Never before has the significance of the words "good neighbor" been so manifest in international relations. Never have the need and benefit of neighborly cooperation in every form of human activity been so evident as they are today. . . .

The essential qualities of a true pan Americanism must be the same as those which constitute a good neighbor, namely, mutual understanding, and, through such understanding, a sympathetic appreciation of the other's point of view. . . . In this spirit the people of every Republic on our continent are coming to a deep understanding of the fact that the Monroe Doctrine, of which so much has been written and spoken for more than a century, was and is directed at the maintenance of independence by the peoples of the continent. It was aimed and is aimed against the acquisition in any manner of the control of additional territory in this hemisphere by any non-American power.

Hand in hand with this pan-American doctrine of continental self-defense, the peoples of the American Republics understand more clearly, with the passing years, that the independence of each Republic must recognize the independence of every other Republic. Each one of us must grow by an advancement of civilization and social well-being and not by the acquisition of territory at the expense of any neighbor.

In this spirit of mutual understanding and of cooperation on this continent you and I cannot fail to be disturbed by any armed strife between neighbors. I do not hesitate to say to you, the distinguished members of the Governing Board of the Pan-American Union, that I regard existing conflicts between four of our sister Republics as a backward step.

Your Americanism and mine must be a structure built of confidence, cemented by a sympathy which recognizes only equality and fraternity. It finds its source and being in the hearts of men and dwells in the temple of the intellect.

We all of us have peculiar problems, and, to speak frankly, the interest of our own citizens must, in each instance, come first. But it is equally true that it is of vital importance to every Nation of this Continent that the American Governments, individually, take, without further delay, such action as may be possible to abolish all unnecessary and artificial barriers and restrictions which now hamper the healthy flow of trade between the peoples of the American Republics. . . .

DISCUSSION QUESTIONS

1   Explain what Roosevelt meant by "good neighbor."

2   How did FDR interpret the Monroe Doctrine?

3   What might have been the implications of this policy shift for the U.S.? For Latin America?

LEADUP TO WORLD WAR II

10–6a | Baldur von Schirach, prayer for Hitler Youth, Germany, 1930s

The Nazi Party first created a youth organization in the early 1920s. One of many such groups in the country at the time, they camped, hiked, and imitated the popular Boy Scout movement (est. 1907). With the rise of the Nazi Party to power, the Hitler Youth, an organization for boys ages ten to fourteen, emphasized paramilitary training, weapons, and fitness. Membership—mandatory by 1936—topped seven million. The goals of Hitler's totalitarian dictatorship became the focus of their education and operation, teaching sacrifice to a greater cause.

Führer, my Führer given me by God,
Protect and preserve my life for long.
You rescued Germany from its deepest need.
I thank you for my daily bread.
Stay for a long time with me, leave me not.
Führer, my Führer, my faith, my light
Hail my Führer.

10-6b | Excerpt from biology textbook lesson for fifth-grade girls, Germany, 1942

In a fascist state, the education system has political goals. The biology textbook excerpted below, *Life Skills for Middle School,* was designed for fifth-grade female students. The lesson, "The Laws of Nature and Humanity," extended principles of natural selection and eugenics to human society and Nazi Germany. Note the ways in which political ideology has been inserted into a discussion of science.

Biology for the Middle School

For 5th Grade Girls

The Laws of Nature and Humanity

I.

We have established that all creatures, plants as well as animals, are in a constant battle for survival. Plants crowd into the area they need to grow. Every plant that fails to secure enough room and light must necessarily die. Every animal that does not secure sufficient territory and guard it against other predators, or lacks the necessary strength and speed or caution and cleverness will fall prey to its enemies. The army of plant eaters threatens the plant kingdom. Plant eaters are prey for carnivores. The battle for existence is hard and unforgiving, but is the only way to maintain life. This struggle eliminates everything that is unfit for life, and selects everything that is able to survive.

We have seen that the laws of nature are built on a struggle for survival. The slow-moving herbivores (e.g., cows) have weapons, the speedier ones (e.g., horses or rabbits) use that speed to escape predators. The rabbit instinctively conceals the traces that lead to his den. As a prey, his eyes are to the sides of his head, while a carnivore's are to the front. The hedgehog has his needles, toads and salamanders have poisonous skins. Predators have keen senses, a powerful spring, sharp teeth, and claws. If we further consider protective coloring, camouflage, and other coloring (above all with young animals), and that each animal has different gifts in seeing and smelling that are appropriate for its needs, we can see everywhere that living creatures are well prepared for the battle for survival. (Compare offensive and defensive characteristics of the various animals!) Animals at our latitude have many characteristics that enable them to survive winter: storing food, hibernation, migration, winter pelts. . . . The same is true for plants. Poisons of various types, irritants, thorns, and needles protect them from herbivores. (Remember the earlier examples!) Seeds that can survive the winter, roots, storage ability (Examples!), enable plants to survive the cold months. By ground leaves, growing high, pyramidal structure, leaf mosaics, climbing, winding, spreading (the dog rose), plants seek the necessary light for their leaves.

All the various habitats are heavily populated; every creature has to fight for its survival and wants to be a winner in this battle. This is summarized in the principle: Each individual wants to maintain its existence in the struggle for survival (self preservation instinct, fighting will, individuality).

Mankind, too, is subject to these natural laws, and has won its dominant position through struggle. This is obvious when we consider the prehistoric hunting age. People then had both to secure their own prey, and protect themselves against the larger carnivores. This old form of the struggle for existence does not, of course, exist in civilized nations any longer. Early man lived in hordes, we live in an ethnic state. The state takes responsibility for territory and much, much more. Nonetheless, each must win his place in his community. As Moltke said, "In the long run, only the hardworking are lucky." True, the larger carnivores are lacking, but bacteria and other tiny carriers of disease are no small danger. Consider the enormous scientific efforts (the struggle for survival!) men have made, and continue to make, to master these enemies, to defeat diseases! Each of us must keep his body strong through exercise and healthy living habits in order to develop his capacities and use them to serve his people. Those who do not do so are unsuitable for the more refined, yet just as relentless, nature of our struggle for life and will perish. Our Führer tells us:

He who wants to live must fight, and he who does not want to fight in this world of perpetual struggle does not deserve to live! (*Mein Kampf*, p. 317)

II.

All living creatures that succeed in the struggle for survival are not satisfied merely with existence, but seek to preserve their species as well. Here, too, is a drive that corresponds to natural law. Without this drive, species would long since have vanished.

The fox builds a den for its helpless young and cares for them. The deer cares for its fawns, and the bat even carries its young with it through the air. Each spring we watch with fascination as the birds cleverly build their nests, hatch their eggs, and untiringly feed their young. Insects place their larvae in certain areas where food is available. Mosquitoes and dragon flies, for example, put them in water, the cabbage moth in cabbages, stag beetles at the base of old oaks. We find the care of the young characteristic of all branches of the animal kingdom (Name all forms of care for offspring with which you are familiar!)

[Here follows a paragraph on insect reproduction.]

Maintaining the species also is a struggle. The deer ruts in the fall and offers battle to other deer in competition for females. The stronger and cleverer deer passes on his inheritance. The rooster defends his status and his hens courageously. The battle for females selects the fittest. Later, we will discuss the laws of inheritance.

[There follows two paragraphs on methods of plant reproduction.]

The drive for maintaining the species is stronger than the instinct for self preservation. Plants sacrifice themselves for their seeds. Most insects die when they have reproduced. The female rabbit defends her young against hawks, often at the cost of her own life. A fox risks its life to secure food for its young. The life of the individual can be sacrificed to assure the continuation of the species. (The law of the species is stronger than that of the individual!)

Among all living creatures, we can see a further natural law: the production of numerous offspring. Nowhere on earth do we find a form of life that produces only one or two offspring (corresponding to the number of the parents). That would inevitably lead to extinction. The elephant has the longest period of procreation, from its 30th to 90th year. It brings about six offspring into the world. A scientist has calculated that even with this slow rate of reproduction, in the absence of the struggle for survival elephants would take over the entire world in a few hundred years. A single pair would produce 19 million descendants in 750 years. The struggle for survival leads most to perish. The blue titmouse has two broods of 10–13 a year, but their number is not increasing. The more threatened a creature is in the struggle for survival, the more offspring it must produce. The greater number of offspring is a necessary means of responding to the hard struggle for survival. Each habitat can disappear from one day to the next (arrival of a new predator, disappearance of a food source).

A large number of offspring are an important means in the struggle for survival of the species. The house mouse can resist the field mouse simply through its larger number of young. In such instances, one can speak of a battle of births.

The second law to which all life is subordinate is: Each life form strives to ensure the survival of its species. The number of offspring must be greater than the number of the parents if the species is to survive (law of the larger number of offspring). Each species strives to conquer new territory. The species goes before the individual.

History provides us with enough examples to prove that mankind, too, is under this law. In the midst of their prosperity, the Romans lost the desire to have children. They sinned against the law of maintaining the species. Their state was undermined and overcome by foreign peoples in a short time. The ethnic traits of the Romans thus vanished. Our nation, too, once hung in the balance. National Socialism restored to the German people the will to have children, and preserved our people from certain decline, which would have been inevitable under the law of species and the law of the greater number of offspring.

Here, too, we can recall the Führer's words:

Marriage, too, cannot be an end in itself, but rather it must have the larger goal of increasing and maintaining the species and the race. That only is its meaning and its task. (*Mein Kampf*, p. 275)
The goal of female education must be to prepare them for motherhood. (*Mein Kampf*, p. 460)

III.

As we have already noted, people do not live as individuals like animals and plants, but as peoples, which largely have come together as ethnic states. We know something similar only with insects. Bees and ants are not only the sum of individuals; each individual shares a united drive in service of the entire group. They do not have an individual will any longer, but rather their actions have only the goal of serving the welfare of the whole, the welfare of the community. The state-building drive in insects has created a higher order from the drives of the individuals. Their species has become a higher order, one will in many parts. The individual member of a beehive does a single task: One may be a worker that carries nectar, another cleans the hive, the third builds on to it, a fourth feeds the larva, a fifth watches the hive's entrance. Each individual activity serves the whole. It is the same with ants. Certain ant species even have a warrior caste that fights in the front lines for the rest; the battle against the enemies of the state here, too, involves the whole group.

The instinctual state of the ants corresponds to the leadership state among mankind; however, the principles of a perfect insect state give people cause to think. They have preserved bees and ants in the struggle for survival and thereby proved their validity. We earlier noted the following truths about ants:

1. The work of the individual has only one purpose: to serve the whole group.

2. Major accomplishments are possible only by the division of labor.

3. Each bee risks its life without hesitation for the whole.

4. Individuals who are not useful or are harmful to the whole are eliminated.

5. The species is maintained by producing a large number of offspring.

It is not difficult for us to see the application of these principles to mankind: We also can accomplish great things only by a division of labor. Our whole economy demonstrates this principle. The ethnic state must demand of each individual citizen that he does everything for the good of the whole, each in his place and with his abilities (Principle 1).

He who loves his people proves it only by the sacrifices he is prepared to make for it. (*Mein Kampf*, p. 474)

If a person acts against the general interest, he is an enemy of the people and will be punished by the law (Principle 4). A look at our history proves that we as a people must defend our territory to preserve our existence.

The world does not exist for cowardly nations. (*Mein Kampf*, p. 105)

Military service is the highest form of education for the Fatherland (Principle 3).

The task of the army in the ethnic state is not to train the individual in marching, but to serve as the highest school for education in service of the Fatherland. (*Mein Kampf*, p. 459)

The fifth principle has already been discussed.

Each citizen of the nation must be ready to do all for the good of the whole, for the will of the Führer, even at the cost sacrificing his own life (the national law). The good of the nation goes before the good of the individual.

These natural laws are incontrovertible; living creatures demonstrate them by their very survival. They are unforgiving. Those who resist them will be wiped out. Biology not only tells us about animals and plants, but also shows us the laws we must follow in our lives, and steels our wills to live and fight according to these laws. The meaning of all life is struggle. Woe to him who sins against this law:

**The person who attempts to fight the iron logic of nature thereby fights the princi-
ples he must thank for his life as a human being. To fight against nature is to bring
about one's own destruction.** (*Mein Kampf*, p. 314)

DISCUSSION QUESTIONS

1 To whom was this prayer addressed? Would you call it religious? Explain.
2 Discuss the connection between politics, science, and education as expressed in the
   textbook lesson.
3 Both these sources target the same group. What was it? What made this group worth
   targeting?

10–7a | Haile Selassie, excerpts from appeal to the League of Nations, Ethiopia, 1936

Haile Selassie I (1892–1975) served as emperor of Ethiopia from 1930 to 1974 and
was a defining figure in modern Ethiopian history. He was leader of the country during
the Second Italo-Ethiopian War (1935–1937) fought between the invading Kingdom of
Italy and the Ethiopian Empire. The defeat of Ethiopia led to the short-lived Italian East
Africa (1936–1941). This Horn of Africa colony included also Italian Somaliland and
Italian Eritrea, territories gained through Italian expansion as far back as the 1880s.
In the Second Italo-Ethiopian War, Selassie appealed to the League of Nations, the
peacekeeping organization that actually included both Italy and Ethiopia as members.
Article X of the Covenant of the League of Nations (1919) called for assistance to be
given to a league member experiencing external aggression. The League of Nations
condemned the invasion and voted to impose economic sanctions, but these were
ineffective due to lack of support.

I, Haile Selassie I, Emperor of Ethiopia, am here today to claim that justice which is due
to my people, and the assistance promised to it eight months ago, when fifty nations
asserted that aggression had been committed in violation of international treaties.

There is no precedent for a Head of State himself speaking in this assembly. But
there is also no precedent for a people being victim of such injustice and being at present threatened by abandonment to its aggressor. Also, there has never before been an
example of any Government proceeding to the systematic extermination of a nation by
barbarous means, in violation of the most solemn promises made by the nations of the
earth that there should not be used against innocent human beings the terrible poison
of harmful gases. It is to defend a people struggling for its age-old independence that
the head of the Ethiopian Empire has come to Geneva to fulfil this supreme duty, after
having himself fought at the head of his armies.

I pray to Almighty God that He may spare nations the terrible sufferings that have just been inflicted on my people, and of which the chiefs who accompany me here have been the horrified witnesses.

It is my duty to inform the Governments assembled in Geneva, responsible as they are for the lives of millions of men, women and children, of the deadly peril which threatens them, by describing to them the fate which has been suffered by Ethiopia.

It is not only upon warriors that the Italian Government has made war. It has above all attacked populations far removed from hostilities, in order to terrorize and exterminate them.

At the beginning, towards the end of 1935, Italian aircraft hurled upon my armies bombs of tear-gas. Their effects were but slight. The soldiers learned to scatter, waiting until the wind had rapidly dispersed the poisonous gases.

The Italian aircraft then resorted to mustard gas. Barrels of liquid were hurled upon armed groups. But this means also was not effective; the liquid affected only a few soldiers, and barrels upon the ground were themselves a warning to troops and to the population of the danger.

It was at the time when the operations for the encircling of Makalle were taking place that the Italian command, fearing a rout, followed the procedure which it is now my duty to denounce to the world. Special sprayers were installed on board aircraft so that they could vaporize, over vast areas of territory, a fine, death-dealing rain. Groups of nine, fifteen, eighteen aircraft followed one another so that the fog issuing from them formed a continuous sheet. It was thus that, as from the end of January, 1936, soldiers, women, children, cattle, rivers, lakes and pastures were drenched continually with this deadly rain. In order to kill off systematically all living creatures, in order to more surely to poison waters and pastures, the Italian command made its aircraft pass over and over again. That was its chief method of warfare.

The very refinement of barbarism consisted in carrying ravage and terror into the most densely populated parts of the territory, the points farthest removed from the scene of hostilities. The object was to scatter fear and death over a great part of the Ethiopian territory.

These fearful tactics succeeded. Men and animals succumbed. The deadly rain that fell from the aircraft made all those whom it touched fly shrieking with pain. All those who drank the poisoned water or ate the infected food also succumbed in dreadful suffering. In tens of thousands, the victims of the Italian mustard gas fell. It is in order to denounce to the civilized world the tortures inflicted upon the Ethiopian people that I resolved to come to Geneva.

None other than myself and my brave companions in arms could bring the League of Nations the undeniable proof. The appeals of my delegates addressed to the League of Nations had remained without any answer; my delegates had not been witnesses. That is why I decided to come myself to bear witness against the crime perpetrated against my people and give Europe a warning of the doom that awaits it, if it should bow before the accomplished fact.

Is it necessary to remind the Assembly of the various stages of the Ethiopian drama? For 20 years past, either as Heir Apparent, Regent of the Empire, or as Emperor, I have never ceased to use all my efforts to bring my country the benefits of civilization, and in particular to establish relations of good neighbourliness with adjacent powers. In particular I succeeded in concluding with Italy the Treaty of Friendship of 1928, which absolutely prohibited the resort, under any pretext whatsoever, to force of arms, substituting for force and pressure the conciliation and arbitration on which civilized nations have based international order. . . .

In October, 1935, the 52 nations who are listening to me today gave me an assurance that the aggressor would not triumph, that the resources of the Covenant would be employed in order to ensure the reign of right and the failure of violence.

I ask the fifty-two nations not to forget today the policy upon which they embarked eight months ago, and on faith of which I directed the resistance of my people against the aggressor whom they had denounced to the world. Despite the inferiority of my weapons, the complete lack of aircraft, artillery, munitions, hospital services, my confidence in the League was absolute. I thought it to be impossible that fifty-two nations, including the most powerful in the world, should be successfully opposed by a single aggressor. Counting on the faith due to treaties, I had made no preparation for war, and that is the case with certain small countries in Europe. . . .

War then took place in the atrocious conditions which I have laid before the Assembly. In that unequal struggle between a Government commanding more than forty-two million inhabitants, having at its disposal financial, industrial and technical means which enabled it to create unlimited quantities of the most death-dealing weapons, and, on the other hand, a small people of twelve million inhabitants, without arms, without resources having on its side only the justice of its own cause and the promise of the League of Nations. What real assistance was given to Ethiopia by the fifty-two nations who had declared the Rome Government guilty of a breach of the Covenant and had undertaken to prevent the triumph of the aggressor? Has each of the States Members, as it was its duty to do in virtue of its signature appended to Article 15 of the Covenant, considered the aggressor as having committed an act of war personally directed against itself? I had placed all my hopes in the execution of these undertakings. . . .

I assert that the problem submitted to the Assembly today is a much wider one. It is not merely a question of the settlement of Italian aggression.

It is collective security: it is the very existence of the League of Nations. It is the confidence that each State is to place in international treaties. It is the value of promises made to small States that their integrity and their independence shall be respected and ensured. It is the principle of the equality of States on the one hand, or otherwise the obligation laid upon small Powers to accept the bonds of vassalship. In a word, it is international morality that is at stake. Have the signatures appended to a Treaty value only in so far as the signatory Powers have a personal, direct and immediate interest involved? . . .

Apart from the Kingdom of the Lord there is not on this earth any nation that is superior to any other. Should it happen that a strong Government finds it may with impunity destroy a weak people, then the hour strikes for that weak people to appeal to the League of Nations to give its judgment in all freedom. God and history will remember your judgment. . . .

I ask the fifty-two nations, who have given the Ethiopian people a promise to help them in their resistance to the aggressor, what are they willing to do for Ethiopia? And the great Powers who have promised the guarantee of collective security to small States on whom weighs the threat that they may one day suffer the fate of Ethiopia, I ask what measures do you intend to take?

Representatives of the World I have come to Geneva to discharge in your midst the most painful of the duties of the head of a State. What reply shall I have to take back to my people?

June, 1936. Geneva, Switzerland.

10–7b | Aurelio Bertiglia, postcard, on Italian conquest of Ethiopia, Italy, ca. 1936

Aurelio Bertiglia (1891–1973) was an Italian caricaturist, painter, and commercial artist. Primary self-taught, he was active in producing postcards from the age of fourteen, producing several anti-Austrian caricatures during the Great War. During the Second Italo-Ethiopian War, Italian dictator Benito Mussolini (1883–1945) directed Bertiglia to produce a series of postcards depicting Ethiopian civilization or Italian soldiers operating in Ethiopia.

SEE COLOR INSERT

DISCUSSION QUESTIONS

1   Why did Emperor Selassie choose to personally address the League of Nations? What arguments did he use to impress upon the League the severity of his nation's situation?

2   Consider the postcard. What might the posture and position of the human figures indicate about how the Italian viewed themselves, the Ethiopians, and the conquest?

3   What made this incident of international significance?

10–8 | Items from the Convention for the Maintenance, Preservation, and Reestablishment of Peace and Additional Protocol, Argentina, 1936

This agreement, signed in Buenos Aires in December 1936, demonstrated the collective concern for peace among the republics of the Americas. It is reflective of the Good Neighbor Policy that President Franklin Roosevelt adopted toward Latin America in 1933. The 1936 agreement, signed by twenty-one countries, drew on two other preceding treaties, the Kellogg-Briand Pact (Treaty of Paris of 1928) and the Saavedra Lamas Pact (Treaty of Non-Aggression and Conciliation of 1933). In Kellogg-Briand, signatory states agreed not to use war to settle "disputes or conflicts of whatever nature or of whatever origin they may be, which may arise among them." The Saavedra Lamas Pact, signed by most Latin American countries and the U.S., promised to settle disputes and disagreements "only by peaceful means" and that the occupation or seizure of territories by armed force would not be acknowledged or considered valid.

ARTICLE 1. In the event that the peace of the American Republics is menaced, and in order to coordinate efforts to prevent war, any of the Governments of the American Republics signatory to the Treaty of Paris of 1928 or to the Treaty of Non-Aggression and Conciliation of 1933, or to both, whether or not a member of other peace organizations, shall consult with the other Governments of the American Republics, which, in such event, shall consult together for the purpose of finding and adopting methods of peaceful cooperation.

ARTICLE 2. In the event of war, or a virtual state of war between American States, the Governments of the American Republics represented at this Conference shall undertake without delay the necessary mutual consultations, in order to exchange views and to seek, within the obligations resulting from the pacts above mentioned and from the standards of international morality, a method of peaceful collaboration; and, in the event of an international war outside America which might menace the peace of the American Republics, such consultation shall also take place to determine the proper time and manner in which the signatory states, if they so desire, may eventually cooperate in some action tending to preserve the peace of the American Continent.

. . .

Additional Protocol Relative to Non-Intervention

ARTICLE 1. The High Contracting Parties declare inadmissible the intervention of any one of them, directly or indirectly, and for whatever reason, in the internal or external affairs of any other of the Parties.

The violation of the provisions of this Article shall give rise to mutual consultation, with the object of exchanging views and seeking methods of peaceful adjustment.

. . .

DISCUSSION QUESTIONS

1   How was this statement a cooperative effort and how was it a unilateral move by the United States? Does it represent a shift from past policy? Why or why not?

2   What additional protocol was added to the convention and what might have made that protocol necessary?

3   How might the timing of this agreement have been important?

10–9 | Mahatma Gandhi, letter to Adolf Hitler, India, 1939

Mahatma Gandhi (1869–1948) was the primary leader of the Indian independence movement and inspiration to movements for civil rights and freedoms around the globe (see chapter 13, 360). His work toward peace encouraged him to write a series of letters to German Chancellor Adolf Hitler in 1939 and 1940, pleading with him to turn from war. He also encouraged the British people to oppose the campaigns of Hitler and Italy's Benito Mussolini through nonviolent means.

As at Wardha, C. P., INDIA,
July 23, 1939
DEAR FRIEND,
Friends have been urging me to write to you for the sake of humanity. But I have resisted their request, because of the feeling that any letter from me would be an impertinence. Something tells me that I must not calculate and that I must make my appeal for whatever it may be worth.

It is quite clear that you are today the one person in the world who can prevent a war which may reduce humanity to a savage state. Must you pay that price for an object however worthy it may appear to you to be? Will you listen to the appeal of one who has deliberately shunned the method of war not without considerable success? Any way I anticipate your forgiveness, if I have erred in writing to you.

I remain,

Your sincere friend,
M. K. Gandhi

HERR HITLER,
BERLIN,
GERMANY

DISCUSSION QUESTIONS

1   What were Gandhi's tone and aim in writing to Hitler?

2   Why did Gandhi believe Hitler the necessary recipient for his message and what methods did Gandhi propose Hitler employ to achieve his ambitions?

10-10a | Carey Orr, political cartoon, "The Only Way We Can Save Her," 1939

Pulitzer Prize-winning cartoonist Carey Orr (1890-1967) captured one aspect of isolationist sentiment toward non-involvement in the war in Europe. Isolationists included both progressives and conservatives as well as business owners and peace activists. In a speech in October 1937, President Franklin D. Roosevelt had called for an international "quarantine" against an "epidemic of world lawlessness" by the aggressive nations of the world. FDR closed with the words, "America hates war. America hopes for peace. Therefore, America actively engages in the search for peace."

Carey Orr. *The Tribune* (Chicago), 1939.

10-10b | Theodor Geisel, cartoon, ". . . and the Wolf chewed up the children and spit out their bones . . . But those were Foreign Children and it really didn't matter," 1941

Known for his children's literature, Theodor Seuss Geisel (1904–1991), or Dr. Seuss, created political cartoons during World War II. He also went on to work for the U.S. Army during the conflict, developing both live-action and animated productions. His *Design for Death,* which depicted the Japanese as victims of seven hundred years of class dictatorship, later won the 1947 Academy Award for Best Documentary Feature. Before America entered the war, however, Geisel's pen drafted a gallery of acerbic criticisms of the isolationists' view of American responsibilities to war-torn Europe.

DISCUSSION QUESTIONS

1   What elements did Orr include in "The Only Way We Can Save Her" to show the direness of the situation facing the United States?

2   Both these cartoons respond to the "America First" approach to the war in Europe. What position did each cartoon take? How did Orr and Geisel make their respective arguments?

11

World War II

STATEMENTS OF PURPOSE IN WWII

Leadership in wartime necessitates some sort of public articulation of the aims and goals of war. Allied and Axis leader in World War II gave such statements frequently, and the themes in them were distributed via propaganda and media to broader audiences. The purposes put forward often depended upon intended audience, and they evolved over the course of the war—especially for nation-states that had remained neutral in the 1930s and joined the war relatively late, such as the Soviet Union and the United States.

Axis leaders, such as Italian Prime Minister Benito Mussolini (1883–1945), Japanese Prime Minister and General Tōjō Hideki (1884–1948), and German Chancellor-Führer Adolf Hitler (1889–1945), could fall back on fascist ideology to explain war aims, as claims to expanded empires were central to political thinking throughout the 1930s.

Allied leaders, such as United Kingdom Prime Minister Winston Churchill (1874–1965), Soviet Premier Josef Stalin (1878–1953), and U.S. President Franklin D. Roosevelt (1882–1945), focused on rallying public support for war and public acquiescence with state demands, though in societies with radically different political systems and memories of World War I. For the Soviet and U.S. populations, especially, leaders needed to explain the move from neutrality to engagement.

Benito Mussolini's Declaration of War on Britain and France, Italy, 1940

Fighters of land, sea and air, Blackshirts of the revolution and of the legions, men and women of Italy, of the empire and of the Kingdom of Albania, listen!

The hour destined by fate is sounding for us. The hour of irrevocable decision has come. A declaration of war already has been handed to the Ambassadors of Great Britain and France.

We take the field against the plutocratic and reactionary democracies who always have blocked the march and frequently plotted against the existence of the Italian people.

Several decades of recent history may be summarized in these words: Phrases, promises, threats of blackmail, and finally, crowning that ignoble edifice, the League of Nations of fifty-two nations.

Our conscience is absolutely clear.

With you, the entire world is witness that the Italy of fascism has done everything humanly possible to avoid the tempest that envelops Europe, but all in vain. It would have sufficed to revise treaties to adapt them to changing requirements vital to nations and not consider them untouchable for eternity.

It would have sufficed not to begin the stupid policy of guarantees, which proved particularly deadly for those who accepted them. It would have sufficed not to reject the proposal of the Fuehrer [Hitler] made last October 6 after the campaign in Poland ended.

Now all that belongs to the past.

If today we have decided to take the risks and sacrifices of war, it is because the honor, interests, and future firmly impose it since a great people is truly such if it considers its obligations sacred and does not avoid the supreme trails that determine the course of history.

We are taking up arms, after having solved the problem of our continental frontiers. We want to break the territorial and military chains that confine us in our sea because a country of 45,000,000 souls is not truly free if it has not free access to the ocean.

This gigantic conflict is only a phase of the logical development of our revolution. It is the conflict of poor, numerous peoples who labor against starvers who ferociously cling to a monopoly of all riches and all gold on earth.

It is a conflict of fruitful, useful peoples against peoples who are in a decline. It is a conflict between two ages, two ideas.

Now the die is cast and our will has burned our ships behind us.

I solemnly declare that Italy does not intend to drag other peoples bordering on her by sea or land into the conflict. Switzerland, Yugoslavia, Greece, Turkey, and Egypt, take note of these words of mine. It depends on them and only on them if these words are rigorously confirmed or not.

Italians, in a memorable mass meeting in Berlin, I said that according to the rules of Fascist morals when one has a friend one marches with him to the end. This we have done and will continue to do with Germany, her people and her victorious armed forces.

On this eve of an event of import for centuries, we turn our thoughts to His Majesty, the King and Emperor, who always has understood the thought of the country.

Lastly, we salute the new Fuehrer, the chief of great allied Germany.

Proletariat, Fascist Italy has arisen for the third time, strong, proud, compact as never before.

There is only one order. It is categorical and obligatory for every one. It already wings over and enflames hearts from the Alps to the Indian Ocean: Conquer!

And we will conquer in order, finally, to give a new world of peace with justice to Italy, to Europe and to the universe.

Italian people, rush to arms and show your tenacity, your courage, your valor.

Tōjō Hideki, Tōgō Shigenori, and Hara Yoshimichi, statements on war, Japan, 1941

Statement by Prime Minister Tōjō Hideki

On the basis of the Imperial Conference decision of November 5, the Army and Navy, on the one hand, devoted themselves to the task of getting everything ready for military operations; while the Government, on the other hand, used every means at its disposal and made every effort to improve diplomatic relations with the United States. The United States not only refused to make even one concession with respect to the position she had maintained in the past but also stipulated new conditions, after having formed an alliance with Great Britain, the Netherlands, and China. The United States demanded complete and unconditional withdrawal of troops from China, withdrawal of our recognition of the Nanking Government, and the reduction of the Tripartite Pact to a dead letter. This not only belittled the dignity of our Empire and made it impossible for us to harvest the fruits of the China Incident, but also threatened the very existence of our Empire. It became evident that we could not achieve our goals by means of diplomacy.

At the same time, the United States, Great Britain, the Netherlands, and China increased their economic and military pressure against us; and we have now reached the point where we can no longer allow the situation to continue, from the point of view of both our national power and our projected military operations. Moreover, the requirements with respect to military operations will not permit an extension of time. Under the circumstances, our Empire has no alternative but to begin war against the United States, Great Britain, and the Netherlands in order to resolve the present crisis and assure survival. . . .

Statement by Foreign Minister Tōgō Shigenori on Japanese-American Negotiations

The United States Government has persistently adhered to its traditional doctrines and principles, ignored realities in East Asia, and tried to force on our Empire principles that she herself could not easily carry out. Despite the fact that we made a number of concessions, she maintained her original position throughout the negotiations, lasting for seven months, and refused to budge even one step. I believe that America's policy toward Japan has consistently been to thwart the establishment of a New Order in East Asia, which is our immutable policy. We must recognize that if we were to accept their present proposal, the international position of our Empire would be reduced to a status lower than it was prior to the Manchurian incident, and our very survival would inevitably be threatened. . . .

Statement by Privy Council President Hara Yoshimichi

In negotiating with the United States, our Empire hoped to maintain peace by making one concession after another. But to our surprise, the American position from beginning to encl was to say what Chiang Kai-shek wanted her to say and to emphasize those ideals that she had stated in the past. The United States is being utterly conceited, obstinate, and disrespectful. It is regrettable indeed. We simply cannot tolerate such an attitude.

If we were to give in, we would give up in one stroke not only our gains in the Sino-Japanese and Russo-Japanese Wars, but also the benefits of the Manchurian incident. This we cannot do. We are loath to compel our people to suffer even greater hardships, on top of what they have endured during the four years since the China incident. But it is clear that the existence of our country is being threatened, that the great achievements of the Emperor Meiji would all come to naught, and that there is nothing else we can do. Therefore, I believe that if negotiations with the United States are hopeless, then the commencement of war, in accordance with the decision of the previous Imperial Conference, is inevitable.

I would like to make a final comment: there is no doubt that initial operations will result in victory for us. In a long-term war, however, it is necessary to win victories, on the one hand, while, on the other hand, we keep the people in a tranquil state of mind. This is indeed the greatest undertaking since the opening of our country in the nineteenth century. We cannot avoid a long-term war this time, but I believe that we must somehow get around this and bring about an early settlement. In order to do this, we will need to start thinking now about how to end the war. Our nation, governed by our magnificent national structure [*kokutai*], is, from a spiritual point of view, certainly unsurpassed in all the world. But in the course of a long-term war, there will be some people who will fall into erroneous ways. Moreover, foreign countries will be actively engaged in trying to undermine the morale of the people. It is conceivable that even patriotic individuals will on occasion attempt to do the same. It will be very difficult to deal with these people. I believe that it is particularly important to pay attention to our psychological solidarity. We must be very concerned about this. Be sure you make no mistakes in handling the inner turmoil of the people.

I believe that the proposal before us cannot be avoided in the light of present circumstances, and I put my trust in officers and men whose loyalty is supreme. I urge you to make every effort to keep the people in a tranquil state of mind, in order to carry on a long-term war.

Concluding Remarks by Prime Minister Tōjō Hideki

I would now like to make one final comment. At this moment our Empire stands at the threshold of glory or oblivion. We tremble with fear in the presence of His Majesty. We subjects are keenly aware of the great responsibility we must assume from this point on. Once His Majesty reaches a decision to commence hostilities, we will all strive to repay our obligations to him, bring the government and the military ever closer together, resolve that the nation united will go on to victory, make an all-out effort to achieve our war aims, and set His Majesty's mind at ease.

I now adjourn the meeting.

[During today's Conference, His Majesty nodded in agreement with the statements being made, and displayed no signs of uneasiness. He seemed to be in an excellent mood, and we were filled with awe.]

Adolf Hitler's speech for Heroes' Memorial Day, Germany, 1941

For the second time we enter this room for a memorial service to our people. Even more than a year ago we appreciate how inadequate are words to express the nation's thankfulness to its heroes. In times of long peace the memory of the terrible experiences of war, out of which rises heroism, gradually grows dim. It even happens that a whole generation knows nothing of war as such and honors its heroes without being in the least worthy of them.

In such a circumstance the greatest sacrifice of man is acknowledged with superficial phrases. There is even danger that, while remembering heroes of times past, the men of the present regard themselves as free of the obligation to conduct themselves with a similar spirit of heroism.

But if the German people in the year 1941 honors its heroes, it does so at a time and under circumstances that give it a right to hold up its head with pride as it pays tribute to men of the near and distant past who sacrificed their lives for the State.

As twelve months ago in this consecrated hall we turned our thoughts to our heroes, there lay behind us the thoroughly successful beginning of a war that Germany did not want, but that was forced on us by the same forces that were responsible before in history for the great war of the peoples in 1914 to 1918.

They were the elements whose goal that time was to rob the German nation of the most primitive right of life, who in the years of the Versailles dictate raised as the dogma of the new world order political enslavement and economic impotence, and now are opposed to the revival of our people with the same hatred with which they once pursued the Second Reich.

In complete misjudgment of the situation, in a sadly false estimate of their own and Germany's power, and in complete ignorance of the will and determination of the new German leadership, they expected a second crushing of our people would be as easy as the first attempt.

The fact that the American General Wood, before the investigation committee of the American Senate, testified that as early as 1936 Churchill told him Germany was getting too strong again and must be destroyed in a new war established firmly in history the real responsibility for present developments.

England and France alone wanted war—not so much the people as a thin stratum of political and financial leadership behind which, wielding its last power, stood international Jewry and its world conspiracies of democracy and Freemasonry.

But it was the hope of these responsible war makers that thrust Poland forward not only to attain outward justification for war but also to make sure in advance that Poland would play its World War role of dividing German strength.

The eighteen-day campaign in Poland was but the precipitous end of these hopes. Under these circumstances the German people were able to enter the year 1940 with proud confidence. But our people did not deceive themselves as to the year lying ahead. The battle in the west, which remains in the memory of every living German World War soldier as an episode of suffering without end, had to be decided.

In exact knowledge of our preparations and plans, in boundless confidence in the German soldier, his armament and leadership and ability and before all in his attitude, I dared on Memorial Day, 1940, to predict that the battle before us would end in the most glorious victory in our history. Eight weeks later this battle started.

But before the defense forces struck in the west, what was probably the most important decision of the war was taken. On April 9, with just a few hours to spare, a dangerous British attempt to strike German defense powers in the heart from the north was anticipated. At dawn on May 10 this perhaps most dangerous threat to our military and political position had been swept aside. So the battle to a decision in the west could begin. It followed a course previously mapped out.

What could not be done in four years of indescribable sacrifice in the World War was accomplished in a few weeks: the crushing of the British-French front.

Despite the conclusion of the guilty British Prime Minister of that time, the year 1940 will go down in history as one of the most decisive and significant. Because in this year there was a shift of power of truly historic importance. If in the year 1918 we could have had only a portion of this success the World War would have been won.

Today German forces stand throughout the world, men and material strengthened to an inconceivable degree, ready to complete joyfully and confidently what was begun in the epochal year 1940.

So we approach with still greater right than in 1940 the German heroes of the past. All of us remember what they accomplished and endured in the World War. But we bow before their sacrifice, ourselves no longer unworthy. As the German divisions started the advance in the West, today's memorial service has its most fitting beginning, because in countless soldiers' cemeteries in the West victorious sons stood for a moment of tribute at the graves of their heroic fathers.

The German people have recovered everything that once was sacrificed in a foolish delusion. So today we can recall with lightened hearts the sacrifice of life in the World War. But in the illustrious events of the present we must not overlook the vast spiritual powers for which the German people and its soldiers must thank the heroism of their ancestors.

The soldiers of the World War did not fall in vain. If at that time the sacrifice was not immediately crowned by success, their heroic conduct left a heritage that an ever worthy German generation will prize with deepest emotion and that paralyzes the memories of our enemies.

It is perhaps this consciousness of strength that enabled the German people today to achieve such greatness. The people feel they are carrying out the will of heroic ancestors.

Beside the dead of the World War lie now the fallen in continuation of this battle. And again, as then, the sons of our people lie in distant places, in the sea everywhere as courageous fighters for their great German home. It is the same German man—be it in World War work or in the present fight that has been thrust upon us—who risks and gives his life to win for his people a greater future, a surer peace, a better organization and human comradeship than that given us by the dictators of Versailles.

But we think also of the Italian soldiers, who as allies also must give up their lives in distant parts of the world. Their ideals and objectives are the same as ours: The world is not here for a few people, and an order based eternally on the distinction between the haves and the have-nots does not exist any more because the have-nots have determined to lay claim to their portion of God's earth.

The home front, too, in this war must make a greater sacrifice than formerly. The heroism of the home front contributes its bit to the most decisive battle in German history. And here it is not only the man who must show the power of his resistance but the woman, too. The nation has become a battling unity. And not because they sought this fight but because it was forced on them.

Behind us lies a Winter of work. What remained to be improved has been done. The German Army is now the strongest military instrument in our history. In the months of this Winter our allies bore the brunt of the whole power of the British attack, but from now on German forces again will resume their share of this load.

No power and no support coming from any part of the world can change the outcome of this battle in any respect. England will fall. The everlasting Providence will not give victory to him who, merely with the object of ruling through his gold, is willing to spill the blood of men.

Germany demanded nothing of England and France. All of the Reich's denunciations, its disarmament and peace suggestions, were vain. International finance and plutocracy want to fight this war to the finish. So the end of this war will and must be its destruction. Then may Providence find a way to lead their people, from whom the chains will be struck, into a better order!

When England and France declared this war, England immediately began a fight against civil life. To the blockade of the World War, that war against women and children, it added this time air and fire war against peaceful villages and cities. In both of these modes of war England will be defeated. The air war that Churchill started will destroy not Germany but England itself. Just so, the blockade will not strike Germany but its inventor.

While the coming of winter limited battle actions on land, the fight in the air and on the sea continued. The heroism of submarine and ship crews goes hand in hand with that of our fliers.

We cannot crown observance of Memorial Day more worthily than to make a renewed determination to change the battle that our international enemies started as a war to our destruction into a final German victory.

So we enter the year 1941, cool and determined to end what started the year before. It is quite immaterial what part of the earth or in which sea or in what air space our German soldiers fight. They will know they battle for fate and freedom and the future of our people forever.

But while we end this battle victoriously we thank our heroes of the past, for we are saving that for which they fell: Germany, our people and its great German Empire.

Winston Churchill, Finest Hour speech, UK, 1940

. . . . I have thought it right upon this occasion to give the House and the country some indication of the solid, practical grounds upon which we base our inflexible resolve to continue the war. There are a good many people who say, "Never mind. Win or lose, sink or swim, better die than submit to tyranny—and such a tyranny." And I do not dissociate myself from them. But I can assure them that our professional advisers of the three Services unitedly advise that we should carry on the war, and that there are good and reasonable hopes of final victory. We have fully informed and consulted all the self-governing Dominions, these great communities far beyond the oceans who have been built up on our laws and on our civilization, and who are absolutely free to choose their course, but are absolutely devoted to the ancient Motherland, and who feel themselves inspired by the same emotions which lead me to stake our all upon duty and honour. We have fully consulted them, and I have received from their Prime Ministers, Mr. Mackenzie King of Canada, Mr. Menzies of Australia, Mr. Fraser of New Zealand, and General Smuts of South Africa—that wonderful man, with his immense profound mind, and his eye watching from a distance the whole panorama of European affairs—I have received from all these eminent men, who all have Governments behind them elected on wide franchises, who are all there because they represent the will of their people, messages couched in the most moving terms in which they endorse our decision to fight on, and declare themselves ready to share our fortunes and to persevere to the end. That is what we are going to do.

We may now ask ourselves: In what way has our position worsened since the beginning of the war? It has worsened by the fact that the Germans have conquered a large part of the coast line of Western Europe, and many small countries have been overrun by them. This aggravates the possibilities of air attack and adds to our naval preoccupations. It in no way diminishes, but on the contrary definitely increases, the power of our long-distance blockade. Similarly, the entrance of Italy into the war increases the power of our long-distance blockade. We have stopped the worst leak by that. We do not know whether military resistance will come to an end in France or not, but should it do so, then of course the Germans will be able to concentrate their forces, both military and industrial, upon us. But for the reasons I have given to the House these will not be found so easy to apply. If invasion has become more imminent, as no doubt it has, we, being relieved from the task of maintaining a large army in France, have far larger and more efficient forces to meet it.

If Hitler can bring under his despotic control the industries of the countries he has conquered, this will add greatly to his already vast armament output. On the other hand, this will not happen immediately, and we are now assured of immense, continuous and increasing support in supplies and munitions of all kinds from the United States; and especially of aeroplanes and pilots from the Dominions and across the oceans coming from regions which are beyond the reach of enemy bombers.

I do not see how any of these factors can operate to our detriment on balance before the winter comes; and the winter will impose a strain upon the Nazi regime, with almost all Europe writhing and starving under its cruel heel, which, for all their ruthlessness, will run them very hard. We must not forget that from the moment when we declared war on the 3rd September it was always possible for Germany to turn all her Air Force upon this country, together with any other devices of invasion she might conceive, and that France could have done little or nothing to prevent her doing so. We have, therefore, lived under this danger, in principle and in a slightly modified form, during all these months. In the meanwhile, however, we have enormously improved our methods of defence, and we have learned what we had no right to assume at the beginning, namely, that the individual aircraft and the individual British pilot have a sure and definite superiority. Therefore, in casting up this dread balance sheet and contemplating our dangers with a disillusioned eye, I see great reason for intense vigilance and exertion, but none whatever for panic or despair.

During the first four years of the last war the Allies experienced nothing but disaster and disappointment. That was our constant fear: one blow after another, terrible losses, frightful dangers. Everything miscarried. And yet at the end of those four years the morale of the Allies was higher than that of the Germans, who had moved from one aggressive triumph to another, and who stood everywhere triumphant invaders of the lands into which they had broken. During that war we repeatedly asked ourselves the question: How are we going to win? and no one was able ever to answer it with much precision, until at the end, quite suddenly, quite unexpectedly, our terrible foe collapsed before us, and we were so glutted with victory that in our folly we threw it away.

We do not yet know what will happen in France or whether the French resistance will be prolonged, both in France and in the French Empire overseas. The French Government will be throwing away great opportunities and casting adrift their future if they do not continue the war in accordance with their Treaty obligations, from which we have not felt able to release them. The House will have read the historic declaration in which, at the desire of many Frenchmen—and of our own hearts—we have proclaimed our willingness at the darkest hour in French history to conclude a union of common citizenship in this struggle. However matters may go in France or with the French Government, or other French Governments, we in this Island and in the British Empire will never lose our sense of comradeship with the French people. If we are now called upon to endure what they have been suffering, we shall emulate their courage, and if final victory rewards our toils they shall share the gains, aye, and freedom shall be restored to all. We abate nothing of our just demands; not one jot or tittle do we recede. Czechs, Poles, Norwegians, Dutch, Belgians have joined their causes to our own. All these shall be restored.

What General Weygand called the Battle of France is over. I expect that the Battle of Britain is about to begin. Upon this battle depends the survival of Christian civilization. Upon it depends our own British life, and the long continuity of our institutions and our Empire. The whole fury and might of the enemy must very soon be turned on us. Hitler knows that he will have to break us in this Island or lose the war. If we can stand up to him, all Europe may be free and the life of the world may move forward into broad, sunlit uplands. But if we fail, then the whole world, including the United States, including all that we have known and cared for, will sink into the abyss of a new Dark Age made more sinister, and perhaps more protracted, by the lights of perverted science. Let us therefore brace ourselves to our duties, and so bear ourselves that, if the British Empire and its Commonwealth last for a thousand years, men will still say, "This was their finest hour."

Joseph Stalin, radio address, Soviet Union, 1941

COMRADES, citizens, brothers and sisters, men of our Army and Navy!
My words are addressed to you, dear friends!

The perfidious military attack by Hitlerite Germany on our Fatherland, begun on June 22, is continuing. In spite of the heroic resistance of the Red Army, and although the enemy's finest divisions and finest air force units have already been smashed and have met their doom on the field of battle, the enemy continues to push forward, hurling fresh forces to the front. Hitler's troops have succeeded in capturing Lithuania, a considerable part of Latvia, the western part of Byelorussia and part of Western Ukraine. . . . Grave danger overhangs our country.

How could it have happened that our glorious Red Army surrendered a number of our cities and districts to the fascist armies? Is it really true that the German-fascist troops are invincible, as the braggart fascist propagandists are ceaselessly blaring forth?

Of course not! History shows that there are no invincible armies and never have been. Napoleon's army was considered invincible, but it was beaten successively by the armies of Russia, England and Germany. Kaiser Wilhelm's German army in the period of the First Imperialist War was also considered invincible, but it was beaten several times by Russian and Anglo-French troops, and was finally smashed by the Anglo-French forces. The same must be said of Hitler's German-fascist army of to-day. This army had not yet met with serious resistance on the continent of Europe. Only on our territory has it met with serious resistance. And if as a result of this resistance the finest divisions of Hitler's German-fascist army have been defeated by our Red Army, this means that it too can be smashed and will be smashed, as were the armies of Napoleon and Wilhelm.

As to part of our territory having nevertheless been seized by the German-fascist troops, this is chiefly due to the fact that the war of fascist Germany against the U.S.S.R. began under conditions that were favourable for the German forces and unfavourable for the Soviet forces. . . . Of no little importance in this respect was the fact that fascist Germany suddenly and treacherously violated the non-aggression pact which she had concluded in 1939 with the U.S.S.R., regardless of the circumstance that she would be regarded as the aggressor by the whole world. Naturally, our peace-loving country, not wishing to take the initiative in breaking the pact, could not resort to perfidy. . . .

That is why the whole of our valiant Red Army, the whole of our valiant Navy, all the falcons of our Air Force, all the peoples of our country, all the finest men and women of Europe, America and Asia, and, finally, all the finest men and women of Germany—denounce the treacherous acts of the German-fascists, sympathize with the

Soviet Government, approve its conduct, and see that ours is a just cause, that the enemy will be defeated, and that we are bound to win.

In consequence of this war which has been forced upon us, our country has come to death grips with its bitterest and most cunning enemy—German fascism. . . . Side by side with the Red Army, the entire Soviet people is rising in defence of our native land.

What is required to put an end to the danger imperilling our country and what measures must be taken to smash the enemy?

Above all it is essential that our people, the Soviet people, should appreciate the full immensity of the danger that threatens our country and give up all complacency, casualness and the mentality of peaceful constructive work that was so natural before the war, but which is fatal to-day, when war has radically changed the whole situation. The enemy is cruel and implacable. He is out to seize our lands watered by the sweat of our brows, to seize our grain and oil secured by the labour of our hands. He is out to restore the rule of the landlords, to restore tsarism, to destroy the national culture and the national existence as states of the Russians, Ukrainians, Byelorussians, Lithuanians, Latvians, Esthonians, Uzbeks, Tatars, Moldavians, Georgians, Armenians, Azerbaijanians and the other free peoples of the Soviet Union, to Germanize them, to turn them into the slaves of German princes and barons. Thus the issue is one of life and death for the Soviet State, of life and death for the peoples of the U.S.S.R.; the issue is whether the peoples of the Soviet Union shall be free or fall into slavery. The Soviet people must realize this and abandon all complacency; they must mobilize themselves and reorganize all their work on a new, war-time footing, where there can be no mercy to the enemy.

Further, there must be no room in our ranks for whimperers and cowards, for panic-mongers and deserters; our people must know no fear in the fight and must selflessly join our patriotic war of liberation against the fascist enslavers. Lenin, the great founder of our state, used to say that the chief virtues of Soviet men and women must be courage, valour, fearlessness in struggle, readiness to fight together with the people against the enemies of our country. These splendid virtues of the Bolshevik must become the virtues of millions and millions of the Red Army, of the Red Navy, of all the peoples of the Soviet Union.

All our work must be immediately reorganized on a war footing, everything must be subordinated to the interests of the front and the task of organizing the destruction of the enemy. The peoples of the Soviet Union now see that German fascism is untamable in its savage fury and hatred of our native country, which has ensured all its working people labour in freedom and prosperity. The peoples of the Soviet Union must rise against the enemy and defend their rights and their land. . . .

The war with fascist Germany cannot be considered an ordinary war. It is not only a war between two armies, it is also a great war of the entire Soviet people against the German-fascist armies. The aim of this national patriotic war in defence of our country against the fascist oppressors is not only to eliminate the danger hanging over our country, but also to aid all the European peoples groaning under the yoke of German fascism. In this war of liberation we shall not be alone. In this great war we shall have true allies in the peoples of Europe and America, including the German people which is enslaved by the Hitlerite misrulers. Our war for the freedom of our country will merge with the struggle of the peoples of Europe and America for their independence, for democratic liberties. It will be a united front of the peoples standing for freedom and against enslavement and threats of enslavement by Hitler's fascist armies. In this connection the historic utterance of the British Prime Minister, Mr. Churchill, regarding aid to the Soviet Union, and the declaration of the United States Government signifying readiness to render aid to our country, which can only evoke a feeling of gratitude in the hearts of the peoples of the Soviet Union, are fully comprehensible and symptomatic.

Comrades, our forces are numberless. The overweening enemy will soon learn this to his cost. Side by side with the Red Army many thousands of workers, collective farmers and intellectuals are rising to fight the enemy aggressor. The masses of our people will rise up in their millions. The working people of Moscow and Leningrad have already begun to form huge People's Guards in support of the Red Army. Such People's Guards must be raised in every city which is in danger of enemy invasion; all the working people must be roused to defend with their lives their freedom, their honour and their country in this patriotic war against German fascism. . . .

All our forces for the support of our heroic Red Army and our glorious Red Navy!

All the forces of the people for the destruction of the enemy!

Forward to victory!

Franklin D. Roosevelt, Four Freedoms speech, United States, 1941

Mr. President, Mr. Speaker, Members of the Seventy-seventh Congress:

I address you, the Members of the Seventy-seventh Congress, at a moment unprecedented in the history of the Union. I use the word "unprecedented," because at no previous time has American security been as seriously threatened from without as it is today.

Since the permanent formation of our Government under the Constitution, in 1789, most of the periods of crisis in our history have related to our domestic affairs. Fortunately, only one of these—the four-year War Between the States—ever threatened our national unity.

Today, thank God, one hundred and thirty million Americans, in forty-eight States, have forgotten points of the compass in our national unity.

It is true that prior to 1914 the United States often had been disturbed by events in other Continents. We had even engaged in two wars with European nations and in a number of undeclared wars in the West Indies, in the Mediterranean and in the Pacific for the maintenance of American rights and for the principles of peaceful commerce. But in no case had a serious threat been raised against our national safety or our continued independence.

What I seek to convey is the historic truth that the United States as a nation has at all times maintained clear, definite opposition, to any attempt to lock us in behind an ancient Chinese wall while the procession of civilization went past. Today, thinking of our children and of their children, we oppose enforced isolation for ourselves or for any other part of the Americas.

That determination of ours, extending over all these years, was proved, for example, during the quarter century of wars following the French Revolution.

While the Napoleonic struggles did threaten interests of the United States because of the French foothold in the West Indies and in Louisiana, and while we engaged in the War of 1812 to vindicate our right to peaceful trade, it is nevertheless clear that neither France nor Great Britain, nor any other nation, was aiming at domination of the whole world.

In like fashion from 1815 to 1914—ninety-nine years—no single war in Europe or in Asia constituted a real threat against our future or against the future of any other American nation.

Except in the Maximilian interlude in Mexico, no foreign power sought to establish itself in this Hemisphere; and the strength of the British fleet in the Atlantic has been a friendly strength. It is still a friendly strength.

Even when the World War broke out in 1914, it seemed to contain only small threat of danger to our own American future. But, as time went on, the American people began to visualize what the downfall of democratic nations might mean to our own democracy.

We need not overemphasize imperfections in the Peace of Versailles. We need not harp on failure of the democracies to deal with problems of world reconstruction. We should remember that the Peace of 1919 was far less unjust than the kind of "pacification" which began even before Munich, and which is being carried on under the new order of tyranny that seeks to spread over every continent today. The American people have unalterably set their faces against that tyranny.

Every realist knows that the democratic way of life is at this moment being directly assailed in every part of the world—assailed either by arms, or by secret spreading of poisonous propaganda by those who seek to destroy unity and promote discord in nations that are still at peace.

During sixteen long months this assault has blotted out the whole pattern of democratic life in an appalling number of independent nations, great and small. The assailants are still on the march, threatening other nations, great and small.

Therefore, as your President, performing my constitutional duty to "give to the Congress information of the state of the Union," I find it, unhappily, necessary to report that the future and the safety of our country and of our democracy are overwhelmingly involved in events far beyond our borders.

Armed defense of democratic existence is now being gallantly waged in four continents. If that defense fails, all the population and all the resources of Europe, Asia, Africa and Australasia will be dominated by the conquerors. Let us remember that the total of those populations and their resources in those four continents greatly exceeds the sum total of the population and the resources of the whole of the Western Hemisphere—many times over.

In times like these it is immature—and incidentally, untrue—for anybody to brag that an unprepared America, single-handed, and with one hand tied behind its back, can hold off the whole world.

No realistic American can expect from a dictator's peace international generosity, or return of true independence, or world disarmament, or freedom of expression, or freedom of religion—or even good business.

Such a peace would bring no security for us or for our neighbors. "Those, who would give up essential liberty to purchase a little temporary safety, deserve neither liberty nor safety."

As a nation, we may take pride in the fact that we are softhearted; but we cannot afford to be soft-headed.

We must always be wary of those who with sounding brass and a tinkling cymbal preach the "ism" of appeasement.

We must especially beware of that small group of selfish men who would clip the wings of the American eagle in order to feather their own nests.

I have recently pointed out how quickly the tempo of modern warfare could bring into our very midst the physical attack which we must eventually expect if the dictator nations win this war.

There is much loose talk of our immunity from immediate and direct invasion from across the seas. Obviously, as long as the British Navy retains its power, no such danger exists.

Even if there were no British Navy, it is not probable that any enemy would be stupid enough to attack us by landing troops in the United States from across thousands of miles of ocean, until it had acquired strategic bases from which to operate.

But we learn much from the lessons of the past years in Europe—particularly the lesson of Norway, whose essential seaports were captured by treachery and surprise built up over a series of years.

The first phase of the invasion of this Hemisphere would not be the landing of regular troops. The necessary strategic points would be occupied by secret agents and their dupes—and great numbers of them are already here, and in Latin America.

As long as the aggressor nations maintain the offensive, they—not we—will choose the time and the place and the method of their attack.

That is why the future of all the American Republics is today in serious danger.

That is why this Annual Message to the Congress is unique in our history.

That is why every member of the Executive Branch of the Government and every member of the Congress faces great responsibility and great accountability.

The need of the moment is that our actions and our policy should be devoted primarily—almost exclusively—to meeting this foreign peril. For all our domestic problems are now a part of the great emergency.

Just as our national policy in internal affairs has been based upon a decent respect for the rights and the dignity of all our fellow men within our gates, so our national policy in foreign affairs has been based on a decent respect for the rights and dignity of all nations, large and small. And the justice of morality must and will win in the end. . . .

Our most useful and immediate role is to act as an arsenal for them as well as for ourselves.

They do not need man power, but they do need billions of dollars worth of the weapons of defense.

The time is near when they will not be able to pay for them all in ready cash. We cannot, and we will not, tell them that they must surrender, merely because of present inability to pay for the weapons which we know they must have.

I do not recommend that we make them a loan of dollars with which to pay for these weapons—a loan to be repaid in dollars.

I recommend that we make it possible for those nations to continue to obtain war materials in the United States, fitting their orders into our own program. Nearly all their materiel would, if the time ever came, be useful for our own defense.

Taking counsel of expert military and naval authorities, considering what is best for our own security, we are free to decide how much should be kept here and how much should be sent abroad to our friends who by their determined and heroic resistance are giving us time in which to make ready our own defense.

For what we send abroad, we shall be repaid within a reasonable time following the close of hostilities, in similar materials, or, at our option, in other goods of many kinds, which they can produce and which we need.

Let us say to the democracies: "We Americans are vitally concerned in your defense of freedom. We are putting forth our energies, our resources and our organizing powers to give you the strength to regain and maintain a free world. We shall send you, in ever-increasing numbers, ships, planes, tanks, guns. This is our purpose and our pledge."

In fulfillment of this purpose we will not be intimidated by the threats of dictators that they will regard as a breach of international law or as an act of war our aid to the democracies which dare to resist their aggression. Such aid is not an act of war, even if a dictator should unilaterally proclaim it so to be.

When the dictators, if the dictators, are ready to make war upon us, they will not wait for an act of war on our part. They did not wait for Norway or Belgium or the Netherlands to commit an act of war.

Their only interest is in a new one-way international law, which lacks mutuality in its observance, and, therefore, becomes an instrument of oppression.

The happiness of future generations of Americans may well depend upon how effective and how immediate we can make our aid felt. No one can tell the exact character of the emergency situations that we may be called upon to meet. The Nation's hands must not be tied when the Nation's life is in danger.

We must all prepare to make the sacrifices that the emergency—almost as serious as war itself—demands. Whatever stands in the way of speed and efficiency in defense preparations must give way to the national need.

A free nation has the right to expect full cooperation from all groups. A free nation has the right to look to the leaders of business, of labor, and of agriculture to take the lead in stimulating effort, not among other groups but within their own groups.

The best way of dealing with the few slackers or trouble makers in our midst is, first, to shame them by patriotic example, and, if that fails, to use the sovereignty of Government to save Government.

As men do not live by bread alone, they do not fight by armaments alone. Those who man our defenses, and those behind them who build our defenses, must have the stamina and the courage which come from unshakable belief in the manner of life which they are defending. The mighty action that we are calling for cannot be based on a disregard of all things worth fighting for.

The Nation takes great satisfaction and much strength from the things which have been done to make its people conscious of their individual stake in the preservation of democratic life in America. Those things have toughened the fibre of our people, have renewed their faith and strengthened their devotion to the institutions we make ready to protect. . . .

In the future days, which we seek to make secure, we look forward to a world founded upon four essential human freedoms.

The first is freedom of speech and expression—everywhere in the world.

The second is freedom of every person to worship God in his own way—everywhere in the world.

The third is freedom from want—which, translated into world terms, means economic understandings which will secure to every nation a healthy peacetime life for its inhabitants—everywhere in the world.

The fourth is freedom from fear—which, translated into world terms, means a world-wide reduction of armaments to such a point and in such a thorough fashion that no nation will be in a position to commit an act of physical aggression against any neighbor—anywhere in the world.

That is no vision of a distant millennium. It is a definite basis for a kind of world attainable in our own time and generation. That kind of world is the very antithesis of the so-called new order of tyranny which the dictators seek to create with the crash of a bomb.

To that new order we oppose the greater conception—the moral order. A good society is able to face schemes of world domination and foreign revolutions alike without fear.

Since the beginning of our American history, we have been engaged in change—in a perpetual peaceful revolution—a revolution which goes on steadily, quietly adjusting itself to changing conditions—without the concentration camp or the quick-lime in the ditch. The world order which we seek is the cooperation of free countries, working together in a friendly, civilized society.

This nation has placed its destiny in the hands and heads and hearts of its millions of free men and women; and its faith in freedom under the guidance of God. Freedom means the supremacy of human rights everywhere. Our support goes to those who struggle to gain those rights or keep them. Our strength is our unity of purpose.

To that high concept there can be no end save victory.

360 DISCUSSION QUESTIONS

1   How did these speakers contextualize the conflict historically? What power does it lend to each position by doing this?

2   How did these statements of purpose frame overall objectives for the Allied as well as Axis cause?

3   Did these statements give suggestions of what the terms of a peace might be?

TOTAL WAR

11–1a | Charles Alston, political cartoon, "December 7th–Remember!" 1943

Charles Henry Alston (1907–1977), African American artist, illustrator, and teacher, was an active force in the Harlem Renaissance, the artistic, intellectual, and social African American movement centered in Harlem, New York, in the 1920s. Alston was also the first African American supervisor for the New Deal's Works Progress Administration's Federal Arts Project. Here, Alston looks back to not only remember the Japanese attack on Pearl Harbor, but also laud the role of Doris "Dorie" Miller, a USS *West Virginia* crewman who, despite no formal training, manned anti-aircraft guns and attended to the wounded. Miller's efforts earned him the Navy Cross, the first African American so awarded. His actions were highly publicized in the black press and his heroism was an inspiration both during and after the war. This cartoon was published the same year Dorie Miller was killed in action when his ship, the USS *Liscome Bay*, was sunk by a Japanese submarine.

11-1b | Frank Curre Jr., excerpts of oral history on experiences at Pearl Harbor, 2009

Frank Curre Jr. (1923–2011) served as a mess cook aboard the USS *Tennessee*, which was moored alongside Miller's USS *West Virginia* in Battleship Row on the morning of the Japanese attack on Pearl Harbor. He was below decks when the attack first began. Here in an oral history interview from 2009, Curre recounts his vivid memories of subsequent events. Curre passed away on December 7, 2011, the seventieth anniversary of the attack on Pearl Harbor.

[T]hey attacked us at seven fifty-five that morning, . . . A big heavyweight wrestler on the ship come running through that passageway. I don't know where he was going, but he was knocking everybody out of the way and he was getting there in a hurry. And then, instantaneously, we hear another one. There was a chief petty officer coming through this time. He'd been in the Asiatic Fleet and spent time over there, knew all those countries, all their flags. He started hollering something about a meatball. Well, to me, I thought he was talking about something to eat. But when he come through we hear another giant blast, and then we go to general quarters.

I'm in a second division forward deck force. First division mans number one turret. We man number two, fourteen-inch gun turret. My battle station is in the lower ammunition handling room. That's right in the bottom of the turret. Next to your turret is your magazine. The boys working in the magazine go in there, close that hatch, and they got a scuttle that they put a bag of powder in, switch it on your side. You take it out, go and put it in another one, send it up to your gun pit. We wasn't down there long when all at once that turret shook like something mad. Boy, it really rattled. We took a 1,760-pound bomb hit. It didn't penetrate, or I wouldn't be here. It hit a glancing blow; hit the middle gun, knocked it out. When it exploded, it killed a captain on the *West Virginia* next to us, blew him almost half in two. We secured all fourteen-inch gun turrets.

As I come out of the overhang, I seen the first of the two god-awful sights I witnessed that day. When I looked over to the right, there's that giant battleship, the *Oklahoma*, already hit and capsized. She was hit so quick with around six torpedoes and went over so quick they didn't have time to flood nothing on the starboard side. I had a chief warrant boatswain by the name of Adkins. He was wanting all us out of number one and number two turret to come aft. He's going to tell us what he wants us to do.

As we're going aft, that's when I watched that bomb that sank the *Arizona*. It come down on the starboard side just right behind turrets number two and number one and exploded. And when that ship exploded, it went twelve to fifteen foot in the air, and the bodies was scattered all over that harbor. If you'd have took a bag of popcorn, went out there in the breeze, come up in the air, that was like the bodies going out all over that harbor.

When she exploded, she caught our fantail on fire, caught the *West Virginia*'s on fire. Both ships is burning. There's a chief petty officer on the *West Virginia*. He's trapped in his quarters. And you can see that fire; it's a roaring inferno. He's got the hatch jammed in there. He can't get out; they can't get to him. He's going to try to get through about a twelve- or fourteen-inch porthole. The old battleships have portholes; the new ones didn't. He got one arm and a head through, and that's all. He couldn't come one way; he couldn't go the other way. Boatswain Adkins had already sent a bunch of us on the *West Virginia* and told us, "Go over there and help them boys, whatever they need. Fight fires. Check below decks. Do whatever the officers tell you."

While we was over there, we hear the old boatswain holler, "Somebody take that man out of his misery," talking about that chief. Somebody took the man out of his misery. Didn't see who did it, didn't want to see who did it, don't care who did it. But I've always said to this day it could not have been one of us teenage kids because I don't think we was mature enough in age to understand fully what that man was asking to be done. Now, at my age, yeah, I know fully what he was asking.

. . .

Then we get out there. The *Solace* motor launch was in. She'd already dropped her barges in the water, and she's picking up dead and wounded. One guy tells us when he's in his barge he goes to pick up one, and the boys in the water is begging him, Don't touch him. He says, "I got to touch him. I got to get him medical help." When he reached to grab him under the arm, what he grabbed ahold of come right out in his hand. Just like you took that body and cooked him. That's what you had to do all during that day, is pick them boys out of that water.

We picked up a survivor that the *Solace* motor launch brought over to us, and he saved his life. He was trapped below decks in the *Oklahoma* in the shipfitter compartment. He'd been on the ship a good while, and he memorized the frames in that ship; that's your ceiling joists. He knew, being in the shipfitter shop, that was frame number so-and-so. And he's in there with another sailor, and you can't see each other. Below decks on a ship you can't see. It's absolute, total darkness. He tells him, "If I can go to frame so-and-so and hold my breath and come back, then we can hold our breath and go all the way. The time we get there we'll be where the lifeline should be, and we'll give ourselves a shove to top of the water." Well, he does what he says. He comes back. He makes it. But he can't get the guy to go with him. He's hysterical. So he leaves, goes on his own, gives himself a shove, and a *Solace* motor launch come by just as his head popped out of that water, bleeding out of eyes, ears, nose, and mouth. Picked him up, and they brought him aboard our ship. He taught me a lesson about them frames.

The *Arizona*, she was a roaring inferno for two and a half days. We had a tug called *Holga*. She pumped water on the *West Virginia*, fantail and everything, and also on the *Arizona*, continuously. When them fires went out, some of us went aboard the *Arizona*, crawled up on there to see what we could find. You could see melted coins—copper, silver. If you got up around a superstructure and went into an area where the wind couldn't have got to, you see piles of ashes where them bodies was cremated right where they stand. They list 1,177 entombed. Many of them, when that bomb blew—spfft!—

they turned to dust, disintegrated. Them poor souls didn't even know they left this earth when that magazine went.

. . .

You react. That's what you do. In no matter what you do, you react. We had three men trapped in the water, burned bad, and we're on the *West Virginia*. They're going to be burned alive because the oil and fire off of that ship and *Arizona* is going to overtake them. I was a excellent swimmer because I grew up in them two rivers down here. I hollered at two guys. I said, "Y'all swim good?" "Yeah." I said, "Let's wet ourselves down, cover up our eyes, and we'll dive through the oil and fire and swim underwater. When we clear it, we'll get them boys out because it's going to catch them, burn them up." They said, Come on, let's do it.

Somebody throwed a hose on us, wet us down. We dove through, went over, and each one of us got one. We was going to try to put them up on our bow and get them in our ship. God, we get around; it looks like it's four miles up there. So we hollered for help on Ford Island. Some boys come down, got them, took them up, put them in their sick bay, but we got them out of the water. Now, whether they lived or died, that we don't know. But, to me, I couldn't live with myself I didn't get in and try to help them. It was going to overtake them.

If a guy goes out here and does something right quick and earns him a Medal of Honor, he didn't do it for the medal. He did what his own conscience dictated him do. He reacted to the moment. He didn't have time to plan nothing. You just do it.

Later in the war, when we'd go to our battle stations, my old heart could beat ninety miles an hour. But the minute I got on that gun and I could see them kamikazes, that bitterness of December 7 set in, and I forgot about being scared. I hated them devils so bad, I couldn't wait to shoot at them. That's the reason I didn't want below decks on a ship. I said, "If they're going to get me, we're going to be looking at each other eyeball to eyeball."

Them guys that come on December 7 wasn't much higher than this ceiling. They'd be in that cockpit, look down, and laugh and smile at you. But when they'd get over to the ships, did their damage, they'd turn and shoot straight up. We ain't figured out yet how they cleared them masts. Them masts on our ships stood 110 foot high. But they'd turn and go straight up. That Zero was a good plane.

For several days you're in a daze, more or less. You still can't figure out what you're looking at has happened. Then you're thinking, What else is going to happen after this? You automatically think about home. You're wanting to be home, and you know you can't. But after that day, you're never a teenage kid again; you're a full-grown man. You create a new sense of values and priorities about your life immediately. You may not know you're doing it, but you do it. You just automatically think different because what you're going through and what you're going to go through is mean stuff.

DISCUSSION QUESTIONS

1   What can these two sources tell us about the experience of the bombing of Pearl Harbor?

2   Discuss how the memory of Pearl Harbor functions differently in the cartoon than in this personal account.

11–2a | The Office of the Coordinator of Inter-American Affairs, motion picture work, 1940

In the 1940s, the Office of the Coordinator of Inter-American Affairs promoted Pan-Americanism, or unity among the countries of the Americas, especially in commercial and economic areas. As Italian and German propaganda spread through Latin America, the U.S. agency worked to counter the influence of Axis messages and subversive activities. Along with purchasing programs, public health projects, and news dissemination, the Office of the Coordinator of Inter-American Affairs also had an active Motion Picture Division.

The Motion Picture Division of CIAA was organized to employ motion pictures as one of the three main media in its information program. In all probability motion pictures, particularly those originating in the United States, provided the most direct approach to the widest audience in the hemisphere, with this being particularly true in the other American republics because of the high rate of illiteracy. In addition, motion picture activities were in a favorable position from the start, for while Axis films presented some competition, in general the technical excellence of those prepared in the United States gave them a definite advantage. Motion picture operations of the agency were to be likewise exceptionally successful because of a high degree of cooperation on the part of the industry. It was also to be a medium very useful in furthering other aspects of the CIAA program, for films dealing with health and sanitation activities were widely used both as a means of popular education and for training purposes. The education divisions of CIAA also utilized motion pictures as a tool. Finally, it was just as successful in the propaganda field. . . .

The first need of the Division upon its inception in 1940 was the establishment of a plan of operation and Mr. Whitney, like Mr. Francisco for radio, made a trip to the field to survey possibilities. By January 1941, the agency had organized its program. . . . A number of Hollywood committees representative of the producers, stars, writers, and directors, who had agreed to cooperate in carrying out the program, were listed; those mentioned were an Executive Committee, one on Visits to South America, another on South American Film Facilities, another on Short Subjects, another on Art Direction, one on Story Material, and one representing the Academy of Motion Picture Arts and Sciences. Plans which were being developed at the time covered such activities as the encouragement of feature films involving Central and South American themes, such as "The Life of Simon Bolivar," "The Road to Rio," and "Blood and Sand." It was hoped also that certain pictures scheduled for production in the near future might be photographed at least in part in Latin America. It was also the plan of the industry to send a number of its leading performers to the other American republics to appear personally at premieres. Another part of the plan involved increased newsreel coverage of events of significance in Latin America. . . .

The Motion Picture Division continued with its orderly plan for increased production of materials dealing with Latin America, and with the coming of war, in common with the other information divisions, laid great emphasis upon subjects connected with the war effort. A summary of objectives as they had developed by 1943 is of interest. The most important specific objectives named were the following:

1. An increase in United States production of feature pictures, short subjects and newsreels about the United States and the other Americas for distribution throughout the Hemisphere;

2. Producing and stimulating the production of pictures in the other Americas, particularly short subjects and newsreels, that could be exhibited effectively in the United States;

3. Eliminating Axis sponsored and produced pictures from exhibition throughout the Hemisphere;

4. Inducing the motion picture industry voluntarily to refrain from producing and/ or distributing in the other Americas pictures that are objectionable in whole or in part; and

5. Persuading producers that it is unwise to distribute in the other Americas pictures that create a bad impression of the United States and our way of life.

. . . The Motion Picture Division also claimed credit for a great increase in the number of feature pictures based on Latin American themes or of particular interest to Latin Americans; in 1943 it was noted that since the inception of the Division in October 1940, about thirty feature pictures on Latin American subjects had been released. These and many other pictures contained Latin American sequences for which CIAA had responsibility. Another area in which the Division was active was the attempt to drive Axis-produced and sponsored pictures from possible distribution and exhibition throughout the hemisphere. This was carried out through the cooperation of United States distributors operating in the other Americas, and by aid from the producers of film and equipment. . . .

An additional field in which the Motion Picture Division was interested was the production of short subjects, prepared on Latin American themes, or those of particular value in regard to United States relations with the other American republics. As early as November 1941, "all major companies accepted commitments to produce a minimum of 24 hemisphere shorts for theatrical release in addition to specially designed travelogues." By 1943 some 61 such shorts had been produced and released at the request of CIAA, without cost to it. Included in the group were such films as "Viva Mexico," "Highway to Friendship," "Gaucho Sports," "Madero of Mexico," "Der Fuehrer's Face," "Cuba, Land of Romance and Adventure," and "Price of Victory."

The Motion Picture Division supplied ideas and story material on Latin American themes to the industry whenever possible. In addition, they were behind many more ambitious projects designed to produce important features and short subjects for distribution. . . .

The Motion Picture Division also worked in close cooperation with the Walt Disney Studios, since the cartoon medium utilized by Mr. Disney was held to be one of the most effective in the field. In 1941 CIAA financed a trip by Mr. Disney and a staff of assistants to the other American republics, with the purpose of affording an opportunity to gain background for a picture or pictures later on. In addition, it served as a good-will tour since the Disney cartoons were extremely popular in the other American republics. Following his return, Mr. Disney completed one feature and several short subjects inspired by the trip. In succeeding years, to further augment its program and to take advantage of the Disney method of visual presentation, CIAA entered into additional contracts with the Walt Disney Studios, Inc., for research on and the production of a series of educational and propaganda films to be distributed throughout the hemisphere. Several of these were designed to further the programs of other divisions of the Office, particularly in the fields of health and sanitation, food supply, and education. . . .

11–2b | Jack Kirby, cover of *Captain America* #1, 1941

Published by Timely Comics, a predecessor of Marvel, Joe Simon and Jack Kirby's Captain America first appeared in March 1941, as can be seen in the image below. He was a patriotic super soldier who often fought agents of the Axis powers in World War II. The popularity of superheroes waned postwar and Captain America was discontinued in 1950 with a short-lived revival in 1953. *Captain America* has continuously been in publication since Marvel revived the character in 1964.

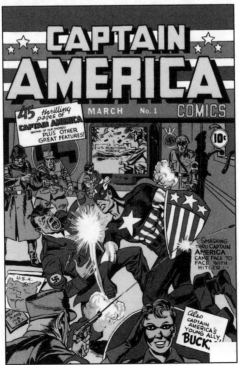

SEE COLOR INSERT

DISCUSSION QUESTIONS

1   Why might motion pictures be an important vehicle for cultivating stronger relationships with Latin America?

2   Discuss how the sources above demonstrate that World War II was truly a "world" war.

3   Consider the interactions between politics, government, corporations, and popular culture in these documents. In what ways do these documents demonstrate the nature of total war?

11–3a | Poster, British Ministry of Health, "She's in the Ranks Too!" UK, 1939–1945

This poster from the British Ministry of Health promoted the broad and vital role women played in the UK war effort. Wartime demands required the entire population to be mobilized. By mid-1943, close to 90 percent of single women and approximately 80 percent of married women were working in factories, in the fields, or with the armed forces. Despite these groundbreaking contributions, propaganda efforts often framed portrayals of women that reinforced more traditional roles.

11–3b | War Manpower Commission, call to women for war job, 1942

Although U.S. women made significant contributions to waging the Great War, the scope and scale of the contributions of women dramatically expanded in the waging of World War II. Besides the approximately 350,000 that served in the armed forces, millions of women engaged in war work. The U.S. War Manpower Commission, created by Executive Order in April 1942, worked to control and balance the labor needs of agriculture, industry, and the military during the war.

IF HITLER CAME TO MOBILE—

Every woman would defend her home with a gun, a knife or her bare fingers.

BUT—

Hitler and his hordes will not come if women help to build ships, more ships to transport our men, tanks, planes and munitions to the battle lines on other Continents—or if women take other jobs directly aiding the war effort.

This folder tells every Mobile woman not now in a war job how she may help win the war. Read it carefully and pass it on to your neighbor. It is an official statement from the War Manpower Commission.

Remember February 22 is an important day in Mobile.

War Manpower Commission

United States Employment Service

11–3c | Photograph, Department of Defense, female shipfitters, 1943

Here, U.S. women shipfitters are shown completing a floor in the engine room of the USS *Nereus*, a Fulton-class submarine tender, a depot ship that supplies and supports submarines. Built in a Mare Island, California, shipyard, just north of San Francisco, it was one of thirty shipyards in the area. Wartime production, seen as critical to the war effort, reached unforeseen levels. In shipbuilding alone, the U.S. went from launching a total of twenty-three ships in the 1930s to commissioning 4,600 ships between 1940 and 1945.

DISCUSSION QUESTIONS

1   Clearly, the war affected women's traditional roles. Looking at these sources, however, what evidence do you see of efforts to preserve them, even in the midst of change?

2   What do these sources tell us about World War II as a total war?

3   How might these experiences affect women and societies after the war?

11–4a | Initial agreement for Bracero Program,
Mexico and United States, 1942

Agreements between the U.S. and Mexico framed the Bracero Program, which began in August 1942. It guaranteed decent living conditions and a 30 cents per hour minimum wage for Mexican laborers sent to the U.S., primarily for railroad and agricultural work. The program became the largest foreign worker program in U.S. history, lasting for twenty-two years and including employment contracts to 5 million laborers in twenty-four states. Despite the scale of the program, it faced resistance in several quarters, most notably in Texas, where it was banned for several years in the mid-1940s due to maltreatment of and discrimination toward Mexican laborers. During World War II, the program was seen as a way for Mexico to support the cause of the Allies.

In order to effect a satisfactory arrangement whereby Mexican agricultural labor may be made available for use in the United States and at the same time provide means whereby this labor will be adequately protected while out of Mexico, the following general provisions are suggested:

1) It is understood that Mexicans contracting to work in the United States shall not be engaged in any military service.

2) Mexicans entering the United States as a result of this understanding shall not suffer discriminatory acts of any kind in accordance with the Executive Order No. 8802 issued at the White House June 25, 1941.

3) Mexicans entering the United States under this understanding shall enjoy the guarantees of transportation, living expenses and repatriation established in Article 29 of the Mexican Labor Law.

4) Mexicans entering the United States under this understanding shall not be employed to displace other workers, or for the purpose of reducing rates of pay previously established.

In order to implement the application of the general principles mentioned above the following specific clauses are established.

(When the word "employer" is used hereinafter it shall be understood to mean the Farm Security Administration of the Department of Agriculture of the United States of America; the word "sub-employer" shall mean the owner or operator of the farm or farms in the United States on which the Mexican will be employed; the word "worker" hereinafter used shall refer to the Mexican farm laborer entering the United States under this understanding.)

Contracts

a. Contracts will be made between the employer and the worker under the supervision of the Mexican Government. (Contracts must be written in Spanish.)

b. The employer shall enter into a contract with the sub-employer, with a view to proper observance of the principles embodied in this understanding. . . .

Transportation

a. All transportation and living expenses from the place of origin to destination, and return, as well as expenses incurred in the fulfillment of any requirements of a migratory nature shall be met by the employer. . . .

Wages and Employment

a. (1) Wages to be paid the worker shall be the same as those for similar work to other agricultural laborers in the respective regions of destination; but in no case shall this wage be less than 30 cents per hour (U.S. currency); piece rates shall be so set as to enable the worker of average ability to earn the prevailing wage.

a. (2) On the basis of prior authorization from the Mexican Government salaries lower than those established in the previous clause may be paid those emigrants admitted into the United States as members of the family of the worker under contract and who, when they are in the field, are able also to become agricultural laborers but who, by their condition of age or sex, cannot carry out the average amount of ordinary work. . . .

d. Work for minors under 14 years shall be strictly prohibited, and they shall have the same schooling opportunities as those enjoyed by children of other agricultural laborers. . . .

f. Housing conditions, sanitary and medical services enjoyed by workers admitted under this understanding shall be identical to those enjoyed by the other agricultural workers in the same localities.

g. Workers admitted under this understanding shall enjoy as regards occupational diseases and accidents the same guarantees enjoyed by other agricultural workers under United States legislation. . . .

i. For such time as they are unemployed under a period equal to 75% of the period (exclusive of Sundays) for which the workers have been contracted they shall receive a subsistence allowance at the rate of $3.00 per day.

For the remaining 25% of the period for which the workers have been contracted during which the workers may be unemployed they shall receive subsistence on the same bases that are established for farm laborers in the United States. . . .

k. At the expiration of the contract under this understanding, and if the same is not renewed, the authorities of the United States shall consider illegal, from an immigration point of view, the continued stay of the worker in the territory of the United States, exception made of cases of physical impossibility. . . .

Mexico City, the 23rd of July 1942. [Entered into force August 4, 1942]

11–4b | Leon Helguera, poster, "Americanos todos: luchamos por la victoria" (Americans All: Let's Fight for Victory), 1943

The U.S. War Information Office (1942–1945) commissioned Leon Helguera (1899–1970), a New York–based commercial artist, to create four "Southwestern" or "Spanish-American" posters for the federal government. With slogans in Spanish and English, these were meant to appeal to Americans of Mexican descent to support the war effort. The message of "Americans All" was designed to have a dual meaning in the 1940s. First, to signify a common bond between countries in the western hemisphere and, second, to inspire a bond and unity among the multi-ethnic groups in the United States. This propaganda to promote common bonds came in an era of outbreaks of violence against newcomers to the U.S., especially Mexican Americans. Immigration-related riots erupted in a dozen U.S. cities in the summer of 1943 alone.

AMERICANOS TODOS
★
LUCHAMOS POR LA VICTORIA

★ AMERICANS ALL ★
LET'S FIGHT FOR VICTORY

SEE COLOR INSERT

DISCUSSION QUESTIONS

1   What protections did the U.S. establish for Mexican workers in the Bracero program? What does that suggest to you about U.S. wartime need for labor?

2   In what ways did Helguera attempt to promote unity between the United States and Mexico in his poster?

3   In what ways were these sources consistent with President Roosevelt's Good Neighbor Policy (chapter 10, item 5)?

11–5 | *LIFE* magazine, advertisement, Schenley Laboratories penicillin production, 1944

World War II saw great advances in medical technology. Penicillin, the first antibiotic, was not employed as a treatment on a patient in the U.S. until March 1942, but quickly found wide use, especially to combat infection among soldiers. Up to World War II, it was not uncommon for the wounded to be more likely to die from infection from a wound than the damage caused by the wound itself. The government's interest in an ample supply of penicillin led more than twenty companies to produce it during the war. By the time of the June 1944 D-Day Invasion, manufacturers generated 100 billion units of penicillin per month. Schenley Laboratories, Inc., which was a whiskey distillery before and after the war, was one of the companies mass-producing penicillin for the war effort.

SEE COLOR INSERT

DISCUSSION QUESTIONS

1   Through text and image, what messages did Schenley Laboratories convey about the war and its contribution to the war to its audience?

2   In what ways can wartime serve as a unique period of innovation and technological breakthrough?

3   What would be the implications of a medical advance like this, for troops, militaries, families, and governments?

11–6a | Sat Ichikawa, map, Crystal City Internment Camp, 1945

Crystal City Internment Camp (1942–1945), originally designed to house internees of Japanese ancestry, confined individuals and families of Japanese, German, and Italian descent throughout World War II. One of the primary confinement facilities for families, the camp housed a population that grew to 3,374 detainees by December 1944. Sat Ichikawa, interned for two years at the camp with his father, mother, and six siblings, hand-drew the map of Crystal City below. Internment camps, justified as an "internal security measure" during World War II, were later deemed "unjust and motivated by racism rather than real military necessity" by the Commission on Wartime Relocation and Internment of Civilians created in 1980.

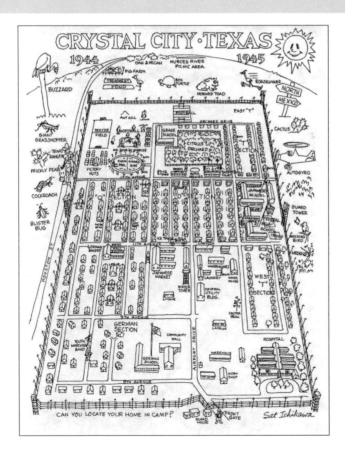

11–6b | Letter from Italian prisoners of war complaining about conditions of Australian internment camp, Australia, 1942

Initially created during the Great War, Internment Camp Gaythorne, near Brisbane, Australia, was expanded to house 1800 prisoners in 1942. During World War II, it originally housed civilian nationals of Germany or Austria, but later housed Indonesian, Finnish, Portuguese, Italian, Chinese, and Albanian internees. Here, Italian prisoners appeal to Switzerland for assistance regarding the conditions of their internment. Switzerland maintained a position of armed neutrality during the war and was seen as a nexus for diplomacy.

COPY   INTERNMENT CAMP,
The Consular Agent of   GAYTHORNE
Switzerland,   7th April, 1942.
BRISBANE.

Dear Sir,
We the undersigned internees wish to lodge a protest against the arrangements and the manner of treatment to us at Stuart Creek gaol. Our complaint is based on the following facts.

1. That the gaol is not a proper and fit place to house internees who are not criminals but only civilians detained for national Security purposes.
2. The food was detestable and consisted of very little boiled rice mornings and afternoon, and little gravy stew at midday.
3. We were there for eleven days, and they did not give us a bath, or sufficient drinking water.
4. The place where we were was very unhealthy.
5. Some things we bought there, we were made to pay four times more than that they are worth.
6. We definitely protest against internees being locked in cells, as in our opinion that puts them on the same level as criminals detained therein.
7. Lastly, we urge you to recommend, to the Commonwealth authorities that an internment camp be made in Townsville as a receiving depot.

Hoping to receive an early, and successful arrangements from you,
Thanking you in anticipation,
We remain, Yours faithfully,
Marlio Signorini, Antonio Sanaceni, M. Tardinai, Giudo Poggioli, Vincenzo Martorona, A. Fantin, E. Goccoli, S. Denaro, C. Cernoia, P. Risitano, E. Paiana, G. Torrisi, F. Dibennedetto, G. Dimarzo, S. Spoto, G. Paganoni, Antonio Passalaegna, Guiseppe

Risitano, A. Stillo, DalleNogare Arturo, E. Fappalando, A. Trovato, A. Caltabairo, G. Merino, F. Volpe, S. Topatiy, P. Hecapisco, R. Serafini, M. Yonna, S. Armanasco, G. Dalla Costa, C. Cacciola / A. Putrino

DISCUSSION QUESTIONS

1   What do you make of Ichikawa's hand-drawn map? What if this were the only source on internment camp life that you had?

2   In what ways could the Italian prisoners' letter of complaint be interpreted? What does it mean that they were able to send such a letter?

3   What do internment camps tell us about personal liberty during wartime?

11–7a | Selected letters from an *Einsatzkommando*, Ukraine, 1942

Einsatzkommandos were a subset of the *Einsatzgruppen*, paramilitary death squads operated by Nazi Germany during World War II. Generally composed of 500–1,000 SS and Gestapo, these mobile killing units trailed the advancing German army. During the invasion of the USSR, *Einsatzkommandos* were first tasked with executing Jewish men of military age and any anti-communist officials. By July 1941, however, the order to kill included all Jewish men, women, and children, initiating the genocide known as the Holocaust. The letters below were written by an *Einsatzkommando* known as Jacob, based in southwestern Ukraine. They were written to an acquaintance, a high-ranking official in the SS.

May 5, 1942

Dear Lieutenant-General,

I have been here in K. for a month. I have long had the intention of sending you a sign of life, but duty never ends. No surprise, really. The area I must supervise with my 23 gendarmes and 500 auxiliary policemen (Ukrainians) is as large as an administrative region in Germany. The policemen cause me the most trouble, those good-for-nothings. No surprise. Yesterday they were half Bolshevik and today they wear the honorable uniform of the police. Some of them are indeed competent fellows. But this percentage is low. In my capacity as post commander, I must also serve as executioner, prosecutor, judge, etc.

Naturally the area is being thoroughly cleansed, especially regarding the Jews. But also the general population must be tightly controlled. One must be watchful all the time. Well, we'll be tough. That way we can go home sooner than would otherwise be the case. The members of my company are very unfortunate. Almost 2 years in Ebersbach and now here in the East on the Romanian border.

I have a nice apartment in a former home for mentally retarded children. A bedroom and a living room with all the furnishings. Am not missing anything except, of course, my wife and the children. You will understand what I mean. My Dieter and my little Line write me very often in their own styles. Sometimes you want to cry when you read their letters. It is not good to be as close of a friend to my children as I was. Hopefully the war and with it my service in the East will soon end.

Jacob, Master of Gendarmerie

June 21, 1942

Dear Lieutenant General Querner,

I simply must reply right away to your kind letter of June 6, 1942. . . . I do thank you for your reminder. Yes, you are right. We men of this new Germany must be tough on ourselves, even if it involves long separations from our families. Especially now as we strive to take care of war criminals once and for all and to create for those coming after us a more beautiful and eternal Germany. We never rest here. Every week there are 3 or 4 actions. Sometimes we deal with gypsies, another time with Jews, partisans, and assorted riffraff. Nice to have a local detachment of the SD here with which cooperation is a breeze. . . . In general we do not mete out arbitrary justice here. But whenever an act requires immediate retribution, we get swiftly in touch with the SD and justice is served right away. In such cases to follow normal legal channels would mean making it impossible to root out an entire family if only the father is the real culprit.

I do not know if you, dear Lieutenant General, ever met in your service in Poland such despicable and pathetic Jews as we do here. I thank destiny that I only had to be confronted with them in recent times. Dealing with them now means to spare our children a horrific experience. People suffering from syphilis, cripples and idiots made up most of them here, and we took care of them. But they remained cunning and materialistic to the very end: "We are specialists—don't shoot us," some of them would venture. They are no human beings, just descendants of the apes.

At this time in Kamenetz Podolsk, only a negligible minority remains of our 24,000 Jewish friends who once populated this place—a tiny percentage. Those who have joined the partisans in the woods likewise figure among our regular customers. Without the least pangs of conscience we resolve those situations according to the popular line, "The waves will do their work and the world will be at peace." [This refers to a Hitler Youth song proclaiming that the waves of the Red Sea will inundate the Jews in their exodus from Egypt to the Promised Land and drown them all.—*translator's note*]

And now a word for my particularly dear friend [Querner's daughter]. She has chosen to be a pharmacist. I wish I had the chance of traveling to Hamburg and buy from her a bag of sour candy for 5 cents. Not sure what that little one of former days would say if she saw me again. Perhaps she would kick me out the door and call me a rotten, miserable ass of times long gone by. . . .

Jacob, Master of Gendarmerie

11–7b | Dr. Franz Blaha, excerpts from testimony about medical experiments at Dachau, Germany, 1946

Medical doctor Franz Blaha, imprisoned at Dachau Concentration Camp from April 1941 to April 1945, testified to the medical experiments conducted on prisoners during his time there. Dachau was the first and most important site at which these medical experiments were performed. Dr. Blaha was the first inmate of a concentration camp to appear as a witness at the Nuremburg Trials. Overseen by judges from the Allied powers, these 1945–1946 tribunals included hearings for twenty-two Nazi war criminals. The Nuremberg tribunals sentenced seven Dachau doctors to death for their crimes.

I, Franz Blaha, being duly sworn, depose and state as follows:

1. I studied medicine in Prague, Vienna, Strasburg and Paris and received my diploma in 1920. From 1920 to 1926 I was a clinical assistant. In 1926 I became chief physician of the Iglau Hospital in Moravia, Czechoslovakia. I held this position until 1939 when the Germans entered Czechoslovakia and I was seized as a hostage and held a prisoner for co-operating with the Czech Government. I was sent as a prisoner to the Dachau Concentration Camp in April 1941 and remained there until the liberation of the camp in April 1945. Until July 1941 I worked in a punishment company. After that I was sent to the hospital and subjected to the experiments in typhoid being conducted by Dr. Muermelstadt. After that I was to be made the subject of an experimental operation and succeeded in avoiding this only by admitting that I was a physician. If this had been known before, I would have suffered, because intellectuals were treated very harshly in the punishment company. In October 1941 I was sent to work in the herb plantation and later in the laboratory for processing herbs. In June 1942 I was taken into the hospital as a surgeon. Shortly afterwards I was directed to conduct a stomach operation on 20 healthy prisoners. Because I would not do this I was put in the autopsy room where I stayed until April 1945. While there I performed approximately 7000 autopsies. In all, 12,000 autopsies were performed under my direction.

2. From the middle of 1941 to the end of 1942 some 500 operations on healthy prisoners were performed. These were for the instruction of the SS medical students and doctors and included operations on the stomach, gall bladder, spleen and throat. These were performed by students and doctors of only 2 years' training, although they were very dangerous and difficult. Ordinarily they would not have been done except by surgeons with at least 4 years' surgical practice. Many prisoners died on the operating table and many others from later complications. I performed autopsies on all of these bodies. The doctors who supervised these operations were Lang, Muermelstadt, Wolter, Ramsauer and Kahr. Standartenführer Dr. Lolling frequently witnessed these operations.

3. During my time at Dachau I was familiar with many kinds of medical experiments carried on there on human victims. These persons were never volunteers but

were forced to submit to such acts. Malaria experiments on about 1,200 people were conducted by Dr. Klaus Schilling between 1941 and 1945. Schilling was personally asked by Himmler to conduct these experiments. The victims were either bitten by mosquitoes or given injections of malaria sporozoites taken from mosquitoes. Different kinds of treatment were applied including quinine, pyrifer, neosalvarsan, antipyrin, pyramidon, and a drug called 2516 Behring. I performed autopsies on bodies of people who died from these malaria experiments. Thirty to 40 died from the malaria itself. Three hundred to four hundred died later from diseases which were fatal because of the physical condition resulting from the malaria attacks. In addition there were deaths resulting from poisoning due to overdoses of neosalvarsan and pyramidon. Dr. Schilling was present at my autopsies on the bodies of his patients.

4. In 1942 and 1943 experiments on human beings were conducted by Dr. Sigmund Rascher to determine the effects of changing air pressure. As many as 25 persons were put at one time into a specially constructed van in which pressure could be increased or decreased as required. The purpose was to find out the effects on human beings of high altitude and of rapid descents by parachute. Through a window in the van I have seen the people lying on the floor of the van. Most of the prisoners used died from these experiments, from internal hemorrhage of the lungs or brain. The survivors coughed blood when taken out. It was my job to take the bodies out and as soon as they were found to be dead to send the internal organs to Munich for study. About 400 to 500 prisoners were experimented on. The survivors were sent to invalid blocks and liquidated shortly afterwards. Only a few escaped.

5. Rascher also conducted experiments on the effect of cold water on human beings. This was done to find a way for reviving airmen who had fallen into the ocean. The subject was placed in ice cold water and kept there until he was unconscious. Blood was taken from his neck and tested each time his body temperature dropped one degree. This drop was determined by a rectal thermometer. Urine was also periodically tested. Some men stood it as long as 24 to 36 hours. The lowest body temperature reached was 19 degrees centigrade, but most men died at 25 or 26 degrees. When the men were removed from the ice water attempts were made to revive them by artificial sunshine, with hot water, by electro-therapy, or by animal warmth. For this last experiment prostitutes were used and the body of the unconscious man was placed between the bodies of two women. Himmler was present at one such experiment. I could see him from one of the windows in the street between the blocks. I have personally been present at some of these cold water experiments when Rascher was absent, and I have seen notes and diagrams on them in Rascher's laboratory. About 300 persons were used in these experiments. The majority died. Of those who survived, many became mentally deranged. Those who did not die were sent to invalid blocks and were killed just as were the victims of the air pressure experiments. I know only two who survived, a Yugoslav and a Pole, both of whom are mental cases. . . .

9. It was common practice to remove the skin from dead prisoners. I was commanded to do this on many occasions. Dr. Rascher and Dr. Wolter in particular asked for this human skin from human backs and chests. It was chemically treated and placed

in the sun to dry. After that it was cut into various sizes for use as saddles, riding breeches, gloves, house slippers, and ladies' handbags. Tattooed skin was especially valued by SS men. Russians, Poles, and other inmates were used in this way, but it was forbidden to cut out the skin of a German. This skin had to be from healthy prisoners and free from defects. Sometimes we did not have enough bodies with good skin and Rascher would say, "All right, you will get the bodies." The next day we would receive 20 or 30 bodies of young people. They would have been shot in the neck or struck on the head so that the skin would be uninjured. Also we frequently got requests for the skulls or skeletons of prisoners. In those cases we boiled the skull or the body. Then the soft parts were removed and the bones were bleached and dried and reassembled. In the case of skulls it was important to have a good set of teeth. When we got an order for skulls from Oranienburg the SS men would say, "We will try to get you some with good teeth." So it was dangerous to have a good skin or good teeth.

10. Transports arrived frequently in Dachau from Stuthof, Belsen, Auschwitz, Mauthausen and other camps. Many of these were 10 to 14 days on the way without water or food. On one transport which arrived in November 1942 I found evidence of cannibalism. The living persons had eaten the flesh from the dead bodies. Another transport arrived from Compiègne in France. Professor Limousin of Clermont-Ferrand who was later my assistant told me that there had been 2,000 persons on this transport when it started. There was food available but no water. Eight hundred died on the way and were thrown out. When it arrived after 12 days, more than 500 persons were dead on the train. Of the remainder most died shortly after arrival. I investigated this transport because the International Red Cross complained, and the SS men wanted a report that the deaths had been caused by fighting and rioting on the way. I dissected a number of bodies and found that they had died from suffocation and lack of water. It was midsummer and 120 people had been packed into each car. . . .

12. Many executions by gas or shooting or injections took place in the camp. The gas chamber was completed in 1944, and I was called by Dr. Rascher to examine the first victims. Of the eight or nine persons in the chamber there were three still alive, and the remainder appeared to be dead. Their eyes were red, and their faces were swollen. Many prisoners were later killed in this way. Afterwards they were removed to the crematorium where I had to examine their teeth for gold. Teeth containing gold were extracted. Many prisoners who were sick were killed by injections while in hospital. Some prisoners killed in the hospital came through to the autopsy room with no name or number on the tag which was usually tied to their big toe. Instead the tag said: "Do not dissect." I performed autopsies on some of these and found that they were perfectly healthy but had died from injections. Sometimes prisoners were killed only because they had dysentery or vomited and gave the nurses too much trouble. Mental patients were liquidated by being led to the gas chamber and injected there or shot. Shooting was a common method of execution. Prisoners could be shot just outside the crematorium and carried in. I have seen people pushed into the ovens while they were still breathing and making sounds, although if they were too much alive they were usually hit on the head first.

DISCUSSION QUESTIONS

1   Discuss the ways in which the letter writer articulated his value and mission.

2   What does Dr. Blaha's testimony reveal about the connection between science and politics in a fascist system?

3   What political and ideological context made the acts described above justifiable for the perpetrators?

11–8 | Hanuš Hachenburg, poem, "Terezín" by thirteen-year-old child, Czech Republic, 1942–1943

Terezín, or Theresienstadt, was a military fortress built in the eighteenth century that consisted of a citadel and adjacent walled garrison town, approximately sixty kilometers from Prague in Czechoslovakia. During World War II, the Nazi SS created a hybrid ghetto and concentration camp at Terezín. The first Czech Jews arrived in November 1941, followed by German and Austrian Jews in June 1942, and Danish Jews in 1943. Approximately 33,000 people died at Theresienstadt, primarily from disease and malnutrition. More than 88,000 were held there on the way to extermination camps or killing sites of the Holocaust. Nazi Germany and its collaborators targeted European Jewry, systematically murdering some six million Jews. Despite the horrors of Terezín, the camp was known for its rich cultural life. Below is a poem from one of Terezín's children, one of approximately fifteen thousand, of which only one hundred survived. Hanuš Hachenburg (1929–1943) was posthumously identified as the author of this piece.

That bit of filth in dirty walls,
And all around barbed wire,
And 30,000 souls who sleep
Who once will wake
And once will see
Their own blood spilled.

I was once a little child,
Three years ago.
That child who longed for other worlds.
But now I am no more a child
For I have learned to hate.
I am a grown-up person now,
I have known fear.

Bloody words and a dead day then,
That's something different than bogie men!

But anyway, I still believe I only sleep today,
That I'll wake up, a child again, and start to laugh and play.
I'll go back to childhood sweet like a briar rose,
Like a bell which wakes us from a dream,
Like a mother with an ailing child
Loves him with aching woman's love.
How tragic, then, is youth which lives
With enemies, with gallows ropes,
How tragic, then, for children on your lap
To say: this for the good, that for the bad.

Somewhere, far away out there, childhood sweetly sleeps,
Along that path among the trees,
There o'er that house
Which was once my pride and joy.
There my mother gave me birth into this world
So I could weep . . .

In the flame of candles by my bed, I sleep
And once perhaps I'll understand
That I was such a little thing,
As little as this song.

These 30,000 souls who sleep
Among the trees will wake,
Open an eye
And because they see
A lot

They'll fall asleep again . . .

DISCUSSION QUESTIONS

1   What marked Hanuš' transition from childhood to adulthood?

2   How did the image of sleep function in the poem? Why is it apt for describing life in a concentration camp?

3   How might a historian use a poem as primary source evidence?

11–9a | Margaret Freyer, excerpts from description of the bombing of Dresden, Germany, 1945

In four raids on February 13–15, 1945, 3,900 tons of high-explosive bombs and incendiary devices were dropped by heavy British and U.S. bombers. The bombing and subsequent firestorm destroyed over 1,600 acres of the city center. With civilian deaths estimated at around 25,000, some historians have questioned the value of Dresden to the German war effort. British and American officials reported it held high strategic significance. World War II would be history's deadliest in terms of total dead, some 75 million people (about 3 percent of the world's population at the time). The high number of civilian deaths, 50 to 55 million, came through the adoption of new weapons, including airpower and the atomic bomb, and the wholesale commitment to total war.

I stood by the entrance and waited until no flames came licking in, then I quickly slipped through and out into the street. I had my suitcase in one hand and was wearing a white fur coat which by now was anything but white. I also wore boots and long trousers. Those boots had been a lucky choice, it turned out.

Because of flying sparks and the fire-storm I couldn't see anything at first. A witches' cauldron was waiting for me out there: no street, only rubble nearly a metre high, glass, girders, stones, craters. I tried to get rid of the sparks by constantly patting them off my coat. It was useless. I stopped doing it, stumbled, and someone behind me called out: "Take your coat off, it's started to burn." In the pervading extreme heat I hadn't even noticed. I took off the coat and dropped it.

Next to me a woman was screaming continually: "My den's burning down, my den's burning down," and dancing in the street. As I go on, I can still hear her screaming but I don't see her again. I run, I stumble, anywhere. I don't even know where I am any more, I've lost all sense of direction because all I can see is three steps ahead.

Suddenly I fall into a big hole—a bomb crater, about six metres wide and two metres deep, and I end up down there lying on top of three women. I shake them by their clothes and start to scream at them, telling them they must get out of here—but they don't move any more. I believe I was severely shocked by this incident; I seemed to have lost all emotional feeling. Quickly, I climbed across the women, pulled my suitcase after me, and crawled on all fours out of the crater.

To my left I suddenly see a woman. I can see her to this day and shall never forget it. She carries a bundle in her arms. It is a baby. She runs, she falls, and the child flies in an arc into the fire. It's only my eyes which take this in; I myself feel nothing. The woman remains lying on the ground, completely still. Why? What for? I don't know, I just stumble on. The fire-storm is incredible, there are calls for help and screams from somewhere but all around is one single inferno. I hold another wet handkerchief in front of my mouth, my hands and my face are burning; it feels as if the skin is hanging down in strips.

On my right I see a big, burnt-out shop where lots of people are standing. I join them, but think: "No, I can't stay here either, this place is completely surrounded by fire." I leave all these people behind, and stumble on. Where to? No idea! But every time towards those places where it is dark, in case there is no fire there. I have no conception of what the street actually looked like. But it is especially from those dark patches that the people come who wring their hands and cry the same thing over and over again:

"You can't carry on there, we've just come from there, everything is burning there!" Wherever and to whomsoever I turn, always that same answer.

In front of me is something that might be a street, filled with a hellish rain of sparks which look like enormous rings of fire when they hit the ground. I have no choice. I must go through. I press another wet handkerchief to my mouth and almost get through, but I fall and am convinced that I cannot go on. It's hot. Hot! My hands are burning like fire. I just drop my suitcase, I am past caring, and too weak. At least, there's nothing to lug around with me any more.

I stumbled on towards where it was dark. Suddenly, I saw people again, right in front of me. They scream and gesticulate with their hands, and then—to my utter horror and amazement—I see how one after the other they simply seem to let themselves drop to the ground. I had a feeling that they were being shot, but my mind could not understand what was really happening. Today I know that these unfortunate people were the victims of lack of oxygen. They fainted and then burnt to cinders. I fall then, stumbling over a fallen woman and as I lie right next to her I see how her clothes are burning away. Insane fear grips me and from then on I repeat one simple sentence to myself continuously: "I don't want to burn to death—no, no burning—I don't want to burn!" Once more I fall down and feel that I am not going to be able to get up again, but the fear of being burnt pulls me to my feet. Crawling, stumbling, my last handkerchief pressed to my mouth. . . . I do not know how many people I fell over. I knew only one feeling: that I must not burn. . . .

I spent all the daylight hours which followed in the town searching for my fiancé. I looked for him amongst the dead, because hardly any living beings were to be seen anywhere. What I saw is so horrific that I shall hardly be able to describe it. Dead, dead, dead everywhere. Some completely black like charcoal. Others completely untouched, lying as if they were asleep. Women in aprons, women with children sitting in the trams as if they had just nodded off. Many women, many young girls, many small children, soldiers who were only identifiable as such by the metal buckles on their belts, almost all of them naked. Some clinging to each other in groups as if they were clawing at each other. . . .

I then went through the Grosser Garten and there is one thing I did realise. I was aware that I had constantly to brush hands away from me, hands which belonged to people who wanted me to take them with me, hands which clung to me. But I was much too weak to lift anyone up. My mind took all this in vaguely, as if seen through a veil. In fact, I was in such a state that I did not realise that there was a third attack on Dresden. Late that afternoon I collapsed in the Ostra-Alle, where two men took me to a friend who lived on the outskirts of the city.

I asked for a mirror and did not recognize myself any more. My face was a mass of blisters and so were my hands. My eyes were narrow slits and puffed up, my whole body was covered in little black, pitted marks. I cannot understand to this day how I contracted these marks, because I was wearing a pair of long trousers and a jacket. Possibly the fire-sparks ate their way through my clothing.

11–9b | Richard Peter, photograph, view from the Rathaus town hall over the destroyed city, Dresden, Germany, 1945

The bombing of Dresden remains controversial, as the moral and military justifications surrounding the event are debated. One factor fueling this was the Nazi government's claims in the immediate aftermath of the Allied action. These claims focused on an exaggerated death toll, the city's cultural importance, the lack of military activity there, and the timing near the end of the war in Europe. Here, from the vantage point of town hall, part of the devastation can be seen.

DISCUSSION QUESTIONS

1   The statue in the right foreground of the photograph is titled "Allegory of Goodness." How does Freyer's testimony add to your understanding of the Dresden photograph?

2   Discuss what total war meant for civilians in World War II, according to these documents.

11-10a | Dr. Marcel Jurod, excerpt from experience as first foreign doctor into Hiroshima after atomic bomb, 1945

Marcel Junod (1904–1961), Swiss doctor and field delegate for the International Committee of the Red Cross, organized the evacuation of POW camps after the Japanese surrender on August 15, 1945. Upon seeing images and descriptions of the conditions in Hiroshima, he organized an assistance mission to the city. On September 8, just over a month after the U.S. dropped the atomic bomb, he became the first foreign doctor to arrive. Dr. Junod spent five days in Hiroshima, visiting major hospitals, distributing supplies, and providing medical care.

At 7.31 the all-clear was given. Feeling themselves in safety people came out of their shelters and went about their affairs and the work of the day began.

Suddenly a glaring whitish pinkish light appeared in the sky accompanied by an unnatural tremor which was followed almost immediately by a wave of suffocating heat and a wind which swept away everything in its path.

Within a few seconds the thousands of people in the streets and the gardens in the centre of the town were scorched by a wave of searing heat. Many were killed instantly, others lay writhing on the ground screaming in agony from the intolerable pain of their burns. Everything standing upright in the way of the blast, walls, houses, factories and other buildings, was annihilated and the debris spun round in a whirlwind and was carried up into the air. Trams were picked up and tossed aside as though they had neither weight nor solidity. Trains were flung off the rails as though they were toys. Horses, dogs and cattle suffered the same fate as human beings. Every living thing was petrified in an attitude of indescribable suffering. Even the vegetation did not escape. Trees went up in flames, the rice plants lost their greenness, the grass burned on the ground like dry straw.

Beyond the zone of utter death in which nothing remained alive houses collapsed in a whirl of beams, bricks and girders. Up to about three miles from the centre of the explosion lightly built houses were flattened as though they had been built of cardboard. Those who were inside were either killed or wounded. Those who managed to extricate themselves by some miracle found themselves surrounded by a ring of fire. And the few who succeeded in making their way to safety generally died twenty or thirty days later from the delayed effects of the deadly gamma rays. Some of the reinforced concrete or stone buildings remained standing but their interiors were completely gutted by the blast.

About half an hour after the explosion whilst the sky all around Hiroshima was still cloudless a fine rain began to fall on the town and went on for about five minutes. It was caused by the sudden rise of over-heated air to a great height, where it condensed and fell back as rain. Then a violent wind rose and the fires extended with terrible rapidity, because most Japanese houses are built only of timber and straw.

By the evening the fire began to die down and then it went out. There was nothing left to burn. Hiroshima had ceased to exist.

The Japanese broke off and then pronounced one word with indescribable but restrained emotion:

"Look."

We were then rather less than four miles away from the Aioi Bridge, which was immediately beneath the explosion, but already the roofs of the houses around us had lost their tiles and the grass was yellow along the roadside. At three miles from the centre of the devastation the houses were already destroyed, their roofs had fallen in and the beams jutted out from the wreckage of their walls. But so far it was only the usual spectacle presented by towns damaged by ordinary high explosives.

About two and a half miles from the centre of the town all the buildings had been burnt out and destroyed. Only traces of the foundations and piles of debris and rusty charred ironwork were left. This zone was like the devastated areas of Tokio, Osaka and Kobé after the mass fall of incendiaries.

At three-quarters of a mile from the centre of the explosion nothing at all was left. Everything had disappeared. It was a stony waste littered with debris and twisted girders. The incandescent breath of the fire had swept away every obstacle and all that remained upright were one or two fragments of stone walls and a few stoves which had remained incongruously on their base.

We got out of the car and made our way slowly through the ruins into the centre of the dead city. Absolute silence reigned in the whole necropolis.

11–10b | Photographs, post–World War II Hiroshima, Japan, 1945–1946

The detonation of a nuclear weapon over Hiroshima on August 6, 1945, killed approximately 80,000 people as a direct result of the blast, and at least another 60,000 would be dead by the end of the year from fallout effects. The U.S. became the first and only nation to use an atomic weapon during wartime, the culmination of a research effort that began in 1940 when U.S. officials learned that Nazi Germany was investigating developing such a device. President Harry Truman authorized the dropping of the atomic bomb, with the consent of the UK, after warnings from advisors on the losses that might result from a mainland invasion of Japan. According to one estimate, Allies may have suffered between 400,000 and 800,000 fatalities, with Japanese deaths projected from five to ten million. Below are some photographs of Hiroshima after the bombing. In the first, blast shadows can be seen on the bridge, created by the intense heat of the initial flash at detonation. In the second, the remains of the Nagarekawa Methodist Church stand among the rubble of Hiroshima.

DISCUSSION QUESTIONS

1   How do Junod's description and the photo provide evidence of the atomic bomb's suddenness and ferocity?

2   To what other locations did Junod compare the appearance of Hiroshima? Why?

3   What were the implications of a weapon this powerful?

POSTWAR

11–11a | Preamble to Charter of the United Nations, 1945

Established after World War II to prevent future wars, the United Nations (UN) succeeded the ineffective League of Nations (1920–1946). Founded through 1944 negotiations among the leading Allied countries, the UN welcomed fifty-one nations to the first meeting of the General Assembly on January 10, 1946. The UN's Security Council is charged with maintaining peace and security among nations. This arm now has fifteen member states, with five permanent members—China, France, Russia, the United Kingdom, and the United States. The other organs of the UN include the Secretariat (administrative), the International Court of Justice (judicial), the Economic and Social Council (economic and social affairs), and the Trusteeship Council (administering trustee territories).

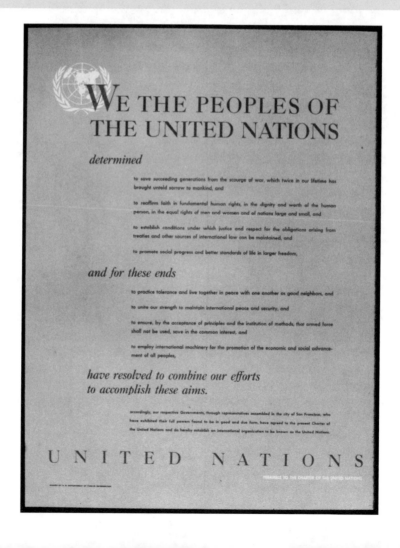

11–11b | Joseph Parrish, political cartoon on the United Nations, "Trojan Horse," 1949

Joseph L. Parrish (1905–1989) was chief cartoonist for the *Chicago Tribune* when he composed this image on the founding of UN headquarters in the United States. Construction began on the New York home of the intergovernmental organization in 1948. Although the strong isolationist sentiment evident after the Great War in the U.S. was missing post–World War II, some elements still questioned the role the United Nations might play in not only the United States' operation in world affairs, but also, as seen in this image, what international elements might make their way to the U.S.

Joseph Parrish. *The Tribune* (Chicago), 1949.

DISCUSSION QUESTIONS

1   Summarize the aims of the United Nations as created. What might have inspired these
    objectives?

2   What does the cartoon express about U.S. concern about internationalism? What is
    the historical context for this?

11–12 | Robert H. Jackson, excerpt from opening statement before the International Military Tribunal, Germany, 1945

Robert H. Jackson (1892–1954) served as U.S. Solicitor General, U.S. Attorney General, and an Associate Justice of the U.S. Supreme Court. Immediately after World War II, he was the Chief United States Prosecutor at the Nuremberg Trials, hearings on the leaders of Nazi Germany under international law and the laws of war. He took a leave of absence from the U.S. Supreme Court for this assignment in 1945–1946. Jackson framed his vigorous prosecution at the tribunals with powerful opening and closing arguments that were widely circulated.

May it please Your Honors:

The privilege of opening the first trial in history for crimes against the peace of the world imposes a grave responsibility. The wrongs which we seek to condemn and punish have been so calculated, so malignant, and so devastating, that civilization cannot tolerate their being ignored, because it cannot survive their being repeated. That four great nations, flushed with victory and stung with injury stay the hand of vengeance and voluntarily submit their captive enemies to the judgment of the law is one of the most significant tributes that Power has ever paid to Reason.

This Tribunal, while it is novel and experimental, is not the product of abstract speculations nor is it created to vindicate legalistic theories. This inquest represents the practical effort of four of the most mighty of nations, with the support of 17 more, to utilize international law to meet the greatest menace of our times—aggressive war. The common sense of mankind demands that law shall not stop with the punishment of petty crimes by little people. It must also reach men who possess themselves of great power and make deliberate and concerted use of it to set in motion evils which leave no home in the world untouched. It is a cause of that magnitude that the United Nations will lay before Your Honors.

In the prisoners' dock sit twenty-odd broken men. Reproached by the humiliation of those they have led almost as bitterly as by the desolation of those they have attacked, their personal capacity for evil is forever past. It is hard now to perceive in these men as captives the power by which as Nazi leaders they once dominated much of the world and terrified most of it. Merely as individuals their fate is of little consequence to the world.

What makes this inquest significant is that these prisoners represent sinister influences that will lurk in the world long after their bodies have returned to dust. We will show them to be living symbols of racial hatreds, of terrorism and violence, and of the arrogance and cruelty of power. They are symbols of fierce nationalisms and of militarism, of intrigue and war-making which have embroiled Europe generation after generation, crushing its manhood, destroying its homes, and impoverishing its life. They have so identified themselves with the philosophies they conceived and with the forces they directed that any tenderness to them is a victory and an encouragement to all the evils which are attached to their names. Civilization can afford no compromise with the social forces which would gain renewed strength if we deal ambiguously or indecisively with the men in whom those forces now precariously survive.

What these men stand for we will patiently and temperately disclose. We will give you undeniable proofs of incredible events. The catalog of crimes will omit nothing that could be conceived by a pathological pride, cruelty, and lust for power. These men created in Germany, under the "Führerprinzip", a National Socialist despotism equalled only by the dynasties of the ancient East. They took from the German people all those dignities and freedoms that we hold natural and inalienable rights in every human being. The people were compensated by inflaming and gratifying hatreds towards those who were marked as "scapegoats". Against their opponents, including Jews, Catholics, and free labor, the Nazis directed such a campaign of arrogance, brutality, and annihilation as the world has not witnessed since the pre-Christian ages. They excited the German ambition to be a "master race", which of course implies serfdom for others. They led their people on a mad gamble for domination. They diverted social energies and resources to the creation of what they thought to be an invincible war machine. They overran their neighbors. To sustain the "master race" in its war-making, they enslaved millions of human beings and brought them into Germany, where these hapless creatures now wander as "displaced persons". At length bestiality and bad faith reached such excess that they aroused the sleeping strength of imperiled Civilization. Its united efforts have ground the German war machine to fragments. But the struggle has left Europe a liberated yet prostrate land where a demoralized society struggles to survive. These are the fruits of the sinister forces that sit with these defendants in the prisoners' dock.

In justice to the nations and the men associated in this prosecution, I must remind you of certain difficulties which may leave their mark on this case. Never before in legal history has an effort been made to bring within the scope of a single litigation the developments of a decade, covering a whole continent, and involving a score of nations, countless individuals, and innumerable events. Despite the magnitude of the task, the world has demanded immediate action. This demand has had to be met, though perhaps at the cost of finished craftsmanship. To my country, established courts, following familiar procedures, applying well-thumbed precedents, and dealing with the legal consequences of local and limited events seldom commence a trial within a year of the event in litigation. Yet less than 8 months ago today the courtroom in which you sit was an enemy fortress in the hands of German SS troops. Less than 8 months ago nearly all our witnesses and documents were in enemy hands. The law had not been codified, no procedures had been established, no tribunal was in existence, no usable courthouse stood here, none of the hundreds of tons of official German documents had been examined, no prosecuting staff had been assembled, nearly all of the present defendants were at large, and the four prosecuting powers had not yet joined in common cause to try them. I should be the last to deny that the case may well suffer from incomplete researches and quite likely will not be the example of professional work which any of the prosecuting nations would normally wish to sponsor. It is, however, a completely adequate case to the judgment we shall ask you to render, and its full development we shall be obliged to leave to historians.

Before I discuss particulars of evidence, some general considerations which may affect the credit of this trial in the eyes of the world should be candidly faced. There is a dramatic disparity between the circumstances of the accusers and of the accused that might discredit our work if we should falter, in even minor matters, in being fair and temperate.

Unfortunately, the nature of these crimes is such that both prosecution and judgment must be by victor nations over vanquished foes. The worldwide scope of the aggressions carried out by these men has left but few real neutrals. Either the victors must judge the vanquished or we must leave the defeated to judge themselves. After the first World War, we learned the futility of the latter course. The former high station of these defendants, the notoriety of their acts, and the adaptability of their conduct to provoke retaliation make it hard to distinguish between the demand for a just and measured retribution, and the unthinking cry for vengeance which arises from the anguish of war. It is our task, so far as humanly possible, to, draw the line between the two. We must never forget that the record on which we judge these defendants today is the record on which history will judge us tomorrow. To pass these defendants a poisoned chalice is to put it to our own lips as well. We must summon such detachment and intellectual integrity to our task that this Trial will commend itself to posterity as fulfilling humanity's aspirations to do justice.

DISCUSSION QUESTIONS

1   According to Jackson, why was this tribunal a necessity?

2   How did Jackson characterize the historical significance of the trial?

3   What might be the significance of a person from the U.S. leading the prosecution in the International Military Tribunal at Nuremberg?

12

The Bipolar World

360

DECLARATIONS OF INDEPENDENCE

Unable to establish Old World empires like the Chinese in East Asia, the Mughals in South Asia, or the Ottoman Turks in the Mediterranean, European states claimed large portions of the New World—specifically, the Americas and Oceania—beginning in the late fifteenth century and accelerating in the seventeenth century. In the late eighteenth and early nineteenth centuries, the first wave of decolonization hit when most of the European colonies in the Americas gained independence, including the U.S., Haiti, and Mexico.

Via naval power, British, Dutch, and French colonial efforts shifted to the Old World, principally South Africa, India, and Southeast Asia. Industrialization created the means for a new age of empire in the 1880s, and new powers, including Germany, Italy, the U.S., and Japan, joined the rush for colonial possessions. This New Imperialism led to massive global empires, especially for the British and French, with negative consequences for native cultures, sovereignty, and identities; the same imperial networks, however, spread Western ideas of nationalism and liberal democracy to colonized peoples.

Promises of self-determination agreed to as a peace aim for the Allies in the Great War were, for the most part, postponed until after World War II, when a second wave of decolonization swept through Africa and Asia. In 1945, approximately 750 million people (almost 1/3 of the global population) lived in lands under colonial powers. That number is now under 2 million in seventeen non-self-governing territories.

Below are representative samples of declarations of independence that appeared in the long process of decolonization.

A Declaration by the Representatives of the United States of America, in General Congress Assembled, 1776

When in the Course of human Events, it becomes necessary for one People to dissolve the Political Bands which have connected them with another, and to assume among the Powers of the Earth, the separate and equal Station to which the Laws of Nature and of

Nature's God entitle them, a decent Respect to the Opinions of Mankind requires that they should declare the causes which impel them to the Separation.

We hold these Truths to be self-evident, that all Men are created equal, that they are endowed by their Creator with certain unalienable Rights, that among these are Life, Liberty, and the Pursuit of Happiness—That to secure these Rights, Governments are instituted among Men, deriving their just Powers from the Consent of the Governed, that whenever any Form of Government becomes destructive of these Ends, it is the Right of the People to alter or to abolish it, and to institute new Government, laying its Foundation on such Principles, and organizing its Powers in such Form, as to them shall seem most likely to effect their Safety and Happiness. Prudence, indeed, will dictate that Governments long established should not be changed for light and transient Causes; and accordingly all Experience hath shewn, that Mankind are more disposed to suffer, while Evils are sufferable, than to right themselves by abolishing the Forms to which they are accustomed. But when a long Train of Abuses and Usurpations, pursuing invariably the same Object, evinces a Design to reduce them under absolute Despotism, it is their Right, it is their Duty, to throw off such Government, and to provide new Guards for their future Security. Such has been the patient Sufferance of these Colonies; and such is now the Necessity which constrains them to alter their former Systems of Government. The History of the present King of Great-Britain is a History of repeated Injuries and Usurpations, all having in direct Object the Establishment of an absolute Tyranny over these States. To prove this, let Facts be submitted to a candid World. . . .

In every stage of these Oppressions we have Petitioned for Redress in the most humble Terms: Our repeated Petitions have been answered only by repeated Injury. A Prince, whose Character is thus marked by every act which may define a Tyrant, is unfit to be the Ruler of a free People.

Nor have we been wanting in Attentions to our British Brethren. We have warned them from Time to Time of Attempts by their Legislature to extend an unwarrantable Jurisdiction over us. We have reminded them of the Circumstances of our Emigration and Settlement here. We have appealed to their native Justice and Magnanimity, and we have conjured them by the Ties of our common Kindred to disavow these Usurpations, which, would inevitably interrupt our Connections and Correspondence. They too have been deaf to the Voice of Justice and Consanguinity. We must, therefore, acquiesce in the Necessity, which denounces our Separation, and hold them, as we hold the rest of Mankind, Enemies in War, in Peace, Friends.

We, therefore, the Representatives of the UNITED STATES OF AMERICA, in GENERAL CONGRESS, Assembled, appealing to the Supreme Judge of the World for the Rectitude of our Intentions, do, in the Name, and by Authority of the good People of these Colonies, solemnly Publish and Declare, That these United Colonies are, and of Right ought to be, FREE AND INDEPENDENT STATES; that they are Absolved from all Allegiance to the British Crown, and that all political Connection between them and the State of Great-Britain, is and ought to be totally dissolved: and that as FREE AND INDEPENDENT STATES, they have full Power to levy War, conclude Peace, contract Alliances, establish Commerce, and to do all other Acts and Things which INDEPENDENT

STATES may of right do. And for the support of this Declaration, on the Protection of divine Providence, we mutually pledge to each ⟨ Fortunes, and our sacred Honor.

Acte de l'Indépendance, Haiti, 1804

Citizens,

It is not enough to have expelled from your country the barbarians who have for ages stained it with blood—it is not enough to have curbed the factions which, succeeding each other by turns, sported with a phantom of liberty which France exposed to their eyes. It is become necessary, by a last act of national authority, to ensure for ever the empire of liberty in the country which has given us birth. It is necessary to deprive an inhuman government, which has hitherto held our minds in a state of the most humiliating torpitude, of every hope of being enabled again to enslave us. Finally, it is necessary to live independent, or die. Independence or Death! Let these sacred words serve to rally us—let them be signals of battle, and of our re-union.

Citizens—Countrymen—I have assembled on this solemn day, those courageous chiefs, who, on the eve of receiving the last breath of expiring liberty, have lavished their blood to preserve it. These generals, who have conducted your struggles against tyranny, have not yet done. The French name still darkens our plains: every thing re-calls the remembrance of the cruelties of that barbarous people. . . .

We have dared to be free—let us continue free by ourselves, and for ourselves; let us imitate the growing child; his own strength breaks his leading-strings, which become useless and troublesome to him in his walk. What are the people who have fought us? what people would reap the fruits of our labours? and what dishonourable absurdity, to conquer to be slaves!

Slaves—leave to the French nation this odious epithet; they have conquered to be no longer free—let us walk in other footsteps; let us imitate other nations, who, carrying their solicitude into futurity, and dreading to leave posterity an example of cowardice, have preferred to be exterminated, rather than be erased from the list of free people. . . .

Peace with our neighbours, but accursed be the French name—eternal hatred to France: such are our principles. . . .

Let us swear to the whole world, to posterity, to ourselves, to renounce France for ever, and to die, rather than live under its dominion—to fight till the last breath for the independence of our country. . . .

Swear then to live free and independent, and to prefer death to every thing that would lead to replace you under the yoke; swear then to pursue for everlasting, the traitors, and enemies of your independence.

He Wakuputanga o te Rangatiratanga o Nu Tireni, New Zealand, 1835

1. We, the hereditary chiefs and heads of the tribes of the Northern parts of New Zea-land, being assembled at Waitangi in the Bay of Islands on this 28th day of October,

eclare the Independence of our Country, which is hereby constituted and de-
_ed to be an Independent State, under the designation of The United Tribes of New
Zealand.

2. All sovereign power and authority within the territories of the United Tribes of
New Zealand is hereby declared to reside entirely and exclusively in the hereditary
chiefs and heads of tribes in their collective capacity, who also declare that they will not
permit any legislative authority separate from themselves in their collective capacity to
exist, nor any function of government to be exercised within the said territories, unless
by persons appointed by them, and acting under the authority of laws regularly enacted
by them in Congress assembled.

3. The hereditary chiefs and heads of tribes agree to meet in Congress at Waitangi
in the autumn of each year, for the purpose of framing laws for the dispensation of
justice, the preservation of peace and good order, and the regulation of trade; and they
cordially invite the Southern tribes to lay aside their private animosities and to consult
the safety and welfare of our common country, by joining the Confederation of the
United Tribes.

4. They also agree to send a copy of this Declaration to His Majesty the King of
England, to thank him for his acknowledgement of their flag; and in return for the
friendship and protection they have shown, and are prepared to show, to such of his
subjects as have settled in their country, or resorted to its shores for the purposes of
trade, they entreat that he will continue to be the parent of their infant State, and that
he will become its Protector from all attempts upon its independence.

Agreed to unanimously on this 28th day of October, 1835, in the presence of His
Britannic Majesty's Resident.

A Declaration of Independence by the Representatives
of the Commonwealth of Liberia, Liberia, 1847

We the representatives of the people of the Commonwealth of Liberia, in Convention
assembled, invested with authority for forming a new government, relying upon the aid
and protection of the Great Arbiter of human events, do hereby, in the name, and on
the behalf of the people of this Commonwealth, publish and declare the said commonwealth a FREE, SOVEREIGN, AND INDEPENDENT STATE, by the name and title of
the REPUBLIC OF LIBERIA. . . .

We recognise in all men, certain natural and inalienable rights: among these are life,
liberty, and the right to acquire, possess, enjoy and defend property. By the practice and
consent of men in all ages, some system or form of government is proven to be necessary to exercise, enjoy and secure those rights; and every people have a right to institute
a government, and to choose and adopt that system or form of it, which in their opinion will most effectively accomplish these objects, and secure their happiness, which
does not interfere with the just rights of others. The right therefore to institute government, and to all the powers necessary to conduct it is an inalienable right, and cannot
be resisted without the grossest injustice.

We the people of the Republic of Liberia were originally the inhabitants of the United States of North America.

In some parts of that country, we were debarred by law from all rights and privileges of men—in other parts, public sentiment, more powerful than law, frowned us down.

We were every where shut out from all civil office.

We were excluded from all participation in the government.

We were taxed without our consent.

We were compelled to contribute to the resources of a country, which gave us no protection.

We were made a separate and distinct class, and against us every avenue to improvement was effectually closed. Strangers from all lands of a color different from ours, were preferred before us.

We uttered our complaints, but they were unattended to, or only met by alledging the peculiar institutions of the country.

All hope of a favorable change in our country was thus wholly extinguished in our bosoms, and we looked with anxiety abroad for some asylum from the deep degradation.

The Western coast of Africa was the place selected by American benevolence and philanthropy, for our future home. Removed beyond those influences which depressed us in our native land, it was hoped we would be enabled to enjoy those rights and privileges, and exercise and improve those faculties, which the God of nature has given us in common with the rest of mankind.

Under the auspices of the American Colonization Society, we established ourselves here, on land acquired by purchase from the Lords of the soil. . . .

Liberia is an asylum from the most grinding oppression.

In coming to the shores of Africa, we indulged the pleasing hope that we would be permitted to exercise and improve those faculties which impart to man his dignity—to nourish in our hearts the flame of honorable ambition, to cherish and indulge those aspirations, which a beneficent Creator had implanted in every human heart, and to evince to all who despise, ridicule, and oppress our race, that we possess with them a common nature; are with them susceptible of equal refinement, and capable of equal advancement in all that adorns and dignifies man.

We were animated with the hope that here we should be at liberty to train up our children in the way they should go—to inspire them with the love of an honorable fame, to kindle within them, the flame of a lofty philanthropy, and to form strong within them, the principles of humanity, virtue, and religion.

Amongst the strongest motives to leave our native land—to abandon forever the scenes of our childhood and to sever the most endeared connexions, was the desire for a retreat where, free from the agitations of fear and molestation, we could in composure and security approach in worship, the God of our fathers.

Thus far our highest hopes have been realized.

Liberia is already the happy home of thousands, who were once the doomed victims of oppression, and if left unmolested to go on with her natural and spontaneous growth; if her movements be left free from the paralysing intrigues of jealous, ambitious and unscrupulous avarice, she will throw open a wider and yet a wider door for thousands, who are now looking with an anxious eye for some land of rest. . . .

Therefore in the name of humanity, and virtue and religion—in the name of the Great God, our common Creator, and our common Judge, we appeal to the nations of Christendom, and earnestly and respectfully ask of them, that they will regard us with the sympathy and friendly consideration, to which the peculiarities of our condition entitle us, and to extend to us, that comity which marks the friendly intercourse of civilized and independent communities.

Tuyên ngộn độc lập, Vietnam, 1945

All men are created equal. They are endowed by their Creator with certain inalienable rights, among these are Life, Liberty and the pursuit of Happiness.

This immortal statement was made in the Declaration of Independence of the United States of America in 1776. In a broader sense, this means: All the peoples on earth are equal from birth, all the peoples have a right to live, to be happy and free.

The Declaration of the French Revolution made in 1791 on the Rights of Man and the Citizen also states: "All men are born free and with equal rights, and must always remain free and have equal rights."

Those are undeniable truths.

Nevertheless, for more than eighty years, the French imperialists, abusing the standard of Liberty, Equality and Fraternity, have violated our Fatherland and oppressed our fellow-citizens. Their have acted contrary to the ideals of humanity and justice.

In the field of politics, they have deprived our people of every democratic liberty.

They have enforced inhuman laws; they have set up three distinct political regimes in the North, the Centre and the South of Viet Nam in order to wreck our national unity and prevent our people from being united.

They have built more prisons than schools. They have mercilessly slain our patriots; they have drowned our uprisings in rivers of blood.

They have fettered public opinion; they have practised obscurantism against our people.

To weaken our race they have forced us to use opium and alcohol.

In the field of economics, they have fleeced us to the back-bone, impoverished our people and devastated our land.

They have robbed us of our ricefields, our mines, our forests and our raw materials. They have monopolized the issuing of bank-notes and the export trade.

They have invented numerous unjustifiable taxes and reduced our people, especially our peasantry, to a state of extreme poverty.

They have hampered the prospering of our national bourgeoisie; they have mercilessly exploited our workers. . . .

Our people have broken the chains which for nearly a century have fettered them and have won independence for the Fatherland. Our people at the same time have overthrown the monarchic regime that has reigned supreme for dozens of centuries. In its place has been established the present Democratic Republic.

For these reasons we, members of the Provisional Government, representing the whole Vietnamese people, declare that from now on we break off all relations of a colonial character with France; we repeal all the international obligation that France has so far subscribed to on behalf of Viet Nam and we abolish all the special rights the French have unlawfully acquired in our Fatherland.

The whole Vietnamese people, animated by a common purpose, are determined to fight to the bitter end against any attempt by the French colonialists to reconquer their country.

We are convinced that the Allied nations which at Teheran and San Francisco have acknowledged the principles of self-determination and equality of nations, will not refuse to acknowledge the independence of Viet Nam.

A people who have courageously opposed French domination for more than eighty years, a people who have fought side by side with the Allies against the fascists during these last years, such a people must be free and independent.

For these reasons, we, members of the Provisional Government of the Democratic Republic of Viet Nam, solemnly declare to the world that Viet Nam has the right to be a free and independent country—and in fact it is so already. The entire Vietnamese people are determined to mobilize all their physical and mental strength, to sacrifice their lives and property in order to safeguard their independence and liberty.

360 DISCUSSION QUESTIONS

1   What were the ideological underpinnings of these declarations of independence? What ideas and ideals were the basis for these statements?

2   These pronouncements span more than a century. What aspects seem consistent and what elements change?

3   How did different cultural traditions or contexts impact the ways in which independence was expressed?

FIGHTING THE COLD WAR

12-1 | Early Cold War rhetoric

Although scholars disagree over the precise beginning of the Cold War—the global struggle for influence and power between the communist and non-communist world from the end of World War II to approximately 1989—these two statements by Churchill and Stalin are among the earliest direct statements of antipathy. Winston Churchill (1874–1965), former UK Prime Minister, delivered this March 1946 speech, titled "The Sinews of Peace," at Westminster College in Fulton, Missouri, with President Harry S. Truman (1884–1972) in attendance. His declarations about the "special relationship" between England and the U.S. and the descent of a communist "iron curtain"—a phrase originating in the 1920s—gained international attention.

Churchill's speech ignited an impassioned response from Josef Stalin (1878–1953), the General Secretary and Premier of the Soviet Union. In *Pravda*, the main press organ of the Communist Party, Stalin responded to Churchill's speech with his own interpretation of events in Eastern Europe and blasted Churchill as a warmongering racist.

12-1a | Winston Churchill, excerpt from "Iron Curtain" speech, UK, 1946

Ladies and gentlemen, the United States stands at this time at the pinnacle of world power. It is a solemn moment for the American democracy. For with this primacy in power is also joined an awe-inspiring accountability to the future. . . . Opportunity is here now, clear and shining, for both our countries. To reject it or ignore it or fritter it away will bring upon us all the long reproaches of the after-time. It is necessary that constancy of mind, persistency of purpose, and the grand simplicity of decision shall guide and rule the conduct of the English-speaking peoples in peace as they did in war. And we must, and I believe we shall prove ourselves equal to this severe requirement.

   . . .

A shadow has fallen upon the scenes so lately lightened—lighted by the Allied victory. No—Nobody knows what Soviet Russia and its Communist international organization intends to do in the immediate future, or what are the limits, if any, to their expansive and proselytizing tendencies. I have a strong admiration and regard for the valiant Russian people and for my wartime comrade, Marshal Stalin. There—There is deep sympathy and goodwill in Britain—and I doubt not here also—towards the peoples of all the Russias and a resolve to persevere through many differences and rebuffs in establishing lasting friendships. We understand the Russian need to be secure on her western frontiers by the removal of all possibility of German aggression.

We welcome Russia to her rightful place among the leading nations of the world. We welcome her flag upon the seas. Above all, we welcome, or should welcome, constant, frequent, and growing contacts between the Russian people and our own peoples on both sides of the Atlantic. It is my duty however, for I am sure you would not wish me to not misstate the facts as I see them to you. It is my duty to place before you certain facts about the present position in Europe.

From Stettin in the Baltic to Trieste in the Adriatic, an iron curtain has descended across the Continent. Behind that line lie all the capitals of the ancient states of central and eastern Europe. Warsaw, Berlin, Prague, Vienna, Budapest, Belgrade, Bucharest, and Sofia, all these famous cities and the populations around them lie in what I must call the Soviet sphere, and all are subject, in one form or another, not only to Soviet influence but to a very high, and in some cases, increasing measure of control from—from Moscow. . . . The Russian-dominated Polish Government has been encouraged to make enormous and wrongful inroads upon Germany, and mass expulsions of millions of Germans on a scale grievous and undreamed-of are now taking place. The Communist parties, which were very small in all these eastern states of Europe, have been raised to preeminence and power far beyond their numbers and are seeking everywhere to obtain totalitarian control. Police governments are prevailing in nearly every case, and so far, except in Czechoslovakia, there is no true democracy.

Turkey and Persia are both profoundly alarmed and disturbed at the claims which are being made upon them and at the pressure being exerted by the Moscow government. An attempt is being made by the Russians in Berlin to build up a quasi-Communist party in their zone of occupied Germany by showing special favors to groups of left-wing German leaders. . . .

If now the Soviet Government tries, by separate action, to build up a pro-Communist Germany in their areas, this will cause new serious difficulties in the British and American zones, and will give the defeated Germans the power of putting themselves up to auction between the Soviets and the Western democracies. Whatever conclusions may be drawn from these facts—and facts they are—this is certainly not the liberated Europe we fought to build up. Nor is it one which contains the essentials of permanent peace.

. . .

In front of the iron curtain which lies across Europe are other causes for anxiety. In Italy the Communist Party is seriously hampered by having to support the Communist-trained Marshal Tito's claims to former Italian territory at the head of the Adriatic. Nevertheless, the future of Italy hangs in the balance. Again one cannot imagine a regenerated Europe without a strong France. . . . However, in a great number of countries, far from the Russian frontiers and throughout the world, Communist fifth columns are established and work in complete unity and absolute obedience to the directions they received from the Communist center. Except in the British Commonwealth, and in the United States, where Communism is in its infancy, the Communist parties or fifth columns constitute a growing challenge and peril to Christian civilization. These are somber facts for anyone to have to recite on the morrow of a victory gained by so much splendid comradeship in arms and in the cause of freedom and democracy; but we should be most unwise not to face them squarely while time remains.

The outlook is also anxious in the Far East, and especially in Manchuria. The agreement which was made at Yalta, to which I was a party, was extremely favorable to Soviet Russia, but it was made at a time when no one could say that the German war might not extend all through the summer and autumn of 1945 and when the Japanese war was expected by the best judges to last for a further eighteen months from the end of the German war. In this country you are all so well-informed about the Far East, and such devoted friends of China, that I do not need to expatiate on the situation there.

. . .

On the other hand, ladies and gentlemen, I repulse the idea that a new war is inevitable—still more that it is imminent. It is because I am sure that our fortunes are still in our hands and that we hold the power to save the future, that I feel the duty to speak out now that I have an occasion to do so. I do not believe that Soviet Russia desires war. What they desire is the fruits of war and the indefinite expansion of their power and doctrines. But what we have to consider here today while time remains, is the permanent prevention of war and the establishment of conditions of freedom and democracy as rapidly as possible in all countries. Our difficulties and dangers will not be removed by closing our eyes to them. They will not be removed by more waiting to see what happens; nor will they be relieved by a policy of appeasement. What is needed is a settlement, and the longer this is delayed, the more difficult it will be and the greater our dangers will become.

From what—what I have seen of our Russian friends and allies during the war, I am convinced that there is nothing they admire so much as strength, and there is nothing for which they have less respect for than weakness, especially military weakness. For that—For that reason the old doctrine of a balance of power is unsound. We cannot afford, if we can help it, to work on narrow margins, offering temptations to a trial of strength. If the Western Democracies stand together in strict adherence to the principles of the United Nations Charter, their influence for furthering these principles will be immense and no one is likely to molest them. If however they become divided or falter in their duty, and if these all-important years are allowed to slip away, then indeed catastrophe may overwhelm us all.

. . .

If—If the population of the English-speaking Commonwealths be added to that of the United States with all such cooperation implies in the air, on the sea, all over the globe and in science and in industry, and in moral force, there will be no quivering, precarious balance of power to offer its temptation to ambition or adventure. On the contrary, there will be an overwhelming assurance of security. If we adhere faithfully to the Charter of the United Nations and walk forward in sedate and sober strength seeking no one's land or treasure, seeking to lay no arbitrary control upon the thoughts of men; if all British moral and material forces and convictions are joined with your own in fraternal association, the highroads of the future will be clear, not only for us but for all; not only for our time, but for a century to come.

12-1b | Joseph Stalin, excerpt from response in *Pravda* to Churchill's "Iron Curtain" speech, Soviet Union, 1946

Q. How do you assess the last speech of Mr. Churchill which was made in the United States?

A. I assess it as a dangerous act calculated to sow the seed of discord among the Allied governments and hamper their cooperation.

Q. Can one consider that the speech of Mr. Churchill is damaging to the cause of peace and security?

A. Undoubtedly, yes. In substance, Mr. Churchill now stands in the position of a firebrand of war. And Mr. Churchill is not alone here. He has friends not only in England but also in the United States of America.

In this respect, one is reminded remarkably of Hitler and his friends. Hitler began to set war loose by announcing his racial theory, declaring that only people speaking the German language represent a fully valuable nation. Mr. Churchill begins to set war loose also by a racial theory, maintaining that only nations speaking the English language are fully valuable nations, called upon to decide the destinies of the entire world.

The German racial theory brought Hitler and his friends to the conclusion that the Germans, as the only fully valuable nation, must rule over other nations. The English racial theory brings Mr. Churchill and his friends to the conclusion that the nations speaking the English language, being the only fully valuable nations, should rule over the remaining nations of the world.

In substance, Mr. Churchill and his friends in England and the United States present nations not speaking the English language with something like an ultimatum: "Recognize our lordship voluntarily and then all will be well. In the contrary case, war in inevitable."

But the nations have shed their blood during five years of cruel war for the sake of liberty and the independence of their countries, and not for the sake of exchanging the lordship of Hitler for the lordship of Churchill.

It is, therefore, highly probable that the nations not speaking English and which, however, make up an enormous majority of the world's population, will not consent to go into a new slavery. . . .

There is no doubt that the set-up of Mr. Churchill is a set-up for war, a call to war with the Soviet Union. . . .

Q. How do you assess that part of Mr. Churchill's speech in which he attacks the democratic regime of the European countries which are our neighbors and in which he criticizes the good neighborly relations established between these countries and the Soviet Union?

A. This part of Mr. Churchill's speech is a mixture of the elements of the libel with the elements of rudeness and lack of tact. Mr. Churchill maintains that Warsaw, Berlin, Prague, Vienna, Budapest, Belgrade, Bucharest, Sofia, all these famous cities and the populations of those areas, are within the Soviet sphere and are all subjected to Soviet influence and to the increasing control of Moscow.

Mr. Churchill qualifies this as the "boundless expansionist tendencies of the Soviet Union." It requires no special effort to show that Mr. Churchill rudely and shamelessly libels not only Moscow but also the above-mentioned States neighborly to the USSR.

To begin with, it is quite absurd to speak of the exclusive control of the USSR in Vienna and Berlin, where there are Allied control councils with representatives of four States, where the USSR has only one-fourth of the voices. . . .

Secondly, one cannot forget the following fact: the Germans carried out an invasion of the USSR through Finland, Poland, Rumania, Bulgaria and Hungary. The Germans were able to carry out the invasion through these countries by reason of the fact that these countries had governments inimical to the Soviet Union.

As the result of the German invasion, the Soviet Union has irrevocably lost in battles with the Germans, and also during the German occupation and through the expulsion of Soviet citizens to German slave labor camps, about 7,000,000 people. In other words, the Soviet Union has lost in men several times more than Britain and the United States together.

It may be that some quarters are trying to push into oblivion these sacrifices of the Soviet people which insured the liberation of Europe from the Hitlerite yoke.

But the Soviet Union cannot forget them. One can ask, therefore, what can be surprising in the fact that the Soviet Union, in a desire to ensure its security for the future, tries to achieve that these countries should have governments whose relations to the Soviet Union are loyal? How can one, without having lost one's reason, qualify these peaceful aspirations of the Soviet Union as "expansionist tendencies" of our Government? . . .

Mr. Churchill further maintains that the Communist parties were very insignificant in all these Eastern European countries but reached exceptional strength. . . .

As is known in Britain at present there is one party which rules the country—the Labor party. The rest of the parties are barred from the Government of the country. This is called by Churchill a true democracy, meanwhile Poland, Rumania, Yugoslavia, Bulgaria, and Hungary are governed by several parties—from four to six parties. And besides, the opposition, if it is loyal, is guaranteed the right to participate in the Government. This, Churchill calls totalitarian and the Government of police. . . .

Churchill would have liked Poland to be ruled by Sosnkowski and Anders, Yugoslavia by Mikhailovich, Rumania by Prince Stirbey and Radescu, Hungary and Austria by some king from the house of Habsburg, and so on.

Mr. Churchill wants to assure us that these gentlemen from the Fascist servants' hall can ensure true democracy. Such is the Democracy of Mr. Churchill. Mr. Churchill wanders around the truth when he speaks of the growth of the influence of Communist parties in eastern Europe. It should, however, be noted that he is not quite accurate. The influence of the Communist parties grew not only in Eastern Europe but in almost every country of Europe where fascism has ruled before: Italy, Germany, Hungary, Bulgaria, Rumania, Finland, and in countries which have suffered German, Italian, or Hungarian occupation. France, Belgium, Holland, Norway, Denmark, Poland, Czechoslovakia, Yugoslavia, Greece, the Soviet Union and so on.

The growth of the influence of communism cannot be considered accidental. It is a normal function. The influence of the Communists grew because during the hard years of the mastery of fascism in Europe, Communists showed themselves to be reliable, daring and self-sacrificing fighters against fascist regimes for the liberty of peoples. . . .

Such is the law of historical development.

Of course, Mr. Churchill does not like such a development of events. And he raised the alarm, appealing to force. . . .

I do not know whether Mr. Churchill and his friends will succeed in organizing after the Second World War a new military expedition against eastern Europe. But if they succeed in this, which is not very probable, since millions of common people stand on guard over the peace, then one confidently says that they will be beaten, just as they were beaten twenty-six years ago.

DISCUSSION QUESTIONS

1   How did Churchill characterize the threat of communism?

2   Why might Churchill's speech and Stalin's response be seen as the start of the Cold War? Provide evidence from both texts.

3   What tactics did Stalin use to counter Churchill's accusations?

12–2a | Excerpts from Marshall Plan, 1947

A U.S. initiative officially known as the European Recovery Program, the four-year operation of the Marshall Plan provided over $12 billion in economic aid to rebuild European economies devastated by World War II. Assistance was roughly divided on a per capita basis among the participating states. Although eighteen European countries received aid, the largest beneficiaries were the UK (26 percent) and France (18 percent). The Soviet Union both refused plan benefits and blocked the participation of some eastern bloc countries. Aid from the Marshall Plan was primarily used for the purchase of U.S. goods, also stimulating the postwar American economy. The role of the program in the rapid recovery of participating war-torn countries has been debated. The aid accounted for about 3 percent of the combined national income for these nations between 1948 and 1951. The plan was named for George Marshall (1880–1959), the U.S. soldier and statesman who served in several posts in the administrations of FDR and Truman. He was Secretary of State when he advocated for this recovery program, for which he received the Nobel Peace Prize in 1953.

I need not tell you gentlemen that the world situation is very serious. That must be apparent to all intelligent people. I think one difficulty is that the problem is one of such enormous complexity that the very mass of facts presented to the public by press and radio make it exceedingly difficult for the man in the street to reach a clear appraisal of the situation. Furthermore, the people of this country are distant from the troubled areas of the earth and it is hard for them to comprehend the plight and consequent reactions of the long-suffering peoples, and the effect of those reactions on their governments in connection with our efforts to promote peace in the world.

In considering the requirements for the rehabilitation of Europe the physical loss of life, the visible destruction of cities, factories, mines and railroads was correctly estimated, but it has become obvious during recent months that this visible destruction was probably less serious than the dislocation of the entire fabric of European economy. For the past ten years conditions have been highly abnormal. The feverish preparation for war and the more feverish maintenance of the war effort engulfed all aspects of national economies. Machinery has fallen into disrepair or is entirely obsolete. Under the arbitrary and destructive Nazi rule, virtually every possible enterprise was geared into the German war machine. Long-standing commercial ties, private institutions, banks, insurance companies and shipping companies disappeared, through loss of capital, absorption through nationalization or by simple destruction. In many countries, confidence in the local currency has been severely shaken. The breakdown of the business structure of Europe during the war was complete. Recovery has been seriously retarded by the fact that two years after the close of hostilities a peace settlement with Germany and Austria has not been agreed upon. But even given a more prompt solution of these difficult problems, the rehabilitation of the economic structure of Europe quite evidently will require a much longer time and greater effort than had been foreseen.

There is a phase of this matter which is both interesting and serious. The farmer has always produced the foodstuffs to exchange with the city dweller for the other necessities of life. This division of labor is the basis of modern civilization. At the present time it is threatened with breakdown. The town and city industries are not producing adequate goods to exchange with the food-producing farmer. Raw materials and fuel are in short supply. Machinery is lacking or worn out. The farmer [or] the peasant cannot find the goods for sale which he desires to purchase. So the sale of his farm produce for money which he cannot use seems to him an unprofitable transaction. He, therefore, has withdrawn many fields from crop cultivation and is using them for grazing. He feeds more grain to stock and finds for himself and his family an ample supply of food, however short he may be on clothing and the other ordinary gadgets of civilization. Meanwhile people in the cities are short of food and fuel. So the governments are forced to use their foreign money and credits to procure these necessities abroad. This process exhausts funds which are urgently needed for reconstruction. [Thus] a very serious situation is rapidly developing which bodes no good for the world. The modern system of the division of labor upon which the exchange of products is based is in danger of breaking down.

The truth of the matter is that Europe's requirements for the next three or four years of foreign food and other essential products—principally from America—are so much greater than her present ability to pay that she must have substantial additional help, or face economic, social and political deterioration of a very grave character.

The remedy lies in breaking the vicious circle and restoring the confidence of the European people in the economic future of their own countries and of Europe as a whole. The manufacturer and the farmer throughout wide areas must be able and willing to exchange their products for currencies the continuing value of which is not open to question.

Aside from the demoralizing effect on the world at large and the possibilities of disturbances arising as a result of the desperation of the people concerned, the consequences to the economy of the United States should be apparent to all. It is logical that the United States should do whatever it is able to do to assist in the return of normal economic health in the world, without which there can be no political stability and no assured peace. Our policy is directed not against any country or doctrine but against hunger, poverty, desperation and chaos. Its purpose should be the revival of a working economy in the world so as to permit the emergence of political and social conditions in which free institutions can exist. Such assistance, I am convinced, must not be on a piece-meal basis as various crises develop. Any assistance that this Government may render in the future should provide a cure rather than a mere palliative. Any government that is willing to assist in the task of recovery will find full cooperation, I am sure, on the part of the United States Government. Any government which maneuvers to block the recovery of other countries cannot expect help from us. Furthermore, governments, political parties or groups which seek to perpetuate human misery in order to profit therefrom politically or otherwise will encounter the opposition of the United States.

It is already evident that, before the United States Government can proceed much further in its efforts to alleviate the situation and help start the European world on its way to recovery, there must be some agreement among the countries of Europe as to the requirements of the situation and the part those countries themselves will take in order to give proper effect to whatever action might be undertaken by this Government. It would be neither fitting nor efficacious for this Government to undertake to draw up unilaterally a program designed to place Europe on its feet economically. This is the business of the Europeans. The initiative, I think, must come from Europe. The role of this country should consist of friendly aid in the drafting of a European program and of later support of such a program so far as it may be practical for us to do so. The program should be a joint one, agreed to by a number, if not all European nations.

An essential part of any successful action on the part of the United States is an understanding on the part of the people of America of the character of the problem and the remedies to be applied. Political passion and prejudice should have no part. With foresight, and a willingness on the part of our people to face up to the vast responsibility which history has clearly placed upon our country, the difficulties I have outlined can and will be overcome.

12–2b | Photograph, Marshall Plan work in West Berlin, West Germany, 1940s

In the aftermath of World War II, the four main allies in Europe—the U.S., UK, USSR, and France—jointly occupied defeated Germany. During this period, 1945–1952, the arrangement evolved into the division of both the country and Berlin, its capital city, into districts containing an eastern and western sector. Mutual distrust of the Soviet Union by the West led to Britain, France, and the U.S. agreeing to a joint occupation of West Germany and West Berlin, while the USSR managed East Germany and East Berlin. West Germany received approximately 11 percent of the aid provided in the Marshall Plan. Military occupation shifted to civilian leadership in 1949 and the country. Germany and its capital, however, would remain divided throughout the Cold War.

DISCUSSION QUESTIONS

1   What do these sources tell us about the aftermath of a total war?

2   What were the U.S. motives behind providing this economic aid to Europe?

3   What might the implications be for participation and non-participation in the European Recovery Program?

12–3a | Gordon Edward George Minhinnick, political cartoon, "The Octopus of Chinese Communism," New Zealand, 1950

The long Chinese Civil War (1927–1949) between the Kuomintang-led government of the Republic of China and the Communist Party of China ended with a Kuomintang retreat to Taiwan and a communist victory over the mainland. Communist Party Leader Mao

Zedong believed socialism would expand and overwhelm all competing ideologies. The transformation of the world's most populous nation to a communist state had wide-ranging global impacts.

12–3b | Senator Joseph R. McCarthy, excerpts from speech to the United States Senate, 1950

Joseph Raymond McCarthy (1908–1957), a Republican U.S. Senator from Wisconsin, emerged as a high-profile and virulent anti-communist politician during the early Cold War. He began his campaign by declaring communist subversion of the federal government, as can be seen below. Later accusations would include the administration of Harry S. Truman, the Voice of America, the U.S. Army, and the film industry. The second Red Scare, underscored by international events like the communist victory in China above, fueled the domestic anti-communist campaigns of the period. With McCarthy as a leading figure, similar campaigns based on unfair allegations and investigations became know as "McCarthyism," a term first coined in 1950. In 1954, the Senate voted to censure McCarthy and his role as a major public figure diminished.

. . . Today we are engaged in a final, all-out battle between communistic atheism and Christianity. The modern champions of communism have selected this as the time. And, ladies and gentlemen, the chips are down—they truly are down. . . .

Six years ago . . . there was within the Soviet orbit 180,000,000 people.

. . . Today, only six years later, there are 800,000,000 people under the absolute domination of Soviet Russia—an increase of over 400 percent. . . . This indicates the swiftness of the tempo of Communist victories and American defeats in the cold war. As one of our outstanding historical figures once said, "When a great democracy is destroyed, it will not be because of enemies from without, but rather because of enemies from within." The truth of this statement is becoming terrifyingly clear as we see this country each day losing on every front.

At war's end we were physically the strongest nation on earth and, at least potentially, the most powerful intellectually and morally. Ours could have been the honor of being a beacon in the desert of destruction, a shining living proof that civilization was not yet ready to destroy itself. Unfortunately, we have failed miserably and tragically to arise to the opportunity.

The reason why we find ourselves in a position of impotency is not because our only powerful potential enemy has sent men to invade our shores, but rather because of the traitorous actions of those who have been treated so well by this Nation. It has not been the less fortunate or members of minority groups who have been selling this Nation out, but rather those who have had all the benefits that the wealthiest nation on earth has had to offer—the finest homes, the finest college education, and the finest jobs in Government we can give.

This is glaringly true in the State Department. There the bright young men who are born with silver spoons in their mouths are the ones who have been worst. . . . I would like to cite one rather unusual case—the case of a man who has done much to shape our foreign policy.

When Chiang Kai-shek was fighting our war [against the Chinese Communists], the State Department had in China a young man named John S. Service. His task, obviously, was not to work for the communization of China. Strangely, however, he sent official reports back to the State Department urging that we torpedo our ally Chiang Kai-shek and stating, in effect, that communism was the best hope of China.

Later, this man—John Service—was picked up by the Federal Bureau of Investigation for turning over to the Communists secret State Department information. Strangely, however, he was never prosecuted. However, Joseph Grew, Under Secretary of State, who insisted on his prosecution, was forced to resign. Two days after Grew's successor, Dean Acheson, took over as Under Secretary of State, this man—John Service—who had been picked up by the FBI and who had previously urged that communism was the best hope of China, was not only reinstated . . . but promoted. And finally, under Acheson, placed in charge of all placements and promotions.

Today, ladies and gentlemen, this man Service is on his way to represent the State Department and Acheson in Calcutta—by far and away the most important listening post in the Far East.

Now, let's see what happens when individuals with Communist connections are forced out of the State Department. Gustave Duran, who was labeled as (I quote) "a notorious international Communist," was made assistant to the Assistant Secretary of State in charge of Latin American affairs. He was taken into the State Department from his job as a lieutenant colonel in the Communist International Brigade. Finally, after intense congressional pressure and criticism, he resigned in 1946 from the State Department—and, ladies and gentlemen, where do you think he is now? He took over a high-salaried job as Chief of Cultural Activities Section in the office of the Assistant Secretary General of the United Nations. . . .

This, ladies and gentlemen, gives you somewhat of a picture of the type of individuals who have been helping to shape our foreign policy. In my opinion the State Department, which is one of the most important government departments, is thoroughly infested with Communists.

I have in my hand 57 cases of individuals who would appear to be either card carrying members or certainly loyal to the Communist Party, but who nevertheless are still helping to shape our foreign policy.

One thing to remember in discussing the Communists in our Government is that we are not dealing with spies who get 30 pieces of silver to steal the blueprints of a new weapon. We are dealing with a far more sinister type of activity because it permits the enemy to guide and shape our policy. . . .

DISCUSSION QUESTIONS

1   How did this political cartoon embody popular fears about the threat of communism?

2   What did McCarthy argue were the roots of communist influence in America?

3   How was the second Red Scare different than the first?

12–4a | Gamal Abdel Nasser, speech nationalizing the Suez Canal Company, Egypt, 1956

When the Middle East became a hotspot of the Cold War in the 1950s, the West had to contend with its long history of imperialism and a newly energized Arab nationalist movement in the region. Gamal Abdel Nasser (1918–1970), President of Egypt from 1954 to 1970, challenged Britain and France by nationalizing the Suez Canal in 1956, sparking the Suez Crisis. Arab nationalists across the Middle East praised Nasser's move, strengthening his position against internal opposition, including the Muslim Brotherhood. When a joint British-French-Israeli military operation attempted to retake the Canal, the U.S. balked at military action, preferring instead to back Egypt's right to the canal in hopes of shoring up an important regional ally in the Cold War.

I began to look at Mr. Black sitting in his chair imagining that I was sitting before Ferdinand de Lesseps.

I recalled the words which we used to read. In 1854, Ferdinand de Lesseps arrived in Egypt. He went to Mohammed Said Pasha, the Khedive. He sat beside him and told him, "We want to dig the Suez Canal. This project will greatly benefit you. It is a great project and will bring excellent returns to Egypt."

While Black was speaking to me, I felt the complexes which his words revived. I was again carried back to Ferdinand de Lesseps.

I told him we have complexes from such matters, and we do not want to see another Cromer governing us again. Loans and interests on these loans have ended in the occupation of our country. I requested him to take this into consideration. We have complexes from de Lesseps and from Cromer, and from political occupation through economic occupation.

That was the picture I had in mind, the picture of De Lesseps who arrived on November 7, 1854. He arrived in Alexandria and began to work cautiously and treacherously. On November 30, 1854, he had already contacted the Khedive and obtained the Concession for the Canal from him. The Concession said. "Our friend De Lesseps has drawn our attention to the benefits which will accrue to Egypt by joining the Mediterranean and the Red Sea by a waterway for the passage of ships. He informed us of the possibility of forming a company for this purpose to comprise the investors of capital. We have approved the idea and have authorised him to form and to operate a company for the digging of the Suez Canal and to exploit it between the two seas."

This was in 1854. In 1856, a hundred years ago, a Firman was issued whereby the company was formed. Egypt got 44 percent of the shares and bound herself with certain obligations to De Lesseps. The De Lesseps company is a private company. It has nothing to do with governments, domination, occupation or imperialism! De Lesseps told the Khedive, "I am your friend, I have come to benefit you and to dig a canal between the two seas for your advantage."

The Suez Canal Company was formed, and Egypt got 44 percent of the shares. Egypt undertook to supply labour to dig the Canal by corvée, of whom 120,000 died without getting paid. We also paid De Lesseps in order that he might give up some concession. We gave up the 15 percent of the profits which we were supposed to get over and above the profits of our 44 percent of the shares. Thus, contrary to the statements made by De Lesseps to the Khedive in which he said that the Canal was dug for Egypt, Egypt has become the property of the Canal.

Article 16 of the agreement concluded on February 22, 1866, stipulated that in view of the fact that the Suez Canal Company is an Egyptian company, it is subject to the country's laws. [But it has been] subject neither to the country's laws nor its regulations. It considers itself a state within a state. The disputes which arise between Egypt and the Company or between individuals of any nationality are to come before Egyptian courts in accordance with the regulations set forth by the laws of the country. Egyptian courts are competent in giving their verdict with regard to disputes which may come up between the Egyptian government and the company according to Egyptian laws.

The result of the words of De Lesseps in 1856, the result of friendship and loans, was the occupation of Egypt in 1882.

Egypt then borrowed money. What happened? Egypt was obliged, during the reign of Ismail, to sell its 44 percent of the shares in the company. Immediately, England sent out to purchase the shares. It bought them for 4 million pounds. Then, Ismail gave up his 5 percent of the company's profits against the ceding of some concessions by the Company which were granted to it.

Then Ismail was obliged to pay to Britain the 5 percent profit which he had relinquished. This amounted to over 4 million pounds. In other words, Britain got Egypt's 44 percent of the Company's shares free. This was the history which took place a century ago.

Is history to repeat itself again with treachery and deceit? Will economic independence . . . or economic domination and control be the cause of the destruction of our political independence and freedom?

Brothers, it is impossible that history should repeat itself.

Today, we do not repeat what happened in the past. We are eradicating the traces of the past. We are building our country on strong and sound bases.

Whenever we turn backwards, we aim at the eradication of the past evils which brought about our domination, and the vestiges of the past which took place despite ourselves and which were caused by imperialism through treachery and deceit.

Today, the Suez Canal where 120,000 of our sons had lost their lives in digging it by corvée, and for the foundation of which we paid 8 million pounds, has become a state within the state. It has humiliated ministers and cabinets.

This Canal is an Egyptian canal. It is an Egyptian Joint Stock Company. Britain has forcibly grabbed our rights, our 44 percent of its shares. Britain still collects the profits of these shares from the time of its inauguration until now. All countries and shareholders get their profits. A state within the state, an Egyptian Joint Stock Company.

The income of the Suez Canal Company in 1955 reached 35 million pounds, or 100 million dollars. Of this sum, we, who have lost 120,000 persons, who have died in digging the Canal, take only 1 million pounds or 3 million dollars. This is the Suez Canal Company, which, according to the Firman, was dug for the sake of Egypt and its benefit.

Do you know how much assistance America and Britain were going to offer us over five years? 70 million dollars. Do you know who takes the 100 million dollars, the Company's income, every year? They take them of course.

It is no shame that I may be poor and borrow money to build my country. It is no shame that I should attempt to get aid for the sake of my country. But, it is shameful that I suck peoples' blood and rights.

We shall not repeat the past. We shall eradicate it by restoring our rights in the Suez Canal. This money is ours. This Canal is the property of Egypt because it is an Egyptian Joint Stock Company.

The Canal was dug by Egypt's sons and 120,000 of them died while working. The Suez Canal Company in Paris is an imposter company. It usurped our concessions.

When De Lesseps came over to Egypt, his arrival was the same as Black who came to Egypt to talk with me. The same action.

But history will never repeat itself. On the contrary, we shall build the High Dam. We shall restore our usurped rights. We shall build the High Dam as we want it. We are determined to do it. 35 million pounds the company gets every year; let Egypt take it. 100 million dollars are collected every year by the company which collects them for the benefit of Egypt. Let it be so, and Egypt will collect the 100 million dollars for the benefit of Egypt.

Thus, today, citizens, when we build the High Dam, we are actually building the dam to defend our dignity, freedom, and pride, and to eradicate humiliation and submission.

Egypt—the whole of Egypt—one national front—one unified and solid front—announces that it will fight to the last drop of its blood. Every one of its sons will be like Salah Mustafa and Mustafa Hafez. We shall all fight to the last drop of our blood for building our country, for the sake of Egypt. We shall not let warmongers, imperialists or those who trade in human beings dominate us. We shall depend on our hands and on our blood. We are rich, but we were careless. We shall restore these rights. The battle continues. We shall restore these rights step by step. We shall realize everything. We shall build a strong and dignified Egypt, the Arab Egypt.

Therefore, I have signed today the following law which has been approved by the Cabinet: [reads text of decree Doc. 18].

Citizens,

We shall not let imperialists or exploiters dominate us. We shall not let history repeat itself once more. We have gone forward to build a strong Egypt. We go forward towards political and economic independence. We go forward towards national economy for the sake of the whole people. We go forward to work. But, whenever we look behind, we do so to destroy the traces of the past, the traces of slavery, exploitation and domination.

Today, citizens, rights have been restored to their owners. Our right in the Suez Canal [has] been restored to us after 100 years.

Today, we actually achieve true sovereignty, true dignity and true pride. The Suez Canal Company was a state within a state. It was an Egyptian Joint Stock Company, relying on imperialism and its stooges.

The Suez Canal was built for the sake of Egypt and for its benefit. But [it] was a source of exploitation and the draining of wealth.

As I said a short while ago, it is no shame to be poor and to work for the building of my country. But it is shameful to suck blood. They used to suck our blood, our rights and take them.

Today, when we regain our rights, I say in the name of the people of Egypt that we shall defend these rights and shall hold fast. We shall sacrifice our lives and our blood in defending them. We shall make up for the past.

Today, when we build the edifice of our dignity, freedom and pride, we feel that it will not be completely sound until we eradicate domination, humiliation and submission. The Suez Canal constituted an edifice of humiliation.

Today, citizens, the Suez Canal Company has been nationalized. This order has been published in the Official Journal. It has become a matter of fact.

Citizens, today we say our wealth has been restored to us.

Citizens. Today, the Suez Canal income is estimated at 35 million pounds or 100 million dollars per annum or 500 million dollars in five years. We shall not seek the 70 million dollar American aid.

Today, fellow-countrymen, by our sweat, our tears, the souls of our martyrs and the skulls of those who died in 1856, a hundred years ago during the corvée, we are able to develop this country. We shall work, produce and step up production despite all these intrigues and these talks. Whenever I hear talk from Washington, I shall [say], "Die of your fury."

We shall build up industry in Egypt and compete with them. They do not want us to become an industrial country so that they can promote the sale of their products and market them in Egypt. I never saw any American aid directed towards industrialization as this would cause us to compete with them. American aid is everywhere directed towards exploitation.

On entering upon the fifth anniversary of the Revolution, as I said at the beginning of my speech, we feel stronger, more resolute and faithful than during the former years.

On embarking upon the fifth year of the Revolution, as Farouk was expelled on July 26, 1952, the Suez Canal Company will depart on the very same day. We are conscious of accomplishing glories and achieving true dignity. Sovereignty in Egypt will belong only to her sons.

We shall march forward united . . . one nation confident in itself, its motherland and its power, one nation relying on itself in work and in the sacred march towards construction, industrialization and creation . . . one nation . . . a solid bloc to hold out treason and aggression and resist imperialism and agents of imperialism.

In this manner, we shall accomplish much and feel dignity and pride and feel that we are building up our country to suit ourselves . . . We build what we want and do what we want with nobody to account to.

When we obtain our usurped and stolen rights, we shall turn towards strength. We shall become stronger each year, and, God willing, next year we shall become more powerful with increased production, work and factories.

Now, while I am speaking to you, fellow countrymen, brothers of yours are taking over the administration and the management of the Canal Company, the Egyptian Canal Company not the foreign Canal Company. They are taking over the Canal Company and its facilities for the direction of navigation in the Canal, the Canal which is situated in the territory of Egypt, cuts through the territory of Egypt, is a part of Egypt and belongs to Egypt. We now perform this task to compensate for the past and build up new edifices for pride and dignity.

May God guide you and peace be with you.

12–4b | Joint Congressional Resolution to Promote Peace and Stability in the Middle East, 1957

Like the Truman Doctrine, the Eisenhower Doctrine (1957) pledged U.S. military assistance to states and peoples threatened by communist aggression. Unlike its predecessor, the Eisenhower Doctrine targeted the Middle East, bringing the region into the United States' sphere of influence with its argument that the fortunes of the two were bound together. In the year following the Suez Crisis of 1956, Congress empowered the Eisenhower administration to act on the promise made to the states of the Middle East. Despite the reluctance of Arab states and Israel to sanction U.S. commitment, the Eisenhower Doctrine marked a turning point in U.S. involvement in the region and initiated long-term American engagement there.

Resolved by the Senate and House of Representatives of the United States of America in Congress assembled, That the President be and hereby is authorized to cooperate with and assist any nation or group of nations in the general area of the Middle East desiring such assistance in the development of economic strength dedicated to the maintenance of national independence.

Sec. 2. The President is authorized to undertake, in the general area of the Middle East, military assistance programs with any nation or group of nations of that area desiring such assistance. Furthermore, the United States regards as vital to the national interest and world peace the preservation of the independence and integrity of the nations of the Middle East. To this end, if the President determines the necessity thereof, the United States is prepared to use armed forces to assist any such nation or group of such nations requesting assistance against armed aggression from any country controlled by international communism: *Provided,* That such employment shall be consonant with the treaty obligations of the United States and with the Constitution of the United States.

SEC. 3. The President is hereby authorized to use during the balance of fiscal year 1957 for economic and military assistance under this joint resolution not to exceed $200,000,000 from any appropriation now available for carrying out the provisions of the Mutual Security Act of 1954, as amended, in accord with the provisions of such Act: *Provided,* That, whenever the President determines it to be important to the security of the United States, such use may be under the authority of section 401 (a) of the Mutual Security Act of 1954, as amended (except that the provisions of section 105 (a) thereof shall not be waived), and without regard to the provisions of section 105 of the Mutual Security Appropriation Act, 1957: *Provided further,* That obligations incurred in carrying out the purposes of the first sentence of section 2 of this joint resolution shall be paid only out of appropriations for military assistance, and obligations incurred in carrying out the purposes of the first section of this joint resolution shall be paid only out of appropriations other than those for military assistance. This authorization is in addition to other existing authorizations with respect to the use of such appropriations. None of the additional authorization contained in this section shall be used until fifteen days after the Committee on Foreign Relations of the Senate, the Committee on Foreign Affairs of the House of Representatives, the Committees on Appropriations of the Senate and the House of Representatives and, when military assistance is involved, the Committees on Armed Services of the Senate and the House of Representatives have been furnished a report showing the object of the proposed use, the country for the benefit of which such use is intended, and the particular appropriation or appropriations for carrying out the provisions of the Mutual Security Act of 1954, as amended, from which the funds are proposed to be derived: *Provided,* That funds available under this section during the balance of fiscal year 1957 shall, in the case of any such report submitted during the last fifteen days of the fiscal year, remain available for use under this section for the purposes stated in such report for a period of twenty days following the date of submission of such report. Nothing contained in this joint resolution shall be construed as itself authorizing the appropriation of additional funds for the purpose of carrying out the provisions of the first section or of the first sentence of section 2 of this joint resolution.

SEC. 4. The President should continue to furnish facilities and military assistance, within the provisions of applicable law and established policies, to the United Nations Emergency Force in the Middle East, with a view to maintaining the truce in that region.

SEC. 5. The President shall within the months of January and July of each year report to the Congress his action hereunder.

SEC. 6. This joint resolution shall expire when the President shall determine that the peace and security of the nations in the general area of the Middle East are reasonably assured by international conditions created by action of the United Nations or otherwise except that it may be terminated earlier by a concurrent resolution of the two Houses of Congress.

Approved March 9, 1957.

DISCUSSION QUESTIONS

1 What reasons did Nasser provide for Egypt's claim on the Suez Canal?
2 What does the congressional resolution allow the U.S. President to do and for how long?
3 Under the conditions of the congressional resolution, would Egypt qualify for U.S. support? Why or why not?

COLD WAR TURNS HOT

12–5a | Harry S. Truman, memoir, section on his initial thoughts on aggression in Korea, 1956

The invasion of South Korea by North Korea launched the Korean War (1950–1953), a regional conflict that had global implications due to its Cold War context. Divided into two states in 1948 with a border at the 38th parallel, both Koreas claimed to be the legitimate government of all Korea and neither accepted the border as permanent. South Korea, supported by the United Nations (principally the U.S.), faced near defeat early in the war as they were overwhelmed by the June 1950 attack by North Korea, supported by China and the USSR. Here, Truman reflects on his thoughts and feelings upon hearing the initial news of the invasion.

The plane left the Kansas City Municipal Airport at two o'clock, and it took just a little over three hours to make the trip to Washington. I had time to think aboard the plane. In my generation, this was not the first occasion when the strong had attacked the weak. I recalled some earlier instances: Manchuria, Ethiopia, Austria. I remembered how each time that the democracies failed to act it had encouraged the aggressors to keep going ahead. Communism was acting in Korea just as Hitler, Mussolini, and the Japanese had acted ten, fifteen, and twenty years earlier. I felt certain that if South Korea was allowed to fall Communist leaders would be emboldened to override nations closer to our own shores. If the Communists were permitted to force their way into the Republic of Korea without opposition form the free world, no small nation would have the courage to resist threats and aggression by stronger Communist neighbors. If this was allowed to go unchallenged it would mean a third world war, just as similar incidents had brought on the second world war. It was also clear to me that the foundations and the principles of the United Nations were at stake unless this unprovoked attack on Korea could be stopped.

12–5b | Ye Shanlu, poster, "Everybody must take precautions against epidemics to smash the germ warfare of American imperialism!" 1952

A United Nations counter-offensive in September 1950 reversed the prospects of the war effort in South Korea. Landing mid-peninsula at Incheon, many North Korean troops became isolated in the south, while others were pushed north. UN forces invaded North Korea and advanced rapidly toward the border with China. On October 19, 1950, the Chinese intervened, sending troops that pushed UN forces back below the 38th parallel. The final two years of the conflict became a war of attrition, with ongoing bombing campaigns, yet a fairly stagnant front line. The conflict, ended not by peace treaty but by a ceasefire, was highly destructive, including approximately 3 million war fatalities and a high civilian death toll.

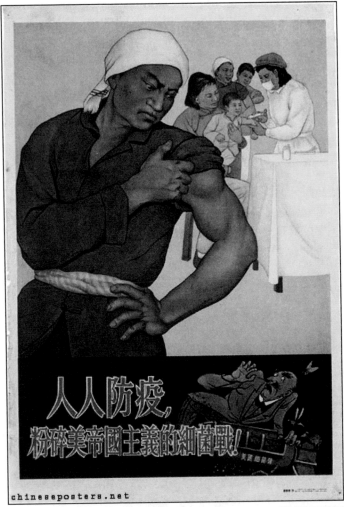

SEE COLOR INSERT

DISCUSSION QUESTIONS

1 How was historical analogy driving Truman's interpretation of events in Korea? What might be the consequences of that?

2 At the time of this poster's creation, the Chinese Communist Party was embarking upon a massive "modern hygiene/health" campaign, encouraging its citizens to be immunized. How might that change the reception of this propaganda? What does that tell us about the interplay between politics and public health?

12-6a | Poster, U.S. Information Agency, Operation Passage to Freedom, South Vietnam, 1954

of the French defeat in the First Indochina War (1946–1954), agreements at the international Geneva Conference in July 1954 gave the Việt Minh control of Vietnam above the 17th parallel and constitutional monarch Bảo Đại the south's State of Vietnam. Operation Passage to Freedom (1954–1955) was a U.S. Navy–assisted resettlement of over 300,000 refugees from communist North Vietnam to South Vietnam. Other countries, including France, may have transported up to 500,000 individuals. The Geneva agreements allowed a 300-day period of free movement until the border was sealed. The relocation was a public relations coup for the U.S. in the early Cold War, as refugees, especially Vietnamese Catholics, fled in great numbers from the communist north. Bảo Đại, the last ruler in the Vietnamese Nguyễn dynasty, would be ousted by Prime Minister Ngô Đình Diệm in 1955 with the creation of the Republic of Vietnam (1955–1975).

Translation: "Move to the South to avoid communism" and "The southern compatriots welcome their northern compatriots with open arms."

SEE COLOR INSERT

12–6b | Nguyen Xuan Phong, excerpt of oral history interview, 2003

Nguyen Xuan Phong (1936–2017), originally from the village of Bac Tri in southern Vietnam, served in a variety of cabinet-level positions in the Republic of Vietnam (South Vietnam) from 1965 to 1975. He was the Minister-of-State in Charge of Negotiations at the Paris peace talks in April 1975 when the political regime in South Vietnam collapsed. After the fall of South Vietnam, Phong was sent for "reeducation," imprisoned outside Hanoi for five years. After release, he worked as a private businessman in Ho Chi Minh City. Here, in an oral history interview in 2003, he reflected on the nature of the war(s) in Vietnam.

. . . after more than a century of French colonial rule and when you came by the end of the Second World War there was a tremendous upsurge all over the world of those former colonies to regain their dignity, to regain their independence, to regain their national sovereignty and so on, even for the ordinary farmers in the countryside, he was also able to feel those things, although he may not understand a lot about those things but that's what he wanted to be, to regain his dignity after more than a century of being you know a second class human being during the French colonial period. And although he did not have any clear idea what independence would mean even now and then with globalization and then what national sovereignty would mean and so on but he wanted to have an end to the foreign presence, to the foreign rule, intervention and so on and that was the things that Ho Chi Minh was very effectively able to use, you see. So it was not really territorial security or fighting battles and get more land, it was to give back those things to the people at that time as anywhere in the world with those former colonies. But then I think that very briefly one may say there were two wars in one in Vietnam, in the '50s, '60s, and '70s. There was a war between the brother enemies, that is the Vietnamese Communists with Ho Chi Minh, his Vietnam Communist Party and those who oppose that without knowing really what they were but then slowly they called themselves the nationalists you know which was equated to be anticommunist but if you asked what the nationalist was they wouldn't be able to define that for you, but the communist Vietnamese would be very able to define you know what the Vietnamese communist was at that time by using the nationalist flag and then Ho Chi Minh was very clever not to project communism per se. He only claimed to be a communist, but being a communist be implied that he was fighting for national independence, for national sovereignty and so on, so for the ordinary people especially in the rural areas who didn't care much to know what communism was but then seeing that in practical terms Ho Chi Minh and his Vietnam Communist Party were fighting, were putting up an effective fight against the foreign presence, against the foreign intervention, so that was not really a fight between the Vietnamese communists and Vietnamese anti-communists you see.

DISCUSSION QUESTIONS

1   What characteristics of North and South Vietnam were highlighted in the poster to encourage emigration?

2   Why might Vietnamese communism have been appealing to the people?

3   How do these two documents broaden the understanding of the conflict in Vietnam to more than a showdown between democracy and communism?

DECOLONIZATION

12–7a | Harold Macmillan, elements of "Winds of Change" speech, UK, 1960

Decolonization of modern empires began in earnest in the years following World War II. Dozens of newly independent states appeared in the postwar period, particularly in Asia and Africa, at the same time that Cold War combatants sought to increase their global influence. Britain began voluntarily dismantling its empire in Africa in the 1950s. While some states, like Ghana (1957), transitioned to independence fairly smoothly, other regions, such as Kenya, South Rhodesia, and South Africa, faced complications due to the large number of white settlers. In 1960, British Prime Minister Harold Macmillan (1894–1986) visited South Africa, a member of the British Commonwealth, and delivered a landmark fifty-minute speech to their Parliament. In it, he very carefully declared two things: British support for African nationalism and British opposition to the apartheid practiced in South Africa. To do otherwise, he believed, risked pushing all emerging states into the arms of Khrushchev and the Soviet Union.

Address by the Right Hon. Harold Macmillan, M.P., to Members of both Houses of the Parliament of the Union of South Africa, Cape Town, 3rd February, 1960

It is . . . a special privilege for me to be here in 1960 when you are celebrating what I might call the golden wedding of the Union. At such a time it is natural and right that you should pause to take stock of your position, to look back at what you have achieved, to look forward to what lies ahead.

. . .

Sir, as I have travelled around the Union I have found everywhere, as I expected, a deep preoccupation with what is happening in the rest of the African continent. I understand and sympathise with your interests in these events and your anxiety about them. Ever since the break up of the Roman empire one of the constant facts of political life in Europe has been the emergence of independent nations. They have come into existence over the centuries in different forms, different kinds of Government, but all have been inspired by a deep, keen feeling of nationalism, which has grown as the nations have grown.

In the twentieth century, and especially since the end of the war, the processes which gave birth to the nation States of Europe have been repeated all over the world. We have seen the awakening of national consciousness in peoples who have for centuries lived in dependence upon some other power. Fifteen years ago this movement spread through Asia. Many countries there of different races and civilisations pressed their claim to an independent national life. To-day the same thing is happening in Africa and the most striking of all the impressions I have formed since I left London a month ago is of the strength of this African national consciousness. In different places it takes different forms but it is happening everywhere. The wind of change is blowing through this continent and, whether we like it or not, this growth of national consciousness is a political fact. We must all accept it as a fact, and our national policies must take account of it.

Of course you understand this better than anyone. You are sprung from Europe, the home of nationalism, and here in Africa you have yourselves created a free nation. A new nation. Indeed, in the history of our times yours will be recorded as the first of the African nationalism, and this tide of national consciousness which is now rising in Africa is a fact for which both you and we and the other nations of the Western world are ultimately responsible. For its causes are to be found in the achievements of Western civilisation, in the pushing forward of the frontiers of knowledge, in the applying of science to the service of human needs, in the expanding of food production, in the speeding and multiplying of the means of communication, and perhaps, above all, the spread of education.

As I have said, the growth of national consciousness in Africa is a political fact and we must accept it as such. That means, I would judge, that we must come to terms with it. I sincerely believe that if we cannot do so we may imperil the precarious balance between the East and West on which the peace of the world depends. The world to-day is divided into three main groups. First there are what we call the Western Powers. You in South Africa and we in Britain belong to this group, together with our friends and allies in other parts of the Commonwealth. In the United States and in Europe we call it the Free World. Secondly there are the Communists—Russia and her satellites in Europe and China whose population will rise by the end of the next ten years to the staggering total of 800 million. Thirdly, there are those parts of the world whose people are at present uncommitted either to Communism or to our Western ideas.

In this context we think first of Asia and then of Africa. As I see it the great issue in this second half of the Twentieth Century is whether the uncommitted peoples of Asia and Africa will swing to the East or to the West. Will they be drawn into the Communist camp? Or will the great experiments in self-government that are now being made in Asia and Africa, especially within the Commonwealth, prove so successful, and by their example so compelling, that the balance will come down in favour of freedom and order and justice?

The struggle is joined and it is a struggle for the minds of men. What is now on trial is much more than our military strength or our diplomatic and administrative skill. It is our way of life. The uncommitted nations want to see before they choose.

12–7b | Nikita Khrushchev, excerpts from address to the meeting of Communist Party organizations, Soviet Union, 1961

Nikita Khrushchev (1894–1971), General Secretary and Premier of the Soviet Union from 1953 to 1964, praised decolonization in Marxist terms, seeking to capitalize on the anti-imperialist wave inspired by independence movements around the world. He pledged support for any wars of liberation, associating the United States' efforts to thwart communism with the imperialist actions of the past. Below is an excerpt from a 1961 speech in which Khrushchev addressed wars of national liberation.

In modern conditions the following categories of wars should be distinguished: World wars, local wars, liberation wars, and popular uprisings. This is necessary to work out the correct tactics with regard to these wars.

Let us begin with the question of world wars. Communists are the most determined opponents of world wars, just as they are generally opponents of wars among states. These wars are needed only by imperialists to seize the territories of others, and to enslave and plunder other peoples....

Imperialists can unleash a war, but they must think hard about the consequences....

In conditions where a mighty socialist camp exists, possessing powerful armed forces, the peoples, by mobilization of all their forces for active struggle against the warmongering imperialist, can indisputably prevent war and this insure peaceful co-existence.

A word or two about local wars.... Certain imperialist circles, fearing that world war might end in the complete collapse of capitalism, are putting their money on un-leashing local wars.

There have been local wars and they may occur again in the future, but oppor-tunities for imperialists to unleash these wars too are becoming fewer and fewer. A small imperialist war, regardless of which imperialist begins it, may grow into a world thermonuclear rocket war. We must therefore combat both world wars and local wars.

. . .

Now a word about national liberation wars. The armed struggle by the Vietnamese people or the war of the Algerian people ... serve as examples of such wars. These wars began as an uprising by the colonial people against their oppressors ... Liberation wars will continue to exist as long as imperialism exists, as long as colonialism exists. These are revolutionary wars. Such wars are not only admissible but inevitable, since the colonialists do not grant independence voluntarily. Therefore, the peoples can attain their freedom and independence only by struggle, including armed struggle.

How is it that the US imperialists, while desirous of helping the French colonialists in every way, decided against direct intervention in the war in Vietnam? They did not intervene because they knew that if they did help France with armed forces, Vietnam would get relevant aid from China, the Soviet Union, and other Socialist countries, which could lead to a world war. . . .

At present, a similar war is taking place in Algeria. . . . It is the uprising of the Arab people in Algeria against the French colonizers. . . . The imperialists in the United States and Britain render assistance to their French allies with arms. . . .

The Algerian people, too, receive assistance from neighboring and other countries that sympathize with their peace-loving aspirations. But it is a liberation war of a people for its independence, it is a sacred war. We recognize such wars, we help and will help the peoples striving for their independence.

Or let us take the Cuban example. A war took place there too. But it also started as an uprising against the internal tyrannical regime supported by US imperialism. . . . However, the United States did not interfere in that war directly with its Armed Forces. The Cuban people, under the leadership of Fidel Castro, have won.

Can such wars flare up in the future? They can. Can there be such uprisings? There can. But these are wars which are national uprisings. . . . What is the attitude of the Marxists toward such uprisings? A most positive one. These uprisings must not be identified with wars among states, with local wars, since in these uprisings the people are fighting for implementation of their right for self-determination, for independent social and national development. These are uprisings against rotten reactionary regimes, against the colonizers. The Communists fully support such just wars and march in the front rank with the peoples waging liberation struggles.

DISCUSSION QUESTIONS

1   How do these two speeches demonstrate the connections between decolonization and the Cold War?

2   What opportunities might wars of independence have presented to both sides in the Cold War?

3   How did Macmillan and Khrushchev articulate the relationship of decolonization/independence movements to the West?

12–8a | Excerpts from the principles of the Bandung Conference, Indonesia, 1955

In 1955, twenty-nine newly independent states of Asia and Africa met in Bandung, Indonesia, to discuss issues common to postcolonial nations and find ways to collaborate with one another. These states self-identified as the Third World—neither part of the capitalist First World or communist Second World—with unique circumstances due to colonial legacies, economic underdevelopment, and their potential as pawns in the Cold War. Laying the foundation for the Non-Aligned Movement, the Bandung participants agreed on principles listed below.

G. Declaration on the Promotion of World Peace and Cooperation

The Asian-African Conference gave anxious thought to the question of world peace and cooperation. It viewed with deep concern the present state of international tension with its danger of an atomic world war. The Problem of peace is correlative with the problem of international security. In this connection, all States should cooperate, especially through the United Nations, in bringing about the reduction of armaments and the elimination of nuclear weapons under effective international control. In this way, international peace can be promoted and nuclear energy may be used exclusively for peaceful purposes. This would help answer the needs particularly of Asia and Africa, for what they urgently require are social progress and better standards of life in larger freedom. Freedom and peace are interdependent. The right of self determination must be enjoyed by all peoples, and freedom and independence must be granted, with the least possible delay, to those who are still dependent peoples. Indeed, all nations should have the right freely to choose their own political and economic systems and their own way of life, in conformity with the purposes and principles of the Charter of the United Nations.

Free from mistrust and fear, and with confidence and goodwill toward each other, nations should practise tolerance and live together in peace with one another as good neighbours and develop friendly cooperation on the basis of the following principles:

1. Respect for fundamental human rights and for the purposes and principles of the Charter of the United Nations.

2. Respect for the sovereignty and territorial integrity of all nations.

3. Recognition of the equality of all races and of the equality of all nations large and small.

4. Abstention from intervention or interference in the internal affairs of another country.

5. Respect for the right of each nation to defend itself singly or collectively, in conformity with the Charter of the United Nations.

6. (a) Abstention from the use of arrangements of collective defence to serve the particular interests of any of the big powers.

   (b) Abstention by any country from exerting pressures on other countries.

7. Refraining from acts or threats of aggression or the use of force against the territorial integrity or political independence of any country.

8. Settlement of all international disputes by peaceful means, such as negotiation, conciliation, arbitration or judicial settlement as well as other peaceful
means of the parties' own choice, in conformity with the Charter of the
United Nations.

9. Promotion of mutual interests and cooperation.

10. Respect for justice and international obligations.

The Asian-African Conference declared its conviction that friendly cooperation in
accordance with these principles would effectively contribute to the maintenance and
promotion of international peace and security, while cooperation in the economic, social and cultural fields would help bring about the common prosperity and well-being
of all.

The Asian-African Conference recommended that the five sponsoring countries
consider the convening of the next meeting of the Conference, in consultation with the
participating countries.

Bandung, 24th April, 1955

12–8b | Richard Wright, excerpts from *The Color Curtain: A Report on the Bandung Conference*, 1956

Civil rights advocate Richard Wright (1908–1960), acclaimed novelist of *Native Son* (1939), *Black Boy* (1945), and other works, traveled to Bandung, Indonesia, from his expat home in Paris as a freelance journalist to cover the conference there in 1955. Intrigued by the idea of black and brown peoples of the world charting their own course, he attended, interacted with Indonesian educated society in Jakarta and Bandung, and produced the first substantive account of the Bandung Conference's proceedings in *The Color Curtain: A Report on the Bandung Conference* (1956), an excerpt of which follows.

Nehru came in in his white Asian cap and the audience stirred. U Nu entered. Sir
John of Ceylon entered. Then Ali Sastroamidjojo, Prime Minister of Indonesia, and
the ideological father of the conference itself, entered, mounted the platform, and took
the chairman's seat. Then came Mohammad Ali, Prime Minister of Pakistan. . . . At last
Sukarno, President of the Republic of Indonesia, mounted the rostrum to deliver the
opening address. . . .

He was a small man, tan of face, and with a pair of dark, deep-set eyes; he moved
slowly, deliberately. He spoke in English with a slight accent; he knew words and how
to use them, and you realized at once that this man had done nothing all his life but
utilize words to capture the attention and loyalties of others. From the very outset, he

sounded the notes of race and religion, strong, defiant; before he had uttered more than a hundred syllables, he declared:

"This is the first international conference of colored peoples in the history of mankind!"

He then placed his finger upon the geographical gateway through which the white men of the West had come into Asia:

"Sisters and Brothers, how terrifically dynamic is our time! I recall that, several years ago, I had occasion to make a public analysis of colonialism, and I drew attention to what I called the 'life line of imperialism.' This line runs from the Strait of Gibraltar, through the Mediterranean, the Suez Canal, the Red Sea, the Indian Ocean, the South China Sea, and the Sea of Japan. For most of that enormous distance, the territories on both sides of this life line were colonies, the people were unfree, their futures mortgaged to an alien system. Along that life line, that main artery of imperialism, there was pumped the lifeblood of colonialism."

In the third paragraph of his address, Sukarno evoked in a solemn manner a reality that Western statesmen refer to only in times of war or dire stress; he paid tribute to the many sacrifices which had made the conference possible. Implied in his recognition of sacrifice was an acknowledgement that it had been only through men willingly surrendering their lives in the past that a bridge had been made to this present moment. He said:

"I recognize that we are gathered here today as a result of sacrifices. Sacrifices made by our forefathers and by the people of our own and younger generations. . . . Their struggle and sacrifice paved the way for this meeting of the highest representatives of independent and sovereign nations from two of the biggest continents of the globe."

For Sukarno and national revolutionaries of his stamp, the present meeting was not merely a lucky stroke of politics, but a gathering whose foundations had been laid long before. He put his finger on the date in modern history when the real struggle against colonialism had begun in earnest:

"I recall in this connection the Conference of the 'League Against Imperialism and Colonialism' which was held in Brussels almost thirty years ago. At that Conference many distinguished delegates who are present here today met each other and found new strength in their fight for independence."

It is hard for the Western world to realize how tenaciously these outsiders cling to and remember each link, each step in their life's struggles; to most of the delegates to whom Sukarno spoke, this meeting was the logical outcome of past sacrificial efforts. And why had they now come together? Sukarno said:

". . . we are living in a world of fear. The life of man today is corroded and made bitter by fear. Fear of the future, fear of the hydrogen bomb, fear of ideologies. Perhaps this fear is a greater danger than the danger itself, because it is fear which drives men to act foolishly, to act thoughtlessly, to act dangerously. . . . And do not think that the oceans and the seas will protect us. The food we eat, the water that we drink, yes, even the very air that we breathe can be contaminated by poisons originating from thousands of miles away. And it could be that, even if we ourselves escaped lightly, the unborn generations of our children would bear on their distorted bodies the marks of our failure to control the forces which have been released on the world."

What strength had Sukarno and Asian and African leaders like him? He was frank about it. He said:

"For many generations our peoples have been the voiceless ones in the world. We have been the unregarded, the people for whom decisions were made by others whose interests were paramount, the peoples who lived in poverty and humiliation. . . . What can we do? The peoples of Asia and Africa wield little physical power. Even our economic strength is dispersed and slight. We cannot indulge in power politics. . . . Our statesmen, by and large, are not backed up with serried ranks of jet bombers."

He then defined the strength of this gathering of the leaders of the poor and backward nations as:

"We, the peoples of Asia and Africa, 1,400,000,000 strong, far more than half of the population of the world, we can mobilize what I have called the *Moral Violence of Nations* in favor of peace. . . ."

And where was this moral violence coming from? . . .

"Religion is of dominating importance particularly in this part of the world. There are perhaps more religions here than in other regions of the globe. . . . Our countries were the birthplace of religions."

And what bound these diverse peoples together? Sukarno said:

"Almost all of us have ties to common experience, the experience of colonialism"

Sukarno was appealing to race and religions; they were the only realities in the lives of the men before him that he could appeal to. And, as I sat listening, I began to sense a deep and organic relation here in Bandung between race and religion, *two of the most powerful and irrational forces in human nature.* Sukarno was not evoking these twin demons; he was not trying to create them; he was trying to organize them. . . . The reality of race and religion was there, swollen, sensitive, turbulent. . . .

It was no accident that most of the delegates were deeply religious men representing governments and vast populations steeped in mystical visions of life. Asian and African populations had been subjugated on the assumption that they were in some way biologically inferior and unfit to govern themselves, and the white Western world that had shackled them had either given them a Christian religion or else had made them agonizingly conscious of their old, traditional religions to which they had had to cling under conditions of imperialist rule. Those of them who had been converted to Christianity had been taught of hope for a freedom and social justice which the white Western world had teasingly withheld. This, a racial consciousness, evoked by the attitudes and practices of the West, had slowly blended with a defensive religious feeling; here, in Bandung, the two had combined into one: *a racial and religious system of identification manifesting itself in an emotional nationalism which was now leaping state boundaries and melting and merging, one into the other.*

. . .

The results of the deliberations of the delegates at Bandung would be, of course, addressed to the people and the statesmen of the Western powers, for it was the moral notions—or lack of them—of those powers that were in question here; it had been against the dominance of those powers that these delegates and their populations had struggled so long. After two days of torrid public speaking and four days of discussions in closed sessions, the Asian-African Conference issued a communiqué. It was a sober document, brief and to the point; yet it did not hesitate to lash out, in terse legal prose, at racial injustice and colonial exploitation.

DISCUSSION QUESTIONS

1   During the Cold War, why would it be important to appeal to national sovereignty and cooperation in the Bandung principles?

2   According to Wright, what characteristics did the nations at Bandung share? How did he see those characteristics interacting?

3   How do these texts connect the repercussions of colonialism with the Cold War?

BIPOLAR CULTURE

12–9a | Film still, *Godzilla*, Japan, 1954

Released in 1954, the Japanese *kaiju* "strange beast" film *Godzilla* launched the world's longest movie franchise, a series that has contained thirty-five films. A product of the early Cold War, the original Godzilla was a 164-foot metaphor of Japanese anxiety in the nuclear age, embodying the fears of postwar Japan following the atomic bombings of Hiroshima and Nagasaki and ongoing nuclear weapon tests in the Pacific. Toho Studios sold the rights to the film to American distributors and a heavily edited and adapted 1956 U.S. version of the film, *Godzilla, King of the Monsters!*, was the Godzilla introduced to worldwide audiences.

12–9b | Tom Lehrer, lyrics, "Who's Next?" 1965

Thomas Andrew Lehrer (born 1928) is a retired American singer-songwriter, satirist, and mathematician. In the 1960s, he wrote and released scores of songs dealing with the social and political issues of the age. He performed the song below as the resident songwriter for the U.S. version of *That Was the Week That Was*, originally a British satirical television show. Lehrer released this song just a few weeks after the U.S. press reported that China had tested a nuclear bomb, making it the fifth country to possess nuclear weapons (U.S., Russia, UK, France, China) at the time.

First we got the bomb and that was good,
'Cause we love peace and motherhood.
Then Russia got the bomb, but that's O.K.,
'Cause the balance of power's maintained that way!
Who's next?

France got the bomb, but don't you grieve,
'Cause they're on our side, I believe.
China got the bomb, but have no fears;
They can't wipe us out for at least five years!
Who's next?

Then Indonesia claimed that they
Were gonna get one any day.
South Africa wants two, that's right:
One for the black and one for the white!
Who's next?

Egypt's gonna get one, too,
Just to use on you know who.
So Israel's getting tense,
Wants one in self defense.
"The Lord's our shepherd," says the psalm,
But just in case, we better get a bomb!
Who's next?

Luxembourg is next to go
And, who knows, maybe Monaco.
We'll try to stay serene and calm
When Alabama gets the bomb!
Who's next, who's next, who's next?
Who's next?

DISCUSSION QUESTIONS

1   How might we understand Godzilla as a product of the Cold War? What might explain his international appeal?

2   How did Lehrer's "Who's Next?" address issues concerning nuclear proliferation?

3   What do these documents tell us about the relationship between politics and pop culture?

12–10 | Declaration of principles from the counterculture movement Provo, Netherlands, 1965

The global counterculture movement of the mid-1960s was comprised of elements of youth disdainful of conformity, alienated by traditional politics, and disenchanted by war. While some chose to drop out of society entirely, others sought to provoke society out of complacency with the status quo by means of action. Provo, a Dutch anarchist counterculture movement, was one of the latter. They staged pranks and happenings designed to attract police attention and public sympathy. By 1966, most Provo happenings involved protests against the Vietnam War; by 1967, Provo dissolved itself, having gained too much respectability and approval to continue its nonconformist ways. The selection below is from Provo's initial declaration of principles in 1965.

PROVO is a monthly sheet for anarchists, provos, beatniks, pleiners, scissor-grinders, jailbirds, Simple Simon stylites, magicians, pacifists, potato-chip chaps, charlatans, philosophers, germ-carriers, grand masters of the queen's horse, happeners, vegetarians, syndicalists, Santa Clauses, kindergarten teachers, agitators, pyromaniacs, assistant assistants, scratchers and syphilitics, secret police, and other riff-raff.

PROVO has something against capitalism, communism, fascism, bureaucracy, militarism, professionalism, dogmatism, and authoritarianism.

PROVO has to choose between desperate resistance and submissive extinction.

PROVO calls for resistance wherever possible.

PROVO realizes that it will lose in the end, but it cannot pass up the chance to make at least one more heartfelt attempt to provoke society.

PROVO regards anarchism as the inspirational source of resistance.

PROVO wants to revive anarchism and teach it to the young.

DISCUSSION QUESTIONS

1   What were the aims of the Provo movement? What tools did they advocate using in pursuit of those objectives?

2   What are some examples of counterculture movements in the U.S. that you are familiar with?

3   What was driving the counterculture movement of the 1960s?

13

The Struggle for Equality

360 | Nonviolent Resistance

Civil Rights

Decolonization

Détente

NONVIOLENT RESISTANCE

The practice of nonviolent resistance—acts of goal-oriented protest, boycotts, civil disobedience, or noncooperation with a commitment to avoiding any kind of violence—has been used by various groups around the world for centuries. In the twentieth century, some of the most famous large-scale campaigns of nonviolent resistance occurred in colonial India, the United States, and South Africa. Mohandas K. Gandhi (1869–1948), leader of the Indian National Congress and arguably the inventor of modern nonviolent resistance, developed his tactics after reading widely, including the works of great Russian author Leo Tolstoy (1828–1910) who wrote extensively on nonviolent resistance. Tolstoy, in turn, was inspired by the writings of American Quakers and American Universalist minister-pacifist-abolitionist Adin Ballou (1803–1890), sponsoring translations of Ballou's work into Russian. Martin Luther King Jr., a minister and leading figure of the civil rights movement in the U.S. in the 1950s and 1960s, learned of Gandhi's methods while a college student, combined them with Christian theology, and made nonviolent resistance the *modus operandi* for many pursuing justice in the U.S., including the Student Nonviolent Coordinating Committee (SNCC). Nelson Mandela, a leader in the African National Congress and its decades of protest against apartheid policies in South Africa, declared his countrymen's movement inextricably connected to that of African Americans in the civil rights era—even though Mandela eventually argued for the necessity of violence in the ANC's fight for justice.

Adin Ballou's catechism of nonviolence, 1844

Q. Whence the term Non-resistance?

A. From the precept, "Resist not evil," Matt. 5:39.

Q. How is the term used?

A. To distinguish the sublime Christian virtue enjoined in the above precept, and the general cause of those who are engaged in urging its importance on the public attention. Such are called Non-resistants.

Q. Is the term Non-resistance to be taken in its most absolute sense, as implying no resistance of evil?

A. No. It must be understood in the precise sense of our Savior's injunction, "Resist not evil"; i.e. resist not injury with injury. Evil must be resisted by every and all righteous means, but never with evil.

Q. How does it appear that Christ meant to be understood—resist not injury with injury?

A. From the context. He says—"Ye have heard that it hath been said, An eye for an eye, and a tooth for a tooth; but I say unto you that ye resist not evil: but whosoever shall smite thee on thy right cheek, turn to him the other also. And if any man will sue thee at the law, and take away thy coat, let him have thy cloak also."

Q. To whom does he refer in the expression "it hath been said"?

A. To the Patriarchs and prophets whose sayings are contained in the Scriptures of the Old Testament, commonly cited by the Jews as "the law and prophets." (He declared he had not come "to destroy the law or the prophets, but to fulfill." That is, he had not come to subvert the essential divine righteousness inculcated in the Old Testament Scriptures, but to promote its perfect fulfillment in spirit and in truth. To effect this, he separated the wheat from the chaff, the divine from the human—the absolute requirements of God from the defective legislation of man intended to enforce those requirements. He aims at the great end by other means. Under their limited inspiration human wisdom found room for its own expedients. They sought the true end, but not by infallible means. He received the Spirit without measure and, correcting their defects, sought the same end by infallible means. His was the unalloyed wisdom of God. Theirs was an admixture of the divine and human. The divine wisdom was sufficient in them to reveal the great end, the essential righteousness to be aimed at, but not sufficient to preserve them from human fallibility as to the best means of attaining that end. Hence the necessity for Christ, and that more glorious Testament of which he is the Mediator. If Noah, Moses, and the prophets had been infallible, there had been no occasion for Christ, and if the first covenant had been faultless, there had been no occasion for the second. It was the glory of the former to predict, foreshadow, and prepare for the latter. And it is the glory of the latter to do away all the defects without impairing, by one jot or tittle, the essential divine excellence of the former.)

Q. To what sayings in particular does Christ refer?

A. To that class in which Noah, Moses, and the prophets authorize the infliction of personal injury on injurers, to punish and suppress evil doing.

Q. Will you quote some of them?

A. "Whoso sheddeth man's blood, by man shall his blood be shed." Gen. 9:6. "He that smiteth a man, so that he die, shall surely be put to death." "And if any mischief follow, then thou shalt give life for life, eye for eye, tooth for tooth, hand for hand, foot for foot, burning for burning, wound for wound, stripe for stripe." Exodus 21:12, 23–25. "He that killeth any man shall surely be put to death. . . . And if any man cause a blemish in his neighbor; as he hath caused a blemish in a man so shall it be done to him. Breach for breach, eye for eye, tooth for tooth." Levit. 21:17, 19, 20. "And the judges shall make diligent inquisition: and, behold, if the witness be a false witness, and hath testified falsely against his brother; then shall ye do unto him, as he had thought to have done unto his brother. . . . And thine eye shall not pity; but life shall go for life, eye for eye, tooth for tooth, hand for hand, foot for foot." Deut. 19: 18–21. These are the sayings referred to by Jesus. (They who murdered, or maimed, or tortured their fellow men did evil. To resist and suppress such evil, the evil doer should be punished with death, or maiming, or some kind of personal torment. Injury should be opposed with injury, murder with murder, torture with torture, evil with evil. So taught Noah, Moses, and the prophets. But Christ negatives all this—I say unto you "Resist not evil," resist not injury with injury, but rather suffer repeated injury from the evil doer. What had been allowed was forbidden, what they had authorized he prohibited, what they had said he unsaid. By understanding what kind of resistance they taught, we know precisely what non-resistance he teaches; for the latter revokes the former, neither more nor less.)

Q. Did the ancients allow both individual and judicial resistance of injury with injury?

A. Yes; and Jesus prohibits both. A Christian has not authority to take life, or inflict injury on injurious fellow man in any case whatsoever.

Q. Could he not kill or maim another in self-defense?

A. No.

Q. Could he not enter a complaint before a magistrate with a view to get his injurer punished?

A. No; for what he does through others he virtually does himself.

Q. Can he not fight in the army or navy of his country against foreign enemies, or against domestic insurrectionists?

A. Certainly not. He can take no part in war or military tactics. He cannot use deadly weapons. He cannot resist injury with injury, alone or in company, by himself or by others.

Q. Then how can he vote for, or appoint, or voluntarily assist the officers of any government, whose constitution obliges the infliction of personal injury by death or otherwise?

A. He cannot consistently do any of these things.

Q. Can he voluntarily contribute money to support a government sustained by military force, capital punishment, or the infliction of personal injuries?

A. No; unless the money were to go for some specific object in itself right, where both the end and the means were benevolent.

Q. Could he pay taxes to such a government?

A. Yes; he ought to do this non-resistingly. The tax is laid and levied by act of government, and demanded without regard to the will of individuals. It cannot be resisted without a final resort to injurious force. This the Christian cannot use; therefore he should submit his property at once to the forceful exaction of the powers that be.

Q. Then why not vote?

A. Voting is an act of government—and assumes all the responsibility of injurious compulsion. Tax paying is submission to compulsion assumed by others. Therefore taxpaying is non-resistance, and voting is the assumption of a power to aggress and resist by deadly force.

Q. Can there not be a government based on Christian principle, which should repudiate all injurious force?

A. Undoubtedly there can be, as soon as individuals combine to institute one. It is only for men to organize society on Christian principles. Then the divine law as expounded by Christ would become their fundamental law—to which all minor regulations must conform, or be declared unconstitutional.

Q. Could such a government use physical force in any case to restrain offenders?

A. It could use any uninjurious physical force, dictated by wisdom. It could confine persons, absolutely dangerous to be at large, in moral hospitals, under keepers capable of restraining them for their good, where they would be surrounded by all the influences necessary to keep them from mischief, and if possible reform them.

Q. Then why cannot individual non-resistants do the same in respect to insane and furious persons in their families and neighborhoods?

A. They can. If it would be right for fifty or fifty thousand of them to use uninjurious physical forces in certain cases, it would be right for a single individual to act on the same principle.

Q. Then Christ does not forbid moral resistance of evil, nor even uninjurious physical resistance of evil, but only resistance of evil with evil—injury with injury?

A. Doubtless his doctrine must be so understood.

Q. What is there then so absurd and unreasonable in the doctrine?

A. Sure enough, what is there? It is one of the most consistent and reasonable doctrines ever taught to mankind. It forbids them to resist evil by doing what will perpetuate and aggravate evil, in order that they may effectually remove the very root of it both from their own and their neighbor's bosom. (He who aggressively injures another fosters hatred, the root of all evil. To injure another because he had injured us, under pretense of suppressing evil, is to repeat the mischief both on him and ourselves: it is to reproduce, or at least nourish, the very same demon we affect to cast out. Satan cannot cast out Satan, nor wrong expurgate wrong, nor evil overcome evil. Therefore true non-resistance is the only effectual resistance of evil. It bruises the serpent's head. It kills out and puts an end to the injurious disposition.)

Q. The theory is unexceptionable, but is it practicable?

A. It is as practicable as any other absolute virtue enjoined in the law of God. Neither this nor any other can be faithfully adhered to under all circumstances, without self-denial, privation, suffering, and in extreme cases loss of life itself. But he who holds this mortal life dearer than duty is already dead to the only life worth possessing. Such an one, in seeking to save his life, loses it. The truth, however, is, that where non-resistance costs the sacrifice of one life, or of any one substantial good of life, its opposite costs thousands. Non-resistance preserves; Resistance destroys. It is incomparably safer to do right than wrong, to forbear than contend injuriously, even in respect to this present life.

Q. If all men were non-resistants, our world would indeed be a happy one. But while only a few act this part, what will become of them?

A. If there were only one, and all the rest should join to crucify him, would he not more gloriously die in the triumph of non-resistant love, praying for his enemies, than he could live wearing the crown of a Caesar, dripping with the blood of the slain? But whether one or one thousand in number, among civilized or savage fellow men, consistence non-resistants have less to fear from the hand of violence than those who trust to injurious forces. The robber, the assassin, the son of Belial, will be more likely to pass them over than they will armed resistants. They that take the sword perish with the sword; but they that seek peace by a friendly, uninjurious, forbearing, forgiving course of conduct, generally enjoy peace; or if they die, they die blessed. So if all were non-resistants, confessedly there would be none to harm or disturb. If the great majority were so, then they would administer a government of love and good will, even to the injurious—never resisting injury with injury—never using an injurious force. If a large majority were non-resistants, they would exert such an ameliorating moral influence on Society, that all extreme and cruel punishments would be discarded, and general peace made the policy of government. If in a small minority, demeaning themselves peaceably, they will seldom experience any thing worse than the contempt of the world; which, without being sensible of it, or grateful for it, will all the time be rendered wiser and better by their testimony. And if at the worst, any of them should be persecuted unto death, they will leave their principles effectually nourished by martyr blood, whilst in heaven their reward will be great. Peace be with them that seek peace, and all conquering love, the imperishable inheritance of every soul that bows willingly to the law of Christ, "resist not injury with injury."

Leo Tolstoy's "A Letter to a Hindu," Russia, 1908

All that exists is One. People only call this One by different names.~THE VEDAS.
God is love, and he that abideth in love abideth in God, and God abideth in him.~I JOHN iv. 16.
God is one whole; we are the parts.~EXPOSITION OF THE TEACHING OF THE VEDAS BY VIVEKANANDA.
. . .

V

Who am I? I am that which thou hast searched for since thy baby eyes gazed wonderingly upon the world, whose horizon hides this real life from thee. I am that which in thy heart thou hast prayed for, demanded as thy birthright, although thou hast not known what it was. I am that which has lain in thy soul for hundreds and thousands of years. Sometimes I lay in thee grieving because thou didst not recognize me; sometimes I raised my head, opened my eyes, and extended my arms calling thee either tenderly and quietly, or strenuously, demanding that thou shouldst rebel against the iron chains which bound thee to the earth.~KRISHNA.

So matters went on, and still go on, in the Christian world. But we might have hope that in the immense Brahman, Buddhist, and Confucian worlds this new scientific superstition would not establish itself, and that the Chinese, Japanese, and Hindus, once their eyes were opened to the religious fraud justifying violence, would advance directly to a recognition of the law of love inherent in humanity, and which had been so forcibly enunciated by the great Eastern teachers. But what has happened is that the scientific superstition replacing the religious one has been accepted and secured a stronger and stronger hold in the East.

In your periodical you set out as the basic principle which should guide the actions of your people the maxim that: "Resistance to aggression is not simply justifiable but imperative, nonresistance hurts both Altruism and Egotism."

Love is the only way to rescue humanity from all ills, and in it you too have the only method of saving your people from enslavement. In very ancient times love was proclaimed with special strength and clearness among your people to be the religious basis of human life. Love, and forcible resistance to evil-doers, involve such a mutual contradiction as to destroy utterly the whole sense and meaning of the conception of love. And what follows? With a light heart and in the twentieth century you, an adherent of a religious people, deny their law, feeling convinced of your scientific enlightenment and your right to do so, and you repeat (do not take this amiss) the amazing stupidity indoctrinated in you by the advocates of the use of violence—the enemies of truth, the servants first of theology and then of science—your European teachers.

You say that the English have enslaved your people and hold them in subjection because the latter have not resisted resolutely enough and have not met force by force.

But the case is just the opposite. If the English have enslaved the people of India it is just because the latter recognized, and still recognize, force as the fundamental principle of the social order. In accord with that principle they submitted to their little rajahs, and on their behalf struggled against one another, fought the Europeans, the English, and are now trying to fight with them again.

A commercial company enslaved a nation comprising two hundred millions. Tell this to a man free from superstition and he will fail to grasp what these words mean. What does it mean that thirty thousand men, not athletes but rather weak and ordinary people, have subdued two hundred million vigorous, clever, capable, and freedom-loving people? Do not the figures make it clear that it is not the English who have enslaved the Indians, but the Indians who have enslaved themselves?

When the Indians complain that the English have enslaved them it is as if drunkards complained that the spirit-dealers who have settled among them have enslaved them. You tell them that they might give up drinking, but they reply that they are so accustomed to it that they cannot abstain, and that they must have alcohol to keep up their energy. Is it not the same thing with the millions of people who submit to thousands' or even to hundreds, of others—of their own or other nations?

If the people of India are enslaved by violence it is only because they themselves live and have lived by violence, and do not recognize the eternal law of love inherent in humanity.

Pitiful and foolish is the man who seeks what he already has, and does not know that he has it. Yes, Pitiful and foolish is he who does not know the bliss of love which surrounds him and which I have given him.~KRISHNA.

As soon as men live entirely in accord with the law of love natural to their hearts and now revealed to them, which excludes all resistance by violence, and therefore hold aloof from all participation in violence—as soon as this happens, not only will hundreds be unable to enslave millions, but not even millions will be able to enslave a single individual. Do not resist the evil-doer and take no part in doing so, either in the violent deeds of the administration, in the law courts, the collection of taxes, or above all in soldiering, and no one in the world will be able to enslave you.

Gandhi, excerpt from *On Nonviolent Resistance*, India, 1916

There are two ways of countering injustice. One way is to smash the head of the man who perpetrates injustice and to get your own head smashed in the process. All strong people in the world adopt this course. Everywhere wars are fought and millions of people are killed. The consequence is not the progress of a nation but its decline. . . . Pride makes a victorious nation bad-tempered. It falls into luxurious ways of living. Then for a time, it may be conceded, peace prevails. But after a short while, it comes more and more to be realized that the seeds of war have not been destroyed but have become a thousand times more nourished and mighty. No country has ever become, or will ever become, happy through victory in war. A nation does not rise that way, it only falls further. In fact, what comes to it is defeat, not victory. And if, perchance, either our act or our purpose was ill-conceived, it brings disaster to both belligerents.

But through the other method of combating injustice, we alone suffer the consequences of our mistakes, and the other side is wholly spared. This other method is satyagraha. One who resorts to it does not have to break another's head; he may merely have his own head broken. He has to be prepared to die himself suffering all the pain. In opposing the atrocious laws of the Government of South Africa, it was this method that we adopted. We made it clear to the said Government that we would never bow to its outrageous laws. No clapping is possible without two hands to do it, and no quarrel without two persons to make it. Similarly, no State is possible without two entities [the rulers and the ruled]. You are our sovereign, our Government, only so long as we consider ourselves your subjects. When we are not subjects, you are not the sovereign either. So long as it is your endeavor to control us with justice and love, we will let you do so. But if you wish to strike at us from behind, we cannot permit it. Whatever you do in other matters, you will have to ask our opinion about the laws that concern us. If you make laws to keep us suppressed in a wrongful manner and without taking us into confidence, these laws will merely adorn the statute-books. We will never obey them. Award us for what punishment you like, we will put up with it. Send us to prison and we will live there as in a paradise. Ask us to mount the scaffold and we will do so laughing. Shower what sufferings you like upon us, we will calmly endure all and not hurt a hair of your body. We will gladly die and will not so much as touch you. But so long as there is yet life in these our bones, we will never comply with your arbitrary laws.

Photograph from the Salt March, India, 1930

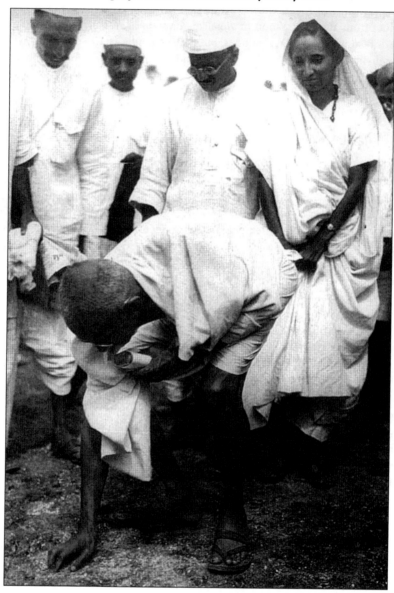

Student Nonviolent Coordinating Committee flyer, "Students Face Mississippi Violence for You!" 1961

STUDENTS face MISSISSIPPI VIOLENCE for YOU!

These high school students in McComb, Mississippi, are marching to the McComb Courthouse to protest the dismissal of a 15-year-old fellow student, Brenda Travis, who had requested service at the local Greyhound Bus Station lunch counter as an interstate traveler. 113 students were arrested the day this picture was taken, and nineteen (19) face trial on October 30. On Monday, October 16, 103 high school students were expelled from their school because they refused to cooperate with injustice and sign statements incriminating themselves.

SNCC student leaders who went to McComb to help local Negroes register to vote have been beaten, jailed, and threatened with death. Three SNCC staff members are currently conducting classes for the expelled students.

SNCC's program in McComb is only part of the expanded program of the Student Non-Violent Coordinating Committee, an independent, Southwide organization, representing stu-

dent protest groups. These young people have taken time out from school and careers because they will not compromise with principle. They know that no American can be truly free until all Americans are free—even in Mississippi.

These courageous young men and women are willing to face Mississippi violence for *you*. What will you do for them? Your contribution will help bring justice and democracy to Mississippi. Please let them know you care!

EXECUTIVE COMMITTEE

Ella Baker

Harry Belafonte

Constance Curry

Charles McDew, *Chairman*

Charles Jones, *Director, Voter Registration*

Robert Moses, *Asst. Director, Voter Registration*

Diane Nash, *Director, Direct Action*

James Bevel, *Asst. Director, Direct Action*

James Forman, *Executive Director*

SEND YOUR CONTRIBUTION TO: The Student Non-Violent Coordinating Committee 197½ Auburn Avenue, Atlanta, Georgia - Telephone 688-0331

A statement from Diane Nash on prison sentence and Mississippi courts, 1962

April 30, 1962
A MESSAGE
FROM: Diane Nash Bevel
TO: Individuals & Organizations Working for Civil Rights
I am surrendering today in Hinds County Court, Jackson, Miss., to serve the sentence imposed on me, on a charge of contributing to the delinquency of minors. This charge was filed last summer after I conducted workshops on the philosophy of nonviolence among Jackson youths, preparing them to go on Freedom Rides.

I have issued a brief statement to the press in which I attempt to explain my basic reason for taking this step. This statement says:

"I have decided to surrender myself, abandon further appeal, and serve my sentence of two years, plus as much additional time as it will take to work out my $2000 fine. To appeal further would necessitate my sitting through another trial in a Mississippi court, and I have reached the conclusion that I can no longer cooperate with the evil and unjust court system of this state. I subscribe to the philosophy of nonviolence; this is one of the basic tenets of nonviolence—that you refuse to cooperate with evil. The only condition under which I will leave jail will be if this unjust and untrue charges against me were completely dropped.

"Some people have asked me how I can do this when I am expecting my first child in September. I have searched my soul about this and considered it in prayer. I have reached the conclusion that in the long run this will be the best thing I can do for my child. This will be a black child born in Mississippi and this wherever he is born he will be in prison. I believe that if I go to jail now it may help hasten that day when my child and all children will be free—not only on the day of their birth but for all of their lives."

This is what I said to the press. To you who also are working in this effort for integration, I would like to say more.

I believe that the time has come, and is indeed long past, when each of us must make up his mind, when arrested on unjust charges, to serve his sentence and stop posting bonds. I believe that unless we do this our movement loses its power and will never succeed.

We in the nonviolent movement have been talking about jail without bail for two years or more. It is time for us to mean what we say.

We sit in, demonstrate and get beaten up. Yet when we are arrested we immediately post bond and put the matter entirely into the hands of the courts even though we know we won't get justice in these courts.

This is first of all immoral, because the Southern courts in which we are being tried are completely corrupt. We say this is a moral battle, but then we surrender the fight into the legal hands of corrupt courts. . . .

Nelson Mandela, excerpts from Rivonia Trial testimony, South Africa, 1964
From court transcript

I have already mentioned that I was one of the persons who helped to form Umkhonto. I, and the others who started the organisation, did so for two reasons. Firstly, we believed that as a result of Government policy, violence by the African people had become inevitable, and that unless responsible leadership was given to canalise and control the feelings of our people, there would be outbreaks of terrorism which would produce an intensity of bitterness and hostility between the various races of this country which is not produced even by war.

Secondly, we felt that without sabotage there would be no way open to the African people to succeed in their struggle against the principle of white supremacy. All lawful modes of expressing opposition to this principle had been closed by legislation, and we were placed in a position in which we had either to accept a permanent state of inferiority, or to defy the Government. We chose to defy the Government. We first broke the law in a way which avoided any recourse to violence; when this form was legislated against, and then the Government resorted to a show of force to crush opposition to its policies, only then did we decide to answer violence with violence.

But the violence which we chose to adopt was not terrorism. We who formed Umkhonto were all members of the African National Congress, and had behind us the ANC tradition of non-violence and negotiation as a means of solving political disputes. We believe that South Africa belonged to all the people who lived in it, and not to one group, be it black or white. We did not want an inter-racial war, and tried to avoid it to the last minute.

. . .

Our fight is against real and not imaginary hardships or, to use the language of the State Prosecutor, "so-called hardships." Basically, My Lord, we fight against two features which are the hallmarks of African life in South Africa and which are entrenched by legislation which we seek to have repealed. These features are poverty and lack of human dignity, and we do not need communists or so-called "agitators" to teach us about these things.

South Africa is the richest country in Africa, and could be one of the richest countries in the world. But it is a land of extremes and remarkable contrasts. The whites enjoy what may well be the highest standard of living in the world, whilst Africans live in poverty and misery. Forty per cent of the Africans live in hopelessly overcrowded and, in some cases, drought-stricken reserves, where soil erosion and the overworking of the soil makes it impossible for them to live properly off the land. Thirty per cent are labourers, labour tenants, and squatters on white farms and work and live under conditions similar to those of the serfs of the Middle Ages. The other thirty per cent live in towns where they have developed economic and social habits which bring them closer in many respects to white standards. Yet most Africans, even in this group, are impoverished by low incomes and high cost of living.

. . .

The complaint of Africans, however, is not only that they are poor and the whites are rich, but that the laws which are made by the whites are designed to preserve this situation.

There are two ways to break out of poverty. The first is by formal education, and the second is by the worker acquiring a greater skill at his work and thus higher wages. As far as Africans are concerned, both these avenues of advancement are deliberately curtailed by legislation.

I ask the Court to remember the present Government has always sought to hamper Africans in their search for education. One of their early acts, after coming into power, was to stop subsidies for African school feeding. Many African children who attended schools depended on this supplement to their diet. This was a cruel act.

There is compulsory education for all white children at virtually no cost to their parents, be they rich or poor. Similar facilities are not provided for the African children, though there are some who receive such assistance. African children, however, generally have to pay more for their schooling than whites.

. . .

The lack of human dignity experienced by Africans is the direct result of the policy of white supremacy. White supremacy implies black inferiority. Legislation designed to preserve white supremacy entrenches this notion.

From written remarks

Africans want to be paid a living wage. Africans want to perform work which they are capable of doing, and not work which the Government declares them to be capable [of]. Africans want to be allowed to live where they obtain work, and not be endorsed out of an area because they were not born there. Africans want to be allowed to own land in places where they work, and not to be obliged to live in rented houses which they can never call their own. Africans want to be part of the general population, and not confined to living in their own ghettoes. African men want to have their wives and children to live with them where they work, and not be forced into an unnatural existence in men's hostels. African women want to be with their menfolk and not be left permanently widowed in the Reserves. Africans want to be allowed out after eleven o'clock at night and not to be confined to their rooms like little children. Africans want to be allowed to travel in their own country and to seek work where they want to and not where the Labour Bureau tells them to. Africans want a just share in the whole of South Africa; they want security and a stake in society.

Above all, we want equal political rights, because without them our disabilities will be permanent. I know this sounds revolutionary to the whites in this country, because the majority of voters will be Africans. This makes the white man fear democracy.

But this fear cannot be allowed to stand in the way of the only solution which will guarantee racial harmony and freedom for all. It is not true that the enfranchisement of all will result in racial domination. Political division, based on colour, is entirely artificial and, when it disappears, so will the domination of one colour group by another. The ANC has spent half a century fighting against racialism. When it triumphs it will not change that policy.

This then is what the ANC is fighting. Their struggle is a truly national one. It is a struggle of the African people, inspired by their own suffering and their own experience. It is a struggle for the right to live.

During my lifetime I have dedicated myself to this struggle of the African people. I have fought against white domination, and I have fought against black domination. I have cherished the ideal of a democratic and free society in which all persons live together in harmony and with equal opportunities. It is an ideal which I hope to live for and to achieve. But if needs be, it is an ideal for which I am prepared to die.

360 DISCUSSION QUESTIONS

1   How do these sources argue for the efficacy of nonviolent resistance over the use of violence? Did they see limits to the approach?

2   How did the different cultural contexts shape concepts of nonviolent resistance?

3   How was the mid-twentieth-century popularization of nonviolent tactics a product of the period?

4   Can you name contemporary examples of the use of nonviolent resistance? In what ways might current popular expressions be different than the examples above?

CIVIL RIGHTS

13-1 | William O. Douglas, excerpt from his memoir on his trip to India, 1951

William O. Douglas (1898–1980), longtime U.S. Supreme Court Justice, spent the court recesses of 1949, 1950, and 1951 traveling through the Middle East and India. Upon his return, he wrote a book—briefly excerpted here—titled *Strange Lands and Friendly People* (1951). Aimed at a general audience, as were many of his books and articles, the book criticized U.S. and British foreign policy in the regions, arguing that Western policies were pushing states there into the arms of extremists. Douglas, who sat on the Supreme Court for thirty-six years, was known as a fierce, though idiosyncratic, civil libertarian and environmentalist, who spoke and wrote frequently on current events and foreign affairs.

This color consciousness is a major influence in domestic and foreign affairs. The treatment of colored peoples of other nations is an important consideration in the warmth of India's relations to the outside world. It is on the tongues of those who meet a new arrival. Thus the first question at my first press conference in New Delhi was, "Why does America tolerate the lynching of Negroes?" The attitude of the United States toward its colored minorities is a powerful factor in our relations with India. . . .

Security for the United States and the other democracies will be found not in the balance of armed might but in the balance of political power. We will be secure only when the bulk of the world is aligned on the democratic front. That is the reason for the tremendous urgency of a *political* rather than a *military* program in Asia.

Such a program to be successful must be geared to the hopes and aspirations of the masses of the people. Dollars and guns cannot build these alliances. Only faith and understanding and ideas that are liberal in their reach will create the conditions under which democratic influence will flourish. Neither wealth nor might will determine the outcome of the struggles in Asia. They will turn on emotional factors too subtle to measure. *Political alliances of an enduring nature will be built not on the power of guns or dollars, but on affection.* The ties that will hold the people of Asia close to each other and close to us will be of that character. We must work at that level, if we want to be partners in the exciting Asian history that is about to be written. We must, in other words, go to the East with warmth and understanding. The rewards will be bitter if we continue to go the other way. It is clear to one who travels the villages of Asia that if we continue to play the role we have played in the last five years, these people will become united in one great crusade—a crusade against America. Nothing would be more needless, nothing more tragic. Yet the anti-American attitude in Asia continues to mount—*for to Asians America is too powerful to cooperate with them and too rich to understand them.*

DISCUSSION QUESTIONS

1   What strategy did Douglas recommend that the U.S. pursue in its relationship with Asia (or the Third World)?

2   How did the views of Douglas align with U.S. actions in the Third World during this period?

3   Discuss the relationship between race relations in the U.S. and U.S. foreign policy.

13–2 | National Union of Ghana Students, letter of support to all jailed sit-in students in York County, SC, Ghana, 1961

The National Union of Ghana Students, founded in the 1930s as a youth group seeking an end to British colonialism, continued its work after Ghanaian independence was achieved in 1957. The Union, representing all students from kindergarten to postgraduate levels, still exists today and advocates for pupils' needs and rights. In 1961, the Union's Secretary for Foreign Affairs drafted this letter of support for the Friendship Nine, nine African American men—eight of whom were college students at Friendship Junior

College–sentenced to 30 days hard labor in jail for staging a sit-in at a segregated McCrory's lunch counter in Rock Hill, South Carolina. The Friendship Nine chose prison instead of paying a fine or posting bail, an approach imitated by many sit-in participants in subsequent protests across the South.

NATIONAL UNION OF GHANA STUDENTS

PRESIDENT	: J.K. FYNN	C/o 157, Queen's Hall
GEN, SECRETARY	: R.N.C. K-QUARSHIE	Kumasi College of Technology,
TREASURER	: MISS M. BLAY	Kumasi,
SEC. FOR INTER-		Ghana.
NATIONAL AFFAIRS	: P.D. VANDER PUIJE	

8th March, 1961.

Dear Friends,

Our hearts go out to you at this time, as you sit in jail for your very brave and selfless fight against color discrimination. We see in your gallant efforts to end racial discrimination in the United States, a bright future for humanity. It is heart-warming in these days of materialism to hear about people, like you, who are prepared to suffer indignity for the sake of establishing such high ideals as the common brotherhood of man.

We know that at such times it is difficult to keep up your spirits and we are aware that many people with less courage will try to make you believe that your effort is serving no useful purpose, but be sure that we, in this part of the world, are with you in spirit although seperated by land, sea and walls.

We sincerely hope that whatever hardships you endure at this time will not discourage you but that these might act as stepping stones to still higher ideals.

Remember the saying "It is darkest before dawn"

With our very best wishes,

Yours sincerely,

P.D. van der Puije
....
P. D. VANDER PUIJE
SECRETARY FOR
INTERNATIONAL AFFAIRS

TO ALL "SIT-IN" STUDENTS IN JAIL
YORK COUNTY JAIL,
YORK,
SOUTH CAROLINA,
U.S.A..

c.c. USNSA.
COSEC.

DISCUSSION QUESTIONS

1   Why might the National Union of Ghana Students express solidarity with civil rights protesters in the United States?

2   The U.S. civil rights movement is sometimes thought of as a domestic issue. How might this letter challenge that view?

13–3a | Robert Altman, photograph, members of Black Panther Party holding up Mao's *Little Red Book* at free Huey Newton rally, 1969

The Black Panther Party (1966–1982), originally the Black Panther Party for Self-Defense, began in Oakland, California, but expanded to include chapters in many major U.S. cities, in the UK, and Algeria. They began as groups of armed citizens monitoring police behavior and progressed to offer social programs, becoming increasingly engaged in political activities. Based on Marxist ideology, the group drew on the larger Black Power movement to argue for community control, economic empowerment, and unification for civil rights. While more mainstream elements of the civil rights movement had focused on the rural South, the Black Panthers worked in inner cities in the North and on the West Coast. Here, members of the BPP hold up copies of *Quotations from Chairman Mao Tse-tung*, commonly known internationally as the *Little Red Book*, a widely distributed and translated collection of statements and speeches by the leader of Communist China.

13–3b | Nguyễn Thị Định, National Liberation Front leader, letter to Black Panther Party, Vietnam, 1970

Madame Nguyễn Thị Định (1920–1992), first female general of the Vietnam People's Army during the Vietnam War, was deputy commander of the National Liberation Front (NLF), the force opposing the U.S. and Republic of South Vietnam. Below is her response to a letter the NLF received from Huey P. Newton, co-founder of the U.S.-based Black Panther Party. Newton's letter had offered Black Panther troops to assist the Vietnamese in "your fight against American imperialism" in the "spirit of revolutionary internationalism, solidarity and friendship."

To: Mr. Huey P. Newton
Minister of Defense
Black Panther Party
Dear Comrade:
We are deeply moved by your letter informing us that the Black Panther Party is intending to send to the National Liberation Front and the Provisional Revolutionary Government of the Republic of South Vietnam an undetermined number of troops, assisting us in our struggle against the U.S. imperialist aggressors.

This news was communicated to all the cadres and fighters of the PLAF in South Vietnam; and all of us are delighted to get more comrades-in-arms, so brave as you, on the very soil of the United States.

On behalf of the cadres and fighters of the SVN PLAF I would welcome your noble deed and convey to you our sincere thanks for your warm support to our struggle against U.S. aggression for national salvation. We consider it as a great contribution from your side, an important event of the peace and democratic movement in the United States giving us active support, a friendly gesture voicing your determination to fight side-by-side with the South Vietnamese people for the victory of the common cause of revolution.

In the spirit of international solidarity, you have put forward your responsibility towards history, towards the necessity of uniting actions, sharing joys and sorrows, participating in the struggle against U.S. imperialism.

You have highly appreciated the close relation between our both uncompromising struggles against U.S. imperialism, our common enemy. It is well known now that the U.S. government is the most warlike, not only oppresses and exploits the American people, especially the Black and the colored ones, but also oppresses and exploits various peoples the world over by all means, irrespective of morality and justice. They have the hunger of dollars and profits which they deprived by the most barbarous ways, including genocide, as they have acted for years in South Vietnam.

In the past years, your just struggle in the U.S. has stimulated us to strengthen unity, and rush forward toward bigger successes.

The U.S. imperialists, although driven by the South Vietnamese and Indochinese people in a defeated position, still have not given up their evil design, still seek to gain the military victories and to negotiate on the position of strength. On the SVN battlefields, they are actively realizing their policy of "Vietnamization" of the war with a view to maintaining the neocolonialism in South Vietnam and prolonging the partition of our country.

The very nature of the policy of "Vietnamization" is prolonging indefinitely the aggressive war at a degree ever so cruel and barbarous. While Nixon puts forward his "initiative for peace," in SVN the aggressive war got harder and harder; after the "urgent pacification" came the "Eagle campaign"; after that, by the "special pacification" in the countrysides and the "for the people" campaign in the towns, Nixon and the Thieu Ky Khiem clique have perpetrated innumerable barbarous crimes towards the people of all strata in SVN.

The five point proposal of Mr. Nixon, put forth on October 7th exposes more clearly his stubborn, perfidious and deceitful nature to U.S. and world opinion. It is clear that Nixon is unwilling to accept a peaceful settlement on the Vietnam problem, but tries to stick to South Vietnam as a neo-colony and U.S. military base, as well as to legalize the U.S. aggression in Indochina as a whole.

The U.S. government must seriously respond to the September 17th statement of the RSVN PRG, for it is the just basis, the reasonable and logical solution of the SVN problem. These are also the urgent aspirations of the whole Vietnamese people, of the progressive Americans and of those the world over who cherish peace, freedom and justice.

Dear Comrades, our struggle yet faces a lot of hardships, but we are determined to overcome all difficulties, unite with all progressive forces, to heighten our revolutionary vigilance, to persist in our struggle, resolutely to fight and win. We are sure to win complete victory.

So are our thinkings: At present, the struggles, right in the United States or on the SVN battlefields, are both making positive contributions for national liberation and safeguarding the world peace. Therefore, your persistent and ever-developing struggle is the most active support to our resistance against U.S. aggression for national salvation.

With profound gratitude, we take notice of your enthusiastic proposal; when necessary, we shall call for your volunteers to assist us.

We are firmly confident that your just cause will enjoy sympathy, warm and strong support of the people at home and abroad, and will win complete victory; and our ever closer coordinated struggle surely stop the bloody hands of the U.S. imperialists and surely contribute winning independence, freedom, democracy and genuine peace.

Best greetings for "unity, militancy, and victory" from the SVN people's liberation fighters.

NGUYEN THI DINH

Deputy Commander of the SVN People's Liberation Armed Forces, Republic of South Vietnam

DISCUSSION QUESTIONS

1   How could Black Panther Party members holding up a copy of the *Little Red Book* be perceived? Be sure to think about multiple viewpoints.

2   How did Nguyễn Thị Định respond to the Black Panther Party's offer of assistance?

3   In what ways are these documents revealing global connections between peoples that identified themselves as part of liberation movements?

13-4 | David Mosley, promotional poster, "The Rumble in the Jungle," Zaire, 1974

With one billion worldwide viewers, the boxing bout between favorite George Foreman and Muhammad Ali has been called "arguably the greatest sporting event of the twentieth century." Don King organized the fight through separate agreements signed by Foreman and Ali to fight if he could get them each a purse of $5 million. Zaire dictator Mobuto Sese Seko (1930–1997) agreed to host the fight, and Libyan dictator Muammar Gaddafi (ca. 1942–2011) came in as the spectacle's primary financial sponsor. Ali upset Foreman with an eighth-round knockout, becoming World Heavyweight Champion for the second time. It was the culmination of a long comeback for Ali, who was stripped of his first heavyweight title after his refusal to be drafted into the U.S. Army during the Vietnam War. David Mosley, the artist of the promotional poster below on the left, produced several iconic drawings of African American figures in the 1960s and 1970s.

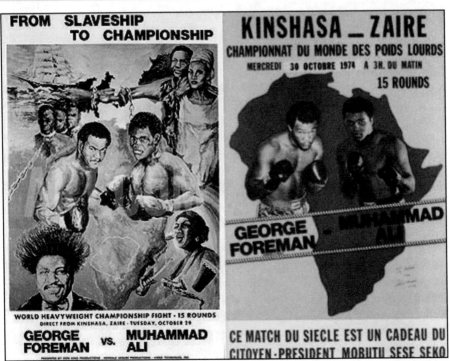

SEE COLOR INSERT

DISCUSSION QUESTIONS

1   Explain the messaging Mosley created in the poster. What symbols, language, and images did he use to accomplish this?

2   To what audience(s) was Mosley attempting to appeal?

3   What might this event tell us about the connection between sports and politics?

DECOLONIZATION

13–5 | Organization of Petroleum Exporting Countries, Statute, Venezuela, 1961

The result of over ten years of negotiation and deal-making between representatives of Venezuela, Iran, Saudi Arabia, Iraq, and Kuwait, the Organization of Petroleum Exporting Countries (OPEC) came into existence in 1960. These five countries founded the intergovernmental organization to counter global domination of oil prices by the seven large multinational oil companies known as "the Seven Sisters." They sought to restore control of natural resources to national groups and to coordinate supply and prices among the world's largest producers of oil. In an era of postwar decolonization and multinational capitalism, OPEC asserted the rights of oil producers over those of imperial powers or foreign petroleum companies. Adopted in 1961, their Statute lays out principles of governance and purpose in six chapters, two of which are excerpted below.

Chapter I. Organization and Objectives

Article 1

The Organization of the Petroleum Exporting Countries (OPEC), hereinafter referred to as "the Organization", created as a permanent intergovernmental organization in conformity with the Resolutions of the Conference of the Representatives of the Governments of Iran, Iraq, Kuwait, Saudi Arabia and Venezuela, held in Baghdad from September 10 to 14, 1960, shall carry out its functions in accordance with the provisions set forth hereunder.

Article 2

A. The principal aim of the Organization shall be the coordination and unification of the petroleum policies of Member Countries and the determination of the best means for safeguarding their interests, individually and collectively.

B. The Organization shall devise ways and means of ensuring the stabilization of prices in international crude oil markets with a view to eliminating harmful and unnecessary fluctuations.

C. Due regard shall be given at all times to the interests of the producing nations and to the necessity of securing a steady income to the producing countries; an efficient, economic and regular supply of petroleum to consuming nations; and a fair return on their capital to those investing in the petroleum industry.

Article 3
The Organization shall be guided by the principle of the sovereign equality of its Member Countries. Member Countries shall fulfill, in good faith, the obligations assumed by them in accordance with this Statute.

Article 4
If, as a result of the application of any decision of the Organization, sanctions are employed, directly or indirectly, by any interested company or companies against one or more Member Countries, no other Member shall accept any offer of a beneficial treatment, whether in the form of an increase in oil exports or in an improvement in prices, which may be made to it by such interested company or companies with the intention of discouraging the application of the decision of the Organization.

Article 5
The Organization shall have its headquarters at the place the Conference decides upon.

Article 6
English shall be the official language of the Organization.

Chapter II. Membership
Article 7
A. Founder Members of the Organization are those countries which were represented at the First Conference, held in Baghdad, and which signed the original agreement of the establishment of the Organization.

B. Full Members shall be the Founder Members as well as those countries whose application for membership has been accepted by the Conference.

C. Any other country with a substantial net export of crude petroleum, which has fundamentally similar interests to those of Member Countries, may become a Full Member of the Organization, if accepted by a majority of three-fourths of Full Members, including the concurrent vote of all Founder Members. . . .

DISCUSSION QUESTIONS
1   How did the Statute define OPEC member obligations, and what powers did the organization possess?
2   What was the message behind the creation of OPEC? Consider the context of decolonization.
3   What might it mean for some Third World countries that, by this period, industrialized states were dependent on fossil fuel?

13-6a | Frantz Fanon, excerpt from *The Wretched of the Earth*, Martinique, 1961

The ideas and writings of Frantz Fanon (1925–1961), a French West Indian psychiatrist, activist, and political thinker, have influenced dozens of national liberation movements and human rights organizers around the world. Born in Martinique and university-educated in France, Fanon experienced both colonial and mainland racism, eventually writing works detailing the psychological toll of colonialism on black people and joining the Algerian National Liberation Front in its war against its imperial ruler, France. Fanon wrote *The Wretched of the Earth* (1961) in the context of the Algerian War (1954–1962). In it, he defends the use of violence by those seeking independence.

National liberation, national renaissance, the restoration of nationhood to the people, commonwealth: whatever may be the headings used or the new formulas introduced, decolonization is always a violent phenomenon. At whatever level we study it—relationships between individuals, new names for sports clubs, the human admixture at cocktail parties, in the police, on the directing boards of national or private banks—decolonization is quite simply the replacing of a certain "species" of men by another "species" of men. Without any period of transition, there is a total, complete, and absolute substitution. It is true that we could equally well stress the rise of a new nation, the setting up of a new state, its diplomatic relations, and its economic and political trends. But we have precisely chosen to speak of that kind of *tabula rasa* which characterizes at the outset all decolonization. Its unusual importance is that it constitutes, from the very first day, the minimum demands of the colonized. To tell the truth, the proof of success lies in a whole social structure being changed from the bottom up. The extraordinary importance of this change is that it is willed, called for, demanded. The need for this change exists in its crude state, impetuous and compelling, in the consciousness and in the lives of the men and women who are colonized. But the I possibility of this change is equally experienced in the form of a terrifying future in the consciousness of another "species" of men and women: the colonizers.

Decolonization, which sets out to change the order of the world, is, obviously, a program of complete disorder. But it cannot come as a result of magical practices, nor of a natural shock, nor of a friendly understanding. Decolonization, as we know, is a historical process: that is to say that it cannot be understood, it cannot become intelligible nor clear to itself except in the exact measure that we can discern the movements which give it historical form and content. Decolonization is the meeting of two forces, opposed to each other by their very nature, which in fact owe their originality to that sort of substantification which results from and is nourished by the situation in the colonies. Their first encounter was marked by violence and their existence together—that is to say the exploitation of the native by the settler—was carried on by dint of a great array of bayonets and cannons. The settler and the native are old acquaintances. In fact, the settler is right when he speaks of knowing "them" well. For it is the settler who has brought the native into existence and who perpetuates his existence. The settler owes the fact of his very existence, that is to say, his property, to the colonial system.

Decolonization never takes place unnoticed, for it influences individuals and modifies them fundamentally. It transforms spectators crushed with their inessentiality into privileged actors, with the grandiose glare of history's floodlights upon them. It brings a natural rhythm into existence, introduced by new men, and with it a new language and a new humanity. Decolonization is the veritable creation of new men. But this creation owes nothing of its legitimacy to any supernatural power; the "thing" which has been colonized becomes man during the same process by which it frees itself.

In decolonization, there is therefore the need of a complete calling in question of the colonial situation. If we wish to describe it precisely, we might find it in the well-known words: "The last shall be first and the first last." Decolonization is the putting into practice of this sentence. That is why, if we try to describe it, all decolonization is successful.

The naked truth of decolonization evokes for us the searing bullets and bloodstained knives which emanate from it. For if the last shall be first, this will only come to pass after a murderous and decisive struggle between the two protagonists. That affirmed intention to place the last at the head of things, and to make them climb at a pace (too quickly, some say) the well-known steps which characterize an organized society, can only triumph if we use all means to turn the scale, including, of course, that of violence. . . .

The uprising of the new nation and the breaking down of colonial structures are the result of one of two causes: either of a violent struggle of the people in their own right, or of action on the part of surrounding colonized peoples which acts as a brake on the colonial regime in question.

A colonized people is not alone. In spite of all that colonialism can do, its frontiers remain open to new ideas and echoes from the world outside. It discovers that violence is in the atmosphere, that it here and there bursts out, and here and there sweeps away the colonial regime—that same violence which fulfills for the native a role that is not simply informatory, but also operative. . . .

We have seen that it takes the form of an armed and open struggle. There is no lack of historical examples: Indo-China, Indonesia, and of course North Africa. But what we must not lose sight of is that this struggle could have broken out anywhere, in Guinea as well as Somaliland, and moreover today it could break out in every place where colonialism means to stay on, in Angola, for example. The existence of an armed struggle shows that the people are decided to trust to violent methods only. He of whom *they* have never stopped saying that the only language he understands is that of force, decides to give utterance by force. In fact, as always, the settler has shown him the way he should take if he is to become free. The argument the native chooses has been furnished by the settler, and by an ironic turning of the tables it is the native who now affirms that the colonialist understands nothing but force. . . .

Not long ago Nazism transformed the whole of Europe into a veritable colony. The governments of the various European nations called for reparations and demanded the restitution in kind and money of the wealth which had been stolen from them: cultural treasures, pictures, sculptures, and stained glass have been given back to their owners.

There was only one slogan in the mouths of Europeans on the morrow of the 1945 V-day: "Germany must pay." Herr Adenauer, it must be said, at the opening of the Eichmann trial, and in the name of the German people, asked once more for forgiveness from the Jewish people. Herr Adenauer has renewed the promise of his people to go on paying to the state of Israel the enormous sums which are supposed to be compensation for the crimes of the Nazis.

In the same way we may say that the imperialist states would make a great mistake and commit an unspeakable injustice if they contented themselves with withdrawing from our soil the military cohorts, and the administrative and managerial services whose function it was to discover the wealth of the country, to extract it and to send it off to the mother countries. We are not blinded by the moral reparation of national independence; nor are we fed by it. The wealth of the imperial countries is our wealth too. On the universal plane this affirmation, you may be sure, should on no account be taken to signify that we feel ourselves affected by the creations of Western arts or techniques. For in a very concrete way Europe has stuffed herself inordinately with the gold and raw materials of the colonial countries: Latin America, China, and Africa. From all these continents, under whose eyes Europe today raises up her tower of opulence, there has flowed out for centuries toward that same Europe diamonds and oil, silk and cotton, wood and exotic products. Europe is literally the creation of the Third World. The wealth which smothers her is that which was stolen from the underdeveloped peoples. The ports of Holland, the docks of Bordeaux and Liverpool were specialized in the Negro slave trade, and owe their renown to millions of deported slaves. So when we hear the head of a European state declare with his hand on his heart that he must come to the aid of the poor underdeveloped peoples, we do not tremble with gratitude. Quite the contrary; we say to ourselves: "It's a just reparation which will be paid to us." Nor will we acquiesce in the help for underdeveloped countries before a program of "sisters of charity." This help should be the ratification of a double realization: the realization by the colonized peoples that *it is their due*, and the realization by the capitalist powers that in fact *they must pay.* . . .

13–6b | Wen Bing, poster, "Awakened Peoples You Will Surely Attain Ultimate Victory!" China, 1963

Like the Soviet Union (see chapter 12, item 7b), the People's Republic of China declared its support for independence movements in the era of decolonization. Asserting itself as a model for newly emerging states, China could call upon its own past experiences with Western imperialism to establish credibility among Third World societies. Using Cold War symbolism, this poster, designed by famed cartoonist and editor Wen Bing (1932–), personified parts of the world and describes them as "awakened" in their quest to throw off imperial rule.

觉醒了的人民，必将得到最后的胜利！

SEE COLOR INSERT

DISCUSSION QUESTIONS

1   Tactically and economically, how did Fanon characterize the relationship between the colonizers and the colonized? Why?

2   Who does each individual represent in the poster above? How are they characterized?

3   What was the role of violence according to these documents?

13–7a | John C. Dreier, diplomat, justifying United States intervention in Guatemala, 1954

John Caspar Dreier (1906–1994) was the U.S. Ambassador to the Organization of American States between 1951 and 1960. The OAS, founded in 1948, was created to promote regional solidarity and cooperation among independent states in the Americas. In 1954, the U.S. Central Intelligence Agency (CIA) launched a covert operation that deposed Guatemalan President Jacobo Árbenz, ending the Guatemalan Revolution (1944–1954). Árbenz ran afoul of the U.S.-based United Fruit Company (UFCO) after his 1951 election due to his implementation of land reform and a new labor code. UFCO, the largest Guatemalan landowner and employer, lobbied the Truman administration to intervene, indicating that Árbenz intended to align Guatemala with the USSR. With Árbenz out, Carlos Castillo Armas became the first in a series of U.S.-backed authoritarian rulers.

I speak today as the representative of one of 10 American countries who have joined in a request that a Meeting of Ministers of Foreign Affairs be convoked to act as Organ of Consultation under articles 6 and 11 of the Inter-American Treaty of Reciprocal Assistance. On behalf of the United States I wish to support this request with all the force and conviction that I can express, feeling profoundly as I and my countrymen do that this is a critical hour in which a strong and positive note of inter-American solidarity must be sounded.

The Republics of America are faced at this time with a serious threat to their peace and independence. Throughout the world the aggressive forces of Soviet Communist imperialism are exerting a relentless pressure upon all free nations. Since 1939, 15 once free nations have fallen prey to the forces directed by the Kremlin. Hundreds of millions of people in Europe and Asia have been pressed into the slavery of the Communist totalitarian state. Subversion, civil violence, and open warfare are the proven methods of this aggressive force in its ruthless striving for world domination. . . .

The first objectives of this new drive for domination were the countries of Eastern Europe and the Balkans. . . .

Communist forces then turned their attention to Asia. Following the fall of China came the stark aggression of the Korean war where once more the united forces of the free world, acting through the United Nations, stemmed the tide of Soviet Communist imperialism.

More recently, we have seen the combination of Communist subversion and political power, backed with weapons from the Communist arsenal, strike deep into Southeast Asia and threaten to engulf another populous area of the world as it emerges from colonialism.

And now comes the attack on America. . . .

There is no doubt, Mr. Chairman, that it is the declared policy of the American States that the establishment of a government dominated by the international Communist movement in America would constitute a grave danger to all our American Republics and that steps must be taken to prevent any such eventuality. . . .

I should like to affirm the fact that there is already abundant evidence that the international Communist movement has achieved an extensive penetration of the political institutions of one American State, namely the Republic of Guatemala, and now seeks to exploit that country for its own ends. This assertion, which my Government is prepared to support with convincing detail at the right time, is clearly warranted by the open opposition of the Guatemalan Government to any form of inter-American action that might check or restrain the progress of the international Communist movement in this continent; by the open association of that Government with the policies and objectives of the Soviet Union in international affairs; by the evidences of close collaboration of the authorities in Guatemala and authorities in Soviet-dominated states of Europe for the purpose of obtaining under secret and illegal arrangements the large shipment of arms which arrived on board the *M/S Alfhem* on May 15, 1954; by the efforts of Guatemala in the United Nations Security Council, in collaboration with the Soviet Union, to prevent the Organization of American States, the appropriate regional organization, from dealing with her recent allegations of aggression, and finally by the vigorous and sustained propaganda campaign of the Soviet press and radio, echoed by the international Communist propaganda machine throughout the world in support of Guatemalan action in the present crisis.

The recent outbreak of violence in Guatemala adds a further sense of urgency to the matter. We well know from experience in other areas into which the international Communist movement has penetrated the tragic proportions to which this inevitable violent conflict may ultimately extend. . . .

Within the last 24 hours it appears that there has been a change in the Government of Guatemala. It is not possible, however, in the opinion of my Government, to arrive at any considered judgment of how this change may affect the problem with which we are concerned. Under the circumstances, it would appear to be essential that we do not relax our efforts at this moment, but proceed with our plans in order to be ready for any eventuality. . . .

I should like to emphasize the fact that the object of our concern, and the force against which we must take defensive measures, is an alien, non-American force. It is the international Communist organization controlled in the Kremlin which has created the present danger. That it is rapidly making a victim of one American State increases our concern for that country and our determination to unite in a defense of all 21 of our American nations. We are confident that the international Communist movement holds no real appeal for the peoples of America and can only subdue them if allowed to pursue its violent and deceitful methods unchecked. Having read the tragic history of other nations seduced by Communist promises into a slavery from which they later could not escape, we wish to leave no stone unturned, no effort unexerted, to prevent the complete subordination of one of our member states to Soviet Communist imperialism. For when one state has fallen, history shows that another will soon come under attack.

13–7b | Juan José Arévalo, excerpt from *The Shark and the Sardines*, Guatemala, 1961

In 1945, Juan José Arévalo (1904–1990) became Guatemala's first democratically elected president. A philosophy professor, Arévalo rose to power in a popular uprising against U.S.-backed dictator Jorge Ubico at the start of the Guatemalan Revolution. Arévalo implemented moderate social reform, including a literacy campaign and an increase in the minimum wage. Despite twenty-five coup attempts, he remained in power until the end of his term, succeeded by the election of Jacobo Árbenz. Here, in comments addressed to the American public, Arévalo introduces his scathing work about U.S. domination of Latin America, *The Shark and the Sardines*.

In your hands you hold a controversial book—a book that speaks out against your State Department's dealings with peoples of Latin America during the Twentieth Century. In it there is intended no insult to, nor offense to, the United States as a nation. The future of your country is identified with the future of contemporary democracy. Neither does this book seek to cast blame on the North American people—who, like us, are victims of an imperialist policy of promoting business, multiplying markets and hoarding money.

Very different was the ideology of the men who first governed your country. It was as thirteen widely varying former colonies inspired by ideals of individual freedom, collective well-being, and national sovereignty that the United States came into existence in the world. Protestants, Catholics and Masons alike, those men of the Eighteenth Century were moved by an ardent sense of dignity that won for them and for their cause the sympathy and the admiration of the entire world. They recognized worth in all kinds of work, they welcomed to their shores foreigners of every origin, and when their crops and their homes were threatened, they defended their crops and their homes just as they defended the privacy of the individual conscience. They went to church with their heads held high and they founded colleges so that their children might advance along the road to self-improvement.

Moral values served as a motivating force in the days of the Independence. Those same values, confirmed by the civilian populace of the young republic, figured among the norms of government. The nation was characterized by its grandeur of spirit and indeed great were the military accomplishments and the thesis of the new law. Amazed, the world applauded.

But as the Twentieth Century was dawning, the White House adopted a different policy. To North America as a nation were transferred the know-how, sentiments and appetites of a financial genius named Rockefeller. Grandeur of spirit was replaced by greed.

The government descended to become simple entrepreneur for business and protector of illicit commercial profits. From then on, Accounting was the Science of Sciences. The logic, the *Novum Organon*. The new instrument of persuasion was the cannon. Now the United States had become different. It was neither a religious state nor a juridic state but, rather, a mercantile state—a gigantic mercantile society with all the apparatus of a great world power. The European juridic tradition was abandoned and North American morality was forgotten. The United States thenceforth was to be a Phoenician enterprise, a Carthaginian republic. Washington and Lincoln must have wept in shame in their graves.

The immediate victim was Latin America. To the North American millionaires converted into government, Latin America appeared an easy prey, a "big business." The inhabitants of this part of the world came to be looked upon as international *braceros*. The multiple-faceted exploitation was carried out with intelligence, with shrewdness, with the precision of clockwork, with "scientific" coldness, with harshness and with great arrogance. From the South the river of millions began to flow Northward and every year it increased.

The United States became great while progress in Latin America was brought to a halt. And when anything or anyone tried to interfere with the bankers or the companies, use was made of the Marines. Panama, 1903. Nicaragua, 1909. Mexico and Haiti, 1914. Santo Domingo, 1916. Along with the military apparatus, a new system of local "revolutions" was manipulated—financed by the White House or by Wall Street—which were now the same. This procedure continued right up to the international scandal of the assault on Guatemala in 1954, an assault directed by Mr. Foster Dulles, with the O.K. of Mr. Eisenhower who was your President at that time.

North American friends, this is history, true history, the briefest possible sketch of history.

We Latin-Americans, who, more than anybody else, suffered from this change in political philosophy and its consequences, could no longer be friends of the government of the United States. The friendship certainly could be re-established. But to do so, it would be necessary for the White House to alter its opinion of us and it would be necessary for conduct to change. We expect a new political treatment. We do not want to continue down this decline that takes us straight to colonial status, however it be disguised. Neither do we want to be republics of traders. Nor do we want to be African *factories*.

We Latin-Americans are struggling to prevent the businessman mentality from being confused with or merged into statesmanship. The North American example has been disastrous to us and has horrified us. We know that a government intimately linked to business and receiving favors from business loses its capacity to strive for the greatest possible happiness for the greatest number of its people. When businessmen are converted into governors, it is no longer possible to speak of social justice; and even the minimum and superficial "justice" of the common courts is corrupted.

In our resistance to the businessman mentality, we are still Spanish, stubbornly Spanish. Also, we have not left off being Catholic nor have we left off being romantic and we cannot conceive of private life without love nor of public life without chivalry nor of our children's education without enlightening ideals.

If you want to be our friends, you will have to accept us as we are. Do not attempt to remodel us after your image. Mechanical civilization, material progress, industrial techniques, fiduciary wealth, comfort, hobbies—all these figure in our programs of work and enjoyment of life. But, for us, the essence of human life does not lie in such things.

These lines, my North American friends, are meant to explain why I wrote the Fable of the Shark and the Sardines. This book was written with indignation—indignation wrapped from time to time in the silk of irony. It declares that international treaties are a farce when they are pacted between a Shark and a sardine. It denounces the Pan-American system of diplomacy—valuable instrument at the service of the Shark. It denounces the Pan-American idea of "allegiance to the hemisphere"—juridic device that will inevitably lead to the establishing of an empire from Pole to Pole. It denounces the relentless and immense siphoning-off of wealth from South to North. It denounces the existence of the terrible syndicate of millionaires, whose interests lie even outside the United States.

It denounces the subordination of the White House to this syndicate. It denounces the conversion of your military into vulgar policemen for the big syndicates. And for the purpose of analysis, it takes up the case of Nicaragua, compelled by the United States to sign (in 1914–1916) a treaty that goes against all written and all moral laws.

This book, friends of the North, has been read all over Latin America. Read it now, yourselves, and accept it as a voice of alarm addressed to the great North American people who are still unaware of how many crimes have been committed in their name.

Juan José Arévalo
Caracas, Venezuela, 1961

DISCUSSION QUESTIONS

1   What rationales did Dreier employ to argue for intervention in Guatemala?

2   In his "briefest possible sketch of history" of U.S.-Latin American relations, what elements did Arévalo choose to include? What did he omit?

3   How had capitalism created a foreign policy framework for U.S.-Latin American relations?

DÉTENTE

13–8a | Photograph, Nixon and Mao ping-pong paddles, 1971

After the communist victory in the Chinese Civil War and the subsequent establishment of the People's Republic of China (1949), the U.S. refused to recognize them, choosing instead to support Taiwan as the legitimate "China." This changed in 1971, when the PRC unexpectedly invited the U.S. ping-pong team to visit mainland China. President Richard Nixon (1913–1994) seized the opportunity to restart a broken relationship via "ping-pong diplomacy," sending envoys to arrange for a presidential visit to China and an American tour for the Chinese ping-pong team in 1972. While deteriorating relations between the Soviets and Chinese had created the possibility of a U.S.-China rapprochement, Nixon was the first U.S. leader to pursue it.

13–8b | Excerpts from the Shanghai Communiqué, China 1972

Arguably one of the most important post–World War II moments in U.S. foreign policy—or perhaps in global affairs—Nixon's visit to China in February 1972 marked a dramatic change in Sino-American relations, China's international position, and Soviet willingness to negotiate with the U.S. The visit was of such obvious significance that the welcome banquet for Nixon and his entourage in Beijing's Great Hall was televised for the American public. The night before Nixon left China, the two countries released a simultaneous statement on U.S.-Chinese agreements now called the Shanghai Communiqué, printed below in full. Of special note were statements on the status of Taiwan, the Vietnam War, Sino-U.S. trade, and cultural exchange.

President Richard Nixon of the United States of America visited the People's Republic of China at the invitation of Premier Chou En-lai of the People's Republic of China from February 21 to February 28, 1972. Accompanying the President were Mrs. Nixon, U.S. Secretary of State William Rogers, Assistant to the President Dr. Henry Kissinger, and other American officials.

President Nixon met with Chairman Mao Tse-tung of the Communist Party of China on February 21. The two leaders had a serious and frank exchange of views on Sino--U.S. relations and world affairs.

During the visit, extensive, earnest, and frank discussions were held between President Nixon and Premier Chou En-lai on the normalization of relations between the United States of America and the People's Republic of China, as well as on other matters of interest to both sides. In addition, Secretary of State William Rogers and Foreign Minister Chi P'eng-fei held talks in the same spirit.

President Nixon and his party visited Peking and viewed cultural, industrial and agricultural sites, and they also toured Hangchow and Shanghai where, continuing discussions with Chinese leaders, they viewed similar places of interest.

The leaders of the People's Republic of China and the United States of America found it beneficial to have this opportunity, after so many years without contact, to present candidly to one another their views on a variety of issues. They reviewed the international situation in which important changes and great upheavals are taking place and expounded their respective positions and attitudes.

The U.S. side stated: Peace in Asia and peace in the world requires efforts both to reduce immediate tensions and to eliminate the basic causes of conflict. The United States will work for a just and secure peace: just, because it fulfills the aspirations of peoples and nations for freedom and progress; secure, because it removes the danger of foreign aggression. The United States supports individual freedom and social progress for all the peoples of the world, free of outside pressure or intervention. The United States believes that the effort to reduce tensions is served by improving communication between countries that have different ideologies so as to lessen the risks of confrontation through accident, miscalculation or misunderstanding. Countries should treat each other with mutual respect and be willing to compete peacefully, letting performance be the ultimate judge. No country should claim infallibility and each country should be prepared to re-examine its own attitudes for the common good. The United States stressed that the peoples of Indochina should be allowed to determine their destiny without outside intervention; its constant primary objective has been a negotiated solution; the eight-point proposal put forward by the Republic of Vietnam and the United States on January 27, 1972 represents a basis for the attainment of that objective; in the absence of a negotiated settlement the United States envisages the ultimate withdrawal of all U.S. forces from the region consistent with the aim of self-determination for each country of Indochina. The United States will maintain its close ties with and support for the Republic of Korea; the United States will support efforts of the Republic of Korea to seek a relaxation of tension and increased communication in the Korean peninsula. The United States places the highest value on its friendly relations with Japan; it will continue to develop the existing close bonds. Consistent with the United Nations Security Council Resolution of December 21, 1971, the United States favors the continuation of the ceasefire between India and Pakistan and the withdrawal of all military forces to within their own territories and to their own sides of the ceasefire line in Jammu and Kashmir; the United States supports the right of the peoples of South

Asia to shape their own future in peace, free of military threat, and without having the area become the subject of great power rivalry.

The Chinese side stated: Wherever there is oppression, there is resistance. Countries want independence, nations want liberation and the people want revolution—this has become the irresistible trend of history. All nations, big or small, should be equal; big nations should not bully the small and strong nations should not bully the weak. China will never be a superpower and it opposes hegemony and power politics of any kind. The Chinese side stated that it firmly supports the struggles of all the oppressed people and nations for freedom and liberation and that the people of all countries have the right to choose their social systems according to their own wishes and the right to safeguard the independence, sovereignty and territorial integrity of their own countries and oppose foreign aggression, interference, control and subversion. All foreign troops should be withdrawn to their own countries.

The Chinese side expressed its firm support to the peoples of Vietnam, Laos, and Cambodia in their efforts for the attainment of their goal and its firm support to the seven-point proposal of the Provisional Revolutionary Government of the Republic of South Vietnam and the elaboration of February this year on the two key problems in the proposal, and to the Joint Declaration of the Summit Conference of the Indochinese Peoples. It firmly supports the eight-point program for the peaceful unification of Korea put forward by the Government of the Democratic People's Republic of Korea on April 12, 1971, and the stand for the abolition of the "U.N. Commission for the Unification and Rehabilitation of Korea." It firmly opposes the revival and outward expansion of Japanese militarism and firmly supports the Japanese people's desire to build an independent, democratic, peaceful and neutral Japan. It firmly maintains that India and Pakistan should, in accordance with the United Nations resolutions on the India-Pakistan question, immediately withdraw all their forces to their respective territories and to their own sides of the ceasefire line in Jammu and Kashmir and firmly supports the Pakistan Government and people in their struggle to preserve their independence and sovereignty and the people of Jammu and Kashmir in their struggle for the right of self-determination.

There are essential differences between China and the United States in their social systems and foreign policies. However, the two sides agreed that countries, regardless of their social systems, should conduct their relations on the principles of respect for the sovereignty and territorial integrity of all states, non-aggression against other states, non-interference in the internal affairs of other states, equality and mutual benefit, and peaceful coexistence. International disputes should be settled on this basis, without resorting to the use or threat of force. The United States and the People's Republic of China are prepared to apply these principles to their mutual relations.

With these principles of international relations in mind the two sides stated that:

—progress toward the normalization of relations between China and the United States is in the interests of all countries;

—both wish to reduce the danger of international military conflict;

—neither should seek hegemony in the Asia–Pacific region and each is opposed to efforts by any other country or group of countries to establish such hegemony; and

—neither is prepared to negotiate on behalf of any third party or to enter into agreements or understandings with the other directed at other states.

Both sides are of the view that it would be against the interests of the peoples of the world for any major country to collude with another against other countries, or for major countries to divide up the world into spheres of interest.

The two sides reviewed the long-standing serious disputes between China and the United States. The Chinese side reaffirmed its position: The Taiwan question is the crucial question obstructing the normalization of relations between China and the United States; the Government of the People's Republic of China is the sole legal government of China; Taiwan is a province of China which has long been returned to the motherland; the liberation of Taiwan is China's internal affair in which no other country has the right to interfere; and all U.S. forces and military installations must be withdrawn from Taiwan. The Chinese Government firmly opposes any activities which aim at the creation of "one China, one Taiwan," "one China, two governments," "two Chinas," and "independent Taiwan" or advocate that "the status of Taiwan remains to be determined."

The U.S. side declared: The United States acknowledges that all Chinese on either side of the Taiwan Strait maintain there is but one China and that Taiwan is a part of China. The United States Government does not challenge that position. It reaffirms its interest in a peaceful settlement of the Taiwan question by the Chinese themselves. With this prospect in mind, it affirms the ultimate objective of the withdrawal of all U.S. forces and military installations from Taiwan. In the meantime, it will progressively reduce its forces and military installations on Taiwan as the tension in the area diminishes.

The two sides agreed that it is desirable to broaden the understanding between the two peoples. To this end, they discussed specific areas in such fields as science, technology, culture, sports and journalism, in which people-to-people contacts and exchanges would be mutually beneficial. Each side undertakes to facilitate the further development of such contacts and exchanges.

Both sides view bilateral trade as another area from which mutual benefit can be derived, and agreed that economic relations based on equality and mutual benefit are in the interest of the people of the two countries. They agree to facilitate the progressive development of trade between their two countries.

The two sides agreed that they will stay in contact through various channels, including the sending of a senior U.S. representative to Peking from time to time for concrete consultations to further the normalization of relations between the two countries and continue to exchange views on issues of common interest.

The two sides expressed the hope that the gains achieved during this visit would open up new prospects for the relations between the two countries. They believe that the normalization of relations between the two countries is not only in the interest of the Chinese and American peoples but also contributes to the relaxation of tension in Asia and the world.

President Nixon, Mrs. Nixon and the American party expressed their appreciation for the gracious hospitality shown them by the Government and people of the People's Republic of China.

DISCUSSION QUESTIONS

1   In what ways could ping-pong be the vehicle through which China and the U.S. established a relationship?

2   What did the U.S. agree to in the Communiqué? What did the PRC agree to in the Communiqué?

3   What might be the ramifications of this newly established relationship?

13–9a | Jimmy Carter, address to the United Nations, 1977

James "Jimmy" Carter (born 1924), President of the United States from 1977 to 1981, worked to reorient the nation's foreign policy toward the issues of human rights, democratic values, arms limitations, and global poverty. Carter held that previous presidential administrations had erred in allowing Cold War concerns and realpolitik to dominate U.S. engagement with the world. Below, in excerpts from his address to the United Nations General Assembly early in his presidency, Carter casts a plan for these new priorities.

It's now eight weeks since I became President. I have brought to office a firm commitment to a more open foreign policy. And I believe that the American people expect me to speak frankly about the policies that we intend to pursue, and it is in that spirit that I speak to you tonight about our own hopes for the future.

I see a hopeful world, a world dominated by increasing demands for basic freedoms, for fundamental rights, for higher standards of human existence. We are eager to take part in the shaping of that world.

But in seeking such a better world, we are not blind to the reality of disagreement, nor to the persisting dangers that confront us all. Every headline reminds us of bitter divisions, of national hostilities, of territorial conflicts, of ideological competition.

In the Middle East, peace is a quarter century overdue. A gathering racial conflict threatens southern Africa, new tensions are rising in the Horn of Africa; disputes in the eastern Mediterranean remain to be resolved.

Perhaps even more ominous is the staggering arms race. The Soviet Union and the United States have accumulated thousands of nuclear weapons. Our two nations now have five times more many missile warheads today than we had just 8 years ago. But we are not five times more secure. On the contrary, the arms race has only increased the risk of conflict.

We can only improve this world if we are realistic about its complexities. The disagreements we face are deeply rooted, and they often raise difficult philosophical as well as territorial issues. They will not be solved easily. They will not be solved quickly. The arms race is now embedded in the very fabric of international affairs and can only be contained with the greatest difficulty. Poverty and inequality are of such monumental scope that it will take decades of deliberate and determined effort even to improve the situation substantially.

I stress these dangers and these difficulties because I want all of us to dedicate ourselves to a prolonged and persistent effort designed first to maintain peace and to reduce the arms race; second, to build a better and more cooperative international economic system; and third, to work with potential adversaries as well as our close friends to advance the cause of human rights. . . .

The search for peace and justice also means respect for human dignity. All the signatories of the U.N. Charter have pledged themselves to observe and to respect basic human rights. Thus, no member of the United Nations can claim that mistreatment of its citizens is solely its own business. Equally, no member can avoid its responsibilities to review and to speak when torture or unwarranted deprivation occurs in any part of the world.

The basic thrust of human affairs points toward a more universal demand for fundamental human rights. The United States has a historical birthright to be associated with this process.

We in the United States accept this responsibility in the fullest and the most constructive sense. Ours is a commitment, and not just a political posture. I know . . . that our own ideals in the area of human rights have not always been attained in the United States, but the American people have an abiding commitment to the full realization of these ideals. And we are determined, therefore, to deal with our deficiencies quickly and openly. We have nothing to conceal. . . .

The United Nations is the global forum dedicated to the peace and well-being of every individual—no matter how weak, no matter how poor. But we have allowed its human rights machinery to be ignored and sometimes politicized. There is much that can be done to strengthen it . . .

Strengthened international machinery will help us to close the gap between promise and performance in protecting human rights. When gross or widespread violation takes place—contrary to international commitments—it is of concern to all. The solemn commitments of the United Nations Charter, of the United Nations Universal Declaration for Human Rights, of the Helsinki Accords, and of many other international instruments must be taken just as seriously as commercial or security agreements. . . .

These then are our basic priorities as we work with other members to strengthen and improve the United Nations.

First, we will strive for peace in the troubled areas of the world; second, we will aggressively seek to control the weaponry of war; third, we will promote a new system of international economic progress and cooperation; and fourth, we will be steadfast in our dedication to the dignity and well-being of people throughout the world. . . .

13–9b | Fritz Behrendt, political cartoon, Camp David Accords, Netherlands, 1978

Fritz Behrendt (1925–2008), a German-Dutch political cartoonist, sketched this interpretation of Carter's accomplishment in brokering the Camp David Accords. Through twelve days of secret negotiations in September 1978, the U.S. hosted meetings of Egyptian President Anwar Sadat and Israeli Prime Minister Menachem Begin that led to two signed agreements, "A Framework for Peace in the Middle East" and "A Framework for the Conclusion of a Peace Treaty between Egypt and Israel." The first outlined a process for Palestinian self-government in Gaza and the West Bank, and the second led to the 1979 Egypt-Israel Peace Treaty. The latter made Egypt the first Arab state to officially recognize Israel. Although much of the Arab world, especially Palestinians, reacted harshly to the agreements, Sadat and Begin shared the 1978 Nobel Peace Prize.

DISCUSSION QUESTIONS

1. How did Carter justify this shift in U.S. foreign policy?

2. What are the tensions evident in the Behrendt cartoon? What forces may have worked against this solution?

3. How did Carter's efforts at Camp David reflect both the opportunities and the challenges of this turn in U.S. foreign policy?

13-10a | Photograph, "The Blue Marble," space, 1972

Taken by the crew of U.S. Apollo 17 approximately 18,000 miles from the surface, this photograph captured the earth from the Mediterranean Sea to Antarctica. With the sun behind the capsule, the image offered a fully illuminated view of the planet from this final mission of NASA's Apollo program, which also represented the last manned mission to the moon. Images such as this contributed to what is known as the "overview effect," the effect of seeing the reality of the Earth in space, in full and free from national boundaries. Apollo 11 astronaut Michael Collins had previously described the power of seeing the planet from this perspective: "it's tiny, it's shiny, it's beautiful, it's home, and it's fragile."

SEE COLOR INSERT

13-10b | James B. Irwin, Apollo 15 astronaut, quote, 1973

James "Jim" Irwin (1930–1991) was the lunar module pilot on Apollo 15 and the eighth person to walk on the moon.

Since I've been back on earth, I feel at home. No matter where I am on earth, I feel completely at home, relaxed. I do not feel foreign, I do not feel alien. I have visited a great many countries around the earth since my return, and I look forward to visiting many more. The experience has literally made me feel a close kinship with everyone. When you see the earth from the perspective of space, you don't see any evidence of the existence of man at all. The human problems do not seem overwhelming, they seem insignificant, puny. All you see is the beauty of the land and the water.

13–10c | Photograph, the Apollo-Soyuz Test Project patch, space, 1975

An important symbol of the détente, or the easing of strained relations, between the U.S. and the USSR in the 1970s, the Apollo–Soyuz Test Project was the first joint U.S.-Soviet space flight. It included shared and separate scientific experiments, but, most importantly, the event marked the end of the highly competitive Space Race between the USSR and U.S. that began with the Soviet launch of Sputnik 1 in 1957.

SEE COLOR INSERT

DISCUSSION QUESTIONS

1   Consider the Blue Marble image. What are your thoughts and feelings upon seeing the Earth from this perspective?

2   How might encountering space shift our notion(s) of humanity?

14

The United States in the World

REVOLUTIONS OF 1989

The end of the twentieth century seemed to signal the worldwide triumph of liberal democracy. The initiation of reform in and eventual collapse of the Soviet Union in the 1980s marked a sociopolitical shift that had repercussions around the globe, most obviously in Eastern Europe, where communist governments—and the Berlin Wall—fell in the autumn of 1989. Though many of these events seemed sudden, even surprising, most democratic movements in totalitarian or authoritarian states had existed for some time. The end of the Cold War acted as a catalyst, creating opportunities and galvanizing mass support for change.

Loosening of restrictions on public discussion in the Soviet Union, or *glasnost*, opened the door for a peaceful protest against the illegal manner in which the USSR claimed the Baltic states in 1939. On August 23, 1989, over two million people held hands across Estonia, Lithuania, and Latvia, challenging the political and moral legitimacy of Soviet rule. Several months earlier, Chinese university students frustrated with corruption, economic inequalities, and limited political voice, launched public protests at Tiananmen Square in Beijing, ultimately squashed by the government on June 4. With the Cold War's end, authoritarian or dictatorial regimes that had enjoyed U.S. support simply because of an anti-communist agenda came under fire with renewed enthusiasm. Examples include the Justice for Aquino, Justice for All (JAJA) Movement in the Philippines, begun in the early 1980s, and the Sebastián Acevedo Movement Against Torture in Chile of the late 1980s, part of a long-term effort opposing the Pinochet regime (1973–1990).

"Hunger strike announcement," China, 1989

In this bright sunny month of May, we are on a hunger strike. In this best moment of our youth, we have no choice but to leave behind us everything beautiful about life. But how reluctant, how unwilling we are!

However, the country has come to this juncture: rampant inflation; widespread illegal business dealings by corrupt officials; the dominance of abusive power; the corruption of bureaucrats; the fleeing of a large number of good people to other countries; and the deterioration of law and order. Compatriots and all fellow countrymen with a conscience, at this critical moment of life and death of our people, please listen to our voice:

This country is our country,

The people are our people.

The government is our government.

Who will shout if we don't?

Who will act if we don't?

Although our shoulders are still tender, although death for us is still seemingly too harsh to bear, we have to part with life. When history demands us to do so, we have no choice but to die.

Our national sentiment at its purest and our loyalty at its best are labeled as "chaotic disturbance"; as "with an ulterior motive"; and as "manipulated by a small gang."

We request all honorable Chinese, every worker, peasant, soldier, ordinary citizen, intellectual, and renowned individuals, government officials, police and those who fabricated our crimes to put their hands over their hearts and examine their conscience: what crime have we committed? Are we creating chaotic disturbances? We walk out of classrooms, we march, we hunger strike, we hide. Yet our feelings are betrayed time after time. We bear the suffering of hunger to pursue the truth, and all we get is the beatings of the police. When we kneel down to beg for democracy, we are being ignored. Our request for dialogue on equal terms is met with delay after delay. Our student leaders encounter personal dangers.

What do we do?

Democracy is the most noble meaning of life; freedom is a basic human right. But the price of democracy and freedom is our life. Can the Chinese people be proud of this?

We have no other alternative but to hunger strike. We have to strike.

It is with the spirit of death that we fight for life.

But we are still children, we are still children! Mother China, please take a hard look at your children. Hunger is ruthlessly destroying their youth. Are you really not touched when death is approaching them?

We do not want to die. In fact, we wish to continue to live comfortably because we are in the prime years of our lives. We do not wish to die; we want to be able to study properly. Our homeland is so poor. It seems irresponsible of us to desert our homeland to die. Death is definitely not our pursuit. But if the death of a single person or a number of persons would enable a larger number of people to live better, or if the death can make our homeland stronger and more prosperous, then we have no right to drag on an ignoble existence.

When we are suffering from hunger, moms and dads, please don't be sad. When we bid farewell to life, uncles and aunts, please don't be heart-broken. Our only hope is that the Chinese people will live better. We have only one request: please don't forget that we are definitely not after death. Democracy is not the private matter of a few individuals, and the enterprise of building democracy is definitely not to be accomplished in a single generation.

It is through death that we await a far-reaching and perpetual echo by others.

When a person is about to die, he speaks from his heart. When a horse is about to die, its cries are sad.

Farewell comrades, take care, the same loyalty and faith bind the living and the dead.

Farewell loved ones, take care. I don't want to leave you, but I have to part with life.

Farewell moms and dads, please forgive us. Your children cannot have loyalty to our country and filial piety to you at the same time.

Farewell fellow countrymen, please permit us to repay our country in the only way left to us. The pledge that is delivered by death will one day clear the sky of our republic.

The reasons of our hunger strike are: first, to protest the cold and apathetic attitude of our government towards the students' strike; second, to protest the delay of our higher learning; and third, to protest the government's continuous distortions in its reporting of this patriotic and democratic movement of students, and their labeling it as "chaotic disturbance."

The demands from the hunger strikers are: first, on equal basis, the government should immediately conduct concrete and substantial dialogues with the delegation of Beijing institutes of higher learning. Second, the government should give this movement a correct name, fair and unbiased assessment, and should affirm that this is a patriotic and democratic students' movement.

The date for the hunger strike is 2:00 P.M., May 13; location, Tiananmen Square.

This is not a chaotic disturbance. Its name should be immediately rectified. Immediate dialogue! No more delays! Hunger strike for the people! We have no choice. We appeal to world opinion to support us. We appeal to all democratic forces to support us.

Image of Baltic Way, Estonia, 1989

Justice for Aquino, Justice for All Movement, Philippines, 1989

Beginnings

"JAJA" is the acronym of the Justice for Aquino, Justice for All Movement. It was launched on August 25, 1983, by organizations advocating the abolition of the Presidential Commitment Order (PCO). When Ninoy Aquino was assassinated, they realized that eliminating the PCO was not enough. They decided to enlarge their cause by creating JAJA. JAJA is growing rapidly: more and more organizations affiliated with it and chapters are being formed throughout the country. As of October 15, less than two (2) months after its creation, JAJA had nearly ninety chapters and member organizations.

JAJA is non-partisan and multi-sectoral. It is an organization of organizations, not of individuals. Its members include civic, business, professional, cultural, farmers', workers', and students' organizations and other action groups devoted to public, religious and humanitarian causes.

Credo

- The Philippines is for Filipinos, not for foreigners. For all Filipinos, not just a few. For all generations of Filipinos, not just the present generation. This can only be achieved through justice, freedom, democracy, and sovereignty.
- As long as the present regime is in power, receiving continuous U.S. military, political, and economic support, genuine freedom and democracy cannot be attained. We have no quarrel with the American people but we oppose the policies of the U.S. Government with respect to the Filipinos.
- Only a united, organized, determined, and militant Filipino people can actualize their hopes and aspirations.
- True democracy requires the active participation and representation in the government of all social sectors and classes.
- Militant, vigilant action based on truth is necessary to attain our people's quest for justice, freedom, democracy and sovereignty.

Objectives

- We demand the immediate resignation of President Marcos, the entire Cabinet, the Executive Committee, members of Batasang Pambansa, and top generals of the military. A responsible transition government composed of men and women of unquestionable integrity should be established to pave the way for the realization of genuine democracy in this country.
- We demand the immediate restoration of the *Writ of Habeas Corpus* throughout the country, the immediate release of all political prisoners, and the grant of unconditional amnesty to all political dissenters and dissidents.
- We demand a fair, open, independent and impartial investigation of the assassination of Ninoy Aquino.
- We demand the complete restoration of freedom of speech, the press, of peaceful assembly, and all other constitutional rights and civil liberties.

- We demand a stop to U.S. or to any other foreign intervention in Philippine affairs.
- We demand an end to the militarization of our society and to repression and terrorism.
- We demand the restoration of the independence and integrity of the judiciary.

Programs

JAJA supports massive multi-sectoral education and information campaigns through:

- Rallies and assemblies, fora, symposia in schools, factories, offices, districts, and neighborhood communities.
- Mass demonstrations, marches, picketing, boycotts, and all forms of militant protests.
- Other forms of concerted actions such as prayer rallies, protest runs, wearing or displaying of protest symbols such as pins, stickers, posters, streamers, and other paraphernalia.
- Organization of JAJA chapters representing all social sectors and classes

Officers

CHAIRMAN—Sen. Lorenzo M. Tañada
SECRETARY GENERAL—Fr. Art R. Balagat
SPOKESPERSONS—Dr. Mita Pardo de Tavera, Sr. Christine Tan

Non-Partisan Nature

JAJA is not a political party. JAJA does not intend to take part in partisan activities. But its members are free to join any political party or movement provided they do so in their individual capacity and do not use the name of JAJA.

Song and chant from Sebastián Acevedo Movement Against Torture, Chile, 1983

I Call You Freedom (Song)

Everyone sings:

For the caged bird
for the fish in the fishbowl
for my friend who's in prison
because he has said what he thinks
for the uprooted flowers
for the trampled grass
for the stripped trees
for the tortured bodies,
I call you freedom.

For the persecuted idea
for the blows received
for the person who doesn't resist

for those in hiding
for the fear they have of you
for the traces of you they monitor
for the way they attack you
for the sons that kill you,
I call you freedom.

I call you in the name of all
by your true name
I call you when it gets dark,
when no one sees me.

I write your name
on the walls of my city. (repeat)

For the clenched teeth
for the restrained anger
for the knot in the throat
for the mouths that don't sing
for the clandestine kiss
for the censured verse
for the exiled youth
for the prohibited names,
I call you freedom.

For the invaded lands
for the conquered peoples
for the suppressed nation
for the exploited men
for the deaths in the flames
for the righteous one executed
for the murdered hero
for the extinguished fires,
I call you freedom.
I call you in the name of all.

Public Denunciation

A Father has sacrificed himself
so that the CNI[1] **would give him back his sons.**
The news impacts the whole world
but the national press pretends nothing is amiss, *El Mercurio*[2] **conceals it.**
10 years we've spent in Chile
    with a servile press that remains silent.

We denounce this press. . . .
This press remains silent about torture and thus **becomes the torturer,**

1   National Intelligence Center.
2   Chilean newspaper.

remains silent about the disappearances and thus **also causes them,**
remains silent about the secret jails and thus **supports them,**
cravenly remains silent about what the CNI does and says
      and thus **collaborates with the CNI.**

We call *El Mercurio* and **the whole national press**
to undertake a campaign **against torture,**
      against the secret jails,
      that the CNI be abolished and dismantled.

If they do not comply, let them definitively forfeit
      the right to claim any of their words have value,
      the right to lend any constructive support

to the establishment of a democracy and **a future for Chile.**

Tomasz Sarnecki, poster, "High Noon," Poland, 1989

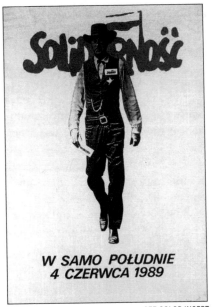

W SAMO POŁUDNIE
4 CZERWCA 1989

SEE COLOR INSERT

360 DISCUSSION QUESTIONS

1   What forms were the protests taking? How was democracy expressed through these forms of protest?

2   What examples of international influence or interaction are evident in the sources?

3   For the protestors, was "democracy" synonymous with "United States"? Why or why not?

COLD WAR: THE FINAL ACT

14-1a | Ronald Reagan, excerpt from "Evil Empire" speech, 1983

Ronald Wilson Reagan (1911–2004) delivered the speech below to a meeting of the National Association for Evangelicals (NAE), a group serving tens of thousands of churches with a constituency in the millions. Evangelicals were an important element in the landslide victory of Reagan in the 1980 presidential election. In his message, he spoke of the Cold War in new stark terms, drawing on concepts that resonated with his audience. This message was part of a round of renewed tensions and heightened rhetoric during the late Cold War.

During my first press conference as president . . . I pointed out that as good Marxist-Leninists, the Soviet leaders have openly and publicly declared that the only morality they recognize is that which will further their cause, which is world revolution. I think I should point out I was only quoting Lenin, their guiding spirit, who said in 1920 that they repudiate all morality that proceeds from supernatural ideas—that's their name for religion—or ideas that are outside class conceptions. Morality is entirely subordinate to the interests of class war. And everything is moral that is necessary for the annihilation of the old, exploiting social order and for uniting the proletariat.

Well, I think the refusal of many influential people to accept this elementary fact of Soviet doctrine illustrates an historical reluctance to see totalitarian powers for what they are. We saw this phenomenon in the 1930s. We see it too often today.

This does not mean we should isolate ourselves and refuse to seek an understanding with them. I intend to do everything I can to persuade them of our peaceful intent, to remind them that it was the West that refused to use its nuclear monopoly in the forties and fifties for territorial gain and which now proposes 50-percent cut in strategic ballistic missiles and the elimination of an entire class of land-based, intermediate-range nuclear missiles.

At the same time, however, they must be made to understand we will never compromise our principles and standards. We will never give away our freedom. We will never abandon our belief in God. And we will never stop searching for a genuine peace. But we can assure none of these things America stands for through the so-called nuclear freeze solutions proposed by some.

The truth is that a freeze now would be a very dangerous fraud, for that is merely the illusion of peace. The reality is that we must find peace through strength.

. . .

Yes, let us pray for the salvation of all those who live in totalitarian darkness—pray they will discover the joy of knowing God. But until they do, let us be aware that while they preach the supremacy of the state, declare its omnipotence over individual man, and predict its eventual domination of all peoples of the earth, they are the focus of evil in the modern world.

It was C. S. Lewis who, in his unforgettable "Screwtape Letters," wrote: "The greatest evil is not done now in those sordid 'dens of crime' that Dickens loved to paint. It is not even done in concentration camps and labor camps. In those we see its final result. But it is conceived and ordered (moved, seconded, carried and minuted) in clear, carpeted, warmed, and well-lighted offices, by quiet men with white collars and cut fingernails and smooth-shaven cheeks who do not need to raise their voice."

Well, because these "quiet men" do not "raise their voices," because they sometimes speak in soothing tones of brotherhood and peace, because, like other dictators before them, they're always making "their final territorial demand," some would have us accept them at their word and accommodate ourselves to their aggressive impulses. But if history teaches anything, it teaches that simple-minded appeasement or wishful thinking about our adversaries is folly. It means the betrayal of our past, the squandering of our freedom.

So, I urge you to speak out against those who would place the United States in a position of military and moral inferiority. You know, I've always believed that old Screwtape reserved his best efforts for those of you in the church. So, in your discussions of the nuclear freeze proposals, I urge you to beware the temptation of pride—the temptation of blithely declaring yourselves above it all and label both sides equally at fault, to ignore the facts of history and the aggressive impulses of an evil empire, to simply call the arms race a giant misunderstanding and thereby remove yourself from the struggle between right and wrong and good and evil.

. . .

I believe we shall rise to the challenge. I believe that Communism is another sad, bizarre chapter in history whose last pages even now are being written. . . .

14–1b | Photograph, anti–arms race protest, West Germany, 1983

Small-scale nuclear protest began as far back as the 1940s with popular participation in the movement growing rapidly in the 1960s and 1970s. Nuclear power also became a prominent public issue, especially after the 1979 accident at Three Mile Island near Harrisburg, Pennsylvania, and the 1986 Chernobyl disaster near Pripyat, Ukraine. The revival of the nuclear arms race in the 1980s garnered widespread global protests, setting records for participation in protest rallies in several countries. Here, in what was a series of 1983 Western European demonstrations, protestors expressed anger over the deployment of medium-range missiles in West Germany and demanded an end to the arms race.

DISCUSSION QUESTIONS

1   How was Reagan characterizing the Cold War? What might the consequences be from employing such rhetoric?

2   How were the location and makeup of the protestors significant in the image above?

3   These two Cold War sources are from the same year. What tension(s) becomes evident in considering these together?

14–2a | National Bipartisan Commission, findings on Central America, 1984

President Ronald Reagan appointed a twelve-member bipartisan commission, chaired by former Secretary of State Henry Kissinger, to recommend foreign policy approaches towards Central America. After a six-month investigation, the commission submitted its report in 1984. Below is the conclusion of that report, reflecting the tension between intervention, aid, and cooperation that had long characterized hemispheric relations and become particularly acute during the Cold War.

We have concluded this exercise persuaded that Central America is both vital and vulnerable, and that whatever other crises may arise to claim the nation's attention the United States cannot afford to turn away from that threatened region. Central America's crisis is our crisis.

All too frequently, wars and threats of wars are what draw attention to one part of the world or another. So it has been in Central America. The military crisis there captured our attention, but in doing so it has also wakened us to many other needs of the region. However belatedly, it did "concentrate the mind."

In the case of this Commission, one effect of concentrating the mind has been to clarify the picture we had of the nations of Central America. It is a common failing to see other nations as caricatures rather than as portraits, exaggerating one or two characteristics and losing sight of the subtler nuances on which so much of human experience centers. As we have studied these nations, we have become sharply aware of how great a mistake it would be to view them in one-dimensional terms. An exceptionally complex interplay of forces has shaped their history and continues to define their identities and to affect their destinies.

We have developed a great sympathy for those in Central America who are struggling to control those forces, and to bring their countries successfully through this period of political and social transformation. As a region, Central America is in mid-passage from the predominantly authoritarian patterns of the past to what can, with determination, with help, with luck, and with peace, become the predominantly democratic pluralism of the future. That transformation has been troubled, seldom smooth, and sometimes violent. In Nicaragua, we have seen the tragedy of a revolution betrayed; the same forces that stamped out the beginnings of democracy in Nicaragua now threaten El Salvador. In El Salvador itself, those seeking to establish democratic institutions are beset by violence from the extremists on both sides. But the spirit of freedom is strong throughout the region, and the determination persists to strengthen it where it exists and to achieve it where it does not.

The use of Nicaragua as a base for Soviet and Cuban efforts to penetrate the rest of the Central American isthmus, with El Salvador the target of first opportunity, gives the conflict there a major strategic dimension. The direct involvement of aggressive external forces makes it a challenge to the system of hemispheric security, and, quite specifically, to the security interests of the United States. This is a challenge to which the United States must respond.

But beyond this, we are challenged to respond to the urgent human needs of the people of Central America. Central America is a region in crisis economically, socially, and politically. Its nations are our neighbors, and they need our help. This is one of those instances in which the requirements of national interest and the commands of conscience coincide.

Through the years, there has been a sort of natural progression in this nation's ties with other parts of the world. At first they were almost exclusively with Europe. Then, without diminishing those ties with Europe, we expanded our trans-Pacific bonds. Now the crisis in Central America has served as a vivid reminder that we need to strengthen our ties to the south, as well as east and west.

Our response to the present crisis in Central America must not be a passing phenomenon. The United States was born of a vision, which has inspired the world for two centuries. That vision shines most brightly when it is shared. Just as we want freedom for ourselves, we want freedom for others. Just as we cherish our vision, we should encourage others to pursue their own. But in fact, what we want for ourselves is very largely what the people of Central America want for themselves. They do share the vision of the future that our ideals represent, and the time has come for us to help them not just to aspire to that vision, but to participate in it.

Our task now, as a nation, is to transform the crisis in Central America into an opportunity: to seize the impetus it provides, and to use this to help our neighbors not only to secure their freedom from aggression and violence, but also to set in place the policies, processes and institutions that will make them both prosperous and free. If, together, we succeed in this, then the sponsors of violence will have done the opposite of what they intended: they will have roused us not only to turn back the tide of totalitarianism but to bring a new birth of hope and of opportunity to the people of Central America.

Because this is our opportunity, in conscience it is also our responsibility.

14–2b | Illustrations and information, the CIA's *The Freedom Fighter's Manual*, 1984

In the context of the Cold War, the United States opposed Marxist governments, political parties, and movements throughout the western hemisphere, preferring instead to empower right-wing, authoritarian dictators or military *juntas* that would cooperate with the U.S. The U.S. Army established the School of the Americas in 1946, training tens of thousands of Latin American military officers, many of whom were later accused of human rights violations, and the Central Intelligence Agency armed, aided, and encouraged nearly any anti-leftist group in the region. In Nicaragua, for example, the Reagan administration imposed hefty economic sanctions, rallied international support against the leftist Sandinista government (1979–1990), and resorted to illegal arms sales to Iran to fund the Contras, a loose conglomeration of right-wing Nicaraguan rebels. Below is an excerpt of a 1983 leaflet dropped by the CIA over Nicaragua, intended for civilians aligned with the Contras.

All Nicaraguans who love their country and cherish liberty—men, women, young and old people, farmers and workers alike—surely ask themselves what they can do with the means at their disposal, in order to participate in the final battle against the usurpers of the authentic sandinista revolution for which the people of Nicaragua have fought and shed their blood for so many years. Some might think that today's armed struggle requires military supplies and economic resources only available to states or terrorist bands armed by Moscow. There is an essential economic infrastructure that any government needs to function, which can easily be disabled and even paralyzed without the use of armaments or costly and advanced equipment, with the small investment of resources and time.

The following pages present a series of useful sabotage techniques, the majority of which can be done with simple household tools such as scissors, empty bottles, screwdrivers, matches, etc. These measures are extremely safe and without risk for those who use them, as they do not require equipment, skill or specialized activities that can draw attention to the doer.

One combatant can perform many of them, without having to turn to collaborators or having to make a detailed plan beforehand. These are acts that can be done practically in an improvised way every time an occasion presents itself. Our sacred cause needs to have more men and women join its ranks in order to perform these sabotage tasks. However, necessary caution should be taken, and only when the task requires it, should another person or persons participate in or have knowledge of a given act. As mentioned above, the techniques found in this manual correspond to the stage of individual sabotage, or at the most cellular—with cells of no more than two individuals—of the clandestine struggle.

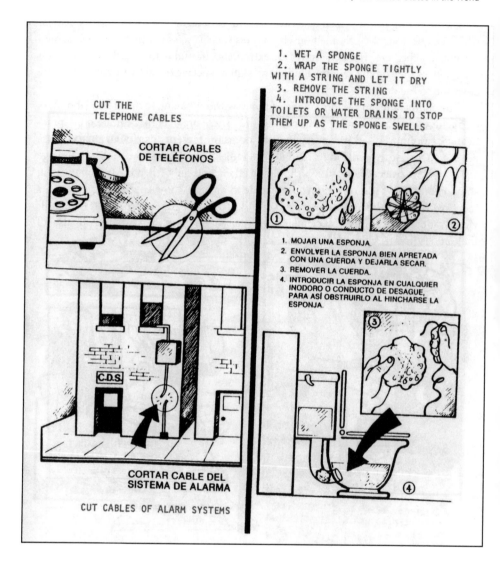

CUT THE
TELEPHONE CABLES

CORTAR CABLES
DE TELÉFONOS

CORTAR CABLE DEL
SISTEMA DE ALARMA

CUT CABLES OF ALARM SYSTEMS

C.D.S.

1. WET A SPONGE
2. WRAP THE SPONGE TIGHTLY
WITH A STRING AND LET IT DRY
3. REMOVE THE STRING
4. INTRODUCE THE SPONGE INTO
TOILETS OR WATER DRAINS TO STOP
THEM UP AS THE SPONGE SWELLS

1. MOJAR UNA ESPONJA.
2. ENVOLVER LA ESPONJA BIEN APRETADA
CON UNA CUERDA Y DEJARLA SECAR.
3. REMOVER LA CUERDA.
4. INTRODUCIR LA ESPONJA EN CUALQUIER
INODORO O CONDUCTO DE DESAGUE,
PARA ASÍ OBSTRUIRLO AL HINCHARSE LA
ESPONJA.

DISCUSSION QUESTIONS

1. According to the Commission's report, why should "crisis" in Central America be considered an American "crisis"?

2. What does the manual suggest about the ways in which the Cold War was being waged?

3. How did the manual's content counter the recommendations of the Bipartisan Commission?

14–3a | Mikhail Gorbachev, excerpts from speech to
the United Nations, Soviet Union, 1988

When Soviet General Secretary Mikhail Gorbachev (b. 1931) appeared at the United Nations in December 1988, he arrived having already dramatically altered the relationship between the Soviet Union and the United States. Gorbachev, a committed communist who came to power in 1985, believed the Soviet system could be renewed, the economy restructured, and the ideology reinvigorated with the right reforms. In order to enact reforms at home, however, he sought to deescalate Cold War tensions abroad, specifically by pursuing nuclear disarmament. In 1987, he and President Ronald Reagan signed the Intermediate-Range Nuclear Forces (INF) Treaty, the first agreement to reduce nuclear arms, to eliminate an entire class of weapons, and to establish on-site inspections. In an address to the UN, Gorbachev suggested next steps in his new approach.

The world in which we live today is radically different from what it was at the beginning, or even in the middle, of this century, and it continues to change, as do all its components.

The advent of nuclear weapons was just another tragic reminder of the fundamental nature of that change. A material symbol and expression of absolute military power, nuclear weapons at the same time revealed the absolute limits of that power. The problem of mankind's survival and self-preservation came to the fore.

. . .

It is obvious, for instance, that the use or threat of force can no longer, and must no longer, be an instrument of foreign policy. This applies, above all, to nuclear arms, but that is not the only thing that matters. All of us, and primarily the stronger of us, must exercise self-restraint and totally rule out any outward-oriented use of force. . . .

. . .

The new phase also requires de-ideologizing relations among States. We are not abandoning our convictions, our philosophy or traditions, nor do we urge anyone to abandon theirs. However, neither do we have any intention to be hemmed in by our values, which would result in intellectual impoverishment, for it would mean rejecting a powerful source of development—the exchange of everything original that each nation has independently created.

In the course of such exchange, let everyone show the advantages of their social system, way of life and their values, not just by words or propaganda, but by real deeds. That would be a fair rivalry of ideologies. But it should not be extended to relations among States, . . .

. . .

Of course, we are far from claiming to be in possession of the ultimate truth, but, on the basis of a thorough analysis of the past and newly-emerging realities, we have concluded that it is on these lines that we should jointly seek the way leading to the supremacy of the universal human idea over the endless multitude of centrifugal forces, and to preserve the vitality of this civilization, which is possibly the only one in the entire universe.

Could this view be a little too romantic? Are we not overestimating the potential and the maturity of the world's social consciousness? We have heard such doubts and such questions, both in our country and from some of our Western partners.

I am convinced that we are not floating above reality. . . .

. . .

Let me now turn to the main issue without which none of the problems of the coming century can be solved: disarmament. . . .

. . .

Today I can report to the General Assembly that the Soviet Union has taken a decision to reduce its armed forces. Within the next two years their numerical strength will be reduced by 500,000 men. The numbers of conventional armaments will also be substantially reduced. This will be done unilaterally, without relation to the talks on the mandate of the Vienna meeting.

By agreement with our Warsaw Treaty allies we have decided to withdraw, by 1991, six tank divisions from the German Democratic Republic, Czechoslovakia and Hungary and to disband them. Assault landing troops and several other formations and units, including assault crossing units with their weapons and combat equipment, will also be withdrawn from the groups of Soviet forces stationed in those countries. Soviet forces stationed in those countries will be reduced by 50,000 men and their armaments by 5,000 tanks.

All Soviet divisions remaining for the time being on the territories of our allies are being reorganized. Their structure will be different from what it is now; after a major cutback of their tanks it will become clearly defensive.

At the same time we shall reduce the numerical strength of the armed forces and the numbers of armaments stationed in the European part of the Soviet Union. In total, Soviet armed forces in this part of our country and in the territories of our European allies will be reduced by 10,000 tanks, 8,500 artillery systems and 800 combat aircraft.

Over these two years we intend to reduce significantly our armed forces in the Asian part of our country too. By agreement with the government of the Mongolian People's Republic a major portion of Soviet troops temporarily stationed there will return home.

In taking this fundamental decision the Soviet leadership expresses the will of the people, who have undertaken a profound renewal of their entire socialist society. We shall maintain our country's defense capability at a level of reasonable and reliable sufficiency so that no one might be tempted to encroach on the security of the Soviet Union and our allies.

By all our activities in favor of demilitarizing international relations we wish to draw the attention of the international community to yet another pressing problem: the problem of transition from the economy of armaments to an economy of disarmament. Is conversion of military production a realistic idea? I have already had occasion to speak about this. We think that it is indeed realistic.

For its part, the Soviet Union is prepared to take the following steps: within the framework of our economic reform to draw up and make public our internal plan of conversion; in the course of 1989 to draw up, as an experiment, conversion plans for two or three defense plants; and to make public our experience in providing employment for specialists from military industry and in using its equipment, buildings and structures in civilian production.

It is desirable that all States, in the first place major military Powers, should submit to the United Nations their national conversion plans to the United Nations. It would be useful also to set up a group of scientists to undertake a thorough analysis of the problem of conversion as a whole and as applied to individual countries and regions and report to the Secretary-General of the United Nations, and subsequently for this matter to be considered at a session of the General Assembly.

Finally, since I am here on American soil, and also for other obvious reasons, I have to turn to the subject of our relations with this great country. I had a chance to appreciate the full measure of its hospitality during my memorable visit to Washington exactly a year ago. Relations between the Soviet Union and the United States of America have a history of five and a half decades. As the world has changed, so have the nature, role and place of those relations in world politics. For too long they developed along the lines of confrontation and sometimes animosity, either overt or covert. But in the last few years the entire world could breathe a sigh of relief, thanks to the changes for the better in the substance and the atmosphere of the relationship between Moscow and Washington.

No one intends to underestimate the seriousness of our differences and the toughness of outstanding problems. We have, however, already graduated from the primary school of learning to understand each other and seek solutions in both our own and common interests.

The USSR and the United States have built the largest nuclear and missile arsenals; but it is those two countries that, having become specifically aware of their responsibility, have been the first to conclude a treaty on the reduction and physical elimination of a portion of their armaments which posed a threat to both of them and to all other countries. Both countries possess the greatest and the most sophisticated military secrets; but it is those two countries that have laid a basis for and are further developing a system of mutual verification both of the elimination of armaments and of the reduction and prohibition of their production. It is those two countries that are accumulating the experience for future bilateral and multilateral agreements.

We value this. We acknowledge and appreciate the contribution made by President Ronald Reagan and by the members of his administration, particularly Mr. George Shultz.

All this is our joint investment in a venture of historic importance. We must not lose that investment, or leave it idle.

The next United States administration, headed by President-elect George Bush, will find in us a partner who is ready—without long pauses or backtracking—to continue the dialogue in a spirit of realism, openness and goodwill, with a willingness to achieve concrete results working on the agenda which covers the main issues of Soviet-United States relations and world politics.

I have in mind, above all, consistent movement toward a treaty on 50-per-cent reductions in strategic offensive arms while preserving the Treaty on the Limitation of Anti-Ballistic Missile Systems (ABM Treaty); working out a convention on the elimination of chemical weapons—here, as we see it, prerequisites exist to make 1989 a decisive year; and negotiations on the reduction of conventional arms and armed forces in Europe.

I also have in mind economic, environmental and humanistic problems in their broadest sense.

. . .

I should like to believe that our hopes will be matched by our joint efforts to put an end to an era of wars, confrontation and regional conflicts, to aggressions against nature, to the terror of hunger and poverty as well as to political terrorism.

This is our common goal and we can only reach it together.

14–3b | Nicholas Garland, political cartoon depicting Gorbachev as Samson, UK, 1991

Though Gorbachev fully intended to repair a broken system, his reforms instead led to the unanticipated but relatively peaceful dissolution of the Soviet Union—an event which had global repercussions. Not only did the Cold War end, but the bipolar world which had existed since World War II lost one of its superpowers. Renowned British political cartoonist Nicholas Garland (b. 1935) published this image in December 1991, as the fate of the USSR became clear.

DISCUSSION QUESTIONS

1   What might have made Gorbachev's address surprising?

2   According to Garland's cartoon, what was Gorbachev's role in the collapse of the USSR? Do you agree with this characterization? Why? Why not?

CHALLENGES OF GLOBAL LEADERSHIP

14–4a | Yasir Arafat, excerpts from press statement on the recognition of Israel, Palestine, 1988

When Yasir Arafat (1929–2004), head of the Palestine Liberation Organization (PLO) and founder of the nationalist, secular political party Fatah, made the 1988 statement excerpted below, his declaration departed from long-held PLO and Fatah stances. Arafat had led armed resistance to the Israeli occupation of Palestine since 1948, the year of Israel's creation. The PLO's acceptance of a "two-state solution," a coexisting Palestine and Israel, led to a series of steps forward in the ongoing regional crisis, culminating in the 1993 Oslo Accords. It also resulted in the splintering of Palestinian and Arab opinion, especially among those who believed Arafat gave too much and got too little from the Israelis.

Let me highlight my views before you. Our desire for peace is a strategy and not an interim tactic. We are bent on peace come what may, come what may.

Our statehood provides salvation to the Palestinians and peace to both Palestinians and Israelis.

Self-determination means survival for the Palestinians and our survival does not destroy the survival of the Israelis as their rulers claim.

Yesterday in my speech I made reference to the United Nations Resolution 181 as the basis for Palestinian independence. I also made reference to our acceptance of Resolution 242 and 338 as the basis for negotiations with Israel within the framework of the international conference. These three resolutions were endorsed by our Palestinian National Council session in Algiers.

In my speech also yesterday, it was clear that we mean our people's rights to freedom and national independence, according to Resolution 181, and the right of all parties concerned in the Middle East conflict to exist in peace and security, and, as I have mentioned, including the state of Palestine, Israel and other neighbors, according to the Resolution 242 and 338.

As for terrorism, I renounced it yesterday in no uncertain terms, and yet, I repeat for the record. I repeat for the record that we totally and absolutely renounce all forms of terrorism, including individual, group and state terrorism.

Between Geneva and Algiers, we have made our position crystal clear. Any more talk such as "The Palestinians should give more"—you remember this slogan?—or "It is not enough" or "The Palestinians are engaging in propaganda games and public-relations exercises" will be damaging and counterproductive.

Enough is enough. Enough is enough. Enough is enough. All remaining matters should be discussed around the table and within the international conference.

Let it be absolutely clear that neither Arafat, nor any for that matter, can stop the intifada, the uprising. The intifada will come to an end only and only when practical and tangible steps have been taken toward the achievement of our national aims and establishment of our independent Palestinian state.

In this context, I expect the E.E.C. to play a more effective role in promoting peace in our region. They have a political responsibility, they have a moral responsibility, and they can deal with it.

Finally, I declare before you and I ask you to kindly quote me on that: We want peace. We want peace. We are committed to peace. We want to live in our Palestinian state, and let live. Thank you.

14–4b | Hamas, excerpts from Charter of the Islamic Resistance Movement of Palestine, Palestine, 1988

Drawing on the decades-old appeal of political Islam as a means of countering colonialism and Western culture, the emergence of Hamas reflected the rise of Islamic fundamentalism in the region that began in 1979 with the Iranian Revolution. In the same year as Arafat's recognition of Israel and renunciation of terror, the Islamic Resistance Movement (Hamas) penned a foundational charter, excerpted below. Founded as an Islamist organization affiliated with the Muslim Brotherhood, Hamas dedicated its efforts to the destruction of Israel through jihad and the construction of an Islamist Palestine. The charter's thirty-six articles detail these goals and repeat several anti-Semitic themes rooted in European anti-Semitism of the previous century. Hamas issued a new charter in 2017 inspired by its party's move into formal politics.

Introduction

All praise is to Allah. We seek His aid, forgiveness, and guidance, and on Him do we rely. We send peace and blessings on Allah's messenger—his family, companions, those who follow him, called with his message and adhered to his way—may the blessing and peace be continued for as long as the heavens and earth last. . . .

This is the charter of *Harakat al-Muqawama al-Islamiyya* (Hamas)[3] [the Islamic Resistance Movement] manifesting its form, unveiling its identity, stating its position, clarifying its expectations, discussing its hopes, and calling for aid, support, and members. Our battle with the Jews is long and dangerous, requiring all dedicated efforts. It is a phase which must be followed by succeeding phases, a battalion which must be supported by battalion after battalion of the divided Arab and Islamic world until the enemy is overcome, and the victory of Allah descends. . . .

Chapter One
Introduction to the Movement

Ideological origin

Article 1: The Islamic Resistance Movement: Islam is its system. From Islam it reaches for its ideology, fundamental precepts, and world view of life, the universe and humanity; and it judges all its actions according to Islam and is inspired by Islam to correct its errors.

The Islamic Resistance Movement's Connection with the Society of the Muslim Brotherhood

Article 2: The Islamic Resistance Movement is a branch of the Muslim Brotherhood chapter in Palestine. The Muslim Brotherhood is an international organization. It is one of today's largest Islamic movements. It professes a comprehensive understanding and precise conceptualization of the Islamic precepts in all aspects of life: concept and belief, politics and economics, education and social service, jurisdiction and law, exhortation and training, communication and arts, the seen and the unseen, and the rest of life's ways.

Structure and Formation

Article 3: The structure of the Islamic Resistance Movement consists of Muslims who gave their loyalty to Allah. They therefore worshipped Him as He truly deserves:
I have only created Jinns and Humans that they may worship Me. Sura 51:Zariyat:56
They knew their obligation towards themselves, their people and their country. They achieved *Taqwa*[4] of Allah in all that [their obligation]. They raised the banner of Jihad in the face of the transgressors to free country and folk from filth, impurity, and evil.
Nay, We hurl the truth against falsehood, and it knocks out its brain, and behold, falsehood doth perish! Sura 21:Anbiya:18
Article 4: The Islamic Resistance Movement welcomes all Muslims who adopt its doctrines and ideology, enact its program, guard its secrets, and desire to join its ranks to perform the obligation and receive their reward from Allah. . . .

Differentiation and Independence

Article 6: The Islamic Resistance Movement is an outstanding type of Palestinian movement. It gives its loyalty to Allah, adopts Islam as a system of life, and works to-

3   *Hamas*: Force and bravery. *al Majam al-wasit*, vol. 1.
4   *Taqwa*: Awareness and fear of Allah, conscious of Allah's watchful gaze.

ward raising the banner of Allah on every inch of Palestine. Therefore, in the shadow of Islam, it is possible for all followers of different religions to live in peace and with security over their person, property, and rights. In the absence of Islam, discord takes form, oppression and destruction are rampant, and wars and battles take place.

The Muslim poet Muhammad Iqbal eloquently declares:

When faith is lost there is no security nor life for he who does not revive religion;
And whoever is satisfied with life without religion then he would have let annihilation be
his partner.

Chapter Two

Goals

Article 9: The Islamic Resistance Movement evolved in a time where the lack of the Islamic Spirit has brought about distorted judgement and absurd comprehension. Values have deteriorated, the plague of evil folk and oppression and darkness have become rampant, cowards have become ferocious. Nations have been occupied, their people expelled and fallen on their faces [in humiliation] everywhere on earth. The nation of truth is absent and the nation of evil has been established; as long as Islam does not take its rightful place in the world arena everything will continue to change for the worse. The goal of the Islamic Resistance Movement therefore is to conquer evil, break its will, and annihilate it so that truth may prevail, so the country may return to its rightful place, and so that the call may be broadcast over the Minarets proclaiming the Islamic state. And aid is sought from Allah. . . .

Chapter Three
Strategy and Means

The Strategy of The Islamic Resistance Movement: Palestine is an Islamic Trust

Article 11: The Islamic Resistance Movement [firmly] believes that the land of Palestine is an Islamic *Waaf* [Trust] upon all Muslim generations till the day of Resurrection. It is not right to give it up nor any part of it. Neither a single Arab state nor all the Arab states, neither a King nor a leader, nor all the kings or leaders, nor any organization—Palestinian or Arab—have such authority because the land of Palestine is an Islamic Trust upon all Muslim generations until the day of Resurrection. And who has the true spokesmanship for all the Muslim generations till the day of Resurrection? . . .

Nation and Nationalism from the Point of View of The Islamic Resistance Movement

Article 12: Nationalism, from the point of view of the Islamic Resistance Movement, is part and parcel of religious ideology. There is not a higher peak in nationalism or depth in devotion than *Jihad* when an enemy lands on the Muslim territories. Fighting the enemy becomes the individual obligation of every Muslim man and woman. *The woman is allowed to go fight without the permission of her husband and the salve without the permission of his master.* . . .

Initiative, Peace Solutions, and International Conferences

Article 13: The initiatives conflict, what are called "Peaceful Solutions" and "International Conferences" to solve the Palestinian problem. As far as the ideology of the Islamic Resistance Movement is concerned, giving up any part of Palestine is like giving up part of its religion. The nationalism of the Islamic Resistance Movement is part of its religion, in that it educates its members, and they perform *Jihad* to raise the banner of Allah over their nation. . . .

There is no solution to the Palestinian Problem except by *Jihad*. The initiatives, options, and international conferences are a waste of time and a kind of child's play. . . .

The Role of the Muslim Woman

Article 17: The Muslim woman has a role in the battle for the liberation which is no less than the role of the man, for she is the factory of men. Her role in directing generations and training them is a big role. The enemies have realized her role: they think that if they are able to direct her and raise her the way they want, far from Islam, then they have won the battle. You'll find that they use continuous spending through mass media and the motion picture industry. They also use the education system by way of their teachers who are part of Zionist organizations—which go by different names and forms, such as [free] Masons, Rotary Clubs, intelligence networks, and other organizations. These are all centers for destruction and destroyers. Those Zionist organizations have great material resources which allow them to play a significant role in society to realize Zionist goals, and enforce the understanding that serves the enemy. These organizations play their role while Islam is absent from the arena and is estranged from its people. The Islamist should play his role in confronting the plans of those destroyers. When the day comes and Islam has its way in directing life, it shall eliminate those organization which are opposed to humanity and Islam. . . .

Social Welfare

Article 20: . . . The Nazism of Jews has included women and children. Terror is for everyone, they frighten people in their livelihood, take their wealth, and threaten their honor. They, with their shocking actions, treat people worse than they treat the worst of war criminals. Deportation from one's land is a form of murder. . . .

Article 21: Part of social welfare is providing aid to everyone who is in need of it, be it material, or spiritual, or collective cooperation to complete some works. . . .

The Powers that Support the Enemy

Article 22: The enemy planned long ago and perfected their plan so that they can achieve what they want to achieve, taking into account effective steps in running matters. So they worked on gathering huge and effective amounts of wealth to achieve their goal. With wealth they controlled the international mass media—news services, newspapers, printing presses, broadcast stations, and more. With money they ignited revolutions in all parts of the world to realize their benefits and reap the fruits of them. They are behind the French Revolution, the Communist Revolution, and most of the revolutions here and there which we have heard of and are hearing of. With wealth they formed secret organizations throughout the world to destroy societies and promote the

Zionist cause; these organizations include the freemasons, the Rotary and Lions clubs, and others. These are all destructive intelligence-gathering organizations. With wealth they controlled imperialistic nations and pushed them to occupy many nations to exhaust their (natural) resources and spread mischief in them.

Concerning the local and international wars, speak with hesitation. They are behind the First World War in which they destroyed the Islamic *Calipha* and gained material profit, monopolized raw wealth, and got the Balfour Declaration. They created the League of Nations so they could control the world through that organization. They are behind the Second World War where they grossed huge profits from their trade of war materials, and set down the foundations to establish their nation by forming the United Nations and Security Council, instead of the League of Nations, in order to rule the world through that organization.

There is not a war that goes on here or there in which their fingers are not playing behind it.

Every time they kindle the fire of war, Allah doth extinguish it; but they (ever) strive to do mischief on earth. And Allah loveth not those who do mischief. Sura 5:Maida:64

Chapter Four

Our Position On: . . .
The Arab Countries and Islam Governments
Article 28: The Zionist invasion is a vicious attack that does not have piety not to use all methods low and despicable to fulfill its obligations; it depends enormously on its penetration of and intelligence operations upon the secret organizations that were offshoots of it—such as the Masons, Rotary, and Lions clubs, and other such networks of spies—and all these secret or public organizations work for the benefit of and with the guidance of the Zionists. Zionists are behind the drug and alcohol trade because of their ability to facilitate the ease of control and expansion. The Arab countries surrounding Israel are requested to open their borders for the *Mujahidin* of the Arab and Islamic countries so they can take their role and join their efforts with their Muslim brothers of Palestine. . . .

The People of Other Faiths
Article 31: The Islamic Resistance Movement is a humanistic movement that takes care of human rights and follows the tolerance of Islam with respect to people of other faiths. Never does it attack any of them except those who show enmity toward it or stand in its path to stop the movement or waste its efforts.

In the shadow of Islam it is possible for the followers of the three religions—Islam, Christianity, and Judaism—to live in peace and harmony, and this peace and harmony is possible only under Islam. The history of the past and present is the best written witness for that. . . .

The Effort to Single Out the Palestinian People
Article 32: World Zionism and Imperialist powers try with audacious maneuvers and well-formulated plans to extract the Arab nations one by one from the struggle with Zionism, so in the end it can deal singularly with the Palestinian people. It already has

removed Egypt far away from the circle of struggle with the treason of "Camp David," and it is trying to extract other countries by using similar treaties in order to remove them from the struggle. . . . Today it's Palestine and tomorrow it will be another country, and then another, the Zionist plan has no bounds, and after Palestine they wish to expand from the Nile River to the Euphrates. When they totally occupy it they will look towards another, and such is their plan in the "Protocols of the Elders of Zion." Their present is the best witness of what is said. . . .

Article 33: The Islamic Resistance Movement goes forth with these general understandings, which are equal and in harmony with the patterns of the universe, like being poured in the river of destiny, to confront the enemy. And their struggle to defend Muslims, Islamic civilization, and religious sanctuaries, of which Masjid al-Aqsa is at the forefront, to ignite the Arab and Islamic people, their governments, and its nationalistic and official organizations, to fear Allah while considering the Islamic Resistance Movement, and its way of dealing with it, should be, as Allah has wished, as supporter and helper spreading its hand to help, with support followed by support until the decision of Allah is manifested. The ranks join the ranks and the *Mujahids* join *Mujahids* and other groups which come forth from everywhere in the Muslim world, answering the call of obligation, repeating "come to *Jihad*"—a call bursting forth into the heights of the Heavens, reverberating until the liberation is complete and the invaders are rolled back and the victory of Allah descends. . . .

DISCUSSION QUESTIONS

1   According to Arafat's statement, why did he and the PLO choose to recognize Israel?

2   According to the Hamas Charter, what key characteristics define an Islamist state?

3   How did Arafat (the PLO) and Hamas, respectively, view Israel, the United Nations, and each other? How do these two sources demonstrate the centrality of the Israel question?

14–5a | George H. W. Bush, excerpts from New World Order speech, 1991

In August 1990, the Iraqi Army invaded and occupied the neighboring country of Kuwait, an action garnering international criticism and economic sanctions from members of the United Nations Security Council. Just over a month later, George H. W. Bush (1924–2018) addressed a joint session of Congress, offering the remarks below. In them, the U.S. President not only addressed the current world crisis but offered a new vision for his country in world affairs in the post–Cold War era.

We gather tonight, witness to events in the Persian Gulf as significant as they are tragic. In the early morning hours of August 2d, following negotiations and promises by Iraq's dictator Saddam Hussein not to use force, a powerful Iraqi army invaded its trusting and much weaker neighbor, Kuwait. Within 3 days, 120,000 Iraqi troops with 850 tanks had poured into Kuwait and moved south to threaten Saudi Arabia. It was then that I decided to act to check that aggression. . . .

. . . tonight I want to talk to you about what's at stake—what we must do together to defend civilized values around the world and maintain our economic strength at home.

Our objectives in the Persian Gulf are clear, our goals defined and familiar: Iraq must withdraw from Kuwait completely, immediately, and without condition.

. . .

As you know, I've just returned from a very productive meeting with Soviet President Gorbachev. And I am pleased that we are working together to build a new relationship . . . Clearly, no longer can a dictator count on East-West confrontation to stymie concerted United Nations action against aggression. A new partnership of nations has begun.

We stand today at a unique and extraordinary moment. The crisis in the Persian Gulf, as grave as it is, also offers a rare opportunity to move toward an historic period of cooperation. Out of these troubled times . . . a new world order—can emerge: a new era—freer from the threat of terror, stronger in the pursuit of justice, and more secure in the quest for peace. An era in which the nations of the world, East and West, North and South, can prosper and live in harmony. A hundred generations have searched for this elusive path to peace, while a thousand wars raged across the span of human endeavor. Today that new world is struggling to be born, a world quite different from the one we've known. A world where the rule of law supplants the rule of the jungle. A world in which nations recognize the shared responsibility for freedom and justice. A world where the strong respect the rights of the weak. This is the vision that I shared with President Gorbachev in Helsinki. He and other leaders from Europe, the Gulf, and around the world understand that how we manage this crisis today could shape the future for generations to come.

The test we face is great, and so are the stakes. This is the first assault on the new world that we seek, the first test of our mettle. Had we not responded to this first provocation with clarity of purpose, if we do not continue to demonstrate our determination, it would be a signal to actual and potential despots around the world. America and the world must defend common vital interests—and we will. America and the world must support the rule of law—and we will. America and the world must stand up to aggression—and we will. And one thing more: In the pursuit of these goals America will not be intimidated.

14–5b | Anthony Lake, excerpts from speech on moving from containment to enlargement, 1993

Anthony Lake (b. 1939) served as National Security Advisor under President Bill Clinton from 1993 to 1997. After the dissolution of the USSR in 1991, the U.S. struggled to find a new strategic and rhetorical vision in its foreign policy. Containment had offered a unifying concept, pulling together priorities in foreign policy, military action, and domestic affairs. Below, Lake offered a new grand vision for U.S. actions in world affairs.

In such a world, our interests and ideals compel us not only to be engaged, but to lead. And in a real-time world of change and information, it is all the more important that our leadership be steadied around our central purpose.

That purpose can be found in the underlying rationale for our engagement throughout this century. As we fought aggressors and contained communism, our engagement abroad was animated both by calculations of power and by this belief: to the extent democracy and market economics hold sway in other nations, our own nation will be more secure, prosperous and influential, while the broader world will be more humane and peaceful.

The expansion of market-based economics abroad helps expand our exports and create American jobs, while it also improves living conditions and fuels demands for political liberalization abroad. The addition of new democracies makes us more secure because democracies tend not to wage war on each other or sponsor terrorism. They are more trustworthy in diplomacy and do a better job of respecting the human rights of their people.

These dynamics lay at the heart of Woodrow Wilson's most profound insights; although his moralism sometimes weakened his argument, he understood that our own security is shaped by the character of foreign regimes. Indeed, most Presidents who followed, Republicans and Democrats alike, understood we must promote democracy and market economics in the world—because it protects our interests and security; and because it reflects values that are both American and universal.

Throughout the Cold War, we contained a global threat to market democracies; now we should seek to enlarge their reach, particularly in places of special significance to us.

The successor to a doctrine of containment must be a strategy of enlargement—enlargement of the world's free community of market democracies.

During the Cold War, even children understood America's security mission; as they looked at those maps on their schoolroom walls, they knew we were trying to contain the creeping expansion of that big, red blob. Today, at great risk of oversimplification, we might visualize our security mission as promoting the enlargement of the "blue areas" of market democracies. The difference, of course, is that we do not seek to expand the reach of our institutions by force, subversion or repression.

We must not allow this overarching goal to drive us into overreaching actions. To be successful, a strategy of enlargement must provide distinctions and set priorities. It must combine our broad goals of fostering democracy and markets with our more traditional geostrategic interests. And it must suggest how best to expend our large but nonetheless limited national security resources: financial, diplomatic and military.

In recent years, discussions about when to use force have turned on a set of vital questions, such as whether our forces match our objectives; whether we can fight and win in a time that is acceptable; whether we have a reasonable exit if we do not; whether there is public and congressional support. But we have overlooked a prior, strategic question—the question of "where"—which sets the context for such military judgments.

I see four components to a strategy of enlargement.

- First, we should strengthen the community of major market democracies—including our own—which constitutes the core from which enlargement is proceeding.
- Second, we should help foster and consolidate new democracies and market economies, where possible, especially in states of special significance and opportunity.
- Third, we must counter the aggression—and support the liberalization—of states hostile to democracy and markets.
- Fourth, we need to pursue our humanitarian agenda not only by providing aid, but also by working to help democracy and market economics take root in regions of greatest humanitarian concern.

A host of caveats must accompany a strategy of enlargement. For one, we must be patient. As scholars observe, waves of democratic advance are often followed by reverse waves of democratic setback. We must be ready for uneven progress, even outright reversals.

Our strategy must be pragmatic. Our interests in democracy and markets do not stand alone. Other American interests at times will require us to befriend and even defend non-democratic states for mutually beneficial reasons.

Our strategy must view democracy broadly—it must envision a system that includes not only elections but also such features as an independent judiciary and protections of human rights.

Our strategy must also respect diversity. Democracy and markets can come in many legitimate variants. Freedom has many faces.

DISCUSSION QUESTIONS

1 According to Bush, how did the crisis in the Persian Gulf present a test for the "new world order"?

2 What elements constituted the new strategy of "enlargement"?

3 How did the end of the Cold War enable these shifts in U.S. foreign policy? What attributes of U.S. influence and power did each speaker emphasize in pursuit of new goals?

14–6 | Mahathir bin Mohamad, excerpts from speech, "Asian Values," Malaysia, 1994

As Prime Minister of Malaysia, Mahathir bin Mohamad (b. 1925) oversaw a significant period of economic growth and rapid modernization in the Southeast Asian country. His administration is also noted for pushback against Western interests, as Mahathir became a leading Third-World advocate and international social activist for developing countries. Here, in a speech given at an international human rights conference, Mahathir responded to the U.S. vision for its role in the world laid out in statements such as Anthony Lake's speech (chapter 14, item 5b), attacking the idea that what was good for the West was good for the world.

3. As the world has numerous communities and the state of their development differs widely, it is natural to expect that their concepts of human rights, of justice, and of obligation to the community to differ and differ widely. . . .

18. Developed countries can do with weak governments or no government. But developing countries cannot function without strong authority on the part of government. Unstable and weak governments will result in chaos, and chaos cannot contribute to the development and well-being of developing countries. Divisive politics will occupy the time and minds of everyone, as we can witness in many a developing country today.

19. The developing countries, by and large, want to practise democracy but must they practise only the liberal forms prescribed by the West, forms which will retard their development and continued independence? But they are continuously being harassed through economic pressures including withdrawal of aid and loans, by carping criticisms and deliberate misinformation by the Western media and by campaigns on the part of Western NGOs, who sometimes finance pressure groups within the country to obstruct the government which they label as undemocratic. Even if the government is replaced, the new government would still be harassed. . . .

22. The record of the democratic governments of the West is not very inspiring. Unless their own interests are at stake, as in Kuwait, they would not risk anything in the cause of democracy. Is it any wonder that many countries are leery of the liberal system propounded by the Western democrats? . . .

27. After the collapse of the Soviet Union and the much vaunted victory over Iraq, the Western powers declared that the independence of nations notwithstanding, they have a right to interfere in the internal affairs of a country if there is evidence of human rights violation. This is very noble but the method is questionable. What qualifies the Western liberal democrats to become both judge and executor of the behaviour of nations and citizens of other countries? If there is to be interference in the internal affairs of nations, should not the U.N. be the right body to lay down the rules and to act? But

the mild objections by insignificant nations were brushed aside. And so, among other things, people in distant lands who unknowingly breach the laws of powerful nations are tried in absentia and sentenced. The implication of this is frightening. When you can be tried under the laws of another country where you have no rights, you have lost your freedom and your independence. You have become colonised again. . . .

31. This then is the reality and irony of Western human rights. On the one hand other Governments are threatened because of some minor breach of human rights; on the other hand, when Western interest is not at stake they are prepared to allow the most brutal violation of human rights to take place before their very eyes.

32. It is rather difficult for us to agree and to accept these double standards. And this unwillingness to accede has brought on a tirade of accusations about Asian recalcitrance. It would seem that Asians have no right to define and practise their own sets of values about human rights. What, we are asked, are Asian values? The question is rhetorical because the implication is that Asians cannot possibly understand human rights, much less set up their own values. . . .

34. No one, no country, no people and no civilisation has a right to claim that it has a monopoly of wisdom as to what constitute human rights. Certainly from the records and the performance of the Western liberals, they are least capable of defining and preaching human rights. Indeed, at the moment they have no right at all to talk of human rights, much less judge others on this issue.

DISCUSSION QUESTIONS

1   Consider the readings in chapter 14, item 5. How do the arguments Mahathir presented compare to U.S. visions for the world?

2   Mahathir stated that the West was "least capable of defining and preaching human rights." From your knowledge of history, what precedents might he have used to support that view?

ACCELERATING GLOBALIZATION

14–7a | Paul Conrad, political cartoon, "Hirohito's Revenge," 1985

By the 1970s, Japan had the world's third-largest gross national product, just behind the U.S. and USSR. The dramatic growth of the Japanese economy in the 1960s and 1970s was, in large part, fueled by heavy manufacturing. Automotive manufacturing comprised one of the largest and most prominent industries of that sector for the Japanese. The growth of the Japanese auto industry over a two-decade period was remarkable, growing from seventh to second in global automotive production by 1970, surpassing the U.S. by 1980, and extending its lead throughout the 1980s. In this image, Pulitzer Prize–winning cartoonist Paul Conrad depicted the enormity of that economic threat, seeing reprisal for the defeat of Japan in World War II.

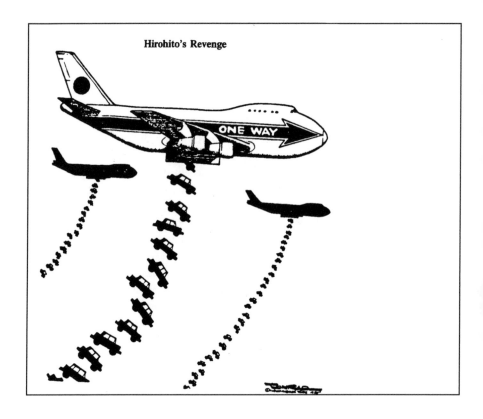

Hirohito's Revenge

14–7b | Maciek Lulko, photograph, Rockefeller Center, 1933

Built in the 1930s, Rockefeller Center was one of the foremost construction projects in New York during the Great Depression. The twenty-two-acre, nineteen-building complex is a fixture of Midtown Manhattan and was recognized as a National Historic Landmark in 1987. In 1989, the Mitsubishi Estate, the real estate arm of the giant Japanese multinational Mitsubishi Group, purchased a controlling interest in Rockefeller Center. It was one of several U.S. trophy acquisitions by the Japanese during the height of their economic power in the 1980s and early 1990s. This list included Firestone Tire & Rubber Co., Columbia Pictures Entertainment, Inc., and MCA Inc.

14-7c | Evan Amos, photograph, Nintendo Entertainment System, Japan, 1980s

Japan's growing influence in the U.S. was much more than economic as elements of Japanese popular culture became commonplace in the 1970s and 1980s. This popularization came in disparate forms, from the adoption of sushi by celebrity clientele in 1970s Hollywood, to the embrace of *anime*, to the 1980 televised epic *Shōgun*, which gave the National Broadcasting Company (NBC) the highest weekly Nielsen ratings in its history. It also came through the early expansion of arcade-based gaming by companies such as Sega and Taito. In 1985, Nintendo remodeled a version of its Family Computer system, or Famicom, for export to the U.S. as an entry into the home-based console gaming market. Dubbed the Nintendo Entertainment System console (1985–1995), NES became the best-selling game console of its time. Introduced on the heels of the North American video game crash of 1983, when market saturation and adoption of personal computers led to a severe recession in the video game console industry, the platform revitalized the industry and sold 35 million units in the U.S.

DISCUSSION QUESTIONS

1   What domestic and international factors contributed to the rising cultural influence of the Japanese in the U.S. in the 1980s?

2   How do these images illustrate the consequences of globalization on the U.S. and Japan?

3   How do these images challenge meanings of "international rivalry" in the context of the Cold War?

14–8 | Elie Wiesel, excerpts from Nobel Peace Prize acceptance speech, 1986

Elie Wiesel (1928–2016) received the Nobel Peace Prize in 1986 for his commitment to human rights and world peace, largely through his ongoing efforts to sustain the memory of the Holocaust and draw attention to those facing injustice. Born in Romania, Wiesel's family suffered at the hands of the Nazis during World War II; while he survived camps at Auschwitz and Buchenwald, Wiesel's parents and sister did not. Wiesel wrote dozens of books, including *Night* (1955), detailing the effects of genocide on humanity and the individual. Further, he spoke out against indifference, seeing a link between the lack of action that allowed the Holocaust to occur in the mid-twentieth century and the lack of action that allows racism, political persecution, and violence to flourish in the current day. Below is his acceptance speech.

It is with a profound sense of humility that I accept the honor you have chosen to bestow upon me. I know: your choice transcends me. This both frightens and pleases me.

It frightens me because I wonder: do I have the right to represent the multitudes who have perished? Do I have the right to accept this great honor on their behalf? . . . I do not. That would be presumptuous. No one may speak for the dead, no one may interpret their mutilated dreams and visions.

It pleases me because I may say that this honor belongs to all the survivors and their children, and through us, to the Jewish people with whose destiny I have always identified.

I remember: it happened yesterday or eternities ago. A young Jewish boy discovered the kingdom of night. I remember his bewilderment, I remember his anguish. It all happened so fast. The ghetto. The deportation. The sealed cattle car. The fiery altar upon which the history of our people and the future of mankind were meant to be sacrificed.

I remember he asked his father: "Can this be true?" This is the twentieth century, not the Middle Ages. Who would allow such crimes to be committed? How could the world remain silent?

And now the boy is turning to me: "Tell me," he asks, "What have you done with my future? What have you done with your life?"

And I tell him that I have tried. That I have tried to keep memory alive, that I have tried to fight those who would forget. Because if we forget, we are guilty, we are accomplices.

And then I explained to him how naive we were, that the world did know and remain silent. And that is why I swore never to be silent whenever and wherever human beings endure suffering and humiliation. We must always take sides. Neutrality helps the oppressor, never the victim. Silence encourages the tormentor, never the tormented. Sometimes we must interfere. When human lives are endangered, when human dignity is in jeopardy, national borders and sensitivities become irrelevant. Wherever men and women are persecuted because of their race, religion, or political views, that place must—at that moment—become the center of the universe.

Of course, since I am a Jew profoundly rooted in my peoples' memory and tradition, my first response is to Jewish fears, Jewish needs, Jewish crises. For I belong to a traumatized generation, one that experienced the abandonment and solitude of our people. It would be unnatural for me not to make Jewish priorities my own: Israel, Soviet Jewry, Jews in Arab land. . . . But there are others as important to me. Apartheid is, in my view, as abhorrent as anti-Semitism. To me, Andrei Sakharov's isolation is as much of a disgrace as Josef Biegun's imprisonment. As is the denial of Solidarity and its leader Lech Walesa's right to dissent. And Nelson Mandela's interminable imprisonment.

There is so much injustice and suffering crying out for our attention: victims of hunger, of racism, and political persecution, writers and poets, prisoners in so many lands governed by the Left and by the Right. Human rights are being violated on every continent. More people are oppressed than free. And then, too, there are the Palestinians to whose plight I am sensitive but whose methods I deplore. Violence and terrorism are not the answer. Something must be done about their suffering, and soon. I trust Israel, for I have faith in the Jewish people. Let Israel be given a chance, let hatred and danger be removed from her horizons, and there will be peace in and around the Holy Land.

Yes, I have faith. Faith in the God and even in His creation. Without it no action would be possible. And action is the only remedy to indifference: the most insidious danger of all. Isn't this the meaning of Alfred Nobel's legacy? Wasn't his fear of war a shield against war?

There is much to be done, there is much that can be done. One person—a Raoul Wallenberg, an Albert Schweitzer, one person of integrity, can make a difference, a difference of life and death. As long as one dissident is in prison, our freedom will not be true. As long as one child is hungry, our lives will be filled with anguish and shame. What all these victims need above all is to know that they are not alone; that we are not forgetting them, that when their voices are stifled we shall lend them ours, that while their freedom depends on ours, the quality of our freedom depends on theirs.

This is what I say to the young Jewish boy wondering what I have done with his years. It is in his name that I speak to you and that I express to you my deepest gratitude. No one is capable of gratitude as one who has emerged from the kingdom of night. We know that every moment is a moment of grace, every hour an offering; not to share them would mean to betray them. Our lives no longer belong to us alone; they belong to all those who need us desperately.

Thank you, Chairman Aarvik. Thank you, members of the Nobel Committee. Thank you, people of Norway, for declaring on this singular occasion that our survival has meaning for mankind.

DISCUSSION QUESTIONS

1 How did memory function in Wiesel's life and peacemaking philosophy? What connections did he make between his own experiences and human rights challenges of the era?

2 To whom was Wiesel speaking? What did he want his audience to do in response to his appeal? In what sense is both the audience and Wiesel's message a product of its context in the late twentieth century?

14–9a | University of California System, poster, "None of These Will Give You AIDS," 1985

U.S. doctors first identified Acquired Immunodeficiency Syndrome (AIDS), caused by infection with the Human Immunodeficiency Virus (HIV), in 1981. Even though the United States' Centers for Disease Control and Prevention (CDC) ruled out casual contact, food, sharing drinks, or environmental surfaces as means of transmission as early as 1983, anxiety about the spread of HIV/AIDS caused public panics, sometimes resulting in protests and violence. Misconceptions about transmission remained a problem well into the new millennium, even with ongoing efforts—such as those pictured below—to educate people about the disease.

SEE COLOR INSERT

14-9b | UNESCO/Aidthi Workshop, poster, AIDS information, India, 1995

HIV/AIDS grew to pandemic proportions by the late 1980s. In 1987, AIDS became the first disease discussed at the United Nations, as the UN tasked the World Health Organization (WHO) with its global efforts to confront the problem. Though major breakthroughs in treatment and understanding of HIV/AIDS occurred in the 1980s and 1990s, AIDS-related complications remained the #4 cause of death in the world and the leading cause of death in Africa by the eve of the new millennium. The U.S. launched PEPFAR, the President's Emergency Plan for AIDS Relief, in 2003 under President George W. Bush, the largest financial commitment to fight a disease in history. To date, PEPFAR has provided $84 billion in treatment, education, and prevention funding. An estimated 37 million people had HIV/AIDS as of 2018.

Translation: Hindi—"neither by eating together,
nor by affection, nor by welcome"

DISCUSSION QUESTIONS

1   What might have been the obstacles to overcoming misconceptions about HIV/AIDS transmission?

2   Who were the respective audiences for each of these posters? In what ways was that evident?

3   Like the Spanish influenza (chapter 8, item 8) and more modern pandemics, how does studying the spread of disease illuminate the phenomenon of globalization?

14–10 | Al Gore, excerpts from speech regarding information superhighways at the International Telecommunications Union, 1994

Albert "Al" Gore Jr. (b. 1948) served as Vice President of the United States under President Bill Clinton from 1993 to 2001. The push to develop the Internet accelerated in the 1990s but dated back to U.S. federally funded research efforts to create computer communication networks in the 1960s. The primary precursor to the modern Internet was the ARPANET (Advanced Research Projects Agency Network), a system that interconnected regional academic and military networks in the 1980s. In this speech at the International Telecommunications Union in Buenos Aires, Argentina, Gore noted the possibilities of a network characterized by the mass connectivity of institutional, personal, and mobile computers. Al Gore Jr. noted the revolutionary nature of these "information superhighways," akin to the ways in which his father, U.S. Senator Al Gore Sr., had championed the interstate highway system a generation before.

I have come here, 8,000 kilometers from my home, to ask you to help create a Global Information Infrastructure. To explain why, I want to begin by reading you something that I first read in high school, 30 years ago.

> "By means of electricity, the world of matter has become a great nerve,
> vibrating thousands of miles in a breathless point of time. The round
> globe is a vast . . . brain, instinct with intelligence!"

This was not the observation of a physicist—or a neurologist. Instead, these visionary words were written in 1851 by Nathaniel Hawthorne, one of my country's greatest writers, who was inspired by the development of the telegraph.

Much as Jules Verne foresaw submarines and moon landings, Hawthorne foresaw what we are now poised to bring into being.

The ITU was created only 14 years later, in major part for the purpose of fostering an internationally compatible system of telegraphy.

For almost 150 years, people have aspired to fulfill Hawthorne's vision—to wrap nerves of communications around the globe, linking all human knowledge.

In this decade, at this conference, we now have at hand the technological breakthroughs and economic means to bring all the communities of the world together. We now can at last create a planetary information network that transmits messages and images with the speed of light from the largest city to the smallest village on every continent.

I am very proud to have the opportunity to address the first development conference of the ITU because the President Clinton and I believe that an essential prerequisite to sustainable development, for all members of the human family, is the creation of this network of networks. To accomplish this purpose, legislators, regulators, and business people must do this: build and operate a Global Information Infrastructure. This GII will circle the globe with information superhighways on which all people can travel.

These highways—or, more accurately, networks of distributed intelligence—will allow us to share information, to connect, and to communicate as a global community. From these connections we will derive robust and sustainable economic progress, strong democracies, better solutions to global and local environmental challenges, improved health care, and—ultimately—a greater sense of shared stewardship of our small planet.

The Global Information Infrastructure will help educate our children and allow us to exchange ideas within a community and among nations. It will be a means by which families and friends will transcend the barriers of time and distance. It will make possible a global information marketplace, where consumers can buy or sell products.

I ask you, the delegates to this conference, to set an ambitious agenda that will help all governments, in their own sovereign nations and in international cooperation, to build this Global Information Infrastructure. For my country's part, I pledge our vigorous, continued participation in achieving this goal—in the development sector of the ITU, in other sectors and in plenipotentiary gatherings of the ITU, and in bilateral discussions held by our Departments of State and Commerce and our Federal Communications Commission.

The development of the GII must be a cooperative effort among governments and peoples. It cannot be dictated or built by a single country. It must be a democratic effort.

And the distributed intelligence of the GII will spread participatory democracy.

To illustrate why, I'd like to use an example from computer science.

In the past, all computers were huge mainframes with a single processing unit, solving problems in sequence, one by one, each bit of information sent back and forth between the CPU and the vast field of memory surrounding it. Now, we have massively parallel computers with hundreds—or thousands—of tiny self-contained processors distributed throughout the memory field, all interconnected, and together far more powerful and more versatile than even the most sophisticated single processor, because they each solve a tiny piece of the problem simultaneously and when all the pieces are assembled, the problem is solved.

Similarly, the GII will be an assemblage of local, national, and regional networks, that are not only like parallel computers but in their most advanced state will in fact be a distributed, parallel computer.

In a sense, the GII will be a metaphor for democracy itself. Representative democracy does not work with an all-powerful central government, arrogating all decisions to itself. That is why communism collapsed.

Instead, representative democracy relies on the assumption that the best way for a nation to make its political decisions is for each citizen—the human equivalent of the self-contained processor—to have the power to control his or her own life.

To do that, people must have available the information they need. And be allowed to express their conclusions in free speech and in votes that are combined with those of millions of others. That's what guides the system as a whole.

The GII will not only be a metaphor for a functioning democracy, it will in fact promote the functioning of democracy by greatly enhancing the participation of citizens in decision-making. And it will greatly promote the ability of nations to cooperate with each other. I see a new Athenian Age of democracy forged in the fora the GII will create. . . .

I opened by quoting Nathaniel Hawthorne, inspired by Samuel Morse's invention of the telegraph.

Morse was also a famous portrait artist in the U.S.—his portrait of President James Monroe hangs today in the White House. While Morse was working on a portrait of General Lafayette in Washington, his wife, who lived about 500 kilometers away, grew ill and died. But it took seven days for the news to reach him.

In his grief and remorse, he began to wonder if it were possible to erase the boundaries of time and space, so that no one would be unable to reach a loved one in time of need. Pursuing this thought, he came to discover how to use electricity to convey messages, and so he invented the telegraph and, indirectly, the ITU.

The Global Information Infrastructure offers instant communication to the great human family.

It can provide us the information we need to dramatically improve the quality of their lives. By linking clinics and hospitals together, it will ensure that doctors treating patients have access to the best possible information on diseases and treatments. By providing early warning on natural disasters like volcanic eruptions, tsunamis, or typhoons, it can save the lives of thousands of people.

By linking villages and towns, it can help people organize and work together to solve local and regional problems ranging from improving water supplies to preventing deforestation.

To promote; to protect; to preserve freedom and democracy, we must make telecommunications development an integral part of every nation's development. Each link we create strengthens the bonds of liberty and democracy around the world. By opening markets to stimulate the development of the global information infrastructure, we open lines of communication

By opening lines of communication, we open minds. This summer, from my country cameras will bring the World Cup Championship to well over one billion people.

To those of you from the 23 visiting countries whose teams are in the Finals, I wish you luck—although I'll be rooting for the home team.

The Global Information Infrastructure carries implications even more important than soccer.

It has brought us images of earthquakes in California, of Boris Yeltsin on a tank in Red Square, of the effects of mortar shells in Sarajevo and Somalia, of the fall of the Berlin Wall. It has brought us images of war and peace, and tragedy and joy, in which we all can share.

There's a Dutch relief worker, Wam Kat, who has been broadcasting an electronic diary from Zagreb for more than a year and half on the Internet, sharing his observations of life in Croatia.

After reading Kat's Croatian diary, people around the world began to send money for relief efforts. The result: 25 houses have been rebuilt in a town destroyed by war.

Governments didn't do this. People did. But such events are the hope of the future.

When I began proposing the NII in the U.S., I said that my hope is that the United States, born in revolution, can lead the way to this new, peaceful revolution. However, I believe we will reach our goal faster and with greater certainty if we walk down that path together. As Antonio Machado, Spanish poet, once said, "Path walker, there is no path, we create the path as we walk."

Let us build a global community in which the people of neighboring countries view each other not as potential enemies, but as potential partners, as members of the same family in the vast, increasingly interconnected human family.

Let us seize this moment.

Let us work to link the people of the world.

Let us create this new path as we walk it together.

DISCUSSION QUESTIONS

1   What functions did Gore foresee for the Global Information Infrastructure (GII)?

2   How might the system Gore described lay a foundation for globalization?

3   Compare the technology of the information superhighway with the technological developments of the Industrial Revolution (chapter 4, items 9 and 12). What do they mean for their respective time periods?

14–11a | Preamble to the North American Free Trade Agreement, Canada, Mexico, and the United States, 1994

Building on the bilateral trade agreement between Canada and the U.S. that began in January 1989, the formation of the North American Free Trade Agreement (NAFTA) created one of the world's largest trade blocs in terms of the gross domestic product (GDP). It tied the U.S., Mexico, and Canada together economically through a compact that provided plans for the elimination of tariffs, duties, and quantitative restrictions on the production and exchange of goods. NAFTA initiated a new era of regional and bilateral free trade agreement within the increasing trend toward globalization.

The Government of Canada, the Government of the United Mexican States and the Government of the United States of America, resolved to:

STRENGTHEN the special bonds of friendship and cooperation among their nations;

CONTRIBUTE to the harmonious development and expansion of world trade and provide a catalyst to broader international cooperation;

CREATE an expanded and secure market for the goods and services produced in their territories;

REDUCE distortions to trade;

ESTABLISH clear and mutually advantageous rules governing their trade;

ENSURE a predictable commercial framework for business planning and investment;

BUILD on their respective rights and obligations under the General Agreement on Tariffs and Trade and other multilateral and bilateral instruments of cooperation;

ENHANCE the competitiveness of their firms in global markets;

FOSTER creativity and innovation, and promote trade in goods and services that are the subject of intellectual property rights;

CREATE new employment opportunities and improve working conditions and living standards in their respective territories;

UNDERTAKE each of the preceding in a manner consistent with environmental protection and conservation;

PRESERVE their flexibility to safeguard the public welfare;

PROMOTE sustainable development;

STRENGTHEN the development and enforcement of environmental laws and regulations; and

PROTECT, enhance and enforce basic workers' rights;

HAVE AGREED as follows:

14–11b | Naomi Klein, excerpt from *No Logo: Taking Aim at the Brand Bullies*, Canada, 1999

Naomi Klein (b. 1970) is a noted Canadian author and social activist. Below is an excerpt from her first book, *No Logo*, for which she became internationally known. Many consider the principles declared in the publication a manifesto for the anti-globalization movement. As a social movement, anti-globalization, or global justice, generally focuses its criticism on the unregulated economic and political power of multinational corporations, arguing against the power and threat they pose as agents of neocolonialism.

Usually, reports about this global web of logos and products are couched in the euphoric marketing rhetoric of the global village, an incredible place where tribespeople in remotest rain forests tap away on laptop computers, Sicilian grandmothers conduct E-business, and "global teens" share, to borrow a phrase from a Levi's Web site, "a world-wide style culture." Everyone from Coke to McDonald's to Motorola has tailored their marketing strategy around this post-national vision, but it is IBM's long-running

"Solutions for a Small Planet" campaign that most eloquently captures the equalizing promise of the logo-linked globe.

It hasn't taken long for the excitement inspired by these manic renditions of globalization to wear thin, revealing the cracks and fissures beneath its high-gloss façade. More and more over the past four years, we in the West have been catching glimpses of another kind of global village, where the economic divide is widening and cultural choices narrowing.

This is a village where some multinationals, far from leveling the global playing field with jobs and technology for all, are in the process of mining the planet's poorest back country for unimaginable profits. . . .

I have become convinced that it is in these logo-forged global links that global citizens will eventually find sustainable solutions for this solid planet. . . . What conditions have set the stage for this backlash? Successful multinational corporations are increasingly finding themselves under attack, whether it's a cream pie in Bill Gates's face or the incessant parodying of the Nike swoosh—what are the forces pushing more and more people to become suspicious of or even downright enraged at multinational corporations, the very engines of our global growth? Perhaps more pertinently, what is liberating so many people—particularly young people—to act on that rage and suspicion? . . .

It is a daunting task but it does have an upside. The claustrophobic sense of despair that has so often accompanied the colonization of public space and the loss of secure work begins to lift when one starts to think about the possibilities for a truly globally minded society, one that would include not just economics and capital, but global citizens, global rights and global responsibilities as well. It has taken many of us a while to find our footing in this new international arena, but thanks in large part to the crash course provided by the brands, we are closer than ever before.

DISCUSSION QUESTIONS

1   How might regional trade agreements serve as building blocks for globalization?

2   In Klein's view, what should be the defining characteristics of a globalized society?

3   According to these sources, what are the benefits and detriments of globalization?

15

The New Millennium

360 | The Digital World

Redefining Security

Globalization

THE DIGITAL WORLD

In the late 1980s, less that 1 percent of the world's data was digital; that number now stands at 99 percent. Behind that dramatic shift is the digital revolution of the last few decades. The shift from the analog age to the digital age developed through the rise of personal computing, digital cellular phones, the growth of the Internet, and the rise of social media. Around the globe, states, societies, and individuals have experienced the widespread changes wrought by expanded and open access to information, new interconnectedness, and easier communication. These developments have been balanced by concerns about surveillance, privacy, social isolation, and media saturation. Despite the ongoing digital revolution, a global digital divide remains, a disparity of computing and information resources between developed and developing countries. In 2014, only three countries, China, the United States, and Japan, hosted 50 percent of the globally installed bandwidth potential. The selections below highlight the ways in which societies and governments around the world have responded to the landscape of the new millennium's digital world.

Chart, technology adoption in U.S. households, 1903–2016

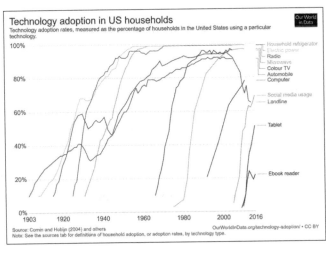

SEE COLOR INSERT

Share of the population using the Internet, 2017

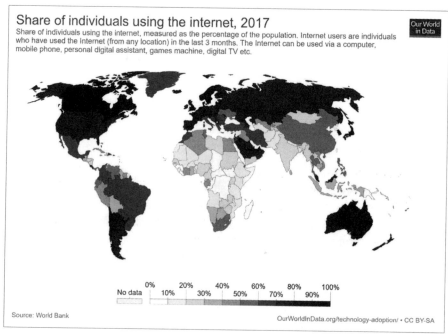

Share of individuals using the internet, 2017

Share of individuals using the internet, measured as the percentage of the population. Internet users are individuals who have used the Internet (from any location) in the last 3 months. The Internet can be used via a computer, mobile phone, personal digital assistant, games machine, digital TV etc.

Our World in Data

No data   0%   10%   20%   30%   40%   50%   60%   70%   80%   90%   100%

Source: World Bank   OurWorldInData.org/technology-adoption/ • CC BY-SA

SEE COLOR INSERT

Ministry of Communications and Information Technology, excerpts from guidelines for cyber cafés, India, 2011

Ministry of Communications and Information Technology

(Department of Information Technology)

Notification

New Delhi, the 11th April, 2011

1. Short title and commencement.—(1) These rules may be called the Information Technology (Guidelines for Cyber Cafe) Rules, 2011. . . .

4. Identification of User.—(1) The Cyber Cafe shall not allow any user to use its computer resource without the identity of the user being established. The intending user may establish his identify by producing a document which shall identify the users to the satisfaction of the Cyber Cafe. Such document may include any of the following:—

(i)   Identity card issued by any School or College; or

(ii) Photo Credit Card or debit card issued by a Bank or Post Office; or

(iii) Passport; or

(iv) Voter Identity Card; or

(v) Permanent Account Number (PAN) card issued by Income-Tax Authority; or

(vi) Photo Identity Card issued by the employer or any Government Agency; or

[vii] Driving License issued by the Appropriate Government; or

[viii] Unique Identification (UID) Number issued by the Unique Identification Authority of India (UIDAI).

(2) The Cyber Cafe shall keep a record of the user identification document by either storing a photocopy or a scanned copy of the document duly authenticated by the user and authorised representative of cyber cafe. Such record shall be securely maintained for a period of at least one year.

(3) In addition to the identity established by an user under sub-rule (1), he may be photographed by the Cyber Cafe using a web camera installed on one of the computers in the Cyber Cafe for establishing the identity of the user. Such web camera photographs, duly authenticated by the user and authorised representative of cyber cafe, shall be part of the log register which may be maintained in physical or electronic form.

(4) A minor without photo Identity card shall be accompanied by an adult with any of the documents as required under sub-rule (1).

(5) A person accompanying a user shall be allowed to enter cyber cafe after he has established his identity by producing a document listed in sub-rule(1) and record of same shall be kept in accordance with sub-rule (2).

(6) The Cyber cafe shall immediately report to the concerned police, if they have reasonable doubt or suspicion regarding any user.

5. Log Register.—(1) After the identity of the user and any person accompanied with him has been established as per sub-rule (1) of rule 4, the Cyber Cafe shall record and maintain the required information of each user as well as accompanying person, if any, in the log register for a minimum period of one year.

(2) The Cyber Cafe may maintain an online version of the log register. Such online version of log register shall be authenticated by using digital or electronic signature. The log register shall contain at least the following details of the user, namely:—

(ii) Name

(iii) Address

(iv) Gender

(v) Contact Number

(vi) Type and detail of identification document

(vii) Date

(vii) Computer terminal identification

(viii) Log in Time

(ix) Log out Time

(3) Cyber Cafe shall prepare a monthly report of the log register showing date-wise details on the usage of the computer resource and submit a hard and soft copy of the same to the person or agency as directed by the registration agency by the 5th day of next month.

(4) The cyber cafe owner shall be responsible for storing and maintaining backups of following log records for each access or login by any user of its computer resource for at least one year:—

(i) History of websites accessed using computer resource al [sic] cyber cafe;

(ii) Logs of proxy server installed at cyber cafe.

Cyber Cafe may refer to "Guidelines for auditing and logging—CISG-2008-01" prepared and updated from time to time by Indian Computer Emergency Response Team (CERT-ln) for any assistance related to logs. This document is available at www.cert-in .org.in

(5) Cyber cafe shall ensure that log register is not altered and maintained in a secure manner for a period of at least one year.

State Council, excerpts from Measures for the Administration of Internet Information Services, China, 2000

Article 3: Internet Information Services are divided into two categories: commercial and noncommercial.

Commercial Internet information providers refers to any service activity whereby one utilizes the Internet to provide information, Web page design, or other services to Internet users through the Internet for compensation.

Non-commercial Internet information providers refers to any service activity whereby one utilizes the Internet to provide public, shared information to Internet users through the Internet without compensation.

Article 4: There will be national implementation of a licensing system for commercial internet information services, and a registration system for non-commercial internet information services.

No one who fails to be licensed or who fails to comply with registration measures may engage in internet information services.

Article 14: Providers of internet information services engaged in journalism, publishing and BBS services shall record all information content and the time it was issued, and the internet address or city name; internet access providers shall record information regarding the amount of time each customer was on the internet, the customer's account number, internet address or city name, primary phone number, etc. Providers of internet information services and internet access providers shall maintain these records for 60 days, and shall make them available to all relevant government agencies examining them pursuant to law.

Article 15: Providers of internet information services may not produce, assist in production of, issue, or broadcast any information:

(i)   opposing the basic principles as they are confirmed in the Constitution;

(ii) jeopardizing the security of the nation, divulging state secrets, subverting state power, or jeopardizing the integrity of the nation's unity;

(iii) harming the honor or the interests of the nation;

(iv) inciting hatred against peoples, racism against peoples, or disrupting the solidarity of peoples;

(v)   disrupting national policies on religion, propagating evil cults and feudal superstitions;

(vi) spreading rumors, disturbing social order or disrupting social stability;

(vii) spreading obscenity, pornography, gambling, violence, murder, terror, or abetting the commission of a crime;

(viii) insulting or defaming third parties, infringing on the legal rights and interests of third parties; and

(ix) containing any other content prohibited by law or administrative rules.

Manoocher Deghati, photograph, art student from the University of Helwan paints the Facebook logo on a mural, Egypt, 2011

SEE COLOR INSERT

Trump Twitter feed, 2018

Donald J. Trump ✔
@realDonaldTrump

45th President of the United States of America🇺🇸

◎ Washington, DC 🔗 Instagram.com/realDonaldTrump 🗓 Joined March 2009

46 Following   **79.1M** Followers

Tweets   Tweets & replies   Media   Likes

Follow

360

360 DISCUSSION QUESTIONS

1   Pick three items from the chart of technology adoption in U.S. households. What might have been some of the influences of these technologies on U.S. society?

2   What might be the significance of the digital revolution for countries that are more open/free societies? What about those that are more closed/controlled?

3   What might be the significance of the global digital divide for both the less connected and more connected societies?

REDEFINING SECURITY

15–1a | Erik Junberger, photograph, National September 11 Memorial

Four coordinated attacks on the morning of September 11, 2001, killed 2,977 individuals, caused approximately $10 billion in property damage, started wars, and led to a significant restructuring of the U.S. government. Two planes flew into the towers of the World Trade Center in the Financial District of Lower Manhattan, New York City, one flew into the Pentagon building in Washington, D.C., with the final plane crashing in a field in Pennsylvania. Intelligence later revealed that the final plane's target was the U.S. Capitol building. The site of the Twin Towers became a site of mourning for the victims of the attacks and the first responders lost in the destruction of the massive structures. The goal of the memorial included the commitment to "respect this place made sacred through tragic loss."

SEE COLOR INSERT

15–1b | George W. Bush, excerpt from address to a joint session of Congress and the American people, 2001

The administration of George W. Bush (b. 1946) launched a War on Terror in response to the September 11 terrorist attacks. The international campaign used military operations, economic measures, and political pressure to target primarily armed Sunni Islamist fundamentalist groups in the Muslim world. Below, in a speech just over a week after the attacks, Bush articulated the American response to the attacks. In the aftermath of 9/11, Bush's approval rate jumped to over 85 percent as the government expanded security and surveillance measures. Since September 11 and with ongoing conflicts related to the War on Terror, the U.S. has remained in a state of national emergency.

Tonight we are a country awakened to danger and called to defend freedom. Our grief has turned to anger, and anger to resolution. Whether we bring our enemies to justice, or bring justice to our enemies, justice will be done.

. . .

On September the eleventh, enemies of freedom committed an act of war against our country. Americans have known wars—but for the past 136 years they have been wars on foreign soil, except for one Sunday in 1941. Americans have known the casualties of war—but not at the center of a great city on a peaceful morning. Americans have known surprise attacks—but never before on thousands of civilians. All of this was brought upon us in a single day—and night fell on a different world, a world where freedom itself is under attack.

Americans have many questions tonight. Americans are asking: Who attacked our country?

The evidence we have gathered all points to a collection of loosely affiliated terrorist organizations known as al-Qaida. They are the same murderers indicted for bombing American embassies in Tanzania and Kenya, and responsible for bombing the U.S.S. *Cole*.

Al-Qaida is to terror what the Mafia is to crime. But its goal is not making money; its goal is remaking the world—and imposing its radical beliefs on people everywhere.

The terrorists practice a fringe form of Islamic extremism that has been rejected by Muslim scholars and the vast majority of Muslim clerics—a fringe movement that perverts the peaceful teachings of Islam. The terrorists' directive commands them to kill Christians and Jews, to kill all Americans, and make no distinctions among military and civilians, including women and children.

This group and its leader—a person named Osama bin Laden—are linked to many other organizations in different countries, including the Egyptian Islamic Jihad and the Islamic Movement of Uzbekistan. There are thousands of these terrorists in more than 60 countries. They are recruited from their own nations and neighborhoods and brought to camps in places like Afghanistan, where they are trained in the tactics of terror. They are sent back to their homes or sent to hide in countries around the world to plot evil and destruction.

. . .

The United States respects the people of Afghanistan—after all, we are currently its largest source of humanitarian aid—but we condemn the Taliban regime. It is not only repressing its own people, it is threatening people everywhere by sponsoring and sheltering and supplying terrorists. By aiding and abetting murder, the Taliban regime is committing murder.

And tonight the United States of America makes the following demands on the Taliban: Deliver to United States authorities all the leaders of al-Qaida who hide in your land. Release all foreign nationals, including American citizens, you have unjustly imprisoned. Protect foreign journalists, diplomats and aid workers in your country. Close immediately and permanently every terrorist training camp in Afghanistan, and hand over every terrorist, and every person in their support structure to appropriate authorities. Give the United States full access to terrorist training camps, so we can make sure they are no longer operating.

These demands are not open to negotiation or discussion. The Taliban must act and act immediately. They will hand over the terrorists or they will share in their fate.

. . .

Americans are asking: Why do they hate us? They hate what they see right here in this chamber—a democratically elected government. Their leaders are self-appointed. They hate our freedoms—our freedom of religion, our freedom of speech, our freedom to vote and assemble and disagree with each other.

DISCUSSION QUESTIONS

1   How did designers choose to memorialize 9/11 at the World Trade Center site? What does that say about the event?

2   In the immediate aftermath of events, what questions did President Bush raise on behalf of the American public? How did he answer those questions?

3   How did September 11 become a foundational event for framing the U.S. view of the world in the twenty-first century?

15–2 | Arcadio Esquivel, political cartoon, "War Code," Costa Rica, 2004

Gerardo Arcadio Esquivel (b. 1959), Costa Rican artist and educator, offered this criticism of the course of U.S. military efforts in the world since the 9/11 attacks. Linked here is the 2003 invasion of Iraq, which, according to President George W. Bush, would disarm Iraq of weapons of mass destruction, end Saddam Hussein's support for terrorism, and free the Iraqi people. The coalition forces that participated in the invasion of Iraq and the war that followed were the U.S., the UK, Australia, Spain, and Poland. This can be contrasted with the thirty-five nations that took part in the Gulf War against Iraq in 1990–1991.

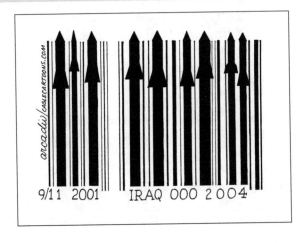

DISCUSSION QUESTIONS

1   Consider the image and text. What was Esquivel saying in his critique of the U.S.?

2   What connection does this piece make between war and economics? How might this relationship have been especially true in the case of the Iraq War?

15–3a | Barack Obama, remarks in eulogy for the Honorable Reverend Clementa Pinckney, 2015

In June 2015, a twenty-one-year-old man from Columbia, South Carolina, shot ten people, killing nine, during a midweek Bible Study at Emanuel African Methodist Episcopal Church in Charleston, South Carolina. Investigators revealed that the killer was a self-radicalized white supremacist who hoped to start a race war. He was influenced by online hate groups and had adopted racist symbols such as the flags of South Rhodesia and apartheid South Africa. A federal court sentenced him to death, and he received life in prison after pleading guilty to state murder charges. One of the victims, Rev. Clementa Pinckney, was pastor of Emanuel AME and a state senator. President Barack Obama (b. 1961) delivered the eulogy at Pinckney's funeral, combining a message on grace with current sociopolitical issues.

THE PRESIDENT: . . . Over the course of centuries, black churches served as "hush harbors" where slaves could worship in safety; praise houses where their free descendants could gather and shout hallelujah—(applause)—rest stops for the weary along the Underground Railroad; bunkers for the foot soldiers of the Civil Rights Movement. They have been, and continue to be, community centers where we organize for jobs and justice; places of scholarship and network; places where children are loved and fed and kept out of harm's way, and told that they are beautiful and smart—(applause)—and taught that they matter. (Applause.) That's what happens in church.

That's what the black church means. Our beating heart. The place where our dignity as a people is inviolate. When there's no better example of this tradition than Mother Emanuel—(applause)—a church built by blacks seeking liberty, burned to the ground because its founder sought to end slavery, only to rise up again, a Phoenix from these ashes. (Applause.) . . .

We do not know whether the killer of Reverend Pinckney and eight others knew all of this history. But he surely sensed the meaning of his violent act. It was an act that drew on a long history of bombs and arson and shots fired at churches, not random, but as a means of control, a way to terrorize and oppress. (Applause.) An act that he imagined would incite fear and recrimination; violence and suspicion. An act that he presumed would deepen divisions that trace back to our nation's original sin. . . .

For too long, we were blind to the pain that the Confederate flag stirred in too many of our citizens. (Applause.) It's true, a flag did not cause these murders. But as people from all walks of life, Republicans and Democrats, now acknowledge—including Governor Haley, whose recent eloquence on the subject is worthy of praise—(applause)—as we all have to acknowledge, the flag has always represented more than just ancestral pride. (Applause.) For many, black and white, that flag was a reminder of systemic oppression and racial subjugation. We see that now.

Removing the flag from this state's capitol would not be an act of political correctness; it would not be an insult to the valor of Confederate soldiers. It would simply be an acknowledgment that the cause for which they fought—the cause of slavery—was wrong—(applause)—the imposition of Jim Crow after the Civil War, the resistance to civil rights for all people was wrong. (Applause.) It would be one step in an honest accounting of America's history; a modest but meaningful balm for so many unhealed wounds. It would be an expression of the amazing changes that have transformed this state and this country for the better, because of the work of so many people of goodwill, people of all races striving to form a more perfect union. By taking down that flag, we express God's grace. (Applause.)

But I don't think God wants us to stop there. (Applause.) For too long, we've been blind to the way past injustices continue to shape the present. Perhaps we see that now. Perhaps this tragedy causes us to ask some tough questions about how we can permit so many of our children to languish in poverty, or attend dilapidated schools, or grow up without prospects for a job or for a career. (Applause.)

Perhaps it causes us to examine what we're doing to cause some of our children to hate. (Applause.) Perhaps it softens hearts towards those lost young men, tens and tens of thousands caught up in the criminal justice system—(applause)—and leads us to make sure that that system is not infected with bias; that we embrace changes in how we train and equip our police so that the bonds of trust between law enforcement and the communities they serve make us all safer and more secure. (Applause.)

Maybe we now realize the way racial bias can infect us even when we don't realize it, so that we're guarding against not just racial slurs, but we're also guarding against the subtle impulse to call Johnny back for a job interview but not Jamal. (Applause.) So that we search our hearts when we consider laws to make it harder for some of our fellow citizens to vote. (Applause.) By recognizing our common humanity by treating every child as important, regardless of the color of their skin or the station into which they were born, and to do what's necessary to make opportunity real for every American—by doing that, we express God's grace. (Applause.)

For too long—

AUDIENCE: For too long!

THE PRESIDENT: For too long, we've been blind to the unique mayhem that gun violence inflicts upon this nation. (Applause.) Sporadically, our eyes are open: When eight of our brothers and sisters are cut down in a church basement, 12 in a movie theater, 26 in an elementary school. But I hope we also see the 30 precious lives cut short by gun violence in this country every single day; the countless more whose lives are forever changed—the survivors crippled, the children traumatized and fearful every day as they walk to school, the husband who will never feel his wife's warm touch, the entire communities whose grief overflows every time they have to watch what happened to them happen to some other place.

The vast majority of Americans—the majority of gun owners—want to do something about this. We see that now. (Applause.) And I'm convinced that by acknowledging the pain and loss of others, even as we respect the traditions and ways of life that make up this beloved country—by making the moral choice to change, we express God's grace. (Applause.) . . .

15–3b | Chart, numbers of deaths from terrorist attacks globally, 1970–2017

The September 11 attacks in 2001 shook the United States, generating long-term changes in policies on national security, privacy, transportation, communication, and immigration, among others. The sense of security enjoyed by the U.S. was also shaken by more recent domestic terrorist attacks, such as the shooting at Emanuel AME Church in Charleston, the Boston Marathon bombing (2013), and the Oklahoma City bombing (1995) which preceded the events of 9/11. Those events illustrate the variety of motives behind domestic terrorism—white supremacy; retribution for U.S. wars on Iraq, Afghanistan, and Islam; and right-wing extremist anger at the U.S. government for raids at Ruby Ridge (1992) and Waco (1993). The graph below places these recent events in international context, providing a visualization related to the human toll of terrorist attacks around the world.

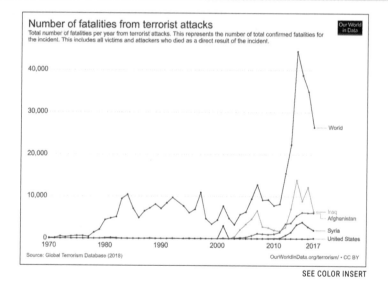

SEE COLOR INSERT

DISCUSSION QUESTIONS

1   How did President Obama characterize the relationship between religion, politics, and society in his eulogy for Reverend Pinckney?

2   What does the chart illustrate about the nature and extent of terrorism?

3   What are the various factors driving acts of violence and terrorism in the United
     States?

15-4 | Word clouds of National Security Strategy statements of the United States of America, 2002, 2010, and 2017

Prepared periodically for the U.S. Congress by the Office of the President, the National Security Strategy outlines the major national security concerns of the U.S. and the White House's strategic vision to address them. In its design, the document is to communicate to both domestic and foreign constituencies and work to create an internal consensus on foreign policy within the executive branch. Although the administrations of Ronald Reagan, George H. W. Bush, and Bill Clinton produced reports, they have taken on an expanded importance in the new millennium. There have been five editions of the National Security Strategy published since 9/11, two under George W. Bush (2002, 2006), two under Barack Obama (2010, 2015), and one by Donald Trump (2017). Below are word clouds or weighted lists of the text from the 2002, 2010, and 2017 National Security Strategies.

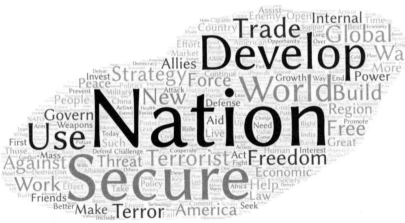

2002

2010

2017

DISCUSSION QUESTIONS

1   What similarities and differences do you observe between each of the word clouds?
2   What factors in 2002, 2010, and 2017 explain why terms appear more or less
    prominently?

15–5 | Akbar Ahmed, excerpt from *The Thistle and the Drone*, Pakistan, 2013

American-Pakistani Akbar Ahmed (b. 1943), a leading authority on contemporary Islam,
is an academic, author, and former diplomat. After the September 11 attacks, Ahmed
wrote a series of pieces on the relationship of the West and Islam post-9/11. Below, in
an introduction from his book, he addressed the use of drones by the U.S. in the ongoing

War on Terror. The recent global effort to fight terrorist groups has seen widespread use of drones, or unmanned combat aerial vehicles, in many theaters of the war, including Pakistan's Waziristan, where Ahmed served as ambassador.

"The Jonas Brothers are here. They're out there somewhere," a smiling and confident President Barack Obama told the expectant and glittering audience attending the White House Correspondents' dinner in Washington on May 1, 2010. "Sasha and Malia are huge fans, but boys, don't get any ideas. I have two words for you: 'predator drones.' You will never see it coming. You think I'm joking?"

Obama's banter may have seemed tasteless, given that he had just been awarded the Nobel Peace Prize, but this was not a Freudian slip. The president was indicating he possessed Zeus-like power to hurl thunderbolts from the sky and obliterate anyone with impunity, even an American pop group. One report said he had a "love" of drones, noting that by 2011 their use had accelerated exponentially. It was also revealed that Obama had a secret "kill list." Having read Saint Augustine and Saint Thomas Aquinas, and their ideas of the "just war" and "natural law," which promote doing good and avoiding evil, did not deter Obama from a routine of going down the list to select names and "nominate" them, to use the official euphemism, for assassination. I wondered whether the learned selectors of the Nobel Peace Prize had begun to have second thoughts.

As its use increased, the drone became a symbol of America's war on terror. Its main targets appeared to be Muslim tribal groups living in Afghanistan, Pakistan, Yemen, and Somalia. Incessant and concentrated strikes were directed at what was considered the "ground zero" of the war on terror, Waziristan, in the Tribal Areas of Pakistan. There were also reports, however, of U.S. drones being used against other Muslim tribal groups like the Kurds in Turkey and the Tausug in the Philippines, and also by the United Kingdom against the Pukhtun tribes of Afghanistan, by France in northern Mali against the Tuareg, and even by Israel in Gaza. These communities—some of the most impoverished and isolated in the world, with identities that are centuries-old—had become the targets of the twenty-first century's most advanced kill technology.

The drone embodied the weaponry of globalization: high-tech in performance, sleek in appearance, and global in reach. It was mysterious, distant, deadly, and notoriously devoid of human presence. Its message of destruction resounded in its names: Predator and Reaper. For its Muslim targets, the UAV, or unmanned aerial vehicle, its official title, had an alliterative quality—it meant death, destruction, disinformation, deceit, and despair. Flying at 50,000 feet above ground, and therefore out of sight of its intended victims, the drone could hover overhead unblinkingly for twenty-four hours, with little escaping its scrutiny before it struck. For a Muslim tribesman, this manner of combat not only was dishonorable but also smacked of sacrilege. By appropriating the powers of God through the drone, in its capacity to see and not be seen and deliver death without warning, trial, or judgment, Americans were by definition blasphemous.

In the United States, however, the drone was increasingly viewed as an absolutely vital weapon in fighting terrorism and keeping America safe. Support for it demonstrated patriotism, and opposition exposed one's anti-Americanism. Thus the debate surrounding the drone rested on its merits as a precisely effective killing machine rather than the human or emotional costs it inflicted. Drone strikes meant mass terror in entire societies across the world, yet little effort was made on the part of the perpetrators to calculate the political and psychological fallout, let alone assess the morality of public assassinations or the killing of innocent men, women, and children. Even those who rushed to rescue drone victims were considered legitimate targets of a follow-up strikes. Nor did Americans seem concerned that they were creating dangerous precedents for other countries.

Instead, boasting with the pride of a football coach, CIA director, and later secretary of defense, Leon Panetta referred to the drones as "the only game in town." Fifty-five members of Congress organized what was popularly known as the Drone Caucus and received extensive funds for their campaigns from drone manufacturers such as General Atomics and Lockheed Martin. The drones' enthusiastic public advocates even included "liberal" academics and self-avowed "hippies" such as philosophy professor Bradley Strawser of Monterey, California. Americans exulted in the fact that the drone freed Americans of any risk. It could be operated safely and neatly from newly constructed high-tech, air-conditioned offices. Like any office worker in suit and tie, the "pilot" could complete work in his office and then go home to take his family bowling or join them for a barbecue in the backyard. The drone was fast becoming as American as apple pie.

Typical of its propensity for excess in matters of security, by 2012 America had commissioned just under 20,000 drones, about half of which were in use. They were proliferating at an alarming rate, with police departments, internal security agencies, and foreign governments placing orders. In September 2012 Iran unveiled its own reconnaissance and attack drone with a range of over 2,000 kilometers. The following month, France announced it was sending surveillance drones to Mali to assist the government in fighting the Tuareg rebels in the north. In October 2012 the United Kingdom doubled its number of armed drones in Afghanistan with the purchase of five Reaper drones from the United States, to be operated from a facility in the United Kingdom. It was estimated that by the end of the decade, some 30,000 U.S. drones would be patrolling American skies alone. There was talk in the press of new and deadly varieties, including the next generation of "nuclear-powered" drones. Despite public interest, drone operations were deliberately obscured.

Ignoring the moral debate, drone operators are equally infatuated with the weapon and the sense of power it gives them. It leaves them "electrified" and "adrenalized"—flying a drone is said to be "almost like playing the computer game Civilization," a "sci-fi" experience. A U.S. drone operator in New Mexico revealed the extent to which individuals across the world can be observed in their most private moments. "We watch people for months," he said. "We see them playing with their dogs or doing their laundry. We know their patterns like we know our neighbors' patterns. We even go to their funerals." Another drone operator spoke of watching people having sex at night through infrared cameras. The last statement, in particular, has to be read keeping in mind the importance Muslim tribal peoples give to notions of modesty and privacy.

The victims are treated like insects: the military slang for a successful strike, when the victim is blown apart on the screen in a display of blood and gore, is "bug splat." Muslim tribesmen were reduced to bugs or, in a *Washington Post* editorial by David Ignatius, cobras to be killed at will. Any compromise with the Taliban in the Tribal Areas of Pakistan, officially designated as the Federally Administered Tribal Areas (FATA), is "like playing with a cobra," he wrote. And do we "compromise" with cobras? Ignatius asked. "No, you kill a cobra." Bugs, snakes, cockroaches, rats—such denigration of minorities has been heard before, and as recent history teaches, it never ends well for the abused people.

DISCUSSION QUESTIONS

1   In what ways does Ahmed see the use of drones as symbolic of the U.S. role in the world in the twenty-first century?

2   What are the moral implications of using such military technology as drones?

3   Recall the sources on the militarization of nuclear technology (chapter 11, item 10; chapter 12, item 9). What common concerns are raised about both nuclear and drone technology?

15–6 | Pew Research Center, chart, "Most Prefer U.S. as World Leader," 2018

China overtook Japan as the world's second-largest economy in 2010, rising from eleventh in 1990. In the last twenty years, the country has also seen a historic rise in both foreign investment in China and Chinese investment overseas. In this Pew Research Center survey of countries from around the globe regarding the current rivalry between China and the United States, almost two-thirds prefer the U.S. as the world's leading power.

Most prefer U.S. as world leader

Having ___ as the world's leading power would be better for the world

	China	U.S.
Japan	8%	81%
Philippines	12	77
Sweden	14	76
South Korea	11	73
Australia	14	72
Canada	15	71
Netherlands	16	71
Poland	6	68
UK	17	67
Israel	13	65
France	21	65
Kenya	30	65
Spain	26	63
Germany	19	58
Nigeria	36	55
Brazil	28	51
Mexico	41	48
Greece	26	46
South Africa	38	45
Hungary	9	45
Indonesia	22	43
Italy	17	37
Argentina	35	33
Tunisia	64	26
Russia	35	13
25-COUNTRY MEDIAN	19	63
U.S.	6	88

Note: "Neither" and "both" volunteered categories not shown.
Source: 2018 Global Attitudes Survey. Q33.

PEW RESEARCH CENTER

DISCUSSION QUESTIONS

1   Globally, which region (Asia, Africa, Europe, South America) favored American leadership the most? Least? Why?

2   Select two countries that differ significantly from the median responses. Explain why the variance might be so great in each case?

3   Can ideology, right or left, be predictive in how each country stated their preference?

GLOBALIZATION

15-7 | The Governments of Mexico, Belize, Honduras, Nicaragua, El Salvador, Panama, Costa Rica, Guatemala, the Dominican Republic and Colombia, "Unauthorized Immigration to the United States," 2006

Accelerating globalization has led to increased migration around the world. The U.S., despite its idealized image as a "melting pot" and "nation of immigrants," has struggled to juggle economic, political, social, and humanitarian aims of immigration regulations throughout its history. The relationship with Latin America has been particularly complex in the last fifty years, as migrants from the region became the major component of the U.S.'s foreign-born population (see chapter 15, item 10) and comprised nearly 75 percent of unauthorized immigrants. In the first decade of the 2000s, most undocumented persons entered via Mexico; thus, much attention has been directed at the U.S.-Mexico border. Foreign ministers of Central America, Colombia, and the Dominican Republic met in Mexico City in January 2006 to draft a response to Washington's heightened debate over illegal immigration.

Joint Declaration of the Meeting of Ministers from Mesoamerican Countries

Mexico City, January 9, 2006

For centuries, men and women have immigrated through borders enriching their communities of origin and to those that welcome them. Even though the flows of people from one country to another or even within the same nation have been constant, never before has the migration phenomenon been studied and discussed in detail as we do now.

Since 1965, the migrant population in the world has maintained constant at around 3 percent of the total representing approximately 175 million of people according to the last count of the United Nations Organization.

However, in reality, the migratory dynamics have acquired more and more importance in world forums and especially in the internal agendas of states, becoming a matter of high sensitivity, since its social, economic and political consequences have manifested themselves more strongly in recent decades.

The reasons for the migration are many and varied and respond to factors present in the recipient countries (economic growth in developing countries and aging populations, among others), on climatic factors, as well as, to the growing contact between already settled communities and their countries of origin.

Nowadays, almost no country or region in the world remains free of the migration phenomenon and its consequences. Population structures among developed countries and those in the process of development, economic asymmetries between nations, growing economic interdependence and the intense relationships and exchanges between countries are variables that encourage the increase of migratory flows and their repercussions.

In this sense, globalization has contributed to the growth of migration and has weakened many of the obstacles for the movement of people through international borders. However, in response to this growth, various countries have implemented a hardening of the rules applicable to migration, which has generated an important gap between the exchange of goods and services and free transit of people.

Population dynamics among the countries that are part of Latin America and the United States, the increasing contact between communities and families and a gap still too deep between income levels, impose the need to improve the administration of the migratory phenomenon. Also, in recent years, faced with new threats to collective security such as terrorism, transnational organized crime, human trafficking and falsification of documents, the binomial migration-security has been placed as one of the greatest challenges of our societies.

The Ministers of Foreign Affairs and senior officials gathered today in Mexico City, taking into account the Declaration of Mar Del Plata: "Create Jobs to Confront Poverty and Strengthen Democratic Governance" on November 5 of 2005:

- We reaffirm that it must be given to all migrants, regardless of their migratory status, the full protection of their human rights and full observance of the labor laws that apply to them;
- We urge to increase the cooperation and dialogue in order to reduce and discourage undocumented migration, as well as promoting migratory processes according to the internal legal order of each state and international law of applicable human rights; and
- We are committed to dialogue in order to reduce the cost and facilitate transfers of remittances, and increase efforts to combat illicit human trafficking of migrants, in accordance with international law of human rights, and facilitate a dignified, orderly and insurance of migrants.

Likewise, the Ministers of Foreign Affairs and senior government officials gathered here today consider:

- That it is convenient to continue strengthening friendships and mutual collaborations among our nations.

- That the international implications of this phenomenon require actions and commitments between regions and neighboring countries, that within the framework of international cooperation, should be guided by the principle of shared responsibility.
- That while a significant number of our nations do not find in their own country an economic and social environment that allows their full development and well-being, there will be conditions to migrate to countries where there is a demand for workers.
- That to the extent that there are sufficient and timely ways in the receiving countries to guarantee a legal, safe, orderly and respectful migration of the rights of the people, dialogue and international cooperation in this area will benefit all countries involved.
- That the growing linkage between migration, security, and borders worldwide is a present reality in our relations; consequently, it is necessary to harmonize these three elements when formulating migration policies.
- That it is the responsibility of all nations to safeguard the integrity, dignity and rights of migrants, so it is imperative to redouble efforts to combat human trafficking, as well as the associated criminal activities and to strengthen cooperation in this matter.
- That, based on the principles of shared responsibility and family unity, the establishment of temporary worker schemes is an essential element to achieve legal migration processes that are safe, orderly, and respectful of human rights. It is also essential to pay attention to the migratory status of the people who are in an undocumented situation in the receiving countries.
- That, respecting the sovereign right of countries to conduct their migration and security policies, partial measures that only contemplate the hardening of migration policies do not represent an integral solution to face the challenges imposed by the migratory phenomenon or take advantage of its opportunities.
- That migrants, regardless of their migratory status, are not and should not be treated as criminals.
- That the borders demanded by the 21st century should be characterized by respect for the rights of individuals, the cooperation, the use of technology and the search for a balance between the legitimate concerns for the security of states and the efficient flow of people and goods.

The Ministers of Foreign Affairs and senior officials gathered today create a working group to exchange views and information on best practices in the field, as well as to work with each other and with other governments in the construction of policies that allow for a better administration of the migratory phenomenon.

DISCUSSION QUESTIONS

1   How might globalization enable migration, both voluntary and involuntary?

2   Human rights emerges as a repeated theme in the document above. How might that
    reflect the concerns of these governments regarding migrants, and what message were
    they sending to the U.S.?

15–8 | Map, density of global shipping routes in the world's oceans, 2012

Approximately 50,000 merchant ships annually transport over 90 percent of the world's
trade, mostly on large container ships, tankers, and bulk carriers. The goods on these
ships are worth about $4 trillion, and the liner shipping industry employs tens of millions
worldwide. The ease and relatively low expense of sea transport is a key element in the
second wave of globalization occurring after World War II, a period in which the value of
world trade has grown by more than thirty times.

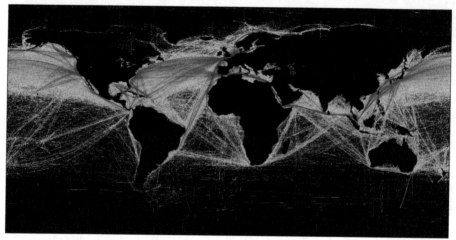

SEE COLOR INSERT

DISCUSSION QUESTIONS

1   What do you note about the pattern(s) of global shipping?

2   What would this pattern mean for those countries in highly trafficked areas? What
    about less trafficked?

15–9a | Graph, global fossil fuel consumption, 1800–2016

While fossil fuels such as coal, oil, and gas have been used for millennia, the Industrial
Revolution created an unprecedented demand for them. According to Our World in Data,
the use of fossil fuels has increased over 1300-fold since 1800. The U.S. is the single

largest consumer of oil and natural gas, while China is the single largest consumer of coal. The burning of fossil fuels has caused increased carbon dioxide in the earth's atmosphere, a primary factor in global warming.

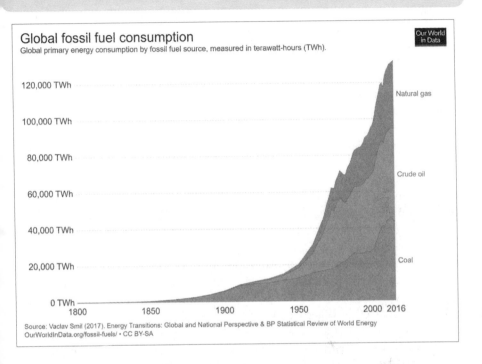

Global fossil fuel consumption
Global primary energy consumption by fossil fuel source, measured in terawatt-hours (TWh).

Our World in Data

Natural gas

Crude oil

Coal

Source: Vaclav Smil (2017). Energy Transitions: Global and National Perspective & BP Statistical Review of World Energy
OurWorldInData.org/fossil-fuels/ • CC BY-SA

15–9b | Mohamed Nasheed, excerpts from speech delivered at the Climate Vulnerable Forum, Maldives, 2009

Mohamed Nasheed (b. 1967), the first democratically elected President of the Maldives, has become a leading advocate for global action to address the effects of climate change. The Maldives are a chain of 2,000 islands in the Indian Ocean, already subject to loss of coastline and contaminated soil and water because of rising ocean waters. Nasheed led the formation of and hosted the first meeting of the Climate Vulnerable Forum, a coalition of eleven—now twenty—developing countries projected to be radically influenced by the effects of rising global temperatures, in November 2009. Soon after, Nasheed appeared at the 2009 United Nations Climate Change Conference in Copenhagen, where he is largely credited with laying the foundations for the 2015 Paris Accord, considered a major step forward in international action on climate change.

We gather in this hall today, as some of the most climate-vulnerable nations on Earth. We are vulnerable because climate change threatens to hit us first; and hit us hardest. And we are vulnerable because we have modest means with which to protect ourselves from the coming disaster.

We are a diverse group of countries. But we share one common enemy. For us, climate change is no distant or abstract threat; but a clear and present danger to our survival. Climate change is melting the glaciers in Nepal. It is causing flooding in Bangladesh. It threatens to submerge the Maldives and Kiribati. And in recent weeks, it has furthered drought in Tanzania, and typhoons in the Philippines. We are the frontline states in the climate change battle.

Ladies and gentlemen, developing nations did not cause the climate crisis. We are not responsible for the hundreds of years of carbon emissions, which are cooking the planet. But the dangers climate change poses to our countries, means that this crisis can no longer be considered somebody else's problem. Carbon knows no boundaries. Whether we like it or not, we are all in this fight together. . . .

Ladies and gentlemen, when we look around the world today, there are few countries showing moral leadership on climate change. There are plenty of politicians willing to point the finger of blame.

But there are few prepared to help solve a crisis that, left unchecked, will consume us all. Few countries are willing to discuss the scale of emissions reductions required to save the planet. And the offers of adaptation support for the most vulnerable nations are lamentable. The sums of money on offer are so low, it is like arriving at a earthquake zone with a dustpan and brush. We don't want to appear ungrateful but the sums hardly address the scale of the challenge. We are gathered here because we are the most vulnerable group of nations to climate change. The problem is already on us, yet we have precious little with which to fight. Some might prefer us to suffer in silence but today we have decided to speak. And so I make this pledge today: we will not die quietly.

DISCUSSION QUESTIONS

1   When did global fossil fuel consumption accelerate exponentially? Why might this be?

2   What was the significance of Nasheed's message coming from a nation such as the Maldives?

3   How do these sources illustrate that climate change is a matter of both physical and political power?

15–10 | Trends in immigration

With buzzwords like "borderlessness" and "mobility," it is perhaps no surprise that accelerating globalization has fostered increased migration around the world over the past fifty years. While migration is praised for meeting labor needs in growing economies and offering opportunities for cultural exchange, critics of globalization often decry perceived threats to domestic labor and way of life posed by large numbers of immigrants. Statistics reflect this tension: according to the Pew Research Center, most Americans (62 percent) hold a positive view of immigrants, while about half the public (51 percent) believes immigration policymaking should be a priority for Congress and the President. Below are two graphs based on U.S. census data indicating longitudinal trends in immigration.

15–10a | Graph, number of immigrants and their share of the total population of the United States, 1850–2018

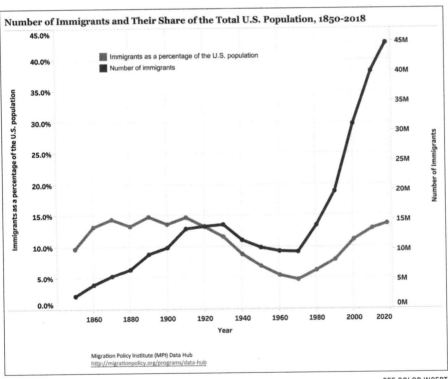

15–10b | Graph, regions of birth for immigrants to the United States, 1960–2018

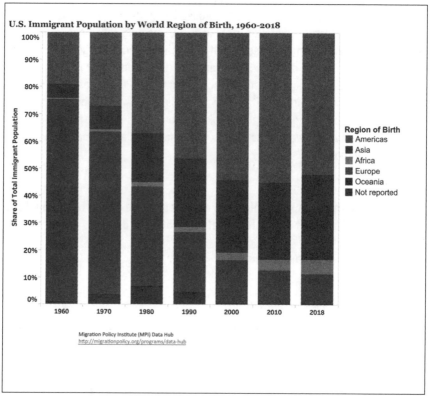

U.S. Immigrant Population by World Region of Birth, 1960-2018

Region of Birth
■ Americas
■ Asia
■ Africa
■ Europe
■ Oceania
■ Not reported

Migration Policy Institute (MPI) Data Hub
http://migrationpolicy.org/programs/data-hub

SEE COLOR INSERT

DISCUSSION QUESTIONS

1   How does the first chart complicate the notion of the nation being "overrun" by immigrants?

2   What do you notice about the origins of the immigrant population over time?

3   What recent immigration trends do you observe? How might these trends influence the U.S. in the future?

SOURCE NOTES

1 | Contact and Colonization

1-360 | Columbian Exchange

- Giuseppe Arcimboldo and Jens Mohr, *Vertumnus*, 1590, photograph via Wikimedia Commons.

- Gabriel Venel, "Chocolate," in *Encyclopédie*, vol. 3, ed. Denis Diderot and Jean le Rond d'Alembert, trans. Philippe Bonin (Paris: Andre Le Breton, 1751–1777), 359–60.

- Sebah & Joaillier, *Café Turc*, 1880–1900, Library of Congress Prints and Photographs Division, https://www.loc.gov/pictures/resource/ppmsca.22268/.

- Recipe for salsa di pomodoro (tomato sauce), 1891, in *La scienza in cucina e l'arte di mangiar bene: manuale pratico per le famiglie*, compiled by Pellegrino Artusi (Florence: Presso l'autore, 1911), recipe 125, pp. 124–25. Available online via HathiTrust at https://catalog.hathitrust.org/Record/011985964. English translation by Jeffrey M. Hunt, © Baylor University Press.

- Ping-Ti Ho, "The Introduction of American Food Plants into China," *American Anthropologist* 57, no. 2, new series: pt. 1 (April 1955): 191.

- Adam Smith, *An Inquiry into the Nature and Causes of the Wealth of Nations* (London: G. Routledge and Son, 1900), 127–28, 196, 432.

1-1   Paolo Toscanelli, "Atlantic Ocean, Toscanelli, 1474," in *A Literary & Historical Atlas of America* (New York: E.P. Dutton & Co., 1911), 1.

1-2   "The Requerimiento [Requirement], Council of Castile, 1510 (Pronouncement to Be Read by Spanish Conquerors to Defeated Indians)," National Humanities Center, https://nationalhumanitiescenter.org/pds/amerbegin/contact/text7/requirement.pdf.

1-3   Jacques Cartier, *The Voyages of Jacques Cartier*, ed. and trans. H. P. Biggar (Ottawa: King's Printer, 1924), 60–64.

1-4a   Theodor de Bry, *The arriual of the Englishemen in Virginia*, in *Wunderbarliche, doch warhafftige Erklärung, von der Gelegenheit vnd Sitten der Wilden in Virginia* . . . [America, pt. 1, German] (Frankfurt: D. Bry, 1590), 40, North Carolina Collection, Wilson Library, University of North Carolina at Chapel Hill, http://dc.lib.unc.edu/cdm/ref/collection/debry/id/57.

1–4b John Smith, *Advertisements for the Unexperienced Planters of New-England, or Anywhere…* (London: Iohn Haviland, 1631), 10–12, Early English Books Online Text Creation Partnership, http://name.umdl.umich.edu/A12458.0001.001.

1–5 Black Bear (Mato Sapo), after Lone Dog, Lakota, dates unknown, *Winter Count*, ca. 1900. Leather, pigment, cotton, glue, newsprint. Frederick Weygold Collection, 1937.68.210, Speed Art Museum, https://www.speedmuseum .org/collections/winter-count/.

1–6 Governor Glen, "Section VIII," in *Historical Collections of South Carolina: Embracing Many Rare and Valuable Pamphlets and Other Documents*, by B. R. Carroll (New York: Harper and Brothers, 1836), 244–47.

1–7a John Nathan Hutchins, *Prospect of the City of New-York*, in *The New-York Pocket Almanack, for the Year 1772* (New York: Hugh Gaine, 1771), John Carter Brown Archive of Early American Images, Brown University, accession number 06-224, record number 06-224-1.

1–7b Andrew Burnaby, *Burnaby's Travels through North American: Reprinted from the Third Edition of 1798*, ed. Rufus Rockwell Wilson and Francis Fauquier (New York: A. Wessels Company, 1904), 88–89, Library of Congress, https:// lccn.loc.gov/04028434.

1–8a "Rolls's Best Virginia in Whites-Alley Chancery-Lane, London" (advertisement), 18th c., The British Museum, https://research.britishmuseum .org/research/collection_online/collection_object_details/collection_image _gallery.aspx?assetId=119435001&objectId=1614805&partId=1.

1–8b Jasper Danckaerts, *The Journal of Jasper Danckaerts, 1679–1680*, ed. Bartlett Burleigh James and J. Franklin Jameson (New York: Charles Scribner's Sons, 1913), 133.

1–9a Phillis Wheatley, "On Being Brought from Africa to America," in *Poems on Various Subjects. Religious and Moral. By Phillis Wheatley, Negro Servant to Mr. John Wheatley, of Boston, in New England* (London: A. Bell, 1773), 18.

1–9b Ottobah Cugoano, "Appendix: Narrative of the Enslavement of Ottobah Cugoano, a Native of Africa; Published by Himself, in the Year 1787," in *The Negro's Memorial, or, Abolitionist's Catechism; by an Abolitionist* (London: Hatchard and Co., and J. and A. Arch, 1825), 120–27. Documenting the American South, University of North Carolina at Chapel Hill, https:// docsouth.unc.edu/neh/cugoano/cugoano.html.

1–10 Natalia Shelikhova, *Russian Oligarch of Alaska Commerce*, ed. Dawn Lea Black, trans. Alexander Yu. Petrov (Fairbanks: University of Alaska Press, 2010), 112–17.

2 | The United States in the Age of Revolution

2–360 | Rights of the Individual

○ National Assembly of France, "Declaration of the Rights of Man," August 26, 1789, Yale Law School, Lillian Goldman Law Library, 2008, https://avalon .law.yale.edu/18th_century/rightsof.asp.

○   U.S. Congress, "Engrossed Bill of Rights," September 25, 1789, Record Group 11, General Records of the United States Government, OurDocuments. gov, https://www.ourdocuments.gov/doc.php?flash=true&doc=13&page= transcript.

○   Marie-Olympe de Gouges, "The Rights of Woman (1791)," in Olympe de Gouges, *Les droits de la femme. A la Reine* (Paris, 1791), 5–12, 13. Available online through the Bibliothèque nationale de France at https://catalogue .bnf.fr/ark:/12148/cb36057180p. English translation by Kel Pero, © Baylor University Press.

○   United Nations General Assembly, "Universal Declaration of Human Rights: General Assembly Resolution 217 A," Documents, United Nations, December 10, 1948, https://www.un.org/en/universal-declaration-human -rights/.

2–1a   John Locke, "Two Treatises of Government," in *The Works of John Locke*, ed. Rod Hay, a new edition, corrected, vol. 5:5 (London: Printed for Thomas Tegg; W. Sharpe and Son; G. Offor; G. and J. Robinson; J. Evans and Co.: also R. Griffin and Co. Glasgow; and J. Gumming, Dublin, 1823), 106–8, 116–18, 125–26. McMaster University Archive of the History of Economic Thought, http://www.yorku.ca/comninel/courses/3025pdf/Locke.pdf.

2–1b   Jean-Jacques Rousseau, "The Social Compact," in *The Social Contract: Or, The Principles of Political Rights*, trans. Rose M. Harrington (New York: G.P. Putnam's Sons, 1893), 19–22.

2–2   Jonathan Mayhew, *A Discourse Concerning Unlimited Submission and Non-Resistance to the Higher Powers, 1790*, 2nd ed. (Boston: Hall & Goss, 1818), 33–34, 40–42.

2–3a   William Pitt, *Correspondence of William Pitt, Earl of Chatham*, ed. John Henry Pringle and William Stanhope Taylor, vol. 2 (London: J. Murray, 1838), 369–73.

2–3b   "The Colonies Reduced—Its Companion," 1767, Library of Congress Prints and Photographs Division, http://hdl.loc.gov/loc.pnp/ppmsca.31019.

2–4a   *Britain, America, at Length Be Friends . . .* , 1774, Library of Congress Rare Book and Special Collections Division, http://hdl.loc.gov/loc.pnp/cph .3a45693.

2–4b   John Adams, "VII. To the Inhabitants of the Colony of Massachusetts-Bay," March 6, 1775, Papers of John Adams, vol. 2, 320, Massachusetts Historical Society, Adams Papers Digital Edition, http://www.masshist.org/ publications/adams-papers/view?&id=PJA02dg5.

2–5a   William L. Stone, *Life of Joseph Brant-Thayendanegea: Including the Border Wars of the American Revolution and Sketches of the Indian Campaigns of Generals Hamar, St. Clair, and Wayne . . . from the Peace of 1783 to the Indian Peace of 1795*, vol. 1 of 2 vols. (New York: G. Dearborn and Co., 1838), 58–63.

2–5b   Benjamin Bussey Thatcher, *Indian Life and Battles: A Minute and Graphic Story of the Early Indian in the United States: A Valuable Compendium to General American History* (New York: D. M. Mac Lellan Book Company, 1910), 190–91.

2–6 Noël Le Mire, *Marquis de Lafayette*, 1781, National Portrait Gallery, Smithsonian Institution, Washington, D.C., https://npg.si.edu/object/npg _NPG.84.126.

2–7a Willis Mason West, ed., "117. Advertisements for Runaway Servants; Newspaper Extracts for the Years 1770–1771, from the New Jersey Archives," in *A Source Book in American History to 1787* (Boston: Allyn and Bacon, 1913), 366–68.

2–7b "Petition for Freedom (Manuscript Copy) to the Massachusetts Council and the House of Representatives, [13] January 1777," Massachusetts Historical Society, Jeremy Belknap Papers, https://www.masshist.org/database/viewer .php?item_id=557&br=1.

2–8 Thomas Jefferson, Letter to J. Banister Jr. (October 15, 1785), in *Memoirs, Correspondence, and Private Papers of Thomas Jefferson, Late President of the United States*, ed. Thomas Jefferson Randolph (London: Henry Colburn and Richard Bentley, 1829), 345–47.

2–9a "It'll Be Okay," *Liberty, Equality, Fraternity*, Roy Rosenzweig Center for History and New Media (George Mason University) and American Social History Project (City University of New York), http://chnm.gmu.edu/ revolution/d/623. English translation by Daniel Watkins, © Baylor University Press.

2–9b "The Levée en Masse, France, 1793," in *The Constitutions and Other Select Documents Illustrative of the History of France, 1789–1907*, by Frank Maloy Anderson, 2nd ed. (Minneapolis: H.W. Wilson, 1908), 184–85.

2–10 *"Incendie du Cap"* [*"Burning of Cap-Français"*]. *"Révolte générale des Négres. Massacre des Blancs"* [*"General revolt of the Blacks. Massacre of the Whites"*], ca. 1815, photograph, Wikimedia Commons.

2–11 Simón de Bolívar, *An Address of Bolivar at the Congress of Angostura (February 15, 1819)*, trans. Francisco Javier Yánes, reprint ordered by the government of the United States of Venezuela, to commemorate the centennial of the opening of the Congress (Washington, D.C.: Press of Byron B. Adams, 1919), 18, 21–23, 25–26, 34, 39.

2–12 Edward Herslet, "No. 188. HATTI-SHERIFF by the Sultan of Turkey, Relative to the Administration of the Ottoman Empire. Gulhané, 3rd November, 1839," in *The Map of Europe by Treaty*, vol. 2 (London: Butterworth, 1875), 1002–5.

3 | The Early Republic and the World

3–360 | Indigenous Peoples

o Supreme Court of the United States, "U.S. Reports: The Cherokee Nation v. the State of Georgia, 30 U.S. (5 Pet.) 1 (1831)," vol. 30, Washington, D.C.: Supreme Court, 1831, Library of Congress, https://www.loc.gov/item/ usrep030001/.

o "Native Lands Act 1865 (29 Victoriae 1865 No. 71)," New Zealand Legal

Information Institute, 2019, New Zealand Acts As Enacted, http://www.nzlii
.org/nz/legis/hist_act/nla186529v1865n71251/.

   o   "Hokkaido Former Natives Protection Law, 1899," in *Reading Colonial Japan: Text, Context, and Critique*, ed. Michele M. Mason and Helen J. S. Lee (Redwood City, Calif.: Stanford University Press, 2012), 57–59. *Ainu Group*, 1904, photograph, Wikimedia Commons.

   o   Kingdom of Norway, "Kingdom of Norway Constitution, 1814 (Rev. 2016), Article 108 (1988)," Constitute: The Comparative Constitutions Project (CCP), 2016, https://www.constituteproject.org/constitution/Norway_2016?lang=en.

   o   United Nations Children's Fund, "United Nations Declaration of the Rights of Indigenous Peoples for Indigenous Adolescents," UNICEF, Human Rights Unit, Programme Division, 2013, http://files.unicef.org/policyanalysis/rights/files/HRBAP_UN_Rights_Indig_Peoples.pdf.

3–1 George Washington, "Washington's Farewell Address (1796)," New York Public Library, 1935, Milstein Division of United States History, The New York Public Library, Astor, Lenox and Tilden Foundation, 105, 136, OurDocuments.gov, https://www.ourdocuments.gov/doc.php?flash=false&doc=15&page=transcript.

3–2a "James Mackay, Instructions for John Thomas Evans, 1796," in *Before Lewis and Clark; Documents Illustrating the History of the Missouri, 1785–1804*, ed. A. P. Nasatir, vol. 2 (St. Louis, Mo.: St. Louis Historical Documents Foundation, 1952), 412–14.

3–2b *Louisiana*, 1804, Library of Congress Geography and Map Division, http://hdl.loc.gov/loc.gmd/g4050.ct000654.

3–3 Norman St. Clair Gurd, "The Council at Old Vincennes [Speech of Tecumseh to William Henry Harrison, 11 Aug 1810]," in *The Story of Tecumseh* (Toronto: William Briggs, 1912), 85–86.

3–4 James Gillray, "The Plumb-pudding in danger;— or—State Epicures taking un Petit Souper," 1805, Library of Congress Prints and Photographs Division, http://hdl.loc.gov/loc.pnp/cph.3g08791.

3–5 John Quincy Adams, "Diary Entry, November 16, 1819," in *Memoirs of John Quincy Adams, Comprising Portions of His Diary from 1795–1848*, ed. Charles Francis Adams, vol. 4 (Philadelphia: J.B. Lippincott & Co., 1875), 438–39.

3–6a James Monroe, "State of the Union Address," in *State of the Union Addresses of James Monroe* (1823), Project Gutenberg, http://gutenberg.readingroo.ms/5/0/1/5014/5014-h/5014-h.htm#dec1823.

3–6b Simón Bolívar, "Letter to Colonel Patrick Campbell, 1829," in *Selected Writings of Bolívar*, by Vicente Lecuna, ed. Harold A. Bierek Jr., trans. Lewis Betrand, 2nd ed. (New York: Colonial Press, 1951), 731–32.

3–7 Hirata Atsutane on the "Land of the Gods," an excerpt from the text *Kodō taii* (古道大意), vol. 1 of 2, volume page 22, line 6 at the top through line 3 at the bottom—volume page 23, line 7 at the top through line 7 at the bottom, from the collection *Hirata Atsutane zenshū*, vol. 1 (Tokyo: Icchidō Shoten, Meiji 44, 1911), ed. Inoue Yorikuni and Tsunoda Tadayuki, and revised by Hirata Moritane and Miki Ioe. Available on HathiTrust at https://hdl .handle.net/2027/uc1.$b377709 (pages 40–41 in the HathiTrust viewer). English translation by Yoshiko Fujii Gaines, © Baylor University Press. Hirata Atsutane on the "art of medicine," an excerpt from the text *Shizu no iwaya* (志都能石屋) / *Meiido taii* (名医道大意), vol. 1 of 2, from the collection *Shinshū Hirata Atsutane zenshū*, vol. 14 (Tokyo: Meicho Shuppan, Shōwa 52, 1977), volume page 444 line 6 at the top through line 3 at the bottom (page 22 within the text *Shizu no iwaya*), ed. Hirata Atsutane Zenshū Kankōkai. English translation by Yoshiko Fujii Gaines, © Baylor University Press.

3–8a　　Gordon Hall and Samuel Newell, *The Conversion of the World: Or The Claims of Six Hundred Millions and the Ability and Duty of the Churches Respecting Them* (Andover, Mass.: Printed for the American Board of Commissioners for Foreign Missions by Flagg & Gould, 1818), 10–15.

3–8b　　Lam Qua, *Portrait No. 02* and *Portrait No. 19*, 1834–1855. Digital Collections, Yale Cushing/Whitney Medical Library, http://library.medicine.yale.edu/ find/peter-parker.

3–9　　Domingo Faustino Sarmiento, *Travels in the United States in 1847.* Translated from *Viajes por Europa, Africa i America 1845–1847*, ed. Javier Fernández, critical edition, 2nd ed. (Madrid; Paris; México; Buenos Aires; São Paulo; Rio de Janeiro; Lima: ALLCA XX, 1996), 290–92, 295, 297, 300–301, 314–15, 336, 426. English translation by Hannah M. Dyar, © Baylor University Press.

3–10　　Xu Jiyu on George Washington and the American political system, from *Ying-huan zhi-lüe: [10 juan / Xu Jiyu zhu]* [*Short Account of the Oceans around Us*] ([China: s.n.]: Daoguang geng xu, 1850). Available via HathiTrust, Hathi viewer pages 811–12, 833–37, 867–68, 870–71, https://babel.hathitrust.org/ cgi/pt?id=coo.31924092367709&view=1up&seq=57. English translation by Benjamin Henry, © Baylor University Press.

4 | Forging a New Industrial Order

4–360 | Comparative Industrialization

◦　　"Convention of Commerce, &c. Balta-Liman, August 16, 1838," in *Treaties, &c. Between Turkey and Foreign Powers, 1535–1855* (London: The Foreign Office, 1855), 276–79.

◦　　Inoue Tankei, *Famous Places in Tokyo: Picture of Azuma Bridge and a Distant View of a Torpedo Explosion*, July 1888, *Throwing Off Asia: Woodblock Prints of Domestic Westernization (1868–1912)*, Museum of Fine Arts, Boston, https://visualizingcultures.mit.edu/throwing_off_asia_01/toa_vis_04.html.

◦　　T. H. Von Laue, "A Secret Memorandum of Sergei Witte on the Industrialization of Imperial Russia," *The Journal of Modern History* 26 (March 1954): 66–67.

o   Max Roser and Esteban Ortiz-Ospina, "Primary and Secondary Education: Primary School Enrollment, 1820–2010," OurWorldInData.org, 2019, https://ourworldindata.org/primary-and-secondary-education.

o   Economic, Financial and Transit Department, League of Nations, "Table 1: Percentage Distribution of the World's Manufacturing, 1870–1938," in *Industrialization and Foreign Trade*, 2nd ed. (United States of America: United Nations, 1948), 13.

4–1   "A Planter's Letter," *The Gentleman's Magazine*, vol. 59 (April 1789), The British Library, https://www.bl.uk/learning/images/makeanimpact/large9003.html.

4–2a   "A Few Plain Questions to Plain Men" (London: S. Bagster Jun. Printer, 1820s), Wilberforce House Museum, The British Library, https://www .bl.uk/learning/histcitizen/campaignforabolition/sources/antislavery/ plainquestions/electionhandbill.html.

4–2b   "The Negro Woman's Appeal to Her White Sisters," ca. 1850, Library of Congress. http://hdl.loc.gov/loc.rbc/rbpe.06500800.

4–3   David Walker, *Walker's Appeal, in Four Articles; Together with a Preamble, to the Coloured Citizens of the World, but in Particular, and Very Expressly, to Those of the United States of America, Written in Boston, State of Massachusetts, September 28, 1829* (Boston: David Walker, 1830), 3–6. Documenting the American South, University of North Carolina at Chapel Hill, https:// docsouth.unc.edu/nc/walker/walker.html.

4–4a   Solomon Northrup, *Twelve Years a Slave: Narrative of Solomon Northrup* (New York: Miller, Orton, Mulligan, 1855), 78–82.

4–4b   *Ship's Manifest, the Schooner Thomas Hunter, Arriving New Orleans, November 11, 1835, from Norfolk, VA*, 1835, Record Group (RG) 36, Preliminary Inventory NC-154, The National Archive and Records Service, https://www .archives.gov/files/research/african-americans/images/m1895R7-hunter-l.jpg.

4–5   Great Britain Ministry of Labour, Great Britain General Register Office, Great Britain Board of Trade, Statistical Dept, and Great Britain Board of Trade, "No. 21-Quantities of Raw Cotton Imported into the United Kingdom," in *Statistical Abstract for the United Kingdom In Each of the Last Fifteen Years From 1856 to 1870*, vol. 18 (London: George E. Eyere and William Spottiswoode, 1871), 58–59.

4–6   Adam Smith, "The Principle of the Mercantile System," in *Select Chapters and Passages from the Wealth of Nations of Adam Smith, 1776* (New York: MacMillan and Co., 1903), 5–7, 16–17, 221–22.

4–7a   J. F. C. Harrison, "Yorkshire Cloth Workers Petition, 1786," in *Society and Politics in England, 1780–1960* (New York: Harper & Row, 1965), 71–72.

4–7b   J. F. C. Harrison, "Letter from Leeds Cloth Merchants, 1791," in *Society and Politics in England, 1780–1960* (New York: Harper & Row, 1965), 72–74.

4–8a   Winslow Homer, "The Bobbin Girl," in *The Song of the Sower*, by William Cullen Bryant, 2nd ed. (New York: D. Appleton, 1881), 29.

4–8b   Harriet H. Robinson and Massachusetts Bureau of Statistics of Labor, *Early Factory Labor in New England: From the Fourteenth Annual Report of the*

Massachusetts Bureau of Statistics of Labor for 1883, ed. Carroll Davidson Wright, repr. ed. (Boston: Wright & Potter Print Co., 1889), 4, 11–12.

4–9a   "Line of American Packets Between N. York & Liverpool," *Evening Post*, October 27, 1817, 2, AMDOCS: Documents for the Study of American History, http://www.vlib.us/amdocs/texts/packets.htm

4–9b   Charles Oscar Paullin, "Transportation: Transportation and Rates of Travel," *Atlas of the Historical Geography of the United States* (New York: Carnegie Institution of Washington and the American Geographical Society of New York, 1932), Digital Collections, University of Denver Penrose Library, http://www.mappingthenation.com/index.php/viewer/index/1.

4–10a   George Iles, "Sketch of McCormick Reaper, Patented January 31, 1845," in *Leading American Inventors* (New York: Henry Holt and Company, 1912), 300. Image, Wikimedia Commons.

4–10b   Reuben Gold Thwaites, "Four Vital Elements and A Radical Departure," in *Cyrus Hall McCormick and the Reaper* (Madison, WI: State Historical Society of Wisconsin, 1909), 240–42.

4–11a   The Working Men's Association, "The People's Charter" (London: H. Hetherington, ca. 1838), The British Library, https://www.bl.uk/learning/histcitizen/21cc/struggle/chartists1/historicalsources/source4/peoplescharter.html.

4–11b   Karl Marx and Frederick Engels, *Manifesto of the Communist Party*, 1848, in *Marx/Engels Selected Works*, trans. Samuel Moore, vol. 1 (Moscow: Progress Publishers, 1969), 98–137.

4–12a   "Map of the 1858 Atlantic Cable Route," *Frank Leslie's Illustrated Newspaper*, August 21, 1858, [Bill Burns'] History of the Atlantic Cable & Undersea Communications: Submarine Cable Route Maps, photograph, Wikimedia Commons.

4–12b   Charles I. Bevans, ed., "General Postal Union; October 9, 1874," in *Treaties and Other International Agreements of the United States of America 1776–1949*, vol. 1, *Multilateral 1776–1917* (Washington, D.C.: Department of State Publication, 1968), 29–38.

4–13   J. Ottmann Lith. Co., *All Nations Use Singer Sewing Machines*, ca. 1892, Library of Congress Prints and Photographs Division, http://hdl.loc.gov/loc.pnp/ppmsca.09488.

5 | Making a Nation

5–360 | National Anthems

o   Claude Joseph Rouget de Lisle, "La Marseillaise," France, 1792.

o   Vicente López y Planes, "Marcha Patriótica (Himno Nacional Argentino)," Argentina, 1812.

o   Francis Scott Key, "The Star-Spangled Banner," United States of America, 1814.

○ Waka Poem, "Kimigayo / His Imperial Majesty's Reign," Japan, 1800. *Kokki oyobi Kokka ni kan suru Hōritsu (Hōritsu dai hyakunijūnana-gō)*, Act on National Flag and Anthem, Act No. 127, 1999-08-13. English translation Christopher Hood, *Japanese Education Reform* (New York: Routledge, 2001).

○ Ibrāhīm Khafājī, "An-Našīd al-Waṭaniyy / The National Anthem," Saudi Arabia, 1984.

○ Naftali Herz Imber, "Hatikvah / The Hope," Israel, 1878.

○ Said Al Muzayin, "Warrior," Palestine, 1996.

○ Enoch Sontonga, C. J. Langenhoven, Jeanne Zaidel-Rudolph, "National Anthem of South Africa," South Africa, 1897.

5–1a   José María Sánchez, "A Trip to Texas in 1828," trans. Carlos E. Castañeda, *Southwestern Historical Quarterly*/Texas State Historical Association, vol. 29, no. 4 (April 1926): 257–60, 283.

5–1b   Eugene C. Barker, "Native Latin Contributions to the Colonization and Independence of Texas," *Southwestern Historical Quarterly*/Texas State Historical Association vol. 46, no. 4 (April 1943): 328–29.

5–2   Charles Wilkes, *Narrative of the United States Exploring Expedition during the Years 1838, 1839, 1840, 1841, 1842*, vol. 5 (Philadelphia: Lea & Blanchard, 1845), Smithsonian Institution, https://library.si.edu/image-gallery/108477.

5–3a   Edwin Williams and Benson J. Lossing, eds., "Polk's First Annual Message," in *The Statesman's Manual: Containing the Presidents' Messages, Inaugural, Annual, and Special, From 1789 to 1858 . . .* , vol. 3 (New York: Edward Walker, 1858), 1555–1560, 1565–1566.

5–3b   J. Distrunell, "Map of the United States of Mexico, According to What Has Been Organized and Defined by the Various Acts of the Congress of Said Republic, Created by the Best Authorities," New York, 1847, General Records of the U.S. Government, The National Archive and Records Service, https://www.archives.gov/publications/prologue/2005/summer/images/mexico-disturnell-l.jpg.

5–4   William Walker, *The War in Nicaragua* (Mobile, Ala.: S. H. Gietzel, 1860), 263, 280, 429–31.

5–5a   "'Caesar Imperator!' Or, The American Gladiators," *Punch*, May 18, 1861, 203.

5–5b   "The Topic: Is the Secession of the Southern States of American from the Union Desirable?" *British Controversialist and Literary Magazine*, 1861, 283–87.

5–6a   United States Department of State, "Annual Message of the President [Alexander Gorchakov to Bayard Taylor, December 1862]," in *Message of the President of the United States, and Accompanying Documents, to the Two Houses of Congress, at the Commencement of the First Session of the Thirty-Eighth Congress* (Washington, D.C.: U.S. Government Printing Office, 1863), 840.

5–6b   "The Russian Fleet, Commanded by Admiral Lisovski, Now in the Harbor of New York," *Harper's Weekly*, October 17, 1863, 664–65.

5–7   An Habituate, *Opium Eating: An Autobiographical Sketch* (Philadelphia: Claxton, Remsen & Haffelfinger, 1876), 49, 54–58, 75–76, 90–91, 116–19.

5–8   Karl Marx, "Address of the International Working Men's Association to Abraham Lincoln, President of the United States of America, January 28, 1865," and "[Charles Francis Adams Response]," in *The Anti-Slavery Reporter*, 3rd ser., vol. 13 (London: Society at No. 27, New Broad Street, 1865), 10, 68.

5–9a   "The Declaration of Sentiments," in *History of Woman Suffrage*, ed. Elizabeth Cady Stanton, Susan Brownell Anthony, and Matilda Joslyn Gage, 2nd ed., vol. 1 (Rochester, N.Y.: Charles Mann, 1889), 70–71.

5–9b   Ernestine L. Rose, *An Address on Woman's Rights: Delivered before the People's Sunday Meeting, in Cochituate Hall, on Sunday Afternoon, Oct. 19th, 1851* (Boston: J.P. Mendum, 1851), 3–7, 19–21. Library of Congress, https://lccn .loc.gov/28018616.

5–10a   Frederick Douglass, *Oration, Delivered in Corinthian Hall, Rochester ["What to the Slave Is the Fourth of July?"]*, July 5, 1852 (Rochester, N.Y.: Lee, Mann & Co., 1852), 10, 14–21. University of Rochester Frederick Douglass Project, http://rbscp.lib.rochester.edu/2945.

5–10b   U.S. Congress, "No. 35-The Black Code of St. Landry Parish, 1865," in *Senate Executive Documents. 39th Congress, 1st Session:1865–1866*, vol. 2 (Washington, D.C.: U.S. Government Printing Office, 1866), 93–94.

5–10c   *Sharecropper Sam Williams with Family Members and Laborers in Cotton Field*, ca. 1908, Library of Congress Prints and Photographs Division, http:// hdl.loc.gov/loc.pnp/cph.3c20752.

5–11a   "Treaty Regulating Immigration from China, November 17, 1880," in *Treaties, Conventions, International Acts, Protocols, and Agreements between the United States and Other Powers*, compiled by William M. Malloy (Washington, D.C.: U.S. Government Printing Office, 1910), 237–38.

5–11b   U.S. Congress, "Chinese Exclusion Act," in *U.S. Statutes at Large*, vol. 22, session 1 (Washington, D.C.: U.S. Government Printing Office, 1882), 58–61.

5–11c   George Frederick Keller, "A Statue for *Our* Harbor," 1881, Online Archive of California, http://cdn.calisphere.org/data/13030/bd/hb809nb2bd/files/ hb809nb2bd-FID4.jpg.

5–12a   "New Mexico," *Harper's Weekly*, April 1, 1876, 262–63.

5–12b   The New Mexico Constitutional Convention, *The Constitution of the State of New Mexico: Adopted by the Constitutional Convention Held At Santa Fe, N. M., From October 3 to November 21, 1910, And As Amended, November 6th, 1911* (Santa Fe, N.M.: La Voz del Pueble Print, 1912), 3–4, 28–29, 43–46.

6 | Western Expansion and Empire

6–360 | Motives for Empire

◦   Jules François Camille Ferry, *Discours sur la politique extérieure et coloniale (2e partie): Affaires tunisiennes (suite et fin), Congo, Madagascar, Égypte, Tonkin*, vol. 5 of *Discours et opinions de Jules Ferry* (Paris: A. Colin & Cie, 1893–1898), 199–200, 209, 210–11, 217–18, 220. Available online through the Bibliothèque nationale de France at http://catalogue.bnf.fr/ark:/12148/cb30431580s. English translation by Kel Pero, © Baylor University Press.

o   John Paton, "British Missionary Letters: Urging the Annexation of the South Sea Islands," in *Accounts and Papers 1883*, vol. 47 (London: HMSO, 1883), 29–30.

o   *Certificate for the American Board of Commissioners for Foreign Missions, Missionary House, Boston, Mass.*, 1857, Historic New England, https://www.historicnewengland.org/explore/collections-access/capobject/?refd=EP001.01.020.01.02.007.

o   Kaiser Wilhelm II, "A Place in the Sun, 1901," in *The German Emperor as Shown in His Public Utterances*, by Christian Gauss (New York: Charles Scribner's Sons, 1915), 180–83.

o   Shigenobu Ōkuma, *Fifty Years of New Japan*, English ed., vol. 2, ed. Marcus B. Huish (London: Smith, Elder, & Co., 1909), 554–55, 571–72, 574–75.

6-1a   Harriet Martineau, "Agriculture," in *Society in America*, vol. 1 (New York: Unders and Otley, 1837), 291–93, Project Gutenberg, https://www.gutenberg.org/files/52621/52621-h/52621-h.htm.

6-1b   *A Kiowa Ledger Drawing Possibly Depicting the Buffalo Wallow Battle in 1874, a Fight between Southern Plains Indians and the U.S. Army during the Red River War*, 1874, photograph, Texas Archeological Research Laboratory, Wikimedia Commons.

6-2   Walker D. Wyman, "California Emigrant Letters," *California Historical Quarterly* 24, no. 4 (December 1945): 361.

6-3a   Samuel Bowles, *Our New West* (Hartford, Conn.: Hartford Publishing Co., 1869), 47–51.

6-3b   Pacific Railway, *Central Pacific Railway Travel Poster: The Great American Panorama*, 1900, Location 68350, Wisconsin Historical Society, https://www.wisconsinhistory.org/Records/Image/IM68350.

6-4   Walt Whitman, "Passage to India," 1870, Academy of American Poets, https://poets.org/poem/passage-india.

6-5   Chicago, Burlington and Quincy Railroad, "Jeden Milion Akru," brochure (in Czech), 1879, trans. Michael Long, and "En Million Akers Nebraska Land" (in Danish), 1879, trans. Davide Zori, Newberry Library, http://www.environmentandsociety.org/exhibitions/railroad/settlement-promotion-burlington-railroad.

6-6a   Francis L. Hawks, ed., "Millard Fillmore, President of the United States of America, to His Imperial Majesty, the Emperor of Japan," in *Narrative of the Expedition of an American Squadron to the China Seas and Japan, Performed in the Years 1852, 1853, and 1854, under the Command of Commodore M. C. Perry, United States Navy, by Order of the Government of the United States*, vol. 1 (Washington, D.C.: A. O. P. Nicholson, 1856), 256–57.

6-6b   *American Warship, Woodblock Print*, ca. 1854, Nagasaki Prefecture, Visualizing Cultures: Massachusetts Institute of Technology, https://

visualizingcultures.mit.edu/black_ships_and_samurai/gallery/pages/06
_065_AmericanWarship.htm. James G. Evans, *U.S. JAPAN FLEET. Com.
PERRY Carrying the 'GOSPEL of GOD' to the HEATHEN*, 1853, Chicago
Historical Society, Visualizing Cultures: Massachusetts Institute of
Technology, https://visualizingcultures.mit.edu/black_ships_and_samurai/
gallery/pages/10_010_GospelOfGod.htm.

6–7a   C. G. Bush, "Spain's 'Sense of Justice,'" 1898, *New York World.*

6–7b   M. Moliné, "La Fatlera Del Oncle Sam," May 23, 1896, photograph, La
Campana de Gràcia, 6, Wikimedia Commons.

6–8a   Rudyard Kipling, "The White Man's Burden," *McClure's Magazine*, February
1889, 290–91.

6–8b   Victor Gillam, "The White Man's Burden (Apologies to Rudyard Kipling),"
Judge, April 1, 1899, The Ohio State University Billy Ireland Cartoon Library
& Museum, photograph, Wikimedia Commons.

6–8c   Udo J. Keppler, "A Trifle Embarrassed," August 3, 1898, Library of Congress
Prints and Photographs Division, http://hdl.loc.gov/loc.pnp/ppmsca.28724.

6–9a   Henri Meyer, "En Chine: Le gateau des Rois et . . . des Empereurs,"
Supplément Illustré du Petit Journal, January 16, 1898, Visualizing Cultures:
Massachusetts Institute of Technology, https://visualizingcultures.mit.edu/
boxer_uprising/gallery/pages/lpj_1898_01_16_meyer_w.htm.

6–9b   J. S. Pughe, "Putting His Foot Down," August 23, 1899, Library of Congress
Prints and Photographs Division, https://cdn.loc.gov/service/pnp/ppmsca/
28500/28534r.jpg.

6–10a   Homer Davenport, "John Bull Presents the Western Hemisphere to Uncle
Sam," *The American Monthly Review of Reviews*, 1902, frontispiece.

6–10b   Theodore Roosevelt, "Theodore Roosevelt's Annual Message to Congress for
1904," 1904, National Archives and Records Administration, OurDocuments.
gov, https://www.ourdocuments.gov/doc.php?flash=false&doc=56&page=
transcript.

6–11a   Andrew Carnegie, "Distant Possessions: The Parting of Ways," *The North
American Review* 167, no. 501 (1898): 239, 241–43, 246.

6–11b   Sen. George Frisbie Hoar, "Subjugation of the Philippines Iniquitous," in *The
World's Famous Orations: America III*, ed. William Jennings Bryan (New
York: Funk and Wagnalls Company, 1906), 220–27.

6–12   "Negros Protest," *Boston Daily Globe*, July 18, 1899.

6–13   Clemencia López, "Women of the Philippines: Address to Annual Meeting of
the New England Woman Suffrage Association, May 29, 1902," *The Woman's
Journal* (June 7, 1902), 184.

6–14   Rubén Darío, "To Roosevelt." Translated from "Á Roosevelt," in *Cantos
de vida y esperanza: Los cisnes y otros poemas* (Barcelona and Madrid: F.
Granada y C.a, 1907), 37–39. English translation by Hannah M. Dyar, ©
Baylor University Press.

6–15	Louis S. Meikle, *Confederation of the British West Indies versus Annexation to the United States of America* (London: Sampson Low, Marston and Co., 1912), 43–44, 62–63, 65, 92.

7 | Constructing the Urban Landscape

7–360 | International Views of Cities in the United States

o	Michel Chevalier and Thomas Gamaliel Bradford, *Society, Manners and Politics In the United States: Being a Series of Letters on North America* (Boston: Jordan and Company, 1839), 190–93, 200–206. Alexis de Tocqueville, *Democracy in America*, trans. Henry Reeve, 2nd ed., vol. 1 (New York: George Adlard, 1838), 270–71.

o	William Redmond Kelly, *An Excursion to California over the Prairie, Rocky Mountains, and Great Sierra Nevada. With a Stroll through the Diggings and Ranches of That Country*, vol. 2 (London: Chapman and Hall, 1851), 255–60. Lord (James) Bryce, "The Menace of Great Cities," in *Housing Problems in America, Proceedings of the Second National Conference on Housing* (Cambridge, Mass.: Harvard University Press, 1912), 20–22.

o	Liang Qichao on New York and poverty in *Journey to the New Continent* [*xin dalu youji*]. Original text available via Taiwan eBook, an eBook repository for the National Central Library of Taiwan, in the sections entitled "New York" (住地低住地面住地頂) and "New York's Dark Side" (黑闇之紐約), https://taiwanebook.ncl.edu.tw/zh-tw/book/NCL-000797670/reader. English translation by Benjamin Henry, © Baylor University Press. D. Tong, "Chinaman's Color a Problem," *Baltimore Sun*, May 15, 1911.

o	Hannah Ritchie and Max Roser, "Share of the Total Population Living in Urban Areas, 1960–2017," and "Global Urban and Rural Population, 1960–2017," OurWorldInData.org, September 2018, https://ourworldindata.org/urbanization.

7–1a	George Edwin Waring, "Modern Methods of Sewage Disposal," in *Modern Methods of Sewage Disposal: For Towns, Public Institutions and Isolated Houses* (New York: D. Van Nostrand Company, 1894), 1–12.

7–1b	George Edwin Waring, "Figures c and d: Morton Street, Corner of Bedford, Looking Toward Bleecker Street, 1893 and 1895," in *Street-Cleaning and the Disposal of a City's Wastes: Methods and Results and the Effect upon Public Health, Public Morals, and Municipal Property* (New York: Doubleday & McClure, 1897), 8–9.

7–2a	Charles J. Bushnell, "Map No. 4 of Chicago Showing the Geographical Relations of the Largest Industries in Some Social Aspects of the Chicago Stock Yards," *The American Journal of Sociology* 7, no. 3 (November 1901): 290–91.

7–2b	Florence Kelley et al., "Nationalities Map No. 1: Hull House Map,1895," Homicide in Chicago, 1870–1930, 2012, http://homicide.northwestern.edu/docs_fk/homicide/HullHouse/NATMAP1.pdf.

7-2c   Jane Addams, *Twenty Years at Hull-House, with Autobiographical Notes* (New York: The Macmillan Company, 1910), 120–27.

7-3   Adams & Lincoln, *Irish Trading Cards: Nos. 1–4*, ca. 1882, Digital Commonwealth: Massachusetts Collections Online, Boston Public Library, https://www.digitalcommonwealth.org/search?utf8=%E2%9C%93&f%5Bcollection_name_ssim%5D%5B%5D=19th+Century+American+Trade+Cards&f%5Binstitution_name_ssim%5D%5B%5D=Boston+Public+Library&q=%22our+new+citizens%22.

7-4a   Cover of *Spalding's Official Baseball Guide*, 1889, General Collections, Library of Congress, https://www.loc.gov/resource/spalding.00145/.

7-4b   Marcellin Auzolle (poster designer), "Cinématographe Lumière," 1895, poster, Wikimedia Commons.

7-5a   Ernesto Galarza, *Barrio Boy* (South Bend: University of Notre Dame Press, 1971), 205–12.

7-5b   Hamilton Holt, *The Life Stories of Undistinguished Americans as Told by Themselves* (New York: James Pott, 1906), 21–32, 38–40, 257–64.

7-6a   Cover of *Le Petit Journal*, "Les 'lynchages' aux États-Unis: Massacre de nègres à Atlanta (Georgie)" ["The Lynchings in the United States: The Massacre of Negroes in Atlanta, Georgia"], October 7, 1906, photograph, Bibliothèque nationale de France, Wikimedia Commons.

7-6b   Liang Qichao, "The Power and Threat of America, 1903," in *Land without Ghosts: Chinese Impressions of America from the Mid-Nineteenth Century to the Present*, ed. R. David Arkush and Leo O. Lees (Berkeley: University of California Press, 1989), 90–91.

7-7a   Edwin Chadwick, "Recapitulation of Conclusions," in *Report to Her Majesty's Principal Secretary of State for the Home Department, from the Poor Law Commissioners, on an Inquiry in the Sanitary Condition of the Labouring Population of Great Britain; with Appendices* (London: Clowes and Sons, 1842), 369–72.

7-7b   Sarah Friedman Dworetz, interview by Leon Stein, June 12, 1958, *Remembering The 1911 Triangle Factory Fire*, The Kheel Center of Cornell University, 2018, https://trianglefire.ilr.cornell.edu/primary/survivorInterviews/SarahDworetz.html.

7-8a   International Workingmen's Association and Institute of Marxism-Leninism of the C.C., C.P.S.U, "Preface to the Rules and Administrative Regulations of the International Working Men's Association," in *The General Council of the First International: Minutes* (Moscow: Progress Publishers, 1964), 265–66.

7-8b   *Solidarity of Labour* (illustration of the proclamation of May 1 as Labour Day), woodcut, 1889, after Walter Crane (1845–1915), colored. Photo: akg-images.

7-9a   Lewis Wickes Hine, *Manuel, the Young Shrimp-Picker, Five Years Old, and a Mountain of Child-Labor Oyster Shells behind Him. He Worked Last Year. Understands Not a Word of English. Dunbar, Lopez, Dukate Company. Location: Biloxi, Mississippi*, February 1911, National Child Labor Committee

Collection, Library of Congress Prints and Photographs Division, https://hdl
.loc.gov/loc.pnp/cph.3a01213.

7–9b   Lewis Wickes Hine, *Exhib[it] Panel*, 1914, National Child Labor Committee
Collection, Library of Congress Prints and Photographs Division, https://hdl
.loc.gov/loc.pnp/nclc.04988.

7–10a   H. D. Lloyd, "The Story of a Great Monopoly," *The Atlantic Monthly*, March
1881, https://www.theatlantic.com/magazine/archive/1881/03/the-story-of
-a-great-monopoly/306019/.

7–10b   Udo J. Keppler, "Next!" September 7, 1904, Library of Congress Prints and
Photographs Division, http://hdl.loc.gov/loc.pnp/cph.3a27007.

7–11   Qiu Jin, excerpts of "An Address to Two Hundred Million Fellow
Countrywomen," from *Jindai Zhongguo nüquan yundong shiliao, 1842–1911*
[*Historical Materials of the Modern Chinese Women's Rights Movement: 1842–
1911*], ed. Li Youning and Zhang Yufa (Taipei: Zhuanji wenxue she, 1975),
423–24. English translation by Benjamin Henry, © Baylor University Press.

7–12a   Ida B. Wells-Barnett, "Mrs. Willie Flake's Story," "Clarrissa Lockett's Story,"
and "Story of James Taylor," in *The East St. Louis Massacre: The Greatest
Outrage of the Century* (Chicago: The Negro Fellowship Herald Press, 1917),
5, 6, 11, 15–16, https://www.siue.edu/artsandsciences/political-science/
about/iur/projects/illinoistown/wells-ida-b-History-part-1.shtml,   made
available through the Northern Illinois University Libraries Digitization
Projects.

7–12b   *Silent Protest Parade in New York [City] against the East St. Louis Riots, 1917*,
ca. 1917, Library of Congress Prints and Photographs Division, https://lccn
.loc.gov/95517074. "Memorandum for N.A.A.C.P. Branches," *The Crisis*,
September 1917, Papers of the National Association for the Advancement of
Colored People, Pt. 7: The Anti-Lynching Campaign, 1912–1955, National
Humanities Center, 2014, https://nationalhumanitiescenter.org/pds/maai2/
forward/text4/silentprotest.pdf.

8 | The Great War

8–360 | Great War Propaganda Posters

○   Harry S. Hopps, "Destroy This Mad Brute: Enlist–U.S. Army," 1918, Library
of Congress Prints and Photographs Division, http://hdl.loc.gov/loc.pnp/
ppmsca.55871.

○   Johnson, Riddle & Co., Ltd., London, "Daddy, what did *YOU* do in the Great
War?" 1915, Library of Congress Prints and Photographs Division, http://hdl
.loc.gov/loc.pnp/cph.3g10923.

○   Sem (artist, 1863–1934), "Pour la Liberté du Monde. Souscrivez à l'Emprunt
National à La Banque Nationale de Crédit," 1917, Library of Congress Prints
and Photographs Division, http://hdl.loc.gov/loc.pnp/cph.3f03869.

○   "They Serve France. How Can I Serve Canada? Buy Victory Bonds," 1915,

Library of Congress Prints and Photographs Division, http://hdl.loc.gov/loc.pnp/cph.3g12692.

○ Pal Sujan, "Landes-Kriegsfürsorge-Ausstellung," 1917, Library of Congress Prints and Photographs Division, http://hdl.loc.gov/loc.pnp/cph.3g11953.

8-1 G. Karl Lehmann-Dumont, *Humoristische Karte von Europa im Jahre 1914*, 1914, Digital Collections, Cornell University Library, 2015, https://digital.library.cornell.edu/catalog/ss:3293872.

8-2 "Telegram from Secretary of State Robert Lansing to the American Embassy, London: Zimmermann Telegram as Received by the German Minister to Mexico," 1917, Record Group 59: General Records of the Department of State, 1763–2002, National Archives and Records Administration. https://catalog.archives.gov/id/302025. "The Ambassador in Great Britain (Page) to the Secretary of State," 1917, Historical Documents, U.S. Department of State: Office of the Historian, https://history.state.gov/historicaldocuments/frus1917Supp01v01/d158.

8-3a Charles J. DaLacy, *UC-5*, 1916, photograph, Wikipedia.

8-3b Woodrow Wilson, "War Messages: Wilson's War Message to Congress, 65th Congress, 1st Session," Senate Document No. 5, Serial No. 7264 (April 2, 1917), 3–8, passim, https://wwi.lib.byu.edu/index.php/Wilson's_War_Message_to_Congress.

8-4a Al Piantadosi and Alfred Bryan, "I Didn't Raise My Boy to Be a Soldier," sheet music, New York, 1915, Digital Collections, Duke University Library, https://library.duke.edu/digitalcollections/hasm_a0665_a0665-1/. "I Didn't Raise My Boy to Be a Soldier," 1915, Digital Collections, Duke University Library, https://library.duke.edu/digitalcollections/hasm_a0665_a0665-1/.

8-4b Theodore Baker, "I Didn't Raise My Boy to Be a Slacker," sheet music (New York: G. Schirmer, 1917), Library of Congress, https://lccn.loc.gov/2013564426. "I Didn't Raise My Boy to Be a Slacker," 1917, Library of Congress, https://lccn.loc.gov/2013564426.

8-5a *Soldiers of the German Colonial Forces*, 1914, Study Collection, National Army Museum, https://collection.nam.ac.uk/detail.php?acc=1987-05-8-3.

8-5b Mohammed Agim, "Excerpt from letter from Mohammed Agim (crossed out) to Subedar Major Firoz Khan (crossed out)," May 28, 1915, British Library, https://www.bl.uk/collection-items/excerpt-letter-from-mohammed-agim-to-subedar-major-firoz-khan.

8-6 *A War Nurse's Diary: Sketches from a Belgian Field Hospital* (New York: The Macmillan Company, 1918), 24–34.

8-7 Wilfred Owen, "Dulce et Decorum Est, 1920," in *Poems by Wilfred Owen with an Introduction by Siegfried Sassoon* (London: Chatto & Windus, 1921), 15.

8-8a William W. Cadbury, "The 1918 Pandemic of Influenza in Canton," *China Medical Journal* 34, no. 1 (January 1920): 15–16.

8-8b Gresham Life Assurance Society (Limited), "A Progressive Year. Influenza Claims Exceed War Claims," *The Times* (London), July 1, 1919, 22.

8–9   "The Syrian Congress at Damascus," in *King-Crane Commission Report in Foreign Relations of the United States Paris Peace Conference*, vol. 12 (Washington, D.C.: U.S. Government Printing Office, 1919), 780–81, https://history.state.gov/historicaldocuments/frus1919Parisv12/pg_780.

8–10a   John T. McCutcheon, "Interrupting the Ceremony," 1918, Digital Collections, The Ohio State University, Billy Ireland Cartoon Library and Museum, 2018, https://hdl.handle.net/1811/44bc752b-4a84-4e0e-a6a2-958e2bfc4cc1.

8–10b   Henry Cabot Lodge, *The Senate and the League of Nations* (New York: Charles Scribner's Sons, 1925), 408–10.

9 | Wrestling with the Modern Age

9–360 | The Modern Woman

○   "Women's Suffrage Mapped," 2018, Cuba Holidays.

○   Margaret H. Sanger, "No Healthy Race without Birth Control" (New York University: The Margaret Sanger Papers Project, March 1921), https://www.nyu.edu/projects/sanger/documents/speech_no_healthy_race_without_bc.php.

○   Tamara de Lempicka, *Die Dame*, July 1, 1929, cover. Kiyoshi Kobayakawa, *Tipsy*, 1930, photograph, Honolulu Museum of Art, Wikimedia Commons.

○   Deng Yingchao's experiences in the May Fourth Movement, ca. 1919. Available via the Chinese news outlet Sina, http://news.sina.com.cn/c/2009-04-21/182217657357.shtml, paragraph 9. English translation by Benjamin Henry, © Baylor University Press. Hu Huaichen, "Shifang binü yi" ["On Freeing Slave Girls"], *Funü Zazhi* [*Women's Magazine*] 6 (January 1920): 1–4. Available via A New Approach to the Popular Press in China: Gender and Cultural Production, 1904–1937, a database of the Heidelberg Research Architecture (HRA), https://kjc-sv034.kjc.uni-heidelberg.de/frauenzeitschriften/public/magazine/page_large.php?magazin_id=4&year=1920&issue_id=360&issue_number=1&img_issue_page=33. English translation by Benjamin Henry, © Baylor University Press.

○   "Afghanistan Royal Proclamation by Queen Soraya (1922)," in *Religious Response to Social Change in Afghanistan, 1919–1929: King Aman-Allah and the Afghan Ulama* (Costa Mesa, Calif.: Mazda, 1999), 221–22.

9–1   Louis C. Fraina, "Application for Membership in the Communist International on Behalf of the Communist Party of America, November 24, 1919," in *Red Radicalism: As Described by Its Own Leaders*, ed. A. Mitchell Palmer (Washington, D.C.: U.S. Government Printing Office, 1920), 5–16.

9–2   Carey Orr, "Close the Gate," *Literary Digest*, July 5, 1919, 29.

9–3a   "Two Soldiers Face Off during the 1919 Riots in Chicago," 1919, *Chicago Tribune*.

9–3b   "Petition from J. A Dewitt Martyn, Secretary of the African Christian Association to Liverpool Lord Mayor," 1920, From Great War to Race Riots, 2019, https://www.greatwar-to-raceriots.co.uk/document-gallery/1920/august-1920.html#!17_08_1920_a.

9–4   "Illustration for Article 'An Alien Antidumping Bill,'" *Literary Digest*, May 7, 1921, 12.

9–5a   Marcus Garvey and the Universal Negro Improvement Association, "Declaration of the Rights of the Negro Peoples of the World: The Principles of the Universal Negro Improvement Association (1920)," in *Negro Year Book: An Annual Encyclopedia of the Negro 1921–1922*, ed. Monroe N. Work (Tuskegee, Ala.: The Negro Year Book Publishing Company, 1922), 59–63.

9–5b   W. E. B. Du Bois, "Credo," *Independent*, October 6, 1904. W. E. B. Du Bois, "The Souls of White Folk," in *Darkwater: Voices from within the Veil* (New York: Harcourt, Brace and Company, 1920), 41–42, 44, 49–50.

9–6a   "The International Jew: The World's Problem." *The Dearborn Independent*, May 22, 1920, Henry Ford Museum, photograph, Wikimedia Commons.

9–6b   Office of United States Chief of Counsel for Prosecution of Axis Criminality, *Nazi Conspiracy and Aggression*, vol. 4 (Washington, D.C.: U.S. Government Printing Office, 1946), 7–10, 636–38.

9–7a   "Statements of U.S. Representative John C. Box: John Box on Immigration Restriction," in *Congressional Record, 70th Congress, 1st Session*, series 69, pt. 3 (Washington, D.C., 1928), 2817–18.

9–7b   Ernesto Galarza, "Life in the United States for Mexican People: Out of the Experience of a Mexican," in *Proceedings of the National Conference of Social Work, 56th Annual Session* (Chicago: University of Chicago Press, 1929), 399–404.

9–8   *Family Listening to the Radio*, ca. 1930, University of Kentucky, Louis Edward Nollau F Series Photographic Print Collection, https://exploreuk.uky.edu/catalog/xt7sf7664q86_4308_1.

9–9a   Daguerre, "King Oliver's Creole Jazz Band," 1923, Tulane University, Hogan Jazz Archive Photography Collection, https://digitallibrary.tulane.edu/islandora/object/tulane%3A29198.

9–9b   "Crickett Smith's Indian Band," ca. 1935, photographer unknown. Photograph courtesy of Jehangir Dalal.

9–10   "Babe Ruth with Young Japanese Baseball Players," 1934, *Japan Today*, November 8, 2018, https://japantoday.com/category/features/lifestyle/babe-ruth-the-sultan-of-swat-visits-japan.

10 | The Search for Solutions

10–360 | Rise of Fascism

  ○   Giovanni Gentile, "Che cosa è il fascismo?" ("What Is Fascism?"), lecture delivered in Florence on March 8, 1925, reprinted in Giovanni Gentile, *Che cosa è il fascismo: Discorsi e polemiche* (Florence: Vellecchi Editore, 1925), 14, 28, 32–33, 36, 38, 63. Translation by Jeffrey M. Hunt, © Baylor University Press.

o   Franz Pfeffer von Salomon, "Zucht. Eine Forderung zum Programm" ("Breeding: A Demand in Relation to the Party Programme"), internal NSDAP memo, 1925, in *Fascism*, ed. Roger Griffin (New York: Oxford University Press, 1995), 118–19.

o   Paula Siber von Groote, excerpt from *Die Frauenfrage und ihre Lösung durch den Nationalsozialismus* (*The Women's Issue and Its National Socialist Solution*) (Wolfenbüttel/Berlin: G. Kallmeyer, 1933), 23–27. Translation by Eric Rust, © Baylor University Press.

o   Antonio Vallejo-Nágera, *Eugenesia de la Hispanidad y Regeneración de la Raza* [*Eugenesis of Spanishness and Regeneration of the Race*] (Editorial Española: Burgos, 1937), 114–18. English translation by Hannah M. Dyar, © Baylor University Press.

o   Nakano Seigō, speech to Far East Society national convention, 1939, from Nakano Yasuo, *Seijika—Nakano Seigō* (*Nakano Seigō the Politician*) (Shinkōukaku Shoten: Tokyo, 1971), ii, 365–66, line 13 at bottom of p. 366 through line 12 at top of p. 367. English translation by Yoshiko Fujii Gaines, © Baylor University Press.

10-1a   "The Single Men's Unemployed Association Parading to Bathurst Street United Church," Toronto, Canada, ca. 1930, photograph, Library and Archives Canada, Wikimedia Commons.

10-1b   Christina D. Romer and Richard H. Pells, "Table 2: Peak-to-Trough Decline in Industrial Production in Various Countries (Annual Data) in Great Depression-Economy," *Encyclopedia Britannica Online*, Encyclopedia Britannica, October 16, 2019, https://www.britannica.com/event/Great-Depression/Sources-of-recovery.

10-2   No-Yong Park, *An Oriental View of American Civilization* (Boston and New York: Hale, Cushman and Flint, 1934), 81–85, 88–89, 91–96, 98–99.

10-3a   Pan African Congress, Executive Committee, "Announcement of the Fourth Pan African Congress," *1927*, 1927, W. E. B. Du Bois Papers, Series 1A, General Correspondence, Special Collections and University Archives, University of Massachusetts Amherst Libraries, http://credo.library.umass.edu/view/pageturn/mums312-b040-i362/#page/1/mode/1up.

10-3b   Hasan al-Banna, *Between Yesterday and Today*, late 1930s, from Ḥasan al-Bannā, *Majmūʿat rasāʾil al-imām al-shahīd Ḥasan al-Bannā* (Beirut: Dār al-Andalus, 1965). English translation by Keegan Terek, © Baylor University Press. For the sake of continuity with other English language scholarship on al-Banna and his written work, the principal section titles in this translation follow verbatim the widely cited translation of these same passages by Charles Wendell (1978).

10-4a   Victor Haya de la Torre, "What Is the APRA?" *The Labour Monthly* (December 1926): 756–59.

10-4b   Carleton Beals, "To the Nicaraguan Border," *Nation*, vol. 126, issue 3268 (February 22, 1928), 204–5; Carleton Beals, "On the Sandino Front," *Nation*, vol. 126, issue 3269 (February 29, 1928), 232–33; Carleton Beals, "On The Trail of Sandino," *Nation*, vol. 126, issue 3270 (March 7, 1928), 260–61; Carleton Beals, "Sandino Himself," *Nation*, vol. 126, issue 3271 (March 14, 1928), 288–89.

10-5 Franklin Delano Roosevelt, *The Public Papers and Addresses of Franklin Delano Roosevelt*, vol. 2 (New York: Random House, 1938), 129–33. https://quod.lib.umich.edu/p/ppotpus/4925381.1933.001?view=toc.

10-6a Baldur von Schirach, "Hitler Youth Prayer," Spartacus Educational, 2016, https://spartacus-educational.com/GERschirach.htm.

10-6b Marie Harm and Hermann Wiehle, "Excerpt from German Biology Textbook for 5th Grade Girls, Germany, 1942," in *Lebenskunde Für Mittelschulen. Fünfter Teil. Klasse 5 Für Mädchen*, trans. Randall Bytwerk (Halle, Germany: Hermann Schroedel Verlag, 1942), 168–73, https://research.calvin.edu/german-propaganda-archive/textbk01.htm.

10-7a Haile Selassie, "Appeal to the League of Nations," in *Selected Speeches of His Imperial Majesty, 1918–1967* (Addis Ababa: Imperial Ethiopian Ministry of Information, Publications & Foreign Languages Press Dept., 1967), 304–6, 310–11, 313–14, 316.

10-7b Aurelio Bertiglia, postcard, [*Children in Colonial Army Uniforms in Ethiopia*], ca. 1936, Library Displays, The Wolfsonian—Florida International University, http://librarydisplays.wolfsonian.org/Youth%20in%20uniform/wall/wyiuwallgroup.htm.

10-8 Charles I. Bevans, ed., "Convention for the Maintenance, Preservation, and Reestablishment of Peace and Additional Protocol, 1936–1937," in *United States Treaties and International Agreements: 1776–1949*, vol. 3, *Multilateral* (Washington, D.C.: U.S. Department of State Publication, 1968), 338–42, https://www.loc.gov/law/help/us-treaties/bevans/m-ust000003-0338.pdf.

10-9 Mahatma Gandhi, "Letter to Adolf Hitler," Bombay Sarvodaya Mandal and Gandhi Research Foundation: Selected Letters, July 23, 1939, https://www.mkgandhi.org/letters/hitler_ltr.htm.

10-10a Carey Orr, "The Only Way We Can Save Her," September 19, 1939, *Chicago Tribune*.

10-10b Theodor Geisel [Dr. Seuss], ". . . and the Wolf chewed up the children and spit out their bones . . . But those were Foreign Children and it really didn't matter," October 1, 1941, Digital Collections, University of California-San Diego, https://library.ucsd.edu/dc/object/bb4642496p.

11 | World War II

11-360 | Statements of Purpose in World War II

o   Benito Mussolini, "A Speech to the People of Rome after Italy's Declaration of War against France and Britain (10 June 1940)," in *Readings in Western Civilization*, ed. George H. Knoles and Rixford K. Snyder (Chicago: J.B.

Lippincott Company, 1951), 830–31. "PM Tōjō Hideki, Foreign Minister Tōgō Shigenori, Privy Council President Hara Yoshimichi, 1 December 1941," in *Japan's Decision for War: Records of the 1941 Policy Conference*, trans. Nobutaka Ike (Redwood City, Calif.: Stanford University Press, 1967), 263, 270, 281–83. "The Text of Hitler's Memorial Day Address," *New York Times*, March 17, 1941.

○ Winston Churchill, "Their Finest Hour," speech presented at the House of Commons, Westminster, UK, June 18, 1940, http://winstonchurchill.org/resources/speeches/1940-the-finest-hour/their-finest-hour. Iosef [Joseph] Stalin, "Radio Address to the Soviet People [Brothers and Sisters!]," July 3, 1941, trans. James von Geldern, Online Archive of Primary Sources, Seventeen Moments in Soviet History, 2019, http://soviethistory.msu.edu/1943-2/the-cult-of-leadership/the-cult-of-leadership-texts/stalin-brothers-and-sisters/. Franklin Delano Roosevelt, "Message to Congress—The State of the Union [Four Freedoms]," January 6, 1941, Franklin D. Roosevelt, Master Speech File, 1898–1945, Franklin D. Roosevelt Presidential Library and Museum, http://www.fdrlibrary.marist.edu/_resources/images/msf/msf01407.

11–1a   Charles Henry Alston, "DECEMBER 7th—REMEMBER!!" 1943, Record Group 208: Records of the Office of War Information, 1926–1951, National Archives and Records Service, https://catalog.archives.gov/id/535613.

11–1b   Stephen M. Sloan, Lois Myers, and Michelle Holland, eds., "Frank Curre, Jr.," in *Tattooed on My Soul: Texas Veterans Remember World War II* (College Station: Texas A&M University Press, 2015), 8–13.

11–2a   United States Office of Inter-American Affairs, *History of the Office of the Coordinator of Inter-American Affairs* (Washington, D.C.: U.S. Government Printing Office, 1947), 67–79.

11–2b   Joe Simon and Jack Kirby, *Captain America* #1, March 1, 1941, Marvel Comics, https://www.marvel.com/comics/issue/7849/captain_america_comics_1941_1.

11–3a   Ministry of Health and Her Majesty's Stationery Office, "SHE'S IN THE RANKS TOO!" 1939–1945, Collections Online, Imperial War Museums, https://www.iwm.org.uk/collections/item/object/19994.

11–3b   "War Manpower Job Flyer Promoting Women to Register for War Jobs," 1942, Women in the Work Force during World War II, National Archives and Records Service, https://www.archives.gov/files/education/lessons//images/wwii-flyer.pdf.

11–3c   *Women Shipfitters Worked on Board the USS NEREUS, and Are Shown as They Neared Completion of the Floor in a Part of the Engine Room. Left to Right Are Shipfitters Betty Pierce, Lola Thomas, Margaret Houston Thelma Mort and Katie Stanfill US Navy Yard, Mare Island, CA*, ca. 1943, Record Group 181: Records of Naval Districts and Shore Establishments, 1784–2000, photograph, National Archives and Records Service, https://catalog.archives.gov/id/296892.

11–4a   United States Department of State, *Treaties and Other International Agreements of the United States of America, 1776–1949*, vol. 9, ed. Charles I.

Bevans (Washington, D.C.: U.S. Government Printing Office, 1968–1976), 1069–75.

11–4b   Leon Helguera, "Americans All: Let's Fight for Victory," 1941–1945, Record Group 44: Records of the Office of Government Reports, 1932–1947, National Archives and Records Service. https://catalog.archives.gov/id/513803.

11–5   Schenley Laboratories, "Thanks to Penicillin . . . He Will Come Home," *LIFE* magazine, August 14, 1944.

11–6a   Sat Ichikawa, *Hand-Drawn Map of Crystal City Internment Camp, Texas*, 1945, M. Nakagawa Family Collection, Densho Digital Repository, http://ddr.densho.org/ddr-densho-64-5/.

11–6b   "[Letter about Prisoner Complaints in Australian Internment Camp, 7 April 1942]," in *Official Visitor's Report—Dated 1st April 1942—Internment Camp Gaythorne*, 1942, 46–47, https://recordsearch.naa.gov.au/SearchNRetrieve/Interface/ViewImage.aspx?B=3381423.

11–7a   Selected letters from an *Einsatzkommando* in Ukraine, 1942, translated from the German text of *Das Dritte Reich und Seine Diener: Dokumente*, ed. Léon Poliakov and Josef Wulf (Berlin-Grunewald: arani Verlags-GmbH, 1956). English translation by Stephanie Hoffman and Eric Rust, © Baylor University Press.

11–7b   "Dr. Franz Blaha Testimony about Medical Experiments at Dachau, 1941–1945," in *The Major War Criminals before the International Military Tribunal, Nuremburg, 14 November 1945–1 October 1946*, vol. 5 (Nuremberg, Germany, 1947), 168–73, https://www.loc.gov/rr/frd/Military_Law/pdf/NT_Vol-V.pdf.

11–8   Hana Volavková, ed., *. . . I Never Saw Another Butterfly . . . : Children's Drawings and Poems from Terezin Concentration Camp 1942–1944*, expanded 2nd ed. by the United States Holocaust Memorial Museum (New York: Schocken Books, 1993), 20–21.

11–9a   Margaret Freyer, "The Bombing of Dresden, 14 February 1945," in *Dresden, 1945: The Devil's Tinderbox*, ed. Alexander McKee (New York: E. P. Dutton, Inc., 1984), 171–75.

11–9b   Richard Peter, view from the town hall tower to the south, 1945, photograph, Saxon State Library/State and University Library Dresden, courtesy of SLUB Dresden/Deutsche Fotothek/Richard Peter sen.

11–10a   Marcel Junod, *Warrior without Weapons*, repr. ed. (Geneva: International Committee of the Red Cross, 1982), 296–97.

11–10b   Photographs of post–World War II Hiroshima from the US National Archives, viewable online in Alan Taylor, "Hiroshima: Before and after the Atomic Bombing," *The Atlantic*, May 12, 2016, https://www.theatlantic.com/photo/2016/05/hiroshima-before-and-after-the-atomic-bombing/482526/#img18.

11–11a   United Nations—Preamble to the Charter of the United Nations, 1942–1945, Records of the Office of Government Reports, 1932–1947, National Archives and Records Service, https://catalog.archives.gov/id/515901.

11–11b   Joseph Parrish, "Trojan Horse," *Chicago Tribune*, 1949.

11–12   Robert H. Jackson, "Second Day, Wednesday, 11/21/1945, Part 04," in *Trial of the Major War Criminals before the International Military Tribunal*, vol. 2, *Proceedings: 11/14/1945–11/30/1945* (Nuremberg, Germany: International Military Tribunal, 1947), 98–102, https://www.roberthjackson.org/speech -and-writing/opening-statement-before-the-international-military -tribunal/.

12 | The Bipolar World

12–360 | Declarations of Independence

○   A Declaration by the Representatives of the United States of America, in General Congress Assembled (Philadelphia, 1776).

○   "Acte de l'Indépendance, Haiti, 1804," in *An Historical Account of the Black Empire of Hayti: Comprehending a View of the Principal Transactions in the Revolution of Saint-Domingo; with Its Ancient and Modern State* (London, 1805), 442–46.

○   "He Wakaputanga o Te Rangatiratanga o Nu Tireni, 1835," in *Fac-Similes of the Declaration of Independence and the Treaty of Waitangi* (Wellington, New Zealand, 1877), 4.

○   "A Declaration of Independence by the Representatives of the People of the Commonwealth of Liberia, 1847," in *The Independent Republic of Liberia; Its Constitution and Declaration of Independence . . . with Other Documents; Issued Chiefly for the Use of the Free People of Color* (Philadelphia, 1848), 8–9.

○   "Tuyên Ngôn Độc Lập, 1945," in *The Declaration of Independence: A Global History* (Cambridge, Mass.: Harvard University Press, 2008), 231–35.

12–1a   Winston Churchill, "The Sinews of Peace," delivered March 5, 1946, Westminster College, Fulton, Missouri, transcribed at American Rhetoric online speech bank, https://www.americanrhetoric.com/speeches/ winstonchurchillsinewsofpeace.htm.

12–1b   "Stalin Interview with *Pravda* on Churchill," transcription, *New York Times*, March 14, 1946.

12–2a   George C. Marshall, "The Marshall Plan Speech [Handout Version]," June 4, 1947, The George C. Marshall Foundation, https://www.marshallfoundation .org/marshall/the-marshall-plan/marshall-plan-speech/.

12–2b   West Berlin, Germany, NWDNS-286-ME-6 (2); ARC #541691, 1948, photograph, Records of the Agency of International Development [AID], National Archives and Records Service, OurDocuments.gov, https://www .ourdocuments.gov/doc_large_image.php?flash=false&doc=82.

12–3a   Gordon Edward George Minhinnick, "The Octopus of Chinese Communism, 1950," in *New Zealand and the Vietnam War: Politics and Diplomacy* by Roberto Rabel (Auckland, New Zealand: Auckland University Press, 2005), 65, https://teara.govt.nz/en/cartoon/34513/the-octopus-of-chinese -communism-1950.

12-3b Joseph R. McCarthy, "Lincoln Day Address," in *Congressional Record, 81st Congress*, vol. 96, part 2 (Washington, D.C.: U.S. Government Printing Office, 1950), 1952–1957.

12-4a Carol A. Fisher and Fred Krinsky, eds., "Nasser Speech Nationalizing the Suez Canal Company, 26 July 1956," in *Middle East in Crisis: A Historical and Documentary Review* (Syracuse, N.Y.: Syracuse University Press, 1959), 136–40, https://surface.syr.edu/supress/4.

12-4b U.S. Congress, Senate and House, Joint Resolution to Promote Peace and Stability in the Middle East, Public Law 85-7, 85th Congress, 1st session, *Congressional Record 71* (March 9, 1957), 5–6, https://www.govinfo.gov/app/details/STATUTE-71/STATUTE-71-Pg5-2/summary.

12-5a Harry S. Truman, *Memoirs by Harry S. Truman*, vol. 2, *Years of Trial and Hope, 1945–1952* (Garden City, N.Y.: Doubleday & Company, Inc., 1956), 332–33.

12-5b Ye Shanlu, *Renren Fangyi, Fensui Mei Diguo Zhuyide Xijunzhan*, June 1952, EAS, International Institute of Social History, https://iisg.amsterdam/en/detail?id=https%3A%2F%2Fiisg.amsterdam%2Fid%2Fitem%2F1057790.

12-6a *Come South*, August 5, 1954, photograph, Record Group 306: Records of the U.S. Information Agency, 1900–2003, National Archives and Records Service, https://catalog.archives.gov/id/6949142.

12-6b Nguyen Xuan Phong, interview by Richard Burks Verrone on June 19, 2003, transcript, The Vietnam Archive (Lubbock: Texas Tech University Press, 2003), 12–13.

12-7a Harold Macmillan, "Address by the Right Hon. Harold Macmillan, M.P., to Members of Both Houses of the Parliament of the Union of South Africa, Cape Town [Winds of Change]," in *Prime Minister's African Tour, January–February 1960* (London: Her Britannic Majesty's Government, 1960), 153–58, http://filestore.nationalarchives.gov.uk/pdfs/small/cab-129-101-c-66.pdf.

12-7b Nikita Khrushchev, "For New Victories of the World Communist Movement," January 6, 1961, printed in U.S. Senate, *Senate Documents*, 87th Congress, 1st Session, vol. 2 Miscellaneous II, Document No. 46, "Appendix III" (Washington: U.S. Government Printing Office, 1962), 63–65.

12-8a George McTurnan Kahin, *The Asian-African Conference: Bandung, Indonesia, April 1955* (Ithaca, N.Y.: Cornell University Press, 1956), 83–85.

12-8b Richard Wright, *The Color Curtain: A Report on the Bandung Conference* (Cleveland: World Pub. Co., 1956), 136–40, 201.

12-9a Ishirô Honda, *Godzilla: The Japanese Original*, 1954.

12-9b Tom Lehrer, "Who's Next?" *The Year That Was*, Reprise/Warner Bros. Records, 1965.

12-10 Provo's declaration of principles, listed in Rudolf de Jong, "Provos and Kabouters," in *Anarchism Today*, ed. David E. Apter and James Joll (Garden City, N.Y.: Doubleday, 1971), 172–73.

13 | The Struggle for Equality

13–360 | Nonviolent Resistance

- Adin Ballou, "'Non-Resistant Catechism' from the *Practical Christian*," August 3, 1844, *Friends of Adin Ballou*, http://www.adinballou.org/catechism .shtml.

- Leo Tolstoy, "A Letter to a Hindu," December 14, 1908, The Literature Network, http://www.online-literature.com/tolstoy/2733/.

- Mahatma Gandhi, "Speech on 'The Secret of Satyagraha in South Africa—July 27, 1916,'" in *The Collected Works of Mahatma Gandhi*, vol. 13, electronic edition (Ahmedabad, India: Navajivan Trust, 1964), 287–91, https://www .gandhiservefoundation.org/about-mahatma-gandhi/collected-works-of -mahatma-gandhi/013-19150109-19171004/. *Salt March*, April 5, 1930, photograph, Wikimedia Commons.

- "'Students Face Mississippi Violence for You!' SNCC Fundraising Flyer for McComb Movement," 1961, Documents, Civil Rights Movement Archive, https://www.crmvet.org/docs/61_sncc_mccomb_fundraiser.pdf. Diane Nash and SNCC, "A Message," April 30, 1962, Documents, Civil Rights Movement Archive, https://www.crmvet.org/docs/620430_sncc_nash_ statement.pdf.

- Nelson Mandela, "I Am Prepared to Die," transcript of audio recording and prepared remarks, Palace of Justice, Pretoria Supreme Court, Pretoria, South Africa, 1964, http://db.nelsonmandela.org/speeches/pub_view.asp?pg=item &ItemID=NMS010&txtstr=prepared%20to%20die.

13–1 William O. Douglas, *Strange Lands and Friendly People* (New York: Harper & Brothers Publishers, 1951), 296, 326.

13–2 National Union of Ghana Students and P. D. Vander Puije, "Support Letter to All 'Sit-in' Students in Jail in York County Jail, SC," March 8, 1961, viewable online in the documents section of the Civil Rights Movement Archive, https://www.crmvet.org/docs/6103_ghana_students.pdf.

13–3a Robert Altman, photograph, members of Black Panther Party holding up Mao's *Little Red Book* at Free Huey Newton rally, May 1969. Courtesy of Robert Altman.

13–3b Letter from Nguyen Thi Dinh to Huey Newton, October 31, 1970, included in *To Die for the People: The Writings of Huey P. Newton*, ed. Toni Morrison (San Francisco: City Lights, 2009), 184–87.

13–4 David Mosley, "The Rumble in the Jungle," 1974.

13–5 OPEC, "The Statute of the Organization of the Petroleum Exporting Countries (OPEC)," *International Legal Materials*, vol. 4, no. 6 (November 1965), 1175–89.

13–6a Frantz Fanon, *The Wretched of the Earth*, preface by Jean-Paul Sartre and trans. Constance Farrington (New York: Grove Press, 1963), 35–37, 70, 83–84, 101–3. Excerpts from THE WRETCHED OF THE EARTH by Frantz Fanon, English translation copyright © 1963 by Présence Africaine. Used by permission of Grove/Atlantic, Inc. Any third party use of this material, outside of this publication, is prohibited.

13–6b Wen Bing, *Awakened Peoples You Will Certainly Attain the Ultimate Victory!* September 1963, EAS, International Institute of Social History, https://iisg .amsterdam/en/detail?id=https%3A%2F%2Fiisg.amsterdam%2Fid%2Fitem %2F1246703.

13–7a U.S. Department of State, "The Guatemalan Problem before the OAS Council," in *Intervention of International Communism in Guatemala*, Department of State Publication 5556 Inter-American Series 48 (Washington, D.C.: U.S. Government Printing Office, 1954), 25–30.

13–7b Juan José Arévalo, *The Shark and the Sardines* (New York: Lyle Stewart, 1961), 9–13.

13–8a Ping-pong paddles with caricatures of U.S. President Richard Nixon and Chinese leader Mao Zedong, Associated Press, 1971.

13–8b Richard M. Nixon, *Richard Nixon: Containing the Public Messages, Speeches and Statements of the President, 1972* (Washington, D.C.: U.S. Government Printing Office, 1974), 70–72.

13–9a Jimmy Carter, *Jimmy Carter: 1977 (in Two Books) Book 1—January 20 to June 24, 1977* (Washington, D.C.: U.S. Government Printing Office, 1977), 444–51.

13–9b Fritz Behrendt, "[Camp David Accords]," *Frankfurter Allgemeine Zeitung, Zeitung Für Deutschland.* Frankfurt/Main, Germany, September 28, 1978, no. 213, https://www.cvce.eu/en/obj/cartoon_by_behrendt_on_the _camp_david_accords_28_september_1978-en-185c0da7-e22e-4ec1-a77d -270e2d22c313.html.

13–10a Harrison Schmitt and Ron Evans, "The Blue Marble," December 7, 1972, photograph, NASA Johnson Space Center, Wikimedia Commons.

13–10b James B. Irwin and William A. Emerson, Jr., *To Rule the Night: The Discovery Voyage of Astronaut Jim Irwin* (Nashville: Broadman Press, 1973), 23–24.

13–10c NASA, *The Apollo–Soyuz Test Project Patch*, 1975, photograph, https:// spaceflight.nasa.gov/gallery/images/apollo-soyuz/apollo-soyuz/hires/s75 -20361.jpg.

14 | The United States in the World

14–360 | Revolutions of 1989

o "'Hunger Strike Announcement,' 12 May 1989," in *Beijing Spring, 1989: Confrontation and Conflict—The Basic Documents*, ed. Michael Oksenberg, Lawrence R. Sullivan, and Marc Lambert (Armonk, N.Y.: ME Sharpe, 1990), 258–60. The Baltic Way human chain of solidarity, photograph courtesy of Rossiya segodnya.

o Aurora Javate de Dios, Petronilo Bn Daroy, and Lorna Kalaw-Tirol, eds., "Primer of the 'Justice for Aquino, Justice for All' Movement," in

Dictatorship and Revolution: Roots of People's Power (Manila: Conspectus, 1988), 566–68.

○ Sebastián Acevedo, "I Call You Freedom" and "Public Denunciation," translated from "Yo Te Nombro Libertad" and "Denuncia Pública," in Hernán Vidal, *El movimiento contra la tortura "Sebastián Acevedo": Derechos humanos y la producción de símbolos nacionales bajo el fascismo chileno* (Edina, Minn.: Society for the Study of Contemporary Hispanic and Lusophone Revolutionary Literatures, 1986), 332–33, 340–41. English translation by Hannah M. Dyar, © Baylor University Press.

○ Tomasz Sarnecki, *High Noon. 4 June 1989*, 1989, viewable on the website of the Victoria and Albert Museum, http://collections.vam.ac.uk/item/O76024/high-noon-4-june-1989-poster-sarnecki-tomasz/.

14–1a Ronald Reagan, "'Evil Empire Speech,' 8 March 1983," in *Ronald Reagan: 1983 (in Two Books). [Book 1]* (Ann Arbor: University of Michigan Library, 2005), 359–64, https://quod.lib.umich.edu/p/ppotpus/4732328.1983.001?view=toc.

14–1b German soldiers in uniform, participating in peace protests in Bonn's Public Gardens in October 1983, photograph © picture alliance/Heinz Wieseler, 1983.

14–2a Henry Kissinger and U.S. National Bipartisan Commission on Central America, *The Report of the President's National Bipartisan Commission on Central America* (Washington, D.C.: Office of the President of the United States, January 1984), 126–27.

14–2b The Central Intelligence Agency, *The Freedom Fighter's Manual: Practical Guide to Liberating Nicaragua from Oppression and Misery by Paralyzing the Military-Industrial Complex of the Traitorous Marxist State without Having to Use Special Tools and with Minimal Risk for the Combatant* (New York: Grove Press, 1985), 1, 6–7.

14–3a Mikhail Gorbachev, "Address to the 43rd UN General Assembly, 7 December, 1988," in *Provisional Verbatim Record of the 72nd Meeting, Held at Headquarters, New York, on Wednesday, 7 December 1988: General Assembly, 43rd Session* (New York: United Nations, 1988), 6, 11–13, 26–31, 33.

14–3b Nicholas Garland, untitled cartoon, *Daily Telegraph* (December 3, 1991), British Cartoon Archive, https://archive.cartoons.ac.uk/Record.aspx?src=CalmView.Catalog&id=NG4886.

14–4a The Associated Press, "Statement by Arafat on Peace in Mideast," *New York Times*, December 15, 1988, https://apnews.com/087f804f64749646db7659ecb8bb53b2.

14–4b "Charter of the Islamic Resistance Movement (Hamas) of Palestine," trans. Muhammad Maqdsi, printed in the *Journal of Palestine Studies* 22, no. 4 (Summer 1993): 122–29, 131–33.

14–5a George H. W. Bush, "Address before a Joint Session of Congress on the Persian Gulf Crisis and the Federal Budget Deficit, September 11, 1990," *Public Papers of the Presidents of the United States: George Bush, 1990*, vol. 2 (Washington, D.C.: U.S. Government Printing Office, 1991), 1218–22, https://quod.lib.umich.edu/p/ppotpus/4733009.1990.002/276?rgn=full+text;view=image.

14–5b   National Security Council, Speechwriting Office, and Antony Blinken, "Tony Lake—'From Containment to Enlargement, 9/21/93," Clinton Digital Library, https://clinton.presidentiallibraries.us/items/show/9013.

14–6   Mahathir bin Mohamad, "Asian Values," speech presented at the Just International Conference on Rethinking Human Rights, Kuala Lumpur, Malaysia, December 6, 1994, http://www.pmo.gov.my/ucapan/?m=p&p=mahathir&id=1206.

14–7a   Paul Conrad, "Hirohito's Revenge," *Los Angeles Times*, March 31, 1985.

14–7b   Maciek Lulko, *Rockefeller Center*, 2014, photograph, Flickr, https://www.flickr.com/photos/lulek/14192146714/in/photolist-nC7sLJ-nC7pym-nSeXUr-nS5Pxv.

14–7c   Evan Amos, *Nintendo Entertainment System with Controller*, 1985, photograph, Vanamo Online Game Museum, Wikimedia Commons.

14–8   Elie Wiesel, "Acceptance Speech, on the Occasion of the Award of the Nobel Peace Prize," The Nobel Foundation, Oslo, Norway, December 10, 1986, https://www.nobelprize.org/prizes/peace/1986/wiesel/26054-elie-wiesel-acceptance-speech-1986/.

14–9a   University of California and American Hospital Association, *None of These Will Give You AIDS*, 1985, HMD Prints & Photos, U.S. National Library of Medicine Digital Collections, https://collections.nlm.nih.gov/catalog/nlm:nlmuid-101438789-img.

14–9b   *[Untitled Poster from India about AIDS]*, 1995, Centre for Community Medicine, AIIMS, New Delhi-110029, https://wellcomecollection.org/works/zz4n6sg4. Translation by Charles Ramsey.

14–10   Al Gore, "Information Superhighways Speech," presented at the International Telecommunications Union Meeting, Buenos Aires, Argentina, March 21, 1994, https://clintonwhitehouse1.archives.gov/White_House/EOP/OVP/html/telunion.html.

14–11a   Organization of American States, "Preamble: North American Free Trade Agreement," Foreign Trade Information System, January 1, 1994, http://www.sice.oas.org/Trade/NAFTA/PREAMBLE.ASP.

14–11b   Naomi Klein, *No Logo: Taking Aim at the Brand Bullies* (Toronto, Ontario: Knopf Canada, 1999), xxxiii, xxxvi–xxxvii, 442. Excerpts from NO LOGO: TAKING AIM AT THE BRAND BULLIES by Naomi Klein. Copyright © 2000, 2002 by Naomi Klein. Reprinted by permission of Picador.

15 | The New Millennium

15–360 | The Digital World

    ◦ Hannah Ritchie and Max Roser, "Technology Adoption in US Households, 1860–2019," OurWorldInData.org, 2019, https://ourworldindata.org/grapher/technology-adoption-by-households-in-the-united-states.

    ◦ Hannah Ritchie and Max Roser, "Share of the Population Using the Internet," OurWorldInData.org, 2017, https://ourworldindata.org/technology-adoption.

○   Ministry of Communications and Information Technology [India], *Guidelines for Cyber Café*, PART II-SEC. 3(i), G.S.R. 315(E), April 11, 2011, https://www.wipo.int/edocs/lexdocs/laws/en/in/in100en.pdf.   [Chinese] State Council, "Measures for the Administration of Internet Information Services (Chinese Text and CECC Partial Translation)," *Congressional-Executive Commission on China*, September 25, 2000, https://www.cecc.gov/resources/legal-provisions/measures-for-the-administration-of-internet-information-services-cecc.

○   AP Photo/Manoocher Deghati, File, March 30, 2011.

○   Donald Trump Twitter Feed, 2020.

15–1a   Erik Junberger, *9/11 Memorial*, December 5, 2015, photograph, Flickr.

15–1b   George W. Bush, "Report on Recovery and Response to Terrorist Attacks on World Trade Center and Pentagon—Message from the President—PM 43," speech, daily ed., September 20, 2001 (Washington, D.C.: The White House, September 20, 2001).

15–2   Arcadio Esquivel, "War Code," August 12, 2004, Politicalcartoons.com, La Prensa, Panama, https://politicalcartoons.com/sku/10543/.

15–3a   Barack Obama, "Remarks by the President in Eulogy for the Honorable Reverend Clementa Pinckney," The White House, Office of the Press Secretary, June 26, 2015, https://obamawhitehouse.archives.gov/the-press-office/2015/06/26/remarks-president-eulogy-honorable-reverend-clementa-pinckney.

15–3b   Hannah Ritchie, Joe Hasell, Cameron Appel, and Max Roser, "Terrorism: Number of Fatalities from Terrorist Attacks," OurWorldInData.org, September 2019, https://ourworldindata.org/terrorism.

15–4   Stephen M. Sloan, "Word Clouds of 2002, 2010, & 2017, National Security Strategies of the United States of America," 2019, National Security Strategy Archive, http://nssarchive.us.

15–5   Akbar Ahmed, *The Thistle and the Drone: How America's War on Terror Became a Global War on Tribal Islam* (Washington, D.C.: Brookings Institution Press, 2013), 1–3. Courtesy of the Brookings Institution Press.

15–6   Pew Research Center, "Table 4: Most Prefer U.S. as World Leader," *Pew Research Center: Global Attitudes & Trends*, September 28, 2018, https://www.pewresearch.org/global/2018/10/01/most-prefer-that-u-s-not-china-be-the-worlds-leading-power/pg_2018-10-1_u-s-image_4-3/.

15–7   The Governments of Mexico, Central America, the Dominican Republic and Columbia, "Unauthorized Immigration to the United States," January 9, 2006. Translated by Elisa Gonzalez.

15–8   B. S. Halpern, T. Hengl, and D. Groll, *Shipping Routes Red Black*, 2008, photograph, University of California, National Center for Ecological Analysis and Synthesis, Wikimedia Commons.

15–9a   Hannah Ritchie and Max Roser, "Fossil Fuels: Global Fossil Fuel Consumption," OurWorldInData.org, 2017, https://ourworldindata.org/fossil-fuels.

15–9b Mohamed Nasheed, "Address by His Excellency President Nasheed [of the Republic of Maldives]," speech presented at the Climate Vulnerable Forum, Malé, Maldives, November 9, 2009, https://presidency.gov.mv/Press/Article/1774?term=4.

15–10a Migration Policy Institute, "Number of Immigrants and Their Share of the Total U.S. Population, 1850–2018," MPI Data Hub: U.S. Immigration Trends, graphic downloaded June 4, 2020, https://www.migrationpolicy.org/programs/data-hub/us-immigration-trends#history.

15–10b Migration Policy Institute, "U.S. Immigrant Population by World Region of Birth, 1960–2018," MPI Data Hub: U.S. Immigration Trends, graphic downloaded June 4, 2020, https://www.migrationpolicy.org/programs/data -hub/us-immigration-trends#history.

Any errors or omissions in the above list are unintentional. The editors and publisher, if notified of an error or omission, will correct at the earliest opportunity.